RICHARD MORRIS'S
PRICK OF CONSCIENCE

EARLY ENGLISH TEXT SOCIETY
O.S. 342
2013

Oxford, Bodleian Library, MS Rawlinson Poet. 175, fo. 53^{v},
printed at 90 per cent of actual size
Reproduced by permission of The Bodleian Libraries,
The University of Oxford

RICHARD MORRIS'S
PRICK OF CONSCIENCE
A CORRECTED AND AMPLIFIED
READING TEXT

PREPARED BY

RALPH HANNA AND SARAH WOOD

Published for
THE EARLY ENGLISH TEXT SOCIETY
by the
OXFORD UNIVERSITY PRESS
2013

OXFORD
UNIVERSITY PRESS

Great Clarendon Street, Oxford OX2 6DP,
United Kingdom

Oxford University Press is a department of the University of Oxford.
It furthers the University's objective of excellence in research, scholarship,
and education by publishing worldwide. Oxford is a registered trade mark of
Oxford University Press in the UK and in certain other countries

First edition published in 2013
Impression: 1

British Library Cataloguing in Publication Data

Data available

Library of Congress Cataloging in Publication Data

Data available

ISBN 978-0-19-968099-3

Typeset by Anne Joshua, Oxford
Printed in Great Britain
on acid-free paper by
TJ International Ltd, Padstow, Cornwall

ACKNOWLEDGEMENTS

We began this edition in a rather modest mode. Whatever one may think of the poem's literary value, *The Prick of Conscience* is a major text and clearly appealed to a broad range of spiritually engaged late medieval readers. Initially, given growing interests in both late medieval spirituality and in 'poetic dullness', we had hoped to reaffirm the importance of the text through a rather cosmetic revision of the only edition, published by Richard Morris in 1863. At that time, we imagined presenting Morris in a photographic facsimile, surrounded by improved annotation to which both of us would contribute, Ralph on matters textual and Sarah on the poet's sources. However, on the basis of trial drafts limited to the poem's first thousand lines, it became clear to us that such a project was doomed. Too many oddments appeared that required off-the-page comment, and Morris's text would have been swamped with corrections. We are grateful to Anne Hudson, who, in her customary wisdom, suggested to us that a new edition detached from Morris's print represented the only proper way forward.

We owe a primary debt to Oxford University Computing Service and its affiliate, the Oxford Text Archive. One of the earliest texts OTA mounted for electronic use (in the early 1980s) was a key-punched transcription of Morris's text, which we have used as the basis from which our edition and commentary have been derived. OTA did not create this electronic document themselves; rather it was 'deposited by the courtesy of Professor Angus McIntosh'. These origins place us happily in the debt of important predecessors; certainly the greatest contributors to studies of *PC* in the last 150 years have been McIntosh and his collaborator, Robert E. Lewis. We are grateful to Bob Lewis for a variety of suggestions and kindnesses as we have gone about our work. In addition, we recall with pleasure a productive epistolary exchange with Derek Britton, who had once projected an edition of *PC* predicated on all the Northern manuscripts.

As with any edition, our expanded treatment of *PC* depends upon the courtesies of librarians, the custodians of the books on which our text is based. We are particularly grateful to the British Library, who preserve both our base-texts (following Morris, our manuscripts **G** and **H**), as well as the finest surviving copy of the poem (**A**). We are similarly indebted to the Bodleian Library, Oxford, for access to both manuscripts and the early printed books that have provided information about the poem's sources. Several collections, less frequently visited by literary scholars, have been unfailingly courteous during sequences of protracted trips to examine their materials, notably Lambeth Palace Library and the Fitzwilliam Museum, Cambridge. We are particularly grateful to Ruth R. Rogers, Special Collections librarian at Wellesley College, for answering numerous queries and for providing a film of the only manuscript we have not examined *in situ*.

We wish very much that there were an active cadre of *PC* scholars whom we might thank for their interest, support, and advice as we worked. Unfortunately (or otherwise), we find ourselves in the position of hoping that our edition might bring such a group into being. Sarah would particularly acknowledge Prof. Chris L. Nighman of Wilfred Laurier University for information about citations analogous to those in *PC* that appear in the florilegium *Manipulus florum*; Marina Kolesnichenko for aid in ploughing through the older German scholarship on the poem; and John Thompson for suggestions and corrections he provided for an earlier version of materials included here. Ralph is grateful to the Radcliffe Institute for Advanced Studies (Cambridge, Mass.), whose 2011–12 fellowship allowed him free time to revise his portion of the script.

All our other debts, besides those we owe one another for support and encouragement, are to the familiar denizens of the Early English Text Society. Our volume has been much improved by Derek Pearsall's meticulous reading, sensitive and supportive of our labours, if not of the object on which we had expended them. (His report, among all its helpful suggestions, describes the poem, on rereading it, as 'excruciatingly boring, relentless in its micro-organisation and repetitiousness'.) Helen Spencer has, as always, been a prescient and painstaking editor. Like our reader, the Society's beloved printer, Anne Joshua, probably thought at many points that she would never see the end of *PC*, and she has thoroughly outdone herself on this occasion. Anne first converted the OTA's antique file into an accessible computer language so that we could work with and on it, and subsequently converted Ralph's last files in Word Perfect 5.1 into Word format. After all that preparation, she has once again produced her typically handsome volume, effortlessly, it would appear, combining three files into a single text-page (as she had earlier with *Speculum Vitae*) as well as handling with aplomb the typical difficulties posed by EETS, characters restricted to one of several languages, an array of fonts, and other oddments. We are very grateful to them all.

R.H.
S.W.

CONTENTS

ABBREVIATIONS x

INTRODUCTION xiii

1. The Poem and Morris's Edition xiii
2. The Manuscripts Used Here xv
3. Authorship and the Poet's Dialect xxxiv
4. The Poet's Verse xlvii
5. The Poet's Sources lii
6. The Aims and Presentation of this Edition lxi

BIBLIOGRAPHY lxxv

RICHARD MORRIS'S
PRICK OF CONSCIENCE 1

COMMENTARY
1. Textual Matters 263
2. Literary Matters, primarily *The Prick of Conscience* and its Sources 287

APPENDICES
1. Unsupported Variants of W, Lines 501–1873 367
2. 'The General Tradition', a Full Substantive Collation of Lines 1–500 in the *b* Tradition 370
3. A Revised List of Manuscripts of *The Prick of Conscience* 378

SELECTIVE GLOSSARY 385

INDEX OF QUOTATIONS AND ALLUSIONS 405

INDEX OF PROPER NAMES 410

PLATE

Oxford, Bodleian Library, MS Rawlinson Poet. 175, fo. 53ᵛ.
Reproduced by permission of The Bodleian Libraries,
The University of Oxford *frontispiece*

ABBREVIATIONS

I. WORKS FREQUENTLY CITED

BL   The British Library, London
BodL   The Bodleian Library, Oxford
Bricquet   Briquet, C.-M., ed. Allan Stevenson, *Les Fili-
                  granes: Dictionnaire historique des marques du
                  papier des leur apparition vers 1292 jusqu'en 1600:
                  A facsimile of the 1907 edition with supplementary
                  material contributed by a number of scholars*, 4 vols.
                  (Amsterdam, 1968).
Britton   Derek Britton, 'Unknown Fragments of *The Prick
                  of Conscience*', *Neuphilologische Mitteilungen*, 80
                  (1979), 327–34
CCCM   Corpus Christianorum, continuatio mediaevalis
CCSL   Corpus Christianorum, series Latina
EETS   Early English Text Society (OS original series, ES
                  extra series, SS supplementary series)
Emmerson   Richard K. Emmerson, *Antichrist in the Middle
                  Ages: A Study of Medieval Apocalypticism, Art,
                  and Literature* (Manchester, 1981)
Hahn   Arnold Hahn, *Quellenuntersuchungen zu Richard
                  Rolles englischen Schriften* (diss., Halle a. S., 1900)
IMEV   Carleton Brown and Rossell Hope Robbins, *The
                  Index of Middle English Verse* (New York, 1943),
                  with Robbins and John L. Cutler, *Supplement to
                  IMEV* (Lexington, Ky., 1965)
Köhler   Reinhold Köhler, 'Quellennachweise zu Richard
                  Rolles von Hampole Gedicht *The Pricke of Con-
                  science*', *Jahrbuch für romanische und englische Lit-
                  eratur*, 6 (1865), 196–212
LALME   Angus McIntosh, M. L. Samuels, and Michael
                  Benskin, *A Linguistic Atlas of Late Mediaeval
                  English*, 4 vols. (Aberdeen, 1986)
Lewis–McIntosh   Robert E. Lewis and Angus McIntosh, *A Descrip-
                  tive Guide to the Manuscripts of the* Prick of

	Conscience, Medium Ævum Monographs, NS 12 (Oxford, 1982)
Lightbown	J. Lightbown, 'The Pricke of Conscience: A Collation of MSS. Galba E IX and Harley 4196', Leeds Studies in English, 4 (1935), 58–61
MET	Middle English Texts (Heidelberg)
Morris	The Pricke of Conscience (Stimulus Conscientiae): A Northumbrian Poem by Richard Rolle de Hampole, ed. Richard Morris (Berlin, 1863)
Les Peines	Robert J. Relihan, Jr., 'A Critical Edition of the Anglo-Norman and Latin Versions of Les Peines de Purgatorie' (Ph.D. diss., University of Iowa, 1978)
PC	The Prick of Conscience
Piccard	Gerhard Piccard, Die Wasserzeichenkartei Piccard im Hauptstadts-Archiv Stuttgart: Findbuch, currently 17 vols. in 25 (Stuttgart, 1961–)
PL	Patrologia Latina
Sharpe	Richard Sharpe, A Handlist of Latin Writers of Great Britain and Ireland before 1540, Publications of the Journal of Medieval Latin, 1 (Turnhout, 1997)
Speculum Vitae	Speculum Vitae: A Reading Edition, ed. Ralph Hanna, using materials assembled by Venetia Somerset, 2 vols., EETS 331–2 (Oxford, 2008)
Walther	Hans Walther, Proverbia sententiaeque Latinitatis medii aevi: Lateinische Sprichwörter und Sentenzen des Mittelalters in alphabetischer Anordnung, 6 vols. (Göttingen, 1963–9). Extended by Proverbia sententiaeque Latinitatis medii ac recentiores aevi: Nova series. Lateinische Sprichwörter und Sentenzen des Mittelalters und der frühen Neuzeit in alphabetischer Anordnung, 3 vols. (Göttingen, 1982–6)

2. MANUSCRIPT SIGLA

A	British Library, MS Additional 33995
a	the agreement of A and W
As	Bodleian Library, MS Ashmole 52

b   the agreement of L, M/As, and S (after line 2850, of L and M/As only)

c   the agreement of G (or H, in the absence of G) and R

G   British Library, MS Cotton Galba E.ix

H   British Library, MS Harley 4196

L   London, Lambeth Palace Library, MS 260

M   Cambridge, Fitzwilliam Museum, MS McClean 131

R   Bodleian Library, MS Rawlinson poet. 175

S   London, Sion College, MS Arch. L.40.2/E.25

W   Wellesley, Mass., Wellesley College, MS 8

INTRODUCTION

I. THE POEM AND MORRIS'S EDITION

The Prick of Conscience remains the *eminence grise* of Middle English studies. Every scholar knows the poem, and virtually none of them knows it. On the one hand, it is hard to remain unaware of a poetic text whose visible circulation appears at least half again as extensive as that of Chaucer's *Canterbury Tales*.[1] On the other, this mid-fourteenth-century originally Northern poem would appear, from the available bibliography, to have attracted very few students and next to no readers.

   Reasons why this ought to be the case are not far to seek. The poem has appeared to many rebarbative, although so within a definable tradition, since it was composed in full consciousness of earlier Yorkshire short-couplet works of spiritual instruction. However unpleasant its doctrinal emphases may appear to modern readers, there are a great many other reasons for the text's obscurity. It, of course, transmits unvarnished 'papist' theology (more intellectually stimulating in the form of the poet's frequently cited Latin source materials). Additionally, it defiantly represents, in origin at least, a regional culture, increasingly in the fifteenth century (and in modern critical tradition) submerged beneath the weight of metropolitan products. Moreover, the long-exploded Victorian fake notoriety of the poem as a work of 'Richard [Rolle] hermit', has increasingly removed it from centres of scholarly interest—and with that removal, the sole edition, Richard Morris's, has become generally unavailable outside major research libraries.[2]

   Yet none of these 'justifications' for ignoring *PC* really any longer merits much respect. Any text that survives in this number of copies must clearly have been central to the interests and aspirations of Middle English literary culture. As Lewis and McIntosh demonstrate,

---

[1] For the many copies (inevitably, the count is not complete), see Lewis–McIntosh. This is the study on which all future efforts must depend; the authors present the basic information on the transmission, with copious references to (much) earlier studies at pp. 5–9. We offer a revised and supplemented list of all the manuscripts as Appendix 3 below.

[2] For manuscripts ascribing the poem to Richard Rolle, five in all, see Lewis–McIntosh, 3 and n. 9 (further 12 n. 32).

the poem was known all over England (not to mention Anglo-Ireland) and even managed, as few Northern texts did, to penetrate, in an important context, metropolitan culture.[3] And, in a critical milieu in which 'fifteenth-century dullness'—and especially fifteenth-century religious writing, the manuscript context in which *PC* most normally appears—has become an increasingly central literary-historical concern, Protestant animadversions about the poem's doctrine appear increasingly short-sighted. But study of the poem and its reception, including a variety of local recensions, have been impeded by the absence of any available text that might properly be used for further analysis.[4]

To fill this gap, we offer this volume, one innovative in the light of past EETS policy and practice. At the centre of this book sits, not our original edition of *PC*, but a corrected and expanded reprinting of Richard Morris's 1863 edition. This was produced by the Philological Society which, at that date, was concerned to generate citations for the projected 'New English Dictionary'. This goal was, of course, one shared by the founders of EETS, among whom Morris was an early stalwart. Morris was typically prescient about what he provided mid-Victorian readers, a print version of quite the best manuscript he could have known, BL, MS Cotton Galba E.ix, with light corrections, in the main derived from other British Museum copies. Only whilst transcription was well under way and some of the volume already typeset, did Morris discover that the Galba manuscript lacked a quire (see iv). He supplied this deficiency (without realizing that the two

---

[3] See Oxford, St John's College, MS 57 (Lewis–McIntosh, 117–18 [MV 85]); and, on its production, Mooney and Matheson, 'The Beryn Scribe and his Texts'. This is a dispersal most unusual for a Northern text after *c*.1330 (when government offices stopped spending substantial periods in York). The only ready analogies are provided by closely related copies of Rolle's 'Form of Living' in Cambridge, Trinity College, MS B.15.17, and San Marino, Huntington Library, MS HM 127; of the prose 'Benjamin Minor' in the latter and the related Cambridge, Mass., Harvard University Library, MS Richardson 22; and of scattered copies of alliterative verse, in the main associated with a single scribe contemporary with HM 127 and Richardson. For the last, see Mooney and Stubbs, 'The HM114 Scribe'.

[4] For a notable beginning with a limited portion of the tradition, see 'Speculum huius vite', ed. Trudel, presenting and discussing the version described by Lewis–McIntosh, 159–61. A more striking example of such revisionary efforts is provided by 'the Lichfield recension', associated with the same group of individuals who also 'midlandized' *Cursor Mundi*, Rolle's English epistles, and *The Northern Homily Cycle*, and whose work underlies, for example, 'the Vernon manuscript'. On these activities, see McIntosh, 'Two Unnoticed Interpolations'; Dareau and McIntosh, 'A Dialect Word'; and R. E. Lewis, 'The Relationship of the Vernon and Simeon Texts'.

manuscripts had been copied side by side, in the same page-, although not quire-, format) from BL, MS Harley 4196. His edition provides an unusually apt, if not always accurate, version of the Northern original, from which all other copies of *PC* descend.

Surrounding this core, we offer annotation designed to render the poem approachable by modern scholars. We offer a variety of qualifications to the text Morris printed, in the main designed to show how his chosen manuscript, **G**, fits within a broader, yet still exclusively Northern, tradition of transmission, from which eventually all copies of *PC* descend. We also provide a much fuller account of the sources which the author laid under contribution, and of analogous Middle English discussions. The edition concludes with a fuller, yet still selective, glossary than Morris gave his readers.

2. THE MANUSCRIPTS USED HERE

Like many early editors, Morris made no effort to examine the full archive, or to produce a critical text. His goal was to provide a representative copy of the poem, in something like what he took to be its original Northern language, in order to support philological (and especially lexicographical) study.[5] But although his knowledge of the poem's tradition was not extensive, it was unusually painstaking and, in certain terms, representatively wide. Like many students of his era, Morris simply began with those copies that were most to hand, ten examples of the text kept in the British Museum. This process, in retrospect, if not thoroughly critical, was unusually prescient, and Morris identified what was, in most respects, the best manuscript he could have chosen in the circumstances. This is an important manuscript of Northern verse texts:

G   BL, MS Cotton Galba E.ix

s. xiv ex. Vellum. Fos. iii (now numbered fos. 1–3) + 110 (numbered 4–113) + i (numbered fo. 114). Overall 335 × 220, usually a little burned around the edges and mounted, the top two or three lines of inner columns shrunk from heat (writing area 258–67 × 170–5, each

---

[5] Cf. Morris's applause for Galba as of 'so much greater philological value' than the other copies, particularly because the book was written in the 'dialect of the district in which Rolle lived—Northumbrian' (i, ii). Morris's pp. i–xxix (of a thirty-three-page introduction) are devoted to phonology, morphology, and lexis.

main scribe a deeper writing area than his predecessors). 47 or 48 lines to the column, in double columns. The original manuscript is the work of four main scribes:

scribe 1 = fos. 4–48^v (texts 1–2, quires 1–4): in anglicana formata (*LALME*'s scribe B). This hand is also probably responsible for BL, MS Cotton Tiberius E.vii, fos. 1–81, mentioned below.

scribe 2 = fos. 48^v–50ra/8 (text 3 and a portion of text 4, added on blank leaves at the end of scribe 1's stint): in rather rough anglicana, perhaps s. xiv/xv (*LALME*'s scribe C);

scribe 3 = fos. 50ra/9–75 (concluding text 4, and continuing on, with texts 5–11, quires 5 and 6): in textura semiquadrata, often approaching textura prescisa (*LALME*'s scribe D). This hand is also responsible for BL, MS Harley 4196, fos. 133ra–164vb (see further below).

scribe 4 = fos. 76–113 (text 12, *The Prick of Conscience*, quires 7–10): in textura semiquadrata (*LALME*'s scribe E).

CONTENTS

Booklet 1 = fos. 4–51

1. Fos. 4ra–25rb: *Ywain and Gawain* (*IMEV* 259).

2. Fos. 25va–48vb: *The Seven Sages*, northern version (*IMEV* 3187C), elsewhere only in BodL, MS Rawlinson poet. 175, described below.

3. Fos. 48vb–49rb: 'Al es bot a fantum þat we with fare' (*IMEV* 189, unique), the text added by scribe 2.

4. Fos. 49rb–50vb: 'Prophecies of Merlin' (*IMEV* 1112). Another scribe 2 addition, with the juncture between his work and that of scribe 3 in mid-text.

5. Fos. 50vb–51rb: 'Sir Penny' (*IMEV* 1480).

6. Fo. 51va: 'Bides a while and haldes ȝoure pais' (*IMEV* 110, a passion lyric, also in Rawlinson, with the next; and in BodL, MS Don. c.13, fos. 165vb–166ra, with the next following directly).

7. Fo. 51^{vab}: 'Man þus on rode . . .' (*IMEV* 2080, another passion lyric, also in Rawlinson and Don. c.13). Most of the final column is blank.

COLLATION. 1–4^{12}. Catchwords under the inner column near the gutter (those of scribes 3 and 4 boxed, those in quires 1–2 informal anglicana); none of the scribes signs his quires.

Booklet 2 = fos. 52–75

8. Fos. 52ra–57va: the eleven historical poems of Lawrence Minot, in order: *IMEV* 3801 (fo. 52ra), 3080 (fo. 52va), 987 (fo. 52va), 709

(fo. 53rb), 2189 (fo. 53vb), 3796 (fo. 54rb), 2149 (fo. 54vb), 585 (fo. 55vb), 3117 (fo. 56ra), 1401 (fo. 56vb), 3899 (fo. 57ra), ed. Hall. On Minot, see Hanna, 'Some North Yorkshire Scribes', 181–4.

9. Fos. 57va–66vb: 'The Gospel of Nicodemus' (*IMEV* 512, also in BL, MS Harley 4196 and Sion College, MS Arch. L.40.2/E.25, both described below; a variant at BL, MS Additional 32578, fo. 116^{v}, copied 1405, probably in Bolton, Lancs.).[6] The final column was mostly blank, now with two additions, in a rather inept imitation insular, s. xvi/xvii (?), *IMEV* 1146 and *IMEV* Sup. 3912.5. The same hand has added, in the same script, derisory marginal comments on *PC* at fos. 96^{v}–98.

10. Fos. 67ra–73va: two large chunks from 'The Book of Shrift' (*IMEV* 694), attached, part or whole, to three early copies of *Cursor Mundi*. The materials here include *Cursor Mundi . . . Part V*, ed. Richard Morris, EETS os 68 (London, 1878), lines 27548–28063+ and 28614–29547+ (1527–51, 1560–86); the marked break between the selections appears on fo. 69rb. The full 'Book of Shrift' only occurs in BL, MS Cotton Vespasian A.iii; excerpts like these also appear in Rawlinson (texts 5 and 9) and Wellesley College, MS 8 (text 3), both described below. For a discussion of these excerpts, see Hanna and Zieman, 'The Transmission of "The Book of Shrift"'.

11. Fos. 73vb–75ra: the Pater Noster, with a metrical exposition (*IMEV* 788), also in *Cursor* manscripts, as lines 25103–402; see *Cursor Mundi . . . Part IV*, EETS os 66 (London, 1877), 1437–45. The remainder of fo. 75 is blank, the verso frame-ruled only.

COLLATION. 5–6^{12}.

Booklet 3 = fos. 76–113

12. Fos. 76ra–113ra: *The Prick of Conscience* (*IMEV* 3428), lacking lines 1538–1729 and 6923–9210, owing to a missing leaf and a lost quire after fo. 110. The remainder of the book was originally blank, fo. 113^{v} unruled.

COLLATION. 7^{12} (–9) 8–9^{12} [missing quire] 10^{4} (–4, probably a cancelled blank).

TEXTUAL PRESENTATION. Headings and Latin in red throughout, but otherwise, the decoration partially parallels the separateness of copying. Thus, scribe 1 and 3 portions introduce the texts with alternate red and blue lombards, the red with violet flourishing, the blue with red flourishing, in scribe 1 portions two-line, in scribe 3

---

[6] This is also a copy of *PC*; see Lewis–McIntosh, 76–7 (MV 43).

portions three-line. At smaller divisions in scribe 1's portion, alternate red and blue paraphs, a bracketlike form only, completed by a dot in the other colour, usually followed by a decorative penwork initial with red and/or ochre slashing. (The latter also appear without the preceding paraph.) The slashed capitals often include pictorial decoration, frequently leaf-shapes but also drawings, e.g. a fully coloured bust of a bearded king (fo. 35rb).

Scribe 3 portions, besides the lombards (two with lions' heads in the flourishing, fos. 54vb and 55va), also continue the provision of decorative penwork initials, with ochre flourishing only, some with leaf-shapes and occasionally faces (e.g. fo. 59rb). In text 8, exaggerated top-line ascenders, especially of the large initial at the opening of the column, all ochre-slashed.

In scribe 4 portions, four-line champs at major divisions, two-line examples at minor ones; these are rather crudely geometrical and not produced by either hand of MS Harley 4196 (see below). At openings of the books of *PC*, these are accompanied by painted column-long spray extensions, three formed from dragons (fos. 76ra, 80vb, 95va). In comparison with the rest of the volume, the text of *PC* is relatively undivided.

LANGUAGE. All the scribes write reasonably identical Northern English. This apparently represents a 'house style', common to all the manuscripts produced with **G** and exemplified in *LALME*'s presentation of Rawlinson, described below.

BINDING. Modern, with three flyleaves at the front, one at the rear. Fo. 1 is a former pastedown; on 1^v, the single note, 'Chaucer exemplar emendate scriptum'. Fo. 2 was the first leaf, with opening of Matins, from a fine *Horae BVM*, s. xiv/xv (good borders and fine large champs, a large illumination of the Annunciation). Fo. 3 is an old flyleaf, with a fragment from the poem added in full on fo. 113^v; below, an added inventory of linen. Also a rear flyleaf, fo. 114, containing runover from two added texts that begin on the final blank verso: fo. 113va 'The [25] Properties of a Horse' (*IMEV* 1176); fos. 113va–114va 'In Iuyl whan the sone schon' (*IMEV* 1497, on the siege of Calais).

PROVENANCE. On fo. 114^v, 'Richard Chawfer' three times, once with a mark (s. xv/xvi); 'Electe bywill of myghte Iene in Ru⟨. . .⟩lroume ⟨ ⟩ Levinge in Chaste diuines Lawe with Sacryd ⟨ ⟩' (s. xvi/xvii).

DESCRIPTIONS. *Ywain*, pp. ix–xi (with a facsimile of scribe 1);

Lewis–McIntosh, 58–9 (MV 27). For further details on the connection of **G** and Harley 4196, see Hanna, 'Yorkshire Writers' and 'Some North Yorkshire Scribes'.

As the description above will indicate, in one respect Morris's choice of **G** as the basis of his edition was unhappy. Morris discovered, but only after his amanuensis had transcribed a quite significant portion of the text, that the manuscript is now missing a quire (see iv). In following **G**, his edition could represent only a portion of the text. Rather than begin again, Morris chose to supplement the transcription of **G** with that of the next best Northern manuscript he knew:

H   BL, MS Harley 4196

s. xiv ex. Fos. 258. Overall 380 × 270 (writing area generally 260–5 × 173–8, scribe 4 routinely slightly shorter columns). 48 lines to the column, in double columns. In textura semiquadrata and quadrata by five scribes:

   scribe 1 = fos. 1ra–6vb (the opening of text 1, quire 1);
   scribe 2 = fos. 7ra–132ra (the remainder of text 1, quires 2–17);
   scribe 3 = fos. 133ra–164vb (the start of text 2, quires 18–21). This scribe also appears, as scribe 3, in **G**.
   scribe 4 = fos. 165ra–205vb (the remainder of text 2, quires 22–6);
   scribe 5 = fos. 206ra–258va (texts 3 and 4, quires 27–33). This individual also occurs elsewhere, as the second scribe copying BodL, MS Rawlinson poet. 175, described below. As in that book (as also his colleague there), not very well prepared ink or parchment and frequently flaking.

   CONTENTS
   Booklet 1 = fos. 1–132
   1. Fos. 1ra–132ra: the temporale of the 'expanded' *Northern Homily Cycle*, ed. Nevanlinna. The texts of the *Cycle* are separately indexed in *IMEV*; see the summary account at 733–6. The remainder of fo. 132 is blank but ruled.
   COLLATION. 1^8 (−1, −7) [scribe 1] ‖ 2–3^8 4^8 (−2, −3) 5–12^8 13^8 (−2) 14^8 [lost quire] 15–16^8 17^{8+1} (+9, fo. 132) [scribe 2]. Regular catchwords, boxed under the inner column (scribe 3 twice, fos. 180^v, 188^v, places them under the outer column). One example, fo. 172^v, within a drawing of a wyvern. Only scribe 2 has regular signatures, many absent, a letter and roman numeral, probably on all leaves in the first half of the quire (quires 3–16 = *c–r*, no signatures

survive in quire *l* and quire *p* lost). There are fragmentary examples of *a–d* in scribe 4's quires 22–5, and one possible scribe 5 signature, '4' on fo. 225.

Booklet 2 = fos. 133–205

2. Fos. 133ra–205vb: the sanctorale of the 'expanded' *Northern Homily Cycle.*

COLLATION. 18–21^8 [scribe 3] ‖ 22–5^8 26^{8+1} (+9, fo. 205) [scribe 4].

Booklet 3 = fos. 206–58

3. Fos. 206ra–215ra: 'The Gospel of Nicodemus' (*IMEV* 512), **G** text 9. The foot of fo. 215ra and the remainder of the side blank.

4. Fos. 215va–258va: *The Prick of Conscience*, lacking lines 2594–3937, owing to missing leaves. The remainder of the final leaf is blank.

COLLATION. 27–8^8 29^8 (–8) 30^8 (–1 to –6) 31–3^8 34^4 [scribe 5].

TEXTUAL PRESENTATION. Headings and Latin in red. There appear to be two programmes, one associated with scribes 1, 2, and 5; the other with scribes 3 and 4. Two different hands (neither the same as that in **G**) supply nice champs, in the first (and superior) hand, three lines at major divisions, two lines at internal breaks (four lines to set off books in *PC*). The second hand four lines and three lines in these positions. In first-hand portions, smaller divisions marked with gold-leaf paraphs with alternate red and blue flourishing, some Latin introduced by a gold-leaf lombard with the same alternate flourishing. As in portions of his stint in **G**, scribe 3 has extended top-line ascenders. Scribe 4's stint is much less extensively decorated than other portions, frequent blank lines around red headings. In scribe 5's text 3, red-slashed cadel capitals at the heads of columns (by the same hand that provides them in *PC* in Rawlinson poet. 175, described below) and, at minor divisions, more ornate initials, red-slashed. What appear decorators' counts of supplied initials at the foot of fos. 38 and 96.

LANGUAGE. The language of all the scribes is nearly identical to the preceding.

BINDING. Modern.

PROVENANCE. An erased inscription beneath the colophon, fo. 258va, s. xv med., appears to include the name 'Margaret ⟨.⟩y⟨.⟩⟨a⟩l . . .'. Early portions of both scribe 2 and scribe 5's work have marginal notations, s. xv ex., identifying the gospel pericopes and (frequently) noting 'good Readyng' (fo. 28rb, etc.). 'Wm Browne 1622' (fo. 1 upper margin); for him, see Edwards, 'Medieval Manu-

scripts', *passim*. Harley acquired the volume, with five other manuscripts, through the middleman activities of the Scottish antiquary
James Anderson (1662–1728) in 1725; see Wright, *Fontes Harleani*,
49. Among the other books that came to Harley's collection through
this transaction was BL, MS Harley 2394, a *Prick of Conscience*
manuscript important in our discussion of dialect below.[7]

DESCRIPTIONS. *The Northern Homily Cycle*, ed. Nevanlinna, i. 5–17
(including description of the book's second partial twin, BL, MS
Cotton Tiberius E.vii, its first seven quires, fos. 1–81, with *Speculum
Vitae*, copied by the first hand of **G**);[8] Lewis–McIntosh, 66–7
(MV 34).

As the description indicates, **H** differs from **G** in presenting its
materials in eight-, rather than twelve-leaf quires. But it remains
surprising that neither Morris nor his amaneunsis appears to have
noted how easily the two books' texts of *PC* might be fitted together.
G and **H** share absolutely identical page contents, and this feature, in
company with their common 'Gospel of Nicodemus', indicates that
they likely reproduced features from the same exemplar. In addition
to their disparate modes of quire-formation, the books also differ, as
indicated above, in the formality and quality of their finishing, **H**
being a significantly more lavish production. Besides these two
manuscripts, a book unknown to Morris, who restricted his atten-
tions to British Museum collections, reflects a similar situation of
production, although this volume is plainer in its production than
the other pair:

R   BodL, MS Rawlinson poet. 175

s. xiv ex. Fos. 134 (numbered 1–133, but there are both fos. 105a and
105b). Overall 270 × 190 (writing area for scribe 1, 205–10 × 150; for
scribe 2, 210 × 148–55), upper corners eaten away by damp late in the
book, damp also causing ink to flake or dissolve sporadically at many
points. 44 lines to the column, in double columns. In textura
quadrata. There are two scribes; the first, in a less consistently
finished hand, copied only *The Prick of Conscience* (text 1), and is
succeeded on fo. 55va (quire 5/leaf 7) by his partner, who is the fifth
scribe of **H**. The two hands are similar enough to believe that they
share common training; ultimately, they are distinguishable by their

---

[7] For this book, see Lewis–McIntosh, 65–6 (MV 33).
[8] For a further description of this book, see *Speculum Vitae*, i, pp. xxxiv–xxxv.

consistency of finishing; by the width of nib, the second considerably wider; and by their forms of *g*, the first a close flat angular loop of s. xiii type, sometimes closed to make an angular trapezoid; the second, a more open and rounded loop.

CONTENTS

1. Fos. 1ra–55rb: *The Prick of Conscience*.

2. Fos. 55va–76ra: the 'expanded' Northern Passion (*IMEV* 170), also in **H** and the associated MS Tiberius E.vii. There the text appears within *The Northern Homily Cycle* temporale account of Good Friday, and the rubric appropriate for that placement is included here. See *The Northern Passion*, 51.

3. Fos. 76rb–80rb: 'Dialogue of St Bernard and the Virgin' (*IMEV* 771), also at Tiberius E.vii, fo. 82, and Sion College, text 3.

4. Fo. 80rb: 'Man þus on rode . . .' (*IMEV* 110, a passion lyric), **G** text 6.

5. Fos. 80va–93rb: 'The Book of Shrift' (*IMEV* 694), with unique inserted poetic Creed (*IMEV* 1375) on fo. 84, **G** text 10.

6. Fo. 93va: 'Bides a while . . .' (*IMEV* 2080, a passion lyric), **G** text 7.

7. Fos. 93vb–94rb: 'Ihesu þi swetnes' (*IMEV* 1781).

8. Fos. 94va–95vb: 'The long charter of Christ' (*IMEV* 1718).

9. Fos. 96ra–108vb: 'The Gast of Gy' (*IMEV* 3028), also at Tiberius E.vii, fo. 90, here including an intercalated bit of text 5. See further Hanna and Zieman, 'The Transmission of "The Book of Shrift"'.

10. Fos. 109ra–131va: *The Seven Sages*, northern version (*IMEV* 3187C), **G** text 2.

11. Fos. 131^vb1–132ra: a version of 'The Vision of St John on the sorrows of the Virgin' (IPMEP 323, a fuller and more accurate account of the manuscripts, at least nine of them, at Hanna, *Index of Middle English Prose*, 12, s.v. HM 127, item 2).

12. Fo. 132ra–vb: 'Luke in his lesson' (*IMEV* 2021). Fo. 133^rv is blank but ruled.

COLLATION. 1–10^12 11^8 (2 and 6 singletons, the stub of the latter preceding fo. 121 [leaf 2]) 12^10 (–6, –7, both stubs; –9, –10, both probably blank). Catchwords, typically boxed, under the inner column, many cut away (one of these, fo. 48^v, with top of an elaborate drawing around the box). The only apparent signatures 'b' and 'R', both in red, fo. 73. The first would mark the second full quire of scribe 2's stint; the second would imply a much larger book, with nine or ten lost quires at the head.

TEXTUAL PRESENTATION. Headings and Latin in red. Cadel capitals at the head of many columns in *PC* (in scribe 1's stint) by a hand that also provided similar decoration in portions of **H** copied by scribe 2 of this manuscript. Two- to five-line red lombards, unflourished, at the heads and internal divisions of texts. Occasionally in scribe 2's stint, internal divisions marked with red paraphs, also unflourished.

LANGUAGE. *LALME*, which does not distinguish the scribes, describes the language as LP 174 and places it near Burneston, North Riding, Yorkshire (coordinates 431/485); see iii. 576–7.

BINDING. Brown reversed calf over millboard, s. xvii, sewn on five thongs.

PROVENANCE. Fo. 133ᵛ has in order (all s. xv ex.): 'Dayme Iohan holme quod Crux in latere'; then, in a single hand, 'Wylliam Asbye', 'Robart Neculson', 'Ihon Freinches'; then 'Ihon Peyrson'. A. I. Doyle identifies ('A Survey', ii. 47–9) the Thomas Gyll, who signed fo. 1, with a chaplain recorded in 1535 as serving in the church of Adwick-le-Street, near Doncaster, and subsequently a schoolmaster and chantry priest in Wragby. There are also seventeenth-century signatures of (?) Raphe Normond' (fo. 132ᵛ) and Christopher Fauell (the latter perhaps associated with the date '1630', also on fo. 133); they are presumably Yorkshiremen, since Richard Rawlinson purchased the book from the library of the Leeds antiquary Ralph Thoresby (d. 1725).

DESCRIPTIONS. *Summary Catalogue*, iii. 321–2 (no. 14667); Lewis–McIntosh, 116–17 (MV 83).

Two closely related manuscripts are now considered to have a better text than any of those described above.[9] Unfortunately, since the first of these was only acquired by the British Museum in 1891, neither was available to Morris. These are:

A   BL, MS Additional 33995

Vellum. s. xiv³ᐟ⁴. Fos. 156 + i (numbered fo. 157). Overall 305 × 205+ (writing area 235 × 150). Except for text 2, usually 40–2 lines (scribe 1) or 44–6 lines (scribe 2) to the column, in double columns. (Text 2 in 40 or so long lines to the page, writing area 255 × 150). Written in two anglicana bookhands (the stints divide at the folio boundary, 101ᵛ/102).

---

[9] See Britton, 328–30 *passim*.

CONTENTS

1. Fos. 1ra–96rb: *Speculum Vitae* (*IMEV* 245), the base text of the Society's earlier edition.

2. Fos. 96^v–101^v: 'Stimulus conscientie minor' (*IMEV* 244); the Wellesley manuscript described below is among the other seven copies (as is also the important Lichfield Rolle anthology, BodL, MS Rawlinson A.389).

3. Fos. 102ra–155ra: *The Prick of Conscience*.

4. Fos. 155rb–156vb: William of Nassington, 'The Band of Love', breaking off at line 329 (*IMEV* 11; the only other copy in Lincoln Cathedral, MS 91, fos. 189–91, copied by Robert Thornton of East Newton, North Riding, Yorkshire).

COLLATION. 1–8^{12} 9^{10} (–10) 10–12^{12} 13$^{?16}$ (–16). Catchwords; from quire 2 and throughout scribe 1's stint, all leaves in the first half of each quire signed with letter and roman numeral (quires 2–9 = *b–i*). The two hands split in the odd 9th quire, probably a production break after *Speculum Vitae*, with the cancel presumably indicating they were working together with the second scribe having already begun *PC* in the following succession of quires and tailoring the opening.

TEXTUAL PRESENTATION. Headings in red, also used for boxes around running titles and marginalia. At textual divisions, two- and three-line red lombards, unflourished. The text is divided by both large extended and one-line red paraphs. In item 1, couplets bracketed in ink; in item 2, in red. A full explanatory programme to *Speculum Vitae*, with both running titles and marginal notations.

LANGUAGE. The scribe of *Speculum Vitae* is not surveyed in *LALME* but identified with 'northwest Yorkshire' (i. 101). The second scribe is *LALME* LP 468 (coordinates 387/491, the Hawes area, North Riding, Yorkshire, an improbable placement, since at this time uninhabited); see iii. 583–4.

BINDING. Modern. Fo. 157 is the retained rear flyleaf from an earlier binding, from a civil law text, s. xiii in.

DESCRIPTIONS. *Catalogue of Additions*, 156–7; Lewis–McIntosh, 77–8 (MV 44); *Speculum Vitae*, i, pp. xxxiii–xxxiv.

W Wellesley, Mass., Wellesley College, MS 8

s. xv in. Paper folded in quarto, each quire usually three full sheets and one half-sheet. There are four different stocks: these have been identified by Valentina S. Grub, in her 2012 Wellesley College BA thesis, as:

Lamb and flag: resembling Briquet 43 (from a damaged mould, 1427 × 1430, the sole stock of quires 1–2);

Fleur-de-lis with fish: Briquet 5895 (1426 × 1438, once 1447); cf. Piccard 13 (Lilie), nos 538–46 (northeast France, 1431 × 1433, the sole stock of quires 3–6)

Flower (and leaves): representative of a type in wide use 1336 × 1431, and not precisely identifiable in Briquet or Piccard 12 (Blatt) (the sole stock of quires 7–8). A similar unidentified mark occurs in a northern book of s. xiv ex., BL, MS Harley 6718; see *Speculum Vitae*, i, p. xxxvii.

Crown: Briquet 4637 (1431); cf. Piccard 1 (Krone), Abt. 1, nos. 311–15 (there associated with a single Piedmontese mill, 1428 × 1468; the sole stock of quires 9–10).

Fos. 126 (paginated 1–252). Overall 215 × 145 (writing area 155 × 95). 29 or 30 long lines to the page. Written in anglicana.

CONTENTS

1. Pp. 1–3: 'Stimulus consciencie minor' (*IMEV* 244), A text 2.

2. P. 4: 'Loverde godd Ihesu cryste . . .' (*IMEV* 1954).

3. Pp. 5–12: 'The Book of Shrift' (*IMEV* 694, also in **G** and **R**), lines 29238–427, 29494–547 only (intervening portions on a leaf now lost).

4. Pp. 13–247: *The Prick of Conscience*, lacking lines 67–127, 1366–1565, 4550–4621, 7418–8571, 9149–9216, owing to missing leaves. The remainder is blank with pen-trials, etc.

COLLATION. [lost quire] 1^{14} (−6, −9) 2^{14} 3^{14} (−1 to −3) 4–5^{14} 6^{14} (−9) 7^{14} 8^{16} [lost quire] 9^{12} (−1, −2, −12) 10^{10} (−9, a cancel). Catchwords only at the ends of quires 7 and 8, the remainder cut away. Quire signatures in arabic numerals on the first rectos.

TEXTUAL PRESENTATION. Headings and Latin (so far as it is recorded) in red, the former frequently picked out with black dots. At heads of texts and major divisions, two-line red lombards, unflourished. Red-slashed capitals at the heads of the verses.

LANGUAGE. Unsurveyed in *LALME* and identified by Lewis–McIntosh as 'fully Northern', but only marginally so. The language is probably that of the southern Vale of York, immediately north of the Humber estuary: earlier long *a* generally *o* (but regular *war*, *yar*, *whar*), words like good/book/sooth with *o* (never *u*), yes/yere (in about equal frequency), eftyr, thorgh (throgh), moght, sal, solde, earlier *-ald* frequently -auld/-awld.

BINDING. Pink sheepskin (shows only on turnins) over wooden

boards, s. xv, rebacked. The whole has been exposed to smoke, the outside (including the edges) severely blackened. Scars in the upper board from two clasp seatings. Intact pastedowns from a choirbook and a document, both s. xv.

PROVENANCE. Following the colophon (p. 247), the erased ex-libris of Byland abbey (OCist, North Riding, Yorkshire),[10] apparently removed to allow the insertion, 'Iste liber constat Ricardo Gardner' (s. xv ex.). Also the signatures, as owner, of William Hotterbrun or Hottebon (s. xv/xvi; pp. 248, 250, the first of which, indicating his ownership, has been cancelled). The opening of an indenture, dated 1534, describing a transaction between Cecilia, wife of Robert Croke 'de skeiby' (Skeeby, North Riding, Yorkshire) and the wife of William Rose or Rofe (p. 252). Further signatures indicate North Yorkshire or Durham ownership down to the eighteenth century; the Bernard Richardson who signed p. 234 (s. xvi), for example, may be connected with a Durham family who owned books originally in the library of the Cathedral priory.

DESCRIPTIONS. Lewis–McIntosh, 128–9 (MV 96). There is no published description; since we know the book only from microfilm, the preceding account depends heavily upon the library's description, supplied by Ruth R. Rogers, the Special Collections Librarian, and upon Valentina Grub's generosity in informing us of and allowing us to cite her researches.

In addition to drawing attention to these important and overlooked copies, Britton's study also presents a *stemma codicum* of the Yorkshire manuscripts of the poem (p. 329). While this highlights the quality of the five manuscripts described above, it equally identifies them as without descendants. None of them, in Britton's account, is the direct ancestor of the general, and very broad, transmission of *PC*. Rather, Britton identifies this as emerging from another family of copies (his *b*). The two copies he places at the head of this line of transmission are:

L London, Lambeth Palace Library, MS 260

s. xv in. (probably 1410–20), excepting the intruded fos. 91–99, of s. xv$^{2/4}$. Fos. 139 (but only 137 medieval, since fos. 100 and 137 are

---

[10] An impressive number of copies of *PC* have similar institutional provenances; in addition to our manuscripts L and S, described below (MV 46 and 49, respectively), see also Lewis–McIntosh MV 2, 11, 40/70, 41, 65, 81; SR 12; E 1, E 7 (? Axholme OCart, Lincs.), L 5, and L 6.

modern insertions). An early foliation, part certainly original, using arabic numerals: fos. 1–101 numbered 1–105 at the top centre of the leaf (including leaves now lost), and fos. 102–36 numbered 1–36 in signature position (actually numbering the openings to facilitate use of the later index). Paper, so far as the marks are legible, of two different stocks:

Crescent: most closely resembling, but not identical with, Briquet 5220 (Italian, 1412 × 1414, the sole stock of quires 1–3);

Dragon: the type of Piccard 10 (Fabeltiere), nos. 869, 880–3, 889–90, 911, 917 (in wide use 1415 × 1424, apparently the remainder). Overall c.275 × 210 (writing area c.230 × 150). About 70 lines to the column, in double columns. Written in a very small anglicana, all but the intrusion (in secretary bookhand), the work of the single scribe 'Wilfrid'.

CONTENTS

Booklet 1 = fos. 1–90

1. Fos. 1ra–63ra: *The Northern Homily Cycle*, the original version, as described, with respect to San Marino, Calif., Huntington Library, MS HM 129, Dutschke, *Guide*, i. 164–73. The Lambeth manuscript has always been taken as the most reliable copy of the full text, which remains very incompletely edited, by Small and Thompson.

2. Fos. 63rb–66vb: *Commune sanctorum exposiciones*, thirteen outlines for sermons on the gospels for these services, followed by a Latin note on tithes and Wilfrid's English verses (*IMEV* 2248).

3. Fos. 67ra–79ra: Robert Holcot, OP's exemplum book, *Convertimini* (Sharpe 554–5).

4. Fos. 79rb–83vb: a further group of thirty exempla, eight of them with English verses; see Hanna, 'Lambeth Palace Library, MS 260', 181–99, where all the English is printed in context.

5. Fos. 84ra–90vb: a series of outlines for Lenten sermons, at least a dozen, the exact number unclear, given missing leaves at the end of this portion. At least some of these have been derived from John Waldeby, OESA of York, *Novum opus dominicale*; see Wenzel, *Latin Sermon Collections*, 40–4, 627–8; Sharpe 336.

COLLATION. 1–7^{12} 8^{12} (–6, –7, –9, –10 to –12, these early cancels). In text 1, catchwords on scrolls towards the gutter, thereafter in the same position but boxed or underlined. In Wilfrid's portion, all leaves in the first half of each quire signed with letter and roman numeral, a good number now absent; quires 1–8 = *a–h*, 11–12 = *b–c*.

Booklet 2 = fos. 91–99 + 100, a modern insertion

6. Fos. 91–99^{v}: John of Holywood (Sacrobosco), *De sphera* (Sharpe 306).

COLLATION. 9^{12+1} (–10 to –12; 13 [fo. 100] an inserted blank modern leaf).

Booklet 3 = fos. 101–39

7. Fos. 101ra–136vb: *The Prick of Conscience*, lacking lines 472–726, owing to a missing leaf. The colophon identifies the text as 'tractus qui vocatur stimulus consciencie interioris per sanctum Ricardum heremitam de hampole', one of five copies with such an ascription. Fo. 137 is an inserted blank modern leaf.

8. Fos. 138ra–139^{vc}: a Latin index to topics treated in *The Prick of Conscience*, in three columns; for discussion, see Hanna, 'Lambeth Palace Library, MS 260', 148–52.[11]

COLLATION. 10^{12} (–3) 11^{12} 12^{12+2} (+13, fo. 136; +14, fo. 137, an inserted blank modern leaf) 13^{2}.

TEXTUAL PRESENTATION. In text 1, headings in the text hand, underlined in red. Three-line red lombards, unflourished, to introduce each homily and to separate out the explication of the gospel and the exempla. In texts 2–5, the lombards alternate, red and blue, some with a little gold, a few with marginal sprays. In text 7, rather crude three-line painted initials, mostly dark green, with painted vine-sprays at the heads of the books. Some readings and marginalia underlined in red.

Wilfrid offered a certain amount of marginal marking (more extensive materials are intruded into the text column), typically notations of the topic and frequent numbering beside divisions of the argument. This has been supplemented much later, in a large textura, probably by Peter Tollar (see below): regular running titles for each occasion in text 1 and for the parts in text 7, extensive marginal signals of textual divisions and of authors cited.

LANGUAGE. LALME identifies the language of *The Northern Homilies* with the area of Beverley, East Riding, Yorkshire (coordinates 499/440); that of *PC*, by the same scribe 'Wilfrid' but presumably drawn from a different exemplar, is mixed, north

---

[11] We would offer some qualifications to the description there. As indicated on that occasion, the index is keyed to the Latin of *PC*. Wilfrid assigned, in sequence, a letter to each Latin section of each opening. However, the majority of these are no longer visible; those for the outer columns of the leaves were lost when the book was planed during its 16th-c. binding, and the surviving index letters are now mostly fragments deep in the gutter. (Very occasional examples along leading edges survive, e.g. fos. 120rb, 124rb).

Yorkshire or south Durham elements among forms of the East Riding. See LPs 361 and 383, iii. 592–3, 663–4 respectively.

BINDING. Blindstamped leather over wood, s. xvi, with scars from two clasps now lost. The original stamps are of Oldham's type RC.b, mainly London and Oxford work of the 1520s to 1540s (see *English Blind-Stamped Book Bindings*, 55), although Oldham provides no example of this particular roll. The later owner Henry Savile updated this, as he did the binding of Cambridge, St John's College, MS B.16 (Henry Daniel on urines, his MS 286, Watson, *Manuscripts*, 71) with his initials, full name, and additional stamps.

PROVENANCE, 'Amen quod T Willson miserere mic⟨ ⟩' (s. xv ex., upside down on fo. 62, foot). Given the signature of Peter Tollar, perhaps the York Dominican Thomas Wilson, who appears four times in ordination records 1487 and 1488; see Emden, *Survey*, 252. 'Robert Bulstede' (s. xv$^{2/2}$, fo. 1 foot). 'Petrus Tollar' (twice, fos. 31^{v} and 32, the latter partly cut off); he was a Dominican of York, ordained to two minor orders in 1534 and after the Dissolution, apparently, rector of Linton in Craven; see Emden, 261; Cross and Vickers, *Monks, Friars and Nuns*, 424, 434. In the later sixteenth century, the book belonged to Henry Savile the elder of Banke (Halifax, West Riding, Yorkshire), his MS 42; see Watson, 26–7. What may be a bit of his shorthand appears in the blank space on fo. 136vb.

DESCRIPTIONS. James and Jenkins, *Descriptive Catalogue*, i. 406–9; Lewis–McIntosh, 79–80 (MV 46). For further discussion, particularly of provenance, see Hanna, 'Lambeth Palace Library MS 260'.

M   Cambridge, Fitzwilliam Museum, MS McClean 131

s. xiv/xv. Vellum. Fos. i + 113 + i. Overall 220 × 145 (writing area 167–75 × 85, to the bounds, but 90–105 in scribe 4 portions). 36 long lines to the page (occasionally 35 in scribe 3 portions and 32–8 in scribe 4 portions). Written mainly in anglicana formata, by four scribes:

scribe 1 = fo. 1^{rv};
scribe 2 = fos. 2–43^{v}/12 (i.e. quire 5, leaf 4^{v});
scribe 3 = fos. 43^{v}/13–85^{v} (i.e. the end of quire 8; the Latin in textura);
scribe 4 = fos. 86–end (i.e. from the head of quire 9; the Latin in textura).

CONTENTS

Fos. 1–113^{v}: *The Prick of Conscience*, lacking lines 1–72, 2861–

3007, 3296–3441, 8396–9062, 9607–end (and 9533 ff. quite fragmentary), owing to missing leaves.

COLLATION. 1^{12} (–1) 2^{12} 3^{10} 4^{10} (–5, –6) 5^{10} (–1, –2) 6–8^{12} 9–10^{10} 11^{10} (–2 to –9) 12^6 (? –5, ? a cancel) $13^{2?}$ (only the fragmentary foot of fo. 113). Red-boxed catchwords, that on fo. 94^v within a drawing of a dragon. Quires 2–4, 6–7 signed accurately with roman numerals on the opening leaf; the only surviving leaf-signatures are roman numerals on all leaves in the first half of quire 2, and *iij.*, *iiij.* on fos. 42^v and 43^v.

TEXTUAL PRESENTATION. Two-line unflourished red lombards at textual divisions; one-line red lombards as versals to introduce the Latin. Scribes 3 and 4 underline the Latin in red. Rhymes yoked in red, usually an arrow shape, early on rectilinear. Scribe 4 has elaborately ornamental rhyme-yokes with beasts and faces, as well as a fair number of marginal drolleries in red.

LANGUAGE. Lewis–McIntosh identify the language as probably that of north-west Yorkshire; *LALME* presents the forms as LP 595, an unmapped example of Lancashire language (iii. 224).

BINDING. Modern, on five bands, but retaining old single flyleaves at front and rear.

PROVENANCE. 'Mr Edward Coples book which I haue in pawne for my book of pp' (fo. i^v, s. xvi).

DESCRIPTIONS. James, *Descriptive Catalogue*, 278; Lewis–McIntosh, 37–8 (MV 5).

As this description will indicate, **M** will not prove entirely helpful in editorial endeavours. As Morris discovered with **G**, the manuscript has significant lacunae and lacks more than 15 per cent of the text. To address this problem, we follow Morris's lead and, in **M**'s absence, supplement its evidence by that provided by a closely related copy:

As   BodL, MS Ashmole 52

s. xiv ex. Fos. i + 65 + i. Overall 175 × 120 (writing area 135 × 100). 36 lines to the column, in double columns (i.e. much the same format as **M**, but presenting a full folio of that manuscript on a single side). Written in textura, at its most formal semiquadrata, but more often unfinished rotunda, with anglicana letter forms (*a*, *w*, *g*, *-s*), þ and *y* not distinguished.

CONTENTS

Fos. 1ra–65ra: *The Prick of Conscience*, substantially complete. There are only seven lines in the final column, most of the lower part of the leaf cut away. Fo. 65^v was originally blank, now very worn, with pen-trials and *IMEV* 3196, a quatrain, s. xv.

COLLATION. 1–7^8 8^{8+1} (+ 9). No catchwords. Quires signed with an arabic or roman numeral on the final versos, many cut away (and the arabic early modern supply); a single possible leaf-signature, mostly abraded (fo. 42). Fos. 35–8 (quire 5, leaves 3–6) appear palimpsest, with erased materials from a liturgical book at the upper edge.

TEXTUAL PRESENTATION. The text is divided by one- to three-line red lombards, unflourished. Line initials set off in a separately ruled column; the Latin set off with red lines. Frequent extended capitals at column openings, many with faces. Some marginalia, sometimes in, or pricked out in, rcd. The first eight lines of fo. 1rb, opposite the opening, left blank, perhaps for an illustration never provided.

LANGUAGE. Lewis–McIntosh comment, 'South Lincolnshire, with traces of features from further west, perhaps Nottinghamshire'. The view is repeated in *LALME*, with the suggestion that the western features might indeed be 'West Midland' (i. 145).

BINDING. Brown calf over pasteboard, s. xvii, with two straps with metal clasps and staples to receive them on the leading edge of the lower board. Front and rear flyleaves with pastedowns, perhaps from an older binding, made from strips from a rent roll, with entries for 30 September and 4 October 1442, turned sideways to form a bifolium.

PROVENANCE. The roll, at the front, has entries for sums paid by Adham Denow for properties in Peynton and by John Cafton kt. for ones in Bywlcomb.

DESCRIPTIONS. Black, *Descriptive, Analytical, and Critical Catalogue*, 91; Lewis–McIntosh, 93–4 (MV 60).

One further book offers significant evidence about the early transmission of *PC*. Because of his sampling procedures, which privileged a passage late in the text, Britton placed this book very low on his *stemma*, as significantly advanced in corruption. But down to about line 2850, where the producers of the volume changed their exemplar, this copy draws faithfully upon a very good manuscript, one often either better (or more carefully transmitted) than that available to either **L** or **M**:

**S   London, Sion College, MS Arch. L.40.2/E.25, currently a
Lambeth Palace Library deposit**

s. xiv/xv. Paper (except the vellum binding leaf, fo. 134). There are
four stocks, all folded in quarto, each quire three full sheets (or three
with a half-sheet), one stock distinctly predominant:

Two circles: visible is Briquet 3194 (Brussels, 1392; although
recorded from a considerably larger sheet than here). But marks of
this type often have a cross, perhaps here obscured in the binding
(compare Briquet 3160–3, or 3227, which appears in BL, MS Arundel
507, copied in Durham, s. xiv ex.): the sole stock of quires 1–3, 7–12
(24 full sheets, including two that have lost a leaf and another that has
lost two leaves, two watermarked half sheets, and two unwatermarked
half sheets; quire 3 also includes a sheet without watermark);

(Bow and?) Arrow: resembles Piccard 9, ii. 1088 et seq.: the sole
stock of quire 4 (one probable full sheet and five single leaves, two
with halves of the mark);

Wheel: not in Briquet: the sole stock of quire 5 (three full sheets);

Pot ?: not in Briquet: the sole stock of quire 6 (three full sheets,
including one that has lost a leaf with half the mark).

Fos. 133 + i (numbered fo. 134); fo. 31 has been mostly torn away and
is now a large stub. Overall 220 × 150 (writing area 180 × 100–5 in
quire 1, up to 190 × 110 in scribe 3 portions). Usually 30–7 lines to
the page (scribe 3, 43–51 lines, partly continued as 40–4 in scribe 2's
quire 10). Written by three scribes, all in anglicana:

scribe 1 = fos. 1–12^v, 48–70 (text 1 and part of text 4, quires 1, 5–6);

scribe 2 = fos. 13–47^v, 102–133^v (texts 2–3 and part of text 4,
quires 2–4, 10–12);

scribe 3 (anglicana formata) = fos. 71–101 (part of text 4, quires 7–9).

CONTENTS

Booklet 1 = fos. 1–12

1. Fos. 1^r–12^v: *Speculum Vitae*, brief and scattered excerpts only,
beginning with a block from line 7799 on (fos. 1^r–3^r), 5595–6004
(with some interpolated material from the 7800s already presented on
fo. 2, fos. 3^r–8^v), then progressively shorter excerpts, especially from
the discussion of Chastity, breaking off with line 15042.

COLLATION. 1^{14} (–1, –2). A single formal catchword, centred in a
red box, fo. 82^v, examples in informal hands, fos. 113^v and 123^v;
scribes 1 and 2 sign all leaves in the first half of each quire with a
roman leaf numeral.

Booklet 2 = fos. 13–38

2. Fos. 13^r–38^v: 'The Gospel of Nicodemus' (*IMEV* 512), **G** text 9 and **H** text 3.

COLLATION. 2^{12} 3^{14} (7, fo. 31, mostly torn away).

Booklet 3 = fos. 39–47

3. Fos. 39^r–47^v: 'Dialogue of St Bernard and the Virgin' (*IMEV* 771), **R** text 3, also Cotton Tiberius E.vii, fo. 82.

COLLATION. 4^{14} (–10 to –14).

Booklet 4 = fos. 48–133

4. Fos. 48^r–133^v: *The Prick of Conscience*; although earlier booklets show connections with Tiberius and related books, with fine copies of this poem, Britton's stemma (p. 329) demonstrates that, at least in later portions, this version is significantly advanced in transmission. The shift in types noted by Lewis–McIntosh (from Type I to Type IV) occurs amidst scribe 3's stint (1582–5446), at line 2850, where there is a division with red lombard. This break may have provided a useful marker for distinguishing two different exemplars, put to use to allow simultaneous copying of the text by three hands.

COLLATION. 5^{12} 6^{12} (–1) 7–8^{12} 9^{12} (–1, –4, –6, –7, –12) 10^{12} 11^{12} (–1 to –3) 12^{12} (–12).

TEXTUAL PRESENTATION Headings in text ink and more formal versions of the text hand, sometimes approaching textura quadrata. At openings, two- to four-line red lombards, unflourished (isolated blue examples with red flourishing, fos. 125, 128). Red boxes around biblical citations in item 4, as well as around marginalia; to fo. 7, rhymes bracketed in red. Line initials red-slashed, similar slashing on some decorative top-line ascenders in scribe 3's portions. Substantial remains of the explanatory programme for *Speculum Vitae*, marginal portions only.

LANGUAGE. *LALME* identifies only two hands. That in quire 1 is associated with the West Riding, Yorkshire (i. 137); that of quire 2 is LP 481 ('Northern' and unmapped); see iii. 670–71.

BINDING. Modern brown leather over millboard; fo. 134 is probably a pastedown from an earlier binding, taken from a missal with musical notation.

PROVENANCE. 'Ryder' (fo. 38^v, lower margin, s. xv); 'Iste liber pertinet Fratri Iohanni Holonde Monacho Westm" (fo. 134), a Westminster monk who said his first mass 1472 and was subprior in 1500.

DESCRIPTIONS. Ker, *Medieval Manuscripts*, i. 289; *Speculum Vitae*, i, pp. xl–xlii; Lewis–McIntosh, 82–3 (MV 49).

3. AUTHORSHIP AND THE POET'S DIALECT

Richard Morris's early edition of *PC*, which predated the first publications of this Society, was an almost overdetermined choice. While medieval evidence for the ascription is sparse, the poem had been associated with a major known author since the dawn of early modern scholarship. The great sixteenth-century bibliographer of native authors, John Bale, ascribed *PC* to the Yorkshire hermit Richard Rolle. Bale's authority was the ascription appended to a Latin prose translation of the text, called *Stimulus conscientiae*, in Oxford, Merton College, MS 68, and his opinion remained unchallenged for more than three centuries.[12] For Morris, *PC* must have seemed irresistible—an English text from a well-known font of spiritual authority, extant in a large number of copies (giving apparent weight to the ascription to an important figure), and written in a scarcely published variety of vernacular language, that of the North.

But Bale had seized upon an ascription unusual in the Middle Ages. As we have already noted, only four further copies—in this case, all of the English verse text—support it, and for most medieval readers, *PC* was a thoroughly anonymous work. Moreover, only one of the manuscript ascriptions, that of our manuscript L, comes from the North itself, and although earlier than that in Merton 68, it is significantly belated, offered after perhaps three-quarters of a century of the poem's transmission.

Moreover, the ascription of the poem to Rolle has little to recommend it. While this Yorkshire holy man is known for verse composition, materials in short couplets are alien to his legitimate output. Moreover, Rolle's interest in basic spiritual instruction of the kind exemplified in the poem could best be described as ephemeral,

---

[12] For the book, see Lewis–McIntosh, 168 (L 6) and the extensive description, Thomson, *A Descriptive Catalogue*, 70–2 (he reports Bale's ascription at 285 [no. 39]). To examples of the ascription noted by Lewis–McIntosh, one should add 'Stimulus consciencie Hampole' in crayon at the foot of fo. 74[vb], in a hand that provides a number of marginal finding notes in the text and running titles elsewhere in the manuscript. Although rich in Northern texts (Waldeby's sermons, for example), this book appears to have been produced along the Norfolk–Suffolk border, *c.*1450–70, a localization consonant with two of the parochial appointments of the donor, Haymond Hadock.

and pursued through brief and slightly developed tracts in prose, for example 'The Ten Commandments' or 'The Seven Gifts'.

Perceptions like these inspired the great Rolle (and nearly originary Middle English manuscript) scholar Hope E. Allen. In her first major publication (1910), Allen thoroughly dismantled the attribution to Rolle and offered a broad logic for dismissing it. Although Wolfgang Riehle has recently revived the traditional ascription, he provides no arguments that undo Allen's persuasive showing.

But, if not Rolle, who or where? The one thing that may be said for Bale's ascription is that it does, quite accidentally, identify the period in which *PC* was composed, for the poem is, even if not of his hand, probably contemporary with the hermit's career. One way of fixing a *terminus ad quem* for composition is provided by the date ascribed to the earliest surviving manuscripts. While palaeographical dating of these books (many in set, and thus difficult to date, texturas) leaves a certain amount of leeway, the earliest copies appear of the mid-fourteenth century (which may mean as late as *c.*1370). And there is ample evidence of copies in circulation, more than a dozen such, at some point *c.*1350–1400—leaving aside extensive evidence of copies made 's. xiv ex.', i.e. after 1370. At the earliest, the poem would appear to have been completed, and transmitted, at a point roughly contemporary with Rolle's death, just at mid-century.

There is a further bit of confirmatory evidence, implying the poem was already in circulation and well known by 1360 or so. This evidence comes from the lengthy conclusion to the poem *Speculum Vitae* (lines 15995–16096). The poet of *Speculum* has modelled his entire envoy upon the parallel materials of *PC* (lines 9482–9621). His borrowings do not simply involve adopting the same order of argument, but a variety of close citations—insistence upon a work for 'lewed men' (*PC* 9544, *Speculum* 16029, 16063), naming the text (*PC* 9548, *Speculum* 16065), references to the work as both read *and* heard (*PC* 9579, etc., *Speculum* 16064, 16071, 16073, etc.). Indeed, the poet of the later poem adapts the language of *PC* in his request for the audience's prayers, whether he is alive or dead (*PC* 9610–18, *Speculum* 16077–84), and the two poems are almost identical in their last four lines. (See further 444–55n in our literary commentary below.) Since *Speculum Vitae* cites extensively Rolle's late epistle 'The Form of Living', it represents a composition of the third quarter of the century, and demonstrates that *PC* was well known by that time.

A *terminus a quo* is somewhat more difficult to establish. But especially in his prologue, the author of *PC* seems aware of the two earlier short-couplet poems of spiritual instruction, *The Northern Homily Cycle* and *Cursor Mundi*.[13] The first of these may well be a work of the very late thirteenth century, but the second is considerably more current. While *Cursor* is traditionally dated '*c*.1300', all four of the central copies of the poem are roughly contemporary, probably of dates in the 1320s or 1330s. On that basis, one should probably place composition of *PC* in the second quarter of the fourteenth century, contemporary with Rolle's works, Latin and English.

The poem's prologue and epilogue provide the primary information that might qualify the poet's anonymity. Both passages insist upon the universal imperative of saving one's soul and associate this process with an equally universal imperative, actively seeking that knowledge which would enable one to be saved. This knowledge will create in the Christian that dreadful (and thus, reverent, loving) obedience which will maximize one's chances for salvation.

But like the prologue to *The Northern Homilies*, which it copiously echoes, that of *PC* recognizes limits to that knowledge. Unlike the prologue to *Cursor Mundi*, which imagines widespread literacy across all England's three languages, the poets of *Homilies* and *PC* insist on the limitations of their audience's access to authoritative knowledge. For both poets, such information is available only through materials in Latin, and their target audience, the 'lewed', while they may be literate in English, do not have access to this learning. The poem exists as English verse for reasons thoroughly pragmatic; that language provides the widest access to the knowledge necessary to salvation, currently enshrouded in works in another language.

Yet the 'lewed' are not a single group. Many may be capable of absorbing knowledge directly from the page. But the *PC*'s imagined target audience includes those potentially 'illiterate' in the modern sense, for the poet persistently imagines the poem as *both* read and heard, available orally/aurally, as well as visually. This audience of

---

[13] Perhaps the most pregnant example is provided by lines 183–6, which one might see as an acknowledgement of the onslaught on romance that opens *Cursor Mundi* (more carefully reprised at *Speculum Vitae* 35–60). Cf. the later attack on wasting one's time on worldly trifles at lines 5644–5724.

hearers, nonetheless, remains capable of reasonably sophisticated internalization of instructional material (a form of 'oral literacy').

Such an insistence upon the audience's 'lewedness' identifies the poet as someone not so, but a trained cleric, with access to Latinate sources of necessary knowledge. Indeed, in terms that again echo the prologue to *The Northern Homilies*, the poet identifies a second imperative, that those possessing knowledge must communicate it, to the needy—and thus undertake the composition of a poem like this one. *PC* itself emphatically executes this responsibility through frequent citation of sources in their original language, authoritative and source-marked materials, frequently rendered in their original Latin. Yet universally, these are made available for lay use through meticulous English translations. Perhaps, given their couplet form, these are designed as mnemonics easily accessible to his audience.

Yet the appeal to unimpeachable Latinate authority scarcely renders the poem lacking in originality. The author's cleverness, especially in the light of contemporary efforts, rests in his insistence upon 'dread' (the biblical 'initium sapientiae, timor Domini', Ecclus. 1: 16 *et alibi*). 'Needful wisdom' here does not rely upon—indeed is predicated upon a model alternative to—the basics instilled by those instructional programmes following upon Lateran IV (and reasserted locally in archbishop John Thoresby's 1357 catechism). Rather, the poem's appeal is a great deal more visceral, frequently relying upon describing the more horrifying aspects of disobedient worldliness and its punitive fruits in the afterlife. The poet quite literally tries to scare the hell out of his audience, and to do so, appeals to the necessity of abandoning worldliness and adopting a humble obedience to general Christian precept. Rather than the meticulously subdivided guide to conduct provided by the later *Speculum Vitae*, he insists upon the ultimate outcome, salvation, and how, through an aversion to all that is not God, one might enhance one's chances of achieving it.[14]

Yet simultaneously, the poem is profuse in offering the audience a great deal of instructional knowledge. Much of this appeals to what one might again see as potentially mnemonic schemata, most evident

---

[14] The disparity between the poem and conventional Lateran catechetics is perhaps best exemplified in the poet's treatment of sin as a generalized category, 'worldliness'. In contrast to Lateran-derived insistence on the Seven Deadly Sins, they appear in *The Prick* only peripherally, e.g. to describe the multiple punishments of Purgatory at 2984–3001. But one might note that the poet here changes his source, *Les Peines*, where the sins are not accurately cited.

in the frequent numbered subdivisions of the argument, e.g. the seven pains of Purgatory (lines 2894 ff.). Equally, the argument engages the audience with materials that might be considered slightly peripheral: does a discussion of the Last Judgement, necessary in the poem's 'four last things' schema, require a lengthy prologue on the reign of Antichrist (lines 4047–4622), for example?

Despite the broad hints offered by the poet's self-presentation in relation to his 'lewed' audience, and in the absence of Rolle as named author, the poem must remain anonymous. The only way of placing its composition more narrowly than the general designation 'Northern' remains linguistic. One must hope that authorial features, ones confirmed by either metre or rhyme, might offer coherent information that would identify a locale in which to place the poet.

The Society's recent edition of *Speculum Vitae* provides an extensive discussion of both the difficulties and the possibilities involved in localising a Northern verse text.[15] Our survey of the evidence provided by the rhymes of *The Prick of Conscience* indicates that its authorial language, in most major respects, is very similar to that there described for *Speculum Vitae*. However, the two poems differ in those features on which the poets choose to rely for their rhymes. Some items well attested in *Speculum Vitae* do not occur at all in the shorter (about 60% of the length) *PC*.[16] Correspondingly, the poet of *PC* often relies upon rhymes unattested in the later work, including several features decidedly recessive in Yorkshire usage. These point toward a narrow and, although adjacent, differing placement for the composition of this poem.

In light of the similarities of usage mentioned above, our presentation initially follows the analysis adopted in the Society's earlier edition. We begin by illustrating, so far as the two poems offer congruent information, the analogous dialectical features of the two texts. This detail, as with *Speculum Vitae*, points toward composition somewhere near or within the northern Vale of York. Having demonstrated this congruence, we pass on to adduce information predicated on rhyme-forms exhibited by *PC*, but foreign to *Speculum Vitae*. These will direct attention to a locale of composition slightly

---

[15] See *Speculum Vitae*, i, pp. lxiii–lxx, with extensive references not here repeated.

[16] In addition, our intuition is that the poet of *The Prick* is considerably less adventurous in his pursuit of rhymes than that of *Speculum Vitae*. For a telling example, compare our discussion of *pare* and *ware* in subsequent paragraphs with the richer array of examples cited in the discussion of the parallel items in *Speculum Vitae*, at i, p. lxiv.

different from that offered in EETS 331 for *Speculum Vitae*. We conclude our demonstration by indicating the fit of features, associated in the Society's edition of *Speculum Vitae* with a different locale, with that here proposed for the composition of *The Prick of Conscience*.

The great majority of the rhymes in *PC* points to general Northern usage. The poem certainly is, as has always been assumed, 'Northern' and very likely from Yorkshire. The rhymes confirm a broad swathe of features which would typify that county:

1. Earlier Old English long *a* has been retained, whether alone, as the product of late Old English 'lengthening groups', or in the *au/ aw*-diphthong (*ou/ow* in most other parts of England, for example *saule/sawle*). For examples of the first (generally Old English words in long *a* rhyming with Middle English long *a* in French words and in open syllables), see *brade:made* 71, *wate:late* 1432, *bare:sare* 1461, *hate:abate* 3088, *waste:maste* 3146. For late Old English/Middle English long *a* before lengthening groups, see the frequent half-rhyme *hald:cald* 988, 1195, 1261, 1401, 1411, etc. And for the diphthong, see *knaw:law* 163, *awe:knawe* 2451, *lawe:sawe* 3063, *saule:Paule* 5033.

This feature indicates that it is highly unlikely that the poet wrote in south-Humbrian Yorkshire, southern portions of the West Riding, where OE long *a* is rounded to long open *o*, as in the rest of England. But the poet's broad extension of the feature would exclude quite substantial southerly portions of the county, broadly any part of the Vale south of the River Wharfe, as well as probably the East Riding. Rhymes confirm that such forms as *wald(e)* 'would', *þare* 'there', and *ware* 'were', at best recessive in these excluded areas, appear universally.[17] See the rhymes *walde:halde* 4395 and *wald:cald* 9546; the repeated *þare:mare* 1069, 2732, 2750, 2770, 3339, etc.; and the similarly repeated *ware:mare* 176, 1921, 2696, 3447, 3477.

Two analogous features, to be discussed more fully below, have no parallel in *Speculum Vitae*. In addition to *þare* and *ware*, *PC* quite persistently rhymes on long *a* a further word with phonetic form analogous to these, the adverb *are* 'previously'. For examples, see *are:mare* 407, 1763, 2850, etc., as well as *ar:þar* 460 and *are:spare* 2398. And, as the forms of *Speculum Vitae* do not, one rhyme here testifies to progressive Northern phonetic developments, an early

---

[17] The analogous form *whare* 'where', well attested in *Speculum Vitae*, does not appear in the rhymes of *PC*.

stage in what would become 'The Great Vowel Shift'. At 6131–2, the poet rhymes historical long *a* with the *ai* diphthong, *gayte* (OE gāt) with *strayt* (OF estreit).[18]

2. The rhymes also confirm those verbal inflections customarily viewed as restricted to Northern use. For *-(e)s* in the present third singular, see 2196, 3561. For *-(e)s* in the present plural, see 1138. The two forms rhyme with one another at 1080–1, 1090–1, and 1112–13. For the present participle in *-and(e)*, see 503, 790, 1490, 1549, 1911, etc. In addition, the poet generally follows the 'Northern personal pronoun rule', whereby a verb with adjacent pronoun has no ending or *-e*; see 28, 194, 293, 296, 343, etc. Rhyme also confirms typical Yorkshire forms for the present of the verb 'to be', third person singular *es* and plural *er*; see 52, 66, 104, 127, 133, etc.; and 1015, 3726, 6426, 7713 respectively.[19]

3. There is substantial evidence that earlier long *o* rhymes with earlier *u*, either short or long. The most persistent evidence concerns the sequence *-ōm*, widely attested in the repeated rhyme *dom:come* (OE cuman), as at 1858, 2601, 2800, 4065, 4979, etc.; as well as the repeated rhyme of the suffix *-dom* with *come*, e.g. 1352, 2643, 7538.[20] There is also extensive evidence for the development in words with earlier *-ōs*, e.g. *use:duse* 3674, 6377, 7630; with earlier *-ōf*, *lufe:byhufe* 70, 945, 1016, etc. (both noun and verb); with earlier *-ōr*, *pur:mesure* 1458, *pure:dore* 3450, *stature:pore* 8255; and with earlier *-ōn*, *Fortune:sone* 1273. The earlier sequence *-ōd*, which is not unambiguously attested in *Speculum Vitae*, appears once, *rude:gude* 9583.[21] The rhyme at 9613, *Ihesu:dru* (OE drōg, drōh) probably attests a related Northern development, the formation of an *iu* diphthong from the earlier sequence *ōg*.

4. Rhyme confirms a wide range of Yorkshire features, although not so extensive a sample as provided by *Speculum Vitae*. These include (we simply present type-spellings indicative of the rhyme evidence): *þa* 'those' (4480, 5017, but also *þas* 6006, to be discussed

---

[18] See Jordan, *Handbuch der mittelenglischen Grammatik*, 69 (par. 44).

[19] *LALME* provides a full mapping for forms of 'are' at ii. 81–3. In contrast, *Speculum Vitae*, whilst showing universal *es*, generally has plural *bene*. The editor of that volume believes the form to be a 'non-native' adaptation in the interests of a broader range of rhymes; see the discussion at i, p. lxvii.

[20] Notice also *dome:Ierome* 4667, *Ierome:come* 4738. A few rhymes appear to rely upon retained *o*, e.g. *done:fone* 2464, 3285; and *do:þarto* 3866, 4055.

[21] See *Speculum Vitae*, i, p. lxv n. 28, and the further discussion below. For the next sentence, see Jordan, *Handbuch der mittelenglischen Grammatik*, 117 (par. 119).

further below), *agayne* 'again' (113, 418, 811, 1723, 1741),[22] *yhit* 'yet'
(21, 4148, 4271, 4735, 7429), *brynne* 'burn' (3148, 3328, 3974, 4921,
4951), *dede* 'death' (487), *rynne* 'run' (781, 7099). *kirke* 'church' and
wirke 'to work' occur in rhyme, but only rhyming with each other,
which renders the rhyme evidence ambiguous (the forms might, after
all, equally represent *chirche:wirche*, etc.).

In the earlier analysis, a narrower placement of *Speculum Vitae*
depended upon a further eight points, all relatively minor features
attested in rhyme. Of these, six reappear in *PC*:[23]

1. In alternation with the customary full forms (e.g. *take* 112, 191;
make 903, 962, 1589; *taken* 1570), the poet relies upon the contracted
forms *mas(e)* 'makes', *tas(e)* 'takes', and *tan(e)* 'taken'. For examples
of the first, see 6374; of the second, 1881, 3294; and of the last 22, 57,
964, 1680, 1994, etc.

2. One rhyme shows the poet's reflex of OE *ĕh* (from 'Anglian
smoothing' of earlier *ĕah/ĕoh*) to be long *e*; see *brest:nest* ('next', OE
neahsta) 8685.

3. In the poet's usage, the suffix OE *-scip* rhymes on long *e*, for
example at 83, 380, 596, 955, 1139 (all with *kepe*).

4. In the poet's usage, the suffix and French morphological element
-is(c)h rhymes on *-s(s)*; cf. *Inglys:specifys* 3560, and the persistent
Crist:peryst at 2942, 3710, 4375, 5105 (with *ravyste* 5027 etc.).

5. The concluding OE sequences *-amb* and *-imb* have been
simplified in the poet's usage, and rhyme on *-am* and *-im*. See
came:wame 463, 515, 836; and *lyms:clyms* 3601.

8. The verbs 'give' and 'live' rhyme, both with each other (e.g.
105–6, 630–1, 922–3) and with other forms in *-eve*, for example, 'give'
at 3860, 4259, 4335, 5568; 'live' at 492, 699, 748, 1731, 2888. This
feature probably provides evidence for 'Northern' lengthening of
short *i* in open syllables (although the prevalence of *geue* would
probably owe a great deal to ON gefa).[24] The development is
otherwise ill-attested in the poem's rhymes, just as it is in *Speculum*

---

[22] The word 'against', frequently in Yorkshire writing (and in *Speculum Vitae*) the same
form as that cited, does not appear in the rhymes of *PC*. However, on the basis of in-line
appearances, the poet's form for 'against' was not identical in form with 'again', since it
must frequently be trisyllabic (as at 4144, 4476, 4488, 5092, 5347, etc.); the usual spelling
recorded in our copy-text is *ogayn(e)s*.

[23] There is no evidence here for points 4, *thredde* 'third'; and 7, *werse* 'worse', adduced
in *Speculum Vitae*.

[24] On such lengthening, see Jordan, *Handbuch der mittelenglischen Grammatik*, 46 (par.
26).

Vitae. Compare repeated examples of the type *wit* ('know', OE witan, not 'Northern' *wete* or *weet(e)*), e.g. 1797, 3763, 4653.

To this point, we have presented information indicating the conformity of the dialect of *The Prick of Conscience* with that of *Speculum Vitae.* However, as we have indicated in passing at several points, *PC* attests a number of rhyming forms alien to the poem earlier edited. We now turn to examine this material.

Six items will attract our attention. They are in no way analogous to one another, except in the fact that all are at best relatively recessive among recorded Yorkshire scribal practices. Each of these can be mapped from the information given in *LALME*'s individual Linguistic Profiles, and some rather tentative isoglosses constructed to indicate areas where these items appear to represent preferred usage. As a result of such study, a quite counterintuitive conclusion emerges: however diverse in nature the items examined, and however different the isoglosses indicating the use of each, all six features overlap, nearly or completely, in but a single place. This is a reasonably small area along the northern edge of the Ordnance Survey's Landranger map 105, including the Howardian Hills and possibly York City, and extending into the southern half of Landranger map 100, northward into the southern Vale of Pickering. The *LALME* LPs most relevant here are 190, 203, 362, 483, 1211, 1232, and 1349, as well as four of the LPs assigned to York itself (145, 1001, 1002, 1352); adjacent, but probably differentiable in detail are LPs 7, 146, 197, 228, and 1348.[25]

The six features on which we predicate this narrow differentiation include:

1. The coalescence of older long *a* and the diphthong *ai*, mentioned above. Evidence for such a feature is of two types. Spellings of older long *a* as *ai/ay*, a 'back-spelling' stimulated by the new fusion of two originally different sounds, might identify this feature, but may simply represent examples of a digraph designed to unambiguously indicate vowel length. This, the most recessive example of the

---

[25] *LALME* provides the full information on these LPs: 7, 146, 190, 197, 203, 483, 1232, 228, and 362 (these last hands in a single manuscript of *PC*, BL, MS Harley 2394) at iii. 574–80, 584–5, 591–4 *passim*; 1349 at iii. 660–1; 145, 1001, 1002, 1348, and 1352 at iii. 565–8; 1211 at iii. 589. LPs 7 and 197 attest only *pure/gude* of the six features introduced below; LPs 146, 228, and 1348 regularly represent earlier long *a* as *o*; LPs 146, 1349, and most York City LPs have -*yng*, rather than -*and*, for the present participle.

features, appears in LP 483 and, proximate to the area identified above, LPs 53, 398, and 476.[26]

A second form of evidence comes from spellings of items historically having the *ai* diphthong but offering, in its stead, spellings in *a*. We have surveyed the two common items 'again/st' and 'their', seeking spellings of the general type *agan-* and *thar(e)/þar(e)*. Examples of the first occur in LPs 1002 and 1211, as well as the proximate LPs 398, 415, and 1355. For examples of the second, see LPs 145, 146, 1232, and the proximate LPs 53, 415, and 1228.[27]

2. A second feature noted above concerns the coalescence of earlier long *o* with *u* in the words 'poor' and 'good'. The first passes unsurveyed in the edition of *Speculum Vitae*, although the form probably appears there; the second cannot be proven part of that poet's rhyming vocabulary. Nine Yorkshire LPs (three of them in the extreme west of the country and eliminable on other grounds) offer spellings like *pure* for 'poor'; two of these are certainly in or adjacent to the area earlier assigned *Speculum Vitae* (LPs 174 and 486); among the remainder are LPs 190 and 197.

As the *Speculum Vitae* edition indicates (see n.21 above), coalescence of earlier *o* and *u* before the consonant *d* is far from a universal feature in Yorkshire. But the spelling *gude* occurs, in most cases as the sole form, in LPs 7, 145, 190, 197, 203, 228, 362, 483, 1002, 1211, 1348, 1349, and 1352, as well as in the adjacent LP 53. So far as the absence of the form from *Speculum Vitae* is concerned, one might note a fairly extensive band of *gode* spellings marking the area just west of that we survey here in detail—which includes portions of that area in which the *Speculum* was probably composed.[28]

3. Although the normal Yorkshire rendition of 'those' is *þa*, the form *þas*, mentioned above, occurs sporadically over a band running east–west across the centre of the county. One of its great concentrations is

---

[26] For *ai/ay*-spellings, see *LALME* iv. 85.

[27] For 'again/st', see *LALME* iv. 66; and for 'their', iv. 15–16, as well as the full mapping of forms at ii. 33–5. In the discussion above, we have mentioned the adverb *are* 'previously' as an item frequent in *PC* but alien to *Speculum Vitae*. This we have finally not included; *LALME* surveys only the parallel conjunction 'ere, before', and although the two should be identical in form (both OE ǣr), we are reluctant to pursue the evidence. The spelling *ar(e)* 'ere, before' is mainly restricted to the Yorkshire–Lincolnshire border; it also occurs in four Nidderdale–Wensleydale LPs, three of them copies of *Speculum Vitae*, LPs 116, 526, 486, and 487. For a full mapping of forms, see *LALME* ii. 159–61.

[28] For *pure*, see *LALME* iv. 237; for *gude*, iv. 87, and the fully mapped forms at ii. 279–81.

[29] For *þas*, see *LALME* iv. 6.

in the area we have designated, where it occurs in LPs 190, 203, 228, 362, 1211, and 1352, as well as in the adjacent LPs 398 and 410.[29]

4. The normal Yorkshire spelling of 'when' shows vocalism identical with the modern form. But where it appears in rhyme in *PC*, 'when' is represented by the distinctly recessive form *whan* (see 1944, 2664). *LALME* reports only eleven mapped Yorkshire LPs with this spelling; of these, four again represent the far west and five more southern areas of Yorkshire already excluded from the discussion. The two remaining examples appear in LPs from the area already identified, LPs 483 and 1349.[30]

5. Quite extensive rhyming evidence identifies the authorial form of 'together' as *togyder* (see 1416, 1861, 2611, 5418, 6013 etc.). In *LALME*'s account, the form is limited to a pair of arcs across eastern portions of the county. Within the area of our concern, it is attested in LPs 190, 362, and 1349, as well as the adjacent LP 398.[31]

6. Evidence for one potentially authorial usage is provided by metre, rather than rhyme. Within the line, the overwhelming evidence suggests that the forms written as *byhoves* and *byhoved* are monosyllabic, i.e. of the type *bus* and *bud*, even though the full forms are required for rhyme (see Textual Commentary, 492n). Contracted forms of this type are attested sporadically across much of south-eastern Yorkshire; within the area with which we are concerned, they appear in LPs 228, 362, and 1349, as well as the adjacent LPs 53 and 410.[32]

The congruence of these results seems to us telling and probably identifying an area from which the *PC* poet drew local forms. There remains one task to perform. In earlier portions of the argument, we have relied upon features evidenced in the rhymes of *Speculum Vitae*; the edition of that work identifies the area in which the poem was probably composed as lying west (and probably slightly south-west) of that identified here as *PC*'s likely place of origin. To complete our demonstration, we offer a tabular account of evidence for the six minor features initially discussed above, but now providing exemplification from within the area posited for composition of *PC*, the Howardian Hills/Vale of Pickering area:

---

[30] For *whan/qwan*, see *LALME* iv. 101–3 and the full mapping of forms at ii. 231–3.
[31] For *togyder*, see *LALME* iv. 269–70, and the fully mapped forms at ii. 351–3.
[32] For *bus/bud*, see *LALME* iv. 130.

1. Contracted forms of 'make' and 'take': *mase* LP 483, *tan* LP 228, as well as *tane* LPs 197 and 1352 (and the adjacent LP 53).

2. Development of earlier *ĕh* to long *e*: *he(e)* 'high' (OE heah) is recorded from LPs 190, 203, and 228; the superlative *heest* from LP 362 (but *heghe* for the positive form); and *een* appears in LP 1349.[33]

3. The suffix *-ship* rhyming on long *e* is recessive in the area, where *-chip* types predominate. But LP 228 has *-chep* and LPs 7 and 197 *-schep*.

4. Development of earlier *-is(c)h* to *-is(s)*: *LALME* offers very little relevant information on this feature. But its records for an analogous form, the representation of the word 'flesh', provide some intriguingly unusual spellings, *flesce* LP 197, *flech* LP 362, *flehsse* LP 483, *flich* LP 1002. With the first in particular, one might compare the routine rendition of the verb 'guess' in our copy-text manuscripts of *PC*, *gesce* (e.g. lines 3928, 4334).

5. Simplification of earlier *-amb* and *-imb*: the adjacent LP 53 has both *amb* and *amm* for the former.

6. Development of earlier *i* to *e* in the verbs 'give' and 'live': Examples from within the area include *gef* LP 362, *lev-* LPs 7 and 1348, and past participle *geuen* LP 1352.[34]

A further authorial detail in the text may add some weight to the placement we propose. In line 1479, the poet offers a pun, presenting the word 'world' as equivalent to 'þe wer elde' 'the worse old age'. On the one hand, this confirms potential retention of the Old English disyllabic form *woruld* (and metre confirms this as well; see p. l). On the other, the pun relies upon a form of this word of either type *war(u)ld* or the type *wer(u)ld*, since the word-play implies that 'worse' should be represented by a form like *war* or *wer*.

This pun may provide evidence to support our proposed localization. *LALME* records no Yorkshire scribe with an overtly disyllabic spelling for 'world'. However, spellings of the type *werld* and *warld* appear sporadically all through the Vale of York, but with a particularly heavy concentration of both alternatives among the profiles we have been examining. However, overt examples of *war* and *wer* as forms of 'worse' only occur on scattered occasions in

[33] For 'eye' (plural) and 'high', see the maps of full forms, *LALME* ii. 261–3 and 285–7 respectively.

[34] The area also provides some evidence for the two *Speculum Vitae* features not reproduced in *PC*: *thred* LPs 203 and 228; *wers* LP 203 and *werst* LP 362 (but see the next two paragraphs).

profiles from the county. But two of the LPs from the area offer at least provocative forms, *wars* in LP 203 and 483 (and *wers* in LP 203).[35] From all this, we conclude that we have a reasonable placement of authorial dialect, similar to, but rather more north-easterly than that for *Speculum Vitae* (cf. LP 1349, here the west-central edge of our probable area of composition, but providing the north-east limit of the area in which the *Speculum* was likely composed).

As we have suggested, the poet's insistence that authoritative materials on his subject are available only in Latin works reserved for clerical use certainly identifies him as a representative of that Latinate cadre. (But given that his primary source, as Allen noted at *Writings Ascribed to Richard Rolle*, 378–9, was Anglo-Norman, the claim is at least partially insincere.) The only narrower specifications one might offer concern the specific 'learned' materials he appears prepared to provide his audience. From the perspective of four-teenth-century lay instruction, the poet would appear particularly widely read, probably with at-hand command of a fairly substantial library (which we elaborate in our discussion of the sources below). While he may have acquired some of his references from such a compendium as the Parisian *Manipulus florum*, a good many texts are so persistently (and continuously) repeated as to insure the author's first-hand knowledge.

Unfortunately, pursuing this line of argument does not allow one to narrow further the designation of the author as 'a North Yorkshire cleric'. There is no extant copy of the Anglo-Norman source, *Les Peines de Purgatoire*, with a clear Northern provenance. (A copy of the derived Latin version, in Oxford, Corpus Christi College, MS 155, was presented to the Cistercian abbey of Rievaulx in the mid-fifteenth century.) The works from which the poet draws those Latinate materials with which he fills out (and 'authorizes') his Anglo-Norman *Peines* simply form the common intellectual stock of four-teenth-century learned men. Bartholomaeus Anglicus and Hugh Ripelin may seem *outré* to us, but Seymour's study testifies to the wide distribution of copies of the former in the later English Middle Ages. And Kaeppeli identifies (*Scriptores*, ii. 260–9) more than thirty pre-1400 copies of Ripelin's *Compendium* from British libraries. While

---

[35] For full mapping of the forms for 'world', see *LALME* ii. 207–9; both *warld* and *werld* types appear together in LPs 7, 190, 197, 203, 228, and 483, *warlde* only in LP 1349. For the less than a dozen recorded Yorkshire examples of *war* or *wer* 'worse', see iv. 291.

the author might have been someone like a York Dominican, he could equally well have been an enthusiastic graduate priest with a parochial living and well-stocked library.

4. THE POET'S VERSE

All the sources of *PC* were composed in Anglo-Norman or Latin prose. However, for their presentation to an English audience, the author chose to render these materials in verse. This decision seems to us far from utterly inevitable and to have required the author's prior decision that verse-form inherently added some important feature to his translations. Further, his fundamentally aesthetic decision was, in later recensions of the poem, received aesthetically as well. 'The Lichfield version', for example, carefully reduces the poem, line by line, into a more familiar octosyllabic verse pattern. Thus, the poem's reception strongly indicates (and reaffirms) the poet's sense that choosing to present a verse rendition was not neutral. Rather, the verse of *PC* (as of other poems in its tradition) must be seen as adding some aesthetic feature not deemed available in prose translation.

The metre of *PC* has received one extensive and important study. In her Edinburgh dissertation, Christine Robinson conclusively demolished the prospect that this poem and *Speculum Vitae* were of common authorship. Central to her demonstration was the differing metrical basis of the two poems. In her account, *PC* is written in French-derived octosyllabic verse depending on the regular alternation of stressed and unstressed syllables, while *Speculum Vitae* routinely shows more irregular verse-patterning and reflects a tradition of 'native four-stress' verse.

Robinson's conclusion is certainly the proper one, and may be demonstrated at any number of points in the poem. As in the Society's earlier edition of *Speculum Vitae* (see pp. lxxiv–lxxix), we offer here an extended, yet relatively brief, metrically marked sample passage to illustrate the poet's technique. Our selected example consists of thirty-eight lines, 1164–1201:[36]

---

[36] Here 'x' indicates a syllable not bearing stress, 'C' one with stress.

```
   x  C    x   C  x  C  x   C
```
He says, 'þe world es nathyng elles
```
    x x   C   xC  x   C    x    C
```
Bot an hard exil, in qwilk men duelles'   1165
```
   x  C x x  C    C x  C
```
And alswa a dym dulful dale
```
  C  x  C  x  C(x)   x   C
```
þat es ful of sorow and bale,
```
   x  x  C   x  C  x   C   x C
```
And a sted of mykel wrechednes,
```
   x  x C   x   C  x   x   C   x  C
```
Of travail and angers, þat here ay es,
```
   x   C    x   C   x  C  xC
```
Of payne, of syn, and of foly,   1170
```
   x   C   x    C  x  CxC
```
Of shenshepe and of velany,
```
   x   C  x  C   x  CxC
```
Of lettyng and of tarying,
```
   x   C x  C   x  C   x  C
```
Of frawardnes and of strivyng,
```
   x   C    x  C   xC x C
```
Of filthe and of corrupcion,
```
   x  Cx  C    x  x  x   C  xC
```
Of violence and of oppression   1175
```
   x  CxC   x  C   x  C
```
Of gil[e]ry and of falshede,
```
   x  C x   C   x    C  x   C
```
Of treson, discorde, and of drede.
```
   x  x   C    x  C    x    C  x  C
```
In þe world, he says, noght elles we se
```
   x   C  x  C   x  CxC
```
Bot wrechednes and vanite,
```
   C    x    C    x  CxC
```
Pride and pompe and covatyse   1180
```
   x   C x   C  x  C   x  C
```
And vayn[e] sleghtes and qwayntyse.
```
   x  C x   C  x   C   x   C
```
þe wor[u]ld, he says, tyl hym drawes
```
   x   C   x   C   x   C   x   C
```
And tilles, and lufes þam þat him knawes,

x   C x x   C   x   C   x C
And many he nuyes and fon avayles;
x   C x C   x   C   x   C
His lufers he desayves and fayles.   1185
x   C x C   x   C x C
His despisers he waytes ay,
x   C   x   x C   x   C x   C
Als shadow to tak þam to his pray.
x C   x   C   x   C x   x   C
Bot þa þat wille him folow, he ledes
x   x   C   x   C x C x   C
And þam scornes and taries in his nedes,
x   C   x   C   x   C   x C
þe whilk a while he here socours   1190
x   x   C   x   C x   C   x C
And þam heghes with ryches and honours.
x   x   C   x x   C   x   C x C
Bot he waytes to bygille þam at þe last,
x   C x   C x x C   x   C
And into povert agayn þam cast;
x   x   C   x   C x   C   x C
Wharfor worldes worshepe may be cald
x   C   x   C xx   x   C x x   C
Noght elles but vanite, and swa I it hald.   1195
x   C   x   C x   C   x x   C
And worldisshe riches, howswa þai come,
x C   x   C   x C   x   x C
I hald noght elles bot filth and fantome.
x   C   x   C x   x   C x x   C
þe world has many with wanite filed
x   x   C   x   C   x   C   x C
And with pride and pompe þam ofte bygyled;
x x x   C x   C   x   C   x   C
þarfor an haly man, als yhe may here,   1200
C   x   x   C   x   C   x C
Spekes to þe world on þis manere:

This selection is sufficient to verify Robinson's contention that the poem is fundamentally octosyllabic, with typically rising/iambic patterns. The basic line typically is of the form 'x C x C x C x C', and in general, the poem is predicated on sustained runs of this pattern. Even in the illustrative passage above, deliberately chosen to illustrate other features, one can point to sequences like lines 1170–4 and 1181–3. In general, this verse-form allows the poet to avoid that feature typical of native four-stress, stress-clash; in the sample it appears once (in 1166). In this case, perhaps significantly, the clash is accompanied by a balancing run of two adjacent unstressed syllables.

Unlike Chaucerian verse, the pattern here is achieved with minimal attention to final syllables, notably -e and -es, neither perhaps a regular feature in the author's spoken Northern Middle English. A certain number of possibly antique full forms are pressed into service, here *gilery* 1176 and *woruld* 1182 (but cf. the ambiguous *worldes* 1194 (either *worulds* or the form with syllabic termination indicated by the spelling?; the disyllabic form *sawol* is testified elsewhere). But the poet, although restrained in their use, is scarcely ignorant of those possibilities Chaucer so readily exploits: line 1181 requires the -e of the plural adjective, the usually suppressed verbal ending -es occurs in 1186, and the nominal plural in -es perhaps in 1191.[37]

However, one might wish to see this strictly octosyllabic pattern as a minimum or ground form, from which frequent variation occurs. This is particularly pronounced at line-openings. As one might expect from later English usage (including Chaucer's), frequently an unstressed syllable preceding the first stress is suppressed (the so-called 'headless line'). This feature occurs in about 10% of the lines above (1167, 1180, 1194, 1201).

But considerably more frequently, poetic lines rely upon extended anacrusis, sequences of unstressed syllables at the line-opening. However, these line-opening variations are most typically succeeded by lines following a normal octosyllabic pattern. In the sample, twice as many lines open with two unstressed syllables as do with the 'headless' option (cf. 1165, 1168, 1169, 1178, 1189, 1191, 1192, 1194, 1199). On one occasion, line 1200, the line opens with a sequence of three unstressed syllables, probably the maximum the poet allows; as most usually, this is succeeded by a standard octosyllabic conclusion.

However, the opening syllabic sequence is not the only locus in the

---

[37] As fairly persistently in Middle English, it is difficult to decide whether this actually represents the abstract noun *richesse*, although the scribes often try to indicate that form explicitly through the spelling *richesce*. Frequent rhymes of the type *cald:hald* (here 1194–5) overtly depend upon suppression of *-ed*; on the other hand, the poet often sounds the inflectional syllable of the infinitive, e.g. *neghë* 1208.

line allowing sequences of unstressed syllables. Line 1195 is notable, and again, probably illustrative of the poet's maximum extent of variation—a full eleven syllables, with sequences of two and three unstressed syllables (although the poet might consider *vanite* metrically dissyllabic). But sequences of more than one unstressed syllable within the line occur with great frequency (cf. lines 1169, 1184 [? elided], 1187, 1188 [? elided], 1192, 1193, 1195, 1196, 1197, and two examples in 1198). And line 1195 is far from unique in tolerating a run of three unstressed syllables (and a line of ten or eleven total), as lines 1175 and 1194 will indicate.

Although various, such a metrical form is far from unusual in England. The poet simply adopts features conventional in the production of earlier Anglo-Norman 'octosyllabic verse'. Although this lacks English stress counting and syllable-weight alteration, it shows the same variety in its syllable counting, and routinely tolerates lines running up to eleven syllables.[38]

But the effective handling of verse involves a great deal more than simply metrical patterning, and the *PC* poet is a supple and more than competent workman. The very brief passage at the head of the sample, lines 1164–9, is fairly typical of his crafting of sense to verse presentation. Although it is a sequence of parallel statements, the poet introduces a good deal of (elegant) variation in the patterning of his grammatically parallel constructions. There are many felicities here, starting with tiny details like possible elisions in alternation with full forms ('And' in lines 1166 and 1168, but perhaps elided 'n' in line 1169); or 'headless' lines mixed with examples of extended anacrusis (line 1167 versus lines 1165 and 1168).

More striking is the relative emphasis upon verbs at the head (carefully enveloping the opening couplet), as opposed to the developing list of nominal epithets for 'world'. The latter forms are presented in various forms of syllabic alternation, sometimes qualified (and sometimes qualified multiply) by pointed adjectives. The full statement comes to rest in its plainest, and most mordant, detail, that 'the world is always with us'. One should not be surprised to learn, on reading further, that this conclusion to line 1169 is actually a 'false rest'.

---

[38] This feature has been noted since Vising, *Anglo-Norman Language and Literature*; see pp. 79–83 (with further early references; one should obviously ignore the emphasis on 'impropriety'). It is worth reopening the question of whether Chaucer did not create the English iambic (hen)decasyllable line as a carefully regularized version of such 'extended octosyllabic' verse, in conjunction with Continental models.

The series of nouns continues for eight additional lines, all with examples of metrical/syntactic variation. Here nouns predominate, but rather than the 'square form' of octosyllabic verse, the line a pair of elements, the continuation begins and ends (lines 1170 and 1177) with lines joining three members. And the length, or metrical weight, of items varies as well, not just expected 'square' disyllabic forms but equally *velany* 1172, *frawardnes* 1173, and *corrupcion* 1174. Whatever his insistence on 'needful knowledge', the poet of *PC* was attentive to offering a pleasing presentation as well.[39]

5. THE POET'S SOURCES

The Prick of Conscience advertises itself as a compilation of 'sere materes drawen / Of sere bukes' (lines 9542–3). Its status as a gathering of earlier sources appears most conspicuously, of course, in the poem's numerous Latin quotations. But the poet's borrowings are far more extensive than these quotations by themselves would indicate. The two early—and still the only comprehensive—studies of the sources by Reinhold Köhler and Arnold Hahn identified most of the poet's important Latin sources (although neither attempted any systematic identification of all the poet's Latin quotations from the Bible and elsewhere). But they also demonstrated that many portions of the poem's English text, too, are quite close translations (often without acknowledgement) of other works.

Any serious investigation of the poet's sources must begin with the important contributions of Köhler and Hahn. But these early researches were limited to Latin source-materials. Both Köhler and Hahn apparently took the poet at his word when he claims at the beginning of the poem that his is a compilation and translation of learned Latin materials for the use of those 'laude' readers unable to cope with Latin ('þat can na Latyn understand', line 339). This claim, however, is quite disingenuous. Indeed, the poet's single most

---

[39] For a further example of rather unobtrusive measured variation, one could compare the handling of the linking 'and of', which appears persistently over about a dozen lines. In line 1170, the stress (as most usually) falls on the preposition, but this is immediately juxtaposed with line 1171, with the much less usual stress on the conjunction. Comparisons with the poet's sources will indicate the active effort at artistic recasting of translated materials into verse. Here see Bartholomaeus Anglicus, *De proprietatibus rerum* 8.1, *in fine*; cf. Trevisa's Englishing, *On the Properties* i. 446/3 ff.

important source is an Anglo-Norman work, *Les Peines de Purgatorie* (probably composed, according to its editor, between 1230 and 1274). Hope E. Allen was the first to recognize that 'Parts of Book III . . . and much of Book IV . . . are founded on the treatise' and that each of Parts 5–7 of *PC* 'has taken (and immensely enlarged) something from the treatise'.[40] Robert Relihan's edition of the Anglo-Norman and Latin versions of *Les Peines* subsequently demonstrated that the Anglo-Norman version provides the source of the long quotation from 'Anselm' in *PC*'s lines 2424–57 (in Part 3); the discussion of the pains of purgatory in Part 4 (lines 2897–3273); the list of venial sins ascribed to Augustine in Part 4 (lines 3440–90); and the enumeration of the fourteen bodily and spiritual joys of heaven and their corresponding pains (ultimately derived from Anselm's *De Similitudinibus*) in Part 7. Relihan showed that our poet worked from the Anglo-Norman, not the Latin version, and that he used a copy related to a specific family of Anglo-Norman manuscripts.[41]

Our investigation largely confirms the views of Allen and Relihan. In addition to the passages discussed by Relihan, *Les Peines* is the source of four (and provides some details for a fifth) of the poet's fourteen pains of hell in Part 6 (lines 6547–7291), as well as of a number of shorter passages in Parts 3, 4, and 5 (lines 2384–423, 2637–42, 2651–73, 2722–5, 2750–83, 3300–8, 3512–59, 5404–21). In total, perhaps about 75 to 80 per cent of the material in *Les Peines* finds corresponding material in *PC* (and the Anglo-Norman author's prologue and the introductions to his chapters account for much of the matter omitted by the English author). This figure contrasts significantly with the poet's much more selective use of particular relevant sections from his other major sources. It seems clear, when one considers the similarity of subject matter and sequence of exposition of the two texts, that *Les Peines* most likely provided our poet with the basic core and inspiration for his work. As Relihan points out, the fundamental similarity of outline appears in the summary the *PC* poet provides of the contents of his treatise in lines 348–69 and the plan of the Anglo-Norman work as described in its prologue:

En ceste compileisoun donc a de primes par la grace de seynte Espirit vous moustroms por quei hom deit sovent penser de quer de sa fin, puis dirrom de la peine de purgatorie; aprés ceo nous toucherom les peynes par les

[40] Allen, *Writings Ascribed to Richard Rolle*, 378–9.   [41] *Les Peines*, 71–86.

queles l'alme est purgé; enaprés nus mustrom pur les queus peccez les almes
sount en purgatorie penez; e aprés nous dirrom certeyne et verreye resoun
pur quei vous devez enterement penser du grant Jour de Jugement, puis
aprés ceo nous dirrom de la grant peine de enfern; au drein nous tucherom
les glories ke les cors e les almes sauvez en averunt e les confusiouns ke les
dampnés averunt saunz fin; e aitant finerom nostre sermon de purgatorie.
(*Les Peines*, ll. 13–26)[42]

The poet of *PC* discusses the Last Things in exactly the same
eschatalogical order as *Les Peines*; as Relihan notes (*Les Peines*, 72),
this is not a particularly common sequence (the *Elucidarium* of
Honorius Augustodunensis, for instance, another of our poet's
sources, presents the pains of hell *before* discussion of the judgement).
The *PC* poet frequently translates the Anglo-Norman text closely,
and is often influenced in his choice of diction by the original.[43] Like
some of his other major sources, *Les Peines* provides a number of our
poet's biblical quotations, which he incorporates into his text in the
same context in which he finds them in the source. The Anglo-
Norman text also supplies one or two of the English poet's more
memorable images, such as the comparison of the superabundant joy
of heaven with a vessel submerged in water and unable to take on any
more liquid (lines 8040–9), or the thirsty in hell sucking the heads of
snakes as the infant sucks the breast of its mother (lines 6763–4).

The Anglo-Norman source, however, provided only a central core
of materials, which the English poet transformed through an
extensive process of *amplificatio* and by imposing his own *ordinatio*.
It will be clear from the outline of *Les Peines* set out in the prologue
quoted above, as well as from the relative length of the two works
(about six hundred lines of prose in Relihan's edition to *PC*'s more
than nine and a half thousand lines of verse), that the English poet
enormously expanded upon the outline provided by the Anglo-
Norman source. To the account of death, purgatory, judgement,

---

[42] 'In this compilation, first of all, by the grace of the Holy Spirit, we will show why a
man ought often to think in his heart about his end; next, we will tell about the pain of
purgatory; after that we will touch upon the pains through which the soul is purged;
afterwards we will show for which sins souls are punished in purgatory; and after we will
tell the certain and true cause why you ought to think thoroughly upon the Day of
Judgement; after this we will tell of the great pain of hell; finally, we will touch upon the
glories which the bodies and the souls of the saved will have and the discomfitures which
the damned will have without end; and with that we will conclude our sermon on
purgatory.'
[43] For example, line 2909, *PC* 'to ravisshe': *Les Peines* 'a ravyr'; line 7950, *PC* 'charged':
Les Peines 'chargés'.

hell, and heaven which he found in *Les Peines*, our poet added two further sections, his Parts 1 and 2 on the wretched life of mankind and on the world, the former largely based on Pope Innocent III's *De Miseria conditionis humanae* and the latter perhaps partially so.[44] He also amplified the original Anglo-Norman source throughout with a large volume of material from a variety of additional (almost exclusively Latin) sources.

The major Latin sources identified by Köhler and Hahn, those that provided materials in more than one book of the poem, are the *Compendium Theologicae veritatis* of Hugh Ripelin of Strasbourg, the *Elucidarium* of Honorius Augustodunensis, Humbert of Romans's *Tractatus de Abundantia exemplorum* (also known as the *Liber de dono timoris*), and Bartholomaeus Anglicus's *De Proprietatibus rerum*. Like Innocent's *De Miseria* (but unlike the Anglo-Norman source, *Les Peines*), the poet used these sources selectively. He borrows from only a few relevant sections of these compendious works, although he often translates from them closely and also frequently takes over their quotations from the Bible and elsewhere. Book 7 of the *Compendium* (together with one chapter from book 4 on the location of purgatory) provides the poet with much of his material on purgatory in Part 4. Together with Adso Dervensis's *De ortu et tempore Antichristi*, this work also supplies the life of Antichrist in Part 5. Two brief passages in Part 7 also derive from the *Compendium* (lines 7780–801 and 8632–43). The *Elucidarium* provides the poet with materials for nine of his fourteen pains of hell in Part 6 and portions of the discussion of heaven in Part 7 (lines 8922–77, 9020–47). It was perhaps also the source of a few further brief passages (see 4328–9, 4609–10, 4895–8, 6017–74nn). The *Tractatus de Abundantia exemplorum* provided the poet with several of his lists: the four reasons why death is to be feared in Part 3 (lines 1818–2598); and, in Part 5, the reasons why the Last Judgement will take place in the Vale of Josephat and the appearance of Christ at the judgement (lines 5181–226, 5279–367); the fifteen accusers at the judgement (lines 5422–611); and the list of things for which account must be rendered at the judgement (lines 5858–959). The poet again used this source selectively, ignoring the text's numerous exempla but, at least in the passages he borrowed in Part 5, pillaging it for its biblical and patristic quotations. His use of Bartholomew's *De*

---

[44] The poet quotes from *De Miseria* directly in Part 2, lines 1506–9. A further brief passage in Part 5, lines 5368–401, is also derived from *De Miseria*.

Proprietatibus was more selective still: this enormous work provided the poet with just two relatively small pieces, his descriptions of the world and the heavens at the openings of Parts 2 and 7 respectively.[45]

As well as vastly amplifying the text with such materials, the *PC* poet also imposed his own *ordinatio* by rationalizing the chapter divisions of the Anglo-Norman text which provided him with his original core. In *Les Peines*, chapter 1 deals with death but also includes some discussion of purgatory, while chapters 2 and 3 discuss respectively the pains of purgatory and the sins for which souls are sent there. Chapter 4 covers the judgement and the pains of hell, while chapters 5 and 6 discuss, respectively, the bodily and the spiritual joys of heaven and their corresponding pains. The English poet clarifies the structure of his text (and thus facilitates, perhaps, readier consultation of individual sections) by dividing into separate parts his discussions of death, purgatory, judgement, hell, and heaven. He also rearranged the sequence of the pains of purgatory as outlined in the Anglo-Norman text, and revised the list of sins and corresponding diseases which forms his fourth pain of purgatory (lines 2982–3001) so that they form a complete seven-sin scheme (*Les Peines* omits gluttony).

The commonplace nature of much of the poet's subject matter makes the definitive identification of further sources difficult, although one may point to a number of broad analogues. The description of heaven in lines 7810–21 and 8646–737, for instance, finds a parallel in book 4 of Hugh of St Victor's *De Anima*. Some version of the materials of the popular *Gospel of Nicodemus* was evidently known to the poet (see lines 6525–42).[46] *PC*'s discussions of purgatory and hell share generic similarities with other-world visions such as the *Visio Sancti Pauli*, *The Vision of Tundale*, and the vision of Fursa related by Bede and in *Les Manuel des Pechiez*, although perhaps closest to *PC*'s treatment is the contemporary Northern

---

[45] The poet's account of the cosmos in these sections, and in the discussion of the location of hell at the beginning of Part 6, was supplemented by additional materials obtained from Moses Maimonides's *Guide for the Perplexed* and from *Sydrac*, an Old French prose compendium of knowledge written in the late 13th c. and cast in the form of a dialogue between the divinely inspired wise man Sidrac and the heathen king Boctus.

[46] Four *PC* manuscripts, BL MS Cotton Galba E.ix, BL MS Harley 4196, BL MS Additional 32578 and Sion College, MS Arch. L.40.2/E.25, also contain an English stanzaic version of this text (see *Harrowing*). The *Gospel of Nicodemus* was also the source, in later 14th-c. Yorkshire, for the Harrowing of Hell in the York Cycle.

English poem *The Gast of Gy*, found together with a copy of *PC* in Oxford, Bodleian Library, MS Rawlinson poet. 175. The poet's discussion of death in Part 3 finds parallels in both the *Legenda Aurea* and the pseudo-Augustinian *Speculum peccatoris* (see 2242–97n).[47] The poem of course has broad generic similarities with a number of *contemptus mundi* themed works like *Speculum peccatoris*, including Richard Rolle's *Expositio super novem lectiones mortuorum*, a commentary on the nine lections (from the book of Job) of the Office of the Dead. The Office of the Dead, to which we return below, forms an important source for our poet, and the generic similarities between *PC* and Rolle's *Super novem lectiones* perhaps make the poem's frequent attribution to Rolle more explicable.[48]

The ultimate sources of much of the poem's material must, then, remain uncertain, despite our poet's fondness for citing the works of named 'authorities', including (pseudo-) Bernard's *Meditationes piissimae de cognitione humanae conditionis*, Jerome's commentary on Joel, Gregory's *Moralia in Job*, and various works of Augustine including *Enarrationes in psalmos*, *De civitate Dei*, and *De disciplina Christiana*. Many of these quotations in fact likely derive from intermediate sources, including florilegia or handbooks as yet unidentified. As already noted, the *PC* poet frequently borrows authoritative citations from his main sources, and several of his quotations from patristic sources appear in forms which seem to have been current in handbooks such as Thomas of Ireland's *Manipulus florum* and *Speculum Christiani*.

Like his patristic quotations, the poet's quotations from the Bible frequently take the form of sequences of citations derived from the major sources already discussed. As with the biblical quotations in *Piers Plowman*, so with our earlier poet: as John Alford puts it, 'The quotations do not come into the poem naked but as liveried servants', drawing the various contexts in which they appear in intermediate sources in their wake.[49] Indeed, the clearest indication of the poet's

---

[47] An English version of *Speculum peccatoris* is edited by Horstmann from Oxford, University College MS 97 in *Yorkshire Writers*, ii. 436–40: for other copies see *Index of Printed Middle English Prose* 213, Jolliffe F. 8.

[48] Rolle possibly also translated an exemplum from one of our poet's major Latin sources, Humbert of Romans's *De Abundantia exemplorum* (edited in *Uncollected Prose and Verse*, 15, no. 6). The exemplum appears, together with an exemplum form of Bede's account of Fursa, in BodL, MS Ashmole 751; see Hanna, *The English Manuscripts of Richard Rolle*, 125–7.

[49] Alford, *Piers Plowman: A Guide*, 16.

use of intermediate sources for many of his biblical quotations comes from his striking habit of incorporating contextual material from his sources into his Latin quotations as if part of the original biblical passage (see, for instance, lines 3164–7, 4057–60, 4171–6, 5494–5, 5682–3). In one case, the poet fails to identify correctly the Bible passage quoted in his source, and presents non-biblical text from this intermediate source as if it were a quotation from the book of Daniel (see 4231–41n).

Where the *PC* poet appears to be supplying his own biblical quotations, it seems likely that he was working from a Bible with commentary. In lines 6595–8, for instance, he incorporates what is evidently a gloss (introduced by the tell-tale phrase, 'id est') into his quotation from Deuteronomy. It seems probable that the poet knew at least the book of Revelation in one of its commentated versions. His moralized description of the architecture of the city of heaven in lines 9048–190 echoes the generic conventions of Apocalypse commentaries such as the *Bible Moralisée*, the *Glossa Ordinaria*, and the popular commentary by Berengaud, although the poet's individual details do not appear to be derived directly from any single such version. Books of the Apocalypse accompanied by commentary (either extracts from Berengaud or an anonymous French prose commentary) and lavish illustration enjoyed considerable popularity in the period between *c*.1250 and 1350. Twenty-seven of these illustrated Apocalypses survive from the fourteenth century, and the poem's description of the architecture of heaven may have been inspired by the pictoral representations such books contained as much as by the text of the Bible itself.[50]

A number of *PC*'s biblical quotations come from one further important source, the Office of the Dead. About half the poet's quotations from the book of Job (those in lines 414–15, 532–3, 710–11, 760–1, 5095–8, 5494–5, 5722, 6819–20, and 6825–6) form part of the nine lections of the Office of the Dead, and the poet quotes various responses from the same Office in lines 2833, 5086–8, 7245–6, and 9128–9. The Office of the Dead may also have influenced the poet's memorable description of the Day of Judgement in lines 6096–113. The various citations from this Office seem particularly apt, not only given the poem's penitential emphasis on inspiring humble dread, but also because of the poet's stress in Part 4 on the efficacy of suffrages for the dead. The poet's use of the Office of the Dead reflects the popularity of the Office as a lay devotion in the later Middle Ages; correspondingly, the many citations from this Office in the poem perhaps in part explain the popularity of *The Prick of Conscience* itself.[51]

In addition to biblical and liturgical sources and the various compendia of theological and scientific knowledge already mentioned, one may point to the poet's use of materials from canon law. During his discussion of purgatory in Part 4, the poet names as authorities on pardons 'Raymund' (of Peñaforte), 'Innocent' (IV), and Hostiensis (see lines 3940–51). Again, however, it seems likely that he knew the works of these authors through some intermediate source, such as William of Pagula's popular *Summa summarum*. Pagula cites all three of the authors mentioned by our poet in his discussion of the efficacy of pardons for those in purgatory, and his *Summa* contains a list of remedies for venial sins that is closer to the version in *PC* lines 3398–411 than those of either Raymund or Hostiensis.

A further intermediate source remains mysterious: we have identified no book 'of sere questyons of divinite' called 'Flos scientie', cited by the poet as his source in line 7202. The ultimate source at this point of the poem is the *Elucidarium*, but it remains possible that the poet found the relevant material in a compilation of the kind his comments here imply. Indeed, the poet's combination of materials throughout the poem may owe something to pre-existing manuscript compilations. In *PC*'s Part 5, for instance, the poet's life of Antichrist, based on Adso Dervensis's *vita*, is followed by an account of the Fifteen Signs before Doomsday (extant in several different versions in the Middle Ages). Adso does not himself discuss the fifteen signs, but in several manuscripts his text is copied with one version or another of the fifteen signs, and it seems quite likely that our poet encountered both sources already combined for his use.[52] Similarly, it appears possible that the poet's combination of an account of death,

---

[51] The Office of the Dead formed a regular part of the immensely popular Books of Hours, described by Wieck as '*the* medieval bestseller' (*Time Sanctified*, 27); of the Latin Sarum-use Books of Hours which survive in the Bodleian Library, all but four include the Office (cf. the descriptions in Van Dijk, *Handlist*). The presence of the Office in Books of Hours implies that lay people regularly recited it privately. For the form of the Office of the Dead, which is the same text in lay Books of Hours as in the Breviary, see Harper, *Forms and Orders*, 105–8.

[52] Thompson, *The* Cursor Mundi, 169 n. 100.

purgatory, judgement, hell, and heaven derived from *Les Peines*, prefaced by an account of the wretchedness of man's bodily life borrowed from Innocent's *De Miseria*, might have been influenced by the manuscript in which he found his major Anglo-Norman source. In several of the manuscripts of the Latin version of *Les Peines*, the text appears together with a copy of Innocent's treatise.[53]

Finally, we must consider briefly an English work that has been proposed as a source for *PC*, the earlier northern English religious compilation *Cursor Mundi*. *PC* shares with *Cursor* (as with other works of the genre, including the later *Speculum Vitae*) a prologue which positions the work in opposition to writings about 'vanytese' (in *Cursor* a specific catalogue of popular romances). Morris, who edited *Cursor* as well as *PC*, believed that several passages of *Cursor* (which he printed in parallel with his text) were direct sources of corresponding discussions of *PC*. We find the evidence for such dependence doubtful. The two poets certainly share a number of themes, and clearly drew on some very similar sources. Among the topics treated by both poems are the conditions of old age, the life of Antichrist, the fifteen signs before doomsday, the account of the harrowing of hell provided by the sons of Simeon in the apocryphal *Gospel of Nicodemus*, and the pains of hell. In most of these cases, however, the *PC* poet has drawn on different versions of the material used by the poet of *Cursor*. Both poets, for instance, include a life of Antichrist based on the account by Adso, but each poet used a distinct textual version of Adso's account, which means their treatments, while superficially similar, differ in numerous details. Thus while the parallels between the two texts are striking, and they occasionally share similar phraseology (see, for instance, 766–99n), we find little conclusive evidence that the *PC* poet drew directly on the earlier English work, except perhaps in the prologue. Nevertheless, the two poets clearly compiled their works from very similar sources, and, in their accounts of the last days, along very similar lines, and it seems impossible that our poet composed in ignorance of the earlier text.[54] We have therefore cited the parallel

---

[53] See *Les Peines*, 104–14, for the Latin manuscripts. The relevant manuscripts are: Oxford, Corpus Christi College, MS 155; London, Lambeth Palace Library, MS 500; BL, MS Additional 33957.

[54] Although, as Thompson shows (*The* Cursor Mundi, 169), *PC* and *Cursor* are not the only texts which share a very similar combination of sources in their accounts of the Last Days: 'There were many other vernacular writers who knew of the Fifteen Signs Legend and incorporated some version of it in their adaptations of either Adso's account of the Antichrist or the textually-related *Elucidarium* treatment of Doomsday.'

passages from *Cursor* where appropriate as illustrative of the tradition of Northern instructional literature in which the *PC* poet was working. We have supplied these together with some analogous passages from the later *Speculum Vitae*, a work which in turn drew on both *Cursor* and *PC*.

6. THE AIMS AND PRESENTATION OF THIS EDITION

The edition below is predicated upon, although it does not reproduce exactly, Morris's. Our reproduction extends to retention of Morris's normalization of his text, where *u* and *v* have been adjusted to confirm to modern usage (although we have removed Morris's analogous, yet sporadic, adjustment of *i* and *j*). We also, even though we have eliminated three Latin passages and inserted an additional fifteen lines overlooked by our predecessor, retain his line numeration, in the main; to adjust it (or to offer a double lineation) would create unnecessary difficulties in referring to past studies. (Our text, including the Latin, as Morris lineated it, usually following the line divisions of **G**, contains the actual 9626 lines usually transmitted in manuscript, not Morris's 9621.)[55]

At the same time, we have not hesitated to correct what Morris printed, to bring this into accord with what he should have reproduced as the text of **G/H**. Morris's printed text includes a large number of substantive errors in reporting the readings of his base manuscripts; a great many, but only a small minority, of these instances were reported by Lightbown long ago, and we cite his discoveries, as relevant, in our collations, where all these substantive errors are recorded.

In addition to substantive errors, we have silently adjusted a greater number of small mistranscriptions. These tend to represent repeated problems, and the 1863 print includes substantial numbers of misrepresentations of presence/absence of *-e*, *es/is/ys*, *-er-/-ir-*, *f/v*, etc. It is unclear whether these forms were produced by Morris's

---

[55] Although numbered to line 9624, Morris's lineation skipped four lines at line 6060 (mislineated 6064), he omitted line 6094, and he made four subsequent (and ultimately self-cancelling) mislineations. Following Britton (317), we have eliminated the Latin at Morris's 1146–51, 6631–2, and 6791–2; in addition, we have restored line 6094, and supplied fourteen lines missing from Morris's edition following 7505 (numbered lines 7505a–n). See further the textual commentary on each of these lections. From line 6060, Morris's lineation is then either three or four ahead of ours.

amaneunsis, by the Berlin typesetters, or by some combination of the two. It is clear, however, that, if proofread against the original manuscripts, corrections were not incorporated in the text as printed. (Had they been, it is hard to imagine missing such a glitch, scarcely without parallel elsewhere, as the reversal of lines 279 and 280 in the published version.) We imagine that Morris trusted both his transcriber and his typesetters and gave the whole only a scan-over sort of reading (the source of a list of errata following the edition at 328) and attended only to immediately visible and clear anomalies.[56]

Reading Morris's text against G and H throws up other oddments, however. To a degree that is not evident from the edition as printed, Morris had fairly frequently emended the manuscripts without, as he sometimes did, offering any indication to his readers that this was the case. Many of these intrusions and excisions are thoroughly anodyne and well taken, as, for example, Morris's silent removal from the heads of lines 2505 and 2993 of G's repetition of the rhyme-word from the previous line. Our text and collations, however, make explicit what Morris apparently felt required no notice; on all such occasions, we mark the text we present and provide notice of G's reading in the collations.

Somewhat surprisingly, given that one goal of the edition was to publicize the language of an extensive, and at the time unparalleled, vernacular text (see n. 5 above), a number of such emendations seems to have been undertaken on linguistic grounds. Morris, it would appear, had a distaste for unusual, if not unsightly, spellings and sought to impose upon his text a certain uniformity of forms (in the event, inconsistently). Overt examples of the tendency appear early on, in the elimination of *is* 'his' 1494 and of *strengh* 'strength' 692 and 702. A century and a half's further linguistic study (and perhaps principally *LALME*'s immense data set) now reveals this pioneering effort as unduly fussy. Hence, we have not hesitated to restore manuscript spellings Morris removed, often silently—and removed even after he should have recognized that they were repeated and thus integral to some Northern *Schriftsprache*, for example *Turgh* 2345,

---

[56] We express our scepticism about Morris's claim that 'the proof sheets in every case hav[e] been read *twice* with the Manuscript' (p. xxxiii, the author's italics). Perhaps the task was delegated, and Morris assumed his instructions had been fulfilled. Cf. further 2172, where the printed text omits a word present in G, and Morris's textual commentary argues that this is an error and suggests inserting the word that actually stands in the manuscript.

Turght 3471, and *thugh* 4350 and 5598. Although such restorations of **GH** forms are scarcely substantive, we again indicate them in our collations.

We have rejected *in toto* only one part of Morris's editorial effort with the poem, his word-division and punctuation. The former is a good deal too dependent on the forms of **G**, and we have simply followed modern usage. Morris's punctuation is unduly heavy by modern standards, and, in its profusion, frequently misleading as to the sense. In Morris's defence, it must be pointed out that the poem frequently rebuffs modern pointing altogether. We have adopted our own punctuation, as seems most fitting, and, in addition to pointing sentences, have replaced Morris's large textual blocks, inherited from **GH**, with modern paragraphing. In this latter procedure, although we have not slavishly followed it, we have frequently been guided by the decisions taken by the scribe of **A**.

Our major editorial contribution exceeds any treatment of the text Morris considered. He was committed to producing a reading text, to offering some entrée into an extensive and important poem. While we join him in this motive through reprinting his work, we pursue an additional interest as well, to consider the value of those readings Morris printed, following **G/H**, in the context of the early Northern promulgation of *The Prick of Conscience*. As a result, we have, considerably more systematically than did Morris, consulted additional copies. And on the basis of the readings these provide, we intervene in the text in many instances to correct errors in **G** which Morris printed.

Our motivation in this activity is not to upstage Morris, whose primary interest, as we have indicated, was to insure that the text was sensible and comprehensible.[57] Rather, we align ourselves with that first generation of students who were inspired by Morris's work, principally Percy Andreae and Karl D. Bülbring. Following Morris's sporadic consultation and citation of British Museum manuscripts, these scholars sought to ascertain the relation of this limited, yet textually diverse, sample of the tradition to the text Morris had provided. Broadly speaking, they affirmed the value of Morris's text as a representative of the best group of Northern copies of *PC*

---

[57] Cf. 'Valuable as is the language of Hampole to the student of our early literature, the matter will be found to be almost as interesting' (p. xxx). By 'matter', Morris has in mind 'curious' medieval beliefs (which include, for a presumed Anglican reader, Purgatory) and glimpses of social history—fairly stock interests of Victorian medieval studies.

(Andreae's 'Z', in Lewis–McIntosh's formulation 'Type I'). And they demonstrated that all versions of *PC*, of whatever type, had descended from this group of copies.

Since these early studies, significant advances in discussing the text have been limited. Pre-eminent here are Lewis–McIntosh's capsule descriptions of the manuscripts, a study filled with valuable information concerning the dialectical profusion of the text types represented by the numerous manuscripts of the poem. The authors make no effort to edit the poem, but their collation of a sequence of scattered sample passages clarifies a great many features of the general transmission. Ultimately, however, whatever their great contribution to understanding the transmission at large, they offer little instruction, beyond what Andreae and Bülbring had already done, into how a text might be constructed, or how exactly the manuscripts might ultimately be related.

The most salient, although very brief, contribution to this discussion remains Derek Britton's impressive and suggestive article. Relying upon a single sample passage for extensive collation and limiting his study to Northern copies (which include a range of genetic forms of the text, not simply 'Z'/'Type I'), Britton offered a tentative *stemma*, a diagramatic indication of the descent of the text (p. 329). The upper reaches of this diagram may be reproduced as:

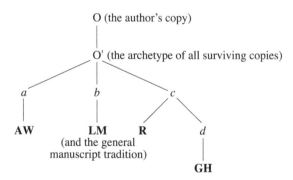

In Britton's account, *PC* descends from three early copies, *a*, *b*, and *c*, each an independent rendition of whatever the author promulgated. These can be identified, and, at least theoretically, their readings reconstructed by the agreement of the seven specific copies indicated above, all among those traditionally identified as

'Z'/'Type I'. Insofar as they address the issue, Lewis–McIntosh confirm Britton's identification of these groups.[58] In addition, since Britton's stemma depends on a relatively late passage (where that manuscript has changed exemplars), he placed **S** very low on his stemma. But spot collations have indicated that, up to line 2850, where, as Lewis–McIntosh indicate, **S** ceases to report 'Z' readings, **S** potentially reports a text more directly derived from *b* than either of **LM**. In contrast, because **H** is **G**'s doublet, derived from the exactly the same copy, and in the same page format, its readings do not need to be considered. One can then reformulate Britton's diagram of the text's descent as:

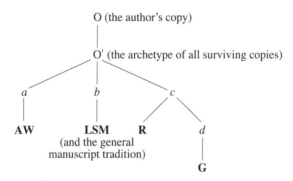

Britton's diagram provides a basic stemmatic logic for investigating the early authorial descent of *The Prick of Conscience*, and thus providing an improved, corrected version of Morris's text. (In Britton's account, although a very good copy, **G**, and with it **H**, proves actually that early copy most distanced from authorial materials, the product of at least three generations of copying, as opposed to the two generations represented by the other six manuscripts.) On the basis of his selective collations, Britton demonstrates the unusual situation (cf. Fourquet, 'Fautes communes'), a trifid textual descent, in which the agreement of any two of the three archetypes (*ab*, *ac*, *bc*) might be presumed to identify the reading of O′.

One can specify the theoretical procedures involved a bit more thoroughly. Wherever *a* agrees in a reading with **G**, one can presume that **R** errs and misrepresents *c*. But similarly, where *a* agrees with **R**, **G** errs (inferentially, in many cases in agreement with its unexamined

---

[58] For **AW**, see 78 and 129; for **GHR**, see 59, 67, and 116.

twin **H**). These erroneous readings represent either mistakes unique to **G** or to *d*, the archetype below, but like **R**, derived from *c*. The readings confirmed by agreements of *a***R** or *a***G** should, but need not necessarily, be confirmed by copies in the *b* tradition.

But equally, readings of *a*, even if unsupported by any of *c*, are potentially authorial. These are particularly likely to be correct against *c* on those occasions when they also are attested in *b* copies. However, outside the *ac* copies, even in quite proximate examples like **LSM**, one can see signs of rather immediate textual degeneration. Readings which appear only in *b*-derived copies, no matter what the profusion of their witness, are extremely unlikely to represent the authorial version. Their combined witness is outweighed by evidence from the two other stemmatic branches, *a* and *c*. On the other hand, they are far from unimportant; especially in cases of profuse witness, they represent the *vulgata* or the 'public form' of the poem, what was widely appreciated in the later Middle Ages as *The Prick of Conscience*. For one intriguing aspect of Britton's stemma concerns the isolation of his *ac* copies. They have no descendants, and would appear to represent 'private' versions, relatively close to the author, but of quite local diffusion.

Our researches depend upon a more extensive (even if still substantially reduced) variant corpus than any published account. We draw our sample for investigating the descent of the poem from an investigation of all variation in **AWRG** (and the parallels to these in **LSM**) over the first fifth of the poem, to line 1850. (In specifically noted instances below, we extend the inquiry further.) This sample is useful, first, because protracted study indicates to us that, as the number of textual notes indicates, the poem's opening is considerably more difficult reading than later portions. In addition, the scribes found this to be the case, and variation among **ARG/H** in the second half of the poem is negligible. (Indeed, over the concluding thousand lines, Morris's amanuensis arguably made more errors in reproducing **G/H** than any of these copies did in reproducing O′ materials.) The first fifth of the poem finds variation at its most profuse, and provides an adequate sample for assessing the early transmission of *PC*.

Our study verifies Britton's suggestions (and thereby the usefulness of his proposed *stemma codicum*). That is, ample evidence of agreement in error attests to the existence of Britton's three descendant archetypes *a*, *b*, and *c*. Most profusely attested are unique agreements in error of **LSM**; these provide unequivocal evidence for *b* and are extremely frequent. They occur twelve times (one every forty or so lines) in *PC* 1–500.[59]

Secondary evidence for *b* is more profuse still. Agreement in error of all three of **LSM** provides unequivocal testimony to the common exemplar, but, in stemmatic terms, agreement in error of any two of the three copies (i.e. the variant groups **LS**, **LM**, or **SM**) *may* indicate descent from the common archetype *b*. (On such occasions, one assumes that the erring pair provides the reading of *b* while the odd manuscript either preserves a correct reading or varies independently.) Such agreements occur extremely frequently; in the first five hundred lines **LS** is testified ten times (two examples per hundred lines), **LM** 26 times (five/100), and **SM** 45 times (nine/100), in total about one variant for every six lines of the text.[60]

However, the evidence of two *b* manuscripts agreeing in error seems to us susceptible to alternative explanations. The three copies show rather skewed propensities to err, as evidenced by those instances when each provides an unsupported erroneous reading. In **L**, such behaviour occurs very frequently, about forty unique errors for every hundred lines. **M** is somewhat more accurate, with about thirty-two unsupported errors per hundred lines, while **S** is comparatively conservative, usually agreeing with *ac* and erring independently perhaps once every ten lines or so.

Britton's *stemma* identifies **L** as the most trustworthy copy in this branch of the tradition. But plainly, the manuscript is not entirely satisfactory in this regard (a fact Britton may signal by placing it on a branch off the main line of transmission?). The scribe Wilfrid is capable of considerable accuracy, and there is a number of ten- to dozen-line segments of his copying that show no variation from the *ac* copies. But among that rich variety of his engagements with the text that we have discussed elsewhere, Wilfrid is capable of manifold intrusive acts of redaction, both minimal rewordings and larger disruptions. The scribe simply responds to the text before him on an individual—and frequently intelligent, if unfaithful—basis.

---

[59] These are the readings provided in Appendix 2 at lines 12, 25, 106, 138, 217, 235, 340, 361, 410, 416, 420, and 467. In addition, the agreements of W*b* at 56 and 467 and of G*b* at 325 may provide attenuated evidence for the group.

[60] For the evidence, see Appendix 2 extensively, as well as a few examples in the main collation: 186 **LM**, 220 **SM**, 234 **LM**, 250, 263, and 333 all **SM**, 470 **LM**. We include in these figures, on occasions when **M** is missing owing to damage (here lines 1–72), readings of **As**. Lewis–McIntosh identify this book as a close relative of **M** (see 38, 94), and our independent investigations confirm that it may stand in for that manuscript.

On the other hand, one should be struck by the unusually accurate behaviour of **S** (and lament that this book's producers apparently chose to represent most of *PC* from inferior, non-'Z' materials).[61] Indeed, **S**'s individual deviations are so infrequent that the scribe's archetypal affiliations down to line 2850 stand out clearly. That is, quite in contrast to either **L** or **M**, **S**'s agreements in error with other books, in this case with **M**, are statistically as strong as the book's propensity to err independently (both about 45 examples in lines 1–500). This showing implies that **SM** actually form a genetic group, constructed subsequent to *b* from the two books' derivation from the same materials. This exemplar, as Britton implies, was apparently more advanced in error than that available to **L**.

This view has a further corollary. Given the relatively high frequency of independent errors in **L** and **M**, the relatively frequent agreement **LM** most likely represents random coincidence. In the light of the trivial nature of errors everywhere in the tradition, **L** and **M** have, in the same context, either hit upon the same relatively commonplace substitutions, or have inherited such coincidental readings circumambient within the *b* tradition.

Evidence for the two other archetypes Britton proposed, while nowhere nearly so strong as that for *b*, is also compelling. Here, given the relative paucity of the evidence, we extend our survey to include all recorded variation in roughly the first third of the poem (to line 3500). **R** varies in isolation quite infrequently, about once every fifty to sixty lines. On that basis, the twenty-one erroneous readings shared with **G** before line 3500 are significant and testify to Britton's *c*; to these may be added an additional seven occasions when **RG** agree in the presence of a single further copy.[62] All told, the two copies **RG** agree in error about once every 125 lines of text, which, given the paucity of their agreements in error, forms a significant showing.[63]

Analysis of the variants reveals evidence for *a* of about the same

---

[61] Indeed, given that the text was copied by a succession of scribes, multiple exemplars may have been necessary in the conditions under which it was reproduced. The scribes may have worked simultaneously on different segments of text, the complete copy arranged after all had concluded their stints, perhaps necessarily using at least two different manuscripts as exemplars.

[62] The agreements occur at 147, 232, 250, 263, 350, 865, 1146–51, 1196, 1448, 1565, 1575, 1677, 2378, 2388, 2444, 2576, 2794, 2891, 2911, 3148, and 3350. More attenuated examples include 1655 W*c*, 2286 M*c*, 2372 W*c*, and 2768, 2771, 2848, 3476 all L*c*.

[63] **G**'s independent errors, all marked in the text, combine readings shared with **H**, that is errors derived from Britton's subarchetype d, as well as a very great deal of context-influenced sloppiness, undue attraction to surrounding copy, in the production of **G** itself.

strength, although perhaps greater persuasiveness, as that for c. **A** is an unusually accurate copy, and it errs independently only once every forty or fifty text-lines. In that context, seventeen erroneous readings shared with **W**, about one every 160–70 lines, have considerable weight. To these may be added a further dozen occasions when **AW** agree in error with one or another isolated copy.[64] Something like 20–25 per cent of **A**'s total variant corpus is shared with **W**, and especially in the context of some distinctive readings (like that at 853) and **A**'s unparallelled accuracy with the text, this is a compelling showing of derivation from a common source, Britton's a.

However, accuracy is not a description easily associated with **W**. Indeed, on the basis of its independent errors, this copy is the least faithful representation of ac; the scribe generates errors (not including his decision to suppress all the poem's Latin from about line 1550) at a rate comparable to **S**, about once every eleven or twelve lines. As a sample of this independent behaviour, our collation reports **W** in full for the first five hundred lines, and Appendix 1 presents all its variants unsupported in those six manuscripts we regularly cite down to line 1873.[65]

However, independent errors do not reveal the full extent of this scribe's vagaries. A full collation of **W** to line 2850, where **S** ceases to offer relevant evidence (the last thousand lines of this sample not reproduced here) shows that **W** frequently agrees with manuscripts securely derived from Britton's archetype b—with all three copies **LSM** on nineteen occasions. It also agrees with individual members of b at a much greater rate: **WL** appears 50 times (about once every 46 lines, given the omissions of the two copies), **WM** 27 times (about once every hundred lines), **WS** 13 times. To these examples, one may add the following agreements of three texts, **W** sharing the same error as two b copies: seventeen agreements of **WSM**, fifteen of **WLM**, four of **WLS**.[66] This evidence quite overwhelms that for **W**'s affiliation with **A** as a.

---

[64] These errors appear at 8, 137, 433, 437, 853, 874, 917, 1029, 1137, 1571, 1834, 2984, 2991, 3011, 3090, 3162, and 3439. For more attenuated evidence, cf. examples of La at 1123, 1761, 3026, 3058, and 3441; Sa at 263, 1580; Ma at 316, 1713, 2461, 3334 (As), 3348 (As).

[65] Given **W**'s omissions, this is about 1,600 lines in all. Our main collations report all **W**'s agreements in error with the remainder of ac, and with b manuscripts' readings for those lections.

[66] For the evidence we print, see the collations: for Wb agreements, 56, 467, 865, 900, 961, 1125, 1629, 1836; for **WL**, see 14, 228, 243, 314, 340, 400, 405, 428, 766, 772, 800, 803, 916, 938, 940, 1077, 1092, 1162, 1191, 1284, 1323, 1568, 1624, 1626, 1651, 1732, 1775,

We account for this behaviour by suggesting that **W** represents a conflated text, one produced by consultation of multiple, here unrelated, copies. Given that **W** represents A's closest textual affiliate, the scribe of **W** must have used as a basic source a manuscript resembling **A** (and thus providing testimony to *a*). However, in addition to a certain sloppiness in reproducing this exemplar, the scribe sought a second source for readings. This appears, from the evidence at our disposal, to have certainly been a *b* manuscript, perhaps one with fairly close relations to the exemplar Wilfrid used (and frequently chose not to represent accurately) in producing **L**.

These discoveries allow us to present a slightly revised version of Britton's diagramme of the textual transmission of *The Prick of Conscience*:

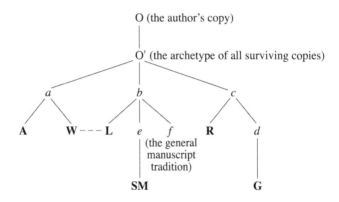

O (the author's copy)

O' (the archetype of all surviving copies)

a   *b*   *c*

A   **W** - - - **L**   *e*   *f*   **R**   *d*

(the general manuscript tradition)

SM   **G**

This revision recognizes our discovery of the partial independence of **SM** and of **W**'s sporadic reliance upon a second copy, in addition to his *a* materials. However, these revisions only 'fine tune' the history of the text, and they primarily ratify Britton's views, as well as, it must be insisted, the inherent prescriptions Britton provided for editing the text.

Our revision of Morris's work attempts to create a text useful for judging the deviations involved in the transmission, both that of advanced 'Z' copies and non-'Z' versions of *PC*. We strive to provide

1781, 1799, 1855, and 1872; for **WM**, 366, 374, 435, 552, 570, 627, 717, 736, 787, 816, 897, 902, 1064, 1101, 1114, 1348, 1699, 1778, 1780, 1849, and 1863; for **WS**, 40, 865, 1365, 1671, 1685, and 1747. For evidence on three-text agreements, see, for **WSM**, 6, 597, 612, 991, 1066, 1075, 1169, 1339, and 1727; for **WLM**, 379, 470, 728, 908, 922, 1573, 1602, 1612, 1628; for **WLS**, 1855.

a stable basis from which further research might proceed. In this context, we use Britton's *stemma codicum* to correct **G** and to produce the form of O′, the last common ancestor of all surviving copies of the poem.

We began this work by producing a complete collation of our seven witnesses for *The Prick of Conscience*, lines 1–500. This initial textual endeavour provided a sufficient demonstration of the advanced nature of transmission in the genetic family *b*. Variation here is profuse and, generally speaking, in the absence of *b*-manuscript agreement in variation with members of either *a* or *c*, of no evidentiary value in constructing O′. While we believe this form of the text extremely important in assessing the general 'public' transmission of *PC*, we ultimately decided to leave this as a task for others to pursue. In Appendix 2, we present the variational evidence for all *b* copies to line 500. After that point, we have only 'spot-collated' these books; we consult them, and record their evidence in our collations, for all readings involving variation among **A**, **R**, and **G**.

As the last sentence implies, we have finally decided to eschew complete collation of **W** as well. Already in the first five hundred lines, the nature of **W**'s text was clear. While already showing provocative agreements with **A**, the manuscript includes a very large number of independent errors (comparable to the most faithful *b*-copy, **S**) and a persistent swathe of agreements with one or more *b* manuscripts. As we have indicated, we have collated **W** fully, down to line 2850, where **S** changes affiliations, and have compared its readings against all of **L**, **S**, and **M**, largely in the hope that some clarity about its relations to the *b* tradition might emerge.[67]

---

[67] To these considerations, we add one further caveat. Britton's identification of *b* is largely determined retrospectively, reading backward from attested manuscript readings (and thus, the distinctive profusion of variation we briefly chronicle in Appendix 2). However, this showing does *not* demonstrate that, in origin, *b* is actually independent of either *a* or *c*. Our investigation of this issue, over the full extent of the poem, has proved inconclusive. We find no compelling evidence that *b* has been derived exclusively from either *a* or *c*; *ab* appears seven times in our full collation and—to discount possible conflation A*b* on six further occasions—*cb* fifteen times. But this may only indicate that *b* itself was an originally eclectic combination of the two. There is somewhat stronger evidence for derivation from individual copies: R*b* occurs thirteen times, and *a*M at least twenty (as well as at least fifteen examples of A**S**, i.e. given the brevity of **S** readings here surveyed, something like fifty examples might be expected), had **S** the full 'Type I' text). The latter at least implies that **SM** may well have been derived, at least in part, from *a* materials, a process perhaps analogous to the production of **W**. Correspondingly, evidence of such derivation of *b* from one of *ac* may be obscured in **L** by Wilfrid's independence in rendering the text.

Most of this evidence we have chosen to suppress here. Our collations report **W** in full to line 500. After that point, we present its readings only selectively. The main collations record, down to line 1873, all those cases where **W** agrees with any of the six other manuscripts collated, and its unique errors appear in Appendix 1. After line 1873, we have treated **W** as we do the three *b* copies and provide its readings only in those cases where **A**, **R**, and **G** vary.

Above, we have indicated the procedures involved in converting Britton's diagram of *PC*'s early transmission into a tool for generating a reliable text. Broadly speaking, we use the agreement of any two archtypes (*ab*, *ac*, *bc*) as identifying a reading likely to have stood in O′. In other situations, particularly cases where some *b* manuscripts share readings with some of *c*, we have been guided by the probabilities underlying manuscript variation. Most discrepancies among the various copies are relatively slight (and grow slighter as the text proceeds). An extremely high percentage of these appear to have been driven by the attraction of surrounding text—an extensive amount of dittography, haplography, and efforts to diminish or strengthen repetition. Thus, an editorial procedure predicated on attestation has routinely been supplemented with our sense of probable scribal behaviour within a specific graphemic context.

Although we generally print O′, occasionally we have felt confident of doing better, and have intruded readings of O, the author's own copy. In these instances, we act without support from our seven manuscripts. Typical examples would include lines 686 and 2791. The first is mandated by the poet's Latin citation, the second (which had occurred to Morris) by a basic point of Christian doctrine which appears to have escaped the majority of the scribes.[68] On several further occasions, which the linked 8969 and 9042–3 may exemplify, we have been guided by the poet's sources. He will have known what they said, and he produces their materials throughout *verbatim*; scribes may not have been so learned as he, and consequently, confused.

We would insist that readings like these have one sobering implication for what we here present. It is, however, not an effect offering any qualification to the edition, conceived as a reproduction of O′, nor to its usefulness for others' further study of *PC*'s transmission. These small readings, where an obvious O lection has

---

[68] And where the two copies that underwrite our conjecture, **W** and **M**, probably both have independently 'corrected' what they recognized was amiss.

been lost, imply that already, before the poem's three archetypes appeared, there had been a substantial transmission, now invisible to us. In this process, a considerable amount of error had already entered the text. This leads us to adopt a certain scepticism at many points about the ultimate accuracy of the text we provide. For example, line 1943 reads unanimously, and we print:

> For his lyf is noght bot als a wyndes blast.

However, we are conscious that suppression of 'als', a variant that occurs in none of our copies, might produce a line more satisfactory. This would be true, both with respect to metre (an octosyllable with anacrusis at the head and one extra syllable, not two, in the third dip) and sense (a provocative metaphor, not a limp simile).

We have not tinkered, however. We allow line 1943—and a great many more like it, including a number where manuscript variation occurs—to stand in the text, as O' readings. Since all these oddments prove part of the later transmission of *PC*, our decision to eschew emendation on these occasions will not diminish the potential value of our text for general transmissional studies. But the reader should understand that the text we print is, as Morris's was, less than a fully critical one.

As we have already signalled, the text that follows is presented with modern word-division and punctuation (including paragraphing). Its lineation follows Morris's, but, unlike the earlier edition, we present a text based on the actual readings reported by **G**. Where we have changed these, we have marked the text. Insertions and adoptions of alternate readings appear in square brackets; omissions are marked with a '+'.

In addition to the text of *PC*, our edition also includes a number of marginal notations, here adopted from **A**. Evidence from *a* and **L** indicates that O' probably included a limited number of marginal notes, designed to offer a reader guidance through a fairly protracted poem. Discussion of variations in these marginal guides—those in **W**, for example, are Latin; those in **L**, often in-text, rather than marginal—does not appear on the text pages, but in the later Textual Commentary.

We also provide foot-of-the-page collations. Those of **G**, **R**, and **A** are complete, the remainder as we have described them above. All variants in the three completely collated manuscripts have been checked against the readings of the remaining four copies, and these books' information reported as well. In presenting the variants, we follow a fixed order of citation, **GRAWLSM**, alternatively *cab*; we signal places where we have emended **G**'s text by a star preceding the line number, or the appropriate variant. The collations also include our substantive variations from Morris's printed text (and a handful of non-substantive readings); we acknowledge, as well, all those emendations Morris suggested, many of which we adopt as well. Our silence may be taken to indicate that Morris reproduces the text of his base manuscript, **G/H**. In general, the procedures here have followed those used in the Society's edition of *Speculum Vitae* and outlined at EETS 331, pp. lxxxvi–lxxxvii.

Besides the three appendices already described, we offer other annotation. This takes three forms. Matters specifically textual are addressed in a section of 'Textual Commentary'. This is succeeded by a separate series of notes addressing the sources of *PC* and the author's handling of them. Our volume concludes with a selective glossary, constructed as an analogue to that in the Society's edition of *Speculum Vitae*.

BIBLIOGRAPHY

I. EDITIONS CITED

Adso Dervensis, *De ortu et tempore Antichristi*, ed. D. Verhelst, CCCM 45 (Turnhout, 1976).

Ancrene Riwle: *The English Text of the Ancrene Riwle: Magdalene College Cambridge MS Pepys 2498*, ed. A. Zetterstein, EETS 274 (Oxford, 1976).

Anselm: *S. Anselmi Opera omnia*, ed. F. S. Schmitt, 6 vols. (Edinburgh, 1946–61).

—— *Memorials of St Anselm*, ed. R. W. Southern and F. S. Schmitt, Auctores Britannici Medii Ævi, 1 (London, 1969).

Antonius Florentius, *Summa theologica*, 4 vols. (Nuremberg, 1477–9).

Apocalypse: *An English Fourteenth-Century Apocalypse Version with Commentary*, ed. Elis Fridner, Lund Studies in English, 29 (Lund, 1961).

The Awntyrs off Arthure at the Terne Wathelyn, ed. Ralph Hanna (Manchester, 1974).

Bartholomaeus Anglicus, *Tractatus de Proprietatibus rerum* (Cologne, 1481); see also Trevisa.

Bede, *Ecclesiastical History of the English People*, ed. Bertram Colgrave and R. A. B. Mynors, Oxford Medieval Texts (Oxford, 1969; repr. 1991).

Bestiary: *A Thirteenth-Century Bestiary in the Library of Alnwick Castle*, ed. Eric G. Millar (Oxford, 1958).

Bible Moralisée, ed. A. de Laborde, 4 vols. (Paris, 1911–21).

The Book of Tribulation, ed. Alexandra Barratt, MET 15 (Heidelberg, 1983).

The Book of Vices and Virtues, ed. W. Nelson Francis, EETS 217 (London, 1942).

Breviarium ad usum Sarum, ed. Francis Procter and Christopher Wordsworth, 3 vols. (Cambridge, 1882–6).

Bromyard, John, *Summa praedicantium* (Nuremberg, 1518).

Caesarius of Arles, *Sermons*, ed. D. Germain Morin, 2 vols., CCSL 103–4 (Turnhout, 1953).

Cato: *Disticha Catonis*, ed. Marcus Boas (Amsterdam, 1952).

Chaucer, Geoffrey, *The Riverside Chaucer*, ed. Larry D. Benson et al. (3rd edn., Boston, 1987).

Cursor Mundi, ed. Richard Morris, 7 vols., EETS os 57, 59, 62, 66, 68, 99, 101 (London, 1874–93).

Dante Alighieri, *The Divine Comedy*, ed. and trans. C. H. Sisson and David D. Higgins (Oxford, 1998).

'Description': Thomas Powell, 'A Description of the Day of Judgement', *Y Cymmrodor*, 4 (1881), 106–38.

The Early South-English Legendary, ed. C. Hortsmann, EETS os 87 (London, 1887).

Elucidarium, see Lefevre.

Fasciculus morum: A Fourteenth-Century Preacher's Handbook, ed. and trans. Siegfried Wenzel (University Park, Pa., 1989).

'The *Gawain*-poet': *The Poems of the Pearl Manuscript* . . . , ed. Malcolm Andrew and Ronald Waldron, rev. edn., Exeter Medieval Texts and Studies (Exeter, 1996, 1999).

Glossa ordinaria: *Biblia Sacra cum Glossa Ordinaria: Facsimile Reprint of the Editio Princeps, Adolph Rusch of Strassburg 1480/81*, ed. Karlfried Froehlich and Margaret T. Gibson, 4 vols. (Turnhout, 1992).

The Gospel of Nicodemus: Gesta Salvatoris, ed. H. C. Kim, Toronto Medieval Latin Texts, 2 (Toronto, 1973).

Gower, John, *The Complete Works of John Gower*, ed. G. C. Macaulay, 4 vols. (Oxford, 1899–1902).

Harrowing: The Middle English Harrowing of Hell and Gospel of Nicodemus, ed. William H. Hulme, EETS es 100 (London, 1907).

Henryson, Robert, *The Poems of Robert Henryson*, ed. Denton Fox (Oxford, 1981).

Hippocrates: *Hippocrates*, ed. and trans. W. H. S. Jones, vol. 2 (London, 1923).

—— *Hippocratis Aphorismi cum commentariolo auctore Martino Lister* (London, 1703).

Honorius, *see* Lefevre.

Hostiensis (Henry de Segusio), *Summa aurea* (Lyon, 1588).

Hugh Ripelin of Strasbourg, *Compendium theologicae veritatis* (Venice, 1588).

Humbert de Romanis, *Liber de abundantia exemplorum ad omnem materiam in sermonibus* (Ulm, *c*.1480).

Hymns to the Virgin and Christ . . . , ed. Frederick J. Furnivall, EETS os 24 (London, 1867).

Innocent III: Lotario dei Segni, *De Miseria condicionis humanae*, ed. Robert E. Lewis, The Chaucer Library (Athens, Ga., 1978).

Innocent IV, *In quinque libros Decretalium* (Venice, 1578).

Isidore of Seville, *Etymologiarum sive originum libri xx*, ed. W. M. Lindsay, 2 vols. (London, 1911).

Jacob's Well: An English Treatise on the Cleansing of Man's Conscience, ed. Arthur Brandeis, EETS os 115 (London, 1900).

Iacopo da Varazze, *Legenda Aurea*, ed. Giovanni P. Maggioni, 2nd edn., Millennio Medievale, 6, Teste 3, 2 vols. (Tavarnuzze [Florence], 1998).

Langland, William, *Piers Plowman: The B Version*, ed. George Kane and E. Talbot Donaldson (London, 1975).

—— *Piers Plowman: The C Version*, ed. George Russell and George Kane (London, 1997).

'The Last Judgement': Robert Reinsch, 'Mittheilungen aus einer franzö-sischen Handschrift des Lambeth Palace zu London', *Archiv für das Studium der neueren Sprachen und Literaturen*, 63 (1880), 51–96.

Lefevre, Yves, *L'Elucidarium et les Lucidaires: Contribution, par l'histoire d'un texte, à l'histoire des croyances religieuses en France au moyen âge* (Paris, 1954).

The 'Liber de Diversis Medicinis' in the Thornton Manuscript, ed. Margaret S. Ogden, EETS 207 (London, 1938).

The Macro Plays . . . , ed. Mark Eccles, EETS 262 (London, 1969).

Maimonides, Moses, *The Guide for the Perplexed*, trans. M. Friedlander (2nd edn., New York, 1956).

'Mandeville': *The Book of John Mandeville*, ed. Tamarah Kohanski and C. David Benson (Kalamazoo, Mich., 2007).

—— *The Defective Version of Mandeville's Travels*, ed. M. C. Seymour, EETS 319 (Oxford, 2002).

Manning, Robert: *Robert of Brunne's Handlyng Synne and its French Original*, ed. Frederick J. Furnivall, 2 vols., EETS os 119, 123 (London, 1901–3).

Medieval English Prose for Women . . . , ed. Bella Millett and Jocelyn Wogan-Browne (Oxford, 1990).

Middle English Sermons: *A Study and Edition of Selected Middle English Sermons*, ed. V. M. O'Mara, Leeds Texts and Monographs, 13 (Leeds, 1994).

Minot, Laurence: *Poems of Laurence Minot*, ed. Joseph Hall (2nd edn., Oxford, 1897).

The Northern Homily Cycle, ed. Anne B. Thompson, TEAMS Middle English Texts Series (Kalamazoo, Mich., 2008).

The Northern Homily Cycle: The Expanded Version . . . , ed. Saara Nevanlinna, 3 vols., Memoires de la Société Néophilologique de Helsinki, 38, 41, 43 (Helsinki, 1972–84).

The Northern Passion (Supplement), ed. Wilhelm Heuser and Frances A. Foster, EETS os 133 (London, 1930).

An Old English Miscellany, ed. Richard Morris, EETS os 49 (London, 1872).

Orologium Sapientiae: K. Horstmann, '*Orologium Sapientiae* or *The Seven Poyntes of Trewe Wisdom* aus MS Douce 114', *Anglia*, 10 (1888), 323–89.

'The Parlement of the Thre Ages', in *Alliterative Poetry of the Later Middle Ages*, ed. Thorlac Turville-Petre, Routledge Medieval English Texts (London, 1989), 67–100.

Peñaforte, Raymund de, *Summa de poenitentia et matrimonio cum glossis Ioannis de Friburgo* (Rome, 1603).

'Le Petit Sermon': Paul Meyer, 'Notice du MS Rawlinson poetry 241', *Romania*, 29 (1900), 1–84.

The Pilgrimage of the Soul: A Critical Edition of the Middle English Dream Vision, Volume I, ed. Rosemarie P. McGerr, Garland Medieval Texts, 16 (New York, 1990).

Preaching in the Age of Chaucer: Selected Sermons in Translation, trans. Siegfried Wenzel (Washington, DC, 2008).

The Prymer or Lay Folks' Prayer Book, ed. Henry Littlehales, 2 vols., EETS os 105, 109 (London, 1895–7).

De quatuordecim partibus beatitudinis (The Fourteen Parts of Blessedness), ed. Avril Henry and D. A. Trotter, Medium Ævum Monographs, NS 17 (Oxford, 1994).

A Revelation of Purgatory by an Unknown Fifteenth-Century Woman Visionary . . . , ed. Marta P. Harley, Studies in Women and Religion (Lewiston, NY, 1985).

The Revelation of the Monk of Eynsham, ed. Robert Easting, EETS 318 (Oxford, 2002).

Rolle, Richard, 'The Form of Living': *Richard Rolle: Prose and Verse*, ed. S. J. Ogilvie-Thomson, EETS 293 (Oxford, 1988), 3–25.

—— *Richard Rolle's Expositio Super Novem Lectiones Mortuorum . . . Volume Two*, ed. Malcolm M. Moyes, Salzburg Studies in English Literature, Elizabethan and Renaissance Studies, 92.12 (Salzburg, 1988).

—— *Richard Rolle: Uncollected Prose and Verse and Related Northern Texts*, ed. Ralph Hanna, EETS 329 (Oxford, 2007).

St Patrick's Purgatory, ed. Robert Easting, EETS 298 (Oxford, 1991).

The Sarum Missal, ed. J. Wickham Legg (Oxford, 1916).

'Sydrac': *Sydrac le philosophe, Le Livre de la fontaine des toutes sciences: Édition des enzyklopädische Lehrdialogs aus dem XIII. Jahrhundert*, ed. Ernspeter Ruhe, Wissenliteratur im Mittelalter, 34 (Wiesbaden, 2000).

Sidrak and Bokkus: A Parallel-Text Edition . . . , ed. T. L. Burton, 2 vols., EETS 311–12 (Oxford, 1998–9).

Small, John, ed., *English Metrical Homilies from Manuscripts of the Fourteenth Century* (Edinburgh, 1862).

Speculum Christiani . . . , ed. Gustaf Holmstedt, EETS 182 (London, 1933).

'Speculum huius vite': Guy Trudel, 'An Edition with Commentary of the *Speculum huius vite*, a Fifteenth-Century Pastoral Manual in English', 2 vols. (D.Phil. thesis; Oxford, 1999).

Speculum sacerdotale, ed. Edward H. Weatherly, EETS 200 (London, 1936).

Spenser, Edmund, *The Works: A Variorum Edition*, ed. Edwin Greenlaw et al., 11 vols. (Baltimore, 1958).

Thomas of Ireland, *Manipulus florum*, ed. Chris L. Nighman, web-mounted at <http://info.wlu.ca/~wwhist/faculty/cnighman/index>.

Three Purgatory Poems: The Gast of Gy, Sir Owain, The Vision of Tundale, ed. Edward E. Foster, TEAMS Middle English Texts Series (Kalamazoo, Mich., 2004).

Treatyse: 'An Edition of *A Treatyse of Gostly Batayle* and *Milicia Christi*', ed. Valerie Murray, 2 vols. (D.Phil. thesis; Oxford, 1970).

Trevisa, John, *Dialogus inter Militem et Clericum* . . . , ed. Aaron J. Perry, EETS 167 (London, 1925).

—— *On the Properties of Things: John Trevisa's Translation of Bartholomaeus Anglicus De Proprietatibus Rerum*, ed. M. C. Seymour et al., 3 vols. (Oxford, 1975–88).

de Voragine. *see* Iacopo

Visio Sancti Pauli: Ein Beitrag zur Visionslitteratur mit einem deutschen und zwei lateinischen Texten, ed. Herman Brandes (Halle, 1885).

The Vision of Tundale, ed. Rodney Mearns, MET 18 (Heidelberg, 1985).

Wimbledon, Thomas, *Wimbledon's Sermon Redde Rationem Villicationis Tue: A Middle English Sermon* . . . , ed. Ione K. Knight, Duquesne Studies, Philological Studies, 9 (Pittsburgh, 1967).

The York Plays: A Critical Edition of the York Corpus Christi Play as recorded in British Library Additional MS 35290, ed. Richard Beadle, EETS ss 23 (Oxford, 2009).

Yorkshire Writers: Richard Rolle of Hampole and his Followers, ed. C. Horstmann, 2 vols. (London, 1895–6).

Ywain and Gawain, ed. Albert B. Friedman and Norman T. Harrington, EETS 254 (London, 1964).

2. SECONDARY WORKS

Aers, David, *Piers Plowman and Christian Allegory* (London, 1975).

Alford, John, 'The Idea of Reason in *Piers Plowman*', *Medieval English Studies Presented to George Kane*, ed. Edward D. Kennedy et al. (Woodbridge, 1988), 199–215.

—— *Piers Plowman: A Glossary of Legal Diction*, Piers Plowman Studies, 5 (Cambridge, 1988).

—— *Piers Plowman: A Guide to the Quotations*, Medieval and Renaissance Texts and Studies, 77 (Binghamton, NY, 1992).

Allen, Hope E., 'The Authorship of the *Prick of Conscience*', *Studies in English and Comparative Literature*, Radcliffe College Monographs, 15 (Boston, 1910), 115–70.

—— 'The *Speculum Vitae*: Addendum', *PMLA* 32 (1917), 133–62.

—— *Writings Ascribed to Richard Rolle Hermit of Hampole and Materials for his Biography* (New York, 1927).

Andreae, Percy, *Die Handschriften des Pricke of Conscience von Richard Rolle de Hampole im Britischen Museum* (Berlin, 1888).

Black, William H., *A Descriptive, Analytical, and Critical Catalogue of the Manuscripts Bequeathed unto the University of Oxford by Elias Ashmole*, Bodleian Library, 'Quarto Catalogues', 10 (Oxford, 1845).

Bloomfield, Morton W., *The Seven Deadly Sins: An Introduction to the History of a Religious Concept* . . . (East Lansing, Mich., 1952).

Brague, Remi, 'Geocentrism as a Humiliation for Man', *Medieval Encounters: Jewish, Christian and Muslim Culture in Confluence and Dialogue*, 3:3 (1997), 187–210.

Britton, Derek, review of Lewis–McIntosh, *Medium Ævum*, 53 (1984), 315–17.

Bülbring, Karl D., 'On Twenty-Five Manuscripts of Richard Rolle's "Pricke of Conscience" . . .', *Transactions of the Philological Society*, 21 (1890), 261–83.

—— 'Zu den Handschriften von Richard Rolle's "Prick of Conscience"', *Englische Studien*, 23 (1897), 1–30.

Burrow, J. A., *The Ages of Man: A Study in Medieval Writing and Thought* (Oxford, 1986).

Bynum, Caroline W., *The Resurrection of the Body in Western Christianity, 200–1336* (New York, 1995).

Catalogue of Additions to the Manuscripts in the British Museum in the Years [1888–1893] (London, 1894).

Coffman, George R., 'Old Age from Horace to Chaucer: Some Literary Affinities and Adventures of an Idea', *Speculum*, 9 (1934), 249–77.

Constable, Giles, 'Twelfth-Century Spirituality and the Late Middle Ages', *Medieval and Renaissance Studies: Proceedings of the Southeastern Institute of Medieval and Renaissance Studies, Summer 1969*, ed. O. B. Hardison, Jr. (Chapel Hill, NC, 1969), 27–60.

Correale, Robert M., and Hamel, Mary, eds, *Sources and Analogues of The Canterbury Tales*, 2 vols. (Cambridge, 2002–5).

Cross, Claire, and Vickers, Noreen, *Monks, Friars and Nuns in Sixteenth-Century Yorkshire*, Yorkshire Archaeological Society Record Series, 150 (Wakefield, 1995).

Dareau, Margaret G., and McIntosh, Angus, 'A Dialect Word in Some West Midland Manuscripts of the *Prick of Conscience*', *Edinburgh Studies in English and Scots*, ed. A. J. Aitken et al. (London, 1971), 20–6.

Dean, Ruth J., *Anglo-Norman Literature: A Guide to Texts and Manuscripts*, Anglo-Norman Text Society Occasional Publications Series, 3 (London, 1999).

D'Evelyn, Charlotte, 'An East Midland Recension of *The Pricke of Conscience*', *PMLA* 45 (1930), 180–200.

Doyle, A. I., 'A Survey of the Origins and Circulation of Theological Writings in English in the 14th, 15th, and Early 16th Centuries with Special Consideration of the Part of the Clergy Therein', 2 vols., (Ph.D. thesis, Cambridge University, 1953).

—— 'Ushaw College, Durham, MS 50: Fragments of the *Prick of Conscience* by the Same Scribe as Oxford, Corpus Christi College, MS

201, of the B Text of *Piers Plowman*', in A. S. G. Edwards et al. (eds.), *The English Medieval Book: Studies in Memory of Jeremy Griffiths* (London, 2000), 43–9.

Dutschke, C. W., *Guide to Medieval and Renaissance Manuscripts in the Huntington Library*, 2 vols. (San Marino, Calif., 1989).

Easting, Robert, *Visions of the Other World in Middle English*, Annotated Bibliographies in Old and Middle English Literature, 3 (Cambridge, 1997).

Edwards, A. S. G., 'Medieval Manuscripts Owned by William Browne of Tavistock (1590/1?–1643/5)', in James P. Carley and Colin G. C. Tite (eds.), *Books and Collectors 1200–1700: Essays Presented to Andrew Watson* (London, 1997), 441–9.

—— and O'Byrne, Theresa, 'A New Manuscript Fragment of the *Prick of Conscience*', *Medium Ævum*, 76 (2007), 305–7.

Emden, A. B., *A Survey of Dominicans in England* . . . (Rome, 1977).

Fourquet, J., 'Fautes communes ou innovations communes?', *Romania*, 70 (1948–9), 85–95.

Gallagher, Edward J., 'The *Visio Lazari*, the Cult, and the Old French Life of Saint Lazarus: An Overview', *Neuphilologische Mitteilungen*, 90 (1989), 331–9.

Gillespie, Vincent A., 'The Literary Form of the Middle English Pastoral Manual with Particular Reference to the *Speculum Christiani* and Some Related Texts', 2 vols. (D.Phil. thesis, Oxford, 1981).

Gilson, Étienne, *The Mystical Theology of Saint Bernard*, trans. A. H. C. Downes (London, 1940).

—— 'Self Knowledge and Christian Socratism', in *The Spirit of Medieval Philosophy*, trans. A. H. C. Downes (London, 1950), 209–28.

Gray, Nick, 'Langland's Quotations from the Penitential Tradition', *Modern Philology*, 84 (1986), 53–60.

Gurevich, Aron, *Medieval Popular Culture: Problems of Belief and Perception*, trans. Janos M. Bak and Paul A. Hollingsworth (Cambridge, 1988).

Hanna, Ralph, *A Descriptive Catalogue of the Western Medieval Manuscripts of St John's College Oxford* (Oxford, 2002).

—— *The English Manuscripts of Richard Rolle: A Descriptive Catalogue* (Exeter, 2010).

—— *The Index of Middle English Prose, Handlist I: A Handlist of Manuscripts Containing Middle English Prose in the Henry E. Huntington Library* (Cambridge, 1984).

—— 'Lambeth Palace Library, MS 260 and the Problem of English Vernacularity', *Studies in Medieval and Renaissance History*, 3rd ser. 5 (2008), 131–99 [2008a].

—— 'Lambeth Palace Library MS 260 and Some Aspects of Northern Book History', *Journal of the Early Book Society*, 9 (2006), 131–40.

—— 'Some Commonplaces of Late Medieval Patience Discussions: An Introduction', in Gerald R. Schiffhorst (ed.), *The Triumph of Patience: Medieval and Renaissance Studies* (Orlando, Fla., 1978), 65–87.

—— 'Some North Yorkshire Scribes and their Context', in Denis Renevey and Graham D. Caie (eds.) *Medieval Texts in Context* (London, 2008), 167–91 [2008b].

—— 'Yorkshire Writers', *Proceedings of the British Academy*, 121 (2003), 91–109.

—— and Zieman, Katherine, 'The Transmission of "The Book of Shrift"', *Journal of the Early Book Society*, 13 (2010), 255–63.

Harley, Marta P., 'Last Things First in Chaucer's *Physician's Tale*: Final Judgement and the Worm of Conscience', *Journal of English and Germanic Philology*, 91 (1992), 1–16.

Harper, John, *The Forms and Orders of Western Liturgy from the Tenth to the Eighteenth Century . . .* (Oxford, 1991).

Harris, William O., *Skelton's Magnificence and the Cardinal Virtue Tradition* (Chapel Hill, NC, 1965).

Heist, William W., *The Fifteen Signs before Doomsday* (East Lansing, Mich., 1952).

Howard, Donald R., *The Three Temptations: Medieval Man in Search of the World* (Princeton, 1966).

Hudson, Anne, *The Premature Reformation: Wycliffite Texts and Lollard History* (Oxford, 1988).

Index of Printed Middle English Prose, ed. R. E. Lewis et al. (New York, 1985).

An Inventory of the Historical Monuments in the City of York, 5 vols. (London, 1962–81).

James, M. R., *A Descriptive Catalogue of the McClean Collection of Manuscripts in the Fitzwilliam Museum* (Cambridge, 1912).

—— and Jenkins, Claude, *A Descriptive Catalogue of the Manuscripts in the Library of Lambeth Palace*, 2 vols. (Cambridge, 1930–2).

Jolliffe, P. S., *A Check-List of Middle English Prose Writings of Spiritual Guidance*, Subsidia Mediaevalia, 2 (Toronto, 1974).

Jordan, Richard, rev. H. Ch. Matthew, *Handbuch der mittelenglischen Grammatik: I. Teil: Lautlehre* (2nd edn.; Heidelberg, 1934).

Kaeppeli, T., *Scriptores Ordinis Praedicatorum Medii Aevi*, 4 vols. (Rome, 1970–93).

Ker, N. R. (vol. 4 with A. J. Piper), *Medieval Manuscripts in British Libraries*, 4 vols. (Oxford, 1969–92).

Kolve, V. A., *Chaucer and the Imagery of Narrative: The First Five Canterbury Tales* (London, 1984).

Le Goff, Jacques, *The Birth of Purgatory*, trans. Arthur Goldhammer (London, 1990).

Lewis, Robert E., 'The Relationship of the Vernon and Simeon Texts of *The Prick of Conscience*', in Michael Benskin and M. L. Samuels (eds.), *So meny people longages and tonges: Philological Essays on Scots and Mediaeval English Presented to Angus McIntosh* (Edinburgh, 1981), 251–64.

Lewis, Suzanne, *Reading Images: Narrative, Discourse and Reception in the Thirteenth-Century Illuminated Apocalypse* (Cambridge, 1995).

McIntosh, Angus, 'Two Unnoticed Interpolations in Four Manuscripts of the *Prick of Conscience*', *Neuphilologische Mitteilungen* 77 (1976), 63–78.

Macray, W. D., rev. R. W. Hunt and A. G. Watson, *Bodleian Library Quarto Catalogues IX: Digby Manuscripts* (Oxford, 1999).

Mann, Jill, 'Allegorical Buildings in Medieval Literature', *Medium Ævum*, 63 (1994), 191–210.

Marks, Richard, *Stained Glass in England during the Middle Ages* (London, 1993).

Mooney, Linne R., and Stubbs, Estelle, 'The HM114 Scribe', paper presented at the Fifth International Piers Plowman Conference, Oxford, 15 April 2011, publication forthcoming.

—— and Matheson, Lister M., 'The Beryn Scribe and his Texts: Evidence for Multiple-Copy Production of Manuscripts in Fifteenth-Century England', *The Library*, 7th ser. 4 (2003), 347–70.

Morgan, Nigel, with a contribution . . . by Michelle Brown, *The Lambeth Apocalypse: Manuscript 209 in Lambeth Palace Library: A Critical Study* (London, 1990).

Oldham, J. Basil, *English Blind-Stamped Book Bindings* (Cambridge, 1952).

Ottosen, Knud, *The Responsories and Versicles of the Latin Office of the Dead* (Aarhus, 1993).

Owst, G. R., *Preaching in Medieval England: An Introduction to Sermon Manuscripts of the Period c. 1350–1450*, Cambridge Studies in Medieval Life and Thought (Cambridge, 1926).

Patch, Howard R., *The Goddess Fortuna in Medieval Literature* (Cambridge, Mass., 1927).

—— *The Other World, according to Descriptions in Medieval Literature*, Smith College Studies in Modern Languages, NS 1 (Cambridge, Mass., 1950).

Pickering, Oliver S., 'Brotherton Collection MS 501: A Middle English Anthology Reconsidered', *Leeds Studies in English*, NS 21 (1990), 141–65.

Post, Gaines, et al., 'The Medieval Heritage of a Humanistic Ideal: "Scientia donum Dei est, unde vendi non potest"', *Traditio*, 11 (1955), 195–234.

Powell, Sue, 'All Saints' Church, North Street, York: Text and Image in the *Pricke of Conscience* Window', in Nigel J. Morgan (ed.), *Prophecy, Apocalypse and the Day of Doom* . . . (Donnington, 2004), 292–316.

Riehle, Wolfgang, 'The Authorship of *The Prick of Conscience* Reconsidered', *Anglia*, 111 (1993), 1–18.

Robbins, Rossell H., 'Signs of Death in Middle English', *Mediaeval Studies*, 32 (1970), 282–98.

Robinson, Christine M., 'A Machine-Readable Edition of the Text of the *Speculum Vitae* as Attested in British Library MS Additional 33995, with Introduction, Glossary, and an Investigation of the Claims for the Common Authorship of the *Speculum Vitae* and the *Prick of Conscience*' (Ph.D. thesis, Edinburgh University, 1987).

Saenger, Paul, *A Catalogue of the Pre-1500 Western Manuscript Books at the Newberry Library* (Chicago, 1989).

Schulz, H. L., 'A Manuscript Printer's Copy for a Lost Early English Book', *The Library*, 4th ser. 22 (1941), 138–44.

—— 'A Middle English Manuscript Used as Printer's Copy', *Huntington Library Quarterly*, 29 (1966), 325–36.

Seiler, Thomas H., 'Filth and Stink as Aspects of the Iconography of Hell', in Clifford Davidson and Thomas H. Seiler (eds.), *The Iconography of Hell*, Early Drama, Art, and Music Monograph Series, 17 (Kalamazoo, Mich., 1992), 132–40.

Seymour, M. C., 'Some Medieval English Owners of *De Proprietatibus Rerum*', *Bodleian Library Record*, 9/3 (Dec. 1974), 156–65.

Shaffern, Robert W., *The Penitents' Treasury: Indulgences in Latin Christendom 1175–1375* (Scranton, Pa., and London, 2007).

Silverstein, Theodore, *Visio Sancti Pauli: The History of the Apocalypse in Latin together with Nine Texts*, Studies and Documents, 4 (London, 1935).

Simpson, James, 'The Role of *Scientia* in *Piers Plowman*', in Gregory Kratzmann and Simpson (eds.), *Medieval English Religious and Ethical Literature: Essays in Honour of G. H. Russell* (Cambridge, 1986), 49–65.

A Summary Catalogue of Western Manuscripts in the Bodleian Library at Oxford, ed. Falconer Madan et al., 7 vols. in 8 (Oxford, 1895–1953).

Swanson, R. N., *Indulgences in Medieval England: Passports to Paradise?* (Cambridge, 2007).

Thompson, John J., *The* Cursor Mundi*: Poem, Texts and Contexts*, Medium Ævum Monographs, NS 19 (Oxford, 1998).

Thomson, R. M., *A Descriptive Catalogue of the Medieval Manuscripts of Merton College, Oxford* (Oxford, 2010).

Van Dijk, S. J. P., *Handlist of the Latin Liturgical Manuscripts in the Bodleian Library Oxford*, vol. 4 (1959).

The Vernon Manuscript: A Facsimile of Bodleian Library, Oxford, MS. Eng. poet. a.1, introd. A. I. Doyle (Cambridge, 1987).

Vising, Johan, *Anglo-Norman Language and Literature* (London, 1923).

Voigt, Max, *Beiträge zur Geschichte der Visionenliteratur im Mittelalter*, Palaestra, 124 (Leipzig, 1924).

Voigts, Linda E., 'A Handlist of Middle English in Harvard Manuscripts', *Harvard Library Bulletin*, 33 (1985), 1–96.

Waters, S. A., 'A History of *Prick of Conscience* Studies', *Studia Neophilologica*, 5 (1983), 147–51.

Watson, Andrew, *The Manuscripts of Henry Savile of Banke* (London, 1969).

Wells, John E., rev. J. Burke Severs et al., *A Manual of the Writings in Middle English 1050–1500*, currently 11 vols. (New Haven, 1967–).

Wenzel, Siegfried, *Latin Sermon Collections from Later Medieval England: Orthodox Preaching in the Age of Wycliffe* (Cambridge, 2005).

—— 'The Pilgrimage of Life as a Medieval Genre', *Mediaeval Studies*, 35 (1973), 370–88.

—— *Preachers, Poets, and the Early English Lyric* (Princeton, 1986).

Whiting, Bartlett J., *Proverbs, Sentences and Proverbial Phrases from English Writings Mainly before 1500* (Cambridge, Mass., 1968).

Wieck, Roger S. et al., *Time Sanctified: The Book of Hours in Medieval Life and Art* (New York, 1988).

Wilson, Edward, 'Langland's "Book of Conscience": Two Middle English Analogues and Another Possible Latin Source', *Notes and Queries*, 228 (1983), 387–9.

Wittig, Joseph S., 'Piers Plowman B, Passus IX–XII: Elements in the Design of the Inward Journey', *Traditio*, 28 (1972), 211–80.

Wood, Sarah, 'A Prose Redaction of *The Prick of Conscience* Book VI in Bodleian Library, MS Laud misc. 23', *Medium Ævum*, 80 (2011), 1–17.

Wright, C. E., *Fontes Harleani: A Study of the Sources of the Harleian Collection . . .* (London, 1972).

THE PRICK OF CONSCIENCE

þe myght of þe Fader almyghty,
þe witt of þe Son al-wytty,
And þe gudnes of þe Hali Gast,
A Godde and lorde of myght mast,
Be wyth us and us help and spede,   5
Now and ever, in al our nede;
And specialy at þis bygynnyng,
And bryng us alle til gude endyng. Amen.
   Befor ar any thyng was wroght,
And ar any bygynnyng was of oght,   10
And befor al tymes, als we sal trow,
þe sam God ay was þat es now,
þat woned ever in his godhede
And in thre persons and anhede.
For God wald ay with þe Fader and þe Son   15 *Howe God was ay in trinite (?) withouten byginnyng*
And wyth þe Hali Gast in anhede won,
Als God in a substance and beyng
Withouten any bygynnyng.
Bygynnyng of hym myght never nan be;
He was ay Godde in Trinite,   20
þat was ay als wys and ful of wytte
And als myghty als he es yhitte,
Was myght and wytte of himselve was tan,
For never na God was bot he alan.
   þe sam God sythyn was þe bygynnyng   25
And þe first maker of alle thyng;   *Howe God was in [þe bygynnyng] and es byginnyg and sal be ende of alle thyng*
And als he is bygynnyng of alle,
Wythouten bygynnyng swa we him calle,
Ende of al wythouten ende—
þus es in haly bokes contende.   30
For als he was ay God in Trinite,
Swa he es, and ay God sal be;
And als he first bygan alle thing,
Swa sal he, [at] þe last, mak endyng
Of alle þing bot of heven and helle   35

M lacks the opening folio and, with it, lines 1–72; As is here cited in its stead, and b represents the agreement of LSAs.   4 Godde and lorde] louerd godd W   myght] myghtes RW*b*
6 in] at WSAs   8 Amen] *om. a*   9 ar] *om.* RW   12 ay was] *trs.* W; *cf.* ay] *om.* As
14 and²] and in W, in L, and an As   15 þe²] *om.* AAs   25 sam] some W
bygynnyng] bygnyng A   27 is] es þe W, was L   34 sal he] *trs.* AS   *at] *om.* G, *Morris's emendation*

And of man and fende and aungelle,
þat aftir þis lyfe sal lyf ay,
And na qwik creature bot þai,
Als men may se in þis boke contende,
þat wille it se or here to þe ende.   40
And God that mad man sal ay be þan,
Als he es now, God and man.
  Alle thyng thurgh 'his' myght made he,
For withouten hym myght nathing be.
Alle thyng þat he bygan and wroght   45
Was byfor þe bygynnyng noght.
Alle thing he ordaynd aftir is wille

[How all creatours sulde
loue God in þair kynde]
f. 76ʳᵇ

In sere kyndes, for certayn skylle;
Wharfor þe creatours þat er dom
And na witt ne skille has, er bughsom   50
To lof hym, als þe boke beres wytnesse,
On þair maner als þair kynd esse.
For ilka thyng þat God has wroght,
þat folowes þe kynd and passes it noght,
Loves his maker and hym worshepes   55
In þat at he þe kynd right kepes.
  Sen þe creatures þat skille has nane
Hym loves in þe kynde þat þai haf tane,
þan aght man, þat has skille and mynde,
Hys creatur worshepe in his kynde,   60
And noght to be of wers condicion
þan þe creatours withouten reson.

Why man awe loue God
byfor alle othir creatours

Mans kynd es to folow Goddes wille
And alle 'hys' comandmentes to fulfille,
For of alle þat God made, mare and les,   65
Man mast principal creature es,
And alle þat he made was for man done,
Als yhe sal here aftirward sone.

Howe God 'made' man
mast digne creature of
all othir

  God to mans kynd had grete lufe
When he ordaynd, for mans byhufe,   70
Heven and herth and þe werld brade
And al other thyng, and man last made

---

40 þe] *om.* WS   41 ay] *om.* R   45 bygan] made W   50 er] here RL, þat are
As   54 þe] hys W   56 þe] hys W*b*   62 creatours] creature W   66 Man]
þan R   *At this point, W is missing a folio and lacks lines 67–127; M begins with line 73.*

Til hys lyknes [in] semely stature;
And made hym mast digne creature
Of al other creaturs of kynde;   75
And gaf hym wytte, skille, and mynde
For to knaw gude and ille;
And þarewith he gaf hym a fre wille
For to chese and for to halde
Gude or ille, wethir he walde.   80
And alswa he ordaynd man to dwelle
And to lyf in erthe, in flesshe and felle,
To knaw his werkes and him worshepe,
And his comandmentes to kepe;
And if he be til God bousom,   85
Til endeles blis at þe last to com;
And, if he fraward be, to wende
Til pyne of helle, þat has nan ende.
    Ilk man þat here lyves, mare and lesse,
God made til his awen lyknesse,   90
Til wham he has gyven witte and skille
For to knaw bathe gude and ille,
And fre wille to chese, als he vouches save,
Gude or ille, + whether he wil have.
Bot he þat his wille til God wil sette,   95
Grete mede þarfor mon he gette;
And he þat tille ille settes his wille   f. 76ᵛᵃ
Grete payne sal have for þat ille.
Wharfor þat man may be halden wode,
þat cheses þe ille and leves þe gude.   100
    Sen God made man of maste dignite
Of alle creatures, and mast fre,
And made him til his awen liknes
In fair stature, als befor sayde es,
And maste has gyven him, and yhit gyves   105
þan til any other creature þat lyves,
And has hight him yit þarto   *Why man aghe to haue*
þe blise of heven, if he uele do;   *in mynde þe benefice þat*
And yhit when he had done mys   *God has done hym*

*73 in] and GS, and in L   89 and] or R   93 to . . . saue] *later, over eras.* G
*94 ille] *repeated* G, *Morris's silent correction*   96 þarfor] þarof AL, *cf.* of it M

And thurgh syn was prived of blys,   110
God tok mans kynd for his sake
And for his love þe dede wald take,
And with his blode boght him agayne
Til þat blisse fra endeles payne,
þus grete lufe God til man kydde,   115
And many benyfices he him dydde.
Wharfor ilk man, bathe lered and lewed,
Suld thynk on þat love þat he man shewed,
And alle þier benefice hald in mynde
þat he þus dyd til mans kynde,   120
And love hym and thank him als he can—
And elles es he an unkynd man—
And serve him, bathe day and nyght,
And þat he has gyven him, use it right,

Why a man suld spend   And his wittes despende in his service –   125
his wittes and his   Elles es he a fole and noght wyse—
vndirstandyng in   And knaw kyndly what God es
gode vse   And what man self es þat es les:
How wayke man es in saul and body,
And how stalworth God es, and how myghty;   130
How man God greves þat dose noght wele,
And what man es worthi þarfor to fele;
How mercyful and gracyouse God es,
And how ful he es of gudenes;
How rightwes God es and how sothefast,   135
And what he has done and sal do at þe last,
And ilk day dos to mankynde.
þis suld ilk man knaw and haf in mynde.

How a man ⟨sulde ta⟩k   For þe right way þat lyggys til blys
þe way to blisse thurgh   And þat ledys a man theder es thys: 140
þe way of w⟨y⟩se⟨dom⟩   þe way of mekenes principaly
And of drede and luf of God almyghty,
þat may be cald þe way of wysdom;
Intyl whilk way na man may com
f. 76ᵛᵇ   Withouten knawyng of God here   145
And of his myght and his werkes sere.

---

110 was] *om.* A, is L   of] of þat RA, *cf.* fra þe L   117 bathe] *later, over eras.* G
121 he] yhe R, þou L   *W returns at line 128.*   129 es] self es A   134 of] of alle W
137 to] vnto W   man-] mans *a*

Bot [a]re he may til þat knawyng wynne,
Hym byhoves knaw himself withinne;
Elles may he haf na knawyng to come
Intil þe forsayde way of wysdome.   150
   Bot som men has wytte to understand,
And yhit þai er ful unkunand
And of som thyng has na knawyng
þat myght styrre þam to gude lyfyng.
Swylk men had nede to lere ilk day   155
Of other men, þat can mare þan þay,
To knaw þat myght þam stir and lede
Til mekenes and til lufe and drede,
þe whilk es way, als befor sayde es,
Til þe blis of heven þat es endeles.   160
In grete perille of saul es þat man
þat has witt and mynde and na gude can
And wil noght lere for to knaw
þe werkes of God and Godes law,
Ne what hymself es þat es lest;   165
Bot lyves als an unskilwys best,
þat nother has skil, witt, ne mynde;
þat man lyfes agayn his kynde.
For a man excuses noght his unkunnyng
þat his wittes uses noght in leryng,   170
Namly, of þat at hym fel to knaw
þat myght meke his hert and make it law.
   Bot he þat can noght suld haf wille
To lere to knaw bathe gude and ille;
And he þat can oght suld lere mare   175
To knaw alle þat hym nedeful ware.
For an unkunnand man thurgh leryng
May be broght til undirstandyng
Of many thynges, to knaw and se
þat has bene and es and yhit sal be,   180
þat til mekenes myght stir his wille
And til lufe and drede and to fle alle ille.
   Many has lykyng trofels to here

---

*147 are] here *c*   164 Godes] gode Morris (Lightbown)   170 wittes] wytte W,
cf. wit (*in rewritten line*) L   leryng] leerenyng W   175 can oght] *trs.* W   176 hym]
to him RW, *om.* L   177 leryng] leernyng W   182 and³] *om.* R   to] *om.* W

And vanites wille blethly lere,
And er bysy in wille and thoght   185
To lere þat þe saul helpes noght.
Bot þat ne[de]ful war to kun and knaw,
To listen and lere þai er ful slaw;
Forþi þai can noght knaw ne se
þe peryls þat þai suld drede and fle,   190
And wilk way þai suld chese and take
And wilk way þai suld lef and forsake.

f. 77ʳᵃ Bot na wonder es, yf þai ga wrang,
For in myrknes of unknawyng þai gang,
Withouten lyght of understandyng   195
Of þat þat falles til ryght knawyng.

þarfor ilk Cristen man and weman
þat has witte and mynd, and skille can,
þat knawes noght þe ryght way to chese,
Ne þe perils þat ilk wise man flese,   200
Suld be bughsom ay and bysy
To here and lere of þam, namely,
þat understandes and knawes by skille,
Wilk es gude way and wilk es ille.
He þat right ordir of lyfyng wil luke   205
Suld bygyn þus, als says þe boke:
To knaw first what hymself es,
Swa may he tyttest com to mekenes,
þat es grund of al vertus to last,
On whilk al vertus may be sette fast.   210
For he þat knawes wele and can se
What himselfe was and es and sal be,
A wyser man [h]e may be talde,
Wether he be yhung man or alde,
þan he þat can alle other thyng   215
And of himself has na knawyng.
For he may noght right God knaw ne fele,
Bot he can first knaw himself wele.
þarfor a man suld first lere

185 er] þe R   186 þat þe] þat at W, þat thyng þat to L, þe thyng þe M   187 þat]
þat at W, to þaas L   *nedeful] neful G, Morris's emendation   191 chese and take]
dreede `cheese' (later?) and take W, dred and quake L   204 es²] om. R   213 A]
om. R   *he may] may he G   218 knaw] om. Morris

To knaw himself prope[r]ly here,   220
For if he hymself knew kyndely,
He suld haf knawyng of God almyghty,
And of his endyng thynk suld he
And of þe day þat last sal be.
He suld knaw what þis worlde es,   225
þat es ful of pompe and lythernes,
And lere to knaw and thynk wythalle
What sal after þis lyf falle.
For knawyng of alle þis shuld hym lede
And mynd wythalle til mekenes and drede,   230
And swa may he com to gude lyvyng,
And atte þe last til + gode endyng;
And when he sal out of þis world wende,
Be broght til þe lyfe þat has na ende.

    þe bygynnyng of alle þis proces   235
Ryght knawyng of a man self es.
Bot som men has mykel lettyng,
þat lettes þam to haf right knawyng
Of þamselfe, þat þai first suld knaw,
þat þam til mekenes first suld draw.   240
And of þat, four thynges I fynd   f. 77rb
þat mase a mans wytt ofte blynd
And knawyng of hymself lettes,
Thurgh wilk four he hymself forgettes.
Of þis saynt Bernard witnes bers   245
And er þa four wryten in þis vers:
    Forma, favor populi, fervor iuvenilis, opesque
    surripuere tibi noscere quid sit homo.
þat es, 'favor of þe folk and fayrnes,
And fervor of [yhouthe] and riches   250
Reves a man sight, skylle, and mynde
To knaw hymself, what he es of kynde'.
    þus þer four lettes his insight
þat he knawes noght himselfe right

---

*220 properly] propely G, a party SM   223 thynk suld] *trs.* (*a later caret after* suld) A   228 falle] befalle WL   *232 gode] a gode *c*   234 þe] þat W, *om.* LM 236 Ryght] þe ryght W   a] *om.* W   243 -self] *add* oft WL   246 er] here R, here hare L   *250 yhouthe] thoght *c*, þe 30wthed L, þe yhouthe SM, *emendation suggested in Morris's note*   253 his] *int., probably original* A, *om.* L

And mas his hert ful hawtayne   255
And ful fraward til his soverayne.
þir four norisches ofte pomp and pride
And other vices þat men can noght hyde,
For in him, in wham ane of þer four es,
Es selden sen any mekenes.   260
Alswa þai lette a man þat he noght sese
þe perils of þe werld ne vanitese;
Ne of þe tym of + dede þat es to com
Thynkes noght, ne of þe day of dom;
Ne he can noght undirstand ne se   265
þe paynes þat after þis lyfe sal be
To synful men þat here lofes foly,
Ne þe blise þat gude men er worthy.
Bot in his delytis settes his hert fast
And fares als þis lyfe suld ay last   270
And gyffes him noght bot to vanite
And to al þat lykyng to hym mygt be.
    Swylk men er noght led with skylle,
Bot þai folow ay þair awen wille
And of noght elles thynkes ne tas hede.   275
What wonder es yf þai haf na drede?
For what þai suld drede, þai knaw noght;
þarfor þai can haf na drede in thoght,
And þat es thurgh defaut of knawyng
Of þat þat myght þam to drede bryng.   280
Yhit som men wille noght understande
þat þat mught mak þam dredande,
For þai wald noght here bot þat þam pays.
þarfor þe prophet in [þe] Psauter says:
    Noluit intelligere   285
    ut bene ageret.
He says, 'he has no wille to fele
Ne to understand for to do wele'.
þis wordes by þam may be sayd here,
þat wil noght undirstand ne lere   290

f. 77va

255 hawtayne] *partly later over eras.* A; *cf.* vngayn M   257 ofte] *om.* W   262 þe²]
þis W   ne] and W   263 þe] *om. aS*   *dede] þe dede *c* (*cf.* of þe] ne of SM)
272 mygt] may AL, *after* lykyng W   275 of] oft W   279–80 *couplet trs.* Morris
(Lightbown)   279 defaut] þe defawte W   *284 in þe] in G

To drede God and to do his wille,
Bot folowes þair likyng and lyves ille.
Som understandes als þai here telle,
Bot na drede in þair hertes may dwelle,
And thurgh defaut of trouthe þat may be;   295
For þai trow nathyng bot þat þa se,
But groches when þai dredful thyng here.
þarfor þe prophet says on þis manere:
    Non crediderunt
    et mu[r]muraverunt.   300
þe prophet say[s] 'þai trowed noght
And groched' and was angred in thoght.
þus er many þat trowes nathyng
þat men þam says ogayn þair likyng,
Bot groches gretly and waxes fraward,   305
When men says oght þat þam thynk hard.
    Som can se in buk swilk thyng and rede,
Bot lightnes of hert reves þam drede,
Swa þat it may noght with þam dwelle,
And þarfor says God þus in þe gospelle: 310
    Quia ad tempus credunt, et in tempore
    temptacionis recedunt.
'Til a tyme', he says, 'som trowes a thyng
And passes þarfra in þe tyme of fandyng'.
Alswa þos says þe prophet David   315
In a psalme þat cordes þarwith:
    Et crediderunt in verbis eius, et lau-
    daverunt laudem eius. Cito fecerunt,
    obliti sunt opera eius.
He says, 'in his wordes trowed þai   320
And loved his lovyng als þai couth say,
But tyte þai had don, and forgat
His werkes' and thogt na mar of þat.
Swilk men er ay swa unstedfast

    296 se] may se W   297–8 *couplet om.* (*added later* [*A*¹] *at the column-foot with signe de*
renvoie) A   297 dredful thyng] of drede A¹   298 þarfor] Forthy A¹, Thare L
300 verbis eius murmurauerunt in tabernaculis suis W   *murmuraverunt] mumurauerunt
G (*i.e.* r¹ *not present*), *Morris's silent correction*   *301 says] sayd *c*L   314 þe] *om.*
WL   316 cordes] acordes *a*M   317 in] *om.* W   319 obliti] et obliti L Morris
(Lightbown)   opera] operum *a*SM   eius] eorum (*corr. later*) A, *om.* M   320 wordes]
worde W   322 and] and sone W   324 er ay swa] here ay are W

þat na drede may with þam [lang] last,   325
For þai er swa wilde, when þai haf quert,
þat na drede þai can hald in hert.
    Bot whaswa can noght drede may lere,
þat þis tretice wil rede or here;
Yf þai rede or here til þe hende   330
þe maters þat er þarin contende,
And undirstand þam al and trow,
Parchaunce þair hertes þan sal bow,
Thurgh drede þat þai sal consayve þarby,
To wirk gude werkes and fle foli.   335
    þarfor þis buke es on Ynglese drawen
f. 77ᵛᵇ Of sere maters þat er unknawen
Til laude men þat er unkunnand,
þat can na Latyn understand,
To mak þam þamself first to knaw   340
And fra syn and vanytese þam draw,
And for to stir þam til right drede,
When þai þis tretisce here or rede.
þat sal prikke þair conscience withyn,
And of þat drede may a lofe bygyn   345
Thurgh comfort of ioyes of heven sere
þat men may aftirwar[d] rede and here.
    þis buk, als itself bers wittenes,
In seven part[y]es divised es.
þe first part[e] to knaw and hafe in mynde   350
Es of þe wrechednes of mans kynde.
þe secunde es of þe condicions sere
And of þe unstabelnes of þis werld here.
þe thred parte es in þis buke to rede
Of þe dede and whi it es to drede.   355
þe ferthe part es of purgatory
Whar saules er clensed of alle foly.
þe fift es of þe day of dome
And of taknes þat befor sal come.

---

*325 lang] *om.* Gb   327 þai] *after* þat W, *after* can L   330 þe] *om.* W
333 þan sal] *trs.* A, ȝit suld (*moved earlier in the line*) L, þan *moved toward the head of the line*
SM   340 þam-] *om.* WL, þaire- R   to²] *om.* Morris, for to W   *347 aftirward]
aftirwar G, *Morris's emendation*   *349 partyes] partes GLM   es] it es W
*350 parte] party *c*   352 secunde] *adds* part W   359 of] of þe W

þe sext es of þe payns of helle   360
þar þe dampned sal evermare dwelle.
þe sevend es of þe ioys of heven.
þer er þe partes of þis buk seven,
And of ilka parte fynd men may
Sere maters in þis buk to say.   365
Ga we now til þat parte þat first es,
þat spekes of mans wrechednes;
For alle þat byfor es wryten to luk,
Es bot als an entre of þis buk.

Here bygynnes þe first part   370
þat es of mans wrechednes.
   First when God made al thyng of noght,
Of þe foulest mater man he wroght.
þat was of erthe for twa skyls to halde:
þe tane es forthy þat God walde   375
Of foul mater mak man in despite
Of Lucifer þat fel als-tyte
Til helle, als he had synned thurgh pride,
And of alle þat with him fel þat tyde.
For þai suld have þan þe mare shenshepe   380
And þe mare sorow, when þai tuk kepe
þat man, of swa foul mater, suld duelle
In þat place fra whilk þai felle.
   þe tother skille es þis to se:
For man suld here þe meker be   385 f. 78ra
Ay when he sese and thynkes in thoght,
Of how foul mater he es wroght.
For God, thurgh his gudnes and his myght,
Wald þat, sen þat place in heven bright
Was made voyde thurgh þe syn of pride,   390
It war filled ogayne on ilka syde
Thurgh þe vertu of mekenes,

362 ioys] ioy W   363 partes] partyse WR   þis buk] þes bokes W   366 þat¹] þe
WM   368 þat] *after* For RL   370–1 *Cf.* De miseria humane condicionis W, Explicit
prologus | Incipit prima pars, *then followed by this rubric, with* mans] mans awn kynd and his
L; Primus pars condicionis humane M   wrechednes] *adds* to se S   374 of] of þe WM
376 mak man] he (*om.* S) made man WS, man mad M   in] for W   379 fel] *after* þat¹
WLM   382 man] men Morris (Lightbown)   391 It] Till it R, That it L

þat even contrary til pryde es.
þan may na man þider come
Bot he þat meke es and boghsome.   395
þat proves þe gospelle þat says us
How God sayd til his disciples þus:

Euangelium   *Nisi efficiamini sicut parvulus, non intrabitis*
              in regnum celorum.

'Bot yhe', he sayde, 'be als a childe',   400
þat es to say, bathe meke and mylde,
'Yhe sal noght entre, be na way
Hevenryke', þat sal last ay.
þan byhoves a man ay here seke
þat may tittest make him meke.   405
    Bot nathyng here may meke him mare
þan to thynk in hert, als I sayde are,
How he was made of a foul matere,
And es noght elles bot herth here.
Forþi says a clerk, als I now say,   410
'What es man bot herth and clay
And poudre þat with þe wynd brekes'?
And þarfor Iob þus to God spekes:

Iob   *Memento, queso, quod sicut lutum feceris*
          me, et in pulverem reduces me.   415

He says, 'Thynk, Laverd, þat als þow made me
Foul erthe and clay here to be,
Right swa þou sal turne me agayne
Til erthe and poudre'; þis es certayn.
þan says our laverd God almyghty   420
Agayne til man þus shortly:
    Memento, homo, quod cinis es,
    et in cinerem reverteris.
'Thynk man', he says, 'askes ertow now,
And into askes agayn turn saltow'.   425
þan es a man noght elles to say
Bot askes and pouder, erthe and clay;
Of þis suld ilk man here haf mynde
And knaw þe wrechednes of [hi]s kynde.

---

398 non] iste non W   399 in] *om.* AR   400 be] *after* yhe WL, be made meke M
405 may tittest] *trs.* WL   406 here may] *trs.* A, *cf.* here *after* hym W   421 til] tyll a W
422–3 *lines om.* W   428 here haf] here (*om.* L) hafe in WL   *429 his] mans G

þat may be sene, als I shewe can,   430
In al þe partys of þe lyfe of man.
Alle mans lyfe casten may be
Principaly in þis partes thre,
þat er thir to our undirstandyng: f. 78rb
Bygynnyng, midward, and endyng.   435
þer thre partes er thre spaces talde
Of þe lyf of ilk man, yhung and alde.
   Bygynnyng of mans lif, þat first es,
Contenes mykel wrechednes;
þarfor I wille, ar [I] forthir pas,   440
Shew yhou waht a man first was.
Som tyme was when a man was noght,
Befor þat he was geten and forth broght.
He was geten aftir, als es knawen,
Of vile sede of man with syn sawen;   445
He was consayved synfully
Within his awen moder body,
Whar his herber within was dight,
Als David says in þe Psauter right: *Dauid*
   Ecce in iniquitatibus conceptus sum, et in   450
   peccatis concepit me mater mea.
'Lo', he says, als mankynd es,
'I am consayved in wykkednes,
And my moder has consayved me
In syn and in caytefte'.   455
þar duelled man in a myrk dungeon
And + a foul sted of corrupcion,
Whar he had na other fode
Bot wlatsom glet and loper[d] blode
And stynk and filthe, als I sayde ar;   460
With ther he was first norisshed þar.
   Aftirwarde, when he out came
Fra þat dungeon, his moder wame,
And was born til þis werldys light,

---

433 partes] partyes *a*   435 midward] þe m. W   and] and þe WM   437 ilk man]
man bath *a (illeg.* R ?), ilk man both L, man S; M *rewrites:* Of mannes life ȝong and alde
*440 I²] *om.* G, *Morris's emendation*   450 iniquitatibus] inquitatibus Morris (*corrected in
his errata*)   456 man] a man W   *457 And] And in GWM (*rubbed and illegible* R)
458 other] *om.* W   *459 loperd] loper G   462 he out] he forthe W, tym L

He ne had nouther strenthe ne myght,   465
Nouther to ga ne yhit to stand,
Ne to crepe with fote, ne with hand.
þan has a man les myght þan a beste
When he es born, and es sene leste;
For a best when it es born, may ga   470
Als-tite aftir, and ryn to and fra.
Bot a man has na myght þarto,
When he es born, swa to do;
For þan may he noght stande ne crepe,
Bot ligge and sprawel and cry and wepe.   475
    For unnethes es a child born fully
þat it ne bygynnes to goule and cry;
And by þat cry men may knaw þan
Whether it be man or weman,
For when it es born it cryes swa.   480
If it be man it says 'a a',
f. 78ᵛᵃ þat þe first letter es of þe nam
Of our formefader Adam.
And if þe child a woman be,
When it es born it says 'e e'.   485
E es þe first letter and þe hede
Of þe name of Eve þat bygan our dede.
þarfor a clerk made on þis manere
þis vers of metre þat es wreten here:
    Dicentes e. vel a. quotquot nascuntur ab Eva.   490
'Alle þas', he says, 'þat comes of Eve,
þat es al men þat here byhoves leve,
When þai er born, whatswa þai be,
þai say outher a a, or e e'.
    þus es here þe bygynnyng   495
Of our lyfe sorow and gretyng,
Til whilk our wrechednes stirres us;
And þarfor Innocent says þus:
Innocencius   *Omnes nascimur eiulantes,*

---

467 with²] *om.* W*b*   470 when it] when *after* For WLM, *and* it *after* born (*the word*
om. LM) W   471 and¹] or W   *L lacks a folio with lines 472–726, and to that point, b here*
represents the agreement of SM.   478 may] *om.* Morris (Lightbown)   483 forme-]
former A, *illeg.* R   489 þis . . . es] þeere . . . are W   490 *adds* In uitam sine ve non
viuit filius Eue W

ut nature nostre miseriam   500
exprimamus.
He says, 'al er we born gretand
And makand a sorowful sembland
For to shew þe grete wrechednes
Of our kynd þat in us es'.   505
Þus when þe tyme come of our birthe,
Al made sorow and na mirthe;
Naked we come hider and bare
And pure – swa sal we hethen fare.
Of þis twa tymes we suld thynk þan,   510
For þus says Iob, þe rightwes man:
   Nudus egressus sum de utero matris   *Iob*
   mee, et nudus revertar illuc.
'Naked', he says, 'first I cam
Hyder, out of my moder wam,   515
And naked I sal turne away';
Swa sal we al at our last day.
  Þus a man es at þe first comyng
Naked and bringes with him nathyng,
Bot a rym þat es ful wlatsom   520
Es his garment when he forth sal com.
Þat `es´ noght bot a blody skyn
Þat he byfor was lapped in,
Whils he in his moder wam lay.
Þe whilk es a foul thyng to say   525
And fouler to here, als says þe buke,
And aldirfoules[t] on to loke.
Þus es a man, als we may se,
In wrechednes borne and caytefte,
And for `to´ life here a fon dayse;   530 f. 78vb
Þarfor Iob þus openly sayse;
   Homo, natus de muliere, brevi vivens   *Iob*
   tempore, repletur multis miserijs.
He says, 'Man þat born es of woman,
Lyfand short time, + fulfild es þan   535

507 made] made we RS   514 first] *after* Naked A   515 Hyder] *om.* A
521 Es] ⟨ ⟩ `es´ A   *527 -foulest] -foules G, *Morris's emendation*   on] opon R
533 repletur . . . miserijs] *om.* W, *cf.* tempore . . . miserijs] *om.* M   *535 time] time to
G, *emendation suggested in Morris's note*

Of many maners of wrechednes'.
þus says Iob, and swa it es.
    Alswa man es borne til noght elles
Bot to travayle, als Iob yhit telles:

Iob   *Homo nascitur ad laborem*   540
             sicut avis ad volatum.
He says, 'Man es born to travaile right
Als a foul es [here] to + flight'.
For littel rest in þis lyf es,
Bot gret travayle and bysynes.   545
Yhit a man es, when he es born,
þe fendes son and fra God es lorn
Ay, til he thurgh grace may com
Til baptem and til cristendom.
þus may a man his bygynnyng se   550
Ful of wrechednes and + caytifte.

    þe tother part of þe lyf men calles
þe mydward, aftir þat it falles,
þe wilk reches fra þe bygynnyng
Of mans lyfe until þe endyng.   555
þe bygynnyng of man, als I talde,
Es vile and wreched to behalde,
Bot how foule es man aftirwarde
Tels þus openly saynt Bernarde:
    Homo nichil aliud est quam sperma   560
    fetidum, saccus stercorum, et esca vermium.
Saynt Bernard says, als þe buke telles,
þat 'Man here es nathyng elles
Bot a foul slyme, wlatsom til men,
And a sekful of stynkand fen   565
And wormes fode' þat þai wald have,
When he es dede and layde in grave.
    Bot som men and women fayre semes
To þe syght withouten, als men demes,
And þat shewes noght elles bot a skyn.   570
Bot whaswa moght se þam within,
Fouler carion moght never be
þan he suld þan of þam se.

þarfor he þat had als sharp syght
And cler eghen and als bright   575
Als has a best þat men lynx calles—
þat may se thurgh thik stane walles—
Littel lykyng suld a man haf þan   f. 79ra
For to behald a faire woman.
For þan mught he se, withouten doute,   580
Als wele within als withoute,
And if he within saw hir right,
Sho war ful wlatsom til his sight.
þus foul within ilk man es,
Als þe buk says and bers witnes.   585
   þan may we se on þis manere
How foul þe kynd of man es here.
Wharfor I hald a man noght witty
þat here es over-prowde and ioly,
When he may ilk day here and se   590
What he es, and was, and sal be.
Bot proud man of þis tas na hede
For him wantes skille þat hym suld lede,
When he es yhung and luffes laykyng,
Or has ese and welth a[t] his lykyng;   595
Or if he be at grete worshepe,
What hymself es þan, he tas na kepe.
Wharfor himself þan knawes he leste
And fares als an unresonabel beste
þat his awen wille folowes, and noght elles,   600
And þarfor þe prophet in þe Psauter telles:
   Homo, cum in honore esset, non intellexit, comparatus   *Dauid*
   est iumentis insipientibus, et similis factus est illis.
'Man when he es til worshepe broght,
Right understandyng has he noght;   605
He may be likend and he es 'lyke' þan
Til bestes, þat na skylle ne witte can'.
   þarfor ilk man þat has witte and mynde
Suld thynk of þe wrechednes of his kynde,
þat es foul and vile and wlatsom,   610

575 And] And 'als' (*later* A) AM, 'And' Als W   580 he] he hyr W, *cf.* he 'se' hyre S,
'he' her M   592 man] men R   *595 at] and GW*b   597 þan] *om.* WSM
602 in] *om.* A   607 skylle . . . witte] *trs. sbs.* W, *cf.* ne witte] *om.* SM   609 of'] on A

For he may se fra his body com,
Bathe fra aboven and fra bynethe,
Alkyn filthe with stynkand brethe.
For mar filthe es nane, hard ne nesshe,
þan es þat comes fra a mans flesshe,   615
And þat may a man bathe se and fele
þat wil byhald himself wele,
How foul he es to mans syght,
And þarfor says saynt Bernard right:

Bernardus   *Si diligenter consideres quid per os,*   620
               quid per nares, ceterosque meatus
               corporis egreditur, vilius sterquilinium
               nuncquam vidisti.

       'If þow wille', he says, 'ententyfly se
       And byhald what comes fra þe,   625
f. 79rb What thurgh mouthe, what thurgh nese como[n]ly,
       And thurgh other overt[ur]es of [þe] body,
       A fouler myddyng saw yhow never nane',
       þan a man es, with flesche and bane.

       Al þe tyme þat a man here lyves,   630
       His kynd na other fruyt gyfes,
       Whether he lyf lang or short while,
       Bot thyng that es wlatsom and vile,
       Als filth and stynk and nathyng elles,
       Als Innocent þus in a boke telles: 635

Innocencius   *Herbas et arbores, inquit, investiga. Ille de se*
               producunt flores, frondes, et fructus; et
               tu de te lendes, pediculos, et l[u]mbricos.
               ille diffundunt oleum, vinum, et balsamum; et
               tu de te sputum, urinam, et stercus. Ille   640
               de se spirant suavitatem odoris; et tu
               de te reddis abhominacionem fetoris.
               qualis est arbor, talis est fructus.

       þis gret clerk telles þus in a buke:
       'Behald', he says, 'Graythely and loke   645

---

612 fra²] *om.* WSM   *626 comonly] commoly G, *Morris's silent correction*
*627 overtures] overtes G   *þe] his G, þi WM, *emendation suggested in Morris's note*
638 lumbricos] limbricos *ca, phrase om.* SM, *Morris's silent correction*   639 diffundunt]
defundunt, *corrected by the scribe from* defendunt R, effundunt W   643 fructus] *adds* eius
W, *phrase om.* M

Herbes and trese þat þou sees spryng
And take gude kepe what þai forth bryng.
Herbes forth bringes floures and sede,
And tres fair fruyt and braunches to sp[r]ede,
And þou forth bringes of þiself here   650
Nites, lyse, and other vermyn sere.
Of herbes and tres springes baum ful gude
And oyle and wyne for mans fude;
And of þe comes mykel foul thyng,
Als fen and uryn and spyttyng.   655
Of herbes and tres comes swete savour,
And of þe comes wlatsom stynk and sour.
Swilk als þe tre es with [þe] bowes,
Swilk es þe fruyt þat on it growes'.
An ille tre may na gude fruyt bere,   660
And þat knawes ilk gude gardynere.
   A man es a tre þat standes noght hard,
Of whilk þe crop es turned donward
And þe rote toward þe firmament,
Als says þe grete clerk Innocent: 665
   Quid est homo secundum formam, nisi quedam   *Innocencius*
   arbor eversa, cuius radices sunt crines?
   truncus est capud cum collo; stipis est pectus cum
   alvo; rami sunt ulne cum tibijs; frondes sunt
   digiti cum articulis. Hoc est folium quod a ven-   670
   to rapitur, et stipula que a sole siccatur.
He says, 'What es man in shap bot a tre
Turned up þat es doun, als men may se,
Of whilk þe rotes þat of it springes   f. 79va
Er þe hare + þat on þe heved hynges?   675
þe stok nest þe rot growand
Es þe heved with [þe] nek folowand;
þe body of þat tre þarby
Es þe brest with þe bely;
þe bughes er þe armes with þe handes   680
And þe legges with þe fete þat standes;
þe braunches men may by skille calle

---

649 braunches] branche A   *sprede] spede G, *emendation suggested in Morris's note*
*658 with þe] with G   663 turned] *om.* A   *675 hare] hares GM (þe^1 *om.* S)
*677 with þe] with G

þe tas and þe fyngers alle.
þis es þe leef þat hanges noght faste,
þat es blawen away thurgh a wynd blaste,   685
And þe body als [str]a of þe tre
þat thurgh þe son may dried be'.
   A man þat es yhung and light,
Be he never swa stalworth and wyght
And comly of shap, lufly and fayre,   690
Angers and yvels may hym appayre
And his beute and his strengh abate,
And mak hym in ful wayk state
And chaunge alle [his] fayre colour
þat son fayles and fades, als dos þe flour.   695
For a flour þat semes fayre and bright
Thurgh stormes fades and tynes þe myght.
   Many yvels, angers, and mescheefes
Oft comes til man þat here lyves,
Als fevyr, dropsy, and iaunys,   700
Tysyk, goute, and other maladys,
þat hym mas strengh and fayrnes tyne,
Als grete stormes dose a flour to dwyne.
þarfor a man may likend be
Til a flour þat es fayre to se;   705
þan son aftir þat it es forth broght,
Welkes and dwynes til it be noght.
þis aught to be ensample til us;
Forwhi Iob in a boke says þus:

Iob   *Homo, quasi flos, egreditur et conteritur et fugit ve-*   710
      lud umbra et nunquam in eodem statu permanet.
'Man', he says, 'Als a flour bright
First forth comes here til þis light,
And es sone broken and passes away
Als a shadu on þe somers day,   715
And never mare in þe same state duelles',
Bot ay passand, als Iob telles.
Of þis þe prophet witnes bers
In a psalme of þe Psauter thurgh þis vers:

---

686 als stra] al(l)swa cS, also a, phrase om. M   692, 702 strengh] strength Morris,
both emendations unnecessary   *694 his] om.* G   695 fayles] fales R   717 ay] ay es
WM

Mane sicut herba transeat; mane floreat   720 *Dauid P⟨salter⟩*
et transeat; vespere decidat, indurat, et arescat.
þe prophet says þus, als writen es,   f. 79vb
'Arely a man passes als þe gres;
Arely at þe bygynnyng of þe day
He floresshe and passes away;   725
At even late he es doun broght,
And fayles and dries and dwynes to noght'.
   In þe first bygynnyng of þe kynd of man
Neghen hundreth wynter man lyfed þan,
Als clerkes in bukes bers witnes.   730
Bot sythen bycom mans lyf les,
And swa wald God at it suld be;
Forwhi he sayd þus til Noe:
   Non permanebit spiritus meus
   in homine in eternum, quia caro   735
   est; erunt dies illius centum
   viginti annorum.
'My gast', he says, 'sal noght ay dwelle
In man, for he es flesshe and felle;
Hys days sal be for to life here   740
An hundreth and twenti yhere'.
Bot swa grete elde may nane now bere,
For sythen mans lyfe bycom shortere,
Forwhi þe compleccion of ilk man
Was sythen febler þan it was þan;   745
Now es it altherfeblest to se.
þarfor mans life short byhoves be,
For ay þe langer þat man may lyfe,
þe mare his lyfe sal hym now griefe,
And þe les him sal thynk his lyf swete,   750
Als in a psalme says þe prophete:
   Si autem in potentatibus octogynta an-
   ni, et amplius eorum labor et dolor.
'If in myghtfulnes four scor yher falle,
Mare es þair swynk and sorow withalle'.   755
For seldom a man þat has þat held
Hele has and himself may weld.

L *returns at* 726.   728 þe²] *om.* WLM   731 Bot] For A   736 est] *om.* WM   *At this*
point, S lacks a folio, with lines 748–820, and to that point, b here represents the agreement of LM.

     Bot now falles yhit shorter mans dayes,
     Als Iob, þe haly man, þus says:
Iob   *Nunc paucitas dierum meorum*   760
     finietur brevi.
     'Now', he says, 'my fon days sere
     Sal enden with[yn] a short tyme here'.
     Fone men may now fourty yhere pas,
     And foner fifty als in som tym was.   765
       Bot als tyte als a man waxes alde,
     þan waxes his kynde wayke and calde.
     þan chaunges his complexcion
     And his maners and his condicion.
f. 80ra þan waxes his hert hard and hevy,   770
     And his heved feble and dysy;
     þan waxes his gaste seke and sare,
     And his face rounclés, ay mare and mare.
     His mynde es short when he oght thynkes,
     His nese ofte droppes, his hand stynkes,   775
     His sight wax[es] dym þat he has,
     His bak waxes croked; stoupand he gas.
     Fyngers and taes, fote and hande,
     And alle his touches er tremblande.
     His werkes forworthes þat he bygynnes,   780
     His hare moutes, his eghen rynnes,
     His eres waxes deef and hard to here,
     His tung fayles, his speche es noght clere.
     His mouthe slavers, his tethe rotes,
     His wyttes fayles, and he ofte dotes;   785
     He is lyghtly wrath and waxes fraward,
     Bot to turne hym fra wrethe it es hard.
     He souches and trowes sone a thyng,
     Bot ful late he turnes fra þat trowyng;
     He es covatous and hard-haldand,   790
     His chere es drery and his sembland.
     He es swyft to spek on his manere
     And latsom and slaw for to here;
     He prayses ald men and haldes þam wyse,

762 fon] schort W, few M   *763 withyn] with G   766 a] *om.* WL (man] men L)
772 gaste] body WL   *776 waxes] wax G   779 And alle] Alle Morris (Lightbown)
787 wrethe] writhe R   hard] full harde WM

And yhung men list him oft despyse; 795
He loves men þat in ald tyme has bene,
He lakes þa men þat now er sene.
He is ofte seke and ay granand
And ofte angerd and ay pleynand.
Alle þir thurgh kynd to an ald man falles 800
þat clerkes propertes of eld calles.
Yhit er þar ma þan I haf talde
þat falles to a man þat es alde.
þus may men se, whaso can,
What þe condicions er of an ald man. 805

  þe last ende of mans lyfe es hard, *þe last ende of þe*
þat es when he drawes to dedward. *lyf of man*
For when he is seke and bedreden lys
And swa feble þat he may noght rys,
þan er men in dout and noght certayn 810
Wethir he sal ever cover agayn.
Bot yhit can som men þat er sleghe
Witte if he sal of þat yvel deghe
By certayn takens, als yhe sal here,
þat byfalles when þe ded es nere. 815
þan bygynnes his frount dounward falle,
And his browes heldes doun wythalle;
þe lefte eghe of hym þan semes les *f. 80*rb
And narower þan þe right eghe es;
His nese at þe poynt es sharp and smalle; 820
þan bygynnes his chyn to falle.
His pouce es stille withouten styringes,
His fete waxes calde, his bely clynges.
And if nere þe dede be a yhung man,
He ay wakes and may noght slepe þan; 825
And an alde man to dede drawand
May noght wake, bot es ay slepand.
Men says al þir takens sere
Er of a man þat þe dede es nere.

  Whiles a man lyves, he es lyke a man; 830
When he es dede, what es he lyke þan?

796 loves] luf (*expunged*) loues R   797 þa] *om.* A, þe L, þese M   800 an ald
man] awlde men WL   803 a] *om.* WL   816 falle] to falle WM   *S returns at line 821*
822 styringes] strynges R

þan may men his liknes se
Chaunged, als it had never bene he;
And when his lyf es broght to þe ende,
þan sal he on þe same wys hethen wende,　　835
Pure and naked, right als he cam
þe first day fra his moder wam.
For he broght with him nathyng þat day,
And noght sal he bere with him away,
Bot it be a wyndyng clathe anely,　　840
þat sal be lapped obout his body.
　　þus wrechedly endes þe lyf of man,
And i[f] we behald what he es þan,
When þe lyf of hym passes oway,
þan es he noght bot erthe and clay　　845
þat turnes til mare corrupcion
þan ever had stynkand carion.
For þe corrupcion of his body,
Yf it suld lang oboven erthe ly,
It myght þe ayr swa corrumpnd mak,　　850
þat men þarof þe dede suld tak,
Swa vile it es and violent.
þarfor þe gret clerk says, Innocent:

Innocencius　　*Quid enim fetidius humano cadavere?*
　　　quid horibilius homine mortuo?　　855
He says, 'whatkyn thyng may fouler be
þan a mans carion es to se?
And what es mar horibel in stede
þan a man es when he es dede'?
Als wa say, nathyng es swa ugly　　860
Als here es a mans dede body.
And when it es in erth layd lawe,
Wormes þan sal it al tognawe
Til þe flesshe be gnawen oway and byten.
Forwhy we fynde [i]n a buk þos writen:　　865

835 on] of ARS　　　　836 right] *om.* AL (*adds* fyrst *after* he L), r⟨hole⟩ R
838 nathyng] noght (*after* broght) W, not L　　　　839 with him] hethen W, *om.* S
*843 if] it G, *Morris's silent correction*　　he es] *trs.* WR　　　853 *added couplet, at the column-foot, later* Tellis in a boke full oppenly | Of þe reicchidness of mannes body A (*marginally, original hand* W)　　860 Als wa] Alswa I L Morris　　863 þan sal] *trs.* W, *cf.* þan] *om.* LM　　864 oway] *before* be W, *om.* LM　　*865 in . . . þos] þos in buk c (a] *om.* Wb buk] bokes W　　þos] *om.* WS)

Cum autem morietur homo, heredita-
bit vermes et serpentes.
þe buk says þus þat 'when a man
Sal dighe, he sal enherite þan
Wormes and nedders', ugly in sight,   870
Til wham falles mans flessh thurgh right.
þarfor in erthe man sal slepe
Oman[g] wormes þat on hym sal crepe
And gnaw on þat stynkand carcays,
Als es wryten in a boke þat says: 875
    Omnes [enim] in pulvere dormient, et
    vermes operient eos.
þat es, 'in pouder sal slepe ilk man,
And wormes sal cover hym þan'.

    For in þis world es nane swa witty,   880
Swa fair, swa strang, ne swa myghty,
Emperour, kyng, duke, ne caysere,
Ne other þat bers grete state here,
Ne riche, ne pure, bond ne fre,
Lered or lawed, whatswa he be,   885
þat he ne sal turne at þe last oway
Til poudre and erthe and vyle clay;
And wormes sal ryve hym in sondre.
And þarfor haf I mykel wondere
þat unnethes any man wille se   890
What he was and what he sal be.
    Bot whaso wald in hert cast
What he was and sal be at þe last
And what he es, whyles he lyves here,
He suld fynd ful litel matere   895
To mak ioy whilles he here duelles,
Als a versifiour in metre þus telles:
    Si quis sentiret, quo tendit et unde venerit,
    nunquam gauderet, sed in omni tempore fleret.
He says, 'whaso wille fele and se   900
Whethen he com and whider sal he,

---

870 nedders] neddes R   *873 Omang] Oman G, *Morris's emendation*
874 gnaw] knaw RL   on] of *a*   *876 enim] *om.* G   et] *om.* R   885 he] it
A, þai LM   897 þus] *before* in WM, vs S, *line om.* L   899 omni] omne Morris
900 wille] wild A, walde W*b*

Suld never be blythe bot ioy forsake
And alle tyme grete and sorow make'.
Wharto þan es man here swa myry
And swa tendre of his vile body   905
þat sal rote and with wormes be gnawen
And swa wgly to syght may be knawen?
Loverd, whaso of him þan had syght,
Aftir þat wormes him swa had dight
And gnawen his flesshe unto þe bane,   910
Swa grysly a sight saw he never nane,
Als he myght se of þat vile carcays.
For saynt Bernard þos in metre says:

Bernardus   *Post hominem, vermis; post vermem, fetor et horror,*
f. 80vb   *et sic in non hominem vertitur omnis homo.*   915

'Aftir man', he says, 'vermyn es,
And aftir vermyn stynkand uglynes,
And swa sal ilk man turned be þan
Fra a man intil na man'.

þos may ilk man in þis parte se,   920
What he was [and] what he sal be
And what he es ay whils he here lyfes
And whatkyn fruyt his kynd here gyfes.
Here may men se, als writen es,
Mikel of mans wrechednes,   925
And mykel mare yhit may men telle;
Bot hereon wille I na langer duelle.
Ga we now forthermar and luke
To þe secund part of þis buke,
In whilk men may haf understandyng   930
Of þe wo'r'ld and of worldysshe lyfyng.

Here bygynnes þe secund part þat
es of þe world.
Al þe world so wyde and brade

902 Suld] He solde WM, Suld he L   904 here] *after* þan W, *om.* L, *after* es S
905 vile] fowle W, *om.* L   907 may] to W, *om. b*   908 had] had a WLM
913 þos] *after* For W, *after* metre L (in metre] *om.* SM)   916 es] he es WL
917 stynkand] *potentially* stynk and *a*   *921 and] *in* G   922 ay] *om.* WLM
931 worldysshe] worldely W, worldes L, þe werldes S, þe worlde M   932–3 þat . . .
world] of mans lyfe L   þat es] *om.* S   þe] þis S   *Cf.* Pars secunda De condicionibus
mundi W, Here begynnes þe secunde of þis bok M

Our Lord speciali for man made,   935
And al other thyng, als clerkes can profe,
He made anly to mans byhove.
Sen he al þe world and alle thynge wroght
Til mans byhove, þan man aght noght
Lufe nowther worldisshe thyng ne bodily,   940
Mare þan our lord God almyghty,
Ne als mykel as God, þogh þat war les;
And whaso dos, unkynd he es.
For God war worthy mare to be lufed
þan any creature, and swa byhufed,   945
Syn he es maker of al thyng
And of alle creatures þe bygynnyng.
    þis say [I] by men þat gyves þam mykel
Til þis world þat es fals and fikel,
And lufes alle thyng þat til it falles;   950
Swilk men worldisshe men men calles,
þat þair luf mast on þe world settes,
And þat luf þe luf of God lettes.
þarfor gude it es þat a man him kepe
Fra worldisshe luf and vany worshepe.   955
For thurgh luf of þis world and vanite,
A man at þe last forbard may be
Of þe blisful world þar al ioy es,
Whar þe lyfe of man sal be endles,
þat dos to God here þat hym falles.   960
þat world þer clerkes 'world of world' calles.
    [By] alle 'þe' world þat God walde make   f. 81ra
For man, of wilk I byfor spake,
þat swa generaly here es tane,
May be undirstanden ma worldes þan ane.   965
For a grete clerk says þat hight Berthelmewe
þat twa worldes er principaly to shewe,
þat þe elementes and al þe hevens
Contenes, als he þam in boke nevens,
And alle þe creatures þat God wroght,   970

938 al] *om.* WL, *cf.* he al] *om.* M   940 worldisshe] worldis AS, worldely WL,
wardly M   *948 I] *om.* G, *cf.* I say L, *Morris's emendation*   951 worldisshe]
worldlysche W, werldes LS, wor⟨d⟩ly M   955 worldisshe] worldly W, werldes LM
luf] *om.* R   958 þar] whare RL   961 world³] worldes W*b*   *962 By] Whi G

Swa þat withouten þa worldes es noght.
þe tan es gastly, invisi[b]le, and clene;
þe tother es bodyly and may be sene.
þe gastly world þat na man may se
Es heven, whar God syttes in Trinite,   975
And þe neghen ordres of angels
And haly spirytes in þat world duelles,
And þider sal we com and þar lyf ay,
If we þederward hald þe right way.
þat world was made for mans wonnyng   980
Omang angels in ioy and lykyng,
Evermare þarin for to duelle,
As men may here þer clerkes telle.
Now hereon wille I na langer stand,
For afterward commes þis mater til hand.   985
    þe tother world, þat men may se,
In twa partes divised may be,
þe whilk alle bodily thyng may hald,
And ayther part may a world be cald,
And bathe men may se and knawe.   990
Bot þe tan es heghe, and þe tother lawe.
þe hegher reches fra þe mon even
Til þe heghest of þe sterned heven;
þat werld es ful bright and fayre,
For þar es na corrupcion, bot cler ayre   995
And þe planettes and sternes shynand,
And sere signes and noght elles þare wonand.
    þe lawer werld, þat lawest may falle,
Contenes haly þe elementes alle
þat on þe erthe and about þe erthe standes,   1000
Whar sere manere of men wonnes in sere landes.
In þis werld es bothe wele and wa,
þat es ofte chaunged to and fra,
þat til som es softe and til sum harde,
Als yhe may here or se aftirwarde.   1005
    þir worldes byfor, als was Goddes wille,
For man was made for certayn skille.
þe heghest world þat passes alle thyng

Was made for mans endles wonnyng,
For ilk man sal hafe þar a place   1010 f. 81ʳᵇ
To wone ay in ioy þat here has grace.
þat world was made to our mast avantage,
For þar falles to be our right heritage.
   þe tother world þat es lawer,
Whare þe sterns and [þe] planetes er,   1015
God ordynd anly for our byhufe
By þis skille, als I can prufe.
þe ayre fra þethen and þe hete of þe son
Sustayns þe erthe here þar we won
And nurisshes alle thyng þat fruyt gyves   1020
And confortes best and man and alle þat lyves;
And tempers our kynde and our complexioun
And settes þe tymes of [þe] yhere in seson
And gyfes us light 'here' whar we duelle,
Elles war þis world myrk als helle.   1025
Yhit þe bodys of þ[at] world in þair kynde
Shewes us forbisens to haf in mynde
How we suld serve God in our kynde here,
Als þai do þar on þair manere.
   þe lawest world was alswa made for man   1030
For þis skylle, als clerkes shew can,
For þat man suld be þarin wonnand
Goddes werkes to se and undirstand,
And his commandmentes and his wille
To knawe and kepe and to fulfille,   1035
And to be proved here in gastly batayls
Of gastly enmys þat man oft assayls,
Swa þat thurgh gastly strenth and victori,
He may be made in þis world worthy
To haf þe coroun of blisse endeles   1040
In þe blisful world þat hegest es.
   Twa worldes here togyder may falle
þat men may erthely worldes calle.
An es þis dale whar we er wonnand;

   1012 mast] *after* made W, *om.* L   1013 For þar] þarfor it R   *1015 and þe]
and G   1021 best] bestes W, herbes S   *1023 of þe] of GSM   1024 whar] þar
aSM, whare þat L   *1026 þat] þe G   1029 þar] *om. a*   1031 als] als þir A
1036 to] for to R, *om.* M   1037 man] men Rb   man oft] *trs.* W, *cf.* oft] *om. b*

Another es man þarin lyfand.   1045
þis dale whar we won thurgh clerkes calde es
þe mare world, and þe man þe les.
Of þe les world wil I noght speke yhit,
For aftirward I sal spek of it;
Bot of þe mare world yhit wil I mare say,   1050
Ar I pas fra þis matir away;
þan wil I aftir shew, als falles,
Skille why men a man world calles.

    þe mar world God wald law on erth sette,
For it suld be til man suggette   1055
For to serve man, and man noght it;
And þus ordand God for mans profit.

f. 81ᵛᵃ Bot now þis world þat man lyfes in
Waxes swa lither and ful of syn
And of welthes þat are bot wayn   1060
þat many mas þe world þair soverayn
And gyves þam þarto al þat þai may
And serves it bysily, nyght and day,
And mas þamself þe worldes tharlles.
þas men worldesshe men men calles,   1065
For about worldisshe thynges þai here travaile
Ful bysily þat at þe last sal fayle.
Bot wald þai do half swilk bysines
Obout goddes of heven, þar al gude es,
þai suld haf alle þat gude es þare   1070
þat never sal faille, bot last ever mare.

    þe world þat es here es noght elles
Bot þe maners of men þat þarin dwelles,
For þis world men may noght [graythely] ken
Bot by þe condicions of + worldis men.   1075
For what mught men by þe world understand
If na worldish men war þarin dwelland?
Alle þas men þat `þe´ world mast dauntes
Mast bisily þe world here hauntes;

1050 wil I] *trs.* A   1063 serves] serue A   1064 worldes] worlde WM
(*construction changed* M)   1065 worldesshe] worldly`s´sche W, werldes LM
1066 worldisshe] worldly WSM, werldes L   1069 goddes] godes W, god *b*
*1074 graythely] *om.* G, *cf.* na man L (*with rewriting*); graytly (*i.e.* noght *om.*) M
*1075 worldis] þe worldis G, worldishe A, worldlyche WSM   1077 worldish]
worldis AM, worldlyche WL

And þas þat `þe´ world serves and loves   1080
Serves þe devel, als þe buk proves.
For þe world here es þe devels servand
þat brynges his servauntes til his hand;
þarfor God him 'prince of þe world' calles,
þat es, of worldis men þat to him falles.   1085
 Forþi þis world es perillius to lufe
By many skilles, as clerkes [can] prove.
þis worlde es fikel and desayvabel
And fals and unsiker and unstabel.
Many men þe world here fraistes,   1090
Bot he es noght wise þat þarin traystes;
For þe world laghes on man and smyles,
Bot at þe last it him bygyles.
þarfor I hald þat man noght witty
þat about þe world es over-bysy,   1095
For a man may noght Goddes servand be,
Bot he þe maners of þe world fle,
Ne lofe God, bot he þe world despise,
For þe godspel says on þis wyse:
 Nemo potest duobus dominis ser-   1100
 vire, quia aut enim unum odio ha-
 bebit et alterum diliget, aut unum
 sustinebit et alterum contempnet.
He says, 'Na man may serve rightly
Twa lordes togedir þat er contrary,   1105
For outher he sal þe tane hate   f. 81vb
And þe tother luf aftir his state,
Or he sal þe tane of þam mayntene
And þe tother despyse'; þus es ofte sene.
 þe world es Goddes enmy by skille   1110
þat contrarius es to Goddes wille,
And swa er al þat þe world luffes,
Als þe apostel says þus and profes:
 Qui vult esse amicus huius mundi,   *Iohannes apostolus*
 inimicus Dei constituitur.   1115

1085 worldis] worldlyche W, worldysch RS, *cf.* þe werlde (men *om.*) L   *1087 can]
om. G   1092 laghes] *after* man WL   on] on a RASM   1101–3 quia . . .
contempnet] *om.* WM   1109 þus] als W, þat L, þis SM   1114 Qui] Quicunque
WM   vult] *perhaps* wlt G (*cf.* 907), vnlt Morris

He says, 'Whaso þe werldes frend wil be,
Goddes enmy þan es he'.
þan suld we noght assent þarto
Ne nathyng þat lykes til þe world do,
For worldisshe men here God + myspays.   1120
þarfor þe apostel yhit þus says:

Apostolus   *Nolite diligere mundum, nec ea*
                 que sunt in mundo.

'Lufes noght þe world here', says he,
'Ne þat þat yhe in world may se'.   1125
For 'Al þat in [þe] world men tel can,
Es outher yhernyng of þe flesshe of man
Or yhernyng of eghe þat may luke
Or pride of lyfe', als says þe buke:

                 Omne quod est in mundo aut   1130
                 est concupiscencia carnis aut
                 concupiscencia oculorum aut
                 superbia vite.

Yhernyng of flesshe es a thyng
þat falles til lust and flesshe-lykyng;   1135
Yhernyng of eghe, als I can gese,
Falles to worldes rychese;
Pride of lyf þat som in hert kepes
Falles `to´ honours and worshepes.
Lust and lykyng þat es flesshely,   1140
Engendres þe syn of lychery;
Worldes riches of grete pryse
Engendres the syn of covatyse;
Honours nuryshes, als men may se,
Vaynglory, vauntyng, and vanite.   1145
+ Sen God made þe world, als says Haly Writ,   1152
To serve man, and noght man to serve it,
f. 82ra Wha[r]`to´ serves man þe world þan

1120 worldisshe] worldys ALM, worldly W   *myspays] mysprays G   1123 sunt]
after mundo *a*L (*adds* etc. W)   1125 in] in þe W*b*   *1126 in þe] in G   1135 flesshe]
flesshly AS (*an original correction in* A)   1137 worldes] worldly *a*, many and sere *after*
rychese L, þe world M   1142 riches] ricchesces A   *1146–51 *an inserted citation:* De
heremita qui quidem sequebatur mundum a se fugientem, et postea fugiebat mundum tunc se
sequentem: 'Munde, vale! Tibi ve! Fugiens me, dum sequerer te; tu sequeris modo me, iam
respuo despiciens te' *c*; Verba cuiusdam solitarij *as sidenote by 1140 and* Munde . . . despiciens
te *here* W   *1154 Wharto] What `to´ (*later corr.*) G, *Morris's silent correction*

And mas hym þe worldes bondman,   1155
When he may serve God and be fre
And oute of servage of þe world be?
   Bot wald a man ryght knaw and fele
What þe world es and byhald it wele,
Hym suld noght lyst, als I understand,   1160
Make þe world na glade sembland.
For lo, what says Barthelmew
þat spekes of þe world, als I wil shew:
He says, 'þe world es nathyng elles
Bot an hard exil, in qwilk men duelles   1165
And alswa a dym dulful dale
þat 'es' ful of sorow and bale,
And a sted of mykel wrechednes,
Of travail and angers, þat here ay es,
Of payne, of syn, and of foly,   1170
Of shens[h]epe and 'of' velany,
Of lettyng and of tarying,
Of frawardnes and of strivyng,
Of filthe and of corrupcion,
Of violence and of oppression,   1175
Of gilry and of falshede,
Of treson, discorde, and of drede.
In þe world', he says, 'Noght elles we se
Bot wrechednes and vanite,
Pride and pompe and covatyse   1180
And vayn sleghtes and qwayntyse.
   'þe world', he says, 'Tyl hym drawes
And tilles, and lufes þam þat him knawes,
And many he nuyes and fon avayles;
His lufers he desayves and fayles.   1185
His despisers he waytes ay,
Als shadow to tak [þam] to his pray.
Bot þa þat wille him folow, he ledes
And þam scornes and taries in his nedes,
þe whilk a while he here socours   1190
And þam heghes with ryches and honours.

1157 of¹] *om.* W, of þe M   1162 says] *add* saynt WL   1163 wil] can A
1165 exil] yle R   1169 angers] anger WSM   *1171 shenshepe] shensepe G,
Morris's emendation   *1187 þam] *om.* G   1191 þam] þaime he WL

Bot he waytes to bygille þam at þe last,
And into povert agayn þam cast';
Wharfor worldes worshepe may be cald
Noght elles but vanite, and swa I it hald.   1195
And worldisshe riches, howswa þai come,
I hald noght elles bot filth and fantome.
   þe world has many with wanite filed
And with pride and pompe þam ofte bygyled;
þarfor an haly man, als yhe may here,   1200
Spekes to [þe] world on þis manere:

f. 82rb   *O munde immunde, utinam [i]ta immundus `esses' ut me*
    non tangeres, aut ita mundus ut
    me non co[in]quinares!

þis es on Inglishe þus to bymene: 1205
'O þou world', he says, 'Unclene,
Whyn mught þou swa unclen be
þat [þou] suld never mare neghe me,
Or be swa clene and nogt vile
þat `þou' suld never mare me file'?   1210
   þe world here, whoso wille

Howe þe world may Unto four thinges may liken by skille.
be likend til þe see First þe world may lykend be
Mast properly unto þe se.
For `þe' se, aftir þe tydes certayn,   1215
Ebbes and flowes and falles agayn,
And waxes ful ken thurgh stormes þat blawes
And castes up and doun many gret wawes.
Swa castes þe world thurgh favour
A man to riches and honour,   1220
And fra þat agayn he castes hym doun
Til povert and to tribulacioun,
And þa er þe grete stormes kene
And þe wawes þat in þe world er sene.

Howe þe world may   Yhit may þe world here þat wyde es   1225
be lykend til + an Be likend to a wildernes,
wildernes þat ful of wild bestes e[s] sene,

1196 worldisshe] worldys A*b*, worldly W, worlisshe Morris (Lightbown)   *1201 þe]
om. G (Lightbown), *Morris's silent supply in accord with the rest*   1202 immunde]
immmunde Morris   *esses] *after* utinam G, *after* immundus W, *om.* M   immundus]
mundus RM   *1204 coinquinares] coquinares G, conquinares R, inquinares S, *Morris's
silent correction*   *1208 þou] *om.* G   1212 liken] lickend W, likend be R, be lykynd *b*
(*with further rewriting* M)   *1227 es] er c*b* (Lightbown)

Als lyons, libardes, and wolwes kene,
þat wald worow men bylyve
And rogg þam in sonder and ryve.   1230
Swa þe world es ful of mysdoers
And of tyrauntes þat men ofte ders,
þe whilk er bisy, nyght and day,
To nuye men in alle þat þai may.
    þe world alswa may lykend be   1235 *Howe þe world may*
Til a forest in a wilde cuntre   *be lykend til a forest*
þat es ful of thefs and outlawes
þat commonly til forestes drawes,
þat haldes pases and robbes and reves
Men of þat þai have, and noght þam leves.   1240
Swa es þe world here þar we duelle
Ful of thefs þat er devels of helle,
þat ay us waytes and er bysy
To robbe us of our gudes gastly.
    þe world may yhit, als yhe sal here,   1245 *Howe þe world may*
Be lykend on þe fierth manere   *be lykend til a felde*
To a feld ful of batailles
Of enemys þat ilk day men assayles.
Forwhy here we er on many wyse
Alle umset with sere enmys   1250
And speciali with enmys thre   f. 82va
Agaynes wham us byhoves [ay] + armed be.
þa er þe world, þe fende, our flesshe,
þat to assayle us here er ay freshe;
And þarfor byhoves us, day and nyght,   1255
Whilles we lif here, agayn þam fight.
    þe world, als clerkes understandes,   *Howe þe world fig⟨h⟩tes*
Agayn us fightes with twa handes,   *ogay⟨n⟩ vs with ⟨twa⟩*
With þe right hand and þe left – þere twa   *handes*
May betaken bathe wele and wa.   1260
þe right hand es welthe, als I halde,
And þe left hand es angre calde.
For þe world assayles sum men awhile

1230 rogg] *after* sonder W, rent M   1239 haldes] hald Morris (Lightbown)
1241 þar] whare R, whare þat L   1246 Be] Bi R   1249 we er] *trs.* A (*the couplet
om.* M)   *1252 ay armed] armend G, armed Morris   1255 -for] *om.* AS   day]
bathe day AL

With þe right hand þam to bygile
(þat es welth, als I sayde before,   1265
Of worldly riches and tresore)
And assayles men, nyght and day,
With þe left hand þam to flay.
þat es with angre and tribulacion
And povert and persecucion,   1270
þe whilk þer clerkes þe left hand calles
Of þe world þat oftesythes falles.
      Bot with þe world comes dam Fortone
þat ayther hand may chaung sone,
For sho turnes obout ay hir whele,   1275
Up and doune, als many may fele.
When sho hir whele lates obout ga,
Sho turnes sum doune fra wele to wa,
And, eft agaynward, fra wa to wele;
þus turnes sho obout oft hir whele,   1280
þe whilk þir clerkes noght elles calles
Bot happe or chaunce þat sodanli falles.
And þat men haldes here noght elles
Bot welthe and angre in whilk men dwelles.
þarfor worldly happe es ay in dout,   1285
Whilles dam Fortune turnes hir whele about.
      Angre men dredes and walde it fle,
And in welthe men wald ay be;
Bot parfit men þat þair lif right ledes
Welthe of þe worlde ay flese and dredes.   1290
For welthe drawes a man fra þe right way
þat ledes til þe blisse þat lastes ay,
Us aght to drede worldly welthe þan
For saynt Ierom says, þe haly man:
Ieronimus   *Quanto in virtutibus crescimus,*   1295
           tanto amplius timere debea-
           mus, ne de sublimiori corruamus.
f. 82ᵛᵇ   'þe mare', he says, 'þat we wax upright
           In welthe and in wordly myght,
           þe mare we suld have drede in thoght,   1300
           þat we fra þe hegher fal noght'.

1267 men] men bothe W, þam S   1269 angre] angers W, angyres sere L
1284 and] or WL   1287 Angre] Angers W, *cf.* Bathe angyrs L

Tyl þis acordes þe wordes of Senek
þat says þus, als yhe here me spek:
   Tunc tibi salubria consilia advoca,   *Seneca*
   cum tibi alludit prosperitas mundi.   1305
Senek on þis maner says:
'When welthe of þe world with þe plays,
+ Sek þan gude consayl wythalle',
For welthe mas men in perils falle.
   þan es worldes welthe to drede þarfor,   1310
Als says þe grete clerk, saynt Gregor:
   Si omnis fortuna timenda est, ma-
   gis tamen prospera quam adversa.
Saynt Gregor says on þis manere:
'If ilka chaunce be to drede here,   1315
Yhit es happe of welthe to drede mare
þan chaunce of angre' þat smertes sare.
For angres mans lyf clenses and proves,
And welthes his lif trobles and droves
And þe saul of man may lightly spille,   1320
For welthes þat men has here at wille
Semes tokenyng of endeles pyn.
For lo! what says here saynt Austyn:
   Sanitas continua et rerum habundan-   *Augustinus*
   cia sunt eterne dampnacionis indicia.   1325
He says, 'Continuel hele here
And plente of worldly gudes sere
Er taknes, als in boke writen es,
Of þe dampnacion þat es endles'.
And to þis wordes, þat sum men myspays,   1330
Acordes saynt Gregor þat þus says:
   Continuus successus temporalium, fu-   *Gregor*
   ture dampnacionis est indicium.
He says, 'Continuel happy commyng
Of worldly gudes es a takenyng   1335
Of þe dampnacion þat sal be'
At þe last day withouten pite.
   Bot þe world prayses nan, bot þa anly

---

*1308 Sek] Senek G, *Morris's silent correction*   1313 tamen] *om.* AL   1321 here]
om. A   1323 here] *om.* WL   1326 here] here (*expunged?*) hele R   1327 worldly]
worldes W, *om.* L

þat til alle worldes welthes er happy
And on worldly thynges settes þair hert   1340
And flese ay þe state of povert.
Swilk men purchaces and gaders fast
And fares als þis lyfe suld ay last;
Til þam þe world es favorabel
In alle þat þam thynk profitabel.   1345
f. 83ʳᵃ   þe world þam lofes, and þai luf it,
And for þai folow þe worldes wit
And mykel can of worldes qwayntys,
þe world þam haldes gude men and + wys.
Til þam commes gudes here manyfalde   1350
To þair dampnacion, als I talde.
Forwhy til heven may na man come
þat folowes þe world and worldes wysdome,
þe quilk, als says wyse men and witty,
Onence God es [noght] bot foly.   1355
       Sapiencia huius mundi est
       stulticia apud Deum.
Many men þe world here fraystes,
Bot he es noght wyse þat þarin traistes,
For it ledes a man with wrenkes and wyles,   1360
And at þe last it hym bygyles.
Bot he may be called witty and wyse
þat þe worlde can fle and dispise
And hates þe maners þat it loffes
And thynkes ay wyder hym byhoves   1365
And on þis lyfe here traystes noght,
Bot on þe tother settes his thoght.
For na syker duellyng fynde we here,
Als þe apostel says on þis manere:
       Non habemus hic manentem civitatem,   1370
       set futuram iniquirimus.
'Na syker wonnyng-sted here haf we,
Bot we seke ane þat sal ay be'.

1339 worldes] worldly WSM   1340 thynges] thyng RM   1348 of] of þe WM,
the couplet om. S   1349 þam haldes] *trs.* W, *cf.* þam] *om.* L   *and] *and* and G
1351 I] I hafe W, are M   1353 and] and þe W, and hys LM, *phrase om.* S   *1355 es
noght] es GL, it is bot M   1358 þe] þis ALS   1365 hym] þat hym WS. *At this point,
W lacks three leaves and with them, lines 1366–1565*   1370 hic] *om.* R Morris
1371 futuram] futurum Morris

For als gestes we here soiourne
A while til we sal hethen tourne;   1375
þat may fal soner þan som wenes,
For we duelle here als aliens
To travail here in þe way our lyms,
Til our countrewarde, als pilgryms.
þarfor þe prophet says til God þus,   1380
Als þis vers in þe Psauter shewes us:
   Ne sileas, quoniam advena ego sum apud   *Dauid Psalter*
   te et peregrinus, sicut omnes patres mei.
'Be noght stille, Loverd', says he,
'For I am a commelyng towarde þe   1385
And pilgrym, als alle my faders was'.
þus may al say þat in þis world sal pas.
þat es to say, be noght swa stille,
þat þow ne make me here knaw þi wille,
And swilk comfort to my saul shew swythe   1390
þat mught make it in þe glade a[n]d blythe;
And say þos to it: 'I am þy hele,
For þou ert my pilgrim lele'.
þis world es þe way and passage,   f. 83rb
Thurgh whilk lyes our pilgrimage;   1395
By þis way byhoves us al gang,
Bot be we war we ga noght wrang.
   For in þis world liggis twa ways,
Als men may fynd þat þam assays;
þe tane es way of the dede calde,   1400
þe tother es way of lyfe to halde.
þe way of dede semes large and eesy,
And þat may lede us over-lightly
Until þe grysly land of mirknes,
þar sorow and pyn evermare es.   1405
þe way of lyf semes narow and harde
þat ledes us til our contrewarde,
þat es þe kyngdom of heven bright,
Whare we sal won ay in Goddes sight
And Goddes awen sons þan be calde,   1410
If we þe way of lyfe here halde.

1382 ego sum] *trs.* R   *1391 and] ad (*i.e. the mark of abbreviation omitted*) G,
Morris's silent correction

þe life of þis world es ful unstable
And ful variand and chaungeable,
Als es sene in contrarius manere
By þe tymes and vedirs and sesons here.   1415
For þe world and worldis life togider
Chaunges and turnes oft hider and þider,
And in a state duelles ful short while,
Unnethes þe space of a myle.
And forþi þat þe worlde es swa unstable,   1420
Alle þat men sese þarin es chaungeable;
For God ordayns here, als es his wille,
Sere variaunce, for certayn skille,
Of þe tyms and wedirs and sesons
In taken of þe worldes condicions,   1425
þat swa unstable er and variande
þat ful short while may in a state stande.
For God wille men se thurgh swilk takens sere
How unstable þis world es here,
Swa þat men suld mare drede and be abayste   1430
Over-mykel in þe world here to trayste.
    Ofte chaunges þe tymes here, als men wele wate,
Als þus: now es arly, now es late;
Now es day, now es nyght;
Now es myrk, now es light.   1435
And þe wedirs chaunges and þe sesons
þus aftir þe worldes condicions,
For now es cald, now es hete;
Now es dry, and now es wete;
Now es snaw, hail, or rayn,   1440
And now es fair wedir agayn;
f. 83ᵛᵃ Now es þe wedir bright and shynand,
And now waxes it alle domland;
Now se we þe lyfte clere and faire,
Now gadirs mystes and cloudes in þe ayre.   1445
    Alle þer variance to understande
May be takens of þis world swa wariande,
And yhit er þar + ma takens sere

1415 here] sere ASM   1416 worldis] wordish R, werld S, þe worldes M
1420 swa] s- *later* A   1438 es¹] cs Morris   1440 Now] For now Morris
1444 lyfte] light ARL, firmament M   *1448 ma] other ma *c*, ma othere SM

Of þe unstablenes of þis lif here.
For now es mirthe, now es murnyng;   1450
Now es laghter and now es gretyng;
Now er men wele, now er men wa;
Now es a man frende, now es he faa;
Now es a man light, now es [he] hevy;
Now es he blithe, now es he drery;   1455
Now haf we ioy, now haf we pyn;
Now we wyn and now we tyn;
Now er we ryche, now er we pur;
Now haf we or-litel, now pas we mesur;
Now er we bigg, now er we bare;   1460
Now er we hale, now seke and sare;
Now haf we rest and now travail;
Now we fande our force, now we fail;
Now er we smert, now er we slawe;
Now er we hegh, now er we lawe;   1465
Now haf we ynogh, now haf we noght;
Now er we aboven, and now doun broght;
Now haf we pees, now haf we were;
Now eese us a thyng, now fele we it dere;
Now lofe we, now hate, now saghtel, now strife.   1470
þer er þe maners here of þis lyfe,
þe whilk er takens of unstabelnes
Of þis worldis lyfe þat chaungeable es.
Bot als þis lyf es ay passand,
Swa es þe worlde ilk day apayrand,   1475
For þe world til þe endewarde fast drawes,
Als clerkes by many takens knawes.
þarfor þe world þat clerkes sees þus helde
Es als mykel to say als 'þe wer elde'.

   Twa erthely worldes til þis life falles,   1480
Als es sayd byfor, þat clerkes calles
þe mare world of erthe and þe les;
Ful chaungeable ayther world es.
þe mare world es þis world brade,

1451 and] om. A   es²] om. RM   1452 now²] and now AS   *1454 he] om. G, the
couplet om. SM, Morris's emendation   1457 and] om. Morris (Lightbown)   we²] om. A
1463 fail] fale R   1469 eese . . . thyng] a thyng eeses vs A, is it gude M   1472 of] of
þe Morris, and L   1478 þus] pus Morris (corrected in his errata)

And þe les es man, for wham it es made,   1485
<Ho>we man <es> þe les   And als the mare world es round sette,
world <ca>lled and es   Swa es þe les world, man, round for to mette.
lyke til <a> man<n..>   For in þe brede of man es contende
                         Als lang space fra þe lang-fynger ende
f. 83ᵛᵇ   Of þe right hande, with armes out spredande,   1490
          Til þe same fynger ende of þe left hande,
          Als fra þe haterel oboven þe croun
          Es sene tyl þe sole of þe fot doun.
          þan if a man is armes out sp[re]de,
          Na mar es þe lengthe þan þe brede.   1495
          Swa may 'men' mette a man withoute
          Als a compas round aboute.
          þos has þe les world, þat man es,
          Shap of þe mare world and liknes.
              Bathe þer worldes, I dar wele say,   1500
          Sal fail atte þe laste and passe away;
          For ay þe mare elde þat þai bere,
          þe mare þai appair and er feblere,
          Als men sees þat til þam tas tent.
          And þarfor says þus Innocent: 1505
Innocencius   Senuit iam mundus, uterque macrocosmos, [id est]
              maior mundus, et microcosmus, [id est] minor mun-
              dus. Et quanto prolixius utriusque senectus producitur,
              tanto deterius utriusque natura turbatur.
          He says þus, als in Latyn es talde,   1510
          'Ayther worlde now waxes alde,
          And þe langer þat þair tym es soght
          And þe elde of ayther of þam forth-broght,
          þe mare in malys and febelnes
          þe kynd of ayther trobled es'.   1515
              Of bathe þer worldes gret outrage we se
          In pompe and pride and vanite,
          In selcouthe maners and sere degyse
          þat now es used of many wyse
          In worldis havyng and beryng,   1520

1493 sene] om. R, sythen S   *1494 sprede] sperde G, Morris's silent correction
*1506 id est] et G, the phrase om. L, om. the quotation SM (at a page boundary M)
*1507 id est] et G   1509 deterius] dexterius Morris (Lightbown)   1513 þam] adds
es A (of þam] om. SM)

In vayn apparail and in weryng
þat tas overmykel vayn costage
And tornes alle intil outrage.
For swilk degises and suilk maners
Als yhong men now hauntes and lers   1525
And ilk day es comonly sen,
Byfor þis tyme ne has noght ben.
For þat somtyme men held velany,
Now yhung men haldes curtasy;
And þat somtym was curtasy cald,   1530
Now wille yhong men velany hald.
Now + may men se ofte chaungyng
Of sere maners of gys of clethyng;
For now wers men short and now syde;
Now uses men narow and now wyde;   1535
Som has þair clethyng hyngand als stoles;
Som gas tatird als tatird foles;
Som gase wrynchand to and fra;   H f. 223ᵛᵃ/1
And som gas hypand als a ka.
þus uses yhong men all new gett,   1540
And þe world þai all awkeward sett
Thurgh swylk uncomly pomp and pryde
þat þai schew, whether þai gang or ryde.
Swa mykell pryde als now es, I wene,
Was never bifore þis tyme sene;   1545
Of whilk comes þir gyses þat we se.
Bot I dred þat þai may takens be
Of gret hasty myscheves to understand
þat tyll þe world er nere comand.
    þarfore in þair gyses þai sall fall,   1550
For þarewyth þai wreth God þat sese all;
And his wreth at þe last sall with þam mete,
Wharfore þus says David þe prophete:
    Et irritaverunt eum in advencionibus suis,   *Dauid Psalter*
    et multiplicata est in eis ruina.   1555
'And þai styrd God tyll wreth', sais he,
'In þair new fyndynges of vanite,

1522 þat] þas Morris   1523 intil] until Morris, into full L   *1532 may]
many G   1546 whilk] swilk Morris   1549 er] es ASM   1552 sall] *after* wreth R,
after þam M

And in þam is fallyng manyfald',
And þat es thurgh pryde þat I of tald;
þis may be said, als þe boke proves,   1560
Be þam þat new gyses controves.
For þai do swa þe world to plese
For pryde, mare þan for þair eese,
And þa þat with swylk gyses God greves
Sall fall in many gre[ef] myscheves.   1565
And for þai will noght be led with skyll,
God lates þam a while have þair will.
    Bot at þe last on þam God will sende
Vengaunce, bot if þai þam here amende.
þan most þai bifore schew som taken   1570
þat God has þam left and forsaken,
And þat may be knawen bi sere gyse.
þarfor says David in þis wyse:
    Et dimisi eos secundum desideria cordis eorum;
    ibunt in + advencionibus suis.   1575
þe prophet David here spekes þus
In Godes name, als þes verses schewes us.
'I left þam', he says, 'out of covert
After þe yhernynges of þair hert;
In þair fyndynges sall þai ga'.   1580
þis may be said be all þa
þat God suffers folow vanytese
After þair lykyng þat þai chese.
þe whilk tyll þe world mase þam gay
And turnes þam fra God oway,   1585
H f. 223ᵛᵇ þai sall at þe last fro hethen wende
In þair syn tyll pyne withouten ende,
Bot þai swylk vanytese forsake
And amendes here betyme make.
    Yhit has þe world, als men sese and heres,   1590
Ma other contrarius maneres.
For now es vertow turned to vyce,

---

*1565 greef] grevos *c*, grete LM, *om.* S   1566 W *returns.*   1568 God will] will
Morris (*the phrase precs.* in þam WL, god *precs.* in þam SM)   1571 has þam] *trs. a*
1573 in] on WLM   *1575 adven-] adinuen- *c*   1580 sall þai] *trs. a*S
1585 þam] þam al Morris   1589 betyme] be tymes A, for þer syn L
1591 maneres] manereres R

And play and bourd untyll malice;
Now es devocyon on som syde
Turned tyll pomp and to pryde;   1595
Now es wysdom halden foly
And turned intyll t[r]echery;
And foly es halden wysdome,
With proud men and unbowsome.

Now es luff turned tyll lychery,   1600
And ryghtwisnes tyll tyrauntry.
þus es þis world turned up þat es doune
Tyll many mans dampnacyoune,
þe whilk folowes þe world swa fraward.
And þarfore þai mon fele payne ful hard   1605
After þis lyfe þat þai here lede,
And þat aght þam gretly to drede.

   Bot it semes þat swilk men er wode,
For þai hald gud thing evell and evell gude;
Wa sall þam be, als we here clerkes tell,   1610
Forwhi Crist says þus in þe gosspell:
   Ve vobis qui dicitis malum bonum   *Euangelium*
   et bonum malum.
He says: 'wa till yhow þat says with will
þat ill es gud and gud es ill';   1615
þat es to say, þam sall be wa
þat here mysturnes þair lyfe swa.
þus es þe world and þe lyfe þarein
Full of vanyte and of syn.

   Bot som men lufes þis lyfe swa mykell   1620
And þe world þat es swa fykell
þat þai wald never part þarfra,
Bot lyfe here ay, if it moght be swa.
For þai luf swa þis worldes vanyte
þat þai wald never other lyfe suld be.   1625
þai will noght knaw þe peryls all

1597 intyll] vnto W, in S   *trechery] thechery H, *Morris's silent correction*
1598 halden] halden now Morris, *cf.* now *after* foly W   1600 luff] lust R
1602 þat es] so WLM   1603 many] many a AR; *cf.* many a man S, many men M
1607 to] *om.* AS   1609 evell²] ille þe W, ill thyg L, *couplet om.* M   1611 says þus]
says Morris, *cf.* þus says *before* Crist SM   1612–13 malum . . . malum] *trs. phrs.* WLM
1614 yhow] þaime W, vs M   1624 swa] so mykell WL   1626 knaw] kenne WL

Of þis lyfe, ne what after sall fall,
Bot for þai life here in delices sere
þai think no heven es bot here.
Bot at þe last, when þair lyfe sall stynt,   1630
þan sall all ioy be fra þam tynt.
　　Bot wald a man understand wele
What þis world es and what he sall fele
H f. 224ʳᵃ When he sall wend fra þis world oway,
Him suld noght lyst, nouther nyght ne day,   1635
Myrthe here ne blythe chere make,
Bot all þe welthes of þis world forsake
And lyf in penaunce and in povert
For þe dred þat he suld have in hert,
If he wald knaw and trow how hard   1640
Him bihoved suffer afterward.
Bot ogayne þat dred yhit moght he
Thurgh hope of hert conforted be,
If he think wele of heven bryght,
Whare he sall won if he here lyf ryght.   1645
þus may ilk man do and thynk,
In whase hert grace of God may synk.
　　And he þat will noght thynk of þis
And yhernes to have nane other blys
Bot þis wreched lyfe þat him thynk gude,   1650
He es outher clomsed or wode;
Or it es a signe of suspecyon
þat he es in way of dampnacyon.
　　Here have I schewed on sere manere
+ þe condicyons of þ[e] world here   1655
And of þe wordes unstabilnes
And of þe maners þat in þe world es.
Now will I pass forthermare
To þe thred part and se what es þare,
For þat part now [I] will begyn   1660
And schew yhow maters þat er within

1628 delices] delytes WLM   1629 þai] þaim W*b*   1644 wele] wille AM
1648 of] on A*b*   1651 or] or elles WL   1652 signe] token W, thyng M
*1655 þe¹] Of þe *c*W, *Morris's silent correction*   *þe²] þis HSM   1658 Now] And now
Morris   *1660 I will] *trs.* HS   1661 And] To RW Morris, And to Lightbown
(*misreporting* H)   er] es A

þat specialy spekes, as I sall rede,
Of þe ded and whi it es to drede.

Here bigynnes þe thred part
þat es of þe ded.   1665
   Ded es þe mast dred thing þat es
In all þis world, als þe boke witnes.
For here es na qwyk creature lyfand
þat it ne es for þe ded dredand
And flese þe ded ay whils it may.   1670
Bot at þe last [it] most be þe dedes pray.
Ded, of all þat it comes to, abates
And chaunges all myghtes and states;
No man may wele ogayn it stand
Whare þat it comes in any land,   1675
þat es to say, bodily ded,
Ogayns þe whilk + may help n[a] red.
For all þat lyf has bihoves it fele;
þat aght ilk man to knaw wele.

   Bot bi þe name of ded may be tane   1680
And understanden ma dedes þan ane,
For als þir clerkes fyndes writen and redes,   *Of thre maners of deds*
Thre maners of dedes er þat men dredes.   H f. 224rb
Ane es bodily ded þat thurgh kynd es,
Aneother gastely, þe thred endeles.   1685
Bodily ded þat is kyndely
Es twynyng betwene þe saule and þe body,
And þat ded es full bytter and hard,
Of whilk I sall schew yhow afterward.

   Gastely ded es a twynyng thurgh syn   1690
Bitwene God and man[s] saule within,
For als þe saule es lyf of þe body,
Swa þe lyfe of þe saule es God allmyghty;
And als þe body, withouten dout,

   1663 it] ded AS   1664–5 þe²] *om.* L; *cf.* De morte Pars tercia W, Tercia pars libri
M, *om.* S   1668 qwyk] `q´whilk (*corr. later*) A, whyk S   *1671 it] he H (*extensively*
rewritten M)   most] behofes WS   *1677 may] no man may H, may nane RA, *cf.* avayles
[na drede] L   na] ne *c*   1679 aght] aghe AS   knaw] knawe it W, knaw full LM
1685 -other] *adds* es WS   1687 þe²] *om.* AL   1688 full] *om.* ASM   1690 a] *om.*
LM Morris (Lightbown)   *1691 mans] man HWS

Es ded when þe saule es passed out,   1695
þe saule of man es ded ryght swa,
When God es departed þarefra.
For whare syn es, es þe devell of hell,
And þare whare þai er [G]od will noght dwell;
For dedely syn and þe devell and he   1700
In a stede may noght togyder be.
þarfor when þe saule es wounded with syn,
God passes out, and þe fende gase in;
þan es þe saule onence God ded,
Ay whils syn and þe devell dwelles in þat stede.   1705
And als þe body may be slayne
Thurgh wapen þat men may ordayne,
Swa es þe saule slane thurgh syn;
Wharfor God and it bihoves twyn.
    þan es gastly ded to dred wele mare   1710
þan bodily ded, þat nane will spare,
In als mykell as þe saule namely
Es better and mare worthy þan þe body.
For all-if þe saul thurgh syn be dede
Fra God allmyghty þat es the hede,   1715
Yhit may it ay lyf and be pyned,
Bot þe body es dedly here thurgh kynde.
Of bodily ded es no gayn-turnyng,
For of erthly lyf it es endyng,
And ryght entre and way it es   1720
Till ioy or payn þat es endeles.
Yhit if þe saule thurgh syn be slayne,
It may thurgh grace qwyken ogayne,
And þe gastly woundes of syn
Thurgh penaunce may be heled within.   1725
    For all-if God be ryghtwyse and myghty,
He es full of gudenes and of mercy,
And to turn him tyll man mare redy es he
þan any man till him will be.
f. 84ra For all-if he þe dede of body that greves   1730
Ordaynd til alle þat here lyfes,

1699 þai er] he es WM   *God will] trs. HS   1705 þat] a R   1713 worthy]
worth aM   1717 Bot] For A   1718 Of] For of W, Of þe SM   1727 of²] om.
WSM

þe dede of saul wild noght he
Of na man, þogh he synful be.
For þe lif of þe saul mare him pays
þan þe dede, for þus himself says: 1735
   Nolo mortem peccatoris, set ut magis
   convertatur et vivat.
'I wille noght þe ded of synful man,
Bot þat he may be turne[d] and lyf þan'.
þan may þe synful þat his saul has slayn   1740
Be turned thurgh grace and lyf agayn.
   Endles dede es þe dede of helle   *Of endeles ded*
That es mast bitter and mast felle.
Helle es halden a full hidos stede,
þe whilk es full of endles dede   1745
And of paynes and sorow þat never sal blyn,
And yhit may nan dighe þat es þarin,
Bot if þai mught dighe, als body here may,
Of alle sorow þan delyverd war þay.
þai sal fele þar many a ded-brayde,   1750
Bot þai sal ay lyf þarwith, als I sayde;
For þe ded of hele es a lif ay dyand
And a ded þat es ay lifand.
Dede of helle es noght elles to say
Bot payns and sorow þat sal last ay,   1755
þe whilk saules sal fele withouten ende,
þat tille þat grisely sted sal wende.
Of þis ded may men rede and luke
Ynoghe in þe sexte part of þis buke
þat spekes of þe payns of helle;   1760
þarfor hereon I wille na langer duelle.
   Bot of bodily dede I wille spek mare,   *Of bodily ded*
þat es entre and way, als I sayd are,
Til lyf or ded þat has nan hende,
Als es aftirward in þis part contende.   1765
Bodily dede here dredes ful many,
For twa skilles principaly.

1732 wild] wyll WL, wald SM   1739 may] rath *later over eras.* A, rather W, mare S,
cf. Bot turne hym son L, But turne fro syn M   *turned] turnes G, *Morris's silent correction*;
cf. turne hym son L   1747 es] are WS   1748 als] als þe W, als a *b*   1750 a ded]
dedes W, ded M   1751 ay lyf] *trs.* A   1761 I wille] *trs. a*L

Twa prin⟨ci⟩pal
sk⟨ylles⟩ why ⟨we sulde⟩
drede bodil⟨y⟩ ded

Ane es for þe payne þat a man has
When þe dede hym assayles and slas.
þe tother es for, when his lif sal here ende,   1770
He what never whider he sal wende;
For in dout he es and uncertayn
Whether he sal til ioy or payn.
Bot howswa he sal aftir fare,
þe payn of dede here es bitter and sare;   1775
þarfor ilk man þat of dede has mynde
Dredes gretely þe dede here thurgh kynde,

f. 84rb And swa it semed, als says þe boke,
That Crist did in manhede þat he toke.
For he byfor, ar he deyghed on þe rode,   1780
For drede of dede he swet blode,
For he wyst, ar he til þe dede suld passe,
What þe payn of þe dede wasse.
þan may we þarby trow right wele
þat þe payn of 'þe' dede es hard to fele.   1785
    Of þe dede here men may thynk wonder,
For alle thyng it brestes in sonder
Als it sculkes by diverse ways.
þarfor þe haly man in boke þus says:
    Mors omnia   1790
    solvit.
'þe dede', he says, 'louses alle thyng'
And of ilk mans lif mas endyng.
þe dede es swa sutil and pryve
þat na man may it properly se,   1795
And forthy þat na man may se it,
þarfor may na man knaw ne witt
Ne ymagyn thurgh witte what it es,
Ne what shappe it has and lyknes.
    Bot what dede es properly to say,   1800
Whaswa wille, shortly wite he may.
Dede es noght elles to telle shortly
Bot a partyng of þe saul and body,

1774 -swa] -soeuer W, *om. b*   1775 of] of þe RA   here es] *trs.* WL (here) *om.* M)
1778 semed] semes WM   1780 þe] *om.* WM   1781 swet] swette þe WL
1791–2 omnia solvit] *trs.* R   1799 and] in WL, ne S, of M   1801 shortly wite] *trs.*
A, *cf.* wille shortly L   1803 and] and þe RWb

Als I byfor aparty sayde.
þis may be calde þe dedis brayde   1805
And a privacion of þe life,
When it partes fra þe body in strife.
And als yhe may se and wate wele
þat myrknes kyndly es noght to fele,
Bot overalle whar na light es   1810
þar es properly myrknes,
Right swa þe dede es noght elles
Bot a privyng of lyf, als clerkes telles.
For wharswaever þe lyf fayles,
þar es þe dede þat ʻþanʼ assayles.   1815
þus þe dede þat men dredes mast
When þe lyf fayles, men byhoves tast.

    Four skilles I fynd writen in som stede   *Howe men suld drede*
Why men suld specialy drede þe dede: *þe ded for four skils*
An es for þe dede-stoure swa felle,   1820
þat es mare payne þan man can telle,
þe whilk ilk man sal fele within,
When þe body and þe saule salle twyn.
Another es for þe sight þat he sal se
Of devels þat about hym þan sal be.   1825
þe thred es for þe acount þat he sal yheld   f. 84ᵛᵃ
Of alle his lyf, of yhouthe and elde.
þe ferth es for he es uncertayne
Whether he sal wend til ioy or payne.
Whaswa wil of þer four take hede,   1830
Hym aght gretely þe dede here to drede.
Of twa of there four byfor I spake;
Now wil I other twa til þam take.
For of twa I spak first generaly,
Now I wille with other twa þam specify.   1835

    First aght men drede þe ded in hert   *þe first skille why ded*
For þe payn of þe dede, þat es swa smert,   *es to drede*
þat es þe hard stour at þe last ende,
When þe saule sal fra þe body wende.
A doleful partyng es þat to telle,   1840

1805 dedis] dede A   1825 be] fle R   1831 here] *after* gretely Morris
(Lightbown), *om.* SM   1832 of²] *om.* A   1833 wil I] *trs.* AS   1834 first] *after*
twa *a, om.* L   1836 þe] *om.* Wb (ded] god L)

For ʼþaiʼ luf ay togyder to duelle.
Nouther of þam wald other forga,
Swa mykel lof es bytwen þam twa;
And þe mare þat twa togyder lufes,
Als a man and his wyfe ofte proves,   1845
þe mare sorow and murnyng
Byhoves be at þair departyng.
Bot þe body and þe saul with þe lyfe
Lufes mare samen þan man and his wyfe,
Whether þai be in gude way or ille,   1850
And þat es for many sere skylle.
    A skylle es, als yhe [n]ow sal se,
Why þai wald ay togyder be:
Forthy þat God, als says Haly Writ,
First body and saul togyder knyt;   1855
Another, for ʼþeʼ tane may noght do,
Bot if þe tother help þarto;
þhe thred for þai bathe togider sal come
Byfor God at þe day of dome;
þe ferthe for when þai er comen theder,   1860
þai sal ay after duel togider.
þarfor þair payne and sorow es mare
When þe tane sal fra þe tother fare.
    þis twynnyng may be cald þe dede
þat fleyghes about fra sted til stede   1865
Thurgh alle landes, fer and nere,
And spares nan of wham he has powere,
For prayer ne gyfte þat men may gyfe.
Whare he comes, he lattes nane lyfe,
Ne for luf ne awe er nane sparde,   1870
For þe dede til na man tas rewarde,
Ne riche ne pover he spars, hegh ne law,
þat he ne þe lyf wil fra þam draw.
f. 84vb þe dede has mercy of na wight,
Als saynt Bernard þus shewes right: 1875

1849 hys] om. WM, þe S   *1852 now sal] trs. GS (adds here, canc.? L)
1855 body] þe body WL, es þe body S   saul] þe sawle WLS   1862 payne . . . sorow]
trs. nouns W, paynes . . . sorows M   1863 sal] after tother WM   1870 er] here es W,
he L, couplet om. SM   1872 he spars] cf. He ne spares at line head W, cf. He spares noþer
at line head L

Non miseretur mors inopie,
non reveretur divicijs, non sa-
piencie, non moribus,
non etati.

He says 'þe dede of povert na mercy has,   1880
Ne to ryches n[a] reward tas,
Ne til wysdom þat wyse men shewes,
Ne til elde of man, ne til gude thewes'.
Dede wil na frendshepe do ne favour
Ne reverence til kyng ne til emperour,   1885
Ne til pape, + til bisshope, ne na prelate,
Ne til nan other man of heghe state,
Ne til religiouse, ne til na seculere,
For dede over al men has powere.
And thurgh þe dede hand al sal pas,   1890
Als Salamon says þat wyse was:
Communionem
mortis scito.   *Salamon*
'Knaw þow', he says, 'þat þe dede es
Comon to al men', bathe mare and les.   1895
þus sal dede visite ilk man,
And yhit na man discryve it can,
For here lyves nan under hevenryke
þat can telle til what þe ded es lyke.
Bot þe payn of dede þat al sal fele   1900   *Howe a philosophir*
A philosopher þus discrived wele.   *discryued þe payne*
For he lykend mans lyf til a tre   *of þe ded*
þat war growand, 'if' it swa mught be,
Thurgh a mans hert and swa shuld sprynge,
þat obout war lapped with þe hert strynge,   1905
And þe croppe out at his mught mught shote,
And to ilka ioynt war fested a rote;
And ilka vayne of þe mans body
Had a rote festend fast þarby,
And in ilka taa and fynger of hand   1910

    *1881 na] ne G, *suggested in Morris's note*   *1886 pape] pape ne GL   na] *om.*
RSM, to L   1887 state] estate Morris (Lightbown)   1888 religiouse] na
religiouse R Morris   1906 mught mught] mouthe mot A, mout suld M, mouth
mught Morris   1909 festend fast] *trs.* A   1910 of] of þe RL, and (*expunged and
canc. in red*) S

War a rote fra þat tre growand;
And ilka lym on ilka syde
With rotes of þat tre war occupyde.
Yf þat tre war tite pulled oute
At a titte with al þe rotes oboute,   1915
þe rotes suld þan rayse þarwith
Ilka vayn and ilka synoghe and lith.
A mare payne couthe na man in hert cast
þan þis war, als lang als it suld last.
And yhit halde I þe payne of dede mare   1920
And mare strang and hard þan þis payn ware.

f. 85ra   þos a philosophir, when he lyfed,
þe payn of þe dede here discrived.
    þarfor ilk man, als I byfor sayde,
Aght to drede þe bitter dedes brayde,   1925
For bathe gode and ille sal it taste.
Bot ille men aght drede it maste,
For dred of ded mast pyns wythin
A man þat here 'es' ful of syn.
þarfor þe prophet says in a stede   1930
And spekes þus until þe dede:

Propheta   *O mors quam amara memoria*
tua homini iniusto.

'O þhou grysely dede', says he,
'Ful bitter es þe mynde of þe,   1935
Until þe synful man' namly,
þat for his syn es paynworthy.
þarfor me thynk he es unsleghe
þat mas hym noght here redy to deghe,
For þe dede es privy and sodayne,   1940
And þe tyme of his commyng uncertayne.
    A man for certayne sal dighe at þe last,
For his lyf is noght bot als a wynd[es] blast,
Bot he wayte never what tyme ne whan;
For swa certayne es here na man   1945
þat can þe tyme of þe dede forluke.
Forþi says saynt Bernard in a boke:

1917 synoghe] syn RW*b*   and²] and ilka R   1920 of] of þe R*a*   1939 noght
here] *trs.* AS, *cf.* hym . . . here] noght hymself L, hym noȝt euer M   *1943 wyndes]
wynd G

Quid in rebus humanis cercius est
morte? Quid incercius hora mortis invenitur?
He says, 'what es til man mare certayn   1950
þan þe dede es', þat es swa sodayn?
'And what es mare uncertayn thyng
þan es þe tyme of the dede commyng'?,
Als wa say nathyng þat may be.
þan may na man here þe dede fle.   1955
þarfor a man hym suld redy make,
Byfor ar þe dede com hym to take,
And put hym byfor and ded byhynde,
Swa þat ded may hym redy fynde.
þarfor saynt Austyn þe haly man   1960
Says þus, als I shew yhow can:
   Nescis qua hora veniat mors.   *Augustinus*
   Semper vigila ut, quod nescis quando
   veniat, paratum te inveniat
   cum venerit; et adhoc forte   1965
   nescis quando veniat, ut semper
   sis paratus.
'Man, þ[ou] knawes noght', says he,
'What tyme þe dedes comyng sal be;
Wake ay als þou had na knawyng   1970 f. 85rb
Of þe tyme of dedys commyng,
þat þe dede may fynd þe, when it sal com,
Ay redy til God and bugh[so]m;
And to þat perchaunce knaw þou ne may
þe commyng, for þou shuld be redy ay'.   1975
þan byhoved us our lyf swa cast
Als ilk day of our lif war þe last;
And ilk day be redy and lif wele,
Als we shuld ilk day þe ded fele,
And byde noght til þe dede us vyset.   1980
þarfor þos says saynt Austyn yhet:
   Latet ultimus dies, ut observentur   *Augustinus*
   omnes dies; sero parantur reme-
   dia cum mortis imminent

1954 Als wa] Alswa (swa I L) GWRL   *1968 þou] þan G, *om.* R   1971 of^2] of
þe *a*RLM   *1973 bughsom] bughm G (*couplet om.* S, *rewrites and avoids the form* M),
Morris's emendation

pericula.   1985
'þe last day of man es hyd', he says,
'For he shuld kepe wele al + other dayes,
For over-late men ordayns remedy,
When perels of dede comes sodanly'.
  For if a man þat unredy es   1990
Be tane with dede in his wykednes,
Turne agayne þan may he noght
For to amend þat he has myswroght.
In þat state þat he es in tane,
He sal be demed when he es gane.   1995
Wharfor a man for drede of lettyng
Shuld noght abyde þe dedes commyng,
Bot make hym redy, ar he fel harde,
And kepe hym ay wele aftirwarde.
For when þe dede es at þe yhate,   2000
þan es he warned over-late.
  þe dede fra a man his mynd reves
And na kyndely witte with hym leves,
For þan sal he fele swilk payn and drede
þat he ne may thynk of na mysdede,   2005
Bot of his payn and of noght elles,
Als þis grete clerk saynt Austyn telles:
    Tymor mortis totam animam sibi vendicat
    ut nec de peccatis tunc libeat cogitare.
'þe drede of + ded, when it sayles a man,   2010
Chalanges al þe saul tyl it þan,
Swa þat hym liste þan haf na thoght
Of his synnes' þat he here has wroght.
þan folowes þat man na wys rede
þat abydes þe commyng of þe dede   2015
And hastes hym noght to clense hym sone
Of al his syns þat [he] has done.
f. 85ᵛᵃ For when þe dede comes til a man,
It es over-late to bygyn þan.
Bot I rede a man he amend hym here,   2020
Or þe dede com or his messangere,

*1987 al] al þe G   1991 with] with þe RAM   1999 ay wele] *trs.* AS
2005 of] on RWLS   *2010 ded] þe ded GAS   sayles] assayles A*b*, fayles Morris
(Lightbown)   *2017 he] *om.* G, *Morris's emendation*

For if he wille swa byfor be war,
þe dede þan wele les drede hym thar.
   His mensangere may be called sekenes
þat comes byfor, als ofte felled es;   2025
For sekenes ofte a man swa pynes
þat thurgh þat payn his mynde he tynes,
For he may than thynk on noght elles
Bot of þe payn þat with hym duelles.
Bot when þe ded comes aftirward   2030
And hym byhoves fele mare hard,
þan sal he be in swylk drede sette
þat he sal God and hymself forget,
And þat es skylle, for he wil noght,
Whyles he has hele, haf God in thoght.   2035
þarfor he sal þan his mynde tyne,
And þarfor [yhit s]ays þus saynt Austyne:

   Hac animaversione percutitur   *Augustinus*
   peccator ut moriens obliviscatur
   sui, qui dum viveret, oblitus   2040
   est Dei.

'þe synful', he says, als es writen,
'With pyne of þe dede es smyten,
þat he', thurgh payn þat him byhoves drighe,
'Hymself forgetis when he sal dighe,   2045
þat whylles he mught lif here bodyly,
Forgatte his God þat es almyghty'.
Many synful has here na grace
To haf tyme of repentance ne space,
For whiles þai lyf, þai have na mynde   2050
Of God, bot forgettes hym ay, als unkynde.
Me thyn[k] þan þat it es skille and right
þat thurgh dede God reve þam mynd and myght;
þus sal þai dyghe and heven-blis tyne
And be putted til endeles pyne   2055
þat til God here er swa uncurtays.

   2024 mensangere] messangere Morris, as R*a*L (*the couplet om.* SM; *Morris's note incorrectly refers to the use in 2021* [Lightbown])   *2037 yhit says þus] þus says (*trs.* L) GLS, þus *after* Austyne M   2051 ay als] als RSM, *trs.* W Morris, þe L *2052 thynk] thyn G, *Morris's emendation*   2053 reve] reues RM   2056 here] *om.* *a*LM, ere S

þarfor David in þe Psauter says:
Vos sicut homines moriemini et
sicut unus de principibus cadetis.
He says, 'Als men yhe sal digh alle   2060
And als ane of þe princes yhe sal falle'.
þat es, yhe sal dighe of þe same manere
Als men dighes in þis world here,
And, als þe spyrites þat fra heven felle,
Be casten don intille helle.   2065

f. 85va   þarfor til a man it war wysdome
To repente hym or þe dede come
And haf God in mynde whyles he lyfes here,
Als þe prophet biddes on þis manere:
Memento creatoris tui antequam ve-   2070
niat tempus visitacionis sue.
'Thynk', he says, 'and hafe [ay] in thoght
Of hym þat made þe first of noght,
Whilles þou lyffes, ar þe tyme sal be
When he with þe dede sal viset þe'.   2075
For when dede here assayles a man,
He may noght thynk wele on God þan,
For þe dede his mynde away than brekes,
And þarfor David þos til God spekes:
Psalter   *Quoniam non est in morte*   2080
qui memor sit tui.
'Lord', he says, 'þat man es noght
In dede, þat of þe here has thoght'.
   Bot men may understand hereby
Dede of saule thurgh syn namly,   2085
For he þat has ay God in thoght
In dede of saul semes he noght;
And he þat of God es myndles
It semes þat he in saul dede es.
   God visites us in ilka stede,   2090
Whare we may fele takens of dede;
And if we couthe understand wele,
Ilk day we may takens of dede fele.
þarfor me thynk alle þis lif here semes

2062 of] one R W*b*   *2072 ay in] *a (later erroneously corr. to ay þi A), in þi GMS, ay
þi R, ay *after* Thynk *and* þi *om.* L

Mar dede þan lyf. þus wys men demes,   2095
For þe boke says, als it beres wyttenes,
þat a man, when he first borne es,
Bygynnes towarde þe dede to draw
And feles here many a dede-thraw,
Als sere yvels and angers, when þai byfalle,   2100
þat men may `þe´ dede-thrawes calle,
And other perils and quathes many
þat commes to men ofte sodanly.
þan es our birthe here bygynnyng
Of þe dede þat es our endyng,   2105
For ay þe mare þat we wax alde,
þe mare our lif may be ded talde.
þarfor whylles we er here lyffand,
Ilk day er we þos dighand;
þan semes our lyf nathyng elles   2110
Bot als a dede, als þe bok telles,
And til other lyf wyn we noght
Til þe dede þis life til ende haf broght.
  Bot when þe dede has made ende,   f. 86ra
þan wate we never whyder we sal wende,   2115
Wether we sal til wele or wa,
Bot til þe tane byhoves us ga.
Forwhy til gude men þe dede es way
Til þe blisse of heven þat lastes ay,
And til ille men yhate and entree   2120
Til þe pyn of helle þat ay sal be.
þarfor David, þat was swa haly,
Spekes þus til God almyghty:
  Qui exaltas me de portis mortis ut an-
  nuntiem omnes laudaciones tuas in portis filie Syon. 2125
'Loverd', says David, 'þou ert he
þat fra þe yhates of dede liftes me
þat I may shew over alle thynges
Specialy alle þi lovynges
In þe yhates of doghter Syon'.   2130
þat, als clerkes says þat can þaron,
Es Haly Kyrk þat God first ches,
Thurgh whilk men commes to þe sight of pes.

  2096 beres] bercs Morris   2102 quathes] quayntyse R   2123 til] vntil *a*SM

By þe yhates of dede, als men may se,
þe dede of helle may understanden be,   2135
Fra wilk God liftes us, day and nyght,
To shewe his lovynges with alle our myght
And to serve hym and his werkes to wyrk
In stedfast trouthe of Haly Kyrk,
Swa þat we may afterwarde wende   2140
Til þe sight of pees þat has nan ende.
Heghe in heven es þat fair sight,
þat alle sal se þat here lyves ryght.

    Bot alle þat sal com til þat stede
Byhoves passe hethen thurgh bodily dede.   2145
For þat dede to þam es noght ille
þat lyffes here after Goddes wille
And in þat lif stedfastly duelles,
And þarfor saynt Austyn þus telles:

Augustinus   *Mala mors putanda non est quam*   2150
    bona vita precessit; neque enim facit
    malam mortem, nisi quod sequitur
    ipsam mortem.

He says, 'Na man ille dede shuld wene
þar whar gude lyf byfor has bene,   2155
For nathyng mas ille dede to tast
Bot þat þat folows þe dede mast',
þat es dedely dedes þat sum wille do,
And yhit says saynt Austyn þos [mare] þarto:

Augustinus   *Non potest male mori qui bene vixerit,*   2160
    et vix bene moritur qui male vixit.

f. 86^(rb) He says, 'He may noght ille dede fele
þat in Goddes laghe has lyfed wele,
And unnethes may men se by skille
þat he dyghes wele þat hafes lyfed ille'.   2165
Bot he þat hates þis lyfes lykyng
Thar noght drede þe dedes commyng,
For aftir his dede na payn hym ders.
þarfor says Caton þus in a vers:
    Non metuit mortem   2170
    qui s[c]it contempnere vitam.

2155 byfor] *om.* A   *2159 þos mare] þos G, mare L, *om.* S   2160 vixerit] vixit
Morris (Lightbown), *quotation om.* W   *2171 scit] sit *c*SM

He says, 'He þat can þis lif despyse
Thar dred þe dede here on na wyse'.
   Swa did martirs þat þe dede soghot,
For by þis lyf sette þai right noght;   2175
And other haly men yherned to dyghe
For to be with God in heven hyghe,
Als þe boke of þair lyfes shewes us,
And swa did saynt Paul þat says þus:
   Cupio dissolvi   2180 *Paulus*
   et esse cum Cristo.
'I yhern', he says, 'be loused away
Fra þis life and be with Crist ay'.
Haly men thogh þis lyf bot wast;
þarfor þair yhernyng til God was mast,   2185
And forþi þat þam thoght alle þis lyfe
Noght bot travail, angre, and strife,
þai yherned þe ende of þair lyf-days,
And þarfor þe haly man þos says:
   Melius est dies mortis   2190
   quam dies nativitatis.
He says. 'Better es þe day of dede
þan þe day of birthe', and mare standes in stede.
Forwhy a gude man dighes to wend to rest
Whare his lyf sal be altherbest   2195
When þe saul fra þe body swippes,
Als saynt Iohan says in þe *Appocalippes*:
   Beati mortui qui in domino   *Ion*
   moriuntur.
'Blissed be alle þas þat in body   2200
Dighes here in God allemyghty'.
For þas þat men sese in gude lyfe ende
Dighes in God, and þai sal wende
Til þe blisse of heven þat es swa hyghe;
Wele es hym þan þat swa may dighe.   2205
   Bot alle-yf haly men may digh wele,
Yhit þe payn of dede byhoves þam fele

2172 þat can] þat S Morris (Lightbown), þat at kan L, can *after* lif M   2174 soghot]
soght Morris, *a silent correction* (similarly 2499)   2182 yhern] yherned AS
2184 thogh] thoght Morris, *a silent correction* (similarly 2436)   2200 Blissed] Blessed
Morris (Lightbown)   2204 es] was A   2206 may] *om.* RM

þat es mare þan man can ymagyn,
When þe body and þe saul sal twyn;
f. 86va þe wilk þam aght dred aparty   2210
Thurgh mans kynd, or elles war ferly.
For sen Crist, als I sayd befor, had dred
Of the ded thurgh kynd of his manhed,
þan aght ilk man, bathe mare and les,
Drede þe dede here þat swa bitter es.   2215
þe se⟨cund⟩ skille wh⟨y⟩   þe secund skil, als byfor es redde,
men dredes þe ded Why þe dede es swa gretely drede,
Es for þe grisly syght of fendes
þat a man sal se when his lyf endes.
For when þe lyf sal pas fra a man,   2220
Devels sal gadir obout hym þan
To ravissche þe saul with þam away
Tyl pyne of helle, if þai may.
Als wode lyons þai sal þan fare
And raumpe on hym and skoul and stare   2225
And grymly gryn on hym and blere
And hydus braydes mak hym to fere.
þai sal fande at his last endyng
Hym into wanhope for to bring
Thurgh thretynges þat þai sal mak   2230
And thurgh þe ferdnes þat he sal tak.
Ful hydus sightes þai sal shew hym
þat his chere sal make grisly and grym;
þat sight he sal se with gastly eghe
With payn of dede þat he most dreghe.   2235
Ieremy Hereof þe prophet Ieremy
Spekes þus in his prophecy:
     Omnes inimici eius apprehenderunt
     eum inter angustias.
He says, 'Omang his grete anguys   2240
Hym þai sal tak al hys enmys'.
Howe þe deuel come til   Na vonder es if þe devels com þan
saynt Martyn at In þe ende obout a synful man
his endyng For to flay hym and tempte and pyn,
When þe devel com to saynt Martyn   2245

In þe tyme of dede at his last day
Hym for to tempte and for to flay.
   And in þe life of saynt Bernard,
We rede þat when he drogh til dedeward,
þat þe devel þat es grisely and grym   2250   *Howe þe deuel come til*
Til hym come and asked hym   *Bernard in þe tyme of*
By what skille he wald and be what ryght   *his ded*
Chalange þe kyngdom of heven bright.
þan answerd Bernard þus mekely
And sayd, 'I knaw þat I am unworthy   2255
Thurgh myn awen desert, to haf it
When I sal out of þis world flit;
Bot my lorde Ihesu Crist ful of myght   f. 86vb
þat it has and weldes thurgh doble ryght—
Thurgh right of his Faders heritage,   2260
And alswa for our grete avauntage
Thurgh right of hys hard passion
þat he tholed for our raunson.
þe ta right frely he granted me
And þe tother til hymself held he,   2265
Of was gyfte I chala[n]ge it by skille,
Als þe lagh of his mercy wille'.
And when þe devel herd hym þus say,
Alle skomfit he vanyst oway;
And þe haly man, when þis was done,   2270
Torned ogayn til hymself sone,
And he yhelded þe gast to God and dyghed
And swa þe saul til heven flyghed.
   And yhit es mare wonder to telle
þat God wald suffer þe devel of helle   2275
Apere til hymself þat es of myght mast,
When he suld dygh and yheld þe gast,
Als docturs says of haly writ
In bukes thurgh whilk men may knaw it.
þan semes it wele þat God wil þus   2280
Suffer þe devel apere til us
In tyme of dede at our last ende,
When we sal out of þis world wende.

Sen haly men þat here liffed right
Mught noght dygh withouten þat sight;   2285
Ne God ys moder þat he loffed mare
Wald noght fra þat syght spare,
Bot þat he graunted at hir askyng
þat in þe tyme of hir passyng
þai suld na power haf hir to dere,   2290
Ne þat þe syght of þam shuld hir fere;
And yhit sen God hymself spard noght,
For at his dede þe devel til hym soght
In his manhede for swa þan he walde,
Als men says þat er gret clerkes calde –   2295
þan er we certayn, withouten were,
þat at our last ende þai sal apere.
　　Bot a gret payne þan til us sal + be
þe sight of þam when we þam se,
For þai er swa grisely, als says þe buke,   2300
And swa blak and foule on to loke
þat al þe men here of mydlerd
Of þat sight [þan] mught be aferd.
For al þe men here of þis lyfe
Swa grysely a sight couth noght descryfe,   2305
f. 87ʳᵃ　Ne thurgh wyt ymagyn ne deme,
Als þai sal in tyme of dede seme.
Ne swa sleygh payntur never nan was,
þogh his sleght mught alle other pas,
þat couthe ymagyn of þair gryslynes   2310
Or paynt a poynt aftir þair liknes.
For in þis lif here may na man
Se þam in þe fourme þat þai haf þan,
For if þai had swa large powere
In swilk forme to shew þam here,   2315
Out of witte þan þai shuld men flay,
Swa orrible and swa foul er þai.
Forwhy swa hardy man here es nane,
Ne þat ever was liffand in flesshe and bane
þat saghe a devel in his fygur right,   2320
þat he ne for ferdnes of þat sight

2286 God ys] godys cM Morris, cryst hys W, ȝit godes L   *2298 sal] sal þis G, sal
it L   *2303 þan] om. Gb   2307 in] in þe RaLS   2317 swa²] om. A

Shuld dighe, or at þe leste tyn his witt
Als son after als he had sene it.
Bot in swilk fourme, als I undirstand,
þai shew þam til na man liffand,   2325
Bot til þam til wham þe dede es nere,
For God has restreyned þai[r] powere
þat þai may na man tempte ne greve
Ferrer forthe þan þai hafe leve.
Bot when þe ded assaylles a man,   2330
In þe foulest figure þai apere þan.
þarfor aght ilk man dredand be
Agayn þe tyme when he sal þam se.
   Bot I wille shew yhow aparty
Why þai er swa foul and grisly,   2335
For sumtyme when þai war bright angels,
Als þa er þat now in heven duels.
Fra þat blisful place thurgh syn þai felle
And bycome þan foule devels of helle,
And horribely defygurd thurgh syn   2340
þat þai war wyth fild and hardend þarin.
For warne syn war, þai had ay bene
Bright aungels, als þai war first sene;
And now er þai made foule and ugly
Turgh fylyng of þair syn anly.   2345
þan es syn mar foule and wlatsome
þan any devel þat out of helle may come,
For a thyng es fouler þat may file
þan þe thyng þat it fyles, and mare vile.
   þarfor says clerkes of grete cunnyng   2350
þat syn es swa foule and swa grisly thyng
þat, if a man mught properly se his syn
In þe kynd lyknes þat it falles be in,
He shuld for ferdnes titter it fle   f. 87rb
þan any devel þat he mught se.   2355
Here may men se and undirstande
How foul es syn and how fylande,
Bot men sese noght ne knawes what it es;

*2327 þair] þai G, *Morris's emendation*   2336 when] *om.* Morris (Lightbown)
2345 Turgh] Thurgh Morris, *a silent correction (cf.* 3471)   2357 how²] howe foule A,
om. S

þarfor men dredes it wele þe les.

Bot if a synful myght se withoute   2360
How foul þe syn es þat he bers oboute,
He suld never make ioy ne haf lykyng
Until he war delyverd of þat foul thyng.
Syn þe devel þus has tane his wglines
Of þe filth of syn þat swa filand es,   2365
þan aght þe saul of synful within
Be ful foule þat es alle sloterd in syn.
þarfor a man aght, warso he wendes,
Mare drede syn þan þe syght of fendes
þat sal aper til hym at his dede-day.   2370
Bot his syn he sal se fouler þan þay,
Of whilk he wald noght [r]ight hym shrife
Ne repent hym here in his lyfe.

þe thred skille why   þe thred skille til our undirstandyng
þe deed es to drede Why us aght drede þe ded[s] commyng   2375
Es for þe acont ful strayt and harde
Of alle our lif þat has bene frawarde,
þat us byhoves yheld in God[des] sight,
Als wele of wrang als of right,
Of alle thyng þat ever we wroght   2380
In werk, in worde, in wille, in thoght,
And of alle þe tymes þat passes oway
Fra our bygynnyng to our last day.
Alle sal þan be shewed and sene,
Bathe gude and ille, foul and clene,   2385
And be reherced, als þe buke telles,
Bytwene grysely fendes and bright angels.
   þai sal dispute þan of [al] our life
With grete discorde and grete strife.
þe aungels sal reherce þe gude,   2390
And þe devels þe yvel with grete mude.
Alle þe uerkes þat we here haf wroght
Bytwene þam þan sal be out soght
And ilka thoght and ilka welle,
Als wele þe gude als þe ille;   2395

2371 se] se þou A, se wele L, see þan S, be M   *2372 right hym] trs. cW, hym LM; noght hym] trs. S   2373 his] þis AS   *2375 deds] dede GWM   *2378 Goddes] god c   *2388 al] om. c   2394 welle] wille Morris, a silent correction

And ilka worde þat spoken haf we,
Gude or ille, whether þai be—
Alle sal be reherced, als I sayde are.
Bytwen þam þan þai sal nan spare,
Bot anly syn þat es wele clensed here   2400
And gude dede þat es don on right manere.
   þan sal we bathe here and se   f. 87va
Al þe privetese þat ever did we.
þarfor says God in þe godspelle
On þis manere, als I wille yow telle: 2405
   Nichil est opertum quod non reveletur, nec   *Euangelium*
   occultum quod non sciatur.
'Nathyng here [es] swa coverd and hydde
þat sal noght þan be shewed and kydde,
Ne swa prive es nathyng þat touches man   2410
þat sal noght be knawen þan'.
þan most us abyde; we may noght fle
Until al our lyf examynd be
And alle our dedys, bathe gude and ille,
Be discussed, after Goddes wille.   2415
þan sal we se alle our syn halely,
And what we er for our syn worthy,
And alle our dedys þat gud here semed
þan sal be discussed haly and demed
Swa þat we may se and knaw by sight,   2420
Wether we þam dide wrang or ryght;
`And wilk we dyd parfitely here,´
And wilk was don on wrang manere.
   þarfor seynt Anselme, als þe buke shewes us,
Spekes tyl þe saul and says þus: 2425
'Wreched saul', he says, 'What may þou say
When þou partes fra þe body away?
þan þe byhoves acounte yhelde
Of alle þi lyf of youthe and elde,
How þow has here led þi lyfe,   2430
And how þow has spendyd þi wittes fife,
Fra þe first day þat [þou] had witte

2399 þai] *om.* A   *2408 here es] here G, is L, is here M   2422-3 *couplet trs.*
Morris (*see note*)   2428 þe byhoves] *trs.* A   2429 of²] *om.* AS, bath in L, in M
*2432 þou] *om.* G, *Morris's emendation* (*the couplet om.* SM)

Unto þe last day + þow shuld hethen flite.
þan sal walaway be þi sang,
For þou here dispended þi tym wrang,   2435
Bathe in werk and word, in thogh and wille,
And yhit when þou mught helpe, þou held þe stille.
þou has done many synful dede;
To greve God þou had na drede.
Bot when þou sese alle þi trespas,   2440
þan sal þou say, "allas! allas!"
When alle þi life sal be thurgh-soght
Unto þe lest thyng þat ever þou wroght,
Whether þou be lered or + lewed,
þi syns sal þan be many shewed   2445
þat þow has done here in þi life,
Of whilk þou couthe þe never shrife.
And þa sal be shewed byfor þe
Ful foule and ugly syns to se,
f. 87vb   Of whilk þou sal haf mare drede and awe   2450
þan of þa þat þou mught here knawe.
Yhit som dedys þat þe thoght here don wele
þou sal þan se foul syns and fele;
þan byhoves þe resayve sone
Efter þi werkes þat þou has done,   2455
þat es to say outher ioy or payne';
þou may on na wyse be þaragayne.
    þos sal ilk man at his endyng
Be putted til an hard rekenyng
And be aresoned, als right es,   2460
Of alle his mysdedys, mare and les.
Na syn þan unrekend sal be,
þogh it war never swa prive.
Alle þe gud dedys þat we haf done
Onence our syns sal þan sem fone,   2465
And yhit we er unsyker in thoght
Wether þai sal be alowed or noght.
For I fynd wryten thre skills why
þat na man may trayste sikerly

*2433 day] R Morris, day þat GAL (Lightbown), day when W (the couplet om. SM)
2435 þi] þe A   2440 þou] you Morris   *2444 or] or þou be c   2447 þe never]
trs. A   2461 mare] bathe mar aM

In hys gude dedys þat he dus here;   2470
þir thre skils er gude to lere.
   Ane es forthy þat alle thynges
þat gude er, anly of God springes;
þan er al gude dedys þat er wroght
Goddes awen dedys and ours noght.   2475
Bot alle our syns þat may be knawen
Commes of ourselven; þa er our awen,
Forwhy withouten God we syn sone,
Bot na gude withouten God es done.
   Another skille es alswa forþi   2480
þat we er comonly mare redy
An hondreth sythes here for to syn
þan anes a gude dede for to bygyn;
Swa may we ay rekken and rede
An hondreth syns agayne a gude dede.   2485
   þe thred skille es þis to shew omang,
For our gude dedys er ofte done wrang,
Noght of right maner als þai suld be
Or parchaunce done oute of charite.
Alle our syns er here certayne   2490
And by right and skille er worthy payne,
Bot for our gude dedys certanly,
We wate noght what we er worthy.
Wharfor our gude dedys we shuld noght prayse,
And þarfor þus saynt Austyn sayse: 2495   *Augustinus*
   Mala nostra sunt pura mala, sed bona
   nostra `non´ sunt pura bona.
He says, 'Our ille dedys er pur ille wroght,   f. 88ra
Bot our gud dedis pur gud er noghot'.
Hereto acordes, als þe buk telles us.   2500
Ysidre þe grete clerk þat says þus:
   Omnes iusticie nostre quasi pannus
   menstruate.
He says, 'Alle our ryghtwysnes er sene
+ Als a clathe filed of thyng unclene'.   2505
Wha[r]for certanly here wate nane

2496 sunt] non sunt Morris, *corrected in his errata*   2496 pura] pura nostra A, *cf.*
mala nostra M   2503 menstruate] menstruale R Morris   *2505 Als] Sene als G,
Morris's silent correction*

How he sal fare, when he es hethen gane.
　Bot comfort of gud hope may he fele
þat here lyves wele to fare wele,
For we awe to trow, withouten were,　　　　　　2510
þat God sal hym yhelde þat dose wele here.
Bot yhit es 'he' noght syker in þir days,
Forwhy þe haly man þos says:
　　Nescit homo utrum dignus sit
　　odio vel amore.　　　　　　2515
'For certayn', he says, 'a man what noght',
þohg he had never swa mykel gude wroght,
'Whether he war worthy after his dede
To hafe luf of God or hatrede'.
And Isidre, als a buke shewes us,　　　　　　2520
Acordes þarto, þat says þus:
Isidre　　*Servus Dei dum bonum agit, utrum*
　　sit ei ad bonum, incertus est.
He says, 'He þat es God servand,
When he gude dus', outher with tung or hand,　　2525
'He es noght certayne yhit in thoght
Wether it be gude til hym or noght'.
　Wharfor our lyfyng here es harde,
Als þe haly man says, saynt Bernarde:
　　Quis sine trepidacione et timore　　　　2530
　　hanc vitam ducere potest?
'Wha', he says, 'may þis lyfe here lede
Withouten tremblyng and drede'?
Als wa say, here may lyf na man
Withouten drede, þat witte can,　　　　　　2535
For al-if a man here afforce hym ay
For to do alle þe gude þat he may,
Yhit may his gude dedis be swa wroght
þat parchaunce God allowes þam noght.
And þarfor saynt Bernard pleyned hym here　　2540
Of his lyf, þat says on þis manere:

Terret me tota vita mea qua, diligenter discussa,
apparet michi aut peccatum aut sterilitas.
et si quis in ea fructus videtur, sic est
aut simulatum, aut imperfectum, aut | alio   2545 f. 88ʳᵇ
modo corruptum, ut possit aut non placere
deo aut displicere.

þer er Bernard wordes þat says,
'Al my lyfe here me flays,
For if it ententyfly discussed be,   2550
It semes noght elles here until me
Bot owther syn þat þe saul mast deres
Or barran thyng þat na fruyt beres.
And if any fruyt þarin seme,
It may be þus be skil to deme   2555
Outher feyned thyng to shew in syght
Or thyng þat es noght alle done ryght
Or on other wyse, corrumped within
(þat es to say, filed with syn)
Swa þat outher þan may it noght   2560
Pay God allemyghty, þat es swa wroght,
Or paraunter it hym myspays'.
þos þe haly man saynt Barnard says.
What may a synful man say þan,
When he þat was swa haly a man,   2565
Couth na fruyt here in his life se?
þan aght þe synful dredand be
Of is life here, þat es unclene,
In whilk na fruyt may be sene.
    þe ferth skille and þe last to telle   2570
Why man dredis þe dede swa felle
Es for he wate noght whether he sal wende
Tylle ioy or payne aftir his lyfes ende.
For swa wyse and witty man es nane
þat wate, when þe dede him has tane,   2575
For certayn wheder + he sal ga,
Whether he sal wend til wele or wa.
þan aght ilk man, bathe yong and alde,

2546 aut] ? autem A, ut L   2558 corrumped] corupt A, ben corrumpt M
2566 his] h *later* A, þis S (*cf. the next*)   2568 is] his ARL, þis SM Morris
*2576 wheder] whederwarde *c*

Haf drede for þis skille þat I talde,
For when þe devels and þe angels   2580
Has desputed our lif, als þe buke telles,
And discucion made, als fals to be,
þan sal we certanly here and se
Our certayne dome þat we sal have,
Wether we sal be dampned or save   2585
And outher þan wend to joy or pyne.
þarfor þe haly man says, saynt Austyne:
  Bene unusquisque de die novissimo
  formidare debet, quia unumquenque
  in quo invenerit suus novissimus dies,   2590
  cum de hoc seculo egreditur, talis in die
  novissimo iudicatur.

f. 88va 'Ilk man', he says, 'þat sal pas away
And shuld haf drede of hys last day,
For in what state swa he be þan,   2595
Swilk als his last day fyndes a man,
When he sal out of þis werld wende,
Swilk mon he be demed at þe ende'.
þarfor our last day þat sal falle
Our day of dome we may [it] calle,   2600
Bot at þe general day of dome
With our bodys we sal come
Byfor Ihesu Cryst, allemyghty kyng,
þat sal þat day deme alle thyng.
þan sal he deme ilka nacyon   2605
And mak a fynal declaracyon
Of alle þe domes byfor shewed
In tyme of dede to lered and lewed.
For þe bodys sal wend to þe same stede
Til whilk þe saul es demed aftir þe dede   2610
And outher þan have ful ioy togyder
Or ful sorow when þai com thyder,
And evermare aftir togyder duelle,
Whethir þai wend to heven or helle.
Bot in erthe sal duelle þe bodis alle   2615
Until þat dredful day sal falle,

2592 iudicatur] indicatur Morris   2598 mon] sal A, bus M   *2600 may it] may
GA, *om.* S   2608 and] or A

When þe dome sal be mast strayt and harde,
Als þis buke shewes aftirwarde.
Bot first, als sone als þe saul namly
Thurgh þe dede es passed fra þe body, 2620
It sal be demed aftir his werkes
Til ioy or payne, als says þer clerkes.
þe synful saul þan gas strik to helle,
In pyne withouten ende to duelle;
þe clene saul þan gas up even, 2625
Withouten lettyng, til þe blis of heven.
    Bot many saules þat er save,
Ar þai com to blis, payne byhoves have
In purgatori and duelle þarin
Until þai be clensed of al syn, 2630
þat er schrywen and noght clensed here,
And þar be fyned als gold þat shynes clere.
For in heven may na saul be sene
Unto it be fyned and clensed clene,
Outher here thurgh penaunce, als clerkes wate, 2635
Or in purgatori thurgh fire hate.
Wharfor þe saul þat es clensed wele
Of al dedely syn and of veniele
Thurgh penaunce here and almusdede,
þe angels als-tit þan sal lede, 2640
When it es passed fra þe body away, f. 88ᵛᵇ
Til þe blis of heven þat sal last ay.
    þarfor whaswa wille folow wysdome,
He suld before, ar he saw þe dede come,
Mak him redy and clense hym clene 2645
Of al spottes of syn þat mught be sene
Thurgh shryfte of mouthe and repentance
And thurgh almusdede and penaunce,
Swa þat dede fynd hym clene of syn,
When þe body and þe saul sal twyn. 2650
And whyles he lyffes til he hethen wende,
Thynk he suld ay of his lyfes hende;
Swa may he hym kepe fra alle folys.
And þarfor says þus Salamon þe wys:

2649 þat] þat þe RA*b*   2653 fra] of A

In omnibus operibus tuis, memorare   2655
novissima tua, et non peccabis
in eternum.

þat es on Inglis þos to say;
He says, 'Thynk on þi endyng day
Ay when þou sal any werk bygyn,   2660
And þan sal þou nevermare syn'.

   And þarfor þou man in þi werk be slyghe
And thynk ay wele þat þou sal dighe;
Thynk þou sal dyghe, þou wate never whan
Ne in what state þou sal be þan,   2665
Ne þou whate never in what stede
þou sal dyghe, ne of what dede.
þarfor at morne, when þou sese lyght,
Thynk als þou sal dygh ar nyght;
When þou gas to slep, if þou be wyse,   2670
Thynk als þou suld noght with þe lyf ryse.
For saynt Austyn says þus in a buke:
'Lat ay þi hert on þi last day luke'.
Whaswa wille thynk ay on þis manere
And be war and make hym redy here   2675
And of alle hys syn clense hym wele,
Ar þe dede com þat hym byhoves fele,
þan may he eschape and passe lightly
þe bitter payn of purgatory
And com til þe blisse of heven bright,   2680
þar ay es day and never nyght.

   Here es þe thred parte of þis buke spedde
þat spekes of þe dede, als I haf redde.
On þis parte I wille na langer stand
Bot passe to another neghest folowand;   2685
þat es þe ferthe part for to specify,
þe whilk spekes of purgatory,
Whar many saules feles ful harde,
Als yhe sal here sone aftirwarde.

2663 wele] *om.* A

[H]ere bygynnes þe ferth part   2690   f. 89ra
þat es of purgatory.

    Many spekes and in buke redes
Of purgatory, but fon it dredes;
For many wate noght what it es—
þarfor þai drede it wele þe les.   2695
Bot if þai knew wele what it ware
Or trowed, þai walde drede it þe mare.
And forthy þat sum has na knawyng
Of purgatory ne undirstandyng,
þarfor I wille now speke aparty   2700
In þis buke of purgatory
And first shew yhow what it es,
And whare it es, als þe buke wittenes;
And whatkyn payns er þarin
And whilk saules gas theder and for what syn;   2705
And alswa what thyng es mast certayn,
þat þam mught help and slake þair payn.
Of þir sex poyntes I wil spek and rede,
And swa I sal þis ferth part spede.

    Purgatory es nathyng elles   2710   *What ⟨is p⟩urgatory*
Bot a clensyng-sted þar saules duelles
þat has synned and had contricyon,
And er in þe way of salvacion
And er noght parfytly clensed here
Of al veniel syns sere.   2715
Bot þar byhoves þam payn fele
Til þai be clensed parfytely and wele
Of alkyn syn þat þai ever wroght
In worde, in dede, in wille, [in] thoght.
For swa pured and fyned never golde was   2720
Als þai sal be, ar þai þethen pas.

    Wharfor þe payn þat þe saul þar hentes
Er mare bitter þan alle þe tourmentes
þat alle þe marters in erthe tholed
Sen God was for us boght and sold.   2725

2690–91 es] spekys L   þat . . . purgatory] of þis buk M (*and inserts a dozen extra lines here*); *cf.* De purgatorio Pars quarta W, *om.* S   *2690 Here] (*unfilled space for initial*)ere G, *Morris's silent correction*   2692 buke] bukes ALM   2699 ne] ne nan A *2719 in] or GWM, and L   2722 saul] saules A, þai M   2723 Er] Es A

For þe lest payn of þe payns þar sere
Es mare þan es þe mast payn here,
Als says a grete clerk þus shortly
In a buke of þe payns of purgatory:
   Minima pena purgatorij est maior   2730
   maxima pena mundi.
He says, 'þe lest payn þat es þare
In purgatori es wele mare
þan þe mast payn þat may be
In al þis werld to fele or se'.   2735
For þe payne þar es mare bitter and felle
þan hert may thynk or tung telle,
Als þe buke says, trow whaswa wille.
   For sum clerkes says and proves by skille
þat bytwen þe payne of helle namly   2740
And þe payn of purgatory
Es na difference bot at þe tane
Has ende, and þe tother has nane.
þe payns of helle sal never sees,
Ne þe saules þarin never haf relees;   2745
Bot in purgatori saules dueles stille
Until þai be clensed of alle ille,
And mare payn fele, als I understande,
þan ever feled man here lyfande.
For þai sal haf a day þare   2750
Als mykel bitter payn or mare
Als a man mught thole here of penaunce
A yhere, and fele als mykel grevaunce;
And als mykel drighe þar fourty days
Als fourty yhere here. þus clerkes says,   2755
Swa es þe payn þar a day to se
Als mykel als here a yhere may be.
Bot ever a day of penance here
May stand in stede þar for a yhere,
Als God says openly and wele   2760
Thurgh þe prophet Ezechyele:
   Diem pro anno
   dedi tibi.

f. 89rb

2727 payn] þayn Morris (*corrected in his errata*)   2728 shortly] sleghely *later over erasure* A, sleghly W

þat es on Inglys þus to say,
'For a yhere I gyf [a] day'.   2765
    þe payn þar þe saules avayles noght
When þai til purgatori er broght
Bot for to clense þe saul[s] of syn
And for na mede in heven to wyn;
þogh þai a thousand yhere war þare,   2770
þair mede in heven shuld never be + mare.
þan serves þat payne þar of noght elles
Bot to clense `þam´ of syn þat þarin duelles.
    Bot penaunce to thole here with gude wille,
Serves + til twa thynges by skille.   2775
Ane es to clense here þe saul wele
Of dedly syn and of veniele;
Another to haf in heven mare mede;
Til þer twa may penaunce us lede.
For þe saul for ilka penaunce here   2780
Sal haf specyel ioy in heven swa clere
þat withouten ende sal laste,
If þai thole payne here with hert stedfast.
Here may men se, als þe buke wittenes,
And understand what purgatori es.   2785
    Now wil I shew yow shortly   f. 89va
Whar, als clerkes says, es purgatory.
þe stede þat purgatory es calde   *Whar purgatory es*
Under þe erthe es, als I halde,
Aboven þe stede, als som clerkes telles,   2790
þar [vn]crysomd + childer duells,
þat fra þe sight of Goddes face
Er putted forever withouten grace.
þat [stede] es neghest oboven hel-pitte
Bytwen purgatory and itte.   2795
þus standes þe stede of purgatory
Oboven þam bathe in þat party.
Alle þat er þar payn byhoves hafe,
Bot þai haf grace and er save.

---

*2765 a] þe G, þe a RL   *2768 sauls] saul cL   *2771 be] be þe cL, be `þe´ S
*2775 til] here til G   *2791 vncrysomd] crysom dede cALS, vncrysomd dede W,
vncristned M, vncrysom dede *suggested Morris textual commentary*   *2794 stede] place c

Bot fra þe other stedes, til þe day of dome,   2800
Sal nevermare saul out come,
For þan sal þai come til þe last iugement
And with þe bodys agayn til helle be hent.
Bot fra purgatory saules may wynne
Til blisse when þai er clensed of synne.   2805
   Aboven þat yhit es þe ferthe stede
þat Crist visited when he was dede,
And þa þat þar war with hym oute tuke
And left nane þaryn, als says þe buke.
Ne fra þat tyme, als we here clerkes telle,   2810
Com never nan yhit þheder to duelle,
Ne never nan forthward sal com;
And þat stede [men] calles *lymbus patrum*,
þe whilk 'a fre preson' on Inglys es
Whare þe haly faders duelled in myrknes.   2815
   Alle þir four stedes men may helle calle,
For þai er closed within þe erthe alle;
And for helle þai may alle be tane,
Of whilk four purgatory es ane.
þarfor Haly Kyrk þat for saules prays   2820
Calles purgatory helle, þat þus says:
   Domine Ihesu Criste, libera animas
   omnium fidelium defunctorum de
   manu inferni.
'Loverd, deliver out of helles hande   2825
Alle Crysten saules þat þar er duellande',
þat es to say, out [of] purgatory,
þar þe saules er clensed parfytely.
Bot fra þe lawest helle, withouten dout,
Na saul may be delyverd out,   2830
For of mercy þar es na hope;
þarfor þus says þe haly man Iobe:
   Quia in inferno nulla est redempcio.
f. 89ᵛᵇ 'In helle', he says, 'es na raunceon',
For na help may be in þat dungeon,   2835
þat es to say in þe lawest helle,

2800 other] tother RS   2807 visited] visit A, wyset L, vyset WS, vysed M
*2813 men] clerkes cSM   2823 fidelium] fldelium Morris (*corrected in his errata*), *Latin*
om. W   2824 inferni] inferi AR   *2827 of] *om.* G, *Morris's emendation*

Whar þe dampned saules sal ay duelle,
Whar messe ne prayer helpes noght
Til þam þat er þeder broght.
For nathyng may abate þair pyne,   2840
And þarfor þus says saynt Austyne:
   Si scirem patrem meum aut matrem
   in inferno, pro eis non orarem.
He says, 'If my fader or moder ware
In helle, and I wist þam þare,   2845
I wald', nouther nyght ne day,
'For þam byd bede here ne pray';
Forwhy almus +, ne messe, ne prayers
Helpes na saul þar, bot parchaunce ders.
  þe twa lawest stedes þat I nevend ar   2850
Er þe helles þat sal last evermar,
Bot purgatory sal noght last ay;
It lastes na langer þan `to´ domesday,
For aftir þat day, als clerkes can se,
Na stede `of´ purgatory sal be,   2855
Bot helle, ful of devels within,
Sal ay last for vengeaunce of syn.
  Now som has wonder and may ask why
God has swa ordaynd purgatory
And helle ymyddes þe erthe swa law;   2860
þe skylle why may be þis to knaw:
þe syn þat es in erthe wroght
Fra erthe unpunyst passes noght;
þan nedly byhoves be punyst syn
Outher opon erthe or within,   2865
þat es outher here þar we duelle
Or in purgatory or in helle.
For syn es swa hevy and swa harde
þat it drawes þe saul ay dunwarde;
Until payn and penaunce haf wasted þat syn,   2870
þe saul may never tylle heven wyn.
  Yhit says þir grete clerkes namly
þat twa stedes er of purgatory;
þe tane es comon, als yhe herd me telle,

*2848 almus] almusdede cL   *At this point, M lacks two folios and lines 2861–3007; until 3007, As is cited instead, and b represents the agreement LAs*

þat within erthe es oboven helle;   2875
And þe tother es speciele thurgh grace
þat es oboven erthe in sere place.
For in þe comon stede som er noght ay
Bot er here punyst, outher nyght or day,
In sere stedes specialy in gast   2880
Whar þai hafe synned in body mast.

f. 90ra And þat may be thurgh helpe and spede
Of prayer of frendes and almusdede,
Til wham þai ofte in gast apere
Thurgh speciel grace in sere stedes here   2885
For to hast þair deliverance
Out of þair payn and þair penaunce
þat, als I ar sayde, gretely greves,
And for warnyng of frendes þat lyefes.
Here may men properly by skille se   2890
Wha[r] purgatory falles to be;
Now wille I rede forthermare
And shew yhow of sum paynes þat er thare.

Of þe payns of   In purgatory, als þe buke wittenes,
purgatory   E[r] diverse payns, som mare, som les,   2895
And many ma þan I can neven.
Bot I fynd wryten payns seven
þat may be called payns of purgatory,
And þa seven I wille here specify,
Of whilk men sal som fele and se   2900
Als tite als þe ded-comyng sal be.

Of þe first payne   þe first payn es of þa seven,
Als yhe herd me byfor neven,
þe grete drede þat þe saul es in
When þe body a[nd] it sal twyn,   2905
For þe saul sese þan about it stande
Grysly devels agayn it raumpande
Als wode lyons to wayt þair pray
And to ravisshe it with þam away.
And þat syght es a payn ful grevous,   2910
For þ[a] devels er swa foul and ydous
þat swa hardy man was never nane

2879 er here] *trs.* RL   *2891 whar] what *c*   *2895 Er] Es G   2896 ma]
mare Morris (Lightbown)   *2905 and] at G   *2911 þa] þe *c*

Lyfand here in flesshe and bane
þat saw þe syght þat þe saul þan sese
þat ne he for ferdelayk is witte shuld lese,   2915
þogh he war never of hert swa balde,
Als in þe thred part of þis boke was talde.
A grete payn aght þis syght to be
Til þe saule þan þat it sal se.
    þe secunde payn neghest folowande   2920 *Of þe secund payne*
Es þe grete drede to understande
þat þe saul sal hafe wyth dole and care
Until þe dome be gyfen, how he sal fare.
For þe angels sal þare redy be
And þe devels swa grisly to se,   2925
þat sal disput of alle his lyfe
Bytwen þam þar with grete stryfe.
His syns sal `þan´ be shewed ful many,
Als I tald byfor in þe thred part namly.
þe saul sal þan bytwene þam stande,   2930 f. 90rb
And þe angels on his ryght hande,
And [þe] devels on þe lefte syde.
þan mot þe saul in grete dred abyde
Until þat stryfe be broght to ende,
And til it witte whyder it sal wende,   2935
And whether it sal be dampned or save.
    þan sal þe saul a grete drede have,
Als a man þat es inmyddes þe se
In grete perille and may noght fle;
When tempestes falles and stormes smert,   2940
þan has þat man grete drede in hert.
He mas þan vowes and cryes on Cryst,
For he es afered þat he `sal´ be peryst.
And þat drede til hym es a grete payn,
For of his lyf he es uncertayn.   2945
And als a man has drede bodily,
When [he] es acouped of felony
Byfor kynges iustice and þe cuntre,
þat charged es if he gilty be—
He wate noght whether he sal be spilt   2950

2930 sal þan] *trs.* L Morris (Lightbown)   *2932 þe¹] *om.* G   2933 mot] most
RWL, mon As   *2947 he] *om.* G, *Morris's silent correction* (Lightbown)

Or be delyverd of þat gilt
Until þai have gyven þair verdite
And outher þarof made hym qwyte,
Als þe laghe walde, or made hym gilty.
If he þan haf drede, it es na ferly,   2955
For in grete dout of lyfe es þat man.
Bot yhit has the saul mare drede þan
Til þe dome by gyven, and `it´ may se
Whether it sal dampned or saufe be.
For if it dome of damp[na]cion here,   2960
It gas til helle withouten recoverere,
And þe saul þat es dampned til þat place
Thar never hope to haf mercy ne grace.
What wonder es þan if `þe´ saule drede have,
þat doutes whethir he sal dampned or save?   2965
Of þes twa maners of payns of drede
Yhe herd me aparty byfor rede,
þe whilk es declared in a stede
In þe thred part þat spekes of þe dede.
Alle þis matere men may se þare;   2970
þarfor here I wil spek þarof na mare.

Of þe thred payne   þe thred payn es a maner of exil
When þe saules here agayn þair wil
Er exild fra þis lyf til payn
Withouten any turnyng agayn.   2975
For þan sal þai haf grete murnyng,
When þai er flemed fra þare lykyng,

f. 90ᵛᵃ   Fra alle þair frendes lefe and dere,
And fra alle þe delyces þat þai had here.
þe murnyng þat þai haf on þis wyse   2980
Til þam sal be grete payn and anguyse.
    þe fereth payn es sere malady
þat þe sauls sal haf in purgatory,
For þai sal haf þar yvels sere
For sere syns þat er unclensed here.   2985
Som for pride þat þai haf herein bene
Sal haf þar als a fever cotidiene,

2960 dampnacion] dampcion G, cf. of d.] be dampned As; Morris's emendation
2958 by] be Morris   2979 delyces] delytes RAs, delyte WL   2984 þar] þair a

þat þe saule sal pyn mar bitterly
þan ever fyver pyned here mans body.
Som sal haf þar for covatyse   2990
Als þe dropsy to grege þair angwyse.
Som sal haf in alle þair lymmes obout
+ For sleuthe als þe potagre and þe gout.
Som for envy sal haf in þair lyms
Als kylles and felouns and apostyms.   2995
Som for yre sal have als þe parlesy;
þat yvel þe saul sal grefe gretely.
Som for glotoni sal haf þare
Als þe swynacy þat greves ful sare.
And som for þe syn of lechery   3000
Sal haf als þe yvel of meselry.
þus sal þe saules, als God vouches save,
For sere syns, sere maledys have,
þat here has hadde repentance
And has noght fulfiled here þair penaunce.   3005
    þir maladies þar þe saul mar greves
þan it dos any body þat here lyves.
Thynk we what payn has þe body
þat has here bot a malady
In þis lif, lastand alle a yhere,   3010
Or noght bot thre days or four here.
þat malady greves þe body sare,
Bot yhit it greves þe saul vele mare
In purgatory, þar it es pynde,
For þe saul es of mare tender kynde.   3015
For als a lytel thyn[g] þin eghe lokand
May greve mare þan it may þi hand,
Swa feles þe saule mare penaunce
þan þe body when it has grevaunce.
    Bot now may som say here-agayne   3020
And aske how þe saul may fele payne,
þat es noght elles bot a spirit
þat may noght be feled, swylk es it.
For it es swa sutil þat aftir þe dede

2991 grege] agrege *a*, encrys L (to] *om*.), eke As   *2993 For] Obout for G, *Morris's
silent correction* sleuthe] sleghthe A þe²] *om*. R   *Here M returns*   3011 here] yhere *a*
3014 it es] *trs*. Morris   *3016 thyng] thynd G, *Morris's suggestion in note*

It may occupy na stede.   3025
f. 90vb Til þis þus men answer may,
Als men may here grete clerkes say:
þe saule þe lyfe of þe body es
Of ilk man here, bathe mare and les;
And withouten þe lyfe is na felyng,   3030
For fclyng may be in na dede thyng.
þan es alle þe felyng halely
In þe saul, and noght in þe body;
For when þe saul es passed away,
þe body es noght bot erthe and clay,   3035
þat es a dede thyng als a stane,
þe whilk may fele nathyng be it ane.
   Alswa yhit may som þos aske mare
How may þe saule þat duelles þare
Be pyned with sere maledy   3040
þat falles til sere lymes of þe body,
Sen it has nouther body ne hede
Ne lym þat may occupy stede.
Til þis, men may answer þus shortly:
þe saule, al-if it haf na body,   3045
It sal be pyned als in lyms sere,
Thurgh whilk it has mast synned here.
Swa sal þe saul fele payn and wa,
And til other saules it sal seme swa.
For ilkan til other sal seme þan   3050
Als þai had shap of body of man;
þus sal ilka saul other se,
For nan of þam may feled be,
Na mar þan here a man ande may,
When it passes fra his mouthe away.   3055
   And þis may be proved be þe godspelle,
Thurgh þe ensampel of þe ryche man in helle
And of Lazar þat he war[n]d mete
þat in Abraham bosom had his sete.
Abraham bosom es nathyng elles   3060
Bot heven þar haly spyrites duelles.
When þe ryche man þat in helle sat lawe

3026 men answer] trs. aL   3051 of²] and R   3058 of] of þe aL   *warnd] ward
G, Morris's suggestion in note

Lazar in Abraham bosom sawe,
He cryed til Abraham and prayed withalle
þat a drope of calde water mught falle   3065
Til his tung fra Lazar fynger ende,
Als es in þe godspel contende.
Bot al-if he þus spak to hym,
Yhit had he na tung no other lym,
Ne Lazar, als yhe sal understande,   3070
Had nouther fynger ne fote ne hande,
For þai bathe war spirites anly
þat nouther had lymmes ne body.
þe tane was in blis soverayne;   f. 91ra
þe tother was in endles payne.   3075
Bot þe ryche man saule feled in helle
Payne, als he had bene in flessche and felle;
And Lazar saule til him semed þan
Als he 'had' body and lymes of man.
    Yhit has men herd som clerkes maynt[en]e   3080
Swilk an opinion, als I wene,
þat a saule þat es in purgatory
Or in helle has of þe ayre a body
For to thole payne in lyms sere,
After þat he has synned here.   3085
Bot whether þe saul haf body or noght,
He sal fele payne after he has wroght.
    þe fifte payne es þe fire hate
þat na maner of þing may abate
Bot almusdede and messe and prayere   3090
þat frendes dus for þe saul here.
To abate þat fire þa thre er best,
For þa thre may bring þe saul to rest.
þat fire is hatter and mare kene
þan al þe fire þat here es sene,   3095
For als þe fire of erthe þar we won
Es hatter þan þe beme of þe son,
Ryght swa þat fire on þe same manere
Es hatter þan þe fire es here.
Alle þe waters þat men may rekken   3100
A spark þarof may noght sleken.

*3080 mayntene] maynte G, *Morris's emendation*   3090 messe] messes *a*

We se þe fire þat here es greves sare
þe body þat standes þarin bare,
Bot mare greves þe fire of purgatory
þe saul, þan þis fire dus þe body.   3105
For þe fire here of strenthe es les
þan þe fire of purgatory es,
And þe body with flesshe and bane
Es harder þan þe saul by it ane,
And þe saul mare tender and nesshe   3110
þan es þe body with þe flesshe.
Sen þat fire es mare hate þare
þan þe fire es here, als I sayd are,
And þe saul es swa tender of kynde,
þan semes it þat it es mare pynde   3115
Thurgh þat fire þan þe body mught be
With alle þe fire of Cristiante.
For a spark of þat fire es mare hate
þan al þe fire of erthe, als clerkes wate.
    Many saules duells in þat fire strang,   3120
Bot sum duelles short wyle, and sum lang,
f. 91rb Aftir þair syn es mare or les
And aftir þair penaunce fulfild es.
Bot na saul may þethen pas
Until it be als clene als it first was,   3125
When he was hoven at funstane
And his Crestendome þar had tane.
    Som clerkes þat spekes of purgatory
Says þat þe fire þare es bodily,
And noght gastly, als þe saule es;   3130
For þe saule, als þe boke bers wytnes,
May be [io]yned with fire bodily,
Als it may be with þe awen body.
Bot þat fire wirkes noght thurgh kynde
In þe saule þat þarwith es pynde,   3135
Als dos þe fire þat brinnes here;
Bot it wirkes on wonderful manere
Als God has ordaynd, forwhy it es
An instrument of Goddes ryghtwysnes,
Thurgh wilk þe saule most clensed be   3140

*3132 ioyned] pyned *cab*

In purgatory, ar it may God se.
   Alle þe fire þat es þarin
Es bot a maner of fyre to wast syn,
And noght divers fires, les and mare,
Bot a maner of fire, als I sayd are,   3145
þat alle veniel syns þan sal waste
þat es unclensed here, lest and maste.
For als [þe] fyre þat caffe son may bryn
Gold may melt þat es lang þarin,
Ryght swa þe fyre þar thurgh lang hete   3150
þat wastes smale syns, may wast grete.
And als þe hete of þe son þat comon es,
Som men greves mare and som men les,
Right swa þe fyre þat es þare
Som sawles pyns les, and som mare.   3155
For þe sawles byhoves duelle þarin,
Aftir þe charge es of þair syn.
   Bot som sawles þar sal be delyver[d] sone
þat large penaunce here has done;
Som sal duel þar many a yhere,   3160
þat litel penaunce has don here
And lang lygyn in þair syn.
And þarfor says þus saynt Austyn:
   Necesse est quod tantum urat dolor,   *Augustinus*
   quantum erat amor; tanto enim quisquis   3165
   torquetur diucius, quanto affectus eius
   ven`i'alibus adherebat forcius.
Saynt Austyn says, 'Nedeful it es
þat sorow war als mykel and na les
For ilka syn and ilka trespas   3170 f. 91va
Als luf and delyte in [þe] syn was'.
And alswa he says on þis manere
þat 'ay þe styflier þat ilk man here
Gyfes his lykyng and [his] wille
Til veniel syns', outher loude or stille,   3175
'þe langer sal he pyned be
In purgatory'; þus says he.

---

  *3148 þe] *om. c,* a *b   *3158 delyverd] delyuer G, *line om.* L, *Morris's emendation*
3162 lang] *om.* a (*adds* heere *after* lygyn W), had lang L   3167 adherebat] ahherebat
Morris   *3171 þe] *om.* G   *3174 his²] *om.* G

þis fire, als byfore wryten es,
Som saules pynes mare, and sum les,
Aftir þat þai þat commes þarin   3180
Brynges ought with þam þat may bryn.
For byfor, ar þai may God se,
Byhoves als thre thynges brinned be,
þat es at say, als wodde and hay
And stubble þat may sone [bryn] away.   3185
þa er veniel synnes þat may falle,
Bathe grete and smale and men withalle.
þe mast veniel syns sal bryn þar langly,
Als wodde brinnes þat es sadde and hevy;
þe lest veniels syns sal brin sone,   3190
Als stobble þat son brinnes and son es done.
Bot swa son brinnes noght þe mene synnes;
þai brin mar slawly, als hay brynnes.
þus sal be brynned and wasted þare
Al[le] veniel syns, bathe les and mare;   3195
And al dedly syns of wilk men er shryven
And þe gilt God has forgyven,
For whilk þe penaunce es noght fulfilled here,
Sal þare be wasted on þe sam manere
And þe saules in þat fire be pyned   3200
Unto þai be als clene als gold fyned.
And when þai er fyned and made bright,
þai sal be broght befor Goddes sight
Til hey paradyse, þat blisful place
Whar ay es rest, ioy, and solace.   3205

The sext payn vj.   þe sext payne es þis to telle,
þat þe saules unclensed þat sal duelle
In purgatory sal be bunden faste
With bandes of syn whilles þai may laste,
Als men þat er bonden in pryson,   3210
þat na man may for gyf[t] ne raunson,
Out of þat hard payn þam wyn,
Until þe fire haf wasted þair bandes of syn.
þus er þai bunden by hend and fete,

---

*3185 bryn] wast G   3190 veniels] veniel, *Morris's silent correction*   *3195 Alle]
Als G   *3211 for gyft] forgyf G, for gyftes W, *Morris's emendation*

Alle byden[e], in þat brinnand hete.   3215
Me thynk þat na payne may be mare
þan þa saules has whyles þai er þare.
Grete dole þay mak somtyme and sarowe,   f. 91vb
For þai may nathyng begg ne borwe
To help þam þat þai war out broght,   3220
Ne þair awen prayer help[s] þam noght.
For þar es nouther stede ne space,
Help ne frenshepe to purchace,
Bot þe gude þat þai did here þai sal þar fele,
Or if þair frendes þat luffes þam wele   3225
For þam here pray or do almusd[ed]e—
Alle þat may help þam in þair nede.
Ful hard payn þar þai fele,
Bot at þai er save þai wate wele;
Bot sumtyme swa mykel pay[n] þai hafe   3230
þat þai tak na kepe þat þai er save.
Wharfor we shuld thynk þat lyves here
What payn it es on þis manere
To be swa pyned and fele swa sare
Fourty wynter, outher les or mare,   3235
Omang devels þat þan has leve
Somtyme to turment þe saules and greve,
Ay whiles þai haf any spot of syn.
For are may þai noght out of payn wyn,
Til þai be clensed and made right clene   3240
Of alle spottes of syn þat may be sene.
And when þai er þus clensed wele,
þan sal þai na mare payn fele,
Bot als-tite þarefter þai sal wende
Tille þe blis þat es withouten ende.   3245
    þe sevend payn of purgatory es   vij.
þat þe saules er als in wildernes,
þar defaut es of alkyn thyng
Of wilk man mught haf lykyng.
þair payn es turned manyfalde;   3250
Now er þai in hete and now in calde,

3215 Alle] Allen Morris (corrected in his errata)   *bydene] bydonen G
*3221 helps] help G   *3226 almusdede] almusde G, Morris's emendation
3229 þai wate] trs. R   *3230 payn] pay G, pyn L, `payn´ M, Morris's emendation

For sumtyme þai sal be pyned lang
With hete and somtyme with cald omang.
þai sal haf þare bathe hunger and threst,
And travayl grete withouten rest.   3255
þai er dungen thare to eke þaire payn
With smert stormes als of wynd and rayn
And with stormes of hayle, sharpe and kene;
Swylk stormes was never [nane] here sene
Als þe sauls sal þar [fel]e and se.   3260
þus sal þai on sere wyse pyned be,
Sum many wynter for þair syn,
Ar þai til þe sight of God may wyn.
Swilk maner of payns þai sal have þare
With other ma þat sal greve sare.   3265
f. 92ra Bot a grete payn yhit þis sal be,
þe grete yhernyng þat þai haf to se
þe face of God þat es swa bright
And þe lang tariyng fra þat syght.
Bot til þat sight þai may never wyn   3270
Until þai be clensed þar of al syn.
     Here haf I talde yhow aparty
Of sum payns of purgatory;
Now I wille shew, als þe boke telles,
Whilk sauls in purgatory duelles.   3275
þe saules þat to purgatory most wend
Aftir þe dede, when þis life has end,
Nedly byhoves dwelle þarin
Unto þai be clensed of al syn,
Thurgh bitter paynes þat er þare.   3280
Bot sum sal fele les, and sum mare,
Aftir þair syn es mare or les,
Als in þis part byfor wryten es,
Or aftir þair syns er many or fone,
And aftir þai haf here penaunce done.   3285
Bot alle saules sal noght duelle in þat stede,
For sum here þat, als-tite aftir þair dede,
Sal wend strykly til heven-blis,

3259 was] war RL, here was M   *nane] *om. cb   *3260 fele] here G
3272 aparty] apare (?) A   3286 Bot] For R   3287 here] er a, ere later with changed
construction L

Als innocentes þat never dyd mys
And other saules of men parfite   3290
þat in nathyng here ha[d] delyte,
Bot anly in God þat boght þam dere,
[And] lyffed ay in penaunce here.
Som þat þe dede here sodanly tas
In dedely syn strik til helle gas;   3295
And þat methynk es na ferly,
Forwhy dedely syn es swa hevy
þat it may within a litel stonde
A saul draw doun til helle-grounde.

   Bot þe saul þat of dedly syn es shryven   3300
Swa þat þe gilt be here forgyven,
If þe penaunce þat es here aioynt
Be noght fulfilled at þe dedes poynt,
And þe saul þat es noght clensed wele
Of smale syns þat er veniele –   3305
þis twa maners of saules er save.
Bot in purgatory þam byhoves have
Ful bitter payn, and duel stil þare
Unto þai be [als] clen, als I sayd are,
Als þai war first when þai had tane   3310
Haly baptem at þe fonstane.

   Yhit says som clerkes on þis manere
þat swa clen of syn es na man here
Ne swa parfite in þe law of Crist,   f. 92rb
Ne yhit a childe, þat es new baptist   3315
þat til heven sal wend aftir þe dede,
þat he ne sal pas forth by þat stede,
And se þe payns þar ilkan.
Bot yhong innocentes sal fele nan,
For þai couthe never na syn wirk   3320
And passes in þe trouthe of Haly Kyrk.
þarfor þai swippe thurgh purgatory
Als a foul þat flyes smertly,
Withouten payn þat may dere
Or any sight þat may þam fere.   3325

*3291 had] has GM   *3293 And] In G, Morris's suggestion in note   At this point, M lacks a further two leaves, to 3441; we cite As instead, and b = the agreement of LAs *3309 als¹] om. G (included in changed construction L)

Bot unnethes any other may
Passe qwyte thurgh purgatory away,
þat þe fire ne sal noght fynd in þam to bryn,
Ar þai passe, thurgh som veniel syn,
Swa strayt þai sal be examynd þan.   3330
For it es nan swa parfite man
þat he ne thynkes somtyme som vayn thoght
þat he lattes pas and charges it noght;
Of swilk hym byhoves clensed be
Or he may þe bright face of God se.   3335
For als gold þat shynes clere and bright
Semes fyned clene ynoghe til mans sight,
Whar it put in fire to fyn mare,
Yhit suld it leve sum dros þare.
Right swa þe saules on þe same manere   3340
Of parfit men þat semes clene here
Of al syn and es to God redy,
Yhit when þai sal pas thurgh purgatory,
þe fire þar þat es within
Sal fynd in þam sum dros of syn,   3345
Als light speche or thoght in vayn,
For whilk þam byhoves fele sum payn.
For swa fyned never na gold here was
Thurgh fire als þai sal be ar þai pas.
    Here haf I shewed + wilk saules sal be   3350
In purgatory, als clerkes can se.
Now wille I som syns here specyfy
For whilk þai duelle in purgatory.
Many maners of syns þat greves
Regnes omang men þat here leves,   3355
Of wilk sum er dedly to fele,
And sum `er´ noght bot veniele.
þa syns þat er cald dedly
Sal noght be purged in purgatory,
Bot þai sal be punyst ay in helle;   3360
And whilk þas er I wil yow telle.

3333 pas] par Morris (*corrected in his errata*)   3334 swilk] whilk *a*As   3348 na]
*om. a*As (gold] *om.* W)   *3350 wilk] swilk *c*, why ylk W   3355 here] *om.* Morris

þir er þa hede-syns þat er dedely: f. 92ᵛᵃ
Pride, hatreden, and envy;
Glotony and sleuthe in Goddes servise,
And lychery and covatyse,   3365
Sacrilege and fals wyttenessyng,
Manslaghter and forsweryng,
Thefte alswa and ravyn—
Ilkan of þir es a dedly syn.
And wreth es dedly syn omang,   3370
If it be halden in hert lang;
And yhit drunkenes es dedly to fele,
If it be over-continuele.
Whaswa feles hym here gylty
In any of þir syns dedly,   3375
Bot if he hym amende ar he hethen wende,
He sal noght aftir his lyfes ende
Wend strek til purgatory,
Bot even til helle withouten mercy.
Bot if he wille hym repent and shrife   3380
Of alle swilk syns here in his lyfe,
Fra helle-pyne þan es he save;
Bot payn and penaunce hym byhoves have
In purgatory, als I wene,
Until he be made of alle syn clene.   3385
Forwhy penaunce for syn, als I sayd are,
Most be fulfilled outher here or þare.
    Syns þat er veniel may dere,
Bot þai er noght swa hevy to bere
Als er dedly, for þai may be here   3390
Fordon on [a] light manere.
For als men heres þer clerkes say,
Ilk man here lyghtly may
Swilk remedys thurgh grace wyn
þat may fordo al veniel syn,   3395
þat es to say, if he clene be
Of dedly syn and wil it fle.
    For I fynd writen ten thynges sere

3362 þa] þe R   3367 Man-] And Morris   3382 es he] *trs.* Ra, *cf.* he is þenne As
3388 er] es A   *3391 a] *om.* G, *couplet om.* As

Ten things þat owaydus
veniel syn⟨s⟩ whar na
dedly syn es

þat veniel syns fordus here;
þas ten er þir þat I now rede: 3400
Haly water and almusdede,
Fastyng and housil of Goddes body,
Prayer of þe Pater Noster namly,
General shrifte þat ilk day may be,
Benyssoun of bisshope of his dignite   3405
And benyssoun of prest þat gyyen es
Namly in þe ende of þe mes;
Knokyng of þe brest of man þat es meke,
Last enoyntyng gyven to þe seke.

f. 92vb   þer ten puttes veniel syns away,   3410
Als men may here þer clerkes say.
   Bot swa many veniel syns sere
May be gadyrd at ans togyder here
þat þai may weghe on þe saul als hevy
Als a syn dus þat es dedly   3415
þat slas þe saul and God myspays;
And þarfor þe poet on þis wyse says:
     De minimis granis fit
     maxima summa caball[i].
Als 'of many `smale´ cornes es made   3420
Til a hors bak a mykel lade',
Right swa may veniel syns many
Mak a mykel syn dedly.
For þai gadir on þe saul ful thyk
And cleves togyder als dos pyk,   3425
Bot if þai swythe be done oway,
Ay als þai com, withouten delay,
For swa parfitely may nane lyf here
Withouten veniel syns sere.
For a man syns [ilk] day þat here duels,   3430
Als þe boke says þat þus tels:
     Septies in die cadit
     iustus.
'Seven sythes at þe lest o þe day
þe ryghtwys falles', þat es to say   3435

---

*3419 caballi] caballo G   3426 þai] þat Morris (*corrected in his errata*)
*3430 ilk] al- G   3434 o] on W*b*, of Morris, *an unnecessary emendation retracted in*
the textual commentary

In sere syns þat er veniel,
Bot sum er mare and sum les to fel.
  In swa many veniel syns we falle
þat na man can reken þam alle;
Bot sum of þam reherce I can,   3440
Als saynt Austyn telles, þe haly man.
For in a boke he reherces som
þat mast es used of custom
And to telle + þa syns he þus bygyns
And says þat þer er veniel syns.   3445
First when a man etes or drinkes mare
Anytime [here] þan myster ware;
When þou may vaile thurgh wytte and skille
And wille noght help, bot haldes þe stylle;
When þou spekes sha`r´ppely til þe pure   3450
þat sum gode askes at þi dore;
When þou erte hale and may wele last
And etes when tym es to fast;
When þe lyst slepe and wil noght ryse
And comes over-late tyl Goddes servise;   3455
Or when þou ert in gude state
And says þi praers [o]ver-late,
Or when þou says praier or orison   f. 93ra
With over-litel devocion;
When a man list dele in bed   3460
With his wyfe þat he has wed,
Hys lust anly for to fulfille,
And to gette a child es noght in wille;
When þou visites men over-late
þat sek er and in febel state,   3465
Or men þat lyes in prison
Or in any tribulacion,
Or men þat er synful and sary,
Or saules þat er in purgatory
(For to visite þam it war grete nede   3470
Turght praier and thurgh almusdede);
When þou paynes þe noght, aftir þi state,

*þir er þe veniele syns
þat saynt Austyn
touches in a buke þat he
made*

3439 can] may *a*   3441 telles] says *a*L   man] men Morris (Lightbown)   *M returns*
*3444 þa] þat G, þais L (*the reading suggested in Morris's note*), þe M, *cf.* þa syns] þaime W
*3447 here þan] þan G, here and L   *3457 over-] euer G

To accorde þam þat er at debate;
When þou spekes over-bitterly
Til any man with noyse or cry;   3475
When þou prayses + a man mare
Thurgh flateryng þan mister ware;
When þou in kirk makes ianglyng
Or thynkes in vayn anythyng
(Be it withouten, be it within,   3480
Yhit it es a veniel syn);
When þou ert over-lyghtly wrathe,
Or sweres and may noght hald þin athe;
When þou bannes any man
In wham þou fyndes na gilt to ban;   3485
When þou supposes any wykkednes
Thurgh suspecion þar na es.
     þir smale syns saynt Austyn telles
Thurgh whilk many saules duelles
In purgatory in payn and wa.   3490
Bot yhit þar er ful many ma
Of veniel syns, be many a score,
Over þas þat I haf tald byfore.
Bot swa witty es nane erthely man
þat alle veniel syns reken can.   3495
For oftesythes of þe day men falles
In syns þat clerkes veniel calles,
Thurgh werk or worde or thoght in vayn,
And ilka syn es worthy payn,
þe whilk most be fordone clenly,   3500
Outher here or in purgatory.
     þarfor I rede ilk man, whyles he lyffes here,
þat he use þa ten thinges sere
þat fordus, als I sayde are,
Alle veniel syns, bathe les and mare.   3505
f. 93rb And if any fal in dedly syn,
Ryse he up and ligg noght lang þarin
And ga to 'þe' prest hym to shrife
And tak his penaunce in his life
And haf he forthynkyng ay in thoght   3510
For þas syns þat he has wroght,

And do he penance with al his myght
And be in prayers, bathe day and night,
And fast and ga wolwarde and wake
And thole hard[n]es for Goddes sake.   3515
   For na man may to heven ga,
Bot if he thole here anger and wa,
And 'when' God sendes a man angwise,
He suld thole it withouten fayntise.
Be it sekenes or oght elles þat greves,   3520
Losse of catelle or of fre[n]des þat lyves,
Or unkyndnes, falsed, or treson,
Or any other tribulacion,
Thole he it mekely and thynk in thoght
þat withouten cause commes it noght,   3525
Bot God wate wele þe cause why.
Parchaunce it es for his foly,
To chasty hym on swilk manere
For his syn þat he dyd here;
Or it may be hym here to prove,   3530
Or to make hym mar drede God and lufe.
þarfor sen God ofte vouches save
þat a man [may] here swilk angers have,
Outher for his syn or hym to fande,
Love he him þan of alle his sande   3535
And take [he] mekely þat God him sendes
And fle alle thyng þat he defendes.
For thurgh nuyes and angers sere,
He makes a man, als his preson here,
Payn to drighe for hys foly   3540
In þis lif, als he es worthy.
And, if he it thole noght grotchand,
In stede of penance it sal hym stand,
And yhit wille God him mare do;
He wil gif him mede þarto   3545
þat his ioy in heven sal heke,
If he thole ang[re]se with hert meke.

---

*3515 hardnes] hardes G   *3521 frendes] fredes G, frynde M, *Morris's emendation*
3522 falsed] falshede Morris, *an unncessary emendation*   3529 syn] syns Morris
(Lightbown)   *3533 may] *om.* G, *after* angers *b*   angers] angre A   *3536 he] *om.* G
3542 it] *om.* A   *3547 angrese] angwyse *c*M

Als þe gude son tholes mekely
þe fader, when he wille hym chasty,
Swa suld ilk man thole and love God ay   3550
And do alle þe gude þat he may—
And specialy almusd[ed]e,
þe naked to clathe and hungry to fede
f. 93ᵛᵃ And other werkes of mercy wirke,
Als theches and preches Haly Kirke –   3555
And kepe him clene to his lyfes ende
Fra syn. þan sal his saul wende
Til blis, and lyghtly pas alle payne
Of purgatori; þis es certayne.

Here haf I shewed yhow on Inglys   3560
Som syns þat saynt Austyn specifys.
Now wil I shew what help es certayne
For þam þat in purgatory has payne
And what may mak þair payn cees
And þam of þair payn to haf relees.   3565
⟨The⟩ help of ⟨fr⟩endes   þe saules þat til purgatory wendes
⟨ ⟩ and ⟨ ⟩ þe dede   May be helped thurgh help of frendes
⟨þat⟩ er in ⟨pur⟩gatory   þat almus for þam dus, and prays,
For þe haly man saynt Austyn says:
Augustinus   Non est negandum spiritus defunctorum, pietate   3570
suorum vivencium, posse relevari.
He says, 'Men shuld noght denye on na manere
þat þe saules of þam þat er dede here,
Of payn may rele[f]ed be
Thurgh frendes lyfand þat has pyte'.   3575
For als þas þat passed, als I sayd are,
Til purgatory er pyned þare
For weniel syns, mare and lesse,
Aparty thurgh Goddes rightwisnesse,
Right swa [þ]ai may thurgh help aparty,   3580
Be rele[f]ed þar thurgh Goddes mercy.
Alle þat men dus here, bathe les and mare,
For þe saules þat duelles þare
Avayles þam noght als to heven-mede,

---

*3552 almusdede] almusde G, *Morris's emendation*   3568 and] or RL
3571 relevari] revelari AL (*corr. later* A)   *3574 relefed] relesed *cab*
*3580 þai . . . help] *trs. phrs. c, cf.* thorow þaim þai may M   *3581 relefed] relesed *cab*

Bot for þare deliverance fra payn to spede.   3585
    Four maners of helpes er general
þat in purgatory availes þam al,
þat es to say, prayer and fastyng
And almusdede and mes-s[yng]yng.
    On twa maners, als clerkes can se,   3590
þe saule fra payn deliverd may be;
þe tane by way of grace es
And þe tother by way of rightwisnes,
By way of grace on twyn manere
Als es writen in þis bok here: 3595
First thurgh prayer of Crist þat es hede,
When he es offerd in fourme of brede
Thurgh prestes hande here at þe mes,
When þe sacrament swa made es.
Alswa thurgh prayer of his lyms,   3600
þat es, of gude men þat toward heven clyms.
þan may þe saules in purgatory,   f. 93vb
By way of grace specialy,
Be deliverd of pyn þat ders
Thurgh messes and rightwis men prayers.   3605
    By way of rightwysnes help may be
On twyn maners, als yhe may se.
First thurgh bihyng of paynes þat greves
With almus, þat men to + pure gyves;
Another es here thurgh assethe-makyng,   3610
Als thurgh penance of fre[n]des and fastyng.
þus may saules, als þe buke beres wytnes,
By helpyd by way of rightwysnes,
þat es to say, þai may in þat nede
Be boght fra payn thurgh almusdede,   3615
Ande thurgh penance for þam here don,
þe dette of payn may be qwitte son.
Right als a man þat duelles in prison
Til he haf payed a certayn raunson,
May be delyverd and broght away   3620
Thurgh a frende þat wille it for hym pay.
On þis wyse may þe saules þat wendes

*3589 mes-syngyng] messyng G, messes-syngyng W   *3609 pure] þe pure GL
*3611 frendes] fredes G, Morris's emendation

Til purgatory, be helped thurgh fre[n]des.
　Bot sum frende[s] may help and som noght,
þe saules þat til purgatory er broght.　　3625
Thurgh þas frendes may þai helped be
þat here lyves [in] ryght charite.
Bot þe help of þam þat charite failles
Til þe saules þat er þar noght availles.
For alle er als lymes of a body,　　3630
þat here er and in purgatory;
And als we may se properly here
A body hafe many lymmes sere,
And ilkan of þam, bathe les and mare,
May help other þat feles sare –　　3635
Bot if a lym dighe and þe myght faile,
þat lym may noght til þe other availe.
Right swa it fars on þe same wyse
By þam [þat] in purgatory lyese
And þat er here, for men may þam calle　　3640
Als lyms of a body alle.
Whaswa in dedly syn es broght
And charite in his hert has noght,
He es als dede in saul within
Ay whiles he es in dedly syn.　　3645
His help vailles noght bot es in vayne,
Als to þe saules þat er in payne.
His help thurgh hymselfe standes in na stede,
For 'he' es als a lym þat es dede.
f. 94ra　　Bot never þe latter, alle-if he swa be　　3650
In syn and out of charite,
Yhit may he help þe saules þus,
If he til pure men gyf almus,
þat þai for þe saules pray specialy,
And [þat] helpes þe saules in purgatory.　　3655
Yhit may þe help and þe travaile
Of sum synful men þe saules avayle,
If it thurgh biddyng done be
Of a frende þat es in charite,

*3623 frendes] fredes G, Morris's emendation　　*3624 frendes] frende c
*3627 in] thurgh c　　*3639 þat] om. G, Morris's emendation　　*3655 þat] om.
G, cf. And] om. M

Or [o]f þe dede self þat has mast nede   3660
Of help of prayer and almusdede.
þat help may avayle þe saules son
For his sake þat biddes it be don,
þat charite in hert has knytt,
And noght for his sake þat dos it.   3665
Forwhy God wille noght do for his sake
þat charite wille noght in hert take.
    þis case ofte falles, als I understande,
Bytwen a loverd and his servande,
Whare þe loverd es gude and rightwys   3670
And þe servand ille, [þat] uses folys.
If þe servand do anythyng
þat es gude at his loverdys bydyng,
Yhit may it availle to a gude use,
Alle-if he be ille þat it duse;   3675
And þat by reson of þe gudenes
Of hym of wham þe by[dd]yng es.
For alle be it onence þe doer dede,
Onence þe bidder it standes in stede;
Bot 'if' þai bathe in charite ware,   3680
þe help til þe dede war wele þe mare.
    Alswa a prest, alle-if he be
Synful and out of charite,
He es Goddes minister and Haly Kirkes,
þat þe sacrament of þe auter wirkes,   3685
þe wilk es never þe les of myght,
Alle-if þe prest here lyf noght right.
For if a prest þat synges mes
Be never swa ful of wykednes,
þe sacrament, þat es swa haly,   3690
May noght apayred be thurgh his foly.
þan may mes saules fra payn bring,
Alle-if a synful prest it syng.
For in Goddes name he synges þe mes,
Under wham in order he es.   3695
Bot speciel prayers with gude entente,

*3660 of] if G, Morris's emendation   At this point, M lacks lines 3666–89.
*3671 þat] and G   *3677 byddyng] bygynnyng GL   3681 þe³] om. a
3685 of] om. R

þat es made besyde þe sacramente,
Of a gude prest er wele better
þan of an ille, and to God swetter.
Bot þe offeryng of Goddis body   3700
Helpes þe saules principaly;
Wharfor it semes þat mes-syngyng
May titest þe saul out of payn bryng,
þat passes hethen in charite
And in purgatory clensed suld be.   3705
   Bot til þam þat er dampned for ay
Na gude dede avayle ne help may,
Nouther almusdede, prayer, ne messe;
For þai er, als þe buke bers witnesse,
Departed halely fra þe body of Criste,   3710
And þa saules for ever er periste.
For als lymmes þat er dede er þai
þat er hewed fra þe body oway.
And als nathyng may help kyndely
þe lymes þat er cutted fra þe body,   3715
Right swa alle helpes þat men can telle
Availles þam noght þat er in helle.
Yhit help of frendes here on sum wyse
Availles þam þat er in paradise
And alswa þam þat in helle duelles,   3720
Als a grete clerk in [a] boke telles.
þan availles 'almus', messe, and bedes
To þe saules þat er in alle thre stedes.
þai availe þe saules in purgatory
To spede þam out mare hastily;   3725
þai vaile þam þat in heven er,
For þai multiplie þar þe titter,
And þe ma þat gaders to þat place,
þe mare þair ioy es, and solace.
þai avail til þam þat er in helle,   3730
For þe foner shuld com þider to duelle,
And þe foner þat þider commes for syn,
þe les payn þai have þat duelles þarin;
And ay þe ma saules þat þider wendes,
þe mare þare payne es, þat never endes.   3735

3711 þa] þe M Morris (Lightbown)   3718 on] of AR   *3721 a²] *om.* G

þus may help here and availe be skille
Til þe saules þat duelles ay in helle stille;
And `til´ þe saules þat er in heven namly,
And til þam þat er in purgatory.
Bot help may na saules out of payn spede   3740
Bot þam þat has charite and nede.
For in helle es na charite,
And in heven na ned may be.
Bot bathe þa twa þe saules has
þat fra hethen til purgatory gas.   3745
 And als a man may here with + hande   f. 94va
Make asethe for another lyfande,
þe whilk es noght of power þarto,
Right swa may a man for þe ded do.
þe saules þat til paradise er gane   3750
Nede of help here haf þai nane;
Bot if for þam war don any gude dede,
It may availe þam, þat of help has nede.
 þe help þat es don here specialy
Availles til þe saules in purgatory,   3755
Bot to som mare and til som les,
Aftir þai er of worthynes
And aftir þe charite es clere
Of þam þat er lyffand here,
þat mast er bysy and dus mare   3760
For sum þan for other þat er þare.
Bot when a man fra þis world sal flitte,
Na man for certayn here may wytte
Whether he sal þan til purgatory wende,
Or to blisse, or to payn withouten ende.   3765
For som semes gude here and parfite
þat aftir þe dede, er dampned als-tite,
For parchaunce þai er ille within
And passes away in dedely syn.
Som semes synful, als þai lyfed mys,   3770
þat er save and er in þe way til blys,
For parchaunce byfor þair endyng,
þai er amended of þair myslyvyng.
Of þis may na man certayn be,

3746 may] *after* here A   *with] with his G   3759 er, here] *trs.* R

For it es Goddes pryvete. 3775
Bot we shuld trow and suppose ay
þat alle er save and in g[u]de way
þat we se here gude werkes wirk
And has þe sacramentes of Hali Kyrk.
Bot whether it be or noght þus, 3780
We suld do þat es in us;
We suld pray, bathe loud and stille,
For al Cristen saules. þus charite wille.
   Now sum may aske why synges men mes
For a yhong child when it dede es, 3785
þat of prayer ne mes has na nede,
For it couth never do synful dede.
þis may be þe right skille why,
For þe lovyng of God principaly
And for usage of Haly Kyrk, 3790
And for þe dedes use þat office to wirk.
And yhit may þe mes in sum case
Help þam in purgatory þat ned hase.

f. 94vb Here haf yhe herde, als þe buke bers witnes,
How almus, penance, praier, and mes, 3795
þat er done thurgh fre[n]des certayne,
May help þe saules þa[t] er in payne.
Now wille I shew yhow yhit mare þarto
What pardon may to þe saules do,
þe whilk þai purchaced on right manere 3800
In clene lif whilles þai liffed here.

Of pardon what it
auailes til þe saule in
purgator⟨y⟩
   Pardon helpes þam, als clerkes says,
þat it has purchased in þair lif-days,
For pardon of papes and bisschopes,
þat es granted here als men hopes, 3805
May availe þair saules in purgatory
þat has purchaced it 'here' worthyly,
If þai of þair syn had contricion
And war shrifen byfor þat pardon.
þan may pardon aftir þair dede 3810
In purgatory þam stand in stede.

*3777 gude] gede G, *Morris's silent correction* (Lightbown)   *3796 frendes] fredes
G, *Morris's emendation*   *3797 þat] þar G, *Morris's emendation*   3800 on] in *a*

For pardon here, þat es certayn,
May þam relese of þe de[tt]e of payn,
Als ferforthe als pardon may reche;
þus haf I herd grete clerkes preche.   3815
    Pardon properly noght elles es
Bot of payn, þat es dette, forgyfnes.
Pardon may nane hafe bot he wil wirke,
For it es of þe tresur of Haly Kirke,
þat es gadirde for nede of pardon   3820
Of þe vertu of Crestes passion,
And of þe worthines of þe dedys
Of his halowes and of þair medys,
And es gaderd on many maners:
First als of marterdom of martires,   3825
Of penance and travail of confessours,
And of þe thechyng of [haly] docturs;
And of chastite of virgyns clene,
þat chast and haly ay has bene;
Of þe fruyt of Haly Kirk werkes,   3830
And of + prayres of gude prestes and clerkes.
Of alle þis, als I shewed byfor,
Es gadird Haly Kirkes tresor,
Of wilk þe pape þe kays bers,
Wharwith he bathe opens and spers.   3835
    þat falles hym 'of' office to halde,
For he es in erthe Godes vicar calde.
þa cays er noght elles to se
Bot playn power of his dignite,
Thurgh whilk he may, be law and skille,   3840
Louse and bynde at his wille.
For þe sam power hym falles to have   f. 95ra
þat Crist til Petre in erthe gave.
For Crist gave to Petre playn powere
And sayd to hym on þis manere: 3845
    Quodcunque ligaveris super terram,
    erit ligatum et in celis, et quodcunque
    solveris super terram, erit solutum

*3813 dette] dede G, *cf.* þat are in M; *Morris's suggestion in note*   3818 wil] wele *a*
3824 And] And it Morris, *an unnecessary emendation*   *3827 haly] *om.* G
*3831 of¹] of þe *c*L   3845 sayd] says Morris (Lightbown)

et in celis.

'Alle þat þou byndes in erthe', says he,   3850
'Sal in heven bonden be,
And alle þat þou lowses in erthe right
Sal be loused in heven bright'.
 þis power til alle papes gaf he,
þat aftir Petre in erthe shuld be,   3855
Als shewes an exposicion
Of þe haly godspelle in a lesson.
þan semes it wele by þis skille here
þat þe pape has swa large powere
To assoyle a man, and hym forgyfe   3860
Alle þe dette of payn þat may greve,
Swa þat he þat þe pape assoyles, fulfille
þat þat þe laghe of þe gospelle wille
And yheld agayn, if he be myghty,
Alle þat he [h]as [tan] wrangwysly.   3865
For when þe pape þat grace wil do,
He byndes hym and alle Haly Kirk þarto
For hym til wham þat grace avayles
To fulfille alle þat in hym failles.
 Bot bischopes here of lagher state   3870
And has les power, als clerkes wate,
Forwhy þair dignite here es les,
And þarfor þair powere restreyned es.
Bot [alle-]if it be noght swa suffishaunt
Als þe papes es, yhit may þai graunt   3875
Of þair power pardon aparty
Til þair hawen underloutes anly;
And yhit most þat, als I sayd befor,
Be gyfen of Haly Kirkes tresor.
 Bot na man may here pardon wyn   3880
Bot [if] he be out of dedly syn,
For he, þat kepyng of þat + tresour has
May noght it dele til Haly Kyrk fas.
And swilk er þai, and nan elles,
þat here in dedly syn duelles;   3885
For out of Haly Kirk er þai.

*3865 has tan] tas G   3870 here] er RaL, are M   *3874 alle-if] if *c*, yf-alle W,
3of-all L, if M   3879 Haly] *om.* R   *3881 if] *om. c*   *3882 þat] þat fair *c, om.* M

þarfor na pardon whyn þai may.
   Bot þe frendes of Haly Kirk may wyn
Pardon, for þai er within;
And swilk er þas þat here er fre   3890 f. 95rb
Of dedly syn + and er in charite,
Til wham pardon sal noght fail
(Bot in purgatory it sal þam avail)
To allege þair saules of payne,
Als fer als it reches of certayne.   3895
þe whilk, als sum says, falles to be sett
For þ[e r]emenand of payns, þat es dett
þat parchaunce es lefte undon here,
And þat may falle on sere manere:
A party for penance þat es ioynt,   3900
þat es noght done at þe dedes poynt;
A party for veniel syns sere,
A party for syns þat er forgeten here;
A party for over-litelle penance
And for over-littelle repentance;   3905
A party for penance eniont and done
Parchaunce over-reklesly and over-sone;
A party for penance þat enioynt es
And es forgeten thurgh reklesnes.
Alle þis may be cald þe remenand   3910
Of þe dette of payn, als I understand,
þe whilk felle to be fulfylled haly,
Outher here or in purgatory.
   Bot alle þis dett may þar be qwytt
Thurgh large pardon, waswa has itt,   3915
In forgyvenes of alle penance soght,
Whethir it be here enioynt or noght.
For swa mykel pardoun may a man
Purches here þat he may þan
In purgatory qwyte alle þe dett   3920
þat hym fra blis may tary or lett.
For swa large es Haly Kirkes tresor
þat it es ynogh to pay þarfor

---

*3891 syn] syns *c*   3894 of] o R   *3897 þe remenand] þemenand G, *Morris's*
emendation payns] payne *a*   3900 ioynt] enioyned M, enioynt Morris   3912 haly]
anely R

And for alle þe paynes þat dett may be
Of alle þe men of Cristante.   3925
   þus pardon in purgatory availles,
Als I tald. Bot som clerkes counsailles
þat we it spare and reserve halely
Until we com til purgatory,
And do here penance whilles we + may.   3930
For a man sal thynk þare a day
Lenger þan hever thogh him here
þe space of alle ane hale yhere.
þan es a day of pardon to gesce
Mare worth[e] þan alle þis worldis riches,   3935
For þe saule had lever, þat in payn dueles
A day of pardon þan anythyng elles.
f. 95ᵛᵃ For alle þe werld, [if] it his ware,
He wald gyf for rest a day þare.
   Of þis maters, þat þus mas mencion   3940
Of help of frendes and of pardon
þat vailles þam þat er in purgatory,
Als I shewed byfor openly,
Spekes Innocent and [Hos]ty[e]n
In bukes, whar + þir maters er sen.   3945
And Raymu[n]d spekes of þe same
In a boke þat es called `h'is name,
And Thomas Alqwyn spekes alswa
Of þis mater and `of' other ma
In a boke, þe whilk made he,   3950
þat hat *Veritas Theologie.*
   Here I have many maters redde
And þe ferthe parte of þis boke spede,
In þe qwilk yhe hafe herd me specify
þe condicions of purgatory: 3955
First what it es to fele and se,
And whar God has ordaynd it to be;
And `what' paynes falles þar to les and mare,

3924 paynes] payne *a*M   *3930 we] we lyf *cb*   3932 thogh] thoȝt M, thoght
Morris   *3935 worthe] worthy *c*M, wrothe L   *3938 if] *om.* G, *Morris's emendation*
*3944 Hostyen] Austyn *cb*   *3945 þir] þair *c*, þe M   *3946 Raymund] raymud G,
Romande M, *Morris's emendation*   3949 of²] *om. a*M   3954 þe] *om.* A   me] me
shewe and *a*

And whilk saules byhoves be pyned þare;
And alswa for what manere of syn   3960
And what may þam help þat er þarin.
Of al þis haf I spoken til þe ende,
And now wille I til þe fifte part wende
þat spekes of þe day of dome
And of takens þat byfor sal come.   3965

Here bygyns þe fifte part þat es of
þe day of dome and of takens þat sal cum byfor.

    In þis part men may of ten þinges rede
þat touches þe grete day of drede,
Of whilk sum byfor þat day sal be   3970
And at þe day, als men sal se.
þe first es of the wonderful takens sere
þat byfor þat day sal be shewed here.
þe secunde es of þe fire þat sal bryn
þe world and al þat es þarin.   3975
þe thred es of þe rysyng generale
Of alle men, `bathe´ grete and smale.
þe ferthe es of Crystes commyng don
Til þe doome in his proper person.
þe fifthe es [of] þe certayn stede   3980
Whar Crist sal deme bathe qwik and dede.
þe sexte es of þe fourme `of´ man
In whilk Crist sal shew hym þan.
þe sevend, of þe accusers many
þat þe synful + sal accuse þar openly.   3985
þe aghtynd, of þe accunt and + rekennyng   f. 95vb
þat þai sal yheld of alle þair lyfyng.
þe neghend, of al men aftir þai haf wroght,
Of wilk som sal be demed, and som noght.
þe tend es of þe grete dome final   3990
þat Crist sal gyf and mak ende of al.
    Of þir sal som falle, als yhe herd me say,
Byfor þat day and sum at þe day.

    3959 byhoves] falles A, falles to W, *after* pyned L   3966–7 þat es] *om.* L, þat
spekes M   and . . . byfor] *om. b*   byfor] *after* takens A   De die iudicij W   3972 of]
om. Ab   3979 his] *om.* Morris   *3980 of] *om.* G   *3985 synful] *adds* saul G,
adds saules R   *3986 and] and þe G, *om.* M

Byfor þe day sere takens sal com,
Of whilk men may here fynd wreten som,   3995
Als of An[ti]crist commyng, and his pouste,
And of other ma þat byfor þat day sal be,
þe whilk takens men sal thynk ful harde,
Als yhe may se and here afterwarde.
And whaswa wille avise hym wele,   4000
He may ilk day here, ʿseʾ, and fele
Takens, warthurgh he may understande,
þat þe day of dome es fast comande.
For wonders þat shuld falle, als I trow,
Agayn þe worldes hende er sene now,   4005
Thurgh whilk wondres grete clerkes knawes
þat þe worlde fast to þe endeward drawes.
Wharfor we shuld make us redy here,
Als þe day of dome war command nere.
Crist disciples, þat yherned haf knawyng   4010
Of sum takens agayns his last commyng,
Spak to Crist, als yhe may here,
In þe godspelle on þis manere:
    ʿDic nobis signum adventus tui et
    consummacionem seculiʾ. Et respondens,   4015
    Ihesus dixit eis, ʿVidete ne quis vos sedu-
    cat. Multi enim venient in nomine
    meo dicentes, "Ego sum Cristus", et multos
    seducent etc. Consurget enim gens
    contra gentem et regnum in regnum,   4020
    et erunt pestilencie et fames, et terre
    motus per loca. Hec autem omnia
    inicia sunt dolorum; et habundabit
    iniquitas, et refrigescet caritas multorum.
ʿSay usʾ, quod þai, ʿof þi commyng   4025
So[m] taken and of þe world endyngʾ.
Crist als-tite answerd þam þan
And sayd, ʿLukes þat yhow desayve na man,
For many sal com in my name,

*3996 Anticrist] ancrist c, ancrystes L, Morris's suggestion in note   3999 se and here]
trs. verbs R, cf. se and] om. M   4010 yherned] adds to RM, aught L   4011 his] þe R
4016 Ihesus] Ihesus Christus Morris   eis] om. A   4025 Say us] Say R, Says us Morris
(Lightbown)   quod] said M, cryed Morris   *4026 Som] Son G, Morris's silent
correction

þat sal say þus, "Crist I am",   4030
And many a man þai sal bygile,
Bot þai sal regne here bot a while.
[M]en ogayne men thurgh strengh sal ryse,   f. 96ra
And rewme ogayne rewme on þe same wyse;
Pestilences and hungers sal be   4035
And erthe-dyns in [sere] contre.
And al þis sal be bygynnyg hard
Of þe sorows þat sal com aftirward;
Wykkednesse sal wax manyfalde,
And charite of many sal wax calde'.   4040
þir takens til his disciples tald he
þat ogayn þe worldes ende shuld be.
   Bot sum of þir takens has bene,
And sum of þam sal yhit be sene.
And of takens þat yhit sal com,   4045
If yhe wille, I sal tel yhow som.
And first of An[ti]crist wille I say,
þat sal com befor domesday
Aftir þe destruccion sal be
Of þe empyre of Rome, þat es yhit fre.   4050
   Somtyme al landes of þe world obout
Was sugette til Rome and underlout,
þat at certayn teremes gaf it trowage,
Als þe custom þan was and þe usage.
þat custom alle landes þan byhoved do,   4055
Bot saynt Paule says þus þarto:
   Quoniam nisi venerit dissencio primum, etc.,
   id est, nisi prius dissenser[i]nt omnia regna
   a Romano imperio, que prius erant sub-
   dita, non antea veniet Anticristus.   4060
He says, 'Bot if first dissension come,
þat es, bot if alle landes hald agayn Rome,
Swa þat it be put til destruccion
Thurgh þam þat first was in subieccion,
Anticrist ar þat tyme sal noght com',   4065

4031 a] *om. a*   *4033-4 *lines trs.* cb   4035 hungers] hunger R*b*
many *c*, som *a*, many sere L, ilke M   *4047 Anticrist] ancrist *c*   *4058 -erint]
-erunt G, *cf.* descenderint L, discenserint M, *Morris's silent correction*   4061 first] *om.*
Morris (Lightbown)

þat sal com byfor þe day of dom.
þat destrucion, als says Haly Writt,
Sal be, bot þat tyme com noght yhitt.
Fra þat tyme sal na land ne contre
In subieccion of Rome langer be,   4070
Ne fra þan sal na man be bughsome
Ne obedient to þe kirk of Rome.
Men sese þat + empire, þat was swa myghty
Es now destruyed a grete party;
Bot at þe last, als I sayd are,   4075
It sal be destruyed wele mare.
Bot þe dignite þat til it sal falle
Sal noght in þat tyme perysshe alle;
It sal stand and duelle, withouten dout,
In alle his regyons obout.   4080

f. 96rb   þos sal þe first taken bygyn at Rome,
For it es heved of al Cristendome;
For when it es put til destrucion,
Alle Haly Kyrk sal be put don.
Som clerkes says þat an sal come   4085
þat sal hald þe empire of Rome
Alle halely, and his croun bere
Wele, and in pees withouten were.
He sal be last emperour þat þare sal be
And mast of alle kynges of pouste,   4090
þe whilk sal wele maynten his state
And þe empire withouten debate,
And it governe thurgh laghe and witte
Als lang als he sal hald itte.
Bot afterwarde at þe last ende   4095
Until Ierusalem he sal wende,
And on þe mount of Olyvette,
He sal þe septre of Rome sette
And his coron he sal lay don alswa,
And lef þam þar and fra þam ga.   4100
þus sal ende þe dignite of Rome,
And alsone aftir [A]nticrist sal come,
Als clerkes says þat has understandyng
Of Daniel and of saynt Paul saying.

*4073 þat¹] þat þe GL   *4102 Anticrist sal] trs. cL

   þan sal Anticrist tyme bygyn,   4105 *Of þe lyf of Anticrist*
þat saynt Paul calles 'þe man of syn'.
For alle-if he be man, neverþeles
He sal be welle of alle wykkednes.
'þe devels son' he sal be cald,
Bot thurgh kynd men shuld him noght swa hald,   4110
Bot thurgh his turnyng fra gode til ille,
+ He sal þe devels wille fulfille.
Alle þe power of þe devel of helle
And alle his witte in hym sal duelle,
In wham al þe tresor of malice   4115
Sal be hidde with alle maner of vice.
He sal til Criste contrarius be
And til alle his lyms þat he sal se,
And heghen hym thurgh pride þat he sal halde
Oboven al þat er paens goddes calde,   4120
þat es to say, Iubiter and Mercury,
And Appolyn and Herculy.
And noght anly obove[n] þa goddes alle
þat þe paens þair goddes sal calle,
Bot he sal heghe himself to be   4125
Aboven þe haly Trinite,
[þat] alle + creatours, bath mare and les,
Shuld honoure over alle thyng þat es.
   Ful synful sal be his bygynnyng,   f. 96ᵛᵃ
And wonderful sal be his lyvyng,   4130
And his endyng sal be sodayn,
For thurgh myght of God he [sal] be slayn.
In his tyme sal be swylk tribulacion
And swa mykel persecucion
þat unnethes any sal dur graunt   4135
þat he es cristen[d] and God servant.
For mare persecucion sal be þan
þan ever was sythen þe world bygan.
   Anticrist es þos mykel at say
Als he þat es ogayn Crist ay.   4140

4105 tyme] þat tyme Morris (Lightbown)   *4112 He] For he *cb*
*4123 oboven] obouem G, *Morris's silent correction*   *4127 þat alle] And alle þe G
*4132 sal] *om.* G, *Morris's emendation*   *4136 cristend] cristen GAM
4139 Anticrist] ancrist R

þan may ilk man be cald by skille
Anticrist þat dos ogayn Goddes wille;
þan may alle þas anticristes be calde
þat ogaynes `Goddes´ laghe will halde.
Bot ma[n]y swilk men may wele knawe   4145
þat mykel dus ogayns Goddes lawe,
Bot [ane] Anticrist, als says haly writ,
Sal com at þe last, þat com noght yhitt,
Als mast tyraunt withouten pyte
þat ever was or ever sal be.   4150
Wharfor I hald þir gret mysdoers
Als Anticrist lyms and his forgangers.
    Now whaswa wille a whyle duelle,
Aparty here I wille hym telle
Of þe maner of Anticrist bygynnyng   4155
And of his lif and of hys endyng.
He sal be geten, als clerkes shew can,
Bytwen a synful man and a woman,
And aftir þat he consayved sal be
þe fende sal entre thurgh his pouste   4160
Within his moder wambe sone;
þus sais a grete clerke sal be done.
Thurgh was myght he sal be forth broght,
And wonders thurgh hym sal be wroght.
He sal be cald 'þe child þat es lorn'   4165
And in Corozaym he sal be born
Of a woman of þe kynred of [D]an,
Bot Cristendome sal he have nan.
He sal be maliciouse and ful of envy,
Als of hym þus spekes þe prophecy: 4170
    Fiat Dan coluber in via, cerastes
    in + semita, mordens ungulas equi,
    ut cadat ascensor eius retro. Hoc est sicut
    serpens in via sedebit et in semita erit,
    ut eos, qui per semitam iusticie ambu-   4175
    lant, feriat et veneno sue malicie occidat.

*4145 many] may G, *the couplet om.* L, *Morris's emendation*   *4147 ane] *om.* GM
*4167 Dan] san(e) cA, Safe L, dane M, *Morris's suggestion in note*   *4171–2 cerastes in]
*repeated G (*the prec.* in *apparently cancelled*), *Morris's silent correction*   4173 est] est
Antichristus Morris

'þe Dan', he says, 'sal þe nedder be,
Sittand in þe way, als men sal se,
And sal byte þe hors by þe hufe harde
And mak þe upstegher fal bakwarde.   4180
And þat es þus mykel at say
Als Anticrist als nedder sal sit in þe way
And smyte þam alle, bathe mare and les,
þat walkes in þe way of rightwysnes,
And sla þam thurght þe venym   4185
Of þe malice þat sal cum of hym'.
    Yhit sal he be circumcid,
And thurgh þat his malice a whyle sal hid.
Alswa til hym sal assygned be
A gude angelle, þat he sal noght se,   4190
Aftir his birthe in his bygynnyng,
þat of him sal haf þe kepyng.
Bot for he agayn þe trouthe þat es
Sal be hardend in wikkednes,
His gude angelle sal fra hym wende   4195
And leve hym in þe kepyng of þe fende.
    He sal be lered, als I understand,
And nurist and mast conversand
In þe cite of Bethsayda;
In Capharnaum he sal regne alswa.   4200
þe whilk Bethsayda and Capharnaum
And Corozaym God weried whilom.
For God spak til þas thre cites þos,
Als þe godspelle here shewes us:
    Ve tibi, Corozaym! Ve tibi, Bethsayda!   4205
    ve tibi, Capharnaum!
He says, 'Wa til þe, Corozaym, mot cum
And til + Bethsayda and Capharnaum'.
For þus in þe first he sal be born and bredde,
And in þe secunde be nuryst, and regne in þe
        thredde.   4210
    He sal gader fast til hym þan
Alle þat of þe devels crafte can,
Als nigremanciens and tregettours,

*4208 til] til þe cM, beth L

Wiches and false enchauntours,
þat þe devels crafte sal hym ken,   4215
Wharthurgh he sal decayve þe men.
Afterwarde thurgh ledyng of þe fende
He sal even to Ierusalem wende
And þar sal he duelle in þat cite
And inmyddes þe temple make his se   4220
And say til alle þat þar sal won
þat he es Crist, Goddes Son,
And mak þe folk hym to honour
And sal say þat he es þair saveour.

f. 97ra   He sal say þat na right Cristen man   4225
Was never byfor his tym bygan,
Bot fals anticristes he sal þam calle
And say þai lyved in fals trowthe alle,
þat has bene fra þe worldes bygynnyng
Until þe tyme of his commyng.   4230
He sal be lusty and lycherous
And desayvabel and trecherous.
He sal hym feyn first als haly
And shew þan appert ypocr[is]y
To desayve Cristen men and lele,   4235
Als says þe prophet Danielle:
    In aperto tum per ypocrisym similabit
    sanctitatem, ut facilius decipere possit.
'First', he says, 'he sal apertely
Feyn halynes thurgh ypocrisy,   4240
þat he mught lightlyer men bygile',
Bot þat tyme sal last bot a while.
    He sal al kynges and princes til hym drawe
And turne þam alle til his lawe,
And thurgh þam þe poples sal turned be   4245
Of ilka land and ilka cuntre.
In alle stedes he sal walk and pas,
þar Crist welk when he in erthe was.
In swylk + presumpcion he sal falle
þat 'he' sal thynk hym loverd of alle.   4250
Thurgh pride he sal ogayn God ryse

*4234 ypocrisy] ypocry G, *Morris's emendation*   4242 bot] noght bot RA
*4249 swylk] swylk a *cb*

And hym sclaunder and his law dispise,
And afforce hym and be bysy
His laghe to chaunge and fordo haly.
He sal turne al poples to his lawe   4255
And til him on four maners þam drawe.
A maner sal be thurgh fals prechyng,
Another thurgh fals miracles shewyng,
þe thred thurgh large gyftes to gyfe,
And þe ferthe thurgh drede of turmentis griefe.   4260
   Thurgh fals prechyng in ilk cuntre
Many til hym sal turned be,
For he sal send thurgh alle þe world wyde
His prechours to preche on ilka syde,
þe qwilk sal preche undir fals colour   4265
And say Cristes lawe es noght bot errour.
And Anticristes lawe þai sal comend
And agayn suthfastnes it defend
And forbede ilk man þat þai noght halde
þe new lawe, þat es Cristes lawe calde;   4270
And his ministres sal swa lette yhit
þat na man sal expound Haly Writ,
þat es to say to right undirstandyng,   f. 97rb
For þai sal say it es bot lesyng,
And make þe pople to trow haly   4275
þat þai sal noght be saved þarby.
þus sal þai bring þe folk in errour
Thurgh þair prechyng with false colour.
Swa his lawes sal pas and his powere
Fra þe est syde til þe west, thurgh þe world here, 4280
And fra þe southe til þe north alswa
His lawes and his power sal ga.
   He sal turne men on another manere
Thurgh fals miracles and wonders sere,
For he sal þan shew wonders many   4285
Thurgh enchauntementes and nygroma[n]cy
Swa gretely þat þe pople sal se.
And þat thurgh myght of þe devel sal be,
Of whilk wondirs I sal tel yhou sum.

*4286 -mancy] -macy G, *Morris's emendation*

He sal do fire fra þe heven don com,   4290
And `þat´ sal be noght bot an ille spirit
þat out of þe ayre sal com doun tite
And omang his disciples don light
And with sere tunges til þam spek ryght,
Als dyd til þe apostels þe Haly Gast.   4295
And þat sal be in mens sight mast,
For `þa´ þat his disciples sal be cald
Sal þam avant and þamself hald
Better of lif and to God mare dere
þan ever war Cristes appostels here.   4300
    Alswa thurgh þe devels crafte and myght,
He sal feyn him ded til mens syght
And on þe thred day thurgh þe devels rede,
He sal feyn hym to ryse fra dede,
And devels aftir sal bere hym up even   4305
Intil þe ayre, als he suld stey til heven.
And als he byfor sal be sene
Als he fra dede rase, men sal wene
þat he es up til heven ravyst
And trow þan þat he es verray Crist.   4310
þus sal Anticrist þan countrefette
þe wondirs of God in erthe swa grete;
    Ma wondirs yhit wirk sal he
þat þe pople sal openly se.
He `sal´ do trese growe and florisshe fayre   4315
And chace þe wyndes about and þe ayre.
Fra heven he sal do falle rayne-shours
And mak waters to ryn ogayn þair cours.
He sal trobel þe se when he wille,
And pees it and make it be stille.   4320
f. 97ᵛᵃ He sal chaung on wonder manere
Divers kyndes in figures sere.
He sal do dede ymages and dome
Speke of thynges þat er `to´ come.
He sal alswa dede men uprays   4325
þat sal gang obout, als þe boke says,
And þat sal be thurgh þe devels quayntis.

4298 avant] avaunce RM   4309 up] *om.* Morris (Lightbown)

For devels sal entre intil þe dede bodys
And bere þa dede bodys obout,
Swa þat parfit men sal be in dout   4330
Whether he es verray Crist or noght,
And þus sal men be in errour broght.
   On þe thred maner he sal bygille
Many thurgh gyftes with'in' short whyle
And turne þam til a fals belyefe   4335
Thurgh large gyftes þat he þam sal gyfe.
For he sal fynde alle þe tresour
þat es or was ever, hidde byfor
Under erthe, or ourwar elles.
þat may noght be gesced, for sum telles   4340
þat mar tresor under erthe es hidde
þan oboven es knawen or kydde.
Of whilk he sal þam alle ryche make,
þat þe lawe of Criste here wille forsake.
þos sal he shew men welth wordly   4345
For to desayve þam þan þarby.
   O[n] þe ferthe maner aftir þan,
He sal turne til hym many a man
And do þam haly folowe his trace
Thugh grete tourmentes and manace   4350
And thurgh drede of dede þat mast may grefe,
For elles he sal noght thole þam lyefe.
Ful grete tribulacions he sal þam shewe,
Als God in þe godspelle sayis thurgh Mathewe:
   Tanta erit tribulacio, ut in errorem   4355 `Matheus´
   inducantur, si fieri potest, eciam electi.
He says, 'Swa mikel tribulacion
Sal be þan' til ilka nacion
Thurghout þe world, ferre and nere,
'þat þas þat God has chosen here   4360
Suld be broght in error sone,
If God wild suffre þat it warre done'.
Bot in þe *Appocalipse* apparty
Es sayd þus ful mistyly:

*4347 On] Of G   4350 Thugh] Thurgh Morris, *Morris, an unnecessary emendation* (*cf. 5598*)   4353 tribulacions] -cion *a*   4356 eciam] et (?) R, effrem L, essencia M   4357 Swa] *om.* Morris (Lightbown)

Pedes eius sunt similes auricalco,   4365
sicut in camino ardente.
　　He says, 'His fete er like latoun bright,
Als in a chymne brynnand light'.
And þis was þat Iohan saw in a vision
Of hym þat semed þe virgyn son.   4370
　　By his fete þat als latoun was semand
Crist last lyms men may undirstand,
þe whilk sal be parfite men in charite,
þat agayne þe worldes ende martird sal be,
þat es to say, in tym of Anticrist,   4375
Thurgh wham many saules sal be perist.
þe chymne, brinand with þe het,
Bytakens þe tribulacion gret
þat sal be when Anticrist sal come,
Thurgh wham many sal thole grete marterdome.   4380
Anticrist sal be þe mast tyraunt
þat ever was, for he sal haunt
Alle þe maners of turmentes kene
In whilk any martirs byfor has bene.
For on sere maners he sal þam turment   4385
þat wille noght til his law assent
And put alle þa to þe dede at þe last,
þat ay duels in þe trouthe stedfast.
Bot alle Cristen men in þat cuntre
þar Crist welk mast tourmented sal be.   4390
And Haymo says, þat a grete clerk was,
'Hys tyrauntry thurgh þe world sal pas'.
　　þe devels þat er now bunden, swa
þat þai may noght 'about' flegh ne ga
Ne nuye als mykel als þai walde,   4395
Sal þan be louse and nathyng þam halde.
þat tyme sal preche na Cresten man,
For þai sal be halden als cursed þan,
Ne nan sal bye with þam ne selle,
Ne felaghshepe hald with þam, ne duelle –   4400
Bot with þas þat had Criste forsaken
And þe merk of Anticrist had taken,
þat men mught knawe and understand
þat þai til Anticrist war assentand.

f. 97vb

For al þas men sal bere his merk.   4405
þat sal forsake to wirk Cristes werk
And sal folowe Anticristes lawe,
By his merk men sal þam knawe,
þe whilk þai sal ber, als I understande,
Outher in þe frount or in þe ryght hande.   4410
Bot other þat wille noght do his rede
Sal be done to vilans dede.
On þis four maners, als I haf shewed,
He sal drawe til hym bathe lered and lewed,
And Crysten law sal be doun layde;   4415
þarfor þus in [þe] *Appocalips* es sayde: *Ion (sic?)*
   Cauda eius terciam partem stellarum   f. 98ra
   celi trahebat et misit eas in terra.
He says, 'With his tayle he droghe don even
þe thred part of þe sternes of heven   4420
And into þe erthe sent þam ryght',
þar þai might noght shyne ne gyf lyght.
   þis was þe taille of þe dragon
þat saynt Iohan saw in a vision.
þe dragon es understanden þe fende   4425
And his taille Anticrist þat folow[s] at þe ende.
And þe thred part of þe sternes bright
Er Cristen men undirstanden right,
þe whilk he sal fra right trowthe draw
And do þam in erthe to hald his law.   4430
þe men of þe worlde þat er covaytous
He sal turne thurgh gyftes precious,
For 'he' sal gyf þam, þat turned wil be
Of gold and silver grete plente.
Alswa men of symple connyng   4435
He sal turne thurgh miracles and prechyng.
Gude men, þat haldes Goddes commandmentes
He sal turne thurgh manace and turmentes.
Many þat semes gude and rightwyse
Sal trow in hym and Crystes trouth despyse.   4440
   First sal Anticrist com in myldnes

4410 or] or els R   *4416 þe] *om.* G   *4426 folows] folowed GL, felous M
4439 semes] sal seme *a*M

And prech ogayn þe right trouth þat es,
And myracles [t]hurgh hym sal be done.
þan sal þe Iewes resayve hym sone
And be turned til hym al haly.   4445
And þat tyme sal com Ennoc and Ely,
Ogayn Anticrist to preche ful harde,
Als yhe may se and here afterwarde.
þan sal Anticrist bygyn felly
To pursue men thurgh tyrauntry;   4450
Gret persecucion þan sal he wyrk
Agayn Cristen men and Haly Kirk.
þan sal he destroye Cristen lawe,
And Gog and Magog til hym drawe.
  þe whilk er halden, als men telles,   4455
þe werst folk þat + in þe world duels.
Som says þat þai er closed haly
By-yhonde þe mountes of Caspy,
Bot þai er noght swa closed obout
þat þai ne mught lightly com out,   4460
Yif a qwene ne war, þat haldes þam in
Thurgh stre[n]gthe, þat þai may noght out wyn,
þat es cald þe qwene of Amazons,
Under whas powere þat folk wons.
f. 98rb Bot at þe last þai sal breke out   4465
And destroy many landes obout.
For þe Iewes has swylk a prophecy
And says þus omang þam commonly
þat þis folk, ogayne þe worldes ende,
Sal com out and til Ierusalem wende   4470
With þair Crist, þat wonders sal wirke
And þan sal þai distroie Haly Kyrke.
  Some clerkes says, als þe glose telles,
þat Go[g] and Magog es noght elles
Bot þe host of Onticrist [þat] sal come   4475
Sodanly ogayn þe day of dome
And ogayne Haly Kyrk werray

---

*4443 myracles] add sal c   *hym sal] hym with sal cancelled? G, hym R, Morris's silent
correction   *4456 þat] þat þat G, Morris's silent correction   4458 mountes]
mountayns RL   *4462 strengthe] stregthe G, Morris's emendation   *4474 Gog]
god G   *4475 þat] om. G, Morris's emendation

For to destroye it if þai may.
þe glose of þe buke says alswa
þat by Gog er understanden alle þa   4480
Thurgh whilk þe devel, our mast enmy,
Sal Cristen men pursue prively.
By Magog may þas understanden be
Thurgh wham openly pursue sal he,
Or þas er understanden þarby   4485
þat in Anticrist tyme first pryvely
And aftirward openly, sal wyrk
Wykkedness ogayne Haly Kyrk.
Gog es als mykel at say als covert,
And Magog es noght elles bot als apert.   4490
    þir twa prophetes, als says som,
Ennok and Hely, byfor sal com
Bytwene þe tyme of þe commyng prive
Of Anticrist, when he [b]orn sal be,
And þe tyme of his oppen commyng,   4495
þat sal be thurgh open prechyng
And thurgh open persecucion
þat he sal do til diverse nacion.
Bytwen þa tymes þa prophetes twa
On sere partes sal preche swa   4500
þat thurgh þair prechyng þai sal drawe
And convert þe Iewes til Cristen lawe,
For þus spekes þe prophete Malachy,
In a boke of þe prophecy:
    Convertent corda patrum   4505
    in filios.
He says, 'þai sal turne thurgh Goddes myght
þe fadirs hertes intil þe sons right',
þat es, þai sal turne þe Iewery
Until right Cristendom halely.   4510
    þan sal Iewes þe sam lawe halde,
þat þai haf, þat er Cristen men calde
And als Cristen men dus swa sal þai do,   f. 98va
Als þe glose says þat acordes þarto:

4483 þas] þus RM, all þai L   4489 covert] couert *with mark of suspension* R
*4494 born sal] *trs. c*   4510 Cristendom] cristen men *a*

Percipient fidem quam   4515
ipsi habuerunt.
'þe Iewes sal tak' þan with hert glade
'þe trouth þat Cristen men byfor hadde'.
Wharfor þe Iewes and Cristen men,
Als þa twa prophetes sal þam ken,   4520
Sal þan thurgh even entencion
Assent in Crist als a religion.
　　þai sal preche, als þe *Appocalips* says,
A thousand and twa hundreth days
And sexti, als men sal se and here,   4525
And als þe glose says – þat es, thre yhere,
Als Crist himself did þat voched safe
To preche þe sam law þat we hafe.
þai sal be, als þe *Appocalips* spekes,
In harde hayres cle[d]de and in sekkes;   4530
þat es, þai sal þan penance preche
And thurgh ensaumple of penance teche.
　　Bot als-tite als Anticrist sal knawe
þat þai turne Iewes til Cristen lawe
Thurgh ensaumple þat þai shew and sarmon,   4535
þan sal he shew grete persecucion
And grevusly þam tourment,
þat til his law wille noght assent,
And do þam to hard dede at þe last,
Yf þai in þe trouthe be stedfast.   4540
Anticrist sal be þan ful wrathe;
He sal do tak þa prophetes bathe
And in Ierusalem thurgh þe devels rede
Hastyly do þam bathe to dede.
þan sal þair bodys, als þe buke says,   4545
In þe stretes ligg stille thre days
And an half, oboven erthe namly,
For na man sal þam dur biry
F[or] drede þat þai sal haf þan
Of Anticrist, þat wikked man.   4550
þair enemys, when þai er slayn,
Of þair dede þai sal be fayn.

*4530 cledde] clende G, Morris's suggestion in note   *4549 For] Fro G, Morris's silent
correction   Here W lacks a folio and, with it, lines 4551–4619

When þai haf liggen dede on þis wyse
Thre days and an half, þai sal ryse,
And þan þair enmys a voce sal here   4555
Until þam spek on þis manere,
'Ely and Ennok, steyes up bathe,
For yhe er passed al maner of wathe'.
And als-tyte when þai haf herd þis steven,
In a cloude þai sal stey up til heven.   4560
þat alle þe pople þan sal se;   f. 98ᵛᵇ
A grete wondre tyl þam þat sal be.
Aftir þair dede, als þe buke says,
Anticrist sal regne yhit fiften days.
þan sal he turne alle til hym haly   4565
þat war turned til Ennok and Hely;
And alle þat til hym wille noght trow þan
Sal þan be don til þe dede, ilk man.
    Anticrist in his grete tyrantry
Sal regne thre yhere and an half fully;   4570
þan sal God abrege his days,
Als Mathew in þe godspel says:
    Nisi breviati fuissent dies, non   *Mattheus*
    erit salva omnis caro.
'Bot his days war abreged', says he,   4575
'Fone men fra þan sal save be',
Bot his tyme God abrege sal þan.
Til þis says saynt Gregore þe haly man:
    Quia nos infirmos aspicit Deus, dies   *Gregor*
    malos quos singulariter intulit, misericorditer breviabit. 4580
He says, 'Forþi þat God sese right
þat we er freyle and feble of myght,
þe days þat er ille and hevy,
þat er putted til sere men singulerly,
Yhit at þe last abrege sal he   4585
Thurgh his gudenes and his pyte'.
Anticrist sal be withouten pere,
And he sal lyf twa and thretty yhere
And an half, als som clerkes says þai se.

4573 fuissent] finissent Morris (Lightbown)   4578 man] ma Morris (*corrected in his errata*)

Of swa many yhere his eld sal be   4590
Fra þe tyme of his first bygynnyng
Until þe tyme of his last endyng.
For sum says he sal lyf als many yhere
Als Crist lifed in mans kynd here,
And when he has þus lang lyfed,   4595
þan sal na ma thurgh him by greved.
   He sal þan son fele Goddes vengeance
And withouten any repentance,
He sal be slayn ful sodanly
Thurgh þe myght of God almyghty,   4600
Opon þe mounte of Olyvett
In þe stede whar Crist his fete sett,
When he stey up til heven bright,
And swa sal he ende thurgh Goddes might.
Som clerkes yhit says alswa   4605
þat saynt Michael sal hym sla
Thurgh Goddes byddyng in þe same stede,
In þe whilk he sal be funden dede.
f. 99ʳᵃ And þe boke says alswa þat he,
Thurgh þe gast of Goddes mouthe slayn sal be.   4610
Bot howswa it be, þis es certayn,
Thurgh Goddes myght þar sal he be slayn.
   Anticrist mynisters, when he is dede,
Sal mak ioy þan in ilka stede,
And haf þair delices nyght and day   4615
And wedden wyfes and þus say:
'Alle-if our prince be dede þus,
We haf pees and welthe plentevus'.
And right als þai sal say þus alle,
Sodanly ded þai sal doun falle   4620
Thurgh þe myght of God almyghty;
þus sal þai enden sodanly.
Bot yhit when þai alle er þus fordone,
þe grete dome sal noght be aftir alsone,
For þe glose of Danyel þus says: 4625
'God sal graunt fyve and fourty days
Til alle þas þat desayved sal be
Thurgh Anticrist and his meyne,

4596 ma] man A, may L

þat þai may amende þam of þair syn
And do penance ar þe dome bygyn'.   4630
þe Iewes sal þan al turned be
Til þat right trouthe, þe whilk haf we.
þan sal God fulfille in þe last days
þis worde þat he in þe godspel says:
    Et fiet unum ovile   4635
    et unus pastor.
He sais, 'Alle f[lok]kes to [a] fald sal falle,
And a hirde sal be' to kepe þam alle.
þat f[lo]k Iewes and Cristen men sal be talde
Under a trouthe in Haly Kirkes falde;   4640
Fra þat tyme forthe sal Hali Kirke be
In pees and rest withouten adverfite.
For þan sal faile alle power of þe fende,
Fra þat tyme unto þe worldes ende,
Swa þat he sal nother tempte ne gryefe   4645
Haly Kirk ne man þat þan sal lyefe.
    Bot how mikel space sal be `fra´ þan
Til þe day of dome, wate na man;
For of al þe prophetes þat men may neven
And alle þe halghes and angels in heven,   4650
Mught never nane witt þat privite,
What tyme þe day of dome sal be.
For God wille þat nane it byfor wytte
Bot himself þat has ordaynt itte.
þarfor Crist til his disciples sayde þus,   4655
Als þe *Boke of Apostels Werkes* shewes us:
    Non est vestrum nosse tempora vel momenta   f. 99rb
    que pater possuit in sua potestate.
'It falles noght yhow knaw þe time prive
þat þe Fadir has sette in his awen pouste'.   4660
þarfor na man suld aske ne say
How mykel we hafe til domesday,
Ne we suld noght yherne it to lere,
[To] witte wether it be ferre or nere.
Bot we suld mak us redy alle,   4665

*4637 flokkes] folkes G, folk *b*   *a] *om.* G   *4639 flok] folk GM   4650 halghes
and angels] *trs. sbs. a,* halouse vndir god M   4651 never] *om.* R   4663 it] yhit A,
om. M   *4664 To] Ne G

Als þe day of dome tomorn suld falle,
And thynk ay on þat dredeful dome,
Als þe haly man dyd, saynt Ierome,
þat ay þaron thoght, bathe nyght and days,
And þarfor þus in a boke he says: 4670
   Sive comedam, sive bibam, sive aliquid
   aliud faciam, semper michi videtur illa
   tuba resonare in auribus meis, 'sur-
   gite mortui, venite ad iudicium'.
He says 'Whether I ette or + drynk,   4675
Or oght elles do, ay me thynk
þat þe beme þat blaw sal on domsday
Sounes in myn eres, þat þus says ay:
"Ryse yhe þat er dede, and come
Unto þe grete dredful dome"'.   4680
  Now haf yhe herd of þe bygynnyng
Of Anticrist, and of his lif and his endyng,
þat men may a werray taken calle,
þat agayne þe day of dome sal falle.
Many ma takens yhit men sal se   4685
Byfor ar þat dre[de]ful day sal be,
Bathe in erthe and yhit in heven,
Als we here Crist in þe gospelle neven,
Whare he spekes of takens sere
þat sal falle and says on þis manere: 4690
   Erunt signa in sole et luna et stellis;
   et in terris pressura gencium pre confusi-
   ione sonitus maris et fluctuum, arescen-
   tibus hominibus pre timore et expectacione, que
   supervenient universo orbi. Nam virtutes   4695
   celorum movebuntur, et tunc videbunt
   filium hominis venientem in nubibus,
   cum potestate magna et maiestate etc.
þir er þe wordes of þe gospelle
þat Crist til his disciples gun telle;   4700
He says þus als he ordaynd be done:
'Takens sal be in þe son and in þe mone,

4669 nyght] nyghtes RM   *4675 or] or I G*b*   4678 þat] and RM
4682 and²] and of R*b*   *4686 dredeful] dreful G, *Morris's emendation*   4687 yhit]
after Bathe *a, om.* M   4688 we] yhe *a*

And in þe sternes þat in heven men may ken;
And in erthe sal be grete thrang of men
For þe mengyng of þe noys of þe se   4705 f. 99va
[And] of þe flodes þat þan sal be.
And men sal wax dry in þat dyn
For drede and for lang bydyng þarin,
þat til al þe world sal com', says he.
'For þe myghtes of heven sal þan styrd be,   4710
And þai sal se þe Son of Man
Comand doun in cloudes þan
With his grete myght and mageste',
And þat tyme sal þe grete dome be.
þir takens er tald aftir þe lettre here,   4715
Bot þe exposicion may be 'on' othir manere.
Alswa God, þat alle thynges knawes wele,
He says þus thurgh þe prophete Ioele:
    Et dabo prodigia in celo sursum et signa   *Ioele*
    in terra deorsum, sanguinem et ignem et   4720
    vaporem fumi; sol convertetur in tenebras et lu-
    na in sanguinem antequam veniat dies Domini
    magnus et manifestus.
He says, 'I sal gyfe wonders sere
Up in heven', als men sal here;   4725
'And takens doun in erthe + on to luke,
þat es blode and fire and brethe of smoke.
þe son sal be turned intil mirknes,
And þe mone intil blode and be lyghtles,
Byfor or þe day of our Lord sal falle,   4730
þat sal be grete and openly shewed til alle'.
þat grete day is þe grete day of dome,
Agayn whilk alle þir takens sal come.
þan may men by swilk takens wytte
þat it es þe mast day þat ever was yhitte,   4735
And þe straytest and þe mast harde,
Als men may se and here aftirwarde.
    Yhit spekes þe haly man saynt Ierome
Of fiften takens þat sal come
Byfor Cristes commyng, als he says,   4740

þe whilk sal falle in xv. days.
Bot whether any other days sal falle
Bytwen þa days, or þai sal alle
Continuely falle, day aftir day,
Saynt Ierom says he can noght say.   4745
And yhit for certayn approves noght he
þat þa fiften days of takens sal be,
Bot he reherces þa takens fiftene
Als he þam fand and writen had sene
In som bokes of þe Ebriens,   4750
þat þa xv. days contens.
Bot saynt Ierome shewes noght ne telles
þat he þam fand writen ourwhar elles,
f. 99ᵛᵇ Bot in þe Hebriens bokes he þam fande
And reherces þam, als he saw þam stande,   4755
Ilka day aftir other even,
Als yhe may here me now neven.

    j.   þe first day of þas fiften days,
þe se sal ryse, als þa bukes says,
Abowen þe heght of ilka mountayne   4760
Fully fourty cubyttes certayne,
And in his stede even upstande
Als an heghe hille dus on þe lande.

  ij. þe secunde day, þe se sal be swa law
þat unnethes men sal it knaw.   4765

 iij. þe thred day, þe se sal seme playn
And stand even in his cours agay[n],
Als it stode `first´ at þe bygynnyng
Withouten mare rysyng or fallyng.

*iiij.*þe fierth day sal swilk a wonder be: 4770
þe mast wondreful fisshes of þe se
Sal com togyder and mak swilk romyng
þat it sal be hydus til mans heryng.
Bot what þat romiyng sal signify
Na man may whit, bot God almyghty.   4775

   v. þe fift day, þe se sal brynne
And alle [þe] watters als þai sal rynne,
And þat sal last fra þe son rysyng

4750 bokes] buke *a*   4759 þa] þe Morris   þa bukes] þe buke R*b*   4765 sal]
may *a*   *4767 agayn] agay G, *Morris's emendation*   *4777 þe] *om.* G

Til þe tyme of þe son doun-gangyng.
  þe sext day, sal spryng a blody dewe   4780 *vj.*
On grisse and tres, als it sal shewe.
þe sevend day, byggyn`s´ doun sal falle   *vij.*
And grete castels and tours withalle.
þe eght day, hard roches and stanes   *viij.*
Sal strik togyder alle attanes,   4785
And ilkan of þam sal other doun cast,
And ilkan agayn other hortel fast,
Swa þat ilka stan, on divers wyse,
Sal sonder other in thre partyse.
þe neghend day, gret erthe-dyn sal be,   4790 *ix.*
Generaly in ilka contre,
And swa gret erth-dyn als `sal´ be þan
Was never hard sythen þe world bygan.
þe tend day þaraftir to neven,   *x.*
þe erthe sal be made playn and even,   4795
For hilles and valeis sal turned be
Intil playn and made even to se.
  þe ellevend day, men sal com out   *xj.*
Of caves and holes, and wend about
Als wode men, þat na witt can,   4800
And nane sal spek til other þan.
þe twelfte day aftir, þe sternes alle   *xij.* f. 100ra
And þe signes fra þe heven sal falle.
þe threted day, sal dede men banes   *xiij.*
Be sett togyder and ryse al attanes   4805
And aboven on þair graves stand;
þis sal byfalle in ilka land.
þe fourtend day, al þat lyves þan   *xiiij.*
Sal dighe, childe, man, and woman,
For þai shalle with þam rys ogayn   4810
þat byfor war dede, outher til ioy or payn.
þe fiftend day þos sal betyde: *xv.*
Alle þe world sal bryn on ilk syde
And þe erthe whar we now duelle
Until þe utter end of alle helle.   4815
þus tels Ierom þer takens fiftene,

4782 byggyns] bygyng L   4784 eght] eghtend RW, eghten L, aght M   4793 þe]
om. A   4804 men] mens A, *om.* L   4810 shalle] suld *a*, þus M   4811 or] or to AL

Als 'he' in þe bokes of Ebriens had sene.
  Bot for alle þa takens þat men sal se,
Yhit sal na man certayn be
What tyme Crist sal come til þe dome,   4820
Swa sodanly he sal doun come.
For als byfel in Noe and Loth days,
Swa sal he com, for Luke in þe godspel says:

Luke   *Et sicut factum est in diebus Noe, ita*
        erit adventus filii hominis: edebant   4825
        et bibebant, uxores ducebant et
        dabantur ad nupcias usque ad diem
        qua intravit Noe in archam. Et
        venit diluvium, et perdidit omnes. Si-
        militer factum est in diebus Loth: ede-   4830
        bant et bibebant, emebant et vendebant,
        plantabant et edificabant,
        qua die autem exiit Loth a Sodomis,
        pluit ignem et sulphur de celo et perdidit
        omnes. Secundum autem hoc erit   4835
        qua die Filius Hominis revelabitur.
þir er þe wordes of þe godspelle,
þat er on Inglissche þus to telle:
'Als was done in þe days of Noe,
Right swa Mans Son sal com', says he.   4840
'Men ete and drank + and war glade
And wedded wyfes and bridalles made,
Until þe day namly þat Noe
Went into þe shippe þat made he,
And sodanly come þe flode þat tyde   4845
And fordid alle þe world swa wyde.
Alswa in þe days of Loth byfelle,
Men ete and drank, shortly to telle,
Ilkan with other, and salde and boght
And planted, and bygged and houses wroght.   4850
f. 100rb And þat day þat Loth yhed out of Sodome,
Sodanly Goddes vengeance come.

4817 had] has RM   4829 diluvium] diliuau*m* ? A, *om. from* nupcias M
4833 Sodomis] *adds* et subito Morris (Lightbown)   4836 revelabitur] *adds* etc. R
4838 er] es Morris (Lightbown)   *4841 drank] drank þan *c*M   4842 bridalles]
brydall R

It rayned fire fra heven and brunstane,
And tynt al þat þare was and spard nane.
Right þus sal falle, als men sal se,   4855
þe `day' [þat] Man[s] Son sal shewed be'.
  [I]n þe ende of þe world byfor þe dome,   *Of þe fire þat sal*
An hydus fire sal sodanly come,   *bryn alle þe world*
þat alle þe world sal haly bryn
And nathyng spare þat es þarin.   4860
For alle þe erthe sal bryn withoute
And þe elementes and + þe ayre oboute,
And alle þat God in þe world has wroght
Sal þan be brynned and wasted to nogoht.
þis fire þat thurgh þe world sal ryse   4865
Sal com þan fra sere partys,
For alle þe fire þat es in þe spere
And under erthe and aboven erthe here
Sal mete togyder attans þan
And bryn alle þat lyves, best and man,   4870
And alle þat growes in erthe and ayre,
Tille alle be clensed and made fayre
Of alle þe corrupcions þat men may se,
þe whilk in þe ayre or in þe erthe may be.
þis fire, als þe buk us says a[nd] lers,   4875
Sal brin and wirk on four maneres.
It sal wirk als þe fir of helle
To punyssche þe synful þat þar sal duelle;
It sal wirk als fire of purgatory
To clense men of veniel syn fully.   4880
It sal wirk als fire of herth here,
þat overalle sal bryn, far and nere,
To wast alle þat on erthe springes
Als gresse and tres and alle other thynges,
And alswa þe bodys of ilk man   4885
To brin haly into askes þan.
It sal wirk als þe fire of þe spere
To make þe elementes clene and clere

*4856 þat Mans] man G   *4857 In] *an unfilled champ and reads* n G, *Morris's silent*
supply   *4862 þe²] alle þe *c*M   4871 in] and *a, om.* L, on þe M   4873 Of]
And *a*   4875 us] *om.* Morris (Lightbown)   *and] als G, *Morris's suggestion in note*
4884 other] erthely *a*

And alle þe ayre bright of hew,
And þe hevens for to seme als new.   4890
Thurght þis fire þat þus sal rayke obout,
þe face of þe erth sal brin without,
And þe shappe of þe world sal fordone be
Als it was first thurgh þe flode of Noe.
And als þat flode passed cubites fiften   4895
Over þe heyghest mount þat ever was sen,
Right swa þe fire als heyghe sal pas
To fordo þe world als it þan was.

f. 100ᵛᵃ And als God byfor his first commyng
Wald here fordo, withouten lettyng,   4900
Alle þe world thurgh water anly
Agayn þe fire of lychery,
Right swa byfor his last commyng,
He sal of þe world mak endyng
Thurgh fire þat sal swa brinnand be   4905
Agayn þe dasednes of charite.
      þe wirkyng of þis fire swa brinnand
Sal conten[e] þir thre short + tymes passand,
þat es bygynnyng, mydward, and ende,
Als in þis bok es here contende.   4910
First þe fire at þe bygynnyng
Sal cum byfor Cristes commyng,
þat þe gude men sal þan clensen and fine
And þe wikked men hard punys and pyne,
þat here luffed syn and thoght it swete,   4915
And þarfor says þus David þe prophete:
      Ignis ante ipsum precedet et inflammabit
      in circuitu inimicos eius.
'þe fir byfor hym' on sere partys
'Sal ga [a]bout `and´ brine his enemys'.   4920
þat fire mens bodys to askes sal brin
And þe world and alle þat es þarine.
þus sal þ[at] fire first byfor come,
Ar Crist com doun til þe dome.
And when þe fire has wasted, als I talde,   4925

4890 seme] serve Morris (Lightbown)   4907 þis] þe Morris (Lightbown)
*4908 contene] contend GAL, *Morris's suggestion in note*   *tymes] tymens G, *Morris's
silent correction*   *4920 and] *int. before* about G, *before* about R   *4923 þat] þe GM

þan sal al men ryse, bathe yhong and alde,
Out of þair graves with saul and body
And come til þe dome þan alle halely.
And our Loverd Crist sal com doun þan
And sit in dome, als domesman,   4930
And deme þan bathe gude and ille,
Als yhe may aftirward here, if yhe wille.
   And yhit þe fire alle þat tyde
Sal brin obout hym, on ilka syde,
Als þe prophete David bers wytnes   4935
In þe Psauter, þar þus writen es:
   Ignis in conspectu eius exardescet,
   et in circuitu eius tempestas valida.
'þe fyre sal brin in his sight', says he,
'And about hym grete tempest sal be'.   4940
And als lang als þat dome sal last
þe fire sal brin on ilk syde fast;
And when þe dome es broght til ende,
þa þat sal be dampned sal wende
With alle þe fire þat swa sal brin   4945
Til helle-pytt and duelle ay þarin.
þan sal alle þe fire be sweped doune   f. 100vb
Intil helle, with alkyn corrupcioune
And alle þe filth of þe world, neshe and hard,
Als in þis bok es writen aftirward.   4950
þus thurgh alle þe world þe fire sal brin
And clense it of al manere of syn
And of alle corrupcions, bath hegh and law,
þat men may now se, here, and knaw.
And when þe fire has wasted al erdly thyng,   4955
þan sal þe hevens sees of movyng.
   Our Lord yhit þan, or he com doun
For to sytte in dome in propre persoun,
Sal send byfor, als þe buke tels,
In four partys his angels   4960
With þair bemes þat þai sal blaw,
þat alle þe world sal here and knaw.
Alle men þai sal þan up calle
And byd þam cum til þe dome alle.
Alle men sal ryse þan þat ever had life,   4965

Man and woman, mayden and wyfe,
Gude and ille, with fleshe and felle,
In body and saul, als clerkes can telle—
And þat in als short whyle als hert may thynk,
Or mans eghe may open or wynk,   4970
Fra þe tyme þat þai þe son sal here,
For þe apostel says on þis manere:

'Apostolus'   *Omnes resurgent in momento, in*
                ictu oculi, in novissima tuba.

He says, 'alle sal 'ryse' in a tym movyng,   4975
Als in þe space of an eghe twynklyng,
When þai here þe dredeful blast
Of þe beme, þat þan sal blaw last'.

    Alle men sal þan tite up ryse
In þe same stature and þe same bodyse,   4980
þat þai had here in þair life-days,
And in non other, als þe buk says.
þan salle alle ryse in þe same eld þan,
þat God had fully here als man,
Namly, when he up rayse thurgh myght   4985
Fra dede, als says saynt Austyn ryght.
þan was he of threty yhere elde and twa
And of thre monethes þarwith alswa.
In þat elde alle sal ryse at þe last,
When þai here þe grete bemes blast,   4990
With þair awen bodys alle hale
And with alle þair lymes, grete and smale.
For alle-if þe bodys of ilka man
Shulde alle be brynned til askes þan,
f. 101ra And yhit þogh alle þe askes of þair bodys   4995
War strew[d] and skaterd in sere partys,
Thurgh ilka lande and ilka cuntre,
þai sal þan togyder alle gader[d] be.
And ilka body sal rise þan halely,
With alle þe lyms, þat falles til þe body   5000
And with alle þe hare of body and hede
Swa þat na hare sal want in na stede.

4979 þan tite] *trs.* R   4984 als] *of* RL, *cf.* as he was M   *4996 strewd] strew G,
a small eyeskip and lacks 4993–5000 M, *Morris's emendation*   *4998 gaderd] gader G,
Morris's emendation

For þare sal na hare be peryste,
Als saynt Luk says þe evaungeli[s]te:
   Capillus de capite   5005 *Luke*
   vestro non peribit.
'Na hare sal perishe ne faile', says he,
'þat falles on þe heved for to be'.
And if any lyms be here unsemely
Thurgh outragiouste of kynd namely,   5010
God sal abate þat outrage thurgh myght
And make þa lyms semely to sight.
And if any lym wanted, þat shuld falle
Til þe body, or any war over-smalle,
Thurgh þe defaut here of kynd God þan wille   5015
Alle þe defautes of þe lyms fulfille,
And þus sal he do namly to alle þa
þat [sal] be save and til blis ga.
For þair bodys sal be semely and bright
With avenand lymes til alle mens sight.   5020
Bot God sal amend on nane wise
Defautes of þe lyms of synful bodys,
For þair bodys sal alle unsemely be
And foul and wgly opon to se.
   Alle þat er gude þan and rightwyse,   5025
þat sal be save, sal first upryse,
And up into þe ayre be ravyste
Agayne þe comyng of Ihesu Criste,
To kepe him when he doun sal come
Als domesman for to sitte in dome.   5030
þe mast perfite men sal Criste first kepe
And alle cum with hym in his felawshepe
And with him ay be in body and saule,
Als þe apostel says, saynt Paule:
   Quoniam ipse Dominus in iussu et voce archangeli   5035 *Paul*
   et in tuba Dei, descendet de celo, et mortui
   qui in Cristo + sunt resurgent primi,
   de`inde´ nos qui vivimus, qui relinquimur, simul
   rapiemur cum illis `in nubibus´

---

*5004 evangeliste] euangelitte G, *Morris's emendation*   *5018 sal] *om.* G
5024 opon] on *a*M, for L   5029 doun sal] *trs. a*M   5035 ipse] Christus
Morris   iussu] iussa Morris   *5037 sunt] mortui sunt *c*

obviam Cristo in aere, sic semper   5040
cum Domino erimus.

He says, 'Our lord sal come doun fra heven,
In Goddis byddyng and archaungel steven
f. 101rb And in þe Son of Goddes awen beme,
Alle þe world þan for to deme.   5045
And þa þat er dede in Crist þan
Sal first uprise, ilka man;
And sythen we on þe sam manere,
þat now lyves and er left here,
Sal þan with þam in cloudes be ravyste   5050
Up intil þe ayre for to mete Criste,
And swa with our lorde ay sal be
Fra þat tyme forward'. þus says he.
    Bot [þ]e synful þat sal rise þat tyde
Bynethe on þe erthe sal Crist abyde   5055
In drede and sorow charged with synne,
For þai may nourwhare away wynne.
þam war lever be depe in helle þan,
þan com byfor þat domesman.
þai wald fayne fle, if þai myght,   5060
Or hide þam fra þat domesman sight
Under erthe or ourwhar elles,
Ion Als saynt Iohan in þe *Apocalips* telles:

Reges terre et principes et tribuni et
+ divites et fortes et omnis   5065
servus et liber + abscondent se in
speluncis et in petris moncium, et
dicent montibus et petris, 'Cadite
super nos'; et collibus, 'abscondite
nos a facie sedentis super tronum   5070
et ab ira agni'.

He says, 'Kynges of þe lande and princes sere
And cheftayns þat er under þam here,
And riche men of divers cuntre
And strenthy men and bond and fre   5075

5046 þa] þai W*b* Morris   *5054 þe] we *c*L, *Morris's suggestion in note*
*5064 tribuni et] *repeats on next line* G, tribuni *canc.* (*but not* et), *Morris's silent correction*
*5066 abscondent] absconderunt *c* (-er- *apparently erased* A)   5067 speluncis]
spelunpcis R, *lacks end of citation* M   5071 agni] igni R, *om.* L

In caves þa[n] wald þam hyde ilkan
And in cragges and in roche[s] of stan;
And sal say til montayns and roches þus,
"Fal opon us now and hyde us
Fra þe face of hym þat syttes in throne   5080
And fra þe wrethe of þe lamb"'. þus tels saynt Iohan.   *Ion*
   Many maner of men sal haf dred þan
To com byfor þat dre[de]ful domesman,
Namely synful men withouten hope,
And yhit says þus þe haly man Iope: 5085 *Iob*
   Domine, quando veneris iudicare terram,
   ubi me abscondam a vultu ire tue, quia
   peccavi nimis [in vita mea]?
'Loverd', he says, 'When þou sal come
To deme þe erthe and sytte in dome,   5090
Whar sal I fra þi wreth hyd me,
Forwhy I haf synd ogaynes þe
Ful gretely in my life here'?   f. 101ᵛᵃ
And yhit says Iob on þis manere:
   Quis michi hoc tribuat   5095
   ut in inferno protegas me
   et abscondas me donec
   pertranseat furor tuus?
'Loverd, wha may gyf to me', says he,
'þat þou in helle mot hyd me   5100
And cover me at þe dredful day
Unto þi wrethe be passed oway'?
þan es it na wondre, als I sayde are,
If þe synful men haf drede and care,
þat sal dampned be and peryst,   5105
For to cum in þe sight of Ihesu Crist,
þat til þam swa wrethful sal seme þan,
When Iob þus says þe haly man.
   Our Lord Crist, thurgh his grete myght,
Sal þan come doun fra heven bright   5110
Als domesman to sit in dome,   *Of commyng of Crist til*
                                                þe dome

*5076 þan] þai *c*   *5077 roches] roche G   5079 Fal] Falles *a*
*5083 dredeful] dreful G, *Morris's emendation*   *5088 in vita mea] etc. G, in vita L,
lacks end of citation M, *Morris's emendation*   5092 ogaynes] til *a*, to M   5100 mot]
moght W, myȝt M, may Morris (Lightbown)   5101 þe] þat *a*M

And with hym grete multitude sal come
Of angels and of archangels
And of + other halghes, als þe buk tels:
　　Ecce Dominus veniet et　　　　　　　　　　5115
　　omnes sancti eius cum eo.
'Lo, our Lord sal com til þe dome,
And alle his halghes sal with him come',
And sodanly he sal hym þan shewe,
Matheus Als says þe godspeller saynt Mathewe:　　　5120
　　Sicut fulgur exijt ab oriente
　　et paret in occidente, ita erit
　　adventus Filij Hominis subitus,
　　choruschans, et terribilis.
'Als þe levennyg out gas in short tyde　　　　　5125
Fra þe est and shewes it in þe west syde,
Right swa þe commyng of Man[s] Son sal be,
Sodayne and bright and dre[de]ful to se'.
He sal com doun; nathyng sal him lett,
Even onence þe mount of Olyvet,　　　　　　　5130
Whar he in manhed stey up even
Fra his disciples til þe Fader in heven.
And in swilk fourme als 'he' stey up þan,
He sal com doune to deme ilk man,
Gude and ille, bathe yong and alde,　　　　　　5135
Als þe angels til his disciples talde:
　　Hic Ihesus, qui assumptus est a vobis
　　in celum, sic veniet + quemadmodum
　　vidistis eum euntem
　　in celum.　　　　　　　　　　　　　　　　　5140
f. 101vb þai sayd, 'Ihesu, þat here es uptane
Fra yhow til heven', with flessch and bane,
'Swa sal he com at þe world ende,
Als yhe saw hym up intil heven wende'.
In þat fourme of man he 'sal' cum þan　　　　　5145
And sitte in dome als domesman.

*5114 of] of al *c*, *om.* M　　　　5125 levennyg] G, levenyng Morris, *a silent correction*
*5127 Mans] man GL　　*5128 dredeful] dreful G, *Morris's emendation*　　　5132 in] of
*a*L　　　5137 vobis] nobis Morris　　　*5138 veniet] veniet et *c*, veniet etc. (*and ends*) M
5141 Ihesu] Ihesus Christ Morris　　　5143 world] worldes *ab*; *at this point, a small eyeskip
and om.* 5155–64 M

When Criste es commen doun to deme

In fourme of man, als he sal seme,
In a place he sal his dome halde,
þat þe vale of Iosaphat es calde, 5150
Whare alle men sal togyder mete,
Als Crist says thurgh Ioel þe prophete:

  Congregabo omnes gentes et
  adducam eas in valle Iosaphat.
He says, 'Alle men I sal togyder calle 5155
And in [þe] vale of Iosaph[a]t lede þam alle'.
And yhit mare to þat he says þus,
Als he thurgh þe prophete shewes us:
  Consurgent et ascendent
  omnes gentes in valle 5160
  Iosephat, quia ibi sedebo
  ut iudicem omnes gentes.
He says, 'Al men sal ryse to þe dome
And into þe vale of Iosaphat come,
For þar', he says, 'I sal sitte namly 5165
To deme alle men', als þai er worthy.
þat vale, þe [na]v[e]le of þe erthe men calles,
For imyd þe erthe withouten it falles;
Iosaphat es þus mykel at say
Als 'stede of dome' at þe last day. 5170
Crist sal noght fully þan doun come
On þe erthe for to sitte in dome,
Bot up in þe ayre he sal sitte
On a whyte cloude, als says Haly Wrytte:
  Ecce apparebit Dominus super 5175
  nubem candidam.
'Lo, our Lorde sal shew hym þan
On a whyte cloude' and sitte als domesman,
Even aboven þat vale namly,
Whare al men sal se his body. 5180
  Bot þe skilles why he sal þare sitte
Men may fynde here þat wille þam witte.
For þe vale of Iosephat es sette
Bytwene þe mount of Olyvet

And Ierusalem on þe [t]other syde,   5185
þat standes imyddes þe world so wyde.
And þar es þe mount of Calvery,
And þe sepulcre of Crist fast þarby,
f. 102ra And in þat cuntre standes Bethleem,
Noght ful ferre fra Ierusalem.   5190
þarfor Crist sal sytte þar þat day,
Onence þe myddes of erth þus for to say:
'Lo, here, als yhe may alle now se
þe vale of Iosaphat under me,
Whare byred was my moder Mary,   5195
Of wham flesshe and blode for yhow tok I'.
He may say, 'Lo, here, als yhe se now,
Bethleem whare I was born for yhow,
And in clotes lapped and layd was
In a cribbe bytwen an ox and an asse'.   5200
    He may say, 'Lo, here yhe may se stande
Ierusalem, þat es nerehande,
Whare I had for yhow many [a] buffet
And with sharp skourges sare was bette,
And fra whethen þe crosse for yhow I bare   5205
þat on my shulder was layd þare'.
He may say also, 'Lo, here þarby,
Als yhe may se, þe mount of Calvery
Whar I was hanged upon þe rode,
Bytwen twa thefes for yhour gode;   5210
Whar my payn for yhow was mast,
And whare I swelt and yhelded þe gast'.
He may say yhit þus alswa,
'Lo, here þe sepulcre a lytel þarfra,
Whar I was layde for yhow als dede,   5215
When I was beryd in þat stede'.
He may say alswa, als here es sett,
'Lo, here þe mount of Olivett,
Whar aungels appered in mens lykenes,
When I stey til even þar blis ay es,   5220
And tald yhow how my commyng shuld be

*5185 þe tother] þe other G, þat oþer *b*   *5203 many a] many *c*L   5204 sare]
hard *a*   5207 Lo] *om.* R   *5220 even] heven Morris, *an unnecessary emendation*
blis ay] *trs. ab*

Tyl þe dome, als yhe may now se'.
  Now haf yhe herd þe skylles why
He sal sitte oboven þat vale namly,
þat men þe vale of Iosaphat calles   5225
þe whilk i[n]my[d]des þe world falles.
Alswa another skille may þis be
Why he sal doun com in þat countre,
For þar was his first commyng doun,
Anly for mans salvacioun,   5230
When he first flessch and blod tok
Of þe mayden Mari, als says [þe] bok.
þus sal 'he' com doun at sitte þare,
To deme al þe world, als I sayde are.
  Crist ful awsterne þan sal be   5235   *Of þe fourm⟨e⟩ of man*
Agayn synful me[n] þat him sal se.   *þa⟨t⟩ Crist sal de⟨me⟩ yn*
+ Dredful and hydus, als says þe boke,   f. 102rb
He sal be to þam, when þai on hym loke,
And ful delitable unto þe syght
Of ryghtwyse men þat lyffed here ryght.   5240
Bot alle þe persons of þe Trinite
And þe godhed sal noght þan shewed be
To ille and gude, þat sal appere þan,
Bot Crist allane in fourme of man,
Goddes Son þat þan sal deme us.   5245
And þarfor saynt Iohan says þus:
  Omne iudicium dedit Filio ut honorifi-   *Ion*
  cent Filium, sicut honorificant Patrem.
'God has gyfen til his Son', says he,
'Alle þe dome þat gyven sal be,   5250
þat men honour þe Son ryght
Als þai honour þe Fadir', ful of myght.
þe gude men sal se hym in manhed þan
With þe godhed, als God and man,
þe whilk he sal noght fra þam hyde;   5255
For þai sal se hym þan glorifide.
And þat sal be a blisful syght,

*5226 inmyddes] imyndes G, ymiddes AM, *Morris's suggestion in note*   *5232 þe²]
om. G, *Morris's emendation*   5233 at] and *ab*   *5236 men] me G, man W, *cf.* þe
synful M, *Morris's emendation*   *5237 Dredful] And dredful G   5241 þe¹] om. A
5248 Filium] illum A   5252 ful] om. aM

Swa fair he sal seme til þam and bryght.
   þe ille men in manhed sal hym se
Anly als he henged on þe rode-tre,   5260
Alle bla and blody als he þan was,
When he deyhed for mans trespas.
þat sight til þam sal be payn and drede,
For þai sal noght se of his godhede;
And for þe godhed es ful of blisse,   5265
þarfor þe syght of it þai sal misse.
Bot in his manhed anly, als I say,
He sal shew hym til þam þat day,
For in fourm of man he sal þan seme
And in his manhede he sal þam deme.   5270
He sal þan at his doun-commyng,
þe taken of þe croys wyth hym bring,
On whilk he boght us fra elle-pyn;
For he wald noght man saul tyn.
þat taken of þe crose alle men sal se,   5275
Bot ful dilitable it sal be
Til rightwys men, and sem fule bright;
And dredful til synful m[e]ns syight.
   þis taken of þe cros sal be shewed þan,
Als þe buk says, and be hyd fra na man: 5280
   Hoc signum crucis erit in celo, cum
   Dominus ad iudicandum venerit.
'þis taken of þe cros in heven sal seme
When our Loverd sal com to deme',
f. 102ᵛᵃ þat es at say, aboven in þe ayre,   5285
þat til gude men sal sem bright and fayre.
þis taken, als I trowe, sal noght be
þe sam cros ne þe sam tre,
On whilk God was nayled fot and hande,
Bot a taken of þat cros semande.   5290
Yhit som trowes, and swa may wel be,
þat þe taken of þe spere men sal þan se
þat staynged Crist until þe hert rote,
And of þe nayles þat hym thurgh hand and fote
Til þe hard rode-tre fast fested,   5295

5266 þai sal] *trs.* RM   *5278 mens] mans G, men M   5285 in] *om.* RL
5293 staynged] stynged RA, stangged W, stekyd L, stong M   until] till R, to *b*

And of þe croun of thornes þat was thrested
On his heved fast, þat þe blode out rane,
When þe thornes hym prikked til þe harn-pane,
And of þe scourges alswa þat brast his hyde,
þat þe blode ran doun on ilk syde.   5300
Alle þer takens sal þan be shewed
Byfor alle men, bathe lerd and lewed,
Bot þe synful, þat dampned sal be,
To þair shenshepe þan sal þam se.
    Crist sal shew þan his woundes wyde,   5305
In heved and fote and in his syde,
þat fressche sal sem and alle bledand
Til þe synful þat bifor hym sal stand.
He sal shew to þar confusioun
Alle þe signes of his passioun,   5310
And þe enchesoun and þe manere
Of his ded þat he tholed here.
And alle þis sal he do þos openly,
To reprove þe synful men þarby.
And þat sal be þair shenchip þan,   5315
For saynt Austyn says þus, þe haly man:
    Fortasse in corpore suo, Dominus cicatrices serva-   Augustinus
    vit ut in iudic[i]o hostibus exprob[r]aret,
    ut convincens eos dicat: 'Ecce homo
    quem crucifixistis; ecce Deus et homo   5320
    quem credere noluistis. Videte vulnera
    que infixistis; agnoscite latus
    quod pupigistis, [quod] propter vos
    apertum est, et intrare noluistis.
He says, 'Our lord, Goddes Son almyghty   5325
Parantere has keped in his body,
þe erres of his wondes sere,
þat he tholed for mans syn here
For to shew þam til his enmys,
When he sal sytte in dome als iustys   5330
To reprove þam at þe last day
And to atteyn þam and þos say;
"Lo, here þe man in flesshe and blode   f. 102vb

5304 þam] þai (þam *altered by expunction*) A, it L, þai M   *5318 iudicio] iudico G
*exprobraret] exprobaret GA, *end of citation om.* M   *5323 quod²] *om.* cL

þe whilk yhe hynged on þe rode;
Lo, her God and man, þat man wroght,   5335
In wham trow wald yhe noght.
Byhalde þe wondes þat yhe styked;
Sese here þe syd þat yhe priked,
þe whilk for yhow was open ay,
And yhe wald entre be ne way"'.   5340
    A, how mikel shenshep sal be
To þe synful þat alle þis sal here and se,
þe whilk til hym dus here na gude agayne,
þat for þam tholed swa mykel payne.
And yhit noght þas þat dos na gud anly,   5345
But oȝer þat er swa ful of felony,
þat ay dos yvel ogayn gude,
And ofte dos Godes Son on [þe] rode
In þat þat in þam es thurgh syn,
Of whilk þai wille never here blyn.   5350
What may þai answer þan and say?
How may þai þam excuse þat day?
In nathyng may þai be excused þan,
Swa rightwys sal be þe domesman.
For þat day, als þe buke wythenes,   5355
Sal noght be shewed but + rightwisnes
Wyth gret reddour, til synful namly,
þat sal be demed als þai her worthy.
þai may defende þam be na ways
For Iohan wyth þe gilden mouth þos says: 5360

Iohannes cum ore aureo   *Non erit tunc locus defensionis,*
                            ubi videbunt Cristum exhibentem
                            testimonia insigniaque sue passionis.

He sais, 'Na sted of defens þar sal be
War þai sal Crist þan openly se   5365
Gyfhand wytnes[yngs] and takens certayn
Of his passioun' and of his payn.
    Alle sal haf gret drede þat day,
Bath gude and ille, als we here clerks say.
þar sal be nouther aungel na man   5370

5344 swa] here swa *a*   5346 oȝer] other Morris, *a silent correction*   *5348 þe]
om. *c*   *5356 -wisnes] -wlisnes G, *Morris's silent correction*   *5366 wytnessyngs]
wytnes *cb*, witnessynge A

þat þai ne sal tremble for drede þan;
Alle-if þai wat þat þai sal be safe,
Yhit sal þai þat day dr[ed]e hafe,
Noght for þamself, for þai er giltles,
Bot for þe gret reddure of ryghtwisnes   5375
And for þe gret austerite
þat Crist sal shew þat day to se,
Agayn þe synful men namly,
þat sal be dampned wythouten mercy.
When rightwys men þat sal be saf,   5380 f. 103ra
And aungels swa mykel dred [sal] haf,
What dred and dole aght synful haf þan?
þarfor þos says þe haly man:
    Si columpne celi contremiscent et
    pavent adventum Cristi,   5385
    et angeli pacis amare flebunt,
    peccatores autem quid facient?
He says, 'If þe pylers of heven bright',
þat er haly men þat has liffed right,
'Sal dred Cristes commyng in manhede,   5390
And þe aungels alswa sal þan haf drede,
And yhit gret ful bitterly þarto,
What sal þe synful men þan do'?
þat sal be dampned, als I sayd are.
And says þe haly man þus mare: 5395
    Si iustus vix salvabitur, impius
    et peccator, ubi parebunt?
'If þe rightwys man', yhit says he,
'Sal unnethes þan saved be,
þe synful and þe wykked man   5400
Whyderward sal þai wend þan'?
    Ryghtwys men, als þe buk telles,
Sal be saf þan and nan elles.
Our Loverd in manhed sal þan sit
Oboune þe synful, als says Haly Writ,   5405
Austerne and wrahte wyth a fel chere,
Wyth þam to threp þat has lyfed ille here.

*5373 drede] dre G, a grete drede M, *Morris's suggestion in note*   *5381 sal] *om.* G
5382 haf] to haf *a*   5390 in] and Morris (Lightbown)   5395 And] And yhit RWM,
Als L   5400 and] þan and *a*   5403 and] ad ? G (similarly 5481 and²)

Helle bynethen, þat es wyde and depe,
Sal þan be open þam to kepe;
þe erthe þat þai sal on stand sal scake   5410
Thurgh þair syn, and tremble and whake,
Swa þat unnethes it sal þam bere,
Swa mykel þair syn þe erth sal dere.
þe world obout þam sal be brinnande;
þe devels on ilk syde þam sal stande.   5415
Gret sorow sal be omang þam þar;
þe heven oboven sal strike þam sar
With thundirs 'dyntes' and levenyngs togyder.
þai wald þan fle and wate never whider;
þai sal be umset swa on ilka side,   5420
þat þai may nouthir fle ne þam hide.
     Many accusers þar sal be þan
To accuse þam byfor þat domesman,
For I fynd written, als yhe sal here,
Fiften maneres of accusours sere,   5425
þat sal accuse in þat dredeful day
þe synful men. þat es to say,
f. 103ʳᵇ Conscience þat es called ynwitt,
And þair awen syns, and Hali Writt,
Gods creatures þat we ken,   5430
Devels and aungels and haythen men,
And martirs þat has feled tourments sere,
And othir þat wranges has tholed here;
Mens sons and doghters unchastyede,
Pover men þat þair nede myght noght hyde,   5435
Suggettes, and benefices receyved here;
þe tourmentes of Cristes passioun sere;
And God hymself and alle þe Trinite.
Alle þere ogayne þe synful sal be.
j. Conscience   First sal þair awen conscience   5440
Accuse þam þan in Cristes presence,
Openly and noght in privete,
For nathyng þan sal hidde be.
Alle thyng sal be shewed þar oppenly,
Daniel For Danyel says þus in his prophecy: 5445

5410 scake] shake R*a*M, *om. in rewritten line* L   5428 yn-] þe *a*, þer in- L, þi M

Sedit iudicium, et libri aperti sunt.
'þe dome sait, and þe bokes er oppen[d] wyde',
And þus sal be sene þat tyde.
þe bokes er conscience and noght elles,
Als þe glose þaron þus telles: 5450
Consciencie omnibus revelabuntur.
'Conscience', it says, 'of ilka thyng
Sal be shewed til alle mens knawyng'.

    þair syns alswa, bathe mare and les,   *ij. Syns*
Sal þam accuse, als þe boke bers wittnes.   5455
For þair syns sal ay witth þam last,
Als þai war bunden obout þair nekes fast.
þe whilk þam sal accuse þat day,
Agayn wham þai sal noght kun say,
And als stolne thyng wreghes a thefe funden,   5460
When it es obout his neke fast bounden,
Right swa þair syns sal wreghe þam þar,
Als þai bunden obout þair nekes war.
And þan sal þair syns say þus
Til ilka synful man, 'þou wroght us,   5465
And [w]e er þin withouten dout,
And þou has lang borne us obout'.

    Alswa accuse sal Haly Writt,   *iij. Haly Writt*
Namly þas men þat knawes it
Or þe poyntes has herde þat falls þarto,   5470
And wald noght aftir Haly Writt do.

    Yhit sal Godes creatures sere   *iiij. Goddes creatures*
Accuse þam on diverse manere,
Als þe son and þe mone and þe sterns
And þe elementes þa[t] us governs.   5475
And alle þe werld sal be þan redy   f. 103va
To accuse þe synful men oppenly,
For alle creatoures hate þam sal,
When he es wrathe þat es maker of alle.

    Alswa devels sal accuse þam þar   5480 *Deuels*
Of alle þair syns, bathe les and mar,
And of þa syns þat þai sal out say
Til whilk þai egged þam, bathe nyght and day,

*5447 oppend] oppen GL, *line (and 5448–51) om.* M   *5466 we] ue G, *Morris's silent
correction   *5475 þat] þa G, *Morris's emendation*

And of þas þai sal þam þar accuse,
Als a thefe his felaghe of theft duse,   5485
þat hym accuses of þe same thyng
þat he with hym did thurgh his eggyng.
þe devels at þe dome sal be redy,
þat to tempte men here [e]r ay bysy.
And þai write alle syns, bathe les and mar,   5490
Of whylk þai may accuse þam þar,
And alle syns þai sal reherce þan,
And þarfor þus says Iob þe haly man:
    Scribis, Domine contra me amaritudines,
      id est, permittis scribi contra me peccata amara.   5495
'Loverd, þou suffers here', says he,
'Be writen bittir syns ogaynes me'.

Aungels   Aungeles alswa, als we here clerkes say,
Sal accuse þe synful men at þat day,
For God þat til þam þair sauls touke   5500
For to kepe here, als says þe buke,
Sal aske of þam at his comyng
Acount to yhelde of þair kepyng.
þan sal þe aungels answere þarto
And say þus, 'Our rede þai wald noght do,   5505
Bot agayne our wille, foly þai wald use'.
þus sal aungels þe synful accuse.

Haythen men   Alswa haythen men, als says þe buke,
þat never baptem ne right trouthe tuke,
Als Iewes and Sarzyns and paens,   5510
þat wate noght what Criestes lawe bymens,
Sal þan accuse, als men sal se,
þe fals Cristen þat dampned sal be.
For þe haythen men at þat grete assys
Sal þan be halden als men rightwys   5515
To regard of þe fals Cristen men
þat wald noght kepe þe comandmentes ten,
Bot spende[d] þair fyve wittes in vayne.
þarfor þai sal have mykel mare payne
In þe pitte of helle þat sal mar griefe   5520

*5489 er ay] *trs.* G, are L, here M   5513 Cristen] *add* men *a* (*the couplet over erasure in the space for a single line* A)   *5518 spended] spendes *c*   5520 þat] *adds* þam Morris (Lightbown)

þan þe haithen men of mysbylyefe.
  þe halghes alswa sal accuse alle þa
þat sal be dampned and to helle ga;
And namly martirs, Godes awen knyghtes,
þai sal accuse þe synful wyghtes,
Als þe tirauntes þat þam pyned and sloghe,
And othir þat þam til tourmentes droghe,
Of wham vengeance til God þai cry,
Als þe *Appocalips* þus shewes þarby:
  Usquequo Domine sanctus et verus, non vindicas
  sanguinem nostrum de hijs qui habitant in terra?
þat es, 'Haly Loverd, sothefast and gude,
How lange sal be ar þow venge our blude
Of our enemys þat in erhte duelles'?
On þis manere þe *Appocalips* telles,
Sen þai to God ay 'vengance' cry,
Of þam þat of þair blude er gilty,
Howe suld þai þan in þe tyme of wreke
Be stille and noght ogayne þam speke?
  Alswa alle þas þat has tholed here
Falsedes and wrangs on sere manere
Sal þat day accuse þam sone,
þat þam has here gret wranges done.
Yhit sons and doghters þat unchastyd war
Sal accuse þar fadirs and modirs þar,
Forþi þat þai war rekles and slawe
To chasty þam and hald þam 'in' awe
And to teche þam gude thewes.
And þarfor þe wys man þus in buke shewes:
  De patre impio conquerentur filij, quoniam
  propter ipsum sunt in opprobrium.
'þe sons sal pleyne þam þan', says he,
'Of þe ille fader and agayn hym be,
For thurgh defaute of hym er þai
In grete reprove', þat es to say,
In defaut of his disciplyne,
Parchaunce be dampned til helle pyne.

þe halghes of heuen and
namly martirs

f. 103vb

5525

5530 Ion

5535

5540 þa þat tholes wranges
be done þam here

5545 Mens sons and doghtirs
vnchastid here

5550

5555

5534 erhte] erthe Morris, *probably a silent correction*   5541 falsedes and] falsede or *a*,
falshedes and Morris, *an unnecessary correction*   5545 þar¹] þair Morris, *an unnecessary*
correction

And þe fader alswa be with þam spilte,
For he es þe cause of þair gilte.
Yhit þe pover sal þam ple[y]ne thurgh right   5560
þe pure men sal Of þe riche men in Godes syght
accuse þe ryche And accuse þam þan ful grevosly,
For þai had of þam na mercy
For to helpe þam here in þair nede,
Nouthir to clathe þam ne to fede,   5565
Bot lete silver and gold on þam rust,
þe whilk þai had in hurde up trust,
And þarof til pure wald noght gyve,
When þai sawe þam at meschyve.
þarfor þe ruste of þat moweld mone   5570
Agayne þam þan sal wittnes be,
f. 104ra And wormes and moghes on þe same manere,
þat in þair clathes has bred here.
þe whilk þai had here over mesur
And of þam wald noght parte til þe pure   5575
Sal þat day be in wittenes broght,
For þe pure þat þai helped noght.
þe suggets ogayne Alswa þa þat suggettes war til man
þair souerayns Sal accuse þair soveraynes þan,
[þat] þam has greved thurgh maystri and myght   5580
And 'of' other wald do þam na right.
þe benefis þat God þe benefices þat God did þam here
had done til man Sal þam accuse on sere manere,
For agayne þam sal Crist allege sone
And shewe þam what he had þam done   5585
And reherce his benefices, mare and les,
To reprove þam of þair unkyndenes.
Yhit þe tourmentes of Cristes passioun,
þat he tholed for mans salvacioun,
Sal þam accuse at þat gret dome,   5590
Ieronimus Forwhy þus says sa[y]nt Ierome:
Crux contra te perorabit; Cristus
per vulnera sua contra te allegabit;
cicatrices contra te loquentur;

*5560 pleyne] plene G, Morris's emendation   5567 þai] þat `þai' (later) A, cf. þat þai
had L   *5580 þat] And G, Morris's suggestion in note   5591 saynt] sanyt G
5592 perorabit] perobit R, portabit te L

clavi de te conquerentur.   5595
He says, 'þe croyce on whilk he dieghed for man
Sal stratly pray ogayne þe þan,
And Crist thugh his wondes wide
Ogayne þe sal allege þat tyde;
þe erres of his wondes sal speke   5600
Ogyne þe and of þe aske wreke;
þe nayles þat in his hend and fete stak,
On þe sal pleyne and gret playnt mak'.

    At þe last, God hymself, mast of myght,   *God and þe Trini⟨te⟩*
And þe Trinite sal accuse þam right,   5605
For þai wrethed God in þair legge pouste,
And alle þe persons of þe Trinite,
Bathe þe Fadir and þe Son and þe Haly Gast.
þarfor þat accusyng sal be mast,
Bot þe secunde person þan alle sale deme,   5610
þat es Crist, Godes Son, þat þan man sal seme.

    Alle þat sal com byfor Crist þat day,
Sal strayt acounte yhelde, ar þai passe away,
Of alle þair lif, howe þai here lyved.   *Of strayt acoun⟨t⟩ þat*
þan sal be sene what þai God gryeved   5615 *man sal yhe⟨lde⟩*
And byfor alle þe werld shewed sal be,
Oppenly and noght in privete;
And byfor halghes and aungels bright,
And byfor devels horribel til mans sight,
And byfor alle wykked men alswa,   5620 f. 104rb
þat sal be dampned til endles wa.

    For alle sal be þan þare, gude and ille,
To deme and be demed als rightwysnes wille;
For Crist, þat rightwyse domesman,
Sal calle alle men byfor hym þan,   5625
Als þe prophet David bers witnes
In [þe] Psauter whare þus writen es:
    Advocavit celum desursum et terram
    discernere populum suum.
He says, 'He sal bifor hym calle   5630
þe heven fra oboven and þe erthe alle
For to deme right his folk þat day'.

5601 Ogyne] Ogayne Morris, *an unnecessary emendation*   *5627 þe] om. G

And þis vers es þus mykel at say,
'He sal calle þan heven byfor hym tit,
þat es to say, haly men and parfit,   5635
þat with hym in dome þan sal sitt
And wyth hym deme, als says Haly Writt'.
Bot þe erthe es noght elles to telle
Bot wykked men and devels of helle,
þe whilk he sal calle at his wille   5640
For to chede out þe gude fra þe ille.
    þan sal ilk man þar of þair lyfyng
Be sette until and hard rekkenyng.
For men sal þan strayte acount yhelde
Of alle þair tyme of yhouthe and elde,   5645
Noght anly of ane or twa yhere,
Bot [of] alle þe tyme þat þai lyfed here,
And specyaly of ilka moment,
Of alle þe tyme þat God þam lent.
A moment of tyme es nan othir thyng   5650
Bot a short space als of a eghe twynklyng.
Na moment sal be unrekend þan,
Als saynt Bernard says, þe haly man:

Bernardus   *Sicut non peribit capillus de capite,*
               ita non erit momentum de toto   5655
               tempore de quo sane
               non conqueratur.

He says, 'Als nan hare of alle þe hed
Sal perisse þat tyme in na sted,
Right swa sal be na moment,   5660
Of alle þe tyme þat God had sent,
Of whilk sal be made na pleynyng'
In þe tyme of þat last rekkenyng.
    Alswa þai sal yhelde acount certayne
Of ilk idel worde spoken in vayne,   5665
þat es to say, þat war fruytles,
Als Haly Writt bers wittnes:

f. 104va   *De omni verbo ocioso in die iudicij*
             reddenda est racio.

5643 and] ane R*a* (*suggested Morris in note*), *the couplet om.* L, a ful M   5645 of²] *om.*
A, bothe W, in *b*   *5647 of] *om.* G   5651 eghe] hegh A   5656 sane] *om.* A
5661 had] has (HM) *suggested Morris in note*

þe buke says shortly on þis manere,   5670
'Of ilkan idel [a]nd vayne word here,
Reson sal be yholden right
At þe day of dome in Godes sight'.
    And noght anely of idel wordes sayd,
Bot of ilk idel thoght þat God noght payd.   5675
For excuse þam may þai noght,
Nouther of idel worde ne of thoght,
þat þai spak or thoght aftir þai had witt,
Of whilk þai war never here qwitt.
[þ]arfor our loverd God allemyghty   5680
Spekes þus thurgh þe prophet Ysay: *Isay*
    Ego cogitaciones eorum venio, ut congregem
    cum gentibus ad iudicandum, sicut iudic[ab]o gentes.
He says 'I com to gadir with men
þe thoghtes of þam þat I ken,   5685
For to deme þam `alle´, mar and les,
Als I sal men deme thurgh rightwysnes'.
Many aght be dredand þarfor,
And yhit sais þus saynt Gregor: *Gregor*
    Ergo sic Deus vias cuiuscunque considerat   5690
    ut nec minutissime cogitaciones, que
    apud vos usu valuerunt, in iudicio
    indiscusse remaneant.
He says 'God', þat alle wysdom kan,
'Swa byhaldes þe wayes of ilk man   5695
þat þe lest thoghtes þat thurgh use had yhe
In þe dome sal noght undiscussed be'.
    And noght anely of + word and thoght,
Bot of alle idel werk þat ever men wroght
þai sal alswa yhit acount yhelde,   5700
Noght anly of gret dedes of elde,
Bot of smale dedes of þair yhouthte
Fra þe tyme þat þai any witt couthe,
þat þai had wroght, bathe nyghtes and days,
And þarfor Salamon þus says: 5705 *Salomon*

---

*5671 and vayne word] word and vayne *c*M   *5680 þar-] Whar- *c*M
*5683 iudicabo] iudico *c*   5686 mar] bathe mar *a*M   *5698 of] of idel *c*, *om.*
L, of ilk idel M   5699 þat] þai Morris

Letare iuvenis in adolescencia tua, et in
bono sit cor tuum in diebus iuventutis tue,
et ambula in vijs cordis tui et intuitu
oculorum tuorum; et scito quod pro
omnibus hijs te adducet   5710
dominus in iudicium.

He says, 'þou yhung man be glad and blithe
In þi yhouthede þat passes swithe,
And þat þi hert in gude be stedfast,
Whilles þe days of þi yhouthe sal last,   5715

f. 104vb   And in þe ways of þi herht ga
And in þe syght of þin eghen twa;
And wytt þou for alle þis of yhouthede,
Our Loverd sal þe into þe dome lede',
Whar resons sa[l] be yholden sere.   5720

Iob   And þarfor says Iob on þis manere:
Et consumere me vis peccatis adolescencie mee?
'Loverd, wil þou waste me to noght
Thurgh þe syns [of yhouthe] þat I haf wroght'?
Alswa men sal þan yhelde acount sone,   5725
Noght anly of þat þat þai wrang had done
Witandly thurgh þair knawyng,
Bot alswa of þat þat þai did thurgh erryng,
Of whilk þai sal noght be excused þan,
Als in buk þus says þe wyse man: 5730
Pro omni errato, sive bonum sive malum
sit, adducetur homo in iudicio.

He says, 'For ilka thyng þat erred es,
Be it gude or ille, mar or les,
Man at þe last day sal be ledde   5735
To þe dome' þat es mast dredde.
And þarfor David, als þe Psauter shewes us,
Was ful dredand, þat says þus:
Et ignorancias meas ne memineris.
'Loverd,' he says, 'Ne mene þou noght   5740
Of my freyle unknawynges of thoght'.
Yhit sal þai yhelde acunt with drede,
Noght anly of ilk apert ille dede,

5716 þi] þe Morris   *5720 sal] sa G, *Morris's silent correction*   *5724 of
yhouthe] *om. cab*   5731 sive (2×)] sine Morris

Bot alswa of ilkan ille dede prive,
þat semed by syght þat gude suld be.   5745
For some dede þat ille es, sems gud here,
For saynt Gregor says on þis manere: *Gregor*
  Interdum sordet in oculis iudicis quod
  fulget in oculis auditoris.
He says, 'Sometyme es foule in þe domesman sight 5750
þat in [þe] eghe of þe herer shynes bright'.
Bot at þe dome sal þat discused be,
Als in þe psalme men may written se:
  Cum accipero tempus,
    ego iusticias iudicabo.   5755
God says þis wordes thurgh þe prophet David
And many othir þat accordes þarwith.
He says, 'When I haf tyme receyved right,
I sal deme rightwysnes' thurgh myght.
  Alswa yhit men byhoves nedly þan   5760
Yhelde acount byfor þe domesman
Noght anely of werkes þat þai had wroght,
Bot alswa of dedes þat þai did noght,
A[ls] of werkes of mercy and of almus   f. 105ra
þat þai noght did, for þe godspelle shewes þus: 5765
  Esurivi, et non dedistis michi manducare;
  sitivi, et non dedidistis michi bibere etc.
þis es, als yhe sal aftirward here,
How God sal say on þis manere:
'I hungerd, and yhe me noght fedde;   5770
I thresed, and yhe me na drynk bedde'.
For þis þai sal be aresoned straytly
And for other werkes noght done of mercy,
And noght anely for þa werkes [un]don,
Bot for þe gude þat þarof myght haf commen son. 5775
  Men byhoves alswa acount yhelde
Of þair saules, þat þam byhoved welde
And haf in kepyng whille þai myght lif,
Of whilk þai sal þan answer gyf.
Now if a kyng of a riche kyngryke   5780
þat had a doghter, þat war hym like

*5751 in þe] in G   *5764 Als] And G, Also M   5767 etc.] *om.* RL Morris
*5774 undon] noght don *c*M

Of bewte and of face and body,
þe whilk he luved specialy
And eghtild to mak hir qwene of worshepe,
Had bytaght hir til his ryfe to kepe,   5785
Yf he þaraftir keped hir mys,
Methyng it war na dout of þis
þat ne þe kyng wald haf rekkenyng
And acount and answer of þat kepyng.
For it semes þat þe kyng had grete encheson   5790
To sette hym for þat kepyng to reson,
And þe mare rek[l]esly þat he hir yhemed,
þe mare grevosly hym aght be demed.
What suld þe kyng of heven do þan
Of a man or of a woman,   5795
Til wham he has bytaght to kepe here
His doghtir þat es hym leve and dere,
þat es man[s] saul, his awen liknes
Whilles it fra dedly syn keped es,
þe whilk he eghteld to coroun qwene   5800
In heven þar ioy sal ay be sene?
Whaswa es rekles and kepes it ille,
He sal be aresoned, and þat es skille,
Of þe kepyng of it þat he tuke.
þarfor þe wyse man says þus in his buke: 5805
    Custodi solicite
    animam tuam.
þat es on Ynglis in þis manere:
He says, 'Kepe þi saul bysily here'.
Bot he es sely þat may sikerly say   5810
In þe tyme of þe dede at his last day,
'I yhelde my saul in þis dede-stour
Til þe Loverd þat es my saveour'.
    Men sal yhit yhelde acount stray[t]ly
Noght of þair saules within anely,   5815
Bot alswa of þair bodys withoute
þat þai had to kepe and bare aboute,

f. 105rb

Howe men sal yhelde
acount noght anely of þe
saules bot of þe bodys

5785 Had] And RM Morris, And he L   *5792 reklesly] rekkesly G, *Morris's*
suggestion in note   *5798 mans] man G   5808 in] on *a*M, to say on L
5812 dede-] deds RA   *5814 straytly] strayly G, *Morris's emendation*

Of whilk þai sal yhelde rekkenyng
Sen þai had þarof þe kepyng.
Ilka mans body may `be´ cald   5820
Als a castelle here for to hald,
þat til man es gyfen of God to kepe
For his profit and Goddes worshepe.
þe enemys ofte assales hard,
And þarfor says saynt Bernard: 5825 *Bernardus*
   Bonum castrum custodit
   qui corpus suum custodit.
'A gude castelle', he says, 'Kepes he
þat his body kepes' in honeste.
   Men sal yhelde acount alswa   5830
At þe dome, ar þai þeþen ga,   *Howe men sal yhelde*
þat stratly of þam sal be tane   *⟨acount⟩ noght ⟨ane⟩ly*
Noght anely of þe saules by þam ane,   *of þe saule be itself ne of*
Ne anely of þair bodys þarby,   *þe body be itself bot of*
Bot of bathe togidre ioyntly.   5835 *bath þe body and þe*
   þat es to say, ilkan sal þan   *sawle togyder ioyntly*
Yhelde acount of alle hale a man,
For a man [m]ay noght proprely be cald,
Bot if þe body and saule togidre hald;
þe saule be itself man es nane,   5840
Ne þe body without saule by it ane,
Bot man may be called on twyn manere,
Whilles þai bathe er knyt togyder here.
For þes clerkes þat + clergy can
Calles man bathe 'inner man' and 'utter man',   5845
Inner man onence þe saule anely
And utter man onence þe body.
Bot þe body and saule bytwene þam twa
Makes bot a man and na ma.
þarfor men sal yhelde acount ioyntly   5850
Of bathe togyder, þe saule and þe body.
And forþi þat God aftir his stature
Made man mast digne and noble creature,

5824 hard] it hard Morris (Lightbown)   5834 þair] þe RW   *5838 may noght
proprely] proprely may noght *c*M, is not propyrly L   5839 body and saule] *trs. sbs.* R
*5844 þat] þat gret *c*M

þarfor if man be til God frawarde
And unkynde and of hym tak na rewarde,   5855
þat ilk dignite of man namely
Sal at þe dome yhelde hym gylty.

Howe men sal yhelde Yhit sal men yhelde acount [noght] anely
acount ⟨noght⟩ anely of Of þareself, bot of other many,
⟨þair⟩self bot of þair
neghbur þat es to say, of ilka neghebur   5860
f. 105va þat men fals to help and to socur.
For God til ilk man commandes right
To helpe his neghebur after his myght,
And þas, þat may helpe and wille noght,
Sal þan til ful strayt acount be broght.   5865

Fadirs and modirs ⟨of⟩ Alswa fadirs and modirs at þat day
þair sones and doght⟨irs⟩ Sal yhelde acount, þat es to say,
Of sons and doghtirs þat þai forthe broght,
þe whilk þai here chastied noght.

Louerdes of þair meigne And loverds alswa of þair meigne,   5870
þe whilk þai lete uniustifyed be,

Maisters of þair And maysters of þair disciples alswa,
discipl⟨es⟩ þat þai lete be unthewed and untaght ga
And chastid þam noght ne þam wald lere.
Forþi says Salamon on þis manere: 5875

Virga discipline fugabit stulticiam
in corde pueri colligatam.

'þe wande', he says, 'Of disciplyne smert
Sal chace foly out of þe childes hert'.
þarfor maysters [u]ses somtyme þe wand   5880
þat has childer to lere undir þair hand.

Prelates of þair suggettes Prelats of ordir and of dignyte
Sal acount yhelde in sere degre
Of þair suggets undir þair powere,
Howe þai þam reweld in þis lyf here,   5885
And answer of þam þat lyfed noght wele,
For þus says þe prophet Ezechiele:

Ecce, ego requiram gregem
meam de manu pastoris.

5855 and of] *trs.* R, *line om.* (*with 5852–7*) L, *rewritten* M   *5858 noght] *om.* G,
Morris's emendation   5874 chastid] chastyed R*a*, chastys M, *cf.* wald not chasty L
*5880 uses somtyme] *trs.* c, *cf.* somtyme] *om.* L   5889 meam] meum R

God says þus thurgh þe prophete,   5890
'Lo, I sal aske my flok of shepe
Of þe hird þat had þam under his hand'.
Of þis word aght prelates be dredand.

   Men sal alswa yhelde rekkenynges sere
Of al gudes þat God has gefen þam here,   5895
Als of gudes of kynde and gudes of graces
And gudes of hap þat men purchases.
þe gudes of kynd er bodily strenthe
And semely shappe of brede and lenthe
And delyvernes and bewte of body;   5900
Swilk gudes of kynd here has many.
Gudes of grace may þir be:
Mynde and witte and sutilte,
And fair shewyng of speche sutille
And knawyng bathe of gude and ille,   5905
Vertus of grete devocioun,
And luf of lyf of contemplacioun.
Gudes of hap er þir to gesce,
Als honours, power, and ryche[sce].
Of alle þir gudes men byhoves   5910
Yhelde acount, als þe buke proves,
And answer straytly of þam alle.
I drede many in arrirage mon falle
And til perpetuele prison gang,
For þai despended þa gudes wrang.   5915
Forwhi God has gyfen here nathyng,
Of whilk he wille noght haf rekkennyng.

   Som sal yhit, als I sayd ar,
Yhelde acount ful straytly þar
Of þe gudes þat þai wald noght bede   5920
Til other þat of þam had nede.
For alle er we als a body here,
For þe appostel says on þis manere:
Omnes enim unum
corpus sumus.   5925

Howe men sal yhelde acount of alle godes þat God has lent, þat es to say, of godes of kynde, of godes of grace, and of godes of happe

f. 105vb

Howe men sal yhelde acount of þe godes þat God sent þam of whilk þai wald noght part til othir þat ⟨of⟩ þam had nede

5893 be] to be RWL, *couplet om.* M   5904 *line om. a* speche] witt R   *after* 5905 *a compensatory line added* And powere to cheese wheþer he wylle W   *5909 rychesce] ryche G, ryches M Morris   5916 Forwhi] Forþi R, *couplet om.* L, For M

He says, 'We er alle als a body'
þat has diverse lyms many.
And als a lym of a body here
Es redy, aftir it has powere,
To serve alle þe other, mar and les,   5930
Of þat office þat gyven it es,
Right swa ilk man þat here lyfes,
Of alle þat God thurgh grace him gyfes,
Suld other serve þat þarof has nede,
Als he wille answere at þe day of drede.   5935
Ful many men lyfes here of þa
þat er halden for to do swa,
Als he þat gret and myghty es,
Es halden to defende þam þat er les;
And þe ryche þat mykel rychesces has,   5940
To gyf þam þat here in povert gas;
And men of laghe alswa to travayle
And to counsaile þam þat askes counsayle;
And leches alswa, if þai wyse ware,
To hele þam þat er seke and sare;   5945
And maysters of þair science to ken
Namly þam þat er unlered men;
And precheours Goddes worde to preche
And þe way of lyf other to teche.
þus es ilk man halden with gude entent   5950
To help other of þat God has þam lent
Frely for Goddes luf and for noght elles.
Wharfor saynt Petre þe appostel þus telles:
   Unusquisque, sicut accipit graciam, in alter-
   utrum illam administrare debet.   5955
f. 106ra He says, 'Ilk man þat grace has here,
Als he resayves grace, on þe same manere
Suld he it ministre and frely bede
Til ilkan other' þat þa[r]of has nede.
And þus es ilk man halden to do,   5960
For in þe godspelle yhit says God mar þarto:
   Quod gratis accepistis,
   gratis date.

5940 rychesces] ryches RW*b*   5948 worde] wordes RL   *5959 þarof] þaiof G,
Morris's suggestion in note

He says, 'þat þat yhe haf of grace fre
And frely resayved, frely gyf yhe'.   5965
   Þus sal men þan yhelde resons sere
Of alle þair lyf, als writen es here,
þat es of alle tymes spended in vayne
And of ilka moment of tyme certayne
And of ilkan idel word and thoght   5970
And of ilkan ydel dede þat þai wroght,
Outher in elde or in þair yhouthe,
Aftir þe tyme þat þai witt first couthe,
And of dedes þat þai thurgh erryng did;
And noght anely of open werkes, bot of hid;   5975
And noght anely of werkes wroght, bot unwroght,
Als of werkes of mercy þat done war noght.
And of þair awen saules þai sal reken þar
And of þair bodys þat þam obout bar;
And noght anly of ayther by þamself þan,   5980
Bot of bathe togyder als of a man;
And yhit noght anely of þamself alle,
Bot of þair neghburs answer þai salle.
And fadirs and modirs sal rekken þat tyde
Of þair sons and doghtirs unchastide;   5985
And loverdes alswa of þair men namly,
þe whilk þai wald noght iustify;
And maysters of þair disciples alswa,
þe whilk þai lete untaght in folis ga;
And prelates and prestes of ilka suggette   5990
þat þai wald noght in right rewel sette;
And alle other þat wrang and in ille entent
þe gudes spended þat God had þam lent,
And of alle wrang haldyngs of gudes sere,
Of whilk þai parted noght til other here   5995
þat of þam had nede, als þai myght se.
Of alle þir thynges men sal aresoned be
At þe day of dome, als God has ordaynd,
Whar nathyng sal be hid ne laynd.
Of alle þir, men sal yhelde acount strayt;   6000
Sal nathyng þan be þar to layt.

5976 bot] bot of R*a*, and L, *passage om.* M   5981 a] *om. a, passage om.* M
5985 and] and þair Morris (Lightbown)

Ful sely es þat man or womman,
þat a gude rekkenyng may yhelde þan,
Swa þat he may pas qwyte and fre
Of alle thyng þat may rekend be. 6005
And swa sely ʻmay' be alle þas,
þat fra hethen in charite gas;
For he þat has here gude endyng,
Sal pas + þar with light rekkenyng.
At þe day of dome, als byfor es talde, 6010
Alle men sal be, bathe yhung and alde
Of men þat sal be demed And gude and ille; alle sal com þider.
and of þas þat sal noght Swa mykel folk com never togyder,
demed be and of þas þat Ne never was sene sythen þe werld bygan,
sal deme and of þas þat Als sal be sene byfor Crist þan, 6015
sal noght deme þat sal be demed aftir þai haf wroght.
Bot som sal deme and sum noght,
For som sal deme with þe domesman,
þat thurgh dome sal noght be demed þan.
Som sal be demed þan ryghtwysly, 6020
þat sal deme on na party.
Bot many other þar sal seme,
þat sal nouther be demed ne deme.
þa þat sal deme and noght demed be
Sal be parfit men with God prive. 6025
Of þa þat demed sal be and deme sal noght,
Sal som til blisse be demed and broght,
And sum sal be demed to helle to wende,
Whar pyn sal be withouten ende.
Bot alle þat trowed noght als trow we 6030
Sal nouther deme ne demed be,
Bot for þai wald noght til our trouthe come,
þai sal wende til helle withouten dome.
First þas þat with Crist sal deme þat day
And noght be demed er namly þai 6035
þat here forsuke þe werldes solace,
And folowed rightly Cristes trace,
Als his apostels and other ma,
þat for his luf tholed angre and wa.

þa sal deme with Crist and nan elles,   6040
Forwhi in þe godspelle þus he telles:
   Vos qui secuti estis me, sedebitis
   super sedes duodecim, iudicantes duodecim
   tribus Israel.
He says, 'Yhe þat folowes me here lyfand   6045
Sal sitt opon twelf setes demand
þe twelf nacions of Israel',
þat es, þas þat God sese here als lele.
   Som sal noght deme, bot demed be
Til blis, als men of grete charite,   6050
þat blethely wirk wald þe werkes of mercy
And keped þam here fra syn dedly.
Som sal noght deme, bot be demed   f. 106va
Til helle and fra God be flemed,
Als þas þat er fals Cristen men,   6055
þat keped noght þe comandmentes ten
And wald noght here forsake þair syn
Bot whils þai lyfed, ay dwelle[d] þarin.
   Som sal noght be demed þat day
þat sal wende to helle and dwelle þar ay,   6060
Als paens and Sarazyns þat had na law,
And Iewes þat never wald Crist knaw.
þarfor þai sal ga til payne endeles
Withouten dome, for þus writen es:
Qui sine lege peccant,   6065
absque lege peribunt.
'þas þat withouten lawe uses syn,
Withouten law sal perysshe þarin'.
And þarfor at þe day of dome namly,
Ilk man sal haf as he es worthy.   6070
   A ful hard day men sal þat day se,
When alle thyng sal þus discussed be.
þat day sal na man be excused
Of nathyng þat he wrang here used,
þat sounes in ille on any manere,   6075
Of whilk he was never delyverd here.

---

*6058 dwelled] dwelle G, dwelle *corr. to* dwelle'd' *later* A   6060 *In Morris's edition,*
this line is misnumbered 6064, and consequently, Morris's lineation is four ahead of that used here
6075 sounes] souned AL, seemed W, soundet M

þe synful sal þare na mercy have,
For nathyng may þam þan save;
Forwhy þai sal þan na help gett
Of sergeaunt ne auturne ne avoket,   6080
Ne of nan other for þam to plede
Ne þam to counsayle ne to rede,
Ne na halghe sal for þam pray.
    þis may be cald a ful harde day,
Forwhi þan, als þe buke bers witnes,   6085
Sal noght be shewed bot rightwy[s]nes
And grete reddure, withouten mercy,
Until alle synful men namely.
þa þat of þair syn here wald noght stynt,
þai sal þat day for ever be tynt   6090
Fra God, with'outen' any recoverere,
And delyverd be til þe devels powere.
Ful wa sal synful + þat day be
For grete reddure þai sal þan se
And til helle pyne be put for ay.   6095
    And þarfor men may calle þat day
þe grete day of delyveraunce,
þe day of wreke and of vengeaunce,
þe day of wrethe and of wrechednes,
þe day of bale and of bitternes,   6100
f. 106ᵛᵇ þe day of pleynyng and accusyng,
þe day of answer and of strait rekkenyng,
þe day of iugement and of iuwys,
þe day of angre and of angwys,
þe day of drede and of tremblyng,   6105
þe day of gretyng and goulyng,
þe day of crying and of duleful dyn,
þe day of sorow þat never sal blyn,
þe day of flaiyng and of af[r]ay,
þe day of departyng fra God away,   6110
þe day of merryng and of myrk[n]es,

6080 avoket] voket R*b*   *6086 -wysnes] -wynes G   6092 til] until Morris
(Lightbown)   *6093 synful] synful men *c*M   þat day be] be þat day Morris
(Lightbown)   6094 *line om.* Morris. *Consequently, from this point, Morris's lineation is*
three ahead of that used in this edition.   6103 iugement] iugements Morris (Lightbown)
*6109 afray] afay G, fray *b*, *Morris's emendation*   *6111 myrknes] myrkes G, *Morris's*
emendation

þe day þat es last and þat mast es,
þe dai when Crist sal make ende of alle.
þus may men discryve þat day and calle.
   Our Loverd þat alle thyng can se and witt   6115
At þe dredeful day of dome sal sitt,
Als kyng and rightwyse domesman
In dome to deme alle þe werld þan
Opon þe setil of his mageste.
þat day sal alle men byfor hym be,   6120
Bathe gude and ille, mare and lesse;
þan sal noght be done bot rightwysnes.
He sal deme al men of ilka degre
Til ioy or payne þat demed sal be,
A[ls] rightwyse domesman and suthefast   6125
And gyf a fynal dome at þe last.
   Bot how he sal deme I sal shewe,
Als telles þe godspelle of Mathewe.
Hys angels þan, aftir his wille,
Sal first departe þe gude fra þe ille,   6130
Als þe hird þe shepe dus fra þe gayte,
þat falles to be putt til pastur strayte.
By þe shepe understand we may
þe gude men þat sal be saved þat day;
By þe gayte understand may we   6135
þe ille men þat þan dampned sal be.
þe gude sal be sette on his right hand,
And þe ille on his lefte syde sal stand.
þan sal our Loverd say þus þat tyde
Til þam þat standes on his right syde: 6140
   Venite, benedicti patris mei,
   possidete paratum vobis regnum
   a constitucione mundi.
He sal say þan, "'Commes now til me,
My Fadir blissed childer fre,   6145
And weldes þe kyngdom þat til yhow es dight
Fra first þat þe werld was ordaynd right".
For I hungred, and yhe me fedde;   f. 107ra

6114 men] nan Morris   *6125 Als] And *c*, He sall sit as L   6135 may we] *trs.*
Morris (Lightbown)   6142 vobis] nobis Morris

I thrested, and + a drynk yhe me bedde.
Of herber grete nede I had;   6150
Yhe herberd me with hert glad.
Naked I was, als yhe myght se;
Yhe gaf me clathes and clad me.
Seke I was and in ful wayke state;
Yhe wisit me, bathe arly and late.   6155
In prisoun when I was halden stille,
Til me yhe come with ful gude wille'.
    þan sal þe rightwys men þat day
Til our Loverd answer þus and say:
'Loverd, when saw we þe hungry,   6160
And to gyf þe mete war we redy?
And when myght we þe thresty se,
And gaf þe drynk with hert fre?
When saw we þe nede of herber have,
And to herber þe vouched save?   6165
When saw we þe naked, and we þe cled?
And when saw we þe seke and in prison sted,
And visited þe with gude wille,
And comforted þe, als was skille'?
Our Loverd sal þan þam answer þus   6170
And say, als þe godspelle shewes us:
'Suthly, I say yhou: swa yhe wroght
þat ilka tyme when yhe did oght
Until ane of þe lest þat yhe myght se
Of my brether, yhe did til me'.   6175
    þan sal our Loverd til alle þas say,
þat þan + on his lefte syde sal stand þat day,
And spek til þam with an austerne chere
þir wordes þat er hydus to here:
    Discedite a me maledicti, in ignem   6180
    eternum, qui preparatus est diablo
    et angelis eius.
'Yhe weryed wyghtes, wende fra my sight
Until þe endeles fire þat es dight
Til þe devel and til his aungels'.   6185
And þan sal he say þus, als þe buke tels:

'I hungred and had defaute of mete,
And yhe wald noght gyfe me at ete;
I thrested and of drynk had nede,
And yhe wald na drynk me bede;   6190
I wanted herber, þat I oft soght,
And alle þat tyme yhe herberd me noght;
Naked withouten clathes I was,
And withouten clathes yhe lete me pas;
Seke I was and bedred lay,   6195
And yhe visite me nouther nyght ne day;
In prison I was, als wele wyst yhe,   f. 107rb
And yhe wald na tyme com til me'.
    þan sal þai answere, als men sal here,
Til our Loverd and say on þis manere: 6200
'Loverd, when saw we þe haf hunger or thrist
Or of any herber haf grete brist?
Or naked or seke or in prison be,
And we nathyng did ne mynystred to þe'?
þan sal our Loverd answer ogayne   6205
And say til þam þir wordes certayne:
'Suthly I say yhou, als falles þarto:
Alle [þe] tyme þat yhe wald noght do
Til ane of lest þat myne er kydde,
Als lang til me yhe noght didde'.   6210
    þus sal our Loverd reherce openly
Til rightwys men þe werkes of mercy,
For to make þam openly kyd
Til grete worshepe of þam þat þam dyd;
And shew til þe synful, als falles þarto,   6215
þair unkyndenes, þat wyld noght do
þe werkes of mercy for his luf
Til þair grete shenshepe and reprove.
    When he has þus sayde and made ende,
þe synful with þe devels sal wende   6220
Until helle-fire þat never sal slake.
A ful hidus cry þan sal þai make,
And say 'Allas, þat we ever war wroght
In mans kynd; whyne war we noght?

*6208 þe] *om.* G

Whyne had God made us swa,   6225
þat us thurt never haf feled wele ne wa?
Now sal we bryn in þe fire of helle,
And withouten ende þarin duelle'.
Helle þan þam sal swelghe als-tite
Withouten any lenger respyte,   6230
And alle þe fire þat þan sal be sene
And alle þe corrupcions þat ever has bene.
And [alle] þe filthe and alle `þe´ stynk
Of alle þe werld þan sal synk
Doun with þam intil þe pitte of helle   6235
To eke þair sorow þat þar sal duelle.
Bot þe ryghtwys men, als þe buke bers wytnes,
Sal wende til blisse, whar lyfe es endel[e]s,
With our Loverd and hys aungels ilkane
Shynand brighter þan ever son shane.   6240
    Now have yhe herd, als es contende
In þis fift part, how þe werld sal ende,
And how Crist at his last commyng
Sal in dome sitte and discusse alle thyng.

f. 107ᵛᵃ   Here may a man read þat has tome   6245

Howe þe processe of þe   A lange proces of þe day of dome,
last dome sal be sped   þat a lang tyme, after I haf redde,
in a moment   Suld contene by skille, ar alle war spedde.
Bot ye sal understand and witte,
Als men may se in haly writte,   6250
þat thurgh þe wysedom and þe vertu
And þe myght of our lord Ihesu,
Alle þe processe þat sal be þat day,
Of whilk any clerk can speke or say,
Sal þan swa shortely be sped and sone,   6255
þat alle sal be in a moment done.
A moment es als of a tyme bygynnyng
Als short als an eghe-twynkelyng.
A grete wondir may þis be kyd
Omang alle [þe] wondirs þat ever God dyd,   6260
þat in swa short tyme at his commyng,
He mught deme and discusse al thyng.

---

*6233 alle¹] om. G   *6238 endeles] endels G, *Morris's silent correction*
6246 lange] large Morris (Lightbown)   *6260 þe] om. cM, *int. later* A   ever God] *trs.* R

Bot of þis suld nane muse, lered ne lewed,
For als grete wo[n]dirs has God shewed;
Als grete a wonder es when he wroght   6265
With a short worde, alle þe werld of noght,
And of þis þe prophete bers wittnes,
þat says þus, als it wryten es:
   Quia ipse dixit et facta sunt,
   ipse mandavit et creata sunt.   6270
'God sayde', says he, 'And alle was done;
He bad, and alle was made sone'.
þus in a short tyme alle thyng made he;
Mare wondir þan þis mught never be,
þan may he als shortly make endyng   6275
Of alle thyng, als he made bygynnyng.
For swa witty and myghty es he
þat nathyng til hym impossibel may be.
þe processe of þat day þat I haf talde,
Al þe men of þe world, bathe yhung and alde,   6280
Sal se and undirstand it alle
In als short tyme als it sal falle.
   Now haf yhe herd me speke and rede
Of þe wondre þat þan sal be and drede.
Bot alleþogh yhe haf herd me rede and say   6285
Of þe reddure, þat sal be done þat day   *Howe men sal be saue*
Untille alle synful men namely,   *at þe day of dome*
þat sal be dampned withouten mercy,   *thurgh mercy purchaced*
Als men may in þis part wryten se,   *in þis lyf*
Na man þarfor suld in dispayre be.   6290
For alle þat has mercy here sal be save,
And alle þat here askes mercy sal it have,
Yf þai it seke whilles þai lyf bodily   f. 107vb
And trewely trayste in Goddys mercy
And amende þam and þair syn fo[r]sake,   6295
Byfor þe tyme ar þe dede þam take,
And do mercy here and charite,
þan gette þai mercy and saved sal be.
Bot if þe dede byfor haf þam tane

*6264 wondirs] wordirs G, wondyr W, *Morris's suggestion in note*   6293 seke] sekes
Morris (Lightbown)   *6295 forsake] fosake G, *Morris's silent correction*
6298 saved] saue *a*M

Ar þai haf mercy, þan gette þai nane,   6300
Bot reddure of rightwysnes anely,
For þan sal be shewed na mercy.
   Here may ilk man, if he wille,
Ha[f] mercy þat dus þat falles þartille;
þoghe he had done never swa mykel syn,   6305
If he amended hym, he myght it wyn.
For þe mercy of God es swa mykel here
And reches overalle, bathe fer and nere,
þat alle þe syn þat + man may do,
It myght sleken, and mare þarto.   6310
And þarfor says saynt Austyn þus
A gude worde þat may comfort us:
   Sicut scintilla ignis in medio maris,
   ita omnis impietas viri ad misericordiam Dei.
'Als a litel spark of fire', says he,   6315
'In mydward þe mykel se,
Right swa alle a mans wykkednes
Unto þe mercy of God es'.
   Here may men se how mykel es mercy
To fordo alle syn and foly,   6320
Forwhy if a man had done here
Als mykel and als many syns sere,
Als al þe men of þe werld has done,
Alle myght his mercy fordo sone.
And if possibel whare, als es noght,   6325
þat ilk man als mykel syn had wroght,
Als alle þe men þat in þe werld ever was,
Yhit mught his mercy alle þair syn pas.
þan semes it wele, als men may se,
þat of his mercy here + es grete plente,   6330
For his mercy spredes on ilka syde
Thurgh alle þe werld, þat es brade and wyde,
And sheues it be many ways.
Dauid And þarfor þe prophete David says:
   Misericordia Domini plena   6335
   est terra.
'þe erthe', he says, 'Es ful of mercy';

*6304 Haf] Has G   *6309 man] a man G, men M   6314 misericordiam] miam
G, miseriam Morris   *6330 here] here he G, *om.* L, here there Morris

þan may men it fynde here plentevously.
And he þat has mercy, ar he hethen wende,
At þe grete dome sal fynde Criste his frende, 6340
Whar rightwysnes anely sal be haunted, f. 108ra
And na mercy þan be graunted.
    Aftir þe grete dome, alle þe werld brade
Sal seme þan als it war new made.
þe erthe sal be þan even and hale 6345 *Of þe world þat sal seme*
And smethe and clere als cristale. *als newe aftir þe dome*
þe ayre obout sal shyne ful bright;
þan sal ay be day and never nyght,
For þe elementes alle sal þan clene be
Of alle + corrupciouns þat we here se. 6350
þan sal alle þe werld in alle partys
Seme als it war a paradys.
þe planetes and þe sternes ilkane
Sal shyne brighter þan ever þai shane;
þe son sal be, als som clerkes demes, 6355
Seven sythe brighter þan it now semes,
For it sal be als bright als it first was,
Byfor ar Adam did trespas.
þe mone sal be als bright and clere
Als þe son es now þat shynes here. 6360
þe son sal [even] þan in þe este stande
Withouten removyng, ay shynande,
And þe mone ogayne it in þe weste
And na mare sal travayle, bot ay reste,
Als þai war sette at þe bigynnyng, 6365
When God made þam and alle thyng.
þai war þan, als men may trow,
Mykel brighter þan þai er now.
    þe movand heve[n]s, withouten dout,
Sal þan ceese o turnyng obout 6370
And na mare obout in course wende,
For of alle thyng þan sal be made ende.
þe movand hevens now obout gas,

6338 it fynde] *trs.* AL, *cf.* here fynd it W, fynd here ful M   *6350 corrupciouns]
corrumpciouns G, corrupcyowne W   *6361 even] *om.* GM, *before* þan R, *om. in
rewritten line* L   *6369 hevens] heues G, of heuen M, *Morris's emendation*   6370 o]
of R*ab*

And þe son and þe mone þair course mas,
And þe othir planetes ilkane   6375
Moves als þai þair course haf tane,
And alle þe elementes kyndely duse
þat þat es nedeful til man[s] use.
þus ordaynd God þam to serve man,
Bot of alle swylk servise þai sal ceese þan.   6380
For alle men aftir domesday
Sal be war þai sal duelle for ay,
þe gude in blis, in rest and peese;
þe ille in payne þat never sal ceese.
What nede war þat þa creatures þan   6385
Shewed swilk servyse mare for man?
    Na qwik creature sal þan be lyfand
Thurghout þe werld in na land,
f. 108rb Ne nathyng sal growe þan, gresse ne tre,
Ne cragges ne roches sal nan þan be,   6390
Ne dale ne hille ne mountayne.
For alle erthe sal be þan even and playne
And be made als clere and fayre and clene
Als any cristal þat here es sene.
For it sal be purged and fyned withoute,   6395
Als alle other elementes sal be oboute,
And na mare be travayled o[n] na side
Ne with na charge mare occupide.
    Now haf yhe herd me byfor rede
Of þe day of dome þat many may drede,   6400
And of þe wondirful takens many,
þat sal falle byfor þat day namly,
And how þe werld þat we now se
Aftir þe dome als new made sal be,
Als here es contened, whaswa wille luke,   6405
In þe fifte part of þis buke.
Hereon now wille I na langer stande
Bot ga til þe sext part neghest folowande,
þat specialy spekes, als writen es,
Of þe paynes of helle þat er endeles,   6410

*6378 mans] man G, *couplet om.* L   6392 For] Bot Morris   6393 clere and
fayre] *trs. adjs. a*, -swa fayre L, clere fayre M   *6397 on] o G   6409 specialy spekes]
trs. a, opynly spekes L

þat alle men, þat here lyf byhoves lede,
Aght specialy mast to drede.
For þa paynes er swa fel and hard,
Als yhe sal here be red aftirward,
þat ilk man may ugge, bathe yhunge and alde,   6415
þat heres þam be reherced and talde.

[*Her begynnes þe sext part
þat es of þe paynes of helle.*]
Many men here spekes of helle,
Bot of þe paynes 'þar' fune can telle.   6420
Bot whaswa here mught wit and k[n]aw wele
What paynes þe synful þar sal fele,
þai suld in grete ferdlayk be broght
Ay when þai on þa paynes thoght;
For þe mynde of þam myght men feer,   6425
Swa bitter and swa horribel þai er.
Bot forþi þat many knawes noght right
What kyn paynes in helle er dight
Withouten ende for synful man,
þarfor I wil shewe yhow, als I can,   6430
Aparty of þa paynes sere,
Als yhe may sone aftirward here.
Bot first I wille shew whare es helle,
Als I haf herd som grete clerkes telle,
And sythen wille I shew yhow mare,   6435
And speke of þe paynes þat er þare.
   Som clerkes says, als þe + buke bers witnes,
þat helle even inmyddes þe erthe es.
For alle erthe by skille may likend be   f. 108va
Til a rounde appel of a tre,   6440
þat even inmyddes has a colke,
And swa it may be tille an egge yholke.
For als a dalk es even imydward
þe yholke of þe egge, when it es hard,

---

*6417–18 *om.* G, *supplied from the forms in* ARL, *cf.* De penis inferni Pars sexta W   es]
spekes L, Hic incipit sexta pars huius libri videlicet penarum infernalium M
*6421 knaw] kaw G, kan W, *cf.* and knaw] *om.* L, *Morris's emendation*   6429 man]
men Morris   6430 wil] sal Morris   *6437 buke] bukes G, buke Morris
(Lightbown)   6439 alle erthe] helle *a, cf.* alle] alle þe M   6443 i-] in- R*a*, in þe L

Ryght swa es helle pitte, als clerkes telles,   6445
Ymyddes þe erthe and nourwhar elles.
And als þe yholk ymyddes þe egge lys,
And þe white obout on þe same wys,
Right swa es þe erthe, withouten dout
Ymyddes þe hevens þat gas obout.   6450
þus may men se by an egge hard dight
How heven and erthe and helle standes right.
    Ful hydus and myrke helle es kyd,
Forwhy it es within þe erthe hyd.
þider þe synful sal be dryven,   6455
Als tyte als þe last dome es gyven,
With alle þe devels ay þar to duelle,
þat now er in þe ayre and in helle.
þar sal þai alle be stoped togider;
Wa sal þam be þat sal wende þider,   6460
For þar es swa mykel sorow and bale,
And swa many paynes withouten tale
þat alle þe clerkes þat ever had wytt,
þat ever was or þat lyfes yhitt,
Couth noght telle ne shew thurgh lare   6465
How mykel sorow and payne er þare.
And if it thurgh kynd myght be swa,
þat an hundreth thousand men or ma
Had an hundreth thousand tunges of stele,
And ilk tung mught speke wysely and wele,   6470
And ilka tung of ilka man
Had bygunnen when þe werld bygan
To spek of helle and swa suld speke ay
Whils þe werld suld last til domesday,
Yhit mught þai noght þe sorow telle   6475
þat to synful es ordaynd in helle.
Forwhy na witt of man may ymagyn
What paynes þar er ordaynd for syn.
    Bot men may fynd, whaswa wil loke,
Som maner of paynes wryten in boke,   6480
Omang all other paynes þat er in helle,
Als men has herd wyse clerkes telle.

6450 Y-] In- RWL   6466 er] es RWL, *rewritten line* M

Bot what man es swa wyse and wytty
þat couthe telle þa paynes proprely,
Bot it war he þat had bene þare   6485
And sene þa paynes bath les and mare?
Bot he þat þar commes, for certayne,   f. 108ᵛᵇ
May noght lightly turne agayne;
He most duelle þar and never oway com,
For þe *Buke* says þus *of Wysdom*:   6490
    Non est agnitus qui reversus
    est ab inferis.
þat es on Ynglisse, 'Men knawes nane
þat turned fra helle þat þider was gane'.
    For alle þat er þar most duelle for ay;   6495
þai may never be broght oway,
Bot it war thurgh miracle anely
And thurgh specyal grace of God almyghty.
Thurgh whilk som, þat in helle has bene
And horrible paynes þar has sene   6500
Has bene broght oway fra alle þat stryf
And bene turned ogayne fra ded til lyf,
Als Lazar was, Mary brother Maudalayne,
þat saw and herd þar many a payne,
þat tyme namly when he was ded,   6505
For his saul was þan at þat sted
Four dayes, als God vouched save,
And swa lang his body lay here in grave,
And at `þe´ last God raysed hym right
Fra ded til lyf thurgh his myght.   6510
Bot þat þat he saw he noght forgatte
And sone þaraftir, als he satte
With Crist at þe meete in Martha hous,
He talde a party of þa paynes hydus.
Bot yhit durst he noght al telle,   6515
F[or] drede of Crist, þat he saw in helle.
Yhit lyfed he aftir fiften yhere,
Bot he lughe never ne made blythe chere
For drede of dede þat he efte most dryghe

6490 þe] þe Morris   6497 it] if Morris (Lightbown)   6506 was þan] *trs.* Morris
(Lightbown)   *6516 For] Fro G, *cf.* Befor Crist L, *Morris's silent correction*
6519 efte most] *trs.* Morris   most] mot *a*, suld L (*with changed construction*), bus M

And of þe paynes þat he saw with eghe.   6520
For how bitter þe dede es nan may witt,
Bot he anely þat has feled itt;
And what paynes in helle er, nane wil wene
Bot he anely þat has þam sene.
    Alswa twa of Symeon sons ryght,   6525
þe whilk Caryn and Leutyn hight,
When þa first war dede and hethen went,
þai saw in helle many a tourment.
And sithen when Crist dighed on þe rode,
þai rase fra ded and obout yhode   6530
And tald how Crist, byfor þat he ras,
Til helle come and tuke out þat his was,
And mykel couthe þai þan telle
Of þe paynes þat þai saw in helle.
f. 109ʳᵃ Bot þai had no leve, als I wene,   6535
To telle alle þat þai þar had sene;
Wharfor þai lyfed here ay in penaunce,
And never aftir made blithe continance.
Of wham es writen in a pistel þus,
þat Pilat sent til Tyberius,   6540
þat þan emperour of Rome was,
For to certifie hym of þis cas.
And yhit many other þat war dede
Has bene sumtyme at þat stede
And sene þar many hydus payne   6545
And thurgh miracle turned til lyf agayne.
    Bot omang alle þat þar has bene sene,
I fynde wryten paynes fourtene,
Thurgh whilk þe synful sal 'be' pyned ay
In body and saule aftir domesday.   6550
þe whilk er als general paynes of helle,
And whilk þas er I sal yhow telle.
þe first es fire swa hate to reken
þat na maner of thyng may it sleken.
þe secunde es calde, als says som,   6555
þat na hete of fire may overcom.
þe thred alswa es filthe and stynk

þat es stranger þan any hert may thynk.
þe ferthe es hunger sharpe and strang.
þe fift es brynnand threst omang.   6560
þe sext es swa mykel myrknes,
þat it may be graped, swa thik it es.
þe seve[n]d es þe horribel sight
Of þe devels þat þar er hydusly dight.
þe eghtend payne es vermyn grete   6565
þat þe synful men sal gnawe and frete.
þe neghend es dyngyng of devels hand
With melles of yren hate glowand.
þe tend payne es gnawyng within
Of conscience þat bites als vermyn.   6570
þe ellevend es hate teres of gretyng
þat þe synful sal scalden in þe dounfallyng.
þe twelfte es shame and shenshepe of syn
þat þai sal haf þat never sal blyn.
þe threttend es bandes of fire brinnand   6575
þat þai sal be bunden with, fote and hand.
þe fourtend payne despayre es cald
þat þe synful sal ay in hert hald.
    Alle þir er generale paynes in helle,
Bot þar er other, ma þan tung may telle,   6580
Or hert may thynk, or eer may here,
Of special paynes þat er sere.
þe whilk many, aftir þai er worthy,   f. 109rb
Sal thole evermare in saule and body;
Bot of alle þa paynes can I noght say,   6585
For na man þam reken ne specyfy may.
Bot yhit wille I speke somwhat mare
Of þe general paynes þat I shewed are,
And with som auctorites þam bynd,
Als men may in sere bukes writen fynd.   6590
    þe first, als I tald, es þe fire hate,   j. Of þe fire of hell
þat nathyng may sleken ne abate;   ⟨and⟩ howe hate it es
Whare þe synful men sal bryn thurgh hete
Of whilk God spekes 'þus' thurgh þe prophete:
    Ignis succensus est in furore   6595

*6563 sevend] seued G, *Morris's emendation*   þe²] *om.* a

meo et ardebit usque ad in-
ferni novissima, id est, usque
in eternum.

'Fyre es kyndeld in my wreth', says he,
'And sal bryn until ende of helle sal be,   6600
þat es evermare', als God vouches save,
For helle sal nevermare ende have.
þat fire es swa hate and ay brynnes,
þat if alle þe waters þat standes or rynnes
On erthe, and alle þe sese withoute,   6605
þat encloses alle þe erthe oboute,
Suld ryn intil þat fire swa hate,
Yhit myght it noght it sleken ne abate,
Na mar þan a drope of water shire,
If alle Rome brend, mught sleken þat fire.   6610
For þe fire of helle, þat es endeles,
Es hatter þan [þe] fire here es,
Right als þe fire þat es brinnand here
Es hatter and of mare powere
þan a purtrayd fire on a waghe,   6615
þat es paynted, outher heghe or laghe,
With a rede coloure til mens sight,
þat nouther brynnes ne gyfes light
Ne on othir manere avales ne ders.
Of þir twa fires I fynde writen twa vers: 6620
    Quam focus est mundi picto fervencior igne,
    tam focus inferni superat fervencia mundi.
'Als þe fire of þe werld hatter es
þan a fire paynted, be it mare or les,
Right swa þe fire of helle passes thurgh hete   6625
Alle þe fires of þe werld', smale and grete.
And forþi þat þe synful brynned ay here
In þe fire of fole yhernyngs sere,
It es right þat þai brynne þare
In þat hate fire for evermare.   6630

f. 109ᵛᵃ   + þe secunde payne es grete calde,   6633
ij. Of þe calde þat þe   þat þe synful sal fele, als I ar talde;
synful sal fele in helle

---

*6612 þe] om. G, þis M   *6630 add Est locus indignis ubi non extinguitur ignis |
Non qui torquetur nec qui torquet morietur c; added to the earlier Latin at 6622 M
6633 es] es þe aM

þat cald sal be swa strang and kene   6635
þat if þe mast roche þat man has sene,
Or þe mast mountayne in any land,
War al attanes in fire brynnand
And even imyddes þat cald war,
It suld frese and turne alle intil yse þar.   6640
And forþi þat þai, omang [þai]r vice,
Brynned ay here in þe calde of malice
And ay was dased in charite,
þarfor it es right þat þai be
In þat strang calde evermare lastand,   6645
Whar þai sal frese, bathe fote and hand.
þe devels sal tak þam fra þat fire
And cast þam, with ful grete ire,
Intil þat cald to eke þair payne
And efte þam cast in þe fire ogayne.   6650
þus sal þai cast þam to and fra,
And evermare þai sal fare swa.
Of þis þe haly man bers wittenes
Iob þat says þus, als writen es: *Iob*
   Ab aquis nivium transibunt   6655
   ad calorem nimium.
'Fra waters of snawes þe synful sal wende
Til þe over-mykel hete' þat has nan ende.
And saynt Austyn says on þis manere
In a buke, als es writen here: 6660 *Augustinus*
   Dicuntur namque mali candere
   exterius calore ut ferrum in for-
   nace, et interius frigore ut
   glacies in yeme.
'þe wikked sal outwith be glowand   6665
Thurgh hete, als iren in fire brynnand
And within thurgh calde sharpe and kene,
Als yse þat es in wynter sene'.
þus sal þai ay be in calde and hete;
þis tourment es ful strang and grete.   6670
  þe thred payne es, als men heres clerkes telle,   *iij. Of þe filt⟨h⟩ and*
þe grete stynk and filthe þat es in helle.   *stynk þat sal be in helle*

6637 Or] Of Morris (Lightbown)   *6641 þair] other *cb*   6662 ferrum] ferum
Morris (Lightbown)   6666 iren] men Morris

Of þis saynt Ierom, þe haly man,
Says þus, als I here shewe yhow can:

Ibi est ignis inextinguibilis   6675
          et fetor intollerabilis.

'þe fire es þar of swa grete pouste
þat it may nevermar slekend be,
f. 109vb And swylk filthe and stynk es in þat ugly hole
          þat nan erthely man mught it thole',   6680
          For na man in erthe may ymagyn
          Swa mykel filthe als sal be þarin.
          Wharfor þar sal be mare stynk
          þan tung may telle or hert thynk.
          þe whilk stynk, with filthe and fen,   6685
          Sal be strang payne til synful men,
          And yhit þe fire, þat bryn þam sal,
          Sal gyfe a st[r]ang stynk withalle,
          For it sal be fulle of brunstane and pyk
          And of other thyng þat es wyk.   6690
          And for þe synful delyted þam here namly
          In þe filthe and stynk of lechery,
          It es right þat þai be ay omang
          þe stynk and filthe in helle swa strang.

iiij. Of þe strang hunger   þe ferthe payne es, als I haf herd say,   6695
     þat sal be in helle   þe strang hunger þat þar sal last ay,
          þe whi[l]k þe synful in helle sal fele
          Evermare, als þir clerkes knawes wele.
          þe strenthe of hungre sal þam swa chace
          þat þair awen flesshe þai sal of race,   6700
          And for hungre þai sal yherne it ete,
          For þai sal gett nan other meete.
          For hungre þai sal be als brayne-wode,
          Bot þe dede þar sal be þair fode,
          Als says þe prophet in a stede,   6705
          'þai sal be fedde with þe dede'.
          Mors depascet
          eos.
          þis es on Inglys þus to rede,

6679 es] *om.* RM, *int. later* A   *6688 strang] stang G, *Morris's emendation*
6694 stynk and filthe] *trs. sbs.* Rb (*with additional rewriting* M)   *6697 whilk] whik G
(*perhaps a legitimate form?*), *Morris's emendation*

'þe dede þam sal dolefuly fede'.   6710
For als he þat has here hungre grete,
Thurgh kynde langes mast aftir mete,
Right swa þe synful þat sal duelle þare
Yhit sal lange aftir þe ded wele mare
þat þai mast hated and drede here,   6715
Bot dighe may þai noght on na manere.
Of þis saynt Ion bers wittnes,
Als in þe *Apocalipse* writen es:
     Disiderabunt mori, et mors
     fugiet ab eis.   6720
'Yherne þai sal to dighe fra þair wa,
And þe ded sal ay fle þam fra'.
And forþy þat þai wald gyf na mete
Til þe poer, þat here [h]ad hunger grete,
Ne of þam had nouther reuthe ne mercy,   6725
Bot used ay outrage and glotony,
It es right þat þai haf þis payne,   f. 110ra
Grete hungre in helle ay þarogayne.

þe fifte payne es, als sal befalle,
Grete threst þat þai sal haf withalle.   6730
Swa mykel in helle sal be þair threst
þat þair hertes sal nere clewe and brest.
Bot þe flaume of fire þai sal drynk,
Menged with brunstan þat foul sal stynk
And with smoke of fyre and wyndes blast   6735
And with other stormes þat ay sal last,
þat alle togider þan sal mete.
And þarfor says David þe prophete:
     Ignis et sulphur et spiritus
     procellarum pars calicis eorum.   6740
He says þus, als we writen fynde,
'Fire and brunstan and stormes with wynde,
A part sal be þar of þair drynk',
And þat sal be menged with smoke and stynk.
Yhit sal þai drynk, ogayne þair wille,   6745
Another maner of drynk þat es ille,
þat sal 'be' bitter and venemus

v. Of þe gret threst þat
þe synful sal haf in helle

---

*6724 had hunger] *trs.* G   6735 of] of þe *a*, and þe M

And be cald þair wyne, for þe prophet says þus:
Fel draconum vinum eorum et venenum
aspidum insanabile.   6750
'Galle of draguns þair wyne sal be,
And wenym of snakes þarwith', says he,
'þat may noght be heled wele',
Swa violent it es to fele.
    þir wordes aftir þe lettre er hard to here,   6755
Bot men may þam take on othir manere.
þai sal swa brynnand threst thole
þat þair hertes sal bryn within als a cole,
For na licour sal þai fynd to fele
þat þair threst mught sleke and þair hertes kele.   6760
þai sal for threst þe hevedes souke
Of þe nedders þat on þam sal rouke,
Als a childe þat sittes in þe moder lappe
And, when it list, soukes hir pappe.
For I fynd þis word in Haly Writt,   6765
Als Iob says þat witnesses it:
    Caput aspidum
    sugent.
'þe heved of nedders' þat on þam sal fest
He says, 'þai sal souke' þan for threst.   6770
Strang payne of threst þan haf þai
When þai sal souke for therst swilk venym ay.
And forþi þat þai wald never blethely
Gyf til poer at drynk þat war thresty
To sleken þair threst, ne on þam thynk,   6775
Ne nouther gyf þam mete ne drynk,
And on þairselven na drynk wald spare
Na day, til þai drunken ware,
It es þan right þat þai in helle fele
Brynnand threst þat never sal kele.   6780
þat sal þai haf when þai com þider
And sharp hungre alswa, bath togydre,
þat never sal ceese, als I [talde] ar;
For þir twa paynes with othir er endel[e]s þar.

f. 110rb (at line 6775)

6764 soukes] souke *a*M   6770 þan] þam R, *om.* L, *line also includes* þaim souke M
6774 at] a *a, om.* L   6779 þat] *repeats* Morris   *6783 talde] sayde GM, say L
*6784, 6790 endeles] endels G, *Morris's emendations*

Of þis saynt Ierom bers wittnes,   6785
þat says þus, als writen es:
   In inferno erit fames infinita   *Ieronimus*
   et sitis infinita.
'In helle sal be', whar never es rest,
'Endel[e]s hungre and endeles threst'.   6790
   + þe sext payne es over-mykel myrknes,   6793 *vj. Of þe ouer-mirknes*
þat in helle sal be ay endeles,   *þat es ⟨in⟩ helle*
þat swa thik es þat men mught it grape,   6795
Fra whilk þe synful sal never eschape.
For na hert may thynk ne tung telle,
Swa mykel mirkenes als es in helle,
Of whilk Iob spekes, als þe buk shewes wele,
And says, 'þe synful sal grape and fele   6800
Myrkenes, als mykel at mydday
Als at mydnyght' þat sal last ay.
   Palpabunt tenebras in meridie,   *Iob*
   sicut in media nocte.
In helle es never day bot ever nyght;   6805
þar brynnes ay fire, bot it gyf[es] na light.
Bot yhit þe synful sal ay se
Alle þe sorowe þat þar sal be
And ilka payne and ilka tourment
Thurgh sparkes of fire þat obout sal sprent.   6810
Bot þat sight sal be til þam þare
Na confort, bot sorowe and kare.
þus to eke þair paynes, þai sal haf sight
Withouten any comfort þar of light,
And forþi þat helle es ay lightles,   6815
It es cald þe land of myrkenes,
þat es depe and myrke and hydus.
þarfor says Iob þe haly man þus: *Iob*
   Ut non revertar ad terram
   tenebrosam.   6820
He says, 'Loverd, þat I noght turne away
Til þe myrke land', whare sorow es ay,
Whare wonyng es ay hydus and ille,   *f.* 110va

6786 es] here es R   *6790 *add* Inferni pene sunt hee (hec Morris) vermes
tenebreque flamma chorus demonum fetor frigusque fames sitis horror *c*   6802 at] a A
*6806 gyfes] gyf G, *Morris's emendation*   6821 noght turne] *trs. a*M, *cf.* be not turnyd L

Iob Als Iob says þat þus spekes mar þartille:
    Ubi nullus ordo, sed sempiternus   6825
    horror inhabitans.
'þar nan ordre wonand es', says he,
'Bot uglynes þat evermare sal be'.
And forþi þat þe synful in þair lyf here
Lufed ay myrknes of syns sere   6830
And wald noght turne þam when þai myght
Fra þat myrknes til Goddes light,
It es right þat þai duelle þare
In þat hidus myrknes evermare,
And nevermare aftir light se.   6835
A strang payne til þam þat sal be.

vij. Of þe hidus sight of   þe sevend payne es of þe fourtene
þe deuels in helle   þe sight of devels þat sal be sene
Omang þe synful þat sal be in helle,
In whas company þai sal ay duelle.   6840
þat sight sal be swa hidus to se
þat alle þe men of Cristiante
Couthe noght thurgh witt ymagyn right
Ne descryve swa hydus a sight,
Als þai þan sal se in helle evermare   6845
Of ugly devels þat sal be þare.
For þan sal be ma devels in helle
þan any tung can reken or telle,
And ilkan sal mare grysely seme
þan any man can ymagyn [or] deme.   6850
For swa hardy es na man ne swa balde
In þis werld, nouther yhung ne alde,
If he myght right consayve in mynde,
How grysely a devel es in his kynde,
þat durst for alle gude of mydlerde   6855
A devel se here. Swa suld he be aferde,
For þe hardyest man in flesshe and bane
þat here lyfes, yf he sawe ane
Of þa devels in þair awen lyknes,
Suld wax wode forferde and be wittles.   6860
Forwhy na witt of man may endure

*6850 or] and G, cf. may deme L   6855 alle] all þe RWb

To se a devel in his propre figure.
    How sal þai fare þan þat ay sal þam se
And ay in company with þam be?
þe synful sal evermare on þam luke,   6865
For þus we fynde wryten in boke:
    In inferno videbunt eos facie ad faciem,
    quorum opera in terris dilexerunt.
'In helle þai sal þam se, face to face,
Whas werkes þai lufed and folowed þe trace,   6870
Whilles þai war here in erthe lyfand'.   f. 110vb
And with þat syght, als I understand,
þai sal duleful criyng and sorow here,
For saynt Austyn says on þis manere:
    Demones igne scintillante   6875   *Augustinus*
    videbunt et miserabilem
    clamorem flencium et la-
    mentancium audient.
'þai sal se þar devels with eghe
Thurgh sparkes þat of þe fire sal fleghe,   6880
And here þarwith on ilka party,
þe wreched synful grete and cry'.
And þe sorow and dule þat þai sal make
Sal nevermare þar cees ne slake;
And forþi þat þai [h]ated here to se   6885
And to here þat þat gude suld be,
+ þarfor it es reson and ryght,
þat þai ay se þat grysely syght
And þat þat heryng haf of duleful dyn
To eke þair payn for þair sin.   6890
    þe aghtend payne, als þe buke says us,   *viij. Of þe horribel*
Es þe horribel vermyn venemus,   *vermyn þat sal seme*
þe whilk sal ay on þe synful rouke   *in helle*
And evermare þam gnawe and souke,
Als ugly draguns and nedders kene   6895
And tades – swa hydus was never here sene—
And other vermyn ful of venym
And wode bestes grysely and grym,

6864 þam] pam Morris   6880 þat] *after* fire *a*   6885 þai] þat Morris   *hated
here] *trs. cb*   *6887 þarfor] And þarfor G, *cf.* Forþi *b*   6892 þe] of R, *om.* M, *cf.* Es
þe] *om.* L   6893 ay] *om.* Morris (Lightbown)

þat with tethe sal [a]y þam gnaw and byte
On alle þair lyms whar þai had delite   6900
Synful werkes here for to wirk,
Agayne þe law of God and of Haly Kyrk.
þus for þai did ay ogayns Goddes lawe,
Vermyn and wode bestes sal þam ay gnawe
For þair syn þat þam thoght here swete.   6905
þarfor God says þus thurgh þe prophete:
    Dentes bestiarum immittam in eos, cum furo-
    re trahencium in terram atque serpencium.
'I sal send in þe synful', says he,
'þe tethe of bestes þat felle sal be,   6910
With wodenes of þam intil erthe drawand
And of nedders' þam fast gnawand.
þus sal wode bestes and vermyn gnaw þam ay
And nevermare pas fra þam oway;
And þat payne þe synful byhoves ay dreghe,   6915
Forwhy þair vermyn sal never dieghe
Bot evermare lyfand with þam duelle.
þar`for´ God says þus in þe godspelle:

H f. 244ᵛᵃ   *Vermis eorum non morietur,*
    et ignis eorum non extinguetur.   6920
'þair vermyn sall never deghe', says he,
'Ne þair fyre sall never slekend be'.
Augustinus And to þat says þus saint Austyne,
þat spekes here of þat vermyne:
    Vermes infernales sunt immortales qui, ut pis-   6925
    ces in aqua, ita vivunt in flamma.
He says, 'Vermyn of hell sall ay lyfe'
And never deghe þe synfull to gryefe,
'The whilk sall lyfe in þe flawme of fyre,
Als fyssches lyfes in water schyre'.   6930
þat vermyn on þam sall ay crepe,
`And´ in þam fest þair clokes full depe;
þai sall umlapp þam all oboute
And gnaw on ilka lym and souke.
With vermyn þai sall all coverd be   6935
Swa þat na lym of þam sall be fre,

And swa þai sall be ay gnawand
On þair lyms, whether þai lyg or stand.
Vermyn in hell sall be þair clethyng,
And vermyn þare sall be þair beddyng.   6940
Na clathes þai sall have to gang in
Ne na beddes to lyg in, bot vermyn.
Wharfor I fynd wryten þare I have red   *Ysay*
How þe prophete discryved swilk a bed
To þe kyng Nabogodonosor   6945
And sayd þus to mak him ferd þarfor:
  Subter te sternetur tinea, et
  operimentum tuum vermes.
He says, 'Of wormes þi bed sall be
þat sall be st[r]ewed thyk under þe,   6950
And þi covertoure on þe sene
Sall be vermyn' full fell and kene.
Swilk beddes er ordaynd in hell
For synfull men þat þare sall dwell.
þus sall þai be pyned for þair syn   6955
Evermare with fyre and vermyn
And with many other payns ma,
For God vouches safe þat it be swa.
For þus fynd we wryten in Haly Wrytt
In a boke of þe Bibell þat hate *Iudyth*:   6960   *Iudith*
  Dabit Dominus ignem et vermes
  in carnes eorum, ut urantur
  et senciant usque in sem-
  piternum.
It says 'Fyre and vermyn þat ay sall lyfe,   6965
Our Lord tyll þe flesch of synfull sall gyfe,
Swa þat þai sall bryn evermare,   H f. 244vb
And ay fele' of vermyn bytyng sare.
þis payn es mare to fele and se
þan all þe paynes þat may be   6970
In þis werld here, mare and les,
Als þe boke openly bers witnes.
  þus sall vermyn in hell be gret payne,
Bot yhit may men say here-ogayne.

6940 þare sall] *trs.* Morris (Lightbown)   6944 discryved] descryed R, dyscries *b*
6949 says] sayde *a*   *6950 strewed] stewed H, *Morris's silent correction*

For men may in som boke wryten se   6975
þat after þe gret dome þat last sall be,
Na quyk creature sall lyf þan,
Bot anely aungell, devell, and man.
How suld in hell þan or ourwhare elles,
Any vermyn lyf, als men telles,   6980
Or any other best þat moght dere?
To þis may men gyf answere
On þis manere, whaswa kan:
þe vermyn þat sall be þan,
Als I understand, noght elles es   6985
Bot devels in vermyn lyknes,
þat sall byte and gnaw þe synfull þare
To eke þair payne and mak it mare.
þus sall þe devels gnaw þam without
In lyknes of vermyn all obout,   6990
And þair conscience als vermyn
Sall gnaw þam overall within,
And þat gnawyng sall be full hard,
Of whilk I sall speke sone afterward.

            þat vermyn in hell sall be mare grysely   6995
þan vermyn here es, and mare myghty.
By vermyn here þan þat greves sare,
Men aght to dred þe vermyn þare;
And forþi þat þe synfull was here namely
Ay full of hateredyn and of envy   7000
And wald noght amend þam of þat syn,
Bot lete it gnaw þam ay within,
It es ryght and skyll thurgh Godes lawe
þat þe vermyn in hell ay þam gnawe.

ix. Of dyngy⟨ng⟩ of   þe neghend payne es to understand   7005
deuels opon þe synful   Dyngyng of devels with hamers glowand.
in helle   For þe devels þe synfull sall ay bete
With glowand hamers huge and grete,
And als smyths strykes on þe yren fast
Swa þat it brekes and brestes at þe last,   7010
Right swa þe devels sall ay dyng
On þe synfull, withouten styntyng,

---

*6981 þat] *repeats* H, *Morris's silent correction*   6987 gnaw] knaw R Morris (*corrected*
in his errata), *couplet om.* M

And with hamers gyf swa gret dyntes,
þat all to powdre moght stryke hard flyntes.
For harder dyntes gaf never engyne   7015   H f. 245ra
þan þai sall gyf, als sais saint Austyne: *Augustinus*
 Sicut machina bellica percutit
 muros opidi, ita demones, ym-
 mo asperius et crudelius, corpora malorum
 et animas flagellabunt post iudicium.   7020
He says, 'Als men may se ane engyne cast
And at þe walles of a castell stryke fast'
With a stane þat es huge and hevy,
'Swa sall devels stryke þa[r] mare felly
þe ill bodyse and saules þat sall dwell,   7025
After þe last gret dome' in hell.
þus sall þai dyng on þam evermare,
With gret glowand hamers, and nane spare.
And þis payne tyll þam sall be endles,
Als þe bok hereof bers witnes;   7030
For þai sall have power ay and leve
þe synfull men to dyng and greve,
Als in a boke es schewed tyll us
þat saynt Austyne made, þare he says þus:
 Parata iudicia blasphematoribus et percu-   7035   *Augustinus*
 cientibus malleis stultorum corpora.
'þe domes sall þan be redy
Till þe sklaunderers of God allmyghty,
And tylle þase þat sall be ay smytand
þe bodyse of synfull with melles in hand'.   7040
And forþi þat þai wald noght take
Haly disciplyne here for Godes sake,
þarfor þe devels sall stryk þam þare
With hevy melles ay, and nane spare.
 þe tend payne es þe gnawyng within   7045   *x. Of gnawyng of þe*
Of þair conscience þat never sall blyn.   *wormes of conscience*
For within þam sall þe worme of conscience frete   *withyn þat þe synful*
Als withouten sall do vermyn grete,   *sal fele in helle*
And swa sall þai evermare, withouten dout,

7017 bellica] bellita Morris *7024 þar] þase H, þar *with last two letters later over*
eras. A, *om.* M, *cf.* and L (*and, in the next line* þe ill] þare) 7030 hereof] hereol Morris
7038 sklaunderers] sclaundres aL (*corr. later* W)

Be gnawen and byten within and without.   7050
Full mykell sorow sall [b]e þan in hell
Omang þe synfull þat þare sall dwell;
For þai sall ever þus cry and say,
'Allas, allas!' and 'walaway!
Whi ne wald we never are trow   7055
What payne and sorow here es now?'
þan sall þai pleyne þam of þair wickednes,
And say þus, als in boke wryten es:

>Quid nobis profuit superbia? Quid divicia-
>rum iactancia? Omnia transierunt velud um-   7060
>bra, et tanquam nuncius precurrens, et tanquam
>navis procedens in fluctuantem aquam, et tan-

H f. 245rb

>[quam] avis transvolans in aere, cuius itineris non
>est invenire vestigium.

'What avayld us pryde?' þai sall say,   7065
'What rosyng of ryches or of ryche aray?
All þat pomp, als we se now,
Es passed oway als a schadow
And als messangere bifore rynand
And als schypp þat gase in water flowand   7070
And als foghel fleghand in þe ayre als wynd,
Of whase gate men may na trace fynd'.
þus sall all þair pomp oway pas
And be als thyng þat never was;
þan sall þam think, when alle es oway,   7075
All þair lyfe here bot als ane howr of a day,
þof þai never so lang had lyfed here.
[þan m]ay þai say on þis manere:
'Right now born we war in þe world to be;
Ryght now in alle our delytes lyfed we;   7080
Ryght now we deghed and passed oway;
Now er we in hell and swa sall be ay'.
þan sall þai knaw how ill þai have lyfed,
When þe worme of conscience þam has greved,

7050 -in] hym/hyn A   *7051 be þan] *trs.* c, *couplet om.* M   7057 sall þai] *trs.*
AL   7058 als] *after* boke A   7061 precurrens] percurrens Morris   *7063 quam]
om. H (*at column boundary*), *Morris's silent supply, om. in truncated citation* M
7069 messangere] messagere A, messaungeres WM, messynger L   7074 thyng]
fhyng ? R   *7078 þan may þai] þai may *c* (þan] þat L)

þat within sall þam ay gnaw and byte   7085
For þai in vanyte had here delyte
And forþi þat conscience styrd þam noght
To forsake þair folyes þat þai wroght,
Bot folowed ay here þair flesschly will.
þarfor it es gud, ryght, and skyll   7090
þat þe worme of conscience within
Evermare in hell þam gnaw for þair syn.
  þe ellevend payne es teres of gretyng
Of þe synfull, þat withouten styntyng
Sall grete evermare, als says þe boke.   7095
Forwhi what for sorow and what thurgh smoke
And what thurgh cald and what thurgh hete
þat þai sall thole, þai sall ay grete,
And þus teres fra þair eghen sall ryn
Evermare and never sall blyn.   7100
Swa mykell water als sall fall þan
Fra a mans eghe may gesce na man;
Forwhi þai sall ay be gretand,
And þair teres sall be ay flowand
And fra þair eghen ryn swa fast,   7105
And þair gretyng swa lang sall last
þat in all þe world here, als I wene,
Es noght swa mykell water sene
Als fra þair eghen sall fall þare,
For þai sall be gretand evermare.   7110
Wharfor saint Austyn says þus,   H f. 245va
Whase wordes er auctentyke tyll us: *Augustinus*
  In inferno plures effundentur lacrime
  quam sunt in mari gutte.
'In hell', he says, 'Out-yhetted sall be   7115
Ma teres þan dropes er in þe see'.
þe synfull sall þare [e]vermare þus grete,
And þair [teres] sall be of swa gret hete
þat þe water þat þan sall doun ryn
Fra þair eghen sall þam schald and bryn.   7120
For it sall be hatter þan ever was

7096 thurgh] for *ab*   7100 Evermare] *possibly* O-H   7102 eghe] eghen A (7099–
7102 *om.* LM)   7117 þare] *om. a*   *evermare þus] *trs. c, cf.* sall . . . mare] þer sall euer *b*
*7118 teres] *om.* H, *Morris's emendation*

Molten led or welland bras,
Als I have herd gret clerkes tell,
þat has descryved þe payns of hell.
And forþi þat þai had here ay lykyng   7125
In þair syn and never forthynkyng
Ne sorow þarfore, for þam thoght it swete,
þarfor þai sall in hell ay grete
And with þair teres be schalded sare
To eke þair payne, als I sayd are.   7130

xij. ⟨Of þe⟩ shame and   þe twel[f]te payne es schame and schenschepe,
shenshipe ⟨þat⟩ þe synful   þat þe synfull sall have in hell swa depe,
⟨sal⟩ haf in helle of þair   Of ilka syn þat ever þai dyd.
⟨syn⟩
Forwhi þare sall be knawen and kyd
All þair syns of thoght, o[f] word, and werk,   7135
Als says saint Austyne, þe gret clerk:

Augustinus   *Omnia in omnibus patebunt et se ab-*
                 scondere non valebunt.

'All þair syns in þam sall schewed be,
And þai may nouther þan þam hyde ne fle'.   7140
þai sall have mare schame of þair syn þare,
And þair schendschepe sall be mare
þan ever had any man here in thoght
For any velany þat ever he wroght;
And þat schame with þam sall last ay   7145
And never sall pas fra þam oway.
þai may say þus þat þare þan dwelles,
Als þe prophete in þe Psauter telles:

Dauid   *Tota die verecundia mea contra me est, et*
            confusio faciei mee cooperuit me.   7150

þat es, 'My schamefulnes', says he,
'Allday es ogayns me,
And þe schenschepe of my face
Sall cover me ever in ilka place'.
þai sall swa schame ay of þair syn   7155
þat þam sall thynk als þai suld bryn
For þe gret schame þat þai sall have þare,

7124 descryved] descryued R*b*   7125 ay] *adds* gret *a*   7130 payne] paynes Morris
(Lightbown)   *7131 twelfte] twefte H   7135 syns of] syn in R, both of M, *cf.* syn]
om. L   *of²] or H, *om. b*   7139 sall schewed] *trs. a*   7141 of] for R, *phrase om. b*
7146 þam] thethen (t¹ *later*) A   7154 ever] *om.* Morris (Lightbown)

þat never sall cese, bot last evermare.
Wharfor if na payne war in hell
Bot þat schame anely, þat I of tell,   7160
It suld be tyll þam + mare payne
þan any man couth here ordayne.
And forþi þat þai here in þair lyfe
Durst never for schame of syn þam schryve,
Bot withouten schame to syn was bald,   7165
It es ryght þat þai have, als I tald,
Schame in hell ay for þair syn,
Of whilk þai wald here never blyn.

   þe threttende + es, als clerkes wate,   *xiij. Of þe bandes of fire*
þe bandes of fyre brynand full hate,   7170 *þat þe synful sal be*
With whilk þe synfull sall be bonden,   *bunden in hel⟨le⟩ with*
Als in som boke wryten es fonden;
And þa bandes of fyre sall never slake.
For þai wald never þair syn forsake,
þai sall be with þa bandes brynand   7175
In hell hard bonden, both fote and hand,
And straytely streyned ilka lym
Thurgh þe devels þat er ugly and grym.
þair wonyng in hell sall be endeles,
Omang stynk and fylth in gret myrknes,   7180
Whare ever es nyght and never[mare] day,
Als men may here gret clerkes say.
þan sall þai fele, when þai þare come,
Godes vengeance thurgh ryghtwise dome
For þair syn þat him here myspays.   7185
Wharfor God þus in þe gosspell says:
   Ligatis manibus et pedibus, mittite
   in tenebras exteriores.
'Lat bynd þair hend and þair fete fast,
And into þe utter myrknes þam cast',   7190
þat es in þe deppest pytt of hell,
Whare mare sorow es þan tong may tell.
þare sall þare hevedes be turned dounward,
And þair fete upward bonden hard,

*7161 þam] þam þare *c*   7165 was] war R*a*   7167 ay] *om.* Morris
*7169 threttende] *add* payne *cb*   7180 in] *and* RL, *couplet om.* M
*7181 -mare] *om.* H*b*

And þair bodyse be streyned bi fete and hed   7195
With brynand bandes glowand red.
þai sall be pyned on þis manere
With other paynes many and sere,
Als a gret clerk says openly
In a boke þat he made thurgh study   7200
Of sere questyons of divinite.
þat es cald *Flos sciencie*,
þat es on Ynglys, *þe Flour of Konyng*,
Whare wryten es many prive thyng.
In þat boke þus he telles   7205
How þai sall hyng þat þare þan dwelles:

H f. 246ra   *Capita, inquit, eorum erunt adinvicem deorsum versa,*
                pedes sursum erecti, et undique penis distenti.

He says in þe grond of hell-dongeoune,
'þe hevedes of synfull sall be turned doune,   7210
And þe fete upward fast knytted,
And in strang payns be streyned and tytted'.
And forþi þat þai war here ay redy
To syn with sere lyms of þair body,
þarfor þai sall be bonden þare   7215
Be diverse lyms, als I sayd are,
With brynand bandes hate glowand,
þat evermare sall be lastand.
And forþi þat þai wald noght God knaw
Na kepe þe ordre here of his law,   7220
Bot turned þam ay fro Godward
And on þe world þair hertes sett hard
And swa mysturned here þair lyfyng
Intyll vanyte and flesschly lykyng,
þarfor it es ryght and resoune   7225
þat þai be turned up-swa-doune
And streyned in hell and bonden fast,
With bandes of fyre þat ay sall last.

xiiij. Of despayre þat   þe fourtente payne es despayre to tell,
þe synful sal euermar   In whilk þe synfull sall ay dwell   7230
duellen in helle   Withouten hope of mercy þan,
For Salamon [þ]us says, þe wise man:

*7232 þus says] trs. HW, sais b

Omnes qui ingrediuntur ad eam non rever-   *Salomon*
tentur, nec apprehendent semitas vite.
He says, 'Alle þase þat tyll hell wendes'   7235
And in despayre sall be omang fendes
'Sall never after turne ogayne,
Ne tak þe ways of lyfe', certayne.
For when þai er dampned thurgh iugement
And with body and saule till hell er sent,   7240
þai sall never after, withouten dout,
Have hope ne thynk to com out,
Bot evermare dwell withouten hope,
For þus says þe haly man Iob:
    Quia in inferno nulla est   7245
     redempcio.
'For in hell', he says, 'Es na redempcyoune'
Thurgh na help of frende. For na devocyoune
Of prayer, ne [of] almusdede, ne [of] messe
May þam help, ne þair payn mak les.   7250
A strang payne sall þis be in hell,
Evermare þus in despayre to dwell,
Withouten hope of recouverere.
þis passes all þe payns of þis lyfe here,
For here has na man payn swa strang   7255   H f. 246rb
þat he ne has somtyme hope omang,
Outher of remedy þat men may kast
Or þat it sall end and noght ay last.
Elles suld þe hert, thurgh sorow and care,
Over-tyte fayle, warn som hope ware,   7260
For in sorow here hope comfortes best,
And men says, 'Warn hope ware, hert suld brest'.
Bot in hell na hope may fall in thoght,
And þair hertes brest may noght,
For þai er ordaynd to lyfe ay þare   7265
Swa þat þai may be pyned evermare.
Bot þe lyfe of þam in þat stede
Es wers and bytterer þan þe dede.
Bot better it war to be fully slayne

7233 ingrediuntur] ingredientur A   eam] infernum Morris (Lightbown)
7248 frende] frendes *a, om. phrs. b*   *7249 ne of¹] ne HA, *om. b*   *ne of²] ne H*b
7252 in] in a A

þan overlang lyfe in strang payne,   7270
Bot þe synfull sall ay þare in payne be,
And na ded may þam sla bot ay þam fle,
Als þe boke openly schewes us,
Whare we may fynd wryten þus:
      Mors fugiet ab eis.   7275
'þe ded', þat here es strang and hard
'Sall ay þare fle fra þamward'.
þe payns of þe ded þai sall ay dreghe,
Bot þai sall nevermare fully deghe;
þai sall ay lyf in sorow and stryfe,   7280
Bot þair lyf sall seme mare ded þan lyfe.
þair lyfe inmydward þe ded sall stand,
For þai sall lyfe evermare deghand
And degh evermare lyfand withall,
Als men dose þat we se in swowne fall.   7285
And forþi þat þai here mykell lufed syn
And thurgh over-mykell hope ay lyfed þarin
And to leve þair syn had never will,
þarfor it es gud, ryght, and skyll
þat þai be ay for þair foly   7290
In hell withouten hope of mercy.
     Now have I schewed yhow, als I couth tell,
þe fourtene generall payns in hell,
Bot yhit es over þase a payne generall,
þat of all other es mast principall.   7295
þat es tharnyng forever of the syght namely
Of our Lord God allmyghty.
For whilk syght þat þai forever have tynt,
þai sall have sorow þat never sall stynt,
And þe sorow þat þarfor sall fall   7300
Sall be mast payne to þam of all.
H f. 246ᵛᵃ For als þe syght of God in heven es
Mast ioy of all other, mare and les,
Right swa þe tharnyng forever of þat syght
Es þe mast payne in hell dyght;   7305
For all þe payns þat in hell may be
Suld noght þam dere, if þai [h]im moght se.

7277 þare] *om.* aM, þan Morris (Lightbown)   7285 swowne] sorow R, swonyg L,
swonynge M   *7307 him moght] *trs.* cb

Yhit sall þare be sere payns many ma,
Als þe boke says, and mare sorow and wa
þan all þe men of erth, ald and yhong,   7310
Moght thynk with hert or tell with tong,
þat þe synfull men þat sall wende
Till hell sall have withouten ende.
þe whilk payns and sorow sall never cees,
For þare sall never be rest ne pees,   7315
Bot travail and stryfe with sorow and care;
Full wa sall þam be þat sall dwell þare.
þai sall thynk on nathyng elles
Bot on þair payns, als som clerkes telles,
And on þair syn þat þai here wroght;   7320
Swa sall payns and sorow troble þar thoght.
For þare sall be þan herd and sene
Alkyn sorow and trey and tene.
þare sall be wantyng of al[le] thyng
In whilk moght be any lykyng,   7325
And defaut of all thyng þat gud moght be,
And of all þat ill es gret plente.
In hell sall be þan + dolefull dyn
Omang þe synfull þat sall dwell þarein,
þat evermare sall þus cry and say: 7330
'Allas, allas!' and 'Walaway!
þat ever we war of wemmen borne,
For we er fra God forever lorne!'
þan sall þai grete and goule and with teth gnayste,
For of help ne mercy thar þam noght trayste.   7335
þe devels obout þam þan in hell
On þam sall evermare rare and yhell;
Swa hydus noyse þai sall þan make
þat all þe world it moght do qwake,
And all þe men lyfand þat herd it   7340
To ga wode for ferd and tyne þair witt.
    þe devils ay omang on þam sall stryke,
And þe synfull þarewith ay cry and skryke;
þare sall be þan mare noyse and dyn

7311 with] in A   *7324 alle] alkyn H, *couplet om.* M   7326 thyng] thynges A,
om. b   *7328 þan] *add* full *c*, fulle M   7337 -mare] *om.* R, þam fast L, *cf.* evermare]
ay M

þan all þe men of erth couth ymagyn,   7345
For þare sall be swilk rareyng and ruschyng
And raumpyng of devels and dyngyng and dusching
And skrykyng of synfull, als I said are,
þat þe noyse sall be swa hydus þare
Omang devels and þase þat sall com þider,   7350
Ryght als heven and erth strake togyder.
Ane hydus thing es it to tell
Of þe noyse þat [þ]an sall be in hell.
þe devels, þat ay sall be full of ire,
Sall stopp þe synfull ay in þe fyre   7355
Swa þat þai sall glowe ay als fyrebrandes
And ay when þai may, weld þair handes;
For sorow þai sall þam hard wryng,
And 'Walaway' þai sall ay syng.

   In hell sall be þan swa gret thrang   7360
þat nane may remow for other ne gang
On na syde, bakward ne forward,
For þai sall be presed togyder swa hard,
Als þai war stopped togyder in ane oven,
Full of fyre bineth and oboven.   7365
Bot neverþeles hell yhit es swa depe
And swa wyde and large þat it moght kepe
Alle þe creatures, les and mare,
Of all þe world, if myster ware.
Ilka synfull sall þare on other prese,   7370
And nane of þam sall other eese,
Bot ever fyght togyder and stryfe,
Als þai war wode men of þis lyfe.
And ilkane scratte other in þe face,
And þair awen flessch of ryve and race,   7375
Swa þat ilkane wald himself fayn sla,
If he moght, swa sall him be wa.
Bot þareto sall þai haf no myght,
For þe ded sall nevermare on þam lyght.
Full fayne þai wald þan ded be,   7380
Bot þe ded sall ay fra þam fle;
After þe ded þai sall yherne ilkone,

*7353 þan sall] *trs.* H, *cf.* sall be þan (*om.* M) *b*   7372 fyght togyder] *trs. a*

Als in þe *Apocalypse* schewes saint Iohan:
  Desiderabunt mori, et
    mors fugit ab eis.   7385
'þai sall yherne', he says, 'To degh ay,
And þe ded sall fle fra þam oway'.
  Omang þam sall ay be debate;
Ilkane of þam sall other hate.
þai sall be full of hateredyn þan;   7390
Ilkane sall other wery and ban
And say, 'Cursed kaytif, wa worth þe',
And 'Weryed mot þou ever be',
And 'Weryed mot þai be evermare,
þat þe gat and þat þe bare,   7395
And þe tyme þat þou was born allswa,
For þi payne [t]yll me es sorow and wa.
It pynes me and greves me sare,   H f. 247ra
Als mykell als myne awen payn or mare,
For my payne it ekes and mase mare grevus'.   7400
Ilkane tyll other þan sall say þus.
  þus ilk mans payne sall other dere,
And nane of þam sall other forbere,
Nouther son ne doghter ne syster ne brother,
Fader ne moder, ne yhit nane other.   7405
For ilkane sall other hate dedly,
And ilkane gryn on other and cry.
Ilkane sall gnaw þair awen tonges in sonder,
And ilkane sall þare on other wonder.
þus in hell sall þai far ay,   7410
And þarwith sklaundre God and say:
'Wharto made God us tyll his lyknes
And lates us now dwell þare sorow ay es?
Bot it semes þat God made us in vayne,
When we er þus putted till endles payne,   7415
Or he us made for noght els to dwell
In erth, bot to be fyrebrandes in hell'.
þai sall wery þe tyme þat þai war wroght
And say 'Allas, whi ne war we noght'?

7392 wa] and wa Morris (Lightbown)   *7397 es] *after* payne *c, cf.* dos me *b*
7406 other hate] *trs. ab*   7410 far] fayre AL, þus fare M   7413 þare] whar *a*, ay
þore M   7418 *At this point, W lacks two quires, and its text resumes at 8572*

þus sall þai sklaundre God omang,   7420
Swa hard þair payns sall be and swa strang.
þai sall ilkane on other stare and gryn,
Als wode men dose here, and make + gret dyn;
Ane hydus thing to here it ware,
Whasa couth tell þe payns þare,   7425
Als properly als þai sall þare be.
    Bot þat couth noght all þe men of Cristiante,
Ne all þe clerkes þat ever had witt
Sen þe world bigan ne þat lyfes yhit
Couth never tell, bi clergy ne arte,   7430
Of þ[e] payns of hell þe thowsand parte.
For þe noumbre of payns þat þare grifes
Passes all þe mens witt þat here lyfes
Or þat ever lyfed in any degre,
And þat may men bi skyll þus se.   7435
For ilka syn þat þe synfull has wroght,
Whar it never swa lytell venyall thoght,
þai sall have certayne payne þare
After þat þe syn es les or mare.
Wha couth þan tell, war he never swa wyse,   7440
All þe syns and all þe folyse,
Both dedly and allswa venyale,
And leve nane untald, gret ne smale,
þe whilk a man has here fallen in,
Fra þe tyme þat he first bigan to syn,   7445
H f. 247ʳᵇ   Both in thoght, in word, and dede?
(Alss wa say, 'nane es þat [þa]me couth rede'.)
And for ilka thing here done in vayne
In hell es ordaynd certayne payne
Till synfull men þat sall dwell þare.   7450
þan bihoves þam, als I sayd are,
For ilka syn þat þai dyd here,
Have certayne payne singulere;
And for ilka manere of syn and foly
Be pyned in hell specyaly.   7455
And als oftsythe als þai here newed þair syn,
Als oftsyth þair payn sall new þare bigyn;

þarfor swa many payns tyll þam sall fall
þat na witt may comprehende þam all;
For na syn þat ever þai here dyd,   7460
Dedly ne veniele, sall `þan´ be hyd,
Bot all openly sene and nane be laynd,
For whilk sall be þare sere payns ordaynd.
Wha moght þan all þe payns tell
þat þe synfull men sall have in hell?   7465
Forwhi if a man fra hethen pass oway
In a dedly syn at his last day,
For ilk venyel syn þat ever dyd he,
He sall þan diversly pyned be;
And als oft renoueld sall be ilk payne,   7470
Als he turned new tyll ilk syn ogayne.
And þe lest payne þare es mare to se
þan all þe payns of þis world may be.
For all þe payns of þis world here,
þat ever was sene, fer or nere,   7475
Als to þe lest payne þare moght noght be tald
Bot als a bathe of water, nouther hate ne cald.
For all þe sorow of þis world, ilka dele,
War noght bot als solace and ioy to fele,
Als to regard of þe lest payne   7480
þat es in hell; þis es certayne.
   Ilk synfull sall haf syght þare
Of all þe payns, both les and mare,
þat all þe synfull men sall dreghe.
þan sall ilkane se þare with eghe   7485
Men and wymmen, many a thowsand,
On ilk syde obout in sere payns dwelland,
And þat syght, þat ilkane [þ]are sall se
Of ilka payne, tyll þam payne sall be.
For all þe payns þat sall fall tyll ilk man   7490
Sall be sorow tyll all þat seese þam þan.
þus sall ilkane dreghe mare payn in hell
þan hert moght ever think or tong tell,
What of payns þat to þamself sall be dyght,   H f. 247ᵛᵃ

7459 comprehende] comprende A   7460 ever þai] *trs.* A Morris (Lightbown), euer
man *b*   7461 þan] here (*expunged*) þan (*later, margin*) H, none M, *om.* Morris
7479 and] or R, *om. phrs. b*   *7488 þare sall] *trs. c*, sall *b*

And what of payns þat þai sall have of syght.   7495
For all þe payns þat þare sall be knawen
Sall greve ilk man als mykell als his awen;
Swilk payns to here, als men may here rede,
Aght to mak ilk man of hell have drede,
For I trow þat here es no man lyfand   7500
Swa hard-herted, þat wald understand
And trow what payns in hell er wroght,
þat he ne suld have gret dred in thoght.
þe whilk suld mak him hate all foly,
Wharfor he war swylk payns worthy.   7505
   þarfor thynkes ay, both yhong and ald,   7505a
On þir payns in hell þat I have tald,   b
How hydus þai er for to dyscryve,   c
And clens yhow here in yhour lyve   d
Of all fylth of syn and of foly   e
And mak yhow to God here swa redy   f
þat yhe be noght worthy to wende   g
Tyll þase hydus payns withouten ende.   h
For he þat couth ryght understand   i
What payns in hell er ay-lastand,   j
Him war lever thole here alkyn payne   k
þat any man couth here ordayne   l
Ar he wald assent tyll any foly   m
Wharfor he war swilk payns worthy.   n
   Bot alle þase þat will þair syn forsake,
Whils þai lyfe here, ar þe ded þam take,
And of all thing have forthynkyng
þat þai have done ogayns Godes bydyng,
And turn þam tyll God fra þair syn   7510
And ask his mercy and trayst þarein
And be lufand tyll him and bowsom,
In þa payns of hell sall never com,
Bot tyll þe blys of heven mon þai wende
And have þare þair [won]yng withouten ende.   7515
   Here have I spoken of þe payns of hell,
Als yhe have herd me openly tell,

---

*7505a–n *om.* Morris *(an eyeskip stimulated by the identical 7505 and 7505n)*
7505d yhour] þis A   7512 tyll] untylle Morris (Lightbown)   *7515 wonyng]
lykyng H Morris, *cf.* won þer ay *(om.* M) *b*

And of þe sext part of þis boke made ende.
Now will I tyll þe sevend part wende,
þat es þe last part of all.   7520
þe whilk spekes, als I schew yhow sall,
Specialy of þe ioyes in heven,
þat er mare þan any tong may neven.
Bot fyrst I will schew yhow whare heven es,
Als clerkes says and þe boke bers witnes,   7525
And efter þat I sall schew yhow mare
And tell yhow of sere ioyes þat er þare.

Here bygyns þe sevend part of þis boke   H f. 247vb
þat es of þe ioyes of heven.
Many þe blys of heven covaytes,   7530
Bot fone þe ryght way þider laytes;
And som thurgh syn er made so blynd
þat þe right way þider þai kan noght fynd;
Som wald be þare, withouten dout,
Bot þai will noght travayl þare-obout.   7535
Bot whasa will tak þe way þiderward
Bihoves in gud werkes travail hard,
For tyll þe kyngdom of heven may no man com
Bot he ga bi þe way of wisdom.
þe way of wysdom es mekenes   7540
And other vertuse, mare and les,
And þat way es cald a gastly way,
Bi whilk men suld here travail ay.
þat es þe way þat ledes men even
Untyll þe hegh kyngdom of heven.   7545
Bi other way may nane, bot he fleghe,
Pass up tyll heven – it es swa heghe.
    For it es þe heghest place þat God wroght
And þe first, when he made all thing of noght.
Na man may gesce swa lang space   7550
Als es fro hethen untyll þat hegh place,
For bitwene us and þat heghe heven
Es all þe firmament to neven,
þ[at] clerkes bi skyll hevens calles,

7522 in] of A*b*   7524 yhow] *om.* R*b*   7526 þat] -ward A, *cf.* sythyn *b*
7545 hegh] haly A   7547 up] vn- RL, *om.* M   *7554 þat] þe H Morris

þe whilk er ay moveand, als falles.   7555
þus er oboven us hevens sere,
Bot all er þai noght olyke clere,
For þe heghest heven es wele bryghter
þan þe other hevens þat er lagher.
For þe heghest has swa mykell bryghtnes   7560
And swa fayre and swa delytable es
þat all þe men of erth couth noght
Swa mykell ymagyn ne thynk in thoght.
Sere hevens God ordaynd for sere thyng,
Bot þe heghest God made for our wonyng.   7565
    Thre hevens er oboven us heghe,
Als clerkes says þat er wise and sleghe.
Ane es þat we þe sterned heven call,
þare þe planetes and þe sternes er all
þat men may se here on nyght schyne.   7570
Ane-other es þat clerkes calles cristallyne,
þat next oboven þe sterned heven es,
And es mare þan þat of wydenes.
Som clerkes it calles on þis manere,
þe water heven, þat es als clere   7575

H f. 248ra   Als cristall, þat hoves oboven þare,
Ryght als water þat frosen ware.
þus telles Berthelmewe in *þe boke*
Of propertese of sere thinges to loke.
þir twa hevens ay obout rynnes,   7580
Both day and nyght, and never blynnes.
þe erth, þat þa hevens obout gase
Es bot als a poynt imyddes a compase,
Swa lytell it es semand without
To regard of þa hevens obout;   7585
And imyddes þe erth es ordaynd hell,
þare þe synfull þat sall be dampned sall dwell,
Als men may before rede and se,
And lawer þan helle may na place be.
    þus both þ[a] hevens obout gase ay   7590

7557 þai] þa Morris (Lightbown)   olyke] ylyke RA, inlyke L, elike M   7559 other]
tother R   7564 thyng] thynges AL   7565 wonyng] wonyngs AL   7566 Thre]
þese Morris (Lightbown)   7571 clerkes] men A   7578 þe] his R, a L
7583, 7586 imyddes] in- Rb   *7590 þa] þe cM, þire L

And never sall ceese untyll domesday.
For clerkes says, þat knawes and sese
Of þir twa hevens þe propretese,
þat if þai moved noght, all suld peryssch,
Both man and beste, foghel and fyssch   7595
And all þat under þam may be
þat lyfes and growes, both gresse and tre.
All suld be smored withouten dout,
Warne þa hevens ay moved obout.
For if þai stode never swa schort while styll,   7600
Alle þat on erth es suld perysch and spyll.
þus telles gret clerkes of clergy
þat has bene lered in astronemy
And knawes þe constellacyouns
And þe heven[s] þat þe erth envirouns.   7605
Of þair moveyng þan have yhe no wonder,
For it noryssch all þat es þareunder,
In wate and drye, in hate and cald,
Ay whils þai move, als I bifore tald.
þir hevens obout gase all erthly thynges   7610
And þam norysches and forth brynges,
For als clerkes says þat to þam tentes,
þai tempre þe strenghe of all þe elementes
Ay als þai move, whils þai obout ga.
Bot þe thred heven es oboven þa twa,   7615
Swa wonderly heghe and swa ferre
þat nathyng may be heghere.
   Yhit som clerkes ma hevens nevens
And says þat þare er other seven hevens
þat semes lawer, als men may se,   7620
þan þe twa hevens falles to be.
Forwhi þe cerk[l]es of þe planetes all
Bi certayne skyll hevens þai call.
And seven planetes er oboven us: H f. 248rb
Fyrst þe mone and Mercury and Venus,   7625
Sythen þe son and þan Mars and Iubiter,
And Saturnus oboven þam þat es hegher.

---

*7605 hevens] heuen H, *cf.* Of heuyn L   7607 noryssch] noryssches Morris, *an unnecessary emendation*   7613 strenghe] strengthe Morris, *an unnecessary emendation*   *7622 cerkles] clerkes H, cerkille M   of] *om.* Morris   7627 þam] þan Morris (Lightbown)

Ilkane þair course obout ay mase
In þair cercles, als God ordaynd hase.
þai styk noght fast, als smale sternes dose;   7630
Ilkane his course mase thurgh use.
Ilka planete falles to be
Hegher þan other in ordre and degre;
þe mone þe fyrst and þe lawest es sene,
And Saturnus þe heghest es, als I wene.   7635
Oboven us er all þe planetes seven,
And þe cercle of ilkane es cald ane heven,
þat er wonderly bryght and fayre.
Yhit ane-other heven es cald þe ayre
þat es lagher, þare þe foghles has flyght,   7640
And þat heven es mast nere our syght,
Bot it es noght swa clere ne clene
Als þe other hevens oboven er sene.
    All þe cercles of þe planetes all
þat we here clerkes þus hevens call   7645
Er bryght and clere, als þe + boke schewes us,
And ilk planete es ferrer þan other fra us.
Fra þe erth untyll þe cercle of þe mone es
þe way of fyve hundreth wynter and na les,
þat es als mykell space at say   7650
Als a man moght ga in playne way
In fyve hundreth yhere fully,
If he moght lyfe swa lang in body,
Als a gret philisophir þat hyght
Rabby Moyses telles ryght   7655
þat thurgh witt mykell couth se.
And over þat allswa says he
þat ilka cercle þat es sene
Of ilka planete may contene,
Als men may fynd wryten here,   7660
þe way of fyve hundreth yhere
Als es gesced in brede and thyknes,
Swa mykell and thyk ilkane es;
þat es at say, als mykell space here

7632 to] for to Morris (Lightbown)   7634 and þe] and Morris (Lightbown)
7642 ne] and A, *phrs. om.* M   7644 cercles] cercle R   *7646 boke] bokes H,
clerkes L

Als a man moght ga in fyve hundreth yhere,   7665
þof þat travaille him suld noght gryfe,
If he here swa lang moght lyfe.
And fra þe poynt of þe erth till Saturnus,
þe heghest planete, may be gesced þus
þe way of seven thowsand yhere   7670
And thre hundreth, als es wryten here.
þat es at say, als es here contende,   H f. 248ᵛᵃ
Als mykell space als a man moght wende
In seven thowsand yhere and playn way gang
And th[r]e hundreth, if he suld lyf so lang –   7675
Swa þat ilk yhere be acounted halely
Of thre hundreth days and fourty,
And þat þe way of ilka day
Be fully of fourty myle of way,
And þat ilka myle fully contene   7680
A thowsand pases or cubites sene.
Raby Moyses says all þis,
þat er noght all my wordes bot his.
   Bot whether all þis be soth or noght,
God wate þat all thyng has wroght,   7685
For he made all thyng thurgh myght and sleght
In certaine noumbre and mesure and weght.
Bot swa sutell and wise may na man be,
þat þat mesuryng knawes swa wele als he;
For nathyng þat may be, mare or les,   7690
Or þat ever was tyll him unknawen es.
Himself fra erth upward met þat way,
When he stey tyll heven on Halghe Thursday;
þat wate he best thurgh wytt and sleght,
What space þat way contene[s] of heght.   7695
Bi all þe hevens had he gane
And passed all þe sternes ilkane
And up tyll þe heghest heven he went,
And all þis way he passed in a moment.
   In þe heghest part of þe sterned heven   7700
Oboven all þe planetes seven,
Standes swa many sternes smale

---

*7675 thre] the H, *cf.* fyfe L (*but in the prec. line,* seven] thre), *Morris's emendation*
7688 man] thyng A   *7695 contenes] contened H   of] on R*b*

þat na man may þam tell bi tale,
þat standes fast þare, als þe boke proves,
And er led obout with þe heven þat moves,   7705
Als nayles er in a whele without
þat with þe whele er turned obout.
Bot þe planetes er noght led swa,
For in þair cercles obout þai ga.
þe sternes semes smale [þare], als we deme,   7710
Bot swa smale er þai noght als þai seme,
For þai er schewed fra us swa fer
þat we may noght se how mykell þai er;
Bot þe lest sterne þare þat we on luke
Es mare þan all erth, als says þe boke.   7715
For clerkes says if all erth in fyre ware
And possibell war þat a man war þare,
Him suld thynk all erth, þof it brynd bryght,
Les þan þe lest sterne þat schynes on nyght.

H f. 248ᵛᵇ   þan aght þat heven gret space contene   7720
þare swa many sternes may be sene.
    All þir hevens here sene may be,
Bot + altherheghest heven may na man se.
Till þat heven couth never clerk thurgh arte
þe space gesce bi ane hundreth thowsand parte,   7725
For it es swa heghe, als Sydrak says,
þat if a stane þat war of pays
Of ane hundreth mens lyftyng
Might falle fro þethen, suld be in fallyng
A thowsand yhere and na les,   7730
Ar it come at þe erth, swa heghe it es.
Bot aungels þat fro heven er sent
May com doune tyll erth in a moment,
And up ogayne tyll heven may flegh
In þe space of a twynkellyng of ane eghe.   7735
And swa may a saule þat es clene and lyght
Com þider fro hethen in als schort a flyght

*7710 þare] om. HL, but as a later marginal corr. H, couplet om. M   7715 all] om.
Morris (Lightbown)   7717 And] And yf A   7718 all erth] om. Morris
*7723 Bot] Bot þe HM   7724 never] om. Morris   7729 suld] it suld Morris
7732 heven] þethen A   7734 heven] erthe A (corrected in a post-medieval hand)
7735 a] om. RL, cf. of a] and M

Thurgh þe myght of God and thurgh noght elles,
And swa has done many þat þare dwelles.
þis may be halden a gret ferly   7740
Omang all þe wonders of God allmyghty,
þat ane aungell may pass swa many myle,
Fra heven tyll hyder in swa schort a while,
And a saule, thurgh Godes mygh and grace,
May fro hethen com þider in swa schort space.   7745
    þis heven es altherheghest of all;
Hegher es nathyng þat may bifall,
þe whilk all thyng contenes of dignyte,
And in nathyng contende may be.
It contenes overall on ilk party   7750
Bath bodily thyng and gastly.
And als hell es lawest place þat may fall,
Swa es þis heven altherheghest place of all;
And als sorow es ay in þe lawest place,
Swa es ay in þe heghest ioy and solace.   7755
And als tyll þe lawest place drawes us syn,
Swa tyll þe heghest may vertuse us wyn.
    þis heven es cald heven empiry,
þat es at say heven þat es fyry,
For it semes all als fyre of gret myght,   7760
þat brynnes noght bot schynes bryght.
þis heven falles noght obout to ga
Ne moves noght, als dose þe other twa,
Bot standes ay styll, for it es þe best
And þe mast worthi place of pees and rest,   7765
þat God has ordaynd for þair wonyng
þat gyfes þam here tyll ryghtwise lyfyng.
þis heven es cald Godes awen see,   H f. 249ra
For þar syttes þe haly Trinite
And all þe orders of aungels,   7770
And + þe blysfull spirites in þ[is] heven dwels
And þe saules of gud men and clene,
þat in þis world ryghtwyse has bene.
And at þe dredfull day of dome,

7746 altherheghest] þe a. place Morris (Lightbown)   7750 contenes] contendes A
7752 es] es þe R   7756 als tyll] *trs.* R, *phrs. om. b*   *7771 And] And all *c*   *in þis]
þat in H, *cf.* in þis heven] þarein L, þat þore M

When all men sall bifor God come,   7775
þan sall all + ryghtwyse men wend þider,
In body and saule both togyder,
þe whilk anely þan sall be save
And full blys in body and saule have.
    þan sall mare ioy be in heven   7780
þan hert may thynk or tong kan neven,
Or ere may here or any eghe se,
þe whilk þai sall have, þat save sall be.
þan passes þat ioy all mens witt,
Als es fonden wryten in Haly Wrytt: 7785
    Quod oculus non vidit, nec
    auris audivit, nec in cor ho-
    minis ascendit, quod preparavit
    deus diligentibus se.
'Eghe moght never se, ne ere here,   7790
Ne intyll mans hert com þe ioyes sere
þat God has ordaynd þare and dyght
Tyll all þat here lufes him ryght'.
For swa mykell ioy þare sall be
þat all þe men of Cristiante,   7795
If ilkane war parfyte in clergy,
In divinite, and in astronomy,
In gemettry and gramer and arte,
Couth noght gese bi þe thowsand parte,
Ne think in hert, ne with tong neven,   7800
þe ioyes þat þan sall be in heven.
For swa wyse here was never man yhit,
Ne swa sleghe ne swa sotell of wytt,
Had he never swa mykell understandyng,
Bot God anely þat knawes all thyng,   7805
þat couth tell a poynt or ymagyn
Of þe ioyes in heven þat never sall blyn,
Als proprely als þai er þare to say,
Bot als þe boke þam schewes, swa we may.
    Alle manere of ioyes er in þat stede: 7810
þare es ay lyfe withouten dede;
þare es yhowth ay withouten elde;

*7776 all] all the *c*   7779 body and saule] *trs. sbs.* A   7781 kan] may A*b*
7802 man] nane A, no man M   7807 in] of RA*b*   7810 manere] maneres A

þare es alkyn welth ay to welde.
þare es rest ay withouten travayle;
þare es alle gudes þat never sal fayle;   7815
þare es pese ay withouten stryfe;   H f. 249ʳᵇ
þare es all manere of lykyng of lyfe;
þare es withouten myrknes lyght;
þare es ay day and never nyght;
þare es ay somer fulle bryght to se   7820
And nevermare wynter in þat contre;
þare es alkyn druryes and rychesce
And mare nobillay þan any man may gesce;
þare es mare worsch[ep]e and honoure
þan ever had kyng here or emperoure;   7825
þare es alkyn power and myght
And endeles wonyng sykerly dyght;
þare es alkyn delyces and eese
And syker peysibilnes and pese;
þare es peysebell ioy ay-lastand   7830
And ioyfull selynes ay lykand;
þare es sely endeles beyng
And endeles blysfulhede in all thyng;
þare es ay blysfull certaynte
And certayne dwellyng ay fre;   7835
þare es laykyng and myrthes sere;
þare es laghyng and lufly chere;
þare es melody and aungels sang
And lovyng and thankyng ay omang;
þare es all frendschepe þat may be   7840
And parfyte luf and charyte;
þare es acorde ay and anehede
And yheldyng of mede for ilk gud dede;
þare es lowtyng and reverence
And boghsomnes and obedience;   7845
þare es all vertuse withouten vyce;
þare es plente of dayntes and delyce;
þare es all þat lykes and may avayle
And nathing þat greves or may fayle;
þare es all þat gud es at will   7850

*7824 worschepe] worsche H, *Morris's emendation*

And nathyng þat may be ill;
þare es all wisdom withouten foly
And honeste withouten vilany;
þare es bryghtnes and bewte
Of all thing þat men sall þare se.   7855
    All þir ioyes er þare generall,
Bot þe mast soverayne ioy of all
Es þe syght of Godes bryght face;
þat passes all other ioyes and solace.
For swa mykell may na ioy be   7860
Als es þe syght of þe Trinite,
þat es Fader and Son and Haly Gaste,
þe syght of whilk sall be ioy maste.

H f. 249ᵛᵃ Forwhi swa mykell ioy and blys
Na ioy may be als es þis.   7865
For all þat þan sall se him ryght
May knaw all thing thurgh þat syght
þat ever was and es and sall be,
Als men may afterward rede and se.
Here have I schewed on a generall manere   7870
þe ioyes of heven, many and sere.

Of þe seuen ⟨bli⟩sses þat   Bot now will I specialy schew yhow mare
falles to þe bod⟨y⟩ þat Of seven maners of blysses þare
sal be saf and of seuen
⟨þat⟩ falles to þe saule And of seven schendschepes in hell allswa,
and also of þe ⟨se⟩uen   þat er even contrary tyll þa –   7875
shenships ⟨þat⟩ falles to And whilk blysses falles specyaly
þe body þat sal ⟨be⟩
dampned ⟨and⟩ of seuen   Tyll þe saule and whilk tyll þe body,
⟨þat⟩ falles ⟨to⟩ þe saule Of þas þat God in heven sall se;
And whilk schendschepes sall appropried be
Tyll þe bodyse of þase þat sall ga   7880
Tyll hell, and whilk till þe saules allswa.
I spak bifore of sere ioyes generaly,
Bot now will I here sere blysses specify
And þair contraryes þat er hard,
Als yhe sall here be red afterward.   7885
Saint Anselme says, þe haly man,
Als I here schew yhow kan,
þat omang all þe ioyes of heven,

Sall be sene speciall blysses seven
þat þe bodyse sall have þat sall be save   7890
And other seven þat þe saules sall have
In þe kyngdome of heven all togyder
After þe dome, when þai com þider.
Bot tyll þe synfull bodyse þare-ogayne,
þat sall be dampned tyll hell payne,   7895
Seven speciall schendschepes sall fall
And other seven tyll þe saules withall
In hell togyder lastand evermare;
Wa es þam þat sall dwell þare.
Heres now, ar I pass ferrer,   7900
Whilk þa specyall blysses er,
þat er appropried tyll þ[e] bodyse
And tyll þe saules of men ryghtwyse,
And þair contraryes, þat I schendschepes call
þat tyll þe synfull bodyse and saules sall fall.   7905
    þe fyrst blys es bryghtnes cald   *j. Of þe blisse of*
þat þe saved bodyse sall ay hald.   *brightnes þat to þe bodye*
For be þair bodyse never swa dym here,   *sal falle in heuen*
In heven þai sall be fayre and clere
And mare schyneand and mare bryght   7910
þan ever þe son was tyll mans syght.
Swa fayre a syght bifore was never sene   H f. 249ᵛᵇ
Als sall be þan, ne swa clene,
When ilka body þat sall be save
Swa mykell bryghtnes þare sall have.   7915
For if a man had eghen swa bryght
And if swa moght be, swa mykell syght
Als has all þe creatures lyfand,
Yhit moght he noght, als I understand,
Ogayne swa mykell bryghtnes loke   7920
Als a body sall have; þus says þe boke.
Bot þe dampned bodyse þare-ogayne   *Of þe shenshipe of*
Sall be foule and stynkand als carayne,   *fou⟨l⟩nes þat þe*
And full myrk and dym sall þai be   *d⟨amp⟩ned bodye sal*
                                                            haue
And full hydus and wlatsom to se.   7925
For swa foul a syght saw never man
Als þe dampned bodyse sall be þan,

7902 appropried] appropred A*b*   *þe] þa H   7918 has] had Morris (Lightbown)

þat with þe saules sall dwell in hell depe.
þis sall to þam be payne and schendschepe.

Of þe blisse of swiftnes   þe secund blys after es swyftnes   7930
þat ilk body sall have þat ryghwise es.
For in les while þan a man may wynke,
þai sall mow fleghe whider þai will thynk,
With body and saule togyder thurgh flyght,
Fra heven tyll erth and ogayne ryght   7935
And fra þe ta syde of þe world wyde,
If þai wyld, tyll þe tother syde.
And whider swa þai þair thoght will sett
Nathyng þam sall ogayne-stand ne lett.
þis may þai do withouten travayle,   7940
And þis swyftnes sall never fayle,
For als þe lyght of þe son thurgh strenthe
May fleghe fra þe est tyll þe west on lenthe,
Ryght swa þai may, whyder þai will fleghe,
In a schort twynkellyng of ane eghe.   7945
For þai sall be als swift þan
Als any thoght es here of man.

Of þe contrary of þat blisshe, þat es shenshipe of heuynes þat þe synful sal haf in helle   Bot þe synfull bodyse sall evermare
On a contrary manere fare.
þai sall be swa hevy, charged with syn   7950
Both withouten and within,
þat þai sall have no myght to stand
Ne unnethes to styr fote ne hand
Ne yhit nane other lym of body;
þair syn sall weghe on þam swa hevy.   7955

iij. Of þe blisshe of strengthe þat þe rightwyse sal haf   þe thred blys es strenthe and myght
þat þe ryghtwise bodyse sall have thurgh ryght.
For þof þai feble here and wayke ware,
Swa mykell myght þai sall have þare
H f. 250ra   And swa mykell strenthe ay-lastand   7960
þat nathyng sall mow ogayne þam stand—
Swa þat þai sall mow remowe at þair will
Ilka mountayne and ilka hill
þat ever was in þe world sene,
And if þai wild, all þe erth bidene,   7965
Withouten any ogayne-standyng

7947 es here] *trs.* A, *cf.* Als is þe thoght of ony man L

Or any lettyng of anythyng,
And in þat dede have no mare swynk
þan a man has here to loke or wynk.
Bot þe synfull bodyse, þat dampned sall be,   7970   *Of þe contrary*
Sall be swa wayke and swa feble to se
þat þai sall unnethes mow stand
Ne myght have anes to lyft þair hand
To wype þe teres fra þare eghen oway,
And þat waykenes sall last with þam ay.   7975

  þe ferth blys allswa es fredome   *iiij. Of þe blisse of*
þat þe saved bodyse sall have þat sall come   *fredom*
Tyll heven, whare alkyn ioyes er,
To do what þai will withouten daunger.
Forwhi þai sall never fele na thyng   7980
Bot þat at sall be at þair lykyng,
And nathing sall þam warn ne lett
To do þair will, whareswa it es sett.
For all thing tyll þam sall be boghand,
And nathing sall ogayne þam stand,   7985
Ne ogayns þam nathing be sett,
þair will ne þair purpose to lett—
Nowther iren ne stele, stane ne tre,
Ne noght elles, swa fre þai sall be.
þai sall mow passe ay whare þai will   7990
And all þair lykyng þan fullfyll.
þis fredom and þis fraunches
Sall be appropried tyll þe saved bodys
With þe saules of þam þat God sall chese,
And þis fredom þai sall never lese,   7995
Bot on contrary manere ogayne þat blys,   *Of þe contrary of þis*
þe dampned bodyse sall fredom mys.   *blisse, þat es shenshipe of*
For þai sall be stresced in hell als thrall   *thraldom*
And all þat may greve thole withall;
þai sall be chaced ogayne þair will   8000
Tyll all manere of thing þat es ill.
þus sall þai in hell in thraldom be,
Fra whilk þai may nevermare fle.

7973 lyft] lyfe R, stere L   7988 iren] men Morris   stane] ne stane Morris
(Lightbown)   7989 þai sall] *trs.* Morris (Lightbown)   7993 appropried] apropred
AM, propyrd L

v. Of þe blisse of hele þe fyft blys, als clerkes wate wele,

Es hele þat þe saved bodyse sall fele, 8005

Withouten seknes or grevaunce

Or angre or payne or penaunce.

H f. 250rb For ivell ne payne sall never þam greve,

Bot in hele and lykyng þai sall ay leve

In heven with ioy on ilka syde, 8010

For þare sall þai be glorifyde.

Of þe contrary of þat blisse, þat es shenshipe of anguys and yuels Bot þe dampned bodyse on other wyse

Sall have strang yvels and angwyse,

Als saules has þat in purgatory dwels

For certayne tyme, als þe boke tels. 8015

Bot swa lang lastes no sekenes þare

Als in hell, for þat lastes evermare;

For purgatory, als wryten es,

Has ende, and hell es endeles.

vj. Of þe blisse of del⟨ite⟩ þe sext blys es þe gret delyte 8020

þat þe saved bodyse sall have swa parfyte

þat no man lyfand kan ne may

Swa mykell yhern here, nyght ne day.

For here moght never man far swa wele,

With swa mykell delyte, als þai sall fele 8025

In all þair wittes, ne swa mykell ioy have,

Als God on þam sall þan vouchesave.

þai sall have swa mykell ioy þare

þat nane of þam sall desyre mare.

For als þe iren þat es glowand 8030

Thurgh strenthe and hete brynand,

Semes better to be fyre-bryght

þan iren, als tyll any mans syght,

Right swa þa þat in heven sall won

Sall seme bryghter þan fyre and schyne als son 8035

And be fullfyld ay in þat place

Of þe luf of God and of his grace

And of all delyces and ioy and blys,

þe whilk þai sall nevermare mys.

And als men here oft has sene 8040

þat a vessell dypped alle bidene

In water or in other lycour thyn,

Be þe vessell never swa wyde wythin,
Has water bath within and without,
Binethen, oboven, and all obout, 8045
And na mare water within may hald,
Ne nane other thing þat lycoure es cald,
Right swa þe ryghtwise sall have ioy, mare
þan þai may think or yhern þare.
Bot þe dampned bodyse ogaynward 8050 *Of þe contrary of þat blisse, þat es shenshipe of sere paynes*
Sall in hell fele [s]trang payne and hard,
For þai sall bryn in fyre ilkane,
þat sall be menged with bronstane
Full hate brynand, and with pyk
And with other thing þat es wyk, 8055
Omang vermyn þat sall þam byte, *H f. 250ᵛᵃ*
And devels þat ay sall þam smyte,
With other payns strang and fell,
Ma þan hert may thynk or tong tell.

þe sevend blys es endeles lyfe 8060 *vij. Of þe blisse of endeles lyf*
þat þe saved sall have, withouten stryfe,
Evermare in heven swa heghe.
For þai sall ay lyf and never deghe
And with God allmyghty þare ay won,
þat es sothfast Fader and sothfast Son 8065
And þe Haly Gast in Trinite,
And in þat lyfe his face þai sall ay se.
Now if a man moght lyf here
In þis world a thowsand yhere,
Yhit suld his lyfe be broght tyll ende 8070
And fra þis world bihoved him wende.
þan suld him thynk, and he toke kepe,
His lyfe noght bot als a dreme in slepe.
þan suld þe lenthe of all his lyfe-days
Seme bot als a day, als þe prophet says: 8075
Quoniam mille anni ante oculos tuos, tanquam
dies hesterna que preterijt.
He says þus, 'Lord, a thowsand yhere
Bifor þine eghen', þat all thyng sese here,
At þe last 'es noght bot als yhisterday, 8080

*8051 strang payne] payns strang H, payn (paynes M) full *b* Morris (Lightbown) 8076 tanquam] tanquum Morris 8079 sese] *possibly* sefe H 8072 þan] Yhit

þat was a while and es passed oway'.
þus when þis lyfe tyll ende es broght,
All þe tyme of it semes als noght;
þan es a day mare in heven swa clere
þan here er many thowsand yhere,   8085
And many thowsand yheres here es les
þan þare a day, als þe boke bers witnes.
þan sall þe lyf be als lang þare
Als þat day lastes, and þat es evermare,
For þare es ay day and never nyght;   8090
þarfor þe prophet says þus ryght:
    Melior est dies una in atrijs
    tuis super milia.
He says, 'Loverd, better es a day lastand
In þi halles þan a thowsand',   8095
þat es, better es in heven a day,
þan a thowsand here þat passes oway.
For all þe days þat here may fall
Passes oway, and þis lyf withall,
And in a day in heven sall be contende   8100
þe tyme þat never sall have ende.
þan sall þat day, als þe boke us leres,
Pass many hundreth thowsand yheres.
And als [lang] in hell sall be nyght,
Als day sall be in heven bryght,   8105
For als men in heven sall ay day se,
Ryght swa sall nyght ay in hell be.
þus sall day in heven be contende,
And nyght in helle, withouten ende.
    Bot se we noght how schort a day es here   8110
To regard of a hundreth yhere?
Yhit es a hundreth yhere les
To regard of þe tyme þat es endeles,
For saint Austyn telles in a sarmon
þat a day here may be a porcyon   8115
Of ane hundreth yhere, als men may se,
All-if þat porcyon full lytell be.
Bot þe space of ane hundreth yhere es

H f. 250vb

8086 es] er RAL, *couplet om.* M   *8104 lang] *om. c*   8110 se we] *trs.* R, *om.*
phrs. b

Na porcyon of endelesnes,
For if a thowsand yhere, þat es mare   8120
Of endlesnes a porcyon ware,
After a thowsand thowsand yheres to kast,
Endlesnes suld sese þan at þe last.
And þat will noght þe reson of endelesnes
Suffer þat it be shorter þan it es,   8125
For if endlesnes any end moght hald,
þan war it endlesnes unproperly cald.
Bot in þat endlesnes es contende
All + tyme þat may have nane ende,
And lyfe in heven sall als lang be   8130
Als men sall tyme þare withouten ende se.
þan semes it wele, als I sayd are,
þat lyfe sall be þare evermare.
    Wharfor ilk man with hert stedfast
Suld seke þat lyfe þat ay sall last,   8135
þe whilk ilk man may lyghtly wyn,
þat here lyfes wele and will fle syn.
And leve noght þat lyf þat lastes ay
For þis lyfe here þat passes oway,
For þat lyfe es syker, and swa es noght þis.   8140
þat lyfe es swa full of ioy and blys
þat a man sall thynk þare a hundreth yhere
In þat lyfe schorter þan a day here.
Till þat ioyfull lyf may all men com
þat meke of hert er here, and bowsom.   8145
þus sall endles lyfe appropryed be
Tyll þe saved bodyse þat ay God sall se.
    Bot þe dampned þat tyll hell sall wende,   *Of þe contrary of*
Sall have ded þare withouten ende,   *þat, [þat] es þe ded*
And þat ded sall ay new þam gryefe.   *withouten ende*
[And] in þat ded þai sall ay lyefe   8150
And swa be pyned, in þair wyttes fyve,   H f. 251ᵣₐ
þat þair lyfe sall seme mare ded þan lyve.
þai sall seme, whether þai lyg or stand,
Als men in transyng, ay deghand;   8155
þai sall ay deghand lyf and lyfand dyghe,

8122 thowsand²] *om.* R*b*   *8129 All] All þe H, A L   8146 appropryed]
apropred A*b*   8148 sidenote þat²] *om.* A   *8151 And] *om.* H

And evermare payns of ded þus dryghe,
And þarewith be tourmented ay omang,
With other bytter payns and strang.
þarfor þe lyfe in hell may be cald   8160
þe secund ded – + swa may we it hald.
þan may þai say, þat sall lyf þare,
'Allas' þat ever moder þam bare.

   Here have I tald, als yhe moght here,
Of seven manere of blysses sere,   8165
þat þe saved bodyse sall have thurgh ryght
With þe saules in heven bryght,
And of þe seven schendschepes allswa
þat er even contrary tyll þa,
þe whilk þe bodyse in hell sall have ay,   8170
þat sall be dampned at domesday.

   Bot I will schew yhow yhit withall
Seven manere of blysses, þat sall fall
Tyll þe saules namely with þe bodyse,
Of all þe men þat er gude and ryghtwise,   8175
þat sall be saved at þat tyde
And in heven be gloryfyde;
And yhit seven schendschepes will I neven
þat er even contrary tyll þa seven,
þe whilk sall fall, withouten ende,   8180
Tyll þ[e] saules of þe synfull þat sall wende
With þe bodyse, untyll hell-pytt,
Als es fonden in Haly Wrytt.

j. Of þe blys of wisdom
þat þe saule sal haue
in heuen
                         þe fyrst blys þat þe saules sall have
                         Of ryghtwyse men þat sall be save   8185
Es wisdom, for þai sall knaw and se
Alle þat was and es and þat yhit sall be.
þai sall have knawyng of God fully
And of þe myght of þe Fader allmyghty;
þai sall knaw þe wytt of þe Son, and taste,   8190
And þe gudenes of þe Haly Gaste.
þus sall þair knawyng parfyte be
In all þe haly Trinite.
þai sall knaw all thing and wytt

*8161 ded] ded and H   8169 er] es Morris (Lightbown)   *8181 þe] þa H
8187 þat²] om. Morris (Lightbown)

þat God has done and sall do yhit,   8195
In heven, in hell, and in erth aywhare.
þus wise þai sall be evermare,
For þai sall have swa mykell grace,
When þai se God face to face,
þat nathyng, þat God ever dyd,   8200 H f. 251rb
Sall be layned fra þam ne hyd,
þat es to say, of þat God vouches save,
þat any creature knawyng may have.
    For saint Austyn, þat mykell couth of clergy,
Says in a sarmon þat he made openly   8205 *Augustinus*
þat in þe syght of God þat þai sall se,
Thre manere of knawyng tyll þam sall be.
For þai sall se him þare, both God and man,
And þamself þai sall se in him þan,
And all men and all thing, less and mare.   8210
þai sall se and knaw in þat syght þare
Als we may thre thynges se here
In a myroure of glas þat es clere:
Ane es þe myrour þat bifor us es,
Aneother es our awene face and lyknes,   8215
And þe thred we may þarin se yhit,
þat es all thyng þat es onence it.
    Right swa men sall se God als he es,
In þe myroure of his bryghtnes,
Als properly als possible may be   8220
Tyll any creature him to se.
þai sall se þamself in him so bryght
And all men togyder, at a syght,
And all other thyng þai sall knawe
And se overall, both hegh and lawe.   8225
All men þan sall se þat þare sall dwell,
All þe creatures in heven and hell.
þare sall be schewed þan tyll þam apertly
Sere privetese of God allmyghty,
þat na man here moght knaw ne wytt   8230
Thurgh clergy ne thurgh Haly Wrytt.
þat es, how God invysible es
And unchaungeable and endles;
And how he was bifor all thing

And withouten any bigynyng;   8235
And how and whi he sall be
Withouten ende, þai sall þan se.
    All thyng þat now es fra þam hyd
Sall þan tyll þam be knawen and kyd.
þai sall þan se þare openly   8240
Of all thynges þe skyll and þe cause whi,
Als whi ane es chosen here and taken,
And ane-other left and forsaken;
Whi ane es uptane tyll a kyngdom,
And ane-other es putted intyll thraldom;   8245
And whi som childer er ded and lorn
In þair moder wambe, ar þai be born.
þai sall knaw allswa, withouten drede,
Skyll whi som deghes in þair barnhede,
And som after when þai mast strenthe weld;   8250
And whi som lyfes tyll þair mast eld.
þai sall yhit sertaine skyll se þan
Whi som er born in fayre schap of man,
And som in uncomly stature;
And whi som er ryche here, and som pore,   8255
And whi som childer geten in hordom
Er baptized, and has Cristendom,
And som þat er in lele wedlayk born
Ar þai be cristend, er ded and lorn.
And whi som by[gy]nnes to be stedfast   8260
To lyfe wele and endes ill at þe last,
And whi som has here ill bigynyng
And at þe last, mase a gud endyng.
Of þir thynges and of other many
þe skylls sall be knawen þan openly   8265
In þe boke of lyfe þat open sall be,
þe whilk es þe syght of þe Trinite.
þus sall all men, þat in heven þan dwelles,
Knaw and witt, als saint Austyn telles,
And in þe bryghtnes of God openly se   8270
All thing þat ever was or yhit sall be,
And all þe soth of ilk thyng and skyll,

HÂ f. 251va [marginal note aligned with line "þai sall knaw allswa, withouten drede,"]

Als ferforth als God vouches safe and will.
   þare sall ilk man als wele knaw other
Als a man here knawes hys syster or brother,   8275
And wyt of what contre þai ware,
And wha þam gatt and wha þam bare.
Ilkane sall knaw þan other[s] thoght
And all þe dedes þat þai ever wroght;
þus wyse sall þai be þat sall come   8280
Tyll þe kyngdom of heven after þe dome.
þai sall be Godes sons and till him lyke
And be made his heyres of hevenryke
And be all als godes of gret myght,
Als þe prophete in þe Psauter says ryght: 8285
   Ego dixi, 'Dij estis et
   filij excelsi omnes'.
He says, 'I sayd, "yhe er godes all,
And Godes sons"'' men sall yhow call.
Wharfore it semes þat when þai com   8290
Tyll heven, þai sall be full of wysdom
And full of myght, lastand evermare,
When þai sall all be als godes þare.
   Bot now may þou ask me and lere
A questyon, and say on þis manere: 8295
'Sall þai oght think, þat sall be safe,   H f. 251vb
On þe syns of whilk þai þam schrafe
Here in þair lyfe and made þam clene,
And of þam assoyled has bene?'
Saint Anselme [þus] answers to þis   8300
And says, + 'þou þat sall have heven-blys,
Sall love God and thank him þare
Of all gudes, both les and mare,
þat he has done tyll þe here
And tyll all other, on þe same manere,   8305
þe whylk at þe day of dome sall be safe
And with þe endles blys sall have.
Gret gud he dose þe, whils þou lyfes,
When he þi syns þe here forgyfes;

8273 vouches] vouche RA, *couplet om. b*   *8278 others] other *cb*   *8300 þus]
om. HM, *cf.* answers] answers þus L   *8301 þou] þat þou *c, cf.* to 30w L   8305 on]
of RA

How moght þou þan, with hert fre,   8310
Thank God of þat þat he has forgyfen þe,
All þe syns þat þou has wroght,
If þou moght thynk on nane in thoght'?
 Bot þou sall þis understand wele,
þat na mare grevance sall þou fele,   8315
Ne na mare payne have ne myslykyng,
When þou has of þi syns meneyng,
þan he has, þat somtyme had in stryfe
A sare wound with swerd or knyfe,
þat parfytely es haled and wele,   8320
Of whilk he may na mare sa[r]e fele.
And als þou now has na schame of þe dede
þat þou dyd in þi barnhede,
Or þat þou dyd in þi dronkennes,
Of whilk tyll þe now na schame es,   8325
Na mare schame sall þou þan have in thoght
Of þi syns þat þou here has wroght,
Of whilk þou ert here schryven parfytely
And þat God has forgyfen here thurgh mercy.
And na mare þan Petre now has schame   8330
Of þat, þat he forsoke our Lord bi name;
Or Mary Maudelayne now has of hir syn
þat scho somtyme delyted hir in,
Na mare schame sall men þan have
Of þair syn here done, þat sall be save.   8335
Bot forþi þat God, þat boght us fre,
Wyld, thurgh his mercy and his pete,
And couth, thurgh his awen wytt clere,
And myght wele, thurgh his awen powere,
Swa gret syns þam frely forgyfe   8340
And þa woundes ha[l]e þat war gryfe,
Wharethurgh þai had deserved wele
þe pyne of hell evermare to fele,
H f. 252ʳᵃ   þarfor þai sall luf him þe mare
And þe mare him love and thank þare,   8345
And als wele for other mens trispas

8315 sall þou] trs. AL, line rewritten M 8317 þi] þis A *8321 sare] sale H,
Morris's emendation 8327 þi] þe Morris 8341 þa] þe Morris *hale] haue H, hele
(with rewriting) M, Morris's emendation

And other mens syn þat he heled has,
Als for þair awen þat þai wroght here.
þarfor says David on þis manere:
   Misericordias Domini   8350
   in eternum cantabo.
He says, 'I sall þe mercyes syng
Of our Loverd ay, withouten cesyng'.
And swa sall all syng withouten ende,
þat tyll þe blys of heven sall wende;   8355
And swa moght þai on nane wise syng,
Warn þai had of þair syns meneyng,
þat þai had done here bodily
And God forgaf thurgh his mercy.
þus sall þe saule be full of wysdom þare   8360
And all thing knaw and se, als I sayd are.

  Bot þe saules þat with þe bodyse sall synk   *Of þe contrary of þat blisse*
Intyll hell, sall on na gud thynk,
Ne have witt ne knaw ne fele
Na dede þat ever was done wele.   8365
Bot on þair payns sall be all þair thoght
And on þair syns þat þai had wroght;
For þai sall on nathyng have meneyng
Bot anely on þair awen wicked lyfyng
And on þair sorow withouten ende   8370
And on þair wrechednes þat sall þam schende,
þe whilk þai sall ay bifor þam se,
And þat syght tyll þam schendschepe sal be.

  þe secund blys þat þe saule sall fele
With þe bodyse, als þir clerkes wate wele,   8375
Sall be frendschepe and parfyte love,
þat es mare þan ever man moght + prove.
For ilkane sall mare luf other þan,   *Of þe blisse of frendship and parfite luf þat þe saule sal haf in heuen*
þan ever lufed here any man,
And als parfytely and als lang   8380
Als he sall luf himself omang.
And þat luf sall be fested swa fast
þat it sall never fayle, bot ay last,

8354 syng] thyng A, *om.* b   8359 forgaf] *adds* þam R, *adds* here L   8377 moght] *add* here *c, add in* herth *b*   *At this point, M lacks eight leaves and lines 8396–9062; to that point, we offer readings of As instead, and* b *represents the agreement of LAs*

For als ilka lym of a body
Lufes all þe other lyms kyndely   8385
And yhernes ay gretly þair hele,
Swa parfyte þat luf sall be and lele.
For þai sall all be of ane assent
And of a will and of ane entent,
For þai sall be þan all als a body   8390
In sere lyms, and als a saule anely;

H f. 252rb And God þair heved sall be þare,
þat sall þam luf als mykell or mare,
Als dose þe heved of þe body þat loves
þe lyms kyndely þat on it moves.   8395
þat clere luf and þat alliance
Sall nevermare fayle thurgh na distance,
Ne thurgh stryfe þat man may make
þat band of luff sall never slake.

Of þe contrary of þat   Bot even þe contrary sall men se   8400
blisse, þat es hatreden Omang þe saules þat dampned sall be,
and enuy   For þai sall be full of felony,
Of hatred, of wreth, and of envy,
Swa þat ilkane w[i]ld with other fyght
And strangell other, if þai myght.   8405
þus sall þai hate and stryfe ilkane,
For pese sall be omang þam nane,
Ne rest ne eese ne worschepe,
Bot travayle and pyne and schendschepe.
Bot God allmyghty, and allswa all his   8410
þat with him sall dwell in heven-blis,
Sall þam in sorow and pyne se
And of þam þai sall have na pete,
Bot hate þam als Godes enmyse.
And þat hateredyn sall þan be ryghtwise,   8415
For þe fader, þat þan sall be save,
Na pete of þe son þare sall have,
þat sall be dampned tyll hell-payne;
Ne þe son, þat sall be saved þare-ogayne,
Sall have na reuthe ne na pyte   8420
Of þe fader þat dampned sall be;

8398 man] men AL   8403 of³] om. AL, in As   *8404 wild] wald HM, sall will L
8405 myght] aught A

Ne þe moder, on þe same manere,
Of þe doghter þat scho lufed here;
Ne þe doghter of þe moder na mare;
Ne þe brother of þe syster þare;   8425
Ne þe syster of þe brother.
Nane of þam sall have reuthe of other,
Ne nane other, þat sall be saved þan,
Sall have reuthe ne pete of dampned man.
    Bot when þe ryghtwyse þe synfull sall se   8430
Pyned in hell, glad þai sall be,
For twa skyls, and ioyfull and fayne.
Ane es forþi þat þai er skaped þat payne;
Aneother es forþi þat Godes vengeance
Es ryghtwise, and his ordinance.   8435
þis proves þe prophete, als þe boke schewes us,
þare he says in þe Psauter þus:
    Letabitur iustus, cum
    viderit vindictam [Domini].
He says þat ilka ryghtwyse man   8440 H f. 252ᵛᵃ
Full glad and blyth sall he be þan,
When þai Godes vengeance se
On þe synfull, þat þan dampned sall be.
    þe thred blys, als men may in boke rede,   *iij. Of þe blis of acorde*
Es veray acord and anehede   8445 *and anhede þat falles to*
þat þe saules sall have in heven, togyder   *þe saule*
With þe bodyse, when þai com þider,
For ilkane sall folow others will,
And ilkane othe[r]s lykyng fullfyll.
And als þine ane eghe folows ryght   8450
þe tother, þare it settes þe syght,
And nouther may turne, hyder ne þider,
Bot þai both ay turne togyder,
Ryght swa sall God acord with all his,
And ilkane with other in þat blys.   8455
And to what thyng þe saule has talent,
To þat þe body sall ay assent;
And whatswa God þan will be done
To þat þai sall assent allsone;

*8439 Domini] *om.* cAs   8441 he] *om.* Morris (Lightbown)   *8449 others]
othes H, oþer b, Morris's emendation

And what thyng swa þai þan will,   8460
þat sall God als-tyte fullfyll.
þis acorde and anehede sall never ceese,
Bot evermare last with rest and peese.
All sall þai be al[s] ane in company
And als a saule and a body.   8465

Of þe contrary of þat blisse   Bot þe dampned þare-ogayne sall stryve,
Ilkane with other, for þair wicked lyve.
For ilkane sall hate other þan,
And ilkane sall wery other and ban;
Ilkane sall yherne with other to fyght,   8470
And ilkane wald sla other if þai myght.
þe body sall hate þe saule bi skylle,
For þe saule here thoght ay þe ill;
þe saule sall ay hate þe body,
For þe body wroght þe foly.   8475
And forþi þat þe saule fyrst syn thoght
And þe body it afterward wroght
And wyld noght leve ne stand þare-ogayne,
Untyll þe ded þe body had slayne,
þarfore bath togyder sall dwell,   8480
Withouten ende in þe pyne of hell.

iiij. Of þe blisse of powere þ⟨at⟩ falles to þe saule   þe ferth blys, omang þe tother all,
þat to þe saules with þe bodyse sall fall,
þe whilk sall be saved, es powere.
For þai sall þare have, both fer and nere,   8485
Swa mykell power and maistry
And lordschip, and be swa myghty

H f. 252ᵛᵇ   þat all thyng þan sall be done
At þair will, hastily and sone,
And whatswa þai will think in thoght,   8490
All sall be at þair will þare wroght.
For all thing sall be tyll [þam] boghand,
And nathyng sall ogayne þam stand,
For God sall fullfyll all þair lykyng
And folow þair will in all thing.   8495
þus sall þai haue þare gret powere

---

*8464 als] all c, om. phrase L, cf. in one As   8471 wald] wild A, om. couplet L
8482 tother] other RA, om. line L   *8492 þam] om. H, Morris's emendation

And heghnes for þare + gret lawnes here,
þat þai had in þare lyfe-days.
And þarfor God in þe gosspell says:
   Qui se humiliat   8500
   exaltabitur.
He says, 'Whaswa here lawes him ryght,
He sall be heghed' in heven bryght.
Bot þe dampned þare-ogayne halely
Sall want alkyn power and maistry,   8505
And þarewith þai sall tharne all thing
Of whilk men moght have lykyng.
þai sall be ay in gret dred and awe
And underfote ay be halden lawe;
þai sall have nathyng at þair wille,   8510
Bot all thing þat sall lyke þam ill.
Mykell sorow þam sall þan bityde
For þair heghenes here and þair pryde,
Als þe bok says þat bers wytnes,
And als in þe same gosspell wryten es: 8515
   Qui se exaltat hu-
   miliabitur.
þat es, 'Whaswa heghe here will him bere,
He sall be lawed' and putted in daungere,
þat es in gret daunger of fendes,   8520
In pyne of helle, þat never endes.
  þe fyft blys þat sall fall alswa
To þe saules, þat with þe bodyse sall ga
Tyll hevenryke, es honoure and worschepe,
Of whilk God himself sall tak kepe.   8525
For þai sall have þare sere honoures
And be coround, als kynges and emperoures,
And sytt in setyls schynand bryght
With alkyn nobelay, rychely dyght.
With bryghtnes of lyght þai sall be cled,   8530
And gret reverence þam sall be bed,
And be honourd als Godes frendes dere
For þe worschepe þat þai dyd him here
In gud werkes, þat tyll him war swete.

Of þe contra⟨ry⟩ of þat blisse, þat `es` tharnyng of alle likyng

v. Of þe bli⟨sse⟩ of þe honour þat þe saule sal receyue in heuen

8497 for] of RAs   *þare] þare awen H, om. phrase L   8498 in] in alle AAs
8506 þai] þat Morris   8508 be ay] trs. Morris (Lightbown)

þarfor þus says David þe prophete: 8535

H f. 253ra   *Nimis honorati sunt*
                        amici tui, Deus.

'þi frendes, Loverd', þat honourd þe
'Er mykell honourd' and swa ay sall be.
Bot þe dampned, þat with syn er fyled,   8540
þare-ogayne sall be revyled
And despysed and ay schent withall
And stresced ogayne þair will als thrall
And pyned with gretter payns sere
þan ever was sene in þis world here.   8545
þai sall [thole] all thyng þat schendschepe es
With payne and sorow þat es endles,
Omang hete and cald, vermyn and stynk,
And alkyn fylth þat hert may think.
And all þe sorow þat þai sall fele   8550
Sall be endles, als þai sall knaw wele.

vj. Of þe blisse   þe sext blys þat to the saules of ryghtwise
of sykernes   Sall be appropryed þan, with þe bodyse
In þe kyngdom of heven, es sykernes
To dwell ay þare whare alkyn ioy es.   8555
For þai sall be þare syker and certayne
To have endeles ioy, and nevermare payne,
And to won ay þare, withouten dout,
Withouten lettyng and putting out,
And withouten all manere of drede,   8560
For of nathyng þare þai sall have nede.
þai sall noght far, als men fares here,
þat lyfes ay in dred and were.
For here both kyng and emperoure
Has dred to tyne þair honoure,   8565
And ilka ryche man has dred allswa
His gudes and ryches to forga,
And ilk man, þat here fares wele,
Has ay dred angers to fele.
Bot þai þat sall com tyll heven-blys   8570

8536 Nimis] Omnis Morris   8539 Er] Es Morris (Lightbown)   *8546 thole]
om. H, *Morris's emendation*   8550 þat þai] *trs.* Morris (Lightbown)
8553 appropryed] appropred AAs, *om. line* L   *W returns at 8572*

Sall never have dred þat ioy to mys,
For þai sall be syker inoghe þare,
þat þair ioy sall last evermare.

   Bot þe dampned men þare-ogayne,
Sall ay be dredand in þair payne,   8575
þat þair payns suld eked be
And be made mare grevous to se.
For þe devels sall ay on þam gang
To and fra, overth[w]ert and endlang;
And omang þam ay ymagyne   8580
How þai may eke þair sorow and pyne;
And þe mare payne þat þai till synfull sall seke,
þe mare þai þair awen payne sall eke.
And, if þai do swa, it es na ferly,
For þai er ay full of ire and envy.   8585
þe devels sall ay opon þam gang,
And ay on þam stamp with þair feth omang
And threst þam doune in fyre and smoke,
And þarfor says Iob þus in a boke:
   Vadent et venient super   8590
   eos horribiles.
He says, 'Grysely devels sall gang and com
On þe synfull', þat tyll God war unbowsom.
þus dredand sall þai ay be þare,
þat þair payne suld be ay mare and mare;   8595
For þai sall be certayne þare þai dwell,
þat þai sall never com out of hell.

   þe sevend blys es ioy parfyte
þat þe saules sall have, with gret delyte,
With þe bodyse þat saved sall be,   8600
And won in heven, whare þai sall ay God se.
Forwhi ilkane [s]all þare þat tyde
In body and saule be gloryfyde,
And full ioy and blys have withall,
With all manere of delyces þat may fall.   8605
Ilkane with other sall be knawen
And fele other mens ioy als þair awen,
And mare ioy and blys moght never be

Of þe contrary of þat blisse, þat es drede (at 8573)

H f. 253rb (at 8584)

vij. Of þe bli⟨sse⟩ of ioye parfite (at 8598)

---

*8579 overthwert] ouerthewrt H   8587 feth] fete R*ab   8591 eos] eos demones
As, *Morris's silent insertion*   *8602 sall þare] trs. c,* þere As

þan ilkane sall þare on other se.
þai sall se, in hevenryke swa wyde,   8610
Many sere ioyes on ilka syde,
For þare sall be ma sere ioyes þan
þan ever couth noumbre erthly man,
Of whilk syght þai sall mare ioy have
þan any man moght yhern or crave.   8615
Ilkane sall be payed swa wele
Of his part of ioy þat he sall fele,
þe whilk he sall parfytely have þare,
þat he sall willen yhern no mare.
þare sall ilkane many thowsandes se   8620
In sere ioyes, als himself sall be,
And þe syght of ilka ioy þan
Sall be swa delytable till ilka man
þat þe ioy of a syght þare sall pas
All þe ioyes þat ever in erth was.   8625
And all þat tyll heven sall be tane
Sall þare þan se þa ioyes ilkane,
And þe syght of ilka ioy þare sall be
Ioy tyll ilka man þat it sall se.
þan sall ilk man have ma ioyes in heven   8630
þan hert may thynk, or tong kan neven;
H f. 253ᵛᵃ   þai sall have ioy, within and without,
Oboven, benethe, and all obout.
Oboven þam þai sall have ioy fully
Of þe syght of God allmyghty;   8635
Binethe þam, of þe sternes and planetes sere
And þe world þat þan sall be bryght and clere;
Obou[t]en þam, of heven, þat þai bryght sall se,
And of other creatures þat fair sall be;
Within þam, of þe glorifying of man,   8640
Of þe body and saule togyder þan;
Withouten þam, of þe blysfull companyse
Of aungels and of men ryghtwise.
Of þe ioyes þat men sal   þai sall have ioy in alle þair wittes
haf in þair fyf wittes   In heven with God þare he syttes.   8645
First þai sall se with þair eghen bryght
Many a fayre blysfull syght;

þai sall þare God apertly se
And all þe thre persons in Trinite,
þe Fader, and Son, and Haly Gaste;   8650   *Of þe ioy of þe sight of*
þat sight sall be þair ioy maste.   *God and þe Trinite*
For als he es, þai sall him se þan,
Sothfast God and sothfast man,
Thurgh whilk syght þai sall knaw
And se all thing, both heghe and law,   8655
And all þe werkes þat ever God wroght,
And ilk mans dede and ilk mans thoght,
And all þat sall in hell be þan,
Ilka devell and ilka man,
And all [þe] payns þat sall be þare,   8660
þai sall se þan, both les and mare;
And all erth and þe hevens obout
And all þat es, within and without.
All sall þai se, thurgh myght and grace,
In þe bryghtnes of Godes face,   8665
Of whilk þai sall evermare have syght,
þat þe mast ioy es in heven bryght.
And for þai sall ay þus God bihald,
þai sall knaw all thyng þat þai knaw wald.
In þis lyfe here men sese him noght   8670
Bot anely thurgh ryght trowth in thoght,
Als thurgh a myroure be lyknes,
Bot þare sall men se him als he es.
Here men him sese gastly thurgh grace,
Bot þare sall men se him face tyll face,   8675
And þat syght þare sall all men have
Withouten ende, þat sall be save.
   þai sall allswa se þare apertly   *Of þe ioy of ⟨þ⟩e sight*
His blysfull moder saint Mary   *⟨of⟩ our le⟨u⟩edy*
þat next syttes God in heven bryght   8680   H f. 253vb
Oboven alle aungels, als es ryght;
For he chese hir tyll his moder dere
And of hir toke flessch and blode here
And vouched safe to souke [of] hir brest,
þarfor it es ryght scho sytt him nest.   8685

8648 God apertly] *trs. a*   8656 And] And se Morris (Lightbown)   *8660 þe]
om. H   8661 þan] *om.* Morris (Lightbown)   *8684 of] *om.* H*b*

Scho es swa fayr þare scho syttes
þat hir fayrnes passes all mens wittes;
A gret ioy þa[re] may be cald
Hir fairnes anely to behald.

Of þe ioy of þe sight of
þe ordres of aungellesþai sall se þare, als þe boke telles,   8690
All þe neghen orders of aungels,
þat er swa fayre on to loke
And swa bryght, als says þe boke,
þat all [þe] fayrnes of þis lyfe here
þat ever was sene, fer or nere,   8695
þat any man myght ordayne defautles,
War noght a poynt to þat fairnes
þat þai sall se þar of þat syght
Of þe ordres of þe aungels bryght.
þai sall se þam full pleysand þan   8700
And servisabyll tyll God and man,
And ilkane ordre in þair degre
Sall do þat þat mast lykand sall be,
Bath tyll God and tyll man ryght.
A gret ioy sall be þare of þat syght,   8705
For ilkane aungell bi him ane
Sall clerer schyne þan ever son schane;
þat syght men may a gret ioy call
To se þe aungels swa bryght all,
þat in heven sall be sene togyder.   8710
þat syght sall all se þat sall com þider.
Swa fayre a syght als þat sall seme
Couth never na wytt here ymagyn ne deme.

Of þe ioy of þe sight of
halghes in heuenþai sall se in heven allswa
Patriarches and prophetes and other ma   8715
And apostels and evaungelistes,
þat folowd nane other lyf bot Cristes.
þai sall se innocentes many ane,
Of whilk som was in Godes name slane;
And other martyrs and confessours   8720
And haly heremytes and doctours,
þat Haly Wryt wald teche and ken;
And many other haly men,

*8688 þare] þat H, it L   8689 to] for to R, þere to As   *8694 þe] om. H
8696 man] om. R, men L

Lered and lewed, þat lyfed wele here,
Both religiouse and seculere.   8725
þai sall se haly virgyns þare
þat here lufed God, ay mare and mare,
And keped þam chast for Godes sake,   H f. 254ʳᵃ
Of whilk som wald þe ded for his luf take.
þai sall se þare in ioy and blys   8730
Other þat God sall chese for his,
Als wedded men þat lyfes wele here
And other many of states sere.
A fayr syght sall be þan to se,
Of all þe fayr folk þat þare sall be,   8735
þat bryghter sall schyne þan ever schane son;
þis syght sall all se þat þare sall won.
    þai sall [þare] allswa apertly se
Ilkane be worscheped in his degre
With gret nobelay, and have sere honours,   8740
And all be als kynges and emperours,
Coround with ryche corouns of blys;
A fulle delytabell syght sall be þis.
þai sall se þare þe gret medes,
þat men sall have þare for þair gud dedes,   8745
After ilkane of þam has lyfed here.
And þas er swa mykell and many and sere—
þat never ende sall have, bot last ay—
þat na man thurgh wytt mesure may
Ne þam reken ne tell þam kan;   8750
Swa many medes þai sall have þan.
þair medes sall be swa precyouse
And swa delitable and plentevouse
þat na man lyfand, als þe boke says,
Couth ne myght þam gesce ne prays.   8755
Bot þa medes sall lyke þam als wele
þat þam ceese, als þam þat sall þam fele.
    þai sall se heven full large and wyde
And round and even on ilka syde
And bryghter schynand þan ever schane son;   8760
Wele sall þam be þat þare sall won.

8732 lyfes] lyfed Morris (Lightbown)   *8738 þare] *om.* Hb, *cf.* also þare W
8748 sall] þai sall Morris (Lightbown)

A delitable syght þat sall be
Tyll þam þat sall dwell in þat contre.
þat contre swa fayre es on to loke
And swa bryght and brade, als says þe boke,   8765
þat all þis world, þare we won yhit,
War noght bot als a myddyng-pytt
To regard of þat contre swa brade,
þat God swa mykell and fayr has made.
þat contre es halden swa large a land   8770
þat within þe space of þat myght stand
Many a thowsand of werldes sere,
þof ilk world war als large als þis here.
And þat land es cald soveraynly
þe kyngdom of God allmyghty,   8775
H f. 254rb þe whilk es made als a cete,
Whare men sall many wonyng-stedes se,
þare all þe haly men sall dwell.
þarfor says Crist þus in þe gospell:
  Multe mansiones sunt,   8780
  in domo patris mei.
He says, 'Wonyng-stedes er many
In þe hows of my fader', God allmyghty.
Our Loverd his 'fader hous' calles
His kyngdom, þat till all his falles,   8785
þe whilk es als a cete bryght
With alkyn ryches dubbed and dyght,
Als says saint Iohan, Godes derlyng dere,
In þe *Apocalyps* on þis manere:
  Vidi sanctam civitatem Ierusalem novam
    descendentem   8790
  de celo, paratam sicut sponsam viro suo ornatam.
'I saw', he says, 'þe haly cete
Of Ierusalem, all new to se,
Comand doun fra heven bryght
Of God allmyghty rychely dyght   8795
Als bryde, made fayre tyll hir brydegome'.
þus says saint Iohan he saw [it] come.
  þis cete es for to understand

8776 als] alle als A   8780 mansiones sunt] *trs.* RA, sunt *after* mei As
8787 ryches] richesce A   *8797 it] him H

Haly Kyrk, þat here es fyghtand
Ogayne þe devell and his myght,   8800
þat it assayles, both day and nyght.
Bot þat fyght sall noght last ay;
It sall last no langer þan tyll domesday.
þan sall Haly Kyrk of fyghtyng cees
And be with God in rest and pees,   8805
For it es bryde, and God + þe brydegome;
þan sall þai both togyder come
And in heven won ay togyder,
And all þair childer sall þan com þider,
þat to þam has bene bowsom and trewe,   8810
And þat bitakens þe cete newe.
For þan sall Haly Kyrk þat tyde
In heven be new gloryfyde
And won ay þare with God allmyghty,
In ioy and myrthe and melody.   8815   *Ecclesia militaris*
Bot yhit Haly Kyrk, þat es Godes bryde,
Bihoves be fyghtand yhit, here to abyde
þe comyng of Crist þat es hir brydegome,
þat ay es myghty for to overcome.   *Ecclesia triumphans*
For Haly Kyrk fyghtes for Godes ryght,   8820
And God overcomes thurgh his myght.
    On twa wise may Haly Kyrk be tane,
And at þe last, sall bath be in ane.
On a manere es cald Haly Kyrk fyghtand;   H f. 254va
On ane-other es Haly Kyrk overcomand.   8825
þir clerkes says, als þe boke beres witnes,
þat Haly Kyrk þat here fyghtand es,
Es noght els bot a gaderyng
Of all Cristen men of lele lyfyng.
Haly Kyrk overcomand es allswa   8830
God with all þe company of þa
þat dwelles with him in his blys,
þe whilk he has hyght tyll all his.
Under Haly Kyrk, þat here fyghtand es,
Er all gud Cristen men, mare and les;   8835
Under Haly Kyrk þat es overcomand

8803 þan] bot R   8806 es] es þe RW   *þe] es þe H, es *b*, *om.* Morris (Lightbown)
8825 On] And on *ab*

Er all haly men in heven wonand.
Bot Haly Kyrk þat here fyghtes fast,
After þe day of dome at þe last,
In þe bryght cete in heven sall won   8840
Evermare with hir spowse, Godes Son.
For þan sall þe noumbre fullfyld be
Of all haly men in þat cete,
Thurgh Haly Kyrk þat es Godes spowse,
And þat cete Crist calles his faders howse.   8845
For þare sall all men þat er ryghtwise and haly
Evermare dwell in aungels company,
And ilkane sall have a blysfull wonyng
And ioy parfyte, withouten endyng.

Of þe cite of heuen   þis cete of heven þat es wyde and brade,   8850
Na man wate properly how it es made
Ne can thurgh wytt ymagyn in thoght
Of whatkyn matere it es wroght.
It es noght made of lyme ne stane
Ne of tre, for swilk matere has it nane,   8855
Als þir erthly cetese er made of here,
þat er made of corruptybell matere.
For nathyng falles to be in þat cete
þat corruptybell or fayland may be.
Bot þe matere þare-of [es], als I trow,   8860
+ Of alle thing þat es of gret vertow.
þis cete was never made with hand,
Bot thurgh þe myght and witt of God all-weldand.
þis cete contenes all hevenryke,
Bot nane wate proprely to what it es lyke.   8865
We fynd wryten þat it es fayre and bryght,
Bot na man kan descryve it ryght,
For swa wyse clerk was never of lyve
þat þe fairnes of it couth proprely descryve.
         Bot all-if I kan noght descryve þat stede,   8870
Yhit will I ymagyn on myne awen hede,

H f. 254vb   For to gyf it a descripcion,
For I have þareto full gret affeccyon,

8852 wytt] wrytt Morris (Lightbown)   8854 ne] and *a*L   8855 for] for of
Morris (Lightbown)   *8860 es] *om.* HL, *before* þareof As   *8861 Of] Es of HL
8868 of] on RW*b*   8873 full] *om.* Morris (Lightbown)

And gret comfort and solace it es to me
To thynk and spek of þat fayr cete.   8875
Þat travaile may greve me nathyng,
For þare-in have I gret lykyng.
Ogayne ryght trowth nathing I do,
If I lyken þe cete þat me langes to,
Þe whilk men may lyken on som party   8880
Bath to bodily thing and gastly.
And forþi þat all thing þat es clere and bryght
Es mast lykand here tyll bodily syght,
Þarfor I will it lyken till bodily thing,
Þat es fayre to syght, with gastly understandyng.   8885
    Þe bryght cete of heven es large and brade,
Of whilk may na comparyson be made
Till na cete þat on erth may stand,
For it was never made with mans hand.
Bot yhit als I ymagyn in my thoght,   8890
I lyken it tyll a cete þat war wroght
Of gold and of precyouse stanes sere
Opon a mote sett of beryll clere,
With walles and wardes and turrettes
And entre and yhates and garettes.   8895
And all þe walles war made, of þat cete,
Of precyouse stanes and ryche perre;
And all þe turrettes of cristall schene,
And þe wardes enamayld and overgylt clene,
And þe yhates of charbucles suld fall,   8900
And þe garettes oboven of rubys and curall.
And at þat cete had lanes and stretes wyde,
And fayr bygynges on ilka syde,
All schynand als gold bryght burnyst
And with alkyn ryches replenyst;   8905
And þat all þe stretes of þe cete and þe lanes
War even paved with precyouse stanes;
And þat þe brede and lenthe of þat cete
War mare þan here es of any contre;
And all manere of melody   8910
Of musyk and of mynstralsy,

8892 and] *om.* Morris (Lightbown)   8906 of þe cete] *om.* a (*placed at the head of the following line*)   8910 And] And þat Morris (Lightbown)

þat moght be schewed with mowthe or hand,
War continuely þare-in sownand,
And þat ilk day on sere manere suld fall
Swa þat na man moght irk withall;   8915
And þat ilka lane and ilka strete
Of þis cete war full of savours swete
Of spycery and of all other thing,
Of whilk any swete savoure moght spryng;
H f. 255ra And þat þar war plente of mete and drynk   8920
And of all other delyces þat man may thynk.
    And þat ilka citesayne þat wonned þare
Had als mykell bewte or mare
Als Absolon, þat swa fayre was,
Whase bewte moght bi skyll pas   8925
þe bewte of all manere of men erthly,
Swa clene he was in lym and body;
And þarewith als mykell strenthe had omang
Als Sampson had, þat was so strang
þat a thowsand men armed clene   8930
He overcome and felled doune all bidene;
And þat ilkane war als swyft to pas
And to ryn, als Assahell of fote was,
[þat] swa swyft was to ryn and ga,
þat thurgh rase wald turne bath buk and ra;   8935
And þat ilkane had þarewith als mykell lykyng
And als mykell þair wille in all thing
Als Salamon had, þat als God vowched save,
þat had all thyng þat he wald have;
And þat ilkane þarwith had als mykell fredome   8940
Als August had, þat was emperour of Rome,
Tyll whame all landes of þe world obout
Served and till him war underlout;
And þat ilkane had withall als continuele hele
Als Moyses had, þat ay was swa lele   8945
þat God wald never with yvell dere him
Bot anely þat he made his eghen dym;
And þat þarewith, if possible ware,
Ilkane moght als lang be lyfand þare
Als Matussale namely dyd here,   8950

*8934 þat] And H   8945 ay] *om.* Morris (Lightbown)

þat lyfed nere[hand] a thowsand yhere;
And þat ilkane moght als mykell wisdom weld
Als Salamon had, þat men swa wise held,
þat thurgh his wisdom had knawyng
Of all thing and understandyng;   8955
And þat ilkane þarewith lufed als wele or mare
And als gud frende ay tyll other ware
Als David tyll Ionathas was kyd,
Wham he lufed als he his awen saule dyd;
And þat ilkane with þat honourd ware   8960
Of all þe other þat wond þare,
Als Ioseph was of þe Egypciens ryght,
Wham þai lowted als loverd of gret myght;
And þarewith þat ilkane war in all thing
Als my[ghty] als was [þ]e gret Alexander kyng   8965
þat conquerd Affryk, Europe, and Asy,
þat contened all þe world halely;
And þat ilkane acorded with other in anehede,   H f. 255rb
Als Li[l]yas with S[cipy]on dyd in dede,
Of whilk nouther wald nathing do   8970
Bot als ayther of þam assented þareto;
And with alle þis, þat ilkane als syker ware
Of þair dwellyng to won lang þare,
Als Ennoc and Hely er on þe same wyse,
þat er syker of þair dwellyng in paradyse,   8975
Fra þe tyme þat þai war þider ravyst
And sall be untyll þe comyng of Anticrist;
And over alle þis, þat ilkane als mykell ioy had
Als he suld have þat war lad
Tyll þe galows, and sodainly in þe gate   8980
War tane and putted till a kynges state;
And þarewith þa[t] tyll ilkane suld fall
All þe ioyes [þat] þai moght have all.
  He þat all þes had, als bifore wryten es,
Suld pass all þe world in worthines.   8985
What man thurgh witt couth tell ioy mare
In þis world to weld þan all þis ware?

*8951 nerehand] nere H   *8965 myghty] mykell H   þe . . . kyng] Alexander þe
gret kyng H, Alexander þe kyng b   *8969 Lilyas . . . Scipyon] Lisyas . . . Sampson cab
8974 er] om. Morris (Lightbown)   *8982 þat] þan H, Morris's suggestion in note
*8983 þat] om. H

For whaswa had all þese, withouten dout,
Had here ioy inoghe, both within and without,
With alkyn delyces þat he moght have here   8990
Specialy in all his wittes sere,
þat es to say, in syght and hereyng
And in smellyng, tastyng, and feleyng.
Bot yhit all þir blysses þat yhe herd me neven
Er als noght + to regard o[f] þe blys of heven,   8995
For als mykell difference, or mare, suld be
Bitwene heven and swilk a cete
Als es bitwene a kynges palays
And a swyn-sty þat es lytell to prays,
And na mare comparyson may be made   9000
Bitwene þe cite of heven, wyde and brade,
And swilk a cete made of gold and perre,
þan bitwene all þe world and a faulde may be.
Allswa all ryches þat may here be sene
War noght bot als muk þat es unclene,   9005
To regard of þe precyouse rychesce
Of þe cete of heven þat na man may gesce.
And all þe melodyse of þe world sere
War noght bot alls sorow to here,
To regard of þe bly[s]full melody   9010
þat in þe cete of heven es ay redy.
And all swete savours þat men may fele,
Of alkyn thing þat here savours wele,
War noght bot als stynk to regard of þ[e] flayre
þat es in þe cete of heven swa fayre.   9015
H f. 255va And all þe worschepe þat here may be
War noght bot als schendschepe to se,
To regard of þe gret worschepe,
Of whilk men sall in heven tak kepe.
    All þe fairnes þat Absolon had in syght   9020
War noght bot laythede in heven bryght;
All þe strenthe of Sampson þat was pereles,
War noght tald þare bot wayknes;
All þe dely[t]es þat had Salomon þe kyng

8995 Er] War Morris   *to] als to H   *of] to H*b*   9004 ryches] ricchesce *a*
*9010 blysfull] blyffull H, blyssfulle Morris   *9014 þe] þat HAs   9017 als] als a *a*
*9024 delytes] delyces H

War noght in heven bot myslykyng;   9025
All þe swyftnes of Assahel þat had he
War noght þare bot slawnes to se;
All þe fredom þat August had whilom
War noght tald þare bot thraldom;
All þe hele þat here had Moyses   9030
War noght tald þare bot als seknes;
All þe eld þat Matussale had here
War les þare þan þe lest day of þe yhere;
All þe wisdom þat Salomon had redy
War noght tald þare bot als foly;   9035
All þe luf þat David Ionathas lufed
War noght þare bot als hatereden proved;
All þe honoure þat þe Egypciens Ioseph dyd
War noght in heven bot schendschip kyd;
All þe myght þat Alexander had aywhare   9040
War noght tald bot wayknes þare;
All þe acord þat Li[l]yas had in his lyfe
With S[cipy]on war [noght] þar bot als stryfe;
All þe sykernes þat had Ennoc and Ely
Of þair dwellyng in paradyse namely   9045
War noght bot als unsykernes
Of wonyng in heven þat es endles.
þus may I lyken, als I ymagyn,
þe cete of heven and þe blys þarein
Tyll a cete of gold and of precyouse stanes sere.   9050
    Bot þe cete of heven es mare bryght and clere,
And es sett on swa heghe a hyll
þat na synfull man may wyn þartyll,
þe whilk hyll I lyken tyll beryll clene,
þat es clerer þan any þat here es sene.   9055
þat hill es noght els bi understandyng
Bot haly thoght and brynand yhernyng,
þat haly men had here to þat stede,
Whils þai lyfed, bifor þair dede.
For God will þat þai als heghe up-pas   9060
Als þair thoght and yhernyng upward was.
    Yhit I lyken, als I ymagyn in thoght,

*9042 Lilyas] Lisyas *cab*   his] þis AL   *9043 Scipyon] Sampson *cab*   noght]
om. H   9049 blys] blyssis RA   9061 upward] vp *a. At this point, M returns*

þe walles of heven tyll walles þat war wroght

Of all manere of precyouse stanes sere,

Cymented with gold full bryght and clere.   9065

[Bot] swa bryght gold ne swa clene

Was never nane in þis world sene,

Ne swa ryche stanes ne swa precyouse

Als obout heven er, ne swa vertuouse.

þe precyouse stanes gastly may be   9070

Gud werkes, and þe gold charyte,

þat obout þase in heven sall schine clere,

þat dose gud werkes in charyte here.

   þe turrettes of heven, gret and small,

I lyken tyll turrettes of clere cristall.   9075

Bot þe turrettes of heven er mare clere shynand

þan ever was cristall in any land.

þa turrettes gastly sere honours may be,

þat gud men in heven sall fele and se.

þe wardes of þe cete of heven bryght   9080

I lyken tyll wardes þat war stalworthly dyght

And clenly wroght and craftily tayled

Of clene sylver and gold, and enamayld.

Bot þa wardes of þe cete of heven

Er mare crafty and strang þan any kan neven,   9085

Bot gastly to speke, þa wardes swa dyght

May be tald strenthe, power, and myght,

þat þas sall have þat in heven sall dwell,

Als yhe moght here me bifore tell.

   þe yhates I lyken of heven swa brade   9090

Tyll yhates þat war of charbukell stanes made,

Bot swa clere charbukell was never sene

Als þa yhates of heven er, ne swa clene.

Bot þa yhates, gastly to speke, er mekenes

And fredom of ryght fayth and bowsomnes,   9095

þat gyfes way and entre tyll men boghsom,

Intyll þe cete of heven for to com.

þe garettes oboven þe yhates bryght

Of þe cete of heven, I lyken þus ryght

Tyll þe garettes of a cete of gold,   9100

*9066 Bot] And H   9082 craftily] ? trastily A, clene M   9085 þan] þam Morris
9087 strenthe] adds and Morris (Lightbown)   9100 a] þe aL

þat wroght war, als I before told,
Of fyne curall and ryche rubys
And of other stanes of gret prys,
With fyne gold wyre all obout frett
And bryght besandes burnyst omang sett.   9105
þe garettes of heven gastly may be
Heghe state and lordschip and dignite,
For all þat sall won in þat cete þare
Sall bere heghe state þare-in evermare.
    þe lanes allswa and þe stretes all,   9110
þat in þe cete of heven may fall,
And þe wonyng-stedes þat er þarin   H f. 256ʳᵃ
I lyken here, after I ymagyn,
Tyll þe lanes and stretes, less and mare,
Of þe cete of gold þat I spak of are,   9115
With þe bygynges on ilk syde standand,
þat of fyne gold war made, bryght schynand.
Bot in na cete þat men may neven
Er st[ret]es and lanes swa bryght als in heven,
Ne swa bryght wonyng-stedes als er þarin,   9120
Can na man thurgh wytt ymagyn,
þe whilk sall schyne, within and without
And on ilka syde [and] alle obout,
Whare all ryghtwyse men sall won at ees
In ioyfull quyete and rest and pese.   9125
And þarfor Haly Kyrk, þat oft prays
For þe saules in purgatory, þus says:
    *Tuam Deus deposcimus pietatem, ut eis tribue-
    re digneris lucidas et quietas mansiones.*
'Loverd God, we ask þi pete,   9130
þat þou vouche safe', als we pray þe,
'To gyf þam wonyng-stedes bryght
And restfull', þat nede has of rest and lyght.
    Na bodily eghe moght never here se
A poynt of swilk bryghtnes als in heven sal be.   9135
Ilka lane in heven and ilka strete
Most schyne bryght bi skyll, for þar sall mete
Aungels and men, bryghter schyneand

---

*9119 stretes] stedes *c*, *cf.* wonnyng-stedes *b*   9120 er] es *a, line rewritten* M
*9123 and²] *om.* HL, *couplet om.* M   9137 Most] Moght R, Sall *b*

þan ever schane þe son in any land.
For þe body of ilk man sall schyne so bryght   9140
þat tyll all a contre, ane moght gyf lyght.
And ilka hare þare, on þair hede
And on þair body on ilka stede,
Sall be als bryght als es þe son,
þat we may se here whare we won   9145
Full bryght schynand oboven us
And þarfor says þe boke þus:
    Fulgebunt iusti sicut sol.
'þe ryghtwis men sall schyne als þe son'
In heven, whare þai sall evermare won.   9150
Now sen a ryghtwis man sall schyne als bright
Als þe son dose, þan mo[t] he gyf lyght
Als fer als þe son dose, and ferrer;
Forwhi he sall þan be wele bryghter.
And yhit sall all þat gret bryghtnes,   9155
þat ryghtwis men sall have þare, be les
þan þe bryghtnes of God allmyghty,
Als sall be knawen þare openly—
Ryght als þe sternes here, whare we won,
Semes als to þe bryghtnes of þe son.   9160
For we sall be þare als sternes in bryghtnes,
And God bryghtest als son of ryghtwisnes.
    Ilka lane and strete þat in heven may be
Es l[ar]ger þan here es any contre,
For þe roume and þe space þat es contende   9165
In þe cete of heven has nane ende.
þa stretes and lanes, gastly to tell,
Er all haly men þat þare sall dwell,
And þair wonyng-stedes may be þe medes,
þat þai sall þare have for þair gud dedes.   9170
In þat cete sall be mare rychesce
þan all þe men of þe world may gesce,
Bot þase ryches, gastly to understand,
Er sere blysses and dely[t]es ay-lastand,

H f. 256rb (margin, beside line 9160)

9143 on²] in R*a*M   *At this point, W lacks a leaf, and with it, lines 9149–9216*
*9152 mot] mon H, mught A, myght L, *9151–4 om.* M   9162 ryghtwisnes]
rightnes A   *9164 larger] lenger HL   9170 þare] *om. b* Morris
*9174 delytes] delyces H

þe whilk all þas, þat tyll heven sall wende,   9175
Sall fele and se þare withouten ende.
    þe pament of heven may lykend be
Till a pament of precyouse stanes and perre.
Bot þe pament of heven sall schyne mar clere
þan ever schane gold or precyouse stanes here,   9180
And þat pament es sett swa fast
þat it sall never fayle bot ay last,
In whilk may na crevyce be sene,
It es swa hale and even and clene.
þis pament of heven als of perre,   9185
Gastly to understand, may be
Parfyte luf and lyfe endeles,
With pese and rest and sykernes,
þat all sall have þat sall won þare,
And þis pament sall last evermare.   9190
þus may a man þat kan and will
All þe cete of heven lyken bi skyll
Tyll bodily thing þat es fayre and bryght
And mast delytabell here to syght,
A[ls] to precyouse stanes of vertow   9195
And to sylver and gold and thing of valow,
þat men may here bodily se,
Bot swilk thinges may nane in heven be.
    Of verray ryches, gret plente es þare,
þat er a hundreth thowsandfald mare   9200
þan all þe ryches of þe world here,
þat ever was sene, fer or nere,
þat fayles and passes [sone] oway.
Bot þe rychesce of heven sall last ay,
þat er all thing, als God vouches save,   9205
þat men in heven yhernes to have.
Oboven þe cete of heven sall noght be sene
Bot bright bemes anly, als I wene,   f. 111ra
þat sal schyne fra Goddes awen face
And sprede obout and over [all] þat place.   9210
His bright face sal alle þas se,
þat sal duelle in þat blisful cite,

*9195 Als] And H   9201 þe²] þis RAL, 9201–6 om. M   *9203 sone] om. H
*9210 all] om. G, cf. all in þat L   W returns at 9217

And þat sight es þe mast ioy of heven,
Als men mught here me byfor neven.
And alle-if þat cite be large and wyde,   9215
Men sal hym se until þe ferrest syde
And als wele þas þat sal be fra hym fer
Als þas þat sal þar til hym be nerrer.
For als men of fer landes may haf sight
Of þe son, þat we se here shyne bright,   9220
And als þe same son þat shynes byyhond þe se
Shewes it here and in ilka cuntre
Alle þe day, aftir þe ryght course es,
Bot when cloudes fra us hydes hir brightnes,
Right swa þe face of God allemyghty   9225
Sal be shewed in heven appertely
Tille alle + men þat þider sal wende,
þogh som suld duelle at þe ferrest ende.
Bot ilk man als he lufes God here
Sal won þar, som fer and som nere,   9230
For som lufes God here mar þan sum,
And som lufes hym les þat til heven sal com.
Alle þas þat God here lufes best,
When þai com þar, sal be hym nerrest,
And þe nerrer þat þai sal hym be,   9235
þe verreylyer þai sal hym se,
And þe mare verraly þai se his face,
þe mare sal be þair ioy and solace.
Bot þa þat here lufs hym les,
þai sal won þar, aftir þare luf es,   9240
Bot ilk man sal se hym in his degre
In what syde of heven swa he sal be.
Here haf yhe herd of many fayre sight,
þat ay sal be sene in heven bright;
Ful glade and ioyful alle þas may be   9245
þat swilk fayre sightes ay þar sal se,
And of mykel ioy may þai `ay´ telle
þat in þat cite of heven sal ay duelle.
    Alswa ilkan sal haf in þair heryng
Grete ioy in heven and grete lykyng,   9250

9218 sal þar] *trs.* R, sall *b*   *9227 alle] alle þe *cb*   9230 and] *om. a*
9231 mar] *after* lufes *a*

For þai sal here þar [ay] aungel sang,
And þe haly men sal ay syng omang
With delitabel voyces and clere.
And with þat, þai sal ay here
Alle other manere of melody   9255
Of + delytable noys of mynstralsy,   f. 111rb
And of alkyn swet tones of musyke
þat til any mans hert mught like.
And of alkyn noyse þat swete mught be,
Ilkan sal here in þat cite,   9260
Withouten instrumentes ryngand
And withouten movyng of mouth or hand
And withouten any travayle,
And þat sal nevermar cese ne fayle.
Swilk melody als þar sal be þan,   9265
In þis werld herd never nan erthely man,
For swa swete sal be þat noyse and shille
And swa delitabel and swa sutille
þat alle þe melody of þis werld here,
þat ever has bene herd, fer and nere,   9270
War noght bot als sorowe and care
Als to þe lest poynt of melody þare.
   Omang þam alswa sal be swete savour;
Swa swete com never of herbe ne flour,
When þai war in seson mast   9275
Or war mast of vertu for to tast.
Ne of spicery mught never spring
Ne yhit of nan othir thyng,
þat thurgh vertu of kynde suld savour wele,
Swa swete savour als þai sal fele,   9280
For na hert may thynk ne tung telle,
How swete sal ilkan til other smelle.
þat savour sal be ful plentevouse
And swa swete and swa delicious
þat alkyn spicery þat men may fele   9285
And + alle othir thyng þat here savours wele
War noght bot als thyng þat stynked sour
Als to regarde of þat delycious savour.

*9251 ay] om. Gb   *9256 Of] Of þe G   9284 swa²] om. R   *9286 And] And
of G

þan sal þat savour þat es swa swete
Be ioy til þam ay when þai samen mete.   9290
Alswa ilkan þat sal won þar
Sal syng with angels, als I sayd ar,
In swilk tones þat sal be swete to here
With ful delitabel voyces and clere.
Bot þai sal love God ay in þair sang   9295
And thank hym of his mercy ay omang,
And ilkan of þat blisful company
Sal speke with othir þar ful swetely,
With laghyng and with lufly sembland,
And say, 'Wele es us þat here er wonnand',   9300
And thank God omang, þat þam gun wysse
Til mekenes, þat þam led til þat blysse
With anger þat þai had in þair lyfdays.

f. 111ᵛᵃ þan may þai say þus als David says:
    Letati sumus pro diebus quibus   9305
    nos humiliasti, annis quibus
    vidimus mala.
'Loverd, ful glad for þe days er we,
In whilk þou made us lawe to be,
In þe yheres in whilk we saw illes';   9310
þus may þai syng and say for sere skilles.
þan sal þair sang and þair spekyng
Be til þam gret ioy and lykyng.
    Alswa þai sal fele worshepes grete,
For ilkan sal be sette in a ryche sete   9315
And als kynges and qwenes corouned be,
With corouns dight with ryche perre
And with stanes of vertu, preciouse to prays,
Als David til God þus spekes and says:
    Posuisti, Domine, super caput eius   9320
    coronam de lapide precioso.
'Loverd, on hys heved þou sette ryght
A coroune of preciouse stane + dight',
Bot swa fayre coroune was never sene
In þis world on kynges heved ne qwene.   9325
þis coroune es þe coroune of blis,

9296 his] *om.* AM   9300 Wele es] weles Morris (Lightbown)   *9323 stane]
stanes *cb*

And þe stane es ioy þat þai sal never mys.
þis worshepe þat þai sal fele, sal pas
Alle þe worshepes þat ever here was,
Of whilk þai sal þar mar ioy have   9330
þan any man can yherne or crave.
    þus sal þai have in þair wittes fyfe
Parfite ioy with endeles lyfe
In þe heghe blisful cite of heven,
Whar sere ioyes er ma þan tung can neven.   9335
For þai sal many hundreth thousand se
Of men and wemen in þat cite,
þat many sere ioyes þar sal haf,
Als þai er worthy and God vouches saf.
And alle þe ioyes þat þai alle sal se,   9340
Sal be ioyes til ilka man þat þar sal be
Withouten his awen ioyes, les and mare,
þat til hymself sal be appropred þare.
For þe sight of ilk ioy þat þai sal se þan,
Sal be ioy þar til ilka man,   9345
For other mens ioyes tham sal like als wele,
Als þai sal þair awen þat þai sal fele.
þan sal a man haf ma ioyes in heven
þan any tung couthe telle or neven,
For ilk man sal haf special ioy and mede   9350
For ilk gude thoght and ilk gude dede,
þat he ever thoght or wroght, open or prive.   f. 111vb
þan may never þair ioys noumbred be,
þat ilk man in heven, when þai com þidir,
Sal in body and saule haf alle togider;   9355
And nevermare of na ioy fele irkyng,
For þai sal ay be new als at þe bigynnyng,
Of whilk þe leste ioy þar to fele and se,
Sal be mar þan alle þe ioyes of the werld may be.
    þai sal be fed þar and cled wele   9360
With ioy of sight þat þai sal fele;
þai sal wirk þar nan othir thyng
Bot love ay God withouten irkyng,
Als a versifiour says in a verse þarby,

9357 at] *om.* RM   9360 fed . . . cled] *trs. verbs* R

þe whilk es made in metre þus shortly: 9365
Visio sit victus, opus est
laus, lumen amictus.
'With þe sight of God þai sal be fed,
And with brightnes of light þai sal be cled,
And þair werk sal be ay lovyng',   9370
In whilk þai sal haf grete likyng.
Bot þair mast ioy in heven sal be
þe blisful sight of þe Trinite,
þe whilk þai sal se evermar.
And þat ioy sal pas alle othir þar,   9375
For ay whilles þai þat sight sal se,
Of alle ioyes þai sal fulfilled be.
And if þai suld þat sight mysse,
þai myght ʻnoghtʼ þan haf parfite blis.
For if a man war pyned in helle,   9380
With ma payns þan tung [couthe] telle,
And he of Goddes face mught se oght,
Alle his payns þan suld gryefe hym noght.
    Now haf I redde here how men sal hafe
Parfite ioy in heven þat sal be safe,   9385
Bot þe dampned men þarogayne
Sal haf ful sorow and parfite payne
Withouten ende for þair wikked lyfe,
For þai sal in alle þair wittes fyfe,
Be turmented on sere manere,   9390
With grysely payns, many and sere,
þat es to say, in syght and heryng,
In smellyng, tastyng, and felyng.
    First þai sal in helle obout þam se
Mare sorow þan ever in þis werld mught be,   9395
And þe sorow þat þai sal se þar
Sal be strang payne til þam evermar.
þair wonyng in helle, als says þe buke,
þai sal se ful of fire and of smoke
f. 112ʳᵃ And ful grisely and myrk and dym,   9400
And obout þam devels ful grym,
þat with sere payns sal pyne þam ay,

*9381 couthe] may GM, moght R, mot L   9383 þan suld] *trs.* Morris (Lightbown)
9402 pyne] payne Morris (Lightbown)

Als men mught here me byfor say.
And alleþogh þai in helle want light,
Yhit sal þai þar of alle payns haf sight   9405
Thurgh þe sparkes of fyre þar, als says saynt Austyn,
Noght til þair comfort bot til þair pyne.
   Yhit mare sorow þam sal bytyde:
þai sal here in helle on ilka syde
Ful hydus noyse and duleful dyn   9410
Of devels and of synful men þaryn.
þai sal here devels þar rare ful hydusly,
And þe synful men goule and cry.
þai sal þar in smellyng fele mare stynk
þan hert may here ymagyn or thynk,   9415
Of brynnand brunstan and of pyk
And of alkyn othir thyng þat es wyk.
þat stynk, als yhe sal understand wele,
Sal be ful strang payne til þam to fele.
Alswa þai sal ilkan other wery   9420
And myssay and sclaundre God allemyghty.
þai sal ay stryfe and be at debate,
And ilkan other sal despice and hate.
Omang þam sal never be pees,
Bot hatreden and stryfe þat never sal cees.   9425
   þair throtes sal ay be filled omang
Of alle thyng þat es bitter and strang,
Of lowe and reke with stormes melled,
Of pyk and brunstane togyder welled,
Of molten bras and lede withalle   9430
And of other welland metalle.
þis sal be strang payne til þam to tast,
Omang alle othir paynes, lest and mast,
With stryf þat sal be omang þam þan,
When ilkan sal other wery and ban.   9435
Alswa þai sal fele, als I byfor talde,
Outrageus hete and outrageouse calde,
For now þai sal frese in yse and now in fire bryn,
And be gnawen, withouten and within:
Within, als yhe sal understand,   9440

9405 þai þar] pai Morris (*corrected in corrigenda*), þai L   9411 þaryn] within R
9419 ful] *om.* Morris (Lightbown)   9432 tast] last Morris (Lightbown)

With wormes of conscience ay bytand.
Withouten, with dragons felle and kene—
Swa hidus was never here nane sene—
With neddirs and tades and othir vermyn
And with many hydus bestes of ravyn,　　　　9445
Als wode wolfes, lyons, and beres felle,
þat sal noght be elles bot devels of helle,
In liknes of hydus bestes and vermyne,
þat sal þam gnaw without to eke þair pyne,
Als in þe sext part of þis boke es wryten.　　9450
þus sal þe synful be gnawen and byten
Withouten thurgh hydus bestes and vermyn,
And thurgh þe worme of conscience within.
　　þe devels alswa sal stryke þam felly,
With glowand hamers, ful huge and hevy,　9455
þat sal seme of iren and stele;
þir payns þai sal with alle other fele.
þus sal þai evermar be pyned þar
In alle þair fife wittes, als I said ar,
With sere payns als es gode skille,　　　　9460
For þai here used þair wittes ille.
Alle þir payns þat yhe [have] herd me tell
And many ma þat sal be in helle,
þai sal thole ay þar þat sal wende þidir,
In body and saule alle togider.　　　　　9465
þus sal þai evermar contynuely
Haf parfite payne þar withouten mercy,
Fra whilk payne and sorow God us shilde
Thurgh prayer of hys moder mylde,
And þe right way of lyf us wysse,　　　　9470
Wharthurgh we may com til heven blysse. Amen.
　　Now es þe last part of þis buke sped,
And alle þe maters þarin haf I red,
þat contenes, als yhe mught here,
Bathe general and special ioyes sere,　　　9475
þat alle þas þat til heven sal comme,
Sal haf aftir þe day of dome;
And sere shendshepes of helle alswa,
þat er even contrary til þa,

f. 112rb In liknes of hydus bestes and vermyne,

*9462 have] om. G, cf. I here b

þe whilk, þas þat sal til helle wende, 9480
Sal haf þar withouten ende.
  Wharfor whaswa of þis wil take hede
May be stird til luf and drede:
Til drede, thurgh mynde of þe hydusnes
Of payne and sorow þat in helle es; 9485
Til luf, thurgh mynd of ioyes and blisse sere
þat God hetes tille alle þat lufes hym here.
Bot þe drede es noght medeful to prufe,
þat accordes noght halely with þat lufe,
For if drede stand by itself anely, 9490
Na mede of God it es [þan] worthy.
þarfor drede suld be lufes brother,
And ayther of þam stand with other,
For whaswa lufes God on ryght manere
He has grete drede to wrethe hym here. 9495
þan lufes he his bydynges to fulfille   f. 112va
And dredes to do oght ogayne his wille;
[He luf]es to be with God ay
And dredes to be put fra hym oway.
For men suld noght drede God anly for payne, 9500
Bot men suld drede to tyn þe ioy soverayne,
þat es, þe syght of God [in] heven,
þe whilk yhe herd me byfor neven;
þa[n] es þat luf ay with þat drede,
And þat dred of God es worthy mede. 9505
For þogh we suld never helle se
Ne syn suld never punyst be,
In purgatory ne in helle
Ne in þis werld here whar we duelle,
Yhit suld we luf God for hymself ryght 9510
And drede to tyne hys luf and of him þe syght.
For sikerly I dar wele say þis,
þat whaswa wyst what ioy and blys
Of þe syght of God in heven war
And als proprely had sene it als it es þar, 9515
He had lever thole here þis payne,

*9491 þan] om. Gb   *9498 He lufes] Delites GL   *9502 in] of G
*9504 þan] þat GL, Morris's suggestion in note   þat²] þat Morris   9507 syn] for syn
Morris, an unnecessary emendation   9509 here] om. Morris (Lightbown)   9515 it²]
om. Morris (Lightbown)

Ilk day anes alle qwi[k]k to be flayne,
Ar he þe syght of his face suld tyne,
þat in heven so bright sal shyne.
Many sere ioys ma þar sal falle,   9520
Bot þat sight es mast principalle ioy of alle,
For þat ioyful sight sal contene
Alle othir ioyes þat sal þar be sene,
Of whilk ioys, þe lest sal pas
Alle þe ioy[s] þat ever here was.   9525
For ioy here es noght bot passand vanite,
And þe ioyes þat er þar evermar sal be,
Til whilk ioyes þat has nan ende,
God us bring when we hethen wende. Amen.
    Now haf I here, als I first undirtoke,   9530
Fulfilled þe seven partes of þis boke,
þat er titeld byfor to have in mynde.
þe first es of þe wrechednes of mans kynde;
þe secunde of þe werldes condicions sere
And of þe unstabelnes of þe werld here;   9535
þe thred es of þe ded þat es bodily;
þe ferthe alswa es of purgatory;
þe fift es of domesday, þe last day of alle
And of þe takens þat byfor sal falle;
þe sext es of þe paynes of helle to neven;   9540
And þe sevend part of þe ioyes of heven.
In þir seven er sere materes drawen
Of sere bukes, of whilk som er unknawen,
f. 112ᵛᵇ Namly til lewed men of Ingland,
þat can noght bot Inglise undirstand.   9545
þarfor þis tretice drawe I wald
In Inglise tung þat may be cald
Prik of Conscience als men may fele.
For if a man it rede and understandes wele
And þe materes þarin til hert wil take,   9550
It may his conscience tendre make
And til right way of rewel bryng it bilyfe,

*9517 qwikk] qwilk G, whik A, whycke W, whikke M, *Morris's emendation*
*9525 ioys] ioy G   9527 And] Bot Morris. *M survives only fragmentarily after
9533, and we cite As instead*   9534 of] es of Morris   9535 þe²] þis *a*   9541 of¹]
es of Morris   9549 understandes] understande Morris (Lightbown)

And his hert til drede and mekenes dryfe
And til luf and yhernyng of heven-blis,
And to amende alle þat he has done mys. 9555
For þe undirstandyng of þir maters seven,
þat men may in þis buke se and neven,
May make a man knawe and hald in mynde
What he es here of his awen kynde
And what he sal be, if he avyse hym wele, 9560
And whar he es for to knaw and fele.
Yhit may he se, when he it redes,
What he es worthy for his dedes;
Whether he es worthy ioy or payne,
þis tretice may make hym be certayne. 9565
For þarin may he many thynges se
þat has bene and es and [yhi]t sal be;
þus may þis tretice, with þe sentence,
Pryk and stirre a mans conscience
And til mekenes and luf and drede it dryfe 9570
For to bring hym til ryght way of lyfe.
    Of alle þeis I haf sere maters soght,
And in seven partes I haf þam broght,
Als es contende in þis tretice here,
þat I haf drawen out of bukes sere 9575
Aftir I had in þam undirstandyng,
Alle-if I be of symple kunnyng.
Bot I pray yhou al *par charite*,
þat þis tretice wil here or se,
Yhe haf me excused at þis tyme, 9580
If ye fynde defaut in þe ryme,
For I rek noght, þogh þe ryme be rude,
If þe maters þarof be gude.
And if any man þat es clerk,
Can fynde any errour in þis werk, 9585
I pray hym he do me þat favour
þat he wille amende þat errour.
For if men may here any errour se,
Or if any defaut in þis tretice be,
I make here a protestacion 9590

9554 of] til *a*, to ȝerne As   *9567 yhit] þat *c*, þat *corr. to* yhit (*later*) A, ay L
9573 partes] partyse RW*b*   9577 Alle-] Als R   of symple] *trs.* R

þat I wil stand til þe correccion
f. 113ra Of `ilk´a rightwyse lered man,
þat my defaut here correcte can.

   þis tretice specialy drawen es
For to stirre lewed men til mekenes   9595
And to make þam luf God and drede.
For whaswa wille it here or rede,
I hope he sal be stirred þarby,
Yf he trow þat God es allemyghty.
And he [þat] sal it here or se   9600
And may noght þarby stirred be,
It semes þat he es wittles
Or over-mykel hardend in wikkednes.
Bot alle þas þat redes it, loud or stille,
Or heres it be red with gode wille,   9605
God graunt þam grace þat þai may
Be stird þarby til ryghtwyse way,
þat es, til þe way of gude lyfyng
And at þe last be broght til gude endyng.

   And yhe þat has herd þis tretice red,   9610
þat now es broght til ende and sped,
For þe luf of our Loverd Ihesu,
Pray for hym specialy þat it dru,
þat if he lyf, God safe hym harmles
And mayntene hys lyf in alle gudenes;   9615
And if he be ded, als falles kyndely,
God of his saule haf mercy
And bryng it til þat bli[s]ful place,
Whar endeles ioy es and solace,
Til whilk place he us alle bryng,   9620
þat for us vouched safe on rode to hyng. Amen.
Explicit tractatus qui dicitur
Stimulus Consciencie.
Here endes þe tretice þat es
Called Pryk of Conscience.

---

*9600 þat] om. c   *9618 blisful] blifful G, *Morris's silent correction*   colophon Amen
As   dicitur] vocatur L   Consciencie] *adds* interioris per sanctum Ricardum heremitam de
Hampole (*with an additional Latin index of the books*) L   Here . . . Conscience] *om.* WL
Pryk] þe pryk R

COMMENTARY

1. TEXTUAL MATTERS

4 *myght*: As *myghtes* WR*b* indicates, the line certainly appears short, but the poet probably sounded dative *-e* following the preposition.

8 *Amen*: Since the word represents extrametrical punctuation, *a*, along with other scribes (here also MS Bodley 99), may have felt free to omit it.

9 *ar*: The WR omission misses the construction, frequently repeated in the poem; translate: 'At the start, before . . .'.

15 *þe²*: A's omission is probably an indifferent reading, although suppressing *þe*, which might have been supplied here on the basis of the example later in the line, certainly is metrically tauter.

A sidenote: These notes run sporadically through the whole text, and are especially frequent in early portions of A and W. As subsequent examples show (see 27, 48, 63, etc.), they also appeared in the exemplar available to L. There the scribe had difficulty recognizing the source and status of these, usually topical, aids to reading. In L, they routinely appear within the text column, undifferentiated from the consecutive verse text, and they have often been edited (especially into the couplet form of the verse text).

In W, all the Latin tends to be added marginally, in textura, but is certainly in the original hand. The A sidenotes here appear as Latin annotation, in this case 'Qualiter Deus erat semper in trinitate sine inicio' by line 13. Such a presentation might point to the sidenotes as originally in Latin; certainly, the scribe of W seems to have perceived them as indicating that all the poem's Latin, elsewhere presented as an integral part of the in-column text, was equally 'marginal marking'. This perception may underwrite W's only sporadic reproduction of the poem's Latin after line 1500, and his omission of it altogether from line 1736.

23 *Was*: The reading of G, Whas *ab, illeg.* R. Although corrected by Morris, *Was* is a legitimate form, an example of G's frequent alternation of *w* and *wh*.

26 *alle*: Since the metre requires disyllabic *allë*, *thyng* represents the uninflected neuter plural. Earlier in the line, *first*[*ë*] also shows inflection, as a weak adjective after the demonstrative.

27 sidenote: Cf. W Quomodo Deus erat est principium et creator omnium et erit finis omnium; L How god is begynnyng withowtyn ˊbeˊgynyng | And endyng withowtyn all thyng (with further disruption, lines 29–30 moved to follow line 32); S omits line 27 and adds after line 28 Withowten ende als be he sall. AW clearly share the same defective form of the note, and we assume a small repetitive phrase has dropped out.

29 *Ende*: The line is essentially parallel to the preceding, but one might note that, in spite of absence of variation, a preceding *And* might have fallen out by haplography. But for a similar suppression of implicit *and*, see 240.

37 *lyfe*: Metre requires the disyllabic inflected infinitive, *lyf[ë]/ly[uë]*. As in *Speculum Vitae* (see the edition, pp. lxxv–lxxvi), the poet of *The Prick* does not suppress *-e* in hiatus; cf. e.g. 694 below.

39–40 *men . . . þat*: The poem, in adjusting sense to fit metrical form, frequently relies upon slightly confusing transpositions of natural word-order like this one. Translate: 'As men who wish to attend to this whole book will see discussed here.' See also 328–9n.

48 sidenote: Here supplied from L, in the forms of A, since A is partly cut away and badly flaking at the edge of the leaf. We have followed W Qualiter omnis creatura Deum laudet in natura sua, in reading *sulde loue* for L's *lowys*.

50 *er*: The RL form *here* is possibly only a spelling variant (cf. 147, 246 below).

56 Translate: 'Insofar as that created thing preserves its nature'.

63 sidenote: Also in W, the Latin Quare homo tenetur laudare Deum pre omnibus alijs creaturis; and in L, with the variant Why man awe] How a man awght L.

69 sidenote: The interlined *made* is a later correction. The parallel materials appear in L after line 80, with an added couplet (see the collation in Appendix 2 below). L's reading, 'How god man . . .', equivalent to the uncorrected A, demonstrates that these notes descend from a common (here erroneous) exemplar; its scribe had skipped, viz. '*ma*de *ma*n'. Additionally, digne] worthy L.

71 *werld*: As routinely, the poet scans 'world' as disyllabic, following OE woruld. For further discussion, see the Introduction, pp. xlv–vi, l.

73 *in*: and GS; given the customary stroke above the tironian *nota* in these hands, a frequent confusion. Cf. 921n.

93 *and fre wille*: Follows from *witte and skille* 91. Such discontinuous parallelism forms a repeated construction through the poem; cf. 229–30n.

94 *ille*: Morris appears to have undertaken silent corrections of a variety of minor readings, here removing the repetition of this word in G.

96 *parfor*: The variation is probably indifferent, although ALM is marginally more difficult, and is apt to have produced independent scribal substitution of the second element on a random basis at many points in the tradition.

101–15 *Sen . . . þus*: The first word, a conjunction, at least in a theoretical way, governs the entire construction to the end of line 114. The *þus* that introduces the following line 115 then slightly obscures the sense, perhaps lost by the poet among his profuse clauses of specification. Translate: 'Since God [did all these things] . . . , he thereby (= *þus*) showed great love . . .'.

106 sidenote: Cf. L following 110, at the foot of f. 110rb: How man aught to hafe in mynde and fle | Vicess and loue þat god þat schewed hym opynly to þe, with four additional lines at the head of the next column (see the collations in Appendix 2).

107 *hight . . . þarto*: Translate 'promised him in addition to that'.

110 *was, of*: The variation reflects two competing scansions of the line. Morris's version, shared by SM, is probably unexceptionable, but the scribes who transmit it may have overlooked the possibility of disyllabic *syn*[*ne*].

116 *benyfices*: After a sibilant, as in *Speculum Vitae*, apocopation of terminal *-es* is routine. Cf. the plural but overtly apocopated form *þier benefice* 'these benefits' 119, and such further examples as *wykkednes* 453 (cf. *iniquitatibus* 450), *þer variance* 1446, or *eese* 1469 'eases'.

121 *he*: In spite of variation in RL, the grammatical sense follows from *ilk man* 117.

129 *es*: A has intruded *self* from the preceding line.

131 Translate: 'How an evil man pains God . . .'.

137 *man*: AW *mans* (i.e. mannes) is probably an effort at avoiding stress-clash, but cf. 128, where *man self* may simplify *mans self*, i.e. *mannes self*.

139 sidenote: A is damaged, with flaking ink, and cut off at the end. Cf. W, more extensive than it appears A can have been: Quomodo homo accipiet viam ad gloriam per viam humilitatis timoris et caritatis Dei que vocatur via sapiencie.

147 *are*: The variation with *here* may not be substantive but a spelling variant (cf. 50, 246, 3287). We emend only in the interests of clarity.

176 *hym*: The form is certainly defensible as an implicit dative, without preposition. But the supply of *to* in WR may offer a more forcefully metrical line. In this form, the poet begins with a lengthy anacrusis and then stresses *alle*, *to*, *nede-*, and *ware*.

182 *And til*: In his textual commentary, Morris suggests, having misunderstood the syntax, reading *Until*.

213 *he may*: Probably the more metrically apt reading.

218 *himself*: As frequently (cf. 207, 243, 254), a metrical line requires the full form *himsel*[*uen*].

229–30 *Knawyng* and *mynd* form the compound subject of *shuld . . . lede*.

232 *gode*: The article *a*, common to the *c* copies, is probably otiose, certainly metrically unnecessary.

246 *er*: L's dittography insures that the scribe has transmitted the appropriate form for an ambiguous spelling.

250 *yhouthe*: In a note, Morris, having printed *c*, identifies the correct reading. *c* has confused ambiguous *y-*, in the written dialect of these manuscripts either representing *þ-* or *ȝ-* (the latter usually rendered unambiguously as *yh-*). The intruded article is an archetypal *b* reading.

   riches: As the rhyme shows, this must be the abstract noun *richesse*, but the form is persistently ambiguous, also representing simple 'riches'. Cf. among many instances, the contrasting uses in 9171 and 9173.

253 *his*: The omission is a small example of homeoarchy, viz. 'lett*is* (*h*)is'.

263 *dede*: The article in *c* has arguably been supplied as an echo of the preceding example. However, the line would be more metrically taut, were one to follow *a*S and omit that example as well. In 263–4 *Ne of . . . Thynkes noght* 'Nor does he think at all of' follows from 261 *þat he noght sese*.

284 *in þe*: The grammatically preferable form.

296 *þa* G is potentially a substantive variant, although given coalescence of earlier *a* and *ai*, possibly only one of spelling.

297–8 The A 'corrector' has derived his readings from a manuscript well advanced in the transmission; here both the variants are attested in MS Bodley 99, a Type II copy of *PC*.

301 *says*: The present is usual in such forms (cf. 284, 287, 298, 310, 313, etc.).

319 *obliti*: L reads *et obliti*, against the other copies and the conventional Vulgate text (Ps. 105: 13). The scribe, as did Morris, may have intruded the conjunction to accord with the translation in the verse; cf. *and* 322.

325 *lang*: With metrical *-ë* on the adverb.

328–9 Another example of the poet's somewhat confusing relative clauses. Translate 'But whoever cannot dread, but who is willing to absorb this treatise, can learn (to dread)'. Cf. 39–40n.

333 In spite of apparent signs of difficulty about what syllables should be stressed, probably an indifferent set of variants.

344 An implicit statement of the poem's title, revealed formally at 9548.

347 In W, followed by the in-column heading Ecce libellus in septem partes.

349 *partyes*: This variant and the next are linked (and the variants in 363 and 433 demonstrate the potential ubiquity of the confusion). Translate 'It is divided into seven chunks. The first part (the term for the poem's divisions, cf. 370) is about . . .'.

379 *of*: i.e. *And in despite of*, to parallel 376–7.

391 *It*: The variants, all clarifications, have been generated by the distance between the governing *Wald* 389 and the clause it introduces. Translate 'Wished that . . . it were filled'.

414 At the head of f. 104rb, A provides a title, a way of facilitating topical consultation: Of þe wrechednes of mans kynde. This is repeated on the next two folios (at 610 and 786, with minor spelling variation). In addition to this signal, the initial leaf of each part has a slit for a string/thread as a finding device; one of these is still intact on the edge of f. 123.

437 The variants probably represent scribal efforts at smoothing and regularizing the metre. In S (and L at 440), the line is followed by an in-column rubric, Off þe begynnyng of mans lyffe (so L); the Latin equivalent Inicium humane vite appears here in W.

458 W sidenote: Nota.

459 *loperd*: G provides the infinitive of this rarely recorded (but in a stockbreeding and dairy culture, predictably commonplace) Scandinavianism. The other scribes recognize the need for a participial adjective.

492 The metre here implies that *byhoves*, as routinely, represents the monosyllable *bus*. Cf. 148, 414, 744, etc., as well as pt. *bud/burd*, e.g. 1641, 1976, 4055. In contrast to this in-line usage, full forms regularly occur in rhyme.

507 *made*: The RS variant *made we*, an attempt to avoid stress-clash, ignores the past plural inflection, *madë*.

552 sidenote: As an in-column rubric S.

553 *aftir . . . falles*: 'in accord with the manner in which it occurs/happens', as the following lines explain.

595 *at*: According to this more challenging reading in AR, ease and riches contribute to pleasure.

626 *comonly*: The scribe misplaced his mark of abbreviation, but presumably intended comonly.

627 *overtures*: G has missed a mark of abbreviation.

628 *yhow*: The G reading is isolated, all others having more transparent þow. Although G's form properly represents 'you', it is probably an acceptable spelling and one with sporadic parallels in all the other copies.

686 *als stra*: All the manuscripts seem to share an error, revealed by the Latin. The universally attested alswa should answer to the *stipula* of poet's citation. Translate: 'And the body of the tree, like straw . . .'.

692, 702 *strengh*: Morris unnecessarily emends G's legitimate form (also in WS, and see *LALME* iv. 78); but cf. strengthe AM, strenkith R.

705 *þat*: Following from *flour* in the preceding line.

763 *withyn*: Probably simplified in G as dittographic, following the scribe's rendition of the full infinitive form *enden*.

775 hand] *c*; cf. ande *a*M, anede L, the more explicit spelling for ON andí, as Morris notes.

776 *waxes*: Given frequent Northern apocopated spellings after sibilants (cf. 116n), probably simply a spelling variant, but one effecting the metre. Note the six surrounding uses of the verb (767, 770, 772, 777, 782, 786), all written as full forms in G, but probably, given the metre, to be construed as apocopated *wax*.

796 *loves*: The variation in R exhibits the frequent hesitation/variation between the two verbs 'to love' (OE lufian) and 'to praise' (OE lofian).

806 sidenote: As in-column heading in rubric R; cf. þis is þe ende of mans lyue L. S returns at 821.

835 *on*: The competing readings represent differing renditions of archetypal *o*.

836 *right*: A attempts to render the line an unproblematic octosyllable; cf. 437.

853 *a*'s added couplet represents another correction predicated upon a manuscript advanced in the tradition; Bodley 99 has the extra couplet and, to accommodate it, must suppress 853 *says*, a reading universal in all the copies we collate.

860 *Als wa*: A alone transmits what was intended; Morris emended to *Alswa I*, a reading here only reproduced in L. Morris construed 'Alswa' as 'also', but one should translate, following A, 'As if he said . . .'. The form essentially reproduces Latin 'quasi diceret', routinely used by glossers to disambiguate rhetorical questions. Cf. 1954, 2534, and 7447, and note the archetypal error cloaked by the spelling *alswa* in 686. For simply one example of the persistent interchange between earlier /w/ and /hw/, cf. *whar* 7437 to represent *war* 'were'.

897 W provides a sidenote: 'Versus', similarly at 913.

900 *wille*: *wild* A is presumably archetypal, and responsible for the remaining variation, since the form is ambiguously both present and past tense, a potential confusion that has generated the *b*-tradition.

907 *wgly*: Here, and on two further occasions (2364, 5024), the scribe renders 'ugly' as *vugly*. We interpret this form on all three occasions as a slightly archaic representation of *wgly*.

921 *and*: G confuses the conjunction and preposition; cf. 73n.

940 *worldisshe*: *worldis* AS is arguably only a spelling variant. All the manuscripts show persistent Northern alternation between earlier *-ish* and

-is, e.g. in the routine spellings for *Ynglis* 'English'. As our discussion of dialect shows (p. xli), forms in *-is* are frequently confirmed in rhyme as authorial. Cf. further the collations for 1075, 1077, 1085, etc. (and note W's persistent effort at finding unambiguous forms).

958 At the head of f. 107rb, A provides an indexing title: Of þe condicions of þe world. This is repeated on the next three folios (at 1134, 1316 with 'condicion', and 1492).

959–60 The second line is a relative clause modifying *man* in the first. Translate: 'Where the life of the man who performs here what is appropriate for God will be endless'.

961 *world of world*: i.e. 'secula seculorum', eternity.

962 *By*: Morris saw that G here erred, but failed to find the relevant reading in other copies. The construction continues with *May be undirst- anden* 965, but is still difficult. The problem is the thoroughly parenthetical line 964, where the poet seeks to indicate that he uses the term 'world' loosely (to indicate all creation), while his discussion proceeds to qualify that broad conceptualization.

971 *withouten*: Here 'outside of'; cf. 2489n.

972 *invisible*: *MED invisile* cites only the G reading, surely, given agreement of the rest, a *lapsus calami* encouraged by the similar strokes involved in writing the sequence *-bl-*.

1006–7 The awkward placement of the adverb obscures the sense; translate: 'As God decreed, these worlds first were made . . .'.

1016 *ordynd*: Although *a*RLS read *ordaynd*, Morris's emendation is probably unnecessary and G's reading (ordaned M) a licit form.

1053 Translate this line: '(I will show) the reason why people call man a world (i.e. the microcosm).'

1067 *þat*: The antecedent of the clause is *worldisshe thynges* in the preceding line.

1069 *goddes*: Probably a permissible form in G, but like H, noted by Morris, AR read godes 'goods' (god *b*).

1085 *of*: i.e. *prince of*, the noun carried over from the title of the preceding line (which translates John 12: 31, 14: 30, 16: 11).

1092 *on*: In spite of majority attestation, GWS are probably metrically preferable.

1100 S provides a sidenote: Dominus dicit in euangelio.

1137 *worldes*: In the trisyllabic form *wor[u]ldly*, the A reading is metrically attractive.

1146–51 At this point, *c* copies (with some support from W) provide a citation, probably based upon the *Vitae patrum*, although our searches have failed to unearth an exact source. This is apparently intrusive, and, together with two other notes restricted to *c* (6630–1, 6791–2), untranslated in the poem's English. The passage does resemble the sort of note one might imagine a poet having left himself for possible expansion, but it may equally reflect an option rejected for the wittier citation at 1202–4.

1202 *esses*: In G, the word has been interlined, by the original hand, but misplaced.

1211–12 Translate: 'Whoever wishes may reasonably compare the world to four things'. The variation we record apparently stems from the scribes' perception of *by* as ambiguous, not clearly either 'by' or 'be', a perception dependent on taking the line as a unit separable from what has preceded.

1212 The sidenote of A appears in S as an in-column heading; for this series, L has generally one-word Latin sidenotes, apparently added by Peter Towler, here Mare.

1225 Sidenote in A: an] and (the symbol *&*).

1227 *es*: The majority reading *er* apparently is the result of construing the line singly, apart from context, where *a wildernes* is the subject.

1235, 1245, 1257 sidenote: All these also appear in R, as in-column rubrics (in 1245 felde] feld ful of batails R).

1398 L has an in-column heading: How twa ways lyggis in þis werld | De duabus vijs in hoc mundo iacentibus | [in the text, not heading, hand:] þe way of dede and of lyfe.

1419 *unnethes . . . myle*: i.e. 'scarcely the length of time required to walk a mile'. Cf. the detailed discussion, derived from Maimonides, at 7672–81, which assumes one could walk forty miles a day (implying literally that things change every ten to fifteen minutes).

1438 *es*[1]: The scribe of G has forgotten the final tongue-stroke of his *e* here, and Morris prints what he could see, as the senseless *cs*. But the scribe's intention is clear, since the curve of the letter is that of *e*, not *c*; a similar reproduction of *e* recurs at *beres* 2096 (*bercs* in Morris).

1443 *domland*: Morris reproduced G's form as *douiland* in the text. However, his textual commentary essentially corrects to the reading we print here, a *hapax legomenon* probably meaning 'dark, murky'.

1444 *lyfte*: In spite of the attestation, ARL surely provide the easier and more predictable reading.

1448 *ma*: The *cb* supply of *other* is otiose and unmetrical, probably dittography generated from the preceding word.

1454 *he*: Omitted in G as the result of haplography; the scribe reproduces only one of two successive examples of *he(-)*. Recurrences of the same error in 1496 and 1815 have attracted the corrector of the manuscript. In the first instance, G dropped the subject in *may me(n) mette* 'may one (the indefinite pronoun) measure'; in the second, he ignored the second of two consecutive words beginning *þa-*.

1479 An etymological pun, 'the worse old age'; see the discussion in the introduction, pp. xlv–vi. Morris's suggestion, in his textual commentary, of *werldes* is simply nonsense.

1494 *is*: Morris's emendation to *his*, even in the presence of *his* AR*b*, is unnecessary. Morris elsewhere prints this form (e.g. 47), and both *h* at the head of words properly beginning with a vowel and its absence from words with *h-* occur frequently in G.

1506, 1507 *id est*: G has confused *.i.* (= id est) with the tironian nota for *et*.

1513 *forth-broght*: We construe as a compound, a calque on the *producitur* of the Latin.

1565 *greef*: A's reading is probably confirmed by the homograph *grete* in *b* copies. This more difficult adjective frequently stimulates such variation; cf. *Speculum Vitae* 4647n, 9207n. Here *c* copies have been attracted by the rhymes in *-ves*, especially the preceding *greves*.

1569 *vengaunce*: Morris again emends unnecessarily; A has his preferred spelling, but RS read as H (vengawnce W), and L reads *veniance*, M *vengans*.

1577 *þes verses*: Most other copies show the ostensibly singular reading *þis vers* AR*b* (*corrected to* verse's' L). But *þis* is ambiguously both singular and plural, and, given northern apocopation of *-ses*, *vers* is both singular and plural also.

1584 *þe whilk*: Precedes its grammatical antecedent, *þai* 1586.

1660 At the head of f. 111rb, A provides an indexing title: Of þe ded and why it es to dre⟨de⟩.

1677 *may help na*: WMS offer the attractive reading 'no counsel may help', as opposed to 'none may help nor advise'. The variation at least begins with varying perceptions of the penultimate word, archetypally *na* '? no/? nor' (cf. the similar difficulty at 1881). Adapting the second, we think erroneous, perception, scribes have attempted to supply a subject.

1682 sidenote: W De tribus generalibus mortis (at 1680), but also at the page foot, following 1684 'Thre maneres of dedes are þat men dredys'; cf. L: 1. De morte corporali 2. De morte spirituali (at 1687), which appear at W 1686 and 1690 as Mors corporalis and Mors spiritualis respectively.

1688 *full*: The omission of the word in ASM creates a headless line.

1691 *mans*: A small bit of haplography, the possessive ending (here providing a metrically necessary syllable) having disappeared before following *s*-.

1742 sidenote: cf. Mors interminabilis W, De morte finali L.

1768 sidenote: Duo principales cause quare timetur mors corporalis W.

1770 *for*: Translate 'The second reason is that he does not know, when his life must end . . .'.

1801 *shortly wite*: The AL variants probably are the result of attraction, the scribes having just copied the word *wille*.

1803 *and*: A*b*'s intrusive *þe* indicates that the scribes missed the poet's customary disyllabic form, from OE sāwol.

1804 *aparty*: This form first appears here, and as a single word (not *a party* 'a portion', e.g. 3900 ff.) on eleven further occasions in the poem. We have let the form stand, with the sense 'in particular, especially, partly'. However, we remain uncertain that all instances are to be so explained; uniquely, at 2334 W offers the variant *apartly*, and G's form *apparty* may imply a similar derivation. At least some examples may well be errors for *a(p)pertly* 'openly, fully'. Although *apertly* seems simple enough, in other Middle English textual traditions, it on occasion gave scribes pause; cf. such renditions of the word as *Piers Plowman* A 1.98 *parfit(ly)*; B 2.100 *aperly* (also a recorded variant at Chaucer, 'Parson's Tale' 294) and *properly*.

1818 sidenote: This also appears in L, with the brief addition *to halde* at the end; cf. Quomodo mors timetur propter quatuor causas W.

1832 At the head of f. 112rb, A provides an indexing title: Of þe condicions of þe ded and wh⟨?⟩y it es to drede, repeated, as 'Of þe ded . . .', on the next four folios (lines 2006, 2180, 2360, 2540).

1836 sidenote: Also in L; cf. Prima causa W.

1840 W provides a sidenote: De amore inter animam et corpus humanum.

1856, 1858, 1860 W provides sidenotes: Secunda causa, Tercia causa, Quarta causa respectively.

1881 *na*: Cf. 1677 above.

1900 sidenote: Cf. the in-column heading Descripcio bona de penis mortis (*with sidenote* Philosophus) L.

1905 *þat*: Logically parallel to *þat* 1903. Translate: 'A tree that was growing . . . and that was wrapped within . . .'.

1906 *mught mught*: Although ungainly, we have let G's forms (= 'mouth might') stand, since there seems no reason to suppose that they are not legitimate spellings.

1958 Translate: 'And value himself (more than death) and (thereby) thwart/hinder death.' *put . . . bifor* may carry connotations of thrusting something forward (here one's spiritual state) for inspection, the *redynes* the passage enjoins.

1971 *of²*: In spite of contrary attestation universally, G is a metrical and headless line. Cf. the variant in 1991.

2024 *mensangere*: Another example of Morris's undue fastidiousness. Although the spelling is uncertainly unusual, it is not unparalleled; cf. the Northern *Ipomadon* 8878.

2056 *here*: In spite of the attestation, the majority reading is probably haplographic.

2096 *beres*: Cf. 1438n.

2102 *quathes*: The more familiar spelling, *wathis*, appears in W*b*.

2154, 2156 *ille dede*: Translate these two uses: '(Should consider) death evil' and '(makes) death evil' respectively. In contrast, as the Latin and the parallel *wele* 2163 indicate, in 2162 *ille* is the adverb 'evilly', and not a predicate adjective.

2159 *sayn*: Morris's *saynt* probably corrects out a perfectly respectable form, although -*t* occurs in all the other copies. However, although universally attested, the word is probably otiose, especially given G's omission later in the line—an error motivated by a line that appears too heavy.

2171 *scit*: This is the form the poet translated (cf. *can* 2172), and in AL, although *sit* may be an acceptable, if confusing, variant spelling.

2174 *soghot*: Although Morris makes the obvious correction to *soght*, the reading of the remainder, a similar form, *noghot*, occurs in 2499 below. The second *o* is a potentially licit epenthetic vowel, breaking a consonant cluster (cf. *Pearl* 11, 326 for 'dewyne'/'dowyne'). Morris thus renders the forms invisible/illegible and makes it impossible to concord them against wider Northern usage. Cf. the similar suppression of a certainly legitimate Yorkshire spelling, *thogh* 'thought', in 2184 and 2436.

2216 sidenote: Cf. Secunda causa quare homines timent mortem L.

2217 *drede*: i.e. *dredde*, the rhyming past tense. Morris's textual commentary misconstrues and suggests reading [*to*] *drede*. This would replace a comprehensible rhyme with at best a half-rhyme.

2235 *With*: The majority reading, with added *þe*, is at least plausible.

2246 *of*: Both variants are probably overspecifying (that in *a* an anticipation of the use of *his* later in the line).

2252 *be*: Morris unnecessarily normalizes the perfectly common GLW spelling to more familiar *bi*; cf. 2555, where he allows the form to stand in the text, whilst noting *bi* H. A further example appears at 2364, where Morris unnecessarily converts G's *Syn* to the spelling *Sen* of *a*R.

2259 *þat*: Although peculiarly placed, the particle parallels *þat* 2255. The underlying structure of the sentence, then, is 'I know I am unworthy . . ., but (also know) that my lord . . .'.

2298 *sal*: In providing *þis/it*, GL read the line in isolation, without recognizing that *þe sight* 2299 is the subject of *sal be*.

2303 *þan*: This *a*R reading relies upon the poet's frequent presentation of *sight[ĕ]* as disyllabic (cf. OE gesihþe). In contrast to this relatively straightforward line, with anacrusis, the other scribes prefer a scansion as a headless line.

2334 L in-column heading: Causa quare demones sunt ita horribiles.

2371 *se*: The variants of ALS appear independent efforts at avoiding an apparent stress-clash, although stress may well fall on *sal*.

2374 *skille*: G may read *skilke*.
  sidenote: Cf. The thyrde skyll to owre vndyrstandyng L.

2391 *grete*: In his textual commentary, Morris suggests reading *eger*, for which there is no support in the manuscripts here consulted.

2408 *here es swa*: A minor bit of haplography in G, the scribe reproducing only one of two consecutive sequences of the letters *es*.

2422–3 The scribe of G initially skipped line 2422, passing from 2421 to the second consecutive line opening with *And wilk*. This error he discovered only at the foot of the column, where he copied line 2449 twice and cancelled the second use. Plainly, just as the scribe of H, he was copying in the same column format as his exemplar and had found here that he was a line short. He then added the line marginally and signalled its insertion at the end of line 2423, rather than at the end of 2421. Morris follows the scribe's direction, but all other copies have the lines in the reverse order.

2433 *day*: In spite of the variation, R is probably wiser than G in omitting the subsequent *þat*. The word has intruded as scribes try to put this line in parallel with the preceding.

2457 *be þaragayne*: Translate: 'raise objections to that' or 'dispute with that'.

2462 L has an in-column heading: Quod non est sperandum presumptuos (?) in bonis operibus triplici de causa.

2489 *oute of*: 'outside of, for reasons extraneous to'; cf. 971n and the use of *within* at 3889 ('inside it').

2508–9 The concluding *to fare wele* follows from *gud hope* in the preceding line, and *he* 2508 is continued in the clause introduced by *þat* 2509. In addition to these syntactic intricacies, natural word order is reversed, so that the object precedes the verb. Translate: 'The man who lives well here may perceive comfort of good hope to continue in a good state.'

2643 G has a later sidenote *nota*.

2649 *þat*: In spite of the weight of attestation, *þat þe*, the reading of AR*b*, is indifferent, probably dittographic.

2692 *buke*: ALM apparently seek an extra syllable, but *buke* has pronounced (if unetymological, cf. OE bēc) -*e*.

2708 L in-column heading: De sex penis purgatorij.

2710 sidenote: Cf. L i. locus purgacionis.

2714 At the head of f. 117rb, A provides an indexing title: Of Purgatory; this reappears on the next four folios, at 2888, 3060, 3234, and 3414.

2750 *a day*: In his textual commentary, Morris suggests prefacing with *in*, which would certainly improve the defective metre. However, the phrase is probably an unmarked dative of time.

2782 *þat*: The poet's source here, *Les Peines*, implies that the antecedent is *ioy*, not *heven*.

2788 sidenote: Cf. Purgatorium ⟨a canc.?⟩ est sub terra W.

2791 *vncrysomd*: There are two problems here. First of all, this limbo is reserved for the *un*baptized, a doctrinal commonplace that may have stimulated W and M in their rendition. Equally, the *ded(e)* that appears later in the line is superfluous (as M again perceived); it has probably been generated as a doublet of the -*ed(e)* of the preceding past participle.

2807 *visited*: The variants are fundamentally non-substantive, but they indicate the contracted form necessary for the metre; this is a headless line.

2813 *men*: The AWL form we print is the unstressed indefinite pronoun *me* 'one, people'.

2889 *for*: Paralleling *For* 2886, although with a shift in the construction from the infinitive to the gerund. Translate: 'they appear to hasten and to warn . . .'.

2894 sidenote: Cf. De diuersis penis (as in-column heading) W.

2902 sidenote: Cf. 1^{a}. pena As.

2920 sidenote: Cf. ij^{a}. pena As.

3004 *þat*: The antecedent is *saules* 3002. Translate: 'the souls that repented, but did not fulfil the conditions of their absolution, shall have various illnesses . . .'.

3102 *þe . . . greves*: Translate: 'The present fire harms.'

3132 *ioyned*: All our manuscripts share the O′ error *pyned*. But Hugh Ripelin had written 'unitur', and we believe it more likely that a scribe early in the tradition misread the form than that the poet read Hugh's text as 'punitur'.

3133 *þe awen body*: i.e. 'its own'.

3169 *war*: Probably to represent the subjunctive *ware* 'should wear (or afflict)'. Hugh Ripelin had written 'durat', not 'urat' (as in 3164, which one might also emend).

3183 *Byhoves*: In his textual commentary, Morris suggests inserting *tham*. But the verb is impersonal and requires no object; indeed, shift from continuing *þai* to the objective would only be confusing. Translate: 'It is fitting that they be burned as . . .'.

3187 *men*: 'Mean, moderate'; cf. 3192.

3190 *veniels*: While the form may simply represent G's dittography before following *s*-, it is defensible as a French adjective marked as plural.

3191 *done*: 'Completed'. But, although there is no support among our copies, the poet may well have written *fordon* 'destroyed'.

3209 *whilles . . . laste*: i.e., until the sin is purged, and the *bandes of syn* thus disappear (3213), and the souls pass to heaven (3244–5).

3213 *haf*: The form is subjunctive, and thus Morris's suggestion, in his textual commentary, of *has/hafes* is unconvincing.

3215 *bydene*: G *bydonen* is unparalleled, here or elsewhere, so far as we can tell, and is probably dittographic.

3287 *þat*: Morris's suggestion, in his textual commentary, of either *here als* or *here er*, misses the construction, in which *here* represents *er/ar*. Translate: 'Some exist who shall, immediately after death, pass . . .'.

3329 *thurgh . . . syn*: To be construed with *ne . . . noght* of the preceding line: 'The fire shall find something, through their venial sin(s), to burn . . .'. The preceding negatives follow from *unnethes* 3326.

3340–2 Translate: 'In exactly the same way, the souls of men who here seem perfect and devoid of all sin . . .'.

3362 G has the later marginal note *mortalia*, and L the in-column heading Peccata mortalia sunt hec.

3419 *summa caballi*: We should probably, following *a mykel lade* 3421, emend the first word as well. Cf. the same proverb, with *sarcina*, at *Speculum Vitae* 5869–70.

3476 *a*: *c*L probably echo the use of *any* in the preceding line.

3487 *na*: In his textual commentary, Morris suggests reading the more explicit *nane*.

3547 *angrese*: The readings—*angwyse* appears in *c*M—seem reasonably equivalent. One of the pair has been derived from the other through confusion of *y* with anglicana *r*.

3574, 3581 *relefed*: As *relevari* 3571 indicates, the archetypal scribe of O'
confused *f* and *s* in producing the now universally attested *relesed*.

3598 At the head of f. 122ʳᵇ, A provides an indexing title: Of Purgatory
And specialy of helpe of frendes fo⟨r⟩ saules þat er in purgatory.

3624 *frendes*: The plural is almost certainly preferable, since the metrical
line depends on reading the parallel plural adjective *som[ë]*. Cf. 3776.

3660 *of þe dede self*: Translate; 'or of the dead person himself'.

3736 *may*: The verb may have absorbed, through haplography in the
archetype of all copies, the unstated subject *þay* (= 'almus, messe, and
bedes' 3722); cf. *þai* 3724, 3726, 3727, 3730.

3776 At the head of f. 123ʳᵇ, A provides an indexing title: Of pardon; the
page still has an intact thread along the leading edge, to facilitate finding it
quickly.

3791 *þat office to wirk*: Follows, a little awkwardly, from *þe right skille why*
3788; translate 'The proper reason for performing that office may be for
. . .'.

3802 sidenote: In L, line 3800 is preceded by the in-column heading Quid
prodest indulgencia animabus existentibus in pena purgatorij.

3813 *dette*: Used a little confusingly over the next two hundred lines to
mean both 'debt' simply and 'what is owing, owed'.

3882 *þat tresour*: For once, a *c* error is not simply a mechanical one, but in
this instance, a metrically otiose overstatement of the obvious. A similar
example appears in 3930.

3944 *Hosteyen*: Most of the scribes have substituted the familiar name of the
great Father for the more obscure commentator on canon law, Hostiensis.
But the subsequent reference to Raymund de Peñaforte, the author of the
great canonical collection *Extra*, as well as of influential materials on
penance, indicates the context of the poet's thinking.

3954 *specify*: Even with the suppression of earlier *þe*, the *a* reading *shewe
and specify* is far too heavy metrically to carry conviction.

3958 At the head of f. 124ʳᵇ, A provides an indexing title: Of þe takens
byfor þe day of dom Of Anticrist. Similar examples, with slightly different
wordings, appear on the next two folios (at lines 4135 and 4317). In the first
instance, Of²] of þe lyf of; and in the third, byfor] ogayne. On ff. 127ʳᵇ
(4495) and 128ʳᵇ (4687), only the first half the note occurs, in the original
form.

3959 *byhoves*: The scribe of *a* has imported the competing reading, *falles*,
from the preceding line.

3985 *synful sal*: The *c* manuscripts intrude *saul(es)*, avoiding the absolute
use of the adjective through a doublet inspired by *sal*.

3996 etc. *Anticrist*: The *c* copies have simply omitted the mark of
abbreviation that should have appeared above *n* in their archetype. In
Latin scripts, *añ* is the normal abbreviation for *ante*. G is particularly prone
to overlooking such markings independently; cf. *chalange* 2266, *warned* 3058,
payn 3230, *frendes* 3521 and 3611.

4028 *na man*: As the Latin shows, the subject. The Middle English word-
order is precise, however, since, were 'you' to be the subject, one would
expect *yhe*, not the object form *yhow*.

4033–4 *a* retains the Latin word-order, and its rendition of the lines avoids
the awkwardness in *cb*, whereby the conjunction that should introduce the
final member appears with that which precedes it.

4036 *sere*: A further archetypal reading which we insert. It is difficult to see
either the *a* or *c* readings as the source of the other, and, given the vapidity
of both, no reason why there should be variation here at all. We suggest that
L, although partially replicating *c*, perhaps as an independent gloss,
preserves the root of the problem. Yet one must acknowledge that *sere* is
scarcely unparalleled in the poem and in general adequately reproduced by
all the scribes.

4102 *alsone*: Analogous to *als-tite*, and representing *als-[s]one*. The form
recurs at 4624 and 8459.

4105 sidenote: Probably originally intended as an in-column heading, for
which no space was left, the same notation appears marginally, in rubric, at
this point in R.

4112 *He*: The *c* copies render the line as a causal statement. In doing so,
they appear to miss the point of the sentence, that Antichrist is not naturally
the evil 'devil's son' (cf. *thurgh kynd* 4110), but that he becomes so by his
own deliberate adoption of evil ways.

4115 *tresor of malice*: i.e. 'the treasury of evil', a locution designed to parody
the papal treasury of grace explained in the preceding part of the poem. The
phrase comes directly from Adso (47/139).

4145–7 The obscure form that this statement takes in G seems predicated
on the confusing centre of line 4145, *swilk men*. The juxtaposition is
confusing, perhaps a stimulus to L omitting the couplet (certainly to W's
replacement of *wele* by *we*), because *men*, the indefinite pronoun 'people', is
actually the subject, whose object is *many swilk*. Translate: 'But people may
easily recognize many such.' G omits, perhaps as independent haplography
(cf. *an an-*), the word crucial to the distinction being drawn: a great many
people may behave in opposition to Christ/God's law, but there is but a
single Antichrist.

4177 *þe Dan*: Although we are dubious as to whether the article could have
been the poet's reading, we have let it stand.

4198 *conversand*: We retain this adjective 'familiar', although Adso here offers 'conseruari' (i.e. nourished and looked after). We take this to be the poet's small mistranslation.

4224 *sal*: Given the suppression of overt expression of this continuing auxiliary (the uses in 4218–19 govern the remainder of the sentence), one might wonder whether it has intruded here from the following line.

4242 *bot²*: AR agreement in 'noght but' is attractive, but the other scribes may transmit a form of the text in which the infinitive *last[ĕ]* is disyllabic.

4307–8 Translate: 'And he shall be seen as he was previously, as if he had risen from death, (so that) men shall . . .'.

4353 *tribulacions*: The singular in *a* may have been derived from the following Latin citation.

4369 *a vision*: As usual, one cannot distinguish between the article plus noun and the more elevated, and perhaps technically specific, noun *avision*.

4596 *by*: Of course, for *be*. *by* and *be* are equally possible spellings of the preposition (modern 'by'), from OE *bī* (stressed) and *be* (unstressed), respectively. G here offers a back-spelling predicated on this analogy.

4865 At the head of f. 129rb, A provides an indexing title: Of þe fiftene takens byfor þe dome þat saynt Ierom of spekes. This particular notation indicates that the scribe intends these guides to identify topics treated on the opening, not the page; the discussion of the 'fifteen signs' occurs on f. 128^vab.

4875 *and*: In G, attracted to the preceding *als*.

5046 At the head of f. 130rb, A provides an indexing title: Of þe general risyng of alle men til þe dom⟨e⟩.

5083 *dredeful*: The first of a sequence of small G errors involving local instances of haplography; see further 5128, 5373.

5167–8 Translate: 'People call that vale "the navel of the world", because it happens (to be) on the surface of the earth, in the middle.' That is, it is placed, as the navel is, in the centre of the body; cf. usual derivation of 'umbilicus' from 'umbus' 'the (central) boss on a shield', e.g. Trevisa, *Properties* 260/2–4.

5168 *imyd*: More or less identical with and representing the fuller form *i(n)myddes* of the other copies collated; cf. 5226, 6443, 6450, etc.

5199 *clotes*: More explicitly *clout(t)es* in the other copies collated.

5220 *even*: i.e. 'heaven'.

5227 At the head of f. 131rb, A provides an indexing title: Of þe commyng of Crist till þe dome Of þe sted whar God sal deme.

5237 *Dredful*: G supplies the connective *And*, not in the other copies. But this sentence deftly reverses the elements of the previous.

5293 *staynged*: Morris cites *stanged* H in note; cf. the discussion of this root, most probably *tang*, at *Speculum Vitae* 9598n, with further references.

5346 *oȝer*: G writes *yogh* (in the form *z*) for *thorn* or *y*.

5408 At the head of f. 132rb, A provides an indexing title: Of þe fourme of man þat Crist sal shewe in þe day of dome.

5418 *thundirs*: As *thonoros* R and *thonowres* W indicate more clearly, an adjective. Translate: 'bolts accompanied by thunder'.

5449 *conscience*: *consciences* AR is more explicit (cf. the Latin plural 5451), a case of apocopated plural after a sibilant (similarly 5452).

5459 Translate: 'not know what to say'.

5469 *þas men*: The direct object of *accuse*.

5482 *þat . . . out say*: The relative clause, 'which they will utter', is largely parenthetical, although the sentence is rather circular in its repetition of information.

5513 *Cristen*: The added *men a* only supplies the obvious, and simply echoes the repeated use of *men* in the surrounding lines. The archetypal *a* scribe may have supplied this complement on the supposition that *Cristen* was unstressed, but the noun is plural, and the adjective *fals*, which is in weak position in any case, represents *fals[ë]*.

5526, 5527 *þam*: i.e. the martyrs. Translate: 'They shall accuse the sinful as having been those tyrants who tortured and slew them.'

5557 *be*: Probably an infinitive following on *er* 5554; translate: 'are to be condemned'.

5566 *þam*: 'Themselves', i.e., as the next line suggests, in the coffers of these rich men, with allusion to Jas. 5: 2–3, which is cited in the source (here Humbert of Romans).

5584 At the head of f. 133rb, A provides an indexing title: Of þe accusurs þat þe synful sal accuse at þe day of dome.

5641 *chede*: To represent *s(c)hede* 'discriminate, separate'. Cf. the widespread Yorkshire representation of the OE suffix *-scip* as *-chep(e)*, as well as sporadic examples of apparent *sh/ch* cross-rhyme in alliterative poems.

5643 *and*: Certainly for *an(e)* and perhaps to be removed as erroneous anticipation of the following word ending in *-d*. But the form is equally likely to be another example of an analogous spelling, since *an* is a widely attested variant of *and*.

5683 *iudicabo*: The AL reading is confirmed by the poet's translation, *sal . . . deme* 5687 (also the reading in the source, Humbert).

5698 *word*: The *c* copies appear to have anticipated the use of *idel* in the following line.

5720 *sal*: A usual small bit of haplography in G. Both *l* and the following *h* begin with the same stroke to form an ascender, and the scribe has provided only one example, not the pair he should have done.

5724 *of yhouthe*: Given the tenor of the discussion beginning at line 5702, the purport of the preceding quotation is to identify, not sins, but sins *of youth*. *Adolescencie* 5722 has no representation in any of our manuscripts, and, although the line-opening *thurgh* could be stressed (a headless line), the line is arguably lacking a stress. This is thus another early archetypal error.

5756 At the head of f. 134rb, A provides an indexing title: Of þe strayt accunt þat men sal yhelde at þe day of dome; it also occurs in the same position on f. 135, at line 5936.

5785 *Had*: The subject is *kyng* 5780, and the construction is governed by *if* in the same line: 'If a king had given his daughter . . . (and) if the reeve . . .'.

5904 The *a* manuscripts omit, apparently having returned to copy, after writing line 5903, at the second example of *sutil-*, rather than the first. W attempts to remedy the omission by supplying an extra line.

6009 *pas*: The *c* addition *mele* is empty padding. It neither helps the metre—the line already has five syllables potentially capable of stress— nor the sense. The intruded word misses (and dissipates) the rhetorical force of *light* 'easy'. The stresses probably fall on *pas*, *light* (with the *-e* of the dative), *rek-*, and *-yng*.

6014 *sythen*: Although not a substantive variant, R provides the metrically more compact form *sen*. The form we print may appear more widely as a way of avoiding the potential confusion of *sen(e) sen(e)*.

6113 At the head of f. 136rb, A provides an indexing title: Of þam þat sal be demed and of þas þat sal noght be demed and of þas þat sal deme and of þas þat sal ⟨n⟩ogh⟨t⟩.

6149 *a drynk*: In the form of G, with *at*, this constitutes a verbal phrase 'offered me (something) to drink'. While this reading may be grammatically more complicated than the simple nominal object, parallel locutions like 6164 and 6190 imply that the simpler reading is apt to be correct. However, cf. 6188, 6774.

6233 *alle*[1]: Probably suppressed in G as repetitive in the context. But without the word, the line is short a stress.

6289 At the head of f. 137rb, A provides an indexing title: Of þe final dome þat Crist sal gyf to þe ?saf.

6324, 6328, etc. *his*: 'God's'.

6397 *on*: Contrast 6370, where the scribe of G may be reproducing archetypal *o*, filled out in the other copies. Here, however, G is apt to be engaging in his frequent haplography, and has elided one part of the repetitive *-n n-*.

6421 *knaw*: G's exemplar may have read *kan* (as in W); however, in copying, the scribe may have become distracted by the subsequent *w-*.

6461 At the head of f. 138rb, A provides an indexing title: Of helle; in the expanded form 'Of þe paynes of hell', it appears in the same position on the next five folios as well (at 6635, 6817, 6997, 7163, and 7336), as well as at the head of f. 143vb (7428).

6516 *þat*: The antecedent is *al* in the preceding line.

6526 *Leutyn*: The form in the Gospel of Nicodemus is 'Leucyus'; the manuscripts may reproduce a spelling assimilated to the common noun *lenten* 'spring' or to the preceding name (in the Gospel 'Carynus').

6630-1, 6791-2 As in the earlier example, lines 1146–51, *c* copies here provide two bits of Latin unparalleled elsewhere. Just as the earlier example, these Latin citations are unique, not simply in their limited transmission but their handling; neither is translated into the poem's English verse. The second, in particular, with its list of nine 'general pains' of hell, looks much more like something associated with the poem's composition than its promulgated text, very like what one imagines the raw materials with which the poet worked. All these may represent then notes intended to be cancelled but inadvertently transmitted through a single archetype of the surviving copies.

6679 *filthe and*: L omits this phrase, very likely wisely. The line appears a good deal too heavy, and the phrase, which does not reproduce the Latin, may represent a sort of 'back-insertion' into the other copies on the basis of lines 6682, 6686, 6692, and 6694.

6732 *clewe*: For *cleve* 'cleave, split'.

6791-2 see 6630-1.

6919 Here G is missing a quire, and we follow Morris in providing, until the omission ends at 9207, the text from G's twin manuscript H.

6932 *clokes*: Morris understood the sense 'claws', but did not know the word, rare in this sense (cf. alliterative *Morte Arthure* 792), but the etymon of modern 'clutch(es)'.

6933-4 *oboute:souke*: A legitimate early English rhyme, with identical vocalism (here long u) and the licence of rhyming any stop with any other having equivalent 'voice' (here both voiceless).

6949 *wormes*: The Latin might suggest rather *moghtes*.

7024 *par*: The majority copies, representing *cb*, here anticipate the need for an object, which the poet had reserved for the succeeding line. While *a* copies provide the superior reading here, at 7038 the previous Latin confirms their error, a small example of haplography (sklaunder*ers*).

7040 *synfull*: Probably adequate, and there are no variants. But given the poet's usual close attention to reproducing the Latin, the word may represent a substitution for *unskylful*, a more expected rendition of *stultorum* 7036.

7093 A here has a sidenote, but it is deep in the gutter and illegible.

7161 *þam*: The *c* copies add *þare*, a blending between the word the archetypal scribe had just copied and the following *mare* he was anticipating.

7211 *knytted*: While the poet may be constrained for rhyme here, this seems a peculiar translation of the transmitted Latin reading *erecti* 'raised'. Possibly the original version had some different reading, e.g. *ligati* or *constricti*. The latter might have been carried over from immediately previous materials in the source here, the *Elucidarium*; cf. 7193–6, reproducing 'per singula membra catenis constricti'.

7328 *dolefull*: The archetypal *c* scribe appears to have anticipated the adjective (or, indeed, *synfull* in the next line) and supplied an extra example of *full*.

7335 *thar . . . trayste*: Translate 'they have no reason to hope (for = *of* earlier in the line)'. OE *þurfan* 'to (have) need', as customarily in the poem, is impersonal.

7357 *weld þair hands*: Translate the line: 'And (yet), whenever they may (in the midst of this cramming and burning), they retain control of their hands'—but only, as the subsequent lines indicate, to wring them in anguish.

7358 *hard*: The adverb 'firmly', which has -*e* and prevents stress-clash.

7423 *make*: This ARL reading is grammatically preferable to *makes* H. In this construction, the verb is in parallel with *stare and gryn* in the preceding line, and not to the preceding *dose* of the subordinate clause. H has arguably been attracted to this verb earlier in the same line.

7505a–n Here Morris's amanuensis made an error reminiscent of a medieval scribe. Having remembered that the last line he had transcribed was *Wharfor he war swylk payns worthy*, he looked back to the manuscript to find that line, only to light upon the poet's verbatim repetition fourteen lines on. As Lightbown first pointed out, the edition consequently omitted these lines from the text.

7510 At the head of f. 144rb, A provides an indexing title: Of þe ioyes of heuen, repeated in the same position of the remaining ten full text leaves (lines 7692, 7884, 8076, 8276, 8474, 8680, 8874, 9064, 9253, and 9446). On ff. 151ra and 152ra, this is supplemented by a second notation, 'Of þe liknes of þe cite of heuen'.

7622 *cerkles*: The scribe of H appears to have missed the suspension indicating unwritten *-er-* and to have assimilated the reading to what, given the context, might be construed the most obvious homeographic noun.

7627–8 The rhyme potentially confirms an authorial *heer* for the superlative, but equally, the rhyme may be provided only by the terminal syllable *-er*.

7732 *heven*: The unsupported A reading *þethen* 'thence, that place' is extremely attractive. The other scribes may have assimilated the form to the use two lines later, but cf. also *hethen* 'hence, this place, earth' 7737, 7745.

7771 We follow the form of the line recorded in A (with important support from R). The *c* copies have intruded *all* from the preceding line, and H*b* have tried to impose full parallelism with earlier members of the sentence.

7776 We emend the line to follow AL, although we suspect that the statement may be otherwise padded out with extra syllables. *men* actually appears the otiose element, but it is universally attested by scribes who may object to the absolute use of the adjective.

7950 (and cf. 7955) *syn*: These are perhaps small archetypal errors, universal in the manuscripts collated here. *Les Peines*, the source here, indicates that the damned are weighed down by their punishments, *pyns*, rather than their *syns*. Although the noun *pyne* historically has a long vowel, and frequently rhymes so, the root does appear rhyming with words in short *i*, in the main proper names (e.g. 2245 *:Martyn*).

8104 *lang*: The archetypal *c* scribe appears to have dropped the word, following the roughly similar strokes of preceding *als*.

8232 *invysible*: Although this reading may appear absurd in a context discussing 'the sight of God', the source here, ps.-Augustine, indicates that it is correct. Cf. 'Tunc justis manifestum est, quomodo Deus est invisibilis, incomparabilis, sine initio et sine fine . . .' (PL 40: 996).

8278 *others*: Although isolated, the explicit A reading clarifies the sense and is paralleled at 8449.

8320, 8341 *haled, hale*: Although Middle English *helen* is a commonplace derivative of OE hǣlan, the poet provides a Middle English reformation based on OE hāl.

8321 *sare*: In H assimilated to the following verb *fele*.

8587 *feth*: The other copies read *fete*, but there are ample parallels in the text for *th* to represent *t*, e.g. *theches* 3555, *thechyng* 3827, *wythenes* 5355.

8697 *war noght a poynt to*: Translate: 'Could not compare in the smallest regard to'.

8815, 8819 A sidenotes: These appear together in R as an in-column heading in rubric preceding line 8816, and are similarly presented in L preceding line 8823.

8860–1 *es als . . . Of:* In H*b*, the verb has been attracted by the use later in the second line; contrast the example at 8906–7, where the archetypal scribe behind *a* apparently has relocated an analogous phrase in an effort to clarify the syntax.

8965 *þe gret . . . kyng:* H reverts to a less problematic prose word-order.

8969, 9042–3 *Lilyas . . . Scipyon:* The archetypal scribe, who presumably read, as in all copies here collated, *Lysias . . . Sampson*, misread what the author had provided. The transmitted reading is plainly nonsense; Samson the judge is a notorious lone wolf, and the author's source (*Elucidarium* 3. 118) provides the reading here bungled, an allusion to Cicero's *De amicitia*. The transmitted *Lysias* is certainly a close homograph of a plausible Middle English form for the name *Laelius*, and the ease of confusing *s* and *l* renders this an easily imaginable scribal rendition of an authorial reading. Laelius's friend was Scipio Africanus the Younger. Even astute scribes encounter difficulty with his name, as for example, in Cambridge University Library, MS Gg.iv.27 of Chaucer's *Parliament of Fowls*. On two occasions (lines 36 and 71), this individual reproduces the name sensibly, but the first time he saw it in his exemplar, he wrote *sothion* (for *sopion*, not *sopion*). Like the archetypal scribe here, he fused *ci* into a vowel written with curved strokes.

9119 *stretes:* The archetypal *c* scribe provides *stedes*, having been attracted to the surrounding uses.

9152 *mot:* H provides *mon*, which is historically plural (OE magon), but is perhaps, following such usages as 96 and 2598, acceptable. Perhaps *mon* echoes the termination of the preceding *þan*.

9203 *sone:* A small example of haplography in H. Faced with the sequence *passes* so*ne* o*way*, the scribe reproduced only one example of the two sequences *so*.

9208 At this point, G returns and provides our copy-text to the end of the poem.

9210 *all:* As the poem nears its end, the scribe of G attempts to reduce potential repetition in adjacent lines; cf. 9251–2, 9524–5.

9218 *nerrer:* The poet's rhyme may not be reflected in the spelling. It may equally represent the contracted *ner* (with close e); cf. the similar *ferre:hegher* (for *heer*?) 7617. See further the full form written at 9234, which may represent the poet's *nest*.

9242 *what . . . swa:* i.e. 'whatever (side)'.

9323 *stane*: The form has the *-e* of the dative, as the Latin and line 9327 show. In *cb*, this has been converted to the more obviously syllabic *-es*.

9342 *withouten*: i.e. 'in excess of'.

9413 *And*: For 'And shall hear', a continuation of the preceding construction.

9486 *blisse*: The universal reading for the obviously plural *blisses*. Customary Northern apocopation here may be re-enforced by the possible haplography at the word-boundary, *blisses sere*.

9488 *es . . . prufe*: Translate: 'That dread (specified in 9489 as that 'which does not accord . . .') may not be demonstrated meritorious/worthy of reward . . .'. Cf. *Speculum Vitae* 399–416 for the traditional distinction between *timor servilis* and *timor filialis*.

9517 *qwikk*: Not only G, but the other manuscripts' variants as well, inscribe confusion with *whilk* 'which', the product of sporadic dialectical fusion of *qw* and *wh* earlier in the manuscript tradition. Cf. *quathes* 2102 for an outstanding example.

9592 *ilka*: Of all the corrections in G, this is one of two proffered by the scribe himself, rather than a corrector.

2. LITERARY MATTERS, PRIMARILY *THE PRICK OF CONSCIENCE* AND ITS SOURCES

Throughout these notes, translations of quotations from the Bible are taken from the Douay–Reims version; square brackets indicate where *PC*'s version differs from the biblical text.

PROLOGUE

The Prologue of *PC* contains a number of echoes of the earlier northern instructional poem *Cursor Mundi* (as well as of *The Northern Homily Cycle*), although there is little clear evidence that the poet used the work directly elsewhere. In its emphasis on self-knowledge, the poem betrays the influence and popularity of Bernard and twelfth-century spirituality during the fourteenth and fifteenth centuries; see 148n.

1–8 The poet begins his work, like many compendious instructional works known to him, including *Cursor*, *The Northern Homily Cycle*, the *Elucidarium* of Honorius Augustodunensis, the *Compendium Theologicae veritatis* of Hugh Ripelin of Strasbourg, and Bartholomaeus Anglicus's *De Proprietatibus rerum*, with God and the Trinity, the origin of the universe. Cf., for instance, *Cursor*, ll. 269–70: 'Tak we our biginning þan / Of him þat al þis world bigan' (all references to *Cursor* are to the text in BL, MS Cotton Vespasian A.iii).

27–8 Cf. *Cursor*, ll. 277–8: 'þof he began al oþer thing / Him self had neuer bigining'.

40 'se or here': Throughout the text is poised, in the poet's presentation, between being read aloud to a communal audience and being read privately and silently; cf. lines 9403n, 9579, 9604–5.

74 'mast digne creature': Although the poet treats man's bodily life with contempt, in common with many twelfth-century works of spirituality, he gives an important emphasis to the dignity of the human soul and its capability to know God through its own likeness to its creator. Unlike any other creature, man has been given a rational soul through which he may apprehend God. The first chapter of the ps.-Bernardian *Meditationes piissimae de cognitione humanae conditionis*, quoted by the poet in lines 247–8 and in Part 1, is entitled 'De dignitate hominis' and similarly emphasizes the dignity of man as created in God's image (*PL* 184: 487–8).

76–80 Cf. *Cursor*, ll. 567–8: 'It has als schilwisnes o will, / þe god to tak and leue þe ill.' Cf. also *Northern Homily Cycle*, Prologue, line 15: 'And gaf him gast of schilwisnes.'

81–2 Cf. *Cursor*, ll. 581–4, also using the doublet 'fless and fell'.

125 'And his wittes despende in his service': Cf. *Northern Homily Cycle*,

Prologue, lines 21–2, 'Forthi suld man in thi servis / Despend his witte and his quaintis.'

139–43 Cf. Ecclus. 1: 16, 'initium sapientiae timor Domini'. Dread of God and the benefits of contemplation upon death are central themes of the *Horologium Sapientiae* of Henry Suso; see especially *Orologium Sapientiae*, 364. Like *PC*, this work was particularly popular in the fifteenth century, with a number of translations of its fifth part on death. See Robert R. Raymo, 'Works of Religious and Philosophical Instruction', in Wells, vii. 2365, 2568 [221]; Valerie M. Lagorio and Michael G. Sargent, 'English Mystical Writings', in Wells, ix. 3125–7, 3466–7 [80]. Cf. also the conclusion, indebted to *PC*, of *Speculum Vitae*, ll. 16001–17 (repeating similar statements at ll. 3493–510).

148 'hym byhoves knaw himself withinne': For the Christian development of the Socratic precept 'Know thyself', see Gilson, 'Self Knowledge and Christian Socratism' and Wittig, 'Piers Plowman B, Passus IX–XII'. Twelfth-century writers like Abelard, Bernard, Hugh of St Victor, and Richard of St Victor all stressed that knowledge of God began with self-knowledge. The popularity of such works of twelfth-century spirituality in the fifteenth century, which saw a revival in the number of manuscripts of twelfth-century texts (discussed by Constable, 'Twelfth-Century Spirituality'), perhaps goes some way towards explaining the apparent popularity of *PC* in the fifteenth century. In its affinity to twelfth-century spirituality, *PC* is similar to other fourteenth-century vernacular works such as *Piers Plowman*, which quotes the opening of the *Meditationes* in B.11.13; see Simpson, 'The Role of *Scientia* in *Piers Plowman*', for discussion.

183–92 Cf. *Cursor*, l. 1 ff., 'Men yhernes rimes for to here'. *PC* does not include *Cursor*'s famous catalogue of romances, probably because, unlike *Cursor*, it is not conceived as a collection of 'gestes' (*Cursor*, l. 123) to rival secular narrative literature. The similarity to the prologue of *Cursor* was not lost on contemporaries: the so-called Lollard sub-group of *PC* manuscripts (for which see Lewis–McIntosh, 6–7 and n. 18) includes interpolated material from *Cursor*'s Prologue.

184 'vanites': Cf. the discussion of the account to be given of 'ilk idel word' in Part 5, lines 5664–73.

205–10 For humility as the virtue which gives man true self-knowledge, see Gilson, *The Mystical Theology of Saint Bernard*, 70–3, citing Bernard's *De gradibus humilitatis*, 1. 2 (*PL* 182: 942).

209 'grund': Cf. *Cursor*, ll. 127–8: 'þar-for þis werc sal i fund / Apon a selcuth stedfast grund'. As the *Cursor* poet 'founds' his work on the Trinity, the origin of the universe, so the *PC* poet 'grounds' his in humility, the most important virtue. Cf. also *Consilia Isidori*, in *Yorkshire Writers*, ii. 369: 'be þou grounded in mekenesse', and *Northern Homily Cycle*, Prologue, lines

81–3, 'Mi speche haf I mint to drawe, / Of Cristes dedes and his sau; / On him mai I best found mi werke'.

247–8 'Beauty, favour of the people, the fervour of youth, and riches deprive you of knowing what man is.' Ps.-Bernard, *Meditationes* 3. 8 (*PL* 184: 490) (Hahn, 16).

285–6 Ps. 35: 4: 'He would not understand that he might do well.'

299–300 Ps. 105: 24–5: 'They believed not . . . and they murmured', with 'murmuraverunt' for biblical 'murmurabant'.

311–12 Luke 8: 13: 'For they believe for a while, and in time of temptation, they fall away', with 'quia' for biblical 'qui'.

316 'þat cordes þarwith': The poet is perhaps thinking of the sermon technique of verbal 'concord', where the preacher would confirm the meanings he derived from the words of his *thema* with authoritative quotations which concorded with his terms either in sense (*concordantia realis*) or in sense and in the actual words (*concordantia realis et vocalis*). See Wenzel, *Preachers, Poets*, 74.

317–19 Ps. 105: 12–13: 'And they believed his words: and they sang his praises. They had quickly done, they forgot his works', with 'opera' for biblical 'operum'.

336–9 Cf. *Northern Homily Cycle*, Prologue, ll. 61–80, where the author explains that both clerks and 'laued man' can understand English, whereas not all men can understand Latin or French. The author of this text distinguishes between clerks, who get their knowledge from Latin books, and 'laud men', who get theirs from hearing. Cf. also *Cursor*, ll. 232–50, also addressing a 'laud' audience. *PC* and *The Northern Homily Cycle* lack *Cursor*'s aggressiveness about the use of English. Cf. also the extensive later discussion, drawing on all three earlier poems, in *Speculum Vitae*, ll. 61–90.

336 'drawen': Cf. *Cursor*, ll. 221–2: 'þis are the maters . . . þat i thynk in þis bok to draw'.

348–69 In its overall design and subject matter, the poem has much in common with works on the theme of *contemptus mundi*, such as the pseudo-Augustinian *Speculum peccatoris*, which complains how few think upon the corruption of the body and the world, the moment of death and the pains of hell (*PL* 40: 985).

The contents (at least of Parts 3–7) and their sequence have significant overlap with *PC*'s main source, *Les Peines*, although the poet's part divisions impose his own *ordinatio* upon the materials he borrows, and he expands on *Les Peines* with a vast amount of additional material.

For the list of contents at the 'entre' of the book, cf. the list of 'poyntes' at the beginning of *Speculum Vitae*, ll. 97–114, and its concluding summary, ll. 16017–46.

PART I

372–4 Cf. Innocent III, *De Miseria*, i. 2. Part 1 is based almost entirely on *De Miseria*, i. 2–9 and 3. 1; Köhler, 197, gives a list of correspondences. The poet perhaps also draws on Innocent's Book 3 in his Part 6, and he quotes from the text again in Part 2, lines 1506–9 and Part 5, lines 5368–401. Chaucer also claims to have translated *De Miseria*, although his translation has not survived. Our poet follows Innocent's order of exposition and typically incorporates biblical quotations in the same sequence as they appear in the source. But he often translates quite freely, and he introduces his own imagery, such as the womb as both the 'herber' and the 'dungeon' of the unborn child in lines 444–57.

A second important source in Part 1 is the ps.-Bernardian *Meditationes*, quoted at lines 560–1, 620–3, 914–15 (as well as at lines 247–8 in the Prologue). It is possible that the poet could have had access to this text in excerpts through some intermediate source; Thomas of Ireland's manual *Manipulus florum*, for instance, includes all the quotations used by the *PC* poet.

The Office of the Dead provides further material for Part 1, as well as being an important source for the poem as a whole. The quotations from the book of Job in lines 414–15, 532–3, 710–11, and 760–1 are all part of the nine lections of the Office of the Dead. At least two of these quotations are probably derived from *De Miseria*, but the quotations from Job in that work perhaps reminded the poet of the Office of the Dead and prompted his inclusion of further passages taken from it (see lines 532–3, 688–727, 710–11nn). For other quotations from the book of Job elsewhere in the poem which are also part of the nine lections of the Office of the Dead, see lines 5095–8, 5494–5, 5722, 6819–20, 6825–6nn.

The poet organizes all these materials around the commonplace threefold division of the ages of man, for which see Burrow, *The Ages of Man*, 5–11. Such a scheme implicitly underlies Innocent's progression in *De Miseria* from the wretchedness of man's conception and birth to the indignities of old age.

372–93 On the creation of man from earth, contrast the rather different account of the creation in *Cursor*, ll. 517–18: 'Of erth allan ne was he noght, / Bot of four elementes worght.' For the question of why God created man from such vile material, compare the account given in the *Elucidarium*, i, 63 (as noted Hahn, 16. All references to the *Elucidarium* are by book and question number). Following Hahn (16), cf. also Rolle, *Super novem lectiones*, ii. 180/1–7. According to Isidore of Seville, the name Adam means 'terra rubra', red earth (*Etymologiae*, 7. 6. 4).

398–9 Matt. 18: 3: 'Unless you . . . become as [a little child], you shall not enter into the kingdom of heaven', with 'parvulus' for biblical 'parvuli'.

410–25 Based upon *De Miseria*, I. 2 (97). As noted by Köhler (p. 198), line 411, although attributed to an anonymous 'clerk', translates Innocent's 'Quid est igitur homo, nisi lutum et cinis?'

414–15 Job 10: 9: 'Remember, I beseech thee, that thou hast made me as the clay, and thou wilt bring me into dust again.' The quotation is taken from *De Miseria*, though it also forms part of the third lection of the Office of the Dead (*Breviarium*, ii. 276; cf. *Prymer*, 60).

422–3 'Remember, man, that you are ashes, and into ashes you will return': cf. Gen 3: 19, 'pulvis es et in pulverem reverteris', and Job 34: 15, 'deficiet omnis caro simul et homo in cinerem revertetur' ('All flesh shall perish together, and man shall return into ashes'). The quotation derives from *De Miseria*, which has 'Cinis es, et in cinerem reverteris'. The same quotation also appears at the beginning of the poem 'Earth into Earth' in Lincoln Cathedral Library, MS 91, where Robert Thornton also provides an extract of lines 438–551 of *PC* (Lewis–McIntosh, E 4).

438–9 Cf. the similarly moralized version of man's birth in 'The Mirror of the periods of Man's Life', ll. 3–8, in *Hymns to the Virgin and Christ*, 58.

444–55 Apparently loosely inspired by *De Miseria*, I. 3 (97–101), which quotes the biblical passage cited here at 450–1. The metaphor of the mother's womb as a 'herber' in line 448, developing the horticultural suggestion of line 445, is the poet's own. Cf. *Speculum Vitae*, ll. 1587–8, apparently echoing the wording of *PC*'s lines 444–60: 'Fra a foul herber he þan came—/þat was fra his moder wame.'

450–1 Ps. 50: 7: 'For behold I was conceived in iniquities; and in sins did my mother conceive me.' The quotation is taken from *De Miseria*.

456–61 Cf. *De Miseria*, I. 4 (101). The English poet's imagery of the womb as a 'myrk dungeon' is his own.

462–75 Cf. *De Miseria*, I. 5 (103).

476–507 Cf. *De Miseria*, I. 6 (103–5).

490 'All are born of Eve saying "E" or "Ah".' Also quoted by Innocent, *De Miseria*, I. 6 (103). See Walther, no. 6845. The Franciscan Nicholas Philip cites the same saying in a sermon from the 1430s; see *Preaching in the Age of Chaucer*, trans. Wenzel, 73.

499–501 'All are born crying in order to express the misery of our nature.' *De Miseria*, I. 6 (103).

508–27 Closely based upon *De Miseria*, I. 7 (105). Line 519 paraphrases the first half of Innocent's quotation from 1 Tim. 6: 7.

512–13 Job 1: 21: 'Naked came I out of my mother's womb, and naked shall I return thither.' The quotation is taken from *De Miseria*.

530–7 Not in *De Miseria*.

532–3 Job 14: 1: 'Man born of a woman, living for a short time, is filled with many miseries', with 'repletur' for biblical 'repletus'. The quotation forms part of the fifth lection of the Office of the Dead (*Breviarium*, ii. 276–7; cf. *Prymer*, 64).

538–45 Perhaps inspired by *De Miseria*, 1. 10 (109), which contains the same quotation from Job as appears in lines 540–1.

540–1 Job 5: 7: 'Man is born to labour [as] the bird to fly.' The quotation is taken from *De Miseria*.

546–629 In moving from man's birth to the second part of his threefold division of the ages of man, the poet leaves *De Miseria* aside to present materials from other sources, particularly ps.-Bernard.

560–1 'Man is nothing other than stinking sperm, a sack of shit, and food for worms'. Ps.-Bernard, *Meditationes* 3. 8 (*PL* 184: 490) (Hahn, 17). Cf. Rolle, *Super novem lectiones*, ii. 129/10–11.

576–7 The story of the ability of the lynx to see through walls seems to have been commonplace: cf. *Bestiary*, pl. 34: 'Oculos habentes murum penetrans' ('having eyes able to pierce through walls'), and Hahn, 17. But our poet might have had this piece of lore from Boethius' *Consolation of Philosophy*, Book 3, Prose 8, since it appears there within a discussion of the mutability of bodily beauty similar to the poet's central theme in Part 1; compare Chaucer's translation, *Riverside Chaucer*, 428/35–49. 'Lynx' in Chaucer's version is the result of a misunderstanding of Boethius' original, really a reference to the Argonaut Lynceus.

592–600 A case in point for the kind of behaviour the poet describes might be Will's sojourn in the Land of Longing in *Piers Plowman* B.11.

592 'proud man': Pride is a common property of middle age (see Burrow, *The Ages of Man*, 46). Pride assaults at twenty years of age in 'The Mirror of the Periods of Man's Life', ll. 113–16, in *Hymns to the Virgin and Christ*, 61.

602–3 Ps. 48: 21: 'Man when he was in honour did not understand: he hath been compared to senseless beasts, and made like to them.' The poet's expansion, 'þat na skylle ne witte can' echoes his earlier discussion (lines 57–82) of how man is made superior to beasts because he is given 'wytte, skille, and mynde' (76) to know good and evil, and free will to choose between them.

620–3 'If you carefully considered what comes from your mouth, what from your nose, and from the other orifices of your body, a viler dung-pit you would never have seen.' Ps.-Bernard, *Meditationes* 3. 7 (*PL* 184: 489). Compare a similar passage in an English sermon quoted by Owst, *Preaching* *in Medieval England*, 341, 'Loke also what fruyt cometh of a man at alle yssues of his body, as at nose, atte mouthe, at eyȝen, and atte alle the other yȝȝues of the body, and of other pryvey membres, and he schall have mater to lowe his herte.'

630–87 The poet quotes, in two blocks, all but the first sentence of *De Miseria*, 1. 8 (105–7).

636–43 'Investigate the plants and the trees, he says: they produce flowers, foliage, and fruit from themselves, and you nits, lice, and worms from yourself. They bring forth oil, wine and balm from themselves, you spittle, urine, and excrement from yourself. They emit a sweetness of smell from themselves, and you give out an abomination of stench from yourself. As is the tree, so is the fruit.' *De Miseria*, 1. 8 (105–7). 'An ille tre may na gude fruyt bere' in 660–1 paraphrases Matt. 7: 18, quoted by Innocent.

666–71 'What is man in his shape but a tree turned upside down? Its roots are the hair, its base is the head along with the neck, its trunk is the chest along with the belly, its branches are the arms along with the legs, its foliage is the fingers and toes along with the joints. This is the leaf that is carried away by the wind and the straw that is dried by the sun.' *De Miseria*, 1. 8 (107) (trans. Lewis, 106). As Köhler notes (p. 200), the idea of man as an inverted tree also appears in Ripelin, *Compendium*, 2. 57.

688–727 The poet's own interpolation into the material he derives from *De Miseria*, apparently influenced by the nine lections of the Office of the Dead. Compare the similar discussion of the flowering of man in his youth and his weakening by disease as his life progresses in Rolle, *Super novem lectiones*, ii. 211/14–212/2.

688–90 On strength and physical beauty in the middle years, compare 'The Mirror of the Periods of Man's Life', ll. 251–2, in *Hymns to the Virgin and Christ*, 66.

695 'son fayles and fades, als dos þe flour': Cf. the refrain in Henryson's 'The Ressoning betuix Aige and Youth', 'O ȝouth, thi flouris fedis ferly sone!' Cf. also Chaucer's *Troilus and Criseyde*, 5. 1841, 'This world that passeth soone as floures faire', and the address to 'yonge, fresshe folkes' in 5. 1835–41. Of course, the idea has biblical precedent: see lines 710–11n.

710–11 Job 14: 2: '[Man] cometh forth like a flower, and is destroyed, and fleeth as a shadow, and never continueth in the same state.' The passage, like that in lines 532–3, forms part of the fifth lection of the Office of the Dead (*Breviarium*, ii. 277; cf. *Prymer*, 64).

720–2 Ps. 89: 6: 'In the morning man shall grow up like grass; in the morning he shall flourish and pass away: in the evening he shall fall, grow dry, and wither', with 'indurat', queried by Morris, for biblical 'induret'.

728–801 Based on *De Miseria*, 1. 9 (107–9). The poet follows the source rather closely, but omits Innocent's quotations from Job 7: 6 and 14: 1 (the latter already quoted in lines 532–3).

734–7 Gen. 6: 3: 'My spirit shall not remain in man for ever, because he is flesh, [and] his days shall be a hundred and twenty years.' The quotation derives from *De Miseria*.

752–3 Ps. 89: 10: 'But if in the strong they be fourscore years: and what is more of them is labour and sorrow.' The quotation derives from *De Miseria*.

760–1 Job 10: 20: '[Now] the fewness of my days [will be] ended shortly.' In the original, the verse is a rhetorical question, 'Shall not the fewness of my days be ended shortly?' The quotation derives from *De Miseria*, though it also forms part of the ninth lection of the Office of the Dead (*Breviarium*, ii. 279; cf. *Prymer*, 69).

764–5 Not to be taken, of course, as a factual statement about the poet's own times: these lines translate Innocent's 'Pauci nunc ad quadraginta, paucissimi ad sexaginta annos pervenient' (107).

766–99 A translation, though not a slavish one, of *De Miseria*, 1. 9 (107–9). Innocent cites as his authority on age Horace's *Ars poetica*, 'Multum senem circumveniunt incommoda'; for the origins of Innocent's catalogue in Horace, see Coffman, 'Old Age', 254. *PC*'s catalogue is very similar, as Coffman indicates (262–7), to the description of Isaac's old age in *Cursor Mundi*, ll. 3555–98. The poet cannot have been working solely from *Cursor*, since he includes several items which seem to be drawn from Innocent and which have no parallel in the English text. It is possible, however, that at some points his wording might have been influenced by the earlier poem: cf. *PC*'s line 775 with *Cursor*, ll. 3572–3: 'þes nese it droppes ai bi-tuine / þe teth to rote, þe aand at stinc' (in Innocent's Latin, 'fetet anhelitus . . . nares effluunt').

This catalogue of the 'propertes of eld' affords a useful opportunity to observe how the poet turns Innocent's Latin prose into English couplets. The poet typically expands by the addition of doublets, so that, for instance, Innocent's 'cor eius affligitur et capud concutitur' becomes 'Than waxes his hert hard and hevy, / And his heved feble and dysy' (lines 770–1); 'facile provocatur' becomes 'lyghtly wrath, and waxes fraward' (line 786).

The poet expands on the catalogue in Innocent by adding a few items of his own: failing wits (line 774; cf. *Cursor*, l. 3583), runny eyes (line 781), slobbery mouth (line 784), and failing speech (line 783). For the latter compare 'Mirror of the Periods of Man's Life', ll. 487–88 in *Hymns to the Virgin and Christ*, 73. For other depictions of age, cf. Humanum Genus in *The Castle of Perseverance*, ll. 2482–91, and *The Parlement of the Thre Ages*, ll. 152–65, in *Alliterative Poetry*. There is a catalogue similar to that in Innocent in *Speculum peccatoris*, from which the poet could have derived some items not included in Innocent's list (*PL* 40: 987).

767 'wayke and colde': In the traditional fourfold scheme of the ages of man based upon the four humours, old age is cold and moist like winter (Burrow, *The Ages of Man*, 12–36). For the coldness of age cf. 'Mirror of the Periods of Man's Life', l. 470, in *Hymns to the Virgin and Christ*, 73; and Henryson's 'The Ressoning betuix Aige and Youth', l. 61 and his portrait of Saturn in his *Testament of Cresseid*, ll. 155–68.

802–29 Not in Innocent. For discussion of the signs of death in 812–29 and a list of known Middle English versions of these signs (which appear in both medical and religious texts), see Robbins, 'Signs of Death in Middle English', esp. 290–1, 293–4. According to Robbins, the signs in *PC* 'are as much medical as religious . . . seven of its eight indications . . . come from vernacular medical texts, and the eighth [that in line 822] . . . from the Latin *Flos Medicinae Schola Salerni*'. Compare the almost identical list in *Liber de Diversis Medicinis*, 58/28–38. Many of the signs, including sharpening of the nose (included in the description of Falstaff's death in *Henry V*), seem to originate ultimately with the *Prognostics* of Hippocrates: see *Hippocrates*, ii (8–9). Cf. also *Hippocratis Aphorismi*, 4. 49.

830–79 Apparently derived from *De Miseria*, 3. 1 (205–7), which contains the quotations in lines 866–7 and 876–7 consecutively, and from which the poet quotes directly in lines 854–5. The poet reverses the order of exposition, however.

854–5 'What indeed is fouler than than a human corpse, what more horrible than a dead man?' *De Miseria*, 3. 1 (207).

866–7 Ecclus. 10: 13: 'For when a man shall die, he shall inherit [worms and serpents]'. The quotation is taken from *De Miseria*.

876–7 Job 21: 26: '[All] shall sleep . . . in the dust, and worms shall cover them.' The quotation is taken from *De Miseria*.

880–919 The poet's own addition. Again, the poet turns from *De Miseria* to materials from elsewhere, including pseudo-Bernard.

898–9 'Anyone who were to perceive where he is heading, and from whence he came, would never make merry, but at all times weep.' Walther, no. 29074.

914–15 'After man, worms, after worms, stench and ugliness. And thus every man turns into no-man.' Ps.-Bernard, *Meditationes* 3. 8 (*PL* 184: 490) (Hahn, 18). The same verses also appear in *Speculum peccatoris* (*PL* 40: 988).

PART 2

The poet's treatment of the world is very broadly similar to that found in Innocent's *De Miseria*, 1. 13–27, and he quotes directly from chapter 25 of that work in lines 1506–9. His account also has much in common with handbooks for preachers, particularly in the comparison of the world to a sea, a wilderness, a forest, and a battlefield; some of the poet's materials may well have been derived from such a handbook.

To these various pulpit commonplaces about the world the poet adds, at the beginning of Part 2, a 'scientific' description drawn from Bartholomaeus Anglicus's encyclopedia, *De Proprietatibus rerum* (see Köhler, 200–2). The poet's 'scientific' accounts of the world and the heavens here and at the beginning of Part 7 (as well as the discussion of the location of hell and the likeness of the world to an apple or an egg in Part 6, lines 6437–52) perhaps seem digressive, giving way to an encyclopedic impulse not entirely in keeping with the poet's stated aim of arousing humble dread. But as Brague, 'Geocentrism', discusses, medieval writers frequently drew from the lowly position of the world in the universe a lesson in humility. Here and in the later discussions in Parts 6 and 7, the poet stresses that the earth, located at the centre of the universe, also stands at its lowest point, made of baser matter than the heavens around it. Hell, at the very centre of the earth, is the lowest place of all (cf. lines 7582–9). This was the typical medieval view of the cosmos, in which those places nearest the centre are coarser in substance than those farthest away. Cf., for instance, in a statement our poet might well have known, Moses Maimonides, *Guide for the Perplexed*, 1. 72 (192): '[The earth's] nobler part surrounds its inferior part . . . For wherever bodies are near the center, they grow dimmer and their substance coarser, and their motion becomes more difficult, while their light and transparency disappear because of their distance from the noble, luminous, transparent, moving, subtle, and simple body—I mean heaven.'

966–1001 According to Bartholomaeus, the lower world stretches from the circle of the moon to the centre of the earth, the higher from the circle of the moon to the planets. The higher parts of the world are nobler, because the matter there is clearer and purer (*De Proprietatibus*, 8. 1; Trevisa, *Properties*, i. 442/13–17, i. 445/17–22). The 'signes' (line 997) of the zodiac are described in *De Proprietatibus*, 8. 9–10. For man as microcosm (lines 1046–7), cf. *De Proprietatibus*, 8. 1 (Trevisa, *Properties*, i. 441/30), although the idea is commonplace.

985 'afterward': That is, in Part 7, lines 7548–79, where the poet discusses the heavens.

1036 'gastly batayls': The prose text *A Treatise of Ghostly Battle*, which appears in BL MS Harley 1706 and six other manuscripts, is closely related in themes and source material to *PC* (see Jolliffe, *A Check-List*, H.3. The text is cited here from *Yorkshire Writers*, ii. 420–36; it has also been edited by Valerie Murray). Relihan argues (*Les Peines*, 61–71, 86–7) that the *Treatise* and *PC* are independently derived from the Anglo-Norman version of *Les Peines de Purgatorie*; cf. also Murray's discussion (*Treatyse*, i. 83–6). Certainly, the descriptions of the pains of purgatory in the *Treatise* and *PC* seem to be, as Relihan and Murray both argue, independently derived from

Les Peines. The *Treatise* reproduces the list of six sins and corresponding diseases from the description in *Les Peines* more or less exactly, whereas *PC* provides a full list of seven sins and alters the diseases associated with each sin (see 2982–3001n and cf. *Yorkshire Writers*, ii. 432). However, there is room for some uncertainty elsewhere. As Relihan points out, the *Treatise* is eclectic in its use of sources (it also draws on *Dives and Pauper*, *Pore Caitif*, and *The Three Arrows on Doomsday*), and it seems to us not impossible that the author of the *Treatise* might have consulted *PC* as well as *Les Peines*, at least for his description of heaven. The *Treatise* includes at this point what appears to be a fairly close translation of *PC* lines 8186–210 (cf. *Yorkshire Writers*, ii. 433). The *PC* poet was himself dependent on *Les Peines* for his own description of heaven, and both the *Treatise* and *PC* contain in their discussions of this topic an image which is ultimately derived from *Les Peines*, ll. 458–63; see 8040–9n. However, in lines 8186–210 the *PC* poet is conflating a second source, the ps.-Augustinian *De triplici habitaculo* (see 8204–73n). Either the author of the *Treatise* was also combining exactly the same materials from *Les Peines* and the ps.-Augustinian source as found in *PC*'s description of heaven, or he was using *PC* itself. In any case, the close connection between the two Middle English texts is clear, and his use of materials from *Les Peines* and *The Three Arrows* indicates that the author of the *Treatise* shared our poet's interest in eschatological themes. See also 2424–57, 7113–14, 7261–6, 7324–7nn.

1049 'aftirward': In lines 1480–1515.

1084 John 12: 31, 14: 30, 16: 11; cf. the allegory of the soul as a castle under siege by 'A proud prikere of Fraunce, *Princeps huius mundi*' in *Piers Plowman* B.9.1–9.

1095 'bysy' is a typical Middle English locution for worldly solicitude; cf. *Piers Plowman* B.7.130.

1100–3 Matt. 6: 24: 'No man can serve two masters. For either he will hate the one, and love the other: or he will sustain the one, and despise the other', intruding 'quia'.

1114–15 Jas. 4: 4: 'Whosoever therefore will be a friend of this world, becometh an enemy of God.' The Vulgate has 'quicumque ergo voluerit amicus esse saeculi huius'.

1122–3 1 John 2: 15: 'Love not the world, nor the things which are in the world.'

1126–45 For medieval ideas about the lust of the flesh, lust of the eyes, and pride of life of 1 John 2: 16, see Howard, *The Three Temptations*, 44–56.

1130–3 1 John 2: 16: 'All that is in the world, is [either] the concupiscence of the flesh, [or] the concupiscence of the eyes, [or] the pride of life.' The

Vulgate has 'concupiscentia carnis et concupiscentia oculorum est et superbia vitae'.

1146–51 In Morris's edition these lines have been removed from the text; see Textual Note. The following note refers to the collations. 'Concerning the hermit who pursued the world when it fled from him, and afterward fled the world when it pursued him: "World, farewell! woe to you! Fleeing me, so long as I follow you, now you pursue me, when I spurn you, hating you".' Source unidentified. A similar passage appears in John Bromyard's *Summa praedicantium, s.v.* mundus, Art. 3. 6: 'Quedam dixisse qui cum de heremo ad episcopatum electus ait, "O munde immunde: quamdiu te secutus sum et fugisti sed nunc fugientem sequeris".' ('A certain man said when he was elected as bishop from his hermitage, "Oh unclean world! As long as I pursued you, you fled me, but now that I flee you, you follow me".')

1152 'als says Haly Writ': In Gen. 1: 28, God gives Adam and Eve the earth and its creatures to rule over.

1164–93 Translated from *De Proprietatibus*, 8. 1 (Trevisa, *Properties*, i. 446/2–21).

1202–4 'O unclean world, would that you were so unclean, that you might not touch me, or so pure, that you might not pollute me.' Source unidentified.

1211–56 The poet's series of comparisons of the world with a sea, a wilderness, a forest, and a battlefield resembles similar comparisons in manuals for preachers, and may have been inspired by such a manual. One source certainly known to our poet, part 7 of Humbert of Romans's *De Abundantia exemplorum*, compares the world to the sea, a desert, a furnace, a dangerous road, a prison, and a ruined house. *Fasciculus morum* compares the world with a sea, a treacherous marketplace, and the Flood; see 5. 27 (556/26–8, 558/52, 558/64–5). John Bromyard compares the world with a shadow, a game of chess, and a game of dice; lovers of the world are compared with horses who carry treasure all day but who sleep at night in a dirty stable (*Summa praedicantium, s.v.* mundus).

1213–14 For the world likened to the sea, compare *Fasciculus morum* 3.21 (282/135, 284/149) and 4.10 (372/36–46); *Manipulus florum, s.v.* mundus, T and U; *Summa praedicantium, s.v.* mundus, Art. 5.17. The world as a sea is of course a commonplace; see Hanna, 'Some Commonplaces', 79–80 n. 3, for tribulation as fire or water as 'a fixed piece of virtue discussions'.

1245–56 For life on earth as a battle, cf. Innocent, *De Miseria*, 1. 18 (125–7), quoting Job 7: 1, the ultimate source of this idea.

1258 'twa handes': Cf. *Speculum Vitae*, ll. 2241–6, 'þe Werlde assaylles on aythir syde / A man þat wil it here habyde. / On þe right syde, als I gesce,

/ It assaylles thurgh welth and ritches; / And on þe left syde alswa, / It assaylles thurgh angre and wa.' For the medieval conception of fortitude as the virtue which involves resistance to the temptations attendant upon both prosperity and adversity, see Harris, *Skelton's Magnificence*, 71–126.

1273–79 For conventional depictions of 'dam Fortone' and her wheel, see Patch, *The Goddess Fortuna*, 35–87, 147–77. For Fortune and her wheel, cf. also *Cursor*, ll. 23719–20.

1282 'happe or chaunce': Cf. the discussion of 'hap' in *Boece*, Book 5, Prose 1 (*Riverside Chaucer*, 457–8).

1295–7 'In so much as we grow in accomplishments, so much the more we ought to fear, that we not fall from higher.' Jerome, *Commentarium in Joelem prophetam*, 1 (*PL* 25: 971).

1304–5 'Then summon to you sound counsel, when worldly good fortune sportively approaches you.' Martin of Braga, *Formula vitae honestae*, 1, 'De prudentia' (*PL* 72: 24), generally attributed to Seneca in the Middle Ages.

1312–13 'If all fortune is to be feared, nevertheless prosperity more so than adversity.' Hahn (19) compares *Twelve Profits of Tribulation* (*Yorkshire Writers*, ii. 46), which cites the same saying of Gregory. In her edition, *The Book of Tribulation*, Alexandra Barratt gives the source as Gregory, *In septem psalmos poenitentiales*, 7 (*PL* 79: 646). Cf. also *Moralia in Job*, 5. 1 (*PL* 75: 679–80).

1324–5, 1332–3 'Continual health and abundance of goods are signs of eternal damnation'; 'A continuous succession of temporal goods is a sign of future damnation' Sources unidentified. As noted by Trudel (*Speculum huius vite*, ii. 422), the two quotations also appear as a pair in *Speculum Christiani*, 205/30–3. The quotation in 1324–5 also appears in *Speculum Vitae*, ll. 7761–4.

1339–41 Cf. *De Miseria* 1. 14: 'Secundum fortunam estimatur persona, cum pocius secundum personam sit estimanda fortuna' ('A person is valued according to his wealth, when wealth should be valued according to the person') (115–17, trans. Lewis, 114–16).

1356–7 1 Cor. 3: 19: 'The wisdom of this world is foolishness with God', with 'sapientia' for biblical 'sapientia enim'.

1362–86 Cf. *De Miseria*, 1. 17 (123–5), which includes both the quotations in lines 1370–1 and 1382–3 in the same order.

1370–1 Heb. 13: 14: 'We have not here a lasting city, but we seek one that is to come', with 'non' for biblical 'non enim'. That this life is a pilgrimage is commonplace, especially in *contemptus mundi* literature; cf. for instance Rolle's *Super novem lectiones*, ii. 124/2–3 and *Speculum peccatoris* (*PL* 40: 986). For the 'pilgrimage of life' as a literary genre in texts including

Deguileville's *Pèlerinage de vie humaine*, see Wenzel, 'The Pilgrimage of Life'.

1382–3 Ps. 38:13: 'Be not silent: for I am a stranger with thee, and a sojourner as all my fathers were', intruding 'ego'.

1432 On the changeableness of time, cf. *De Proprietatibus*, 9. 2 (Trevisa, *Properties*, i. 517/35–518/37.

1481 'als es sayd byfor': In lines 1046–7.

1486–99 As Hahn notes (p. 19), the comparison resembles *Compendium*, 2. 57.

1506–9 'The world has already grown old, both the macrocosm, the greater world, and the microcosm, the lesser world; and the longer the old age of each is extended, the more severely the nature of each is disturbed.' *De Miseria*, 1. 25 (137). *De Miseria* reads 'Senuit iam mundus uterque, megacosmus et microcosmus, et quanto . . .'.

1554–5 Ps. 105: 29: 'And they provoked him with their inventions: and destruction was multiplied among them', with 'irritaverunt' for biblical 'inritaverunt' and 'advencionibus' for biblical 'adinventionibus'.

1574–5 Ps. 80: 13: 'So I let them go according to the desires of their heart: they shall walk in their own inventions', with 'eos' for biblical 'illos' and 'advencionibus' for biblical 'adinventionibus'.

1612–13 Isa. 5: 20: 'Woe to you that call evil good, and good evil', intruding 'vobis' (for which cf. Matt. 23: 16).

PART 3

The first chapter of the Anglo-Norman *Les Peines de Purgatorie* supplies *PC*'s lines 2384–2457 and 2651–73, including the long quotation from 'Anselm' in lines 2424–57. The poet's list of 'four special reasons why death is feared' was probably adapted from the list presented under the heading 'De timore mortis' in part 5 of the *Tractatus de Abundantia exemplorum* by Humbert of Romans, also used by the poet in Part 5. However, our poet presents only four from a list of eight in the source, and he fills out each item with his own materials, including the speech of Bernard in lines 2255–67, perhaps taken from Jacobus de Voragine's *Legenda Aurea*. It is possible that the poet derived some of his other materials, especially earlier in Part 3, from a handbook for preachers of some kind. Several of his patristic quotations, including those in lines 1982, 2160, and 2588, appear in forms which differ from the original sources but which appear to have been current citation forms, attested in manuals such as *Speculum Christiani* and *Manipulus florum*; the quotations in 2008 and 2038 also appear as a pair in the former work.

1736–7 'I desire not the death of the [sinner], but that [rather he] turn . . .

and live.' Cf. Ezek. 33: 11, 'nolo mortem impii sed ut revertatur impius a via sua et vivat'.

1758–9 The poet describes the living death of hell in lines 7267–85.

1790 'Death releases everything.' Walther, no. 38355.

1818–31 A similar, though more extensive, list appears in Humbert of Romans's *De Abundantia exemplorum*, part 5, 'De timore mortis'. The poet, if he indeed made use of this source, selected only four items from an original list of eight, and those he included he elaborated with his own materials. However, the poet's items appear in the same sequence as in *De Abundantia exemplorum*, and several details suggest that this was indeed the basis for the English poet's list: see 1844–7, 2002–19, and 2242–97nn.

1832 'byfor I spake': In lines 1766–73, where the poet originally introduced the first two items in this list of four, the pain of death and the uncertainty about one's eternal fate.

1840–3 Cf. *Cursor*, ll. 17009–12.

1844–7 As Hahn indicates (p. 19), this comparison with a husband and wife was probably derived from *De Abundantia exemplorum*, part 5, 'De timore mortis', the major source of the poet's list of causes to fear death: 'vt patet in uiro et uxore' ('as appears in the case of a husband and wife'). Our poet expands on the source in setting out four reasons why the body and soul would not be parted.

1876–9 'Death does not pity poverty, nor respect riches, or wisdom, or morality, or age.' Bernard, *De conversione ad clericos*, 7 (*PL* 182: 843) (Hahn, 20).

1892–3 Ecclus. 9: 20: 'Know it to be a communication with death.'

1900–23 As Hahn indicates (p. 20), there is a similar comparison between the death of a man and the felling of a tree in Antoninus Florentinus, *Summa theologica*, 4. 14. 8.

1932–3 Ecclus. 41: 1: 'Oh death, how bitter is the remembrance of thee to [the unjust man]', with 'iniusto' for biblical 'pacem habenti in substantiis suis'. Cf. *Orologium Sapientiae*, 358: 'O deth, how bitter is þy mynde to a likynge herte and norisched vp in delyces!'

1948–9 'What in human affairs is more certain than death; what more uncertain than the hour of death's coming?' Bernard, *De conversione ad clericos*, 7 (*PL* 182: 843) (Hahn, 20).

1962–7 'You do not know in which hour death will come: always keep watch, so that, since you do not know when he will come, he may find you ready when he comes. Perhaps, too, it is for this reason that you do not know when he will come, that you may always be prepared.' Augustine, *Enarratio in psalmos*, 120 (*PL* 37: 1606).

1982–5 'The last day is hidden, that all days might be attended to; remedies are prepared too late, when the dangers of death are imminent.' 'Latet . . . omnes dies': Augustine, *Sermones*, 39. 1 (*PL* 38: 241); 'sero . . . pericula': *Glossa Ordinaria*, 2, on Esther 7: 1. Chris Nighman (private communication) points out to us that this pairing of sources as one quotation also occurs in Thomas of Ireland, *Manipulus Florum*, *s.v.* mors M.

2002–19 *De Abundantia exemplorum*, part 5, 'De timore mortis', also discusses how death inhibits thoughts of making amends for sin, although here citing the authority of Gregory. On the paralysing fear accompanying death, compare also *Orologium Sapientiae*, 360.

2008–9 'The fear of death claims the whole soul to itself, so that one is unable to think about one's sins.' Unidentified. Trudel (*Speculum huius vite*, ii. 424) notes that the same passage is also quoted and attributed to Augustine in *Speculum Christiani*, 209/9–10.

2038–41 'The sinner is struck with this perception, so that dying he forgets himself, who while living forgot God.' Ps.-Augustine; really Caesarius of Arles, *Sermones*, i. 277; cf. *PL* 39: 2153, 2221. The same quotation appears, following the previous one in lines 2008–9, in *Speculum Christiani*, 209/10–11. The quotation also appears, though there attributed to Gregory, in *De Abundantia exemplorum*, part 5, 'De timore mortis'.

2058–9 Ps. 81: 7: 'You like men shall die: and shall fall like one of the princes', with 'vos' for biblical 'vos autem'.

2070–1 Eccles. 12: 1: 'Remember thy creator . . . before the time of [his visitation] come.' The Vulgate has 'memento creatoris tui in diebus iuuentutis tuae, antequam veniat tempus adflictionis'.

2080–1 Ps. 6: 6: 'For there is no one in death, that is mindful of thee.'

2096–111 Cf. Rolle, *Super novem lectiones*, ii. 213/7–8: 'Quanto enim puer ad statum hominis crescit, tanto proprius ad non hominis statum uenit' ('For as far as the boy grows towards the condition of a man, the closer he comes to the condition of non-man').

2124–5 Ps. 9: 15: 'Thou that liftest me up from the gates of death, that I may declare all thy praises in the gates of the daughter of Sion.'

2133 'þe sight of pes': The poet alludes to the Hebrew etymology of 'Jerusalem'.

2150–3 'A bad death is not to be thought of where a good life precedes, for only what follows death makes death evil.' Augustine, *De Civitate Dei*, 1. 11 (*PL* 41: 25–6) (Hahn, 21).

2160–1 'He who has lived well cannot die badly, and scarcely can he die well who has lived badly.' The first half of the quotation is Augustine, *De Disciplina Christiana*, 12 (*PL* 40: 676) (Hahn, 21). The second half we have not located in Augustine, though it is quoted, as here, in Thomas of Ireland,

Manipulus florum, s.v. mors S, and in *Speculum Christiani*, 49/24–5 and 209/1–2.

2170–1 'He who scorns to live does not fear death.' *Disticha Catonis*, 4. 22 (Hahn, 21).

2180–1 Phil. 1: 23: '[I desire] to be dissolved and to be with Christ/.' The Vulgate reads 'desiderium habens dissolvi'.

2190–1 Eccles. 7: 2: 'The day of death [is better than] the day of one's birth', intruding 'quam'.

2198–9 Rev. 14: 13: 'Blessed are the dead, who die in the Lord.'

2216–19 'þe secund skil': Cf. *De Abundantia exemplorum*, part 5, 'De timore mortis': 'Aliud est occursus demonum' (in the source, the fourth reason why death is to be feared). See Gurevich for the death-bed scene, in which the dying man is confronted by devils, as 'a favourite theme of medieval art' (*Medieval Popular Culture*, 186). For devils in popular literature, see ibid. 186–94. *The Gast of Gy*, a poem very similar to *PC* in its treatment of purgatory (for which see notes to Part 4), describes the sight of devils as the greatest trouble at the time of death; see ll. 599–608, in *Three Purgatory Poems*.

2238–9 Lam. 1: 3: 'All [his enemies] have taken [him] in the midst of straights', with 'inimici' for biblical 'persecutores' and 'eum' for biblical 'eam'.

2242–97 There is a very similar passage on how the devil tried to impede the soul of St Martin on its journey to heaven and how the Blessed Virgin asked that she be spared the sight of devils at her death in *Speculum peccatoris* (*PL* 40: 990). Here the poet would have found already combined accounts of the deaths of Martin and the Blessed Virgin, although he may also have known these, as Hahn suggests (p. 21), from the *Legenda Aurea* (ii. 1150, ii. 780). In the latter source, he could have found Bernard's life immediately following the Assumption of the Virgin (ii. 818–19). The speech of Bernard in lines 2255–67 directly translates a speech which appears both in the *Legenda Aurea* and in two lives of Bernard (*PL* 185: 491, 258) (cf. Hahn, 21).

The original suggestion for the poet's discussion of the appearance of devils at the deaths of Martin, Bernard, Mary, and Christ probably came, however, from *De Abundantia exemplorum*; cf. lines 2242–7 with part 5, 'De timore mortis': 'Quid autem mirum si adueniunt ad mortem impii affuit dyabolus etiam in obitu Martini et ipsius Christi?' ('why should anyone wonder that they come at the death of the wicked when the devil also appeared at the death of Martin and of Christ himself?'). As throughout his list of reasons why death is to be feared, the poet seems to have used *De Abundantia exemplorum* as a framework into which he inserted his own selection of materials from other sources.

2374–569 The 'representatio' each soul must make before God at the time of death is the fifth reason why death should be feared in *De Abundantia exemplorum*. Our poet's account derives chiefly, however, from that in *Les Peines*. The idea that angels and devils would dispute over the fate of the individual soul at the time of death was a common one in popular visionary literature and, as in *PC*, this belief was not felt to be incompatible with the apparently contradictory official doctrine concerning the Last Judgement of all souls at the end of time (treated by our poet in Part 5). See Gurevich, *Medieval Popular Culture*, 119–22, 138–40.

2384–457 Cf. *Les Peines*, ll. 45–74. The author of *PC* follows the similar account in *Les Peines* of angels and devils disputing for man's soul fairly closely, using the same verb, 'dispute' (2388) for the Anglo-Norman 'desputer' ('ut disputent' in the Latin version of *Les Peines*). Only lines 2400–1 of this initial description of the 'dispute' between angels and devils seem to have no direct parallel in *Les Peines*. *PC* cites, in the same order, the two authorities—Luke 12: 2 and Anselm's *Meditatio* 1—also found in *Les Peines*. In both these quotations, as discussed below, the author of *PC* seems to be working from *Les Peines* rather than directly from the original sources.

2404–11 *Les Peines* also provides a translation of the biblical passage cited here (Luke 12: 2), and then quotes the Latin original (*Les Peines*, ll. 52–7). The poet seems to be working from the Anglo-Norman translation in *Les Peines* rather than directly from the biblical original, since he writes 'swa covered and hydde . . . swa prive', apparently imitating the Anglo-Norman 'si privement . . . si celes', rather than the straightforward 'opertum' and 'occultum' in the Vulgate original. PC poet's 'prive' echoes 'privement muscee' in *Les Peines*.

2424–57 The ultimate source is Anselm's *Meditatio* 1, but Relihan argues persuasively (*Les Peines*, 72–5) that the poet worked from *Les Peines*, ll. 57–74, which contains exactly the same extract from Anselm immediately following its quotation from Luke 12: 2. An independent English translation of the whole meditation (edited from Oxford, University College MS 97 in *Yorkshire Writers*, ii. 443–5) appears alongside an excerpt from *PC* rendered into prose in BodL, MS Laud misc. 23 (see Wood, 'A Prose Redaction'). *A Treatise of Ghostly Battle* also contains a brief extract from the same Anselmian source (*Yorkshire Writers*, ii. 429); for this text and its relation to *PC*, see 1036n.

    That *PC* derives from *Les Peines* and not directly from Anselm can be seen by comparing their treatment of the passage in which Anselm describes how many sins will be revealed before us at death (our account here follows Relihan): 'Certe plura et fortassis terribiliora his quae nunc vides' ('certainly more and perhaps more frightful than those which you see now') (*Opera omnia*, iii. 77). *Les Peines* expands Anselm's 'plura et fortassis terribiliora' to 'plus e, par aventure, plus a doter *e plus oribles*' ('more and, perhaps, more fearful *and more horrible*') (ll. 69–70). *PC* follows this expansion by referring to '*foule and ugly* syns . . . / of whilk þou sal haf mare drede and awe, / þan of þa þat þou mught here knawe' (2449–51) (our emphasis). Cf. also *PC*'s lines 2452–3 with *Les Peines*, ll. 71–3, and lines 2453–6 with *Les Peines*, ll. 73–4, in both cases omitting the same material from the original Anselmian text. 'Efter þi werkes' (2455) translates 'solom vos fez' in the Anglo-Norman version of *Les Peines* (l. 73), a phrase which has no equivalent in the Latin version.

2496–7 'Our bad deeds are entirely bad, but our good deeds are not entirely good.' Cf. the similar statement in Gregory, *Moralia in Job*, 35. 22 (*PL* 76: 780).

2502–3 'All our justices as the rag of a menstruous woman'. As Hahn indicates (p. 22), actually Isa. 64: 6, with 'omnes' for biblical 'universae'.

2514–15 'Man does not know whether he is worthy of hatred or love.' Ps.-Augustine, Sermo 44 (*PL* 40: 1321).

2522–3 'When the servant of God does good, he does not know whether it be good for him or not.' Isidore of Seville, *Sententiarum* 3. 9 (*PL* 83: 694) (Hahn, 22).

2530–1 'Who, without trepidation and fear, may lead this life?' Source unidentified.

2542–7 My whole life terrifies me, which fully considered appears to me either sinful or useless; and if anything in it seems fruitful, it is either illusory, or imperfect, or in some other way corrupted, so that it would either not be acceptable to God, or else displease him.' Ps.-Bernard, *Tractatus de interiori domo seu de conscientia*, 19 (*PL* 184: 525).

2570 'þe ferth skille': Cf. *De Abundantia exemplorum*, part 5, 'De timore mortis': 'Aliud est ignote regionis ingressus' (here sixth in the list of fearful accompaniments to death).

2588–92 'Well ought everyone to fear his last day, because as each shall be found in his last day, when he goes out of the world, so shall he be judged in the last day.' Augustine, *Epistola* 199. 1 (*PL* 33: 905). The poet in fact presents a paraphrase of the original passage. As Chris Nighman points out to us (private communication), an identical paraphrase occurs in *Manipulus florum*, *s.v.* mors P.

2618 'aftirwarde': In the poet's account of the Judgement in Part 7, lines 4957–6240. See especially line 6071 for the Judgement as a 'ful hard day'.

2637–42 From *Les Peines*, ll. 74–7.

2651–73 The end of *PC*'s Part 3 closely translates the beginning of chapter 1 of *Le Peines*, ll. 28–39. *PC* includes the same citations from Ecclus. 7: 40 and Augustine—although the *PC* poet evidently felt able to supply, from

memory or consultation, the Latin of the passage from Ecclus. 7: 40, which
Les Peines provides only in French translation.

2655–7 Ecclus. 7: 40: 'In all thy works remember thy last end, and thou
shalt never sin.' The passage is the incipit of *Les Peines* and appears in many
contemptus mundi themed texts.

2673 Cf. ps.-Augustine, Sermo 48 (*PL* 40: 1331–2), quoting Ecclus. 7: 40.
The quotation is taken from *Les Peines*, ll. 35–7.

PART 4

Part 4 is unusual in that the poet provides quite detailed information about
several of his sources in lines 3940–51. Köhler (p. 203) and Hahn (p. 23)
discuss the *Compendium Theologicae veritatis* of Hugh Ripelin of Strasbourg
(named by title in lines 2730–1, although attributed there to Thomas
Aquinas) as the major source of the poet's treatment of purgatory. This
text the poet refers to as 'a buke of þe payns of purgatory' in lines 2728–36.
However, the poet's most important source, never named in the text, is
perhaps once again *Les Peines*. The Anglo-Norman work probably provided
the poet's basic framework for this part, and it is certainly the source of the
poet's list of venial sins in lines 3440–95 and the main source of his list of
the pains of purgatory. Other sources named by the poet are 'Innocent'
(probably Innocent IV, not Innocent III, as Köhler, 202, had believed),
'Hostiensis' and 'Raymund'. These three commentators on canon law the
poet consulted (either directly or in a compilation such as William of
Pagula's *Summa summarum*) for his discussion of indulgences at the end of
Part 4. Our poet was undoubtedly familiar, too, with popular visions of the
other world, but he does not dwell on the physical terrors of purgatory in
the same way that many of these texts do. His rather more restrained
treatment, which is most interested in expounding orthodox doctrine on the
subject, is closest in spirit to the contemporary English poem *The Gast of
Gy*, which appears together with a copy of *PC* in BodL, MS Rawlinson
poet. 175 (and is quoted here from the edition in *Three Purgatory Poems*).

2710–15 By the twelfth century purgatory was established as 'the place of
purgation for two sinful situations: venial sins and sins regretted and
confessed but for which penance had yet to be completed' (Le Goff, *The
Birth of Purgatory*, 219). Cf. the explanation offered in *Gy*, ll. 331–5: 'For ilk
a man both more and myn / Sall suffer penaunce for their syn / In this erth
here, whare thai dwell, / Or els in Purgatori or in Hell.'

2722–5 Cf. *Les Peines*, ll. 82–4.

2730–1 'The smallest pain of purgatory is greater than the greatest pain of
earth.' *Compendium*, 7. 3 (noted Köhler, 203). The idea that the pains of
purgatory would be greater than any earthly pain originates with

Augustine's commentary on Ps. 37 in his *Enarratio in psalmos*; see Le Goff, *The Birth of Purgatory*, 68.

2750–83 Cf. *Les Peines*, ll. 86–99. The two texts include the same quotation from Ezek. 4: 6, 'Diem pro anno dedi tibi.' *PC*'s 'specyel ioy' (2781) echoes 'especial joye' in the Anglo-Norman ('speciale gaudium' in the Latin). On time in purgatory, see Le Goff, *The Birth of Purgatory*, 294–5. Stays in purgatory were usually brief because time seemed to pass so slowly there. For a day's pain in purgatory as equivalent to a year on earth, compare *Gy*, ll. 411–12 and *A Revelation of Purgatory*, 81/726–9. According to *Horologium Sapientiae*, the bitterness of the pains of purgatory is equivalent to a hundred years of suffering on earth (*Orologium Sapientiae*, 363). For discussions of time in popular visionary literature, see Gurevich, *Medieval Popular Culture*, 133–6.

2762–3 Ezek. 4:6: 'A day for a year . . . I have appointed to thee.' The quotation is taken from *Les Peines*.

2786–828 Based on *Compendium*, 4. 22 (Köhler, 203; Hahn, 23). This chapter of the *Compendium* is cross-referenced in *Compendium*, 7. 3, the poet's major source in this part of the poem.

2790–819 'Aboven þe stede . . . neghest aboven hel-pitte', etc: In his account of the four different locations which may be described as 'hell' (2816–19), the poet is following the precise geography of the other world set out in the *Compendium*: 'Item prout Infernus sumitur pro loco poenae, quadrupliciter distinguitur. Vnus est Infernus damnatorum . . . Supra hunc est limbus puerorum . . . supra hunc locum est purgatorius . . . Supremus locus inter haec est limbus sanctorum patrum' ('likewise just as "hell" is taken for a place of punishment, it is distinguished in four ways. One is the the hell of the damned . . . above that is the limbo of children . . . above that place is purgatory . . . the highest place between these is the limbo of the holy patriarchs'). The location of purgatory, together with the nature of purgatorial fire, was one of the two great questions debated about purgatory. The idea that purgatory was a specific place seems to have evolved only relatively slowly. Twelfth-century writers often expressed doubts about its location, and there was some hesitation about whether purgatory should be located on earth or in the upper reaches of hell. Even into the thirteenth century, Bonaventure hesitated to assign one specific location to purgation after death. On the other hand, the geography of purgatory, and its relationship to the earth, was elsewhere described very precisely, as in the accounts of Saint Patrick's purgatory and those which placed the mouth of purgatory at Mount Etna. Dante places purgatory in the southern hemisphere, opposite Jerusalem in the northern hemisphere (*Inferno*, 34). The geography of the other world in the *Compendium* resembles that of Albert the Great, who held that purgatory was located near hell. See Le Goff, *The Birth of Purgatory*, 134, 144, 150, 159, 200–4, 242–4, 252–4, 257, and *passim*.

2799 'Bot þai haf grace and er save': The *Compendium* has a more complex scheme distinguishing 'poena damni' and 'pena sensus' and interior and exterior 'darkness' in each of the places of the other world. Those in purgatory have 'pena sensus, et damni ad tempus, and sunt ibi tenebrae exteriores et non interiores; quia *per graciam* habent lucem interiorem, *quia vident se esse saluandos*' ('sensory pain, and the pain of loss for a time, and they are in that place in exterior darkness but not interior darkness, because *through grace* they have interior light, *because they know themselves to be saved*') (our emphasis). The *Compendium* is apparently indebted here to Albert the Great, who argued that those in purgatory have the light of faith and the light of grace. See Le Goff, *The Birth of Purgatory*, 257.

2804–5 Cf. *Compendium*, 7.2. From Augustine onwards it was established that purgation after death would not last beyond doomsday. See Le Goff, *The Birth of Purgatory*, 75–6. Elsewhere the *PC* poet, like many other writers on purgatory, makes it clear that doomsday is the maximum sentence: the individual soul will leave purgatory as soon as it is purged. See lines 2868–71 and n.

2809 'als says þe buke': The harrowing of hell is described in the apocryphal *Gospel of Nicodemus*; see 6525–42n.

2822–4 'Lord Jesus Christ, release from the hand of hell the souls of all the faithful dead.' Offertorium in the Mass for the Dead; see *Sarum Missal*, 433. The quotation is taken from the *Compendium* (which reads 'de poenis inferni').

2827–8 The poet's overt gloss depends upon a similar clarification in *Compendium* 4: 22: 'infernus ibi sumitur pro purgatorio' ('"hell" here is taken as "purgatory"').

2833 'For in hell there is no redemption.' The *Compendium*'s quotation from the Mass for the Dead triggers a quotation from the Office of the Dead, the response of the seventh lection (*Breviarium*, ii. 278; *Prymer*, 68). Cf. Job 7: 9, 'qui descenderit ad inferos non ascendet'. *PC*'s form of the quotation is widely dispersed and also appears in *Piers Plowman* B.18.149a. Gray ('Langland's Quotations', 58) discusses various other examples in penitential literature; see also Alford, *Piers Plowman: A Guide*, 110. The same passage is quoted again in lines 7245–6. The quotation here from the Office of the Dead is particularly apt, given the emphasis later placed in this part of the poem on the efficacy of suffrages for the dead.

2842–3 'If I knew my father or mother to be in hell, I would not pray for them.' Unlocated in Augustine, but the same quotation appears, also attributed to Augustine, in *De Abundantia exemplorum*, part 2, 'De carentia bonorum in damnatis' (as noted Hahn, 23), as well as in *Speculum Christiani*, 121/24–6. Cf. also *Cursor*, ll. 23333–50.

2868–71 For this account of the heaviness of the soul burdened by sin, cf.

the *Compendium*'s explanation of why the purged soul ascends straight to heaven (7. 2). Hugh of St Victor wrote that it was appropriate that heaven should be above the earth and hell below because sins weigh down the soul; see Le Goff, *The Birth of Purgatory*, 143.

2872–89 For these two purgatories the poet follows *Compendium*, 7. 3 (Köhler, 203; Hahn, 23). The phrases 'comon . . . speciele thurgh grace' echo the *Compendium*'s 'secundum legem communem . . . secundum dispensationem specialem'.

2877 'in sere place': In the *Compendium*, 'in diversis locis'. Earlier writers had often suggested that purgation might be carried out, or at least begin, on earth. Augustine held that purgation was begun in this life, and Gregory provided anecdotes about the dead undergoing purgation on earth and appearing to the living. Thomas Aquinas would not rule out the idea of souls being punished on earth. The presentation in the *Compendium* and *PC* is closer, however, to the argument of Albert the Great: he said that the reason that Gregory and others had claimed purgatory was on earth was because souls in purgatory could appear on earth by special dispensation to warn the living. See Le Goff, *The Birth of Purgatory*, 70, 93–4, 270–2, 257. Compare *Gy*, ll. 536–8: 'Thare er Purgatoryes sere: / Ane is comon to mare and les, / And departabill ane other es.' *Gy*'s spirit appears in the place where he sinned most when alive, the bedroom he shared with his wife.

2897–3273 'payns seven': These seven pains are the same as those presented in *Les Peines*, ll. 102–88 but in a different order. In *Les Peines* the discussion of purgatorial fire comes before the discussion of diseases, and exile, *PC*'s third pain, is the sixth pain in *Les Peines*. On the relative rarity of the sevenfold scheme found in *Les Peines* and *PC*, and for *PC*'s dependence on *Les Peines* here, see Relihan's discussion (*Les Peines*, 55–6, 82–5). While *Les Peines* furnishes the main source for the poet's treatment, however, the English poet expands, as throughout his poem, with materials taken from elsewhere, including, in lines 3128–85, the discussion of purgatorial fire from the *Compendium*, 7. 3.

2902–9 Cf. *Les Peines*, ll. 115–19. *PC*'s 'to ravisshe' (2909) echoes 'a ravyr' in the Anglo-Norman *Peines* ('rapiant' in the Latin version).

2917 'in þe thred parte of þis boke was talde': In lines 2216–373, where the poet described the fearful appearance of devils around the dying man.

2920–45 Cf. *Les Peines*, ll. 120–5. *PC*'s wording seems to be influenced by that of *Les Peines*, the English poet's 'dole' (2922), equivalent to the Anglo-Norman 'dolur' (or 'dolor' in the Latin version). But the *PC* poet expands *Les Peines*'s discussion of the dispute between angels and devils. The comparison with the man on the sea in a storm derives from *Les Peines*, but the *PC* poet adds the following comparison (2946 ff.) with the man charged with felony. Not all writers on purgatory thought that the souls there would be doubtful of their future state: Thomas Aquinas insisted that the souls in purgatory know they will be saved (Le Goff, *The Birth of Purgatory*, 273), and Dante claims that those in purgatory are happy because they hope eventually to join the blessed in heaven (*Inferno*, 1, ll. 118–20).

2929 'in þe thred part namly': Cf. lines 2374–401.

2966–71 The poet discussed the soul's doubt about its future state in lines 2570–86 (as the fourth reason why death is to be feared) and the dispute between angels and devils over the soul in lines 2374–401. The first pain listed here, sight of devils, was also discussed in the third part of the poem, in lines 2216–373; see 2917n.

2972–81 Cf. *Les Peines*, ll. 173–6. *PC* seems to be derived from the Anglo-Norman version of *Les Peines* since the Latin has no equivalent for 'amis' (l. 174), *PC*'s 'frendes' (2978).

2982–3001 Cf. *Les Peines*, ll. 139–51. There was, as Bloomfield notes (*The Seven Deadly Sins*, 221), an 'age-old equation of sin and sickness'. The sins were also frequently associated with the four humours (imbalances of which caused sickness), as, for instance, in *Speculum sacerdotale*, 93. See Bloomfield, 23, 71, 164, 195–6, 208, 212–13, 220–1, 242, 355 n. 6, 430 n. 6, 437 n. 213 for references and discussion, upon which the notes below are based.

　　PC's list of diseases differs from that presented in *Les Peines*, chapter 2, but *Les Peines* probably provided the poet's major inspiration; the lines which follow the list of diseases (3002–19) are also apparently derived from *Les Peines*. There is a list of sins and corresponding diseases in *PC*'s other major source in Part 4, the *Compendium*, 3. 14, but *PC* does not follow this list (although it shares with it the association of avarice and 'dropsy'). The associations between specific sins and diseases were, however, various, and the *PC* poet could easily be conflating several different such schemes, or inventing one of his own.

2986–7 'fever cotidiene': *Les Peines* has 'apostumes e . . . agüe' (boils and fever) as the disease for pride. *Les Peines* lists pride last, but the *PC* poet presents this sin, as more typically in medieval listings, first. The poet follows the traditional Gregorian order (for which see Bloomfield, *The Seven Deadly Sins*, 72–3) with some modifications. Fever could also be associated with envy, as in Gower's *Mirour de l'omme*, *Works*, i, ll. 3817 ff.

2990–1 'þe dropsy': Cf. *Les Peines*, l. 143: 'idropesye por coveitise' ('dropsy for covetousness'). Dropsy is associated with avarice in Gower's *Mirour de l'omme*, *Works*, i, l. 7603, as well as in *Compendium*, 3. 14, as noted above. In Spenser's *Faerie Queene* Gluttony has a 'dry dropsie' (*Works*, i, Book 1, Canto 4, 23, line 6).

2992–3 'þe potagre and þe gout': *Les Peines* lists 'pareleseye' (palsy) for sloth, as does Grosseteste's *Templum Domini* (for which see Bloomfield, *The*

Seven Deadly Sins, 437 n. 213). Spenser's Avarice has 'A grieuous goute' (29, line 7).

2994–5 'kylles and felouns and apostyms': *Les Peines* gives 'jauniz' (jaundice) for envy. Spenser's Envy has a 'leprous mouth' (22, line 8). Langland's Envy has 'þe palsy' (*Piers Plowman* B.5.77), which is the disease associated with wrath in *PC*.

2996–7 'parlesy': *Les Peines* lists fever for ire; palsy is the disease for sloth in this text. Spenser's Wrath has spleen, frenzy, 'shaking Palsey' and 'St Fraunces fire' (35, lines 8–9). Langland's Wrath is 'neuelynge wiþ þe nose' and has a flux (*Piers Plowman* B.5.136, 179).

2998–9 'glotoni . . . swynacy': *Les Peines* omits gluttony from its list of sins and their corresponding diseases. Gluttony could be associated with leprosy, as in Grosseteste's *Templum Domini* (see Bloomfield, *The Seven Deadly Sins*, 233).

3000–1 'meslry': *Les Peines* gives 'meneison e . . . flux' (diarrhoea and discharge) for lechery. Gower also linked leprosy with lechery in *Mirour de l'omme*, *Works*, i, l. 9639, but it was also sometimes linked with envy. Henryson's Cresseid is perhaps the most famous literary case of leprosy in the Middle Ages.

3002–19 Cf. *Les Peines*, ll. 151–8. As Relihan indicates (*Les Peines*, 84), the Latin version of *Les Peines* lacks anything corresponding to the phrase 'pur deus jours ou treis' reflected in *PC*'s 'thre days, or four' (3011), suggesting that the English poet was using the Anglo-Norman rather than the Latin version. Relihan also shows that the discussion of how the soul feels more pain than the body, just as a small object lodged in the eye causes more pain than the same object would cause the hand, also suggests that the *PC* poet was using the Anglo-Norman rather than the Latin version, since the Latin lacks half the comparison.

3020–87 *Les Peines* does not go on to consider, as the *PC* poet does in these lines, the question of how the soul is able to feel pain after its separation from the body at death. *PC*'s discussion might have been inspired by the examination of the same question in a source he certainly knew, the Old French encyclopedia *Sydrac*, question 71 (66–7). According to this source, souls will receive after death either a 'vestement de grace et de glorie' ('clothe of grace' in the later English verse translation, *Sydrak and Bokkus*, Laud misc. 559 text, question 23, l. 1630) or a 'vestement de paine et de dolour' ('clothe of sorowe', *Sydrak and Bokkus*, l. 1632). Our poet does not employ the clothing metaphor, however. In *Gy*, the Prior who questions Gy's spirit also asks how it is that souls can be tormented by bodily pains like fire (ll. 1706–58). Virgil tells Dante that God allows souls to suffer from the pains of heat and cold, but does not see fit to reveal how; Statius returns to the same question later on (*Purgatorio*, 3, ll. 31–3, 35, ll. 88–108). In medieval otherworld visions souls typically appear to possess physical characteristics; see Gurevich, *Medieval Popular Culture*, 141–2.

The parable ('ensampel') of the rich man and Lazarus recounted in Luke 16: 19–25 (cf. lines 3056–79) was also employed by Peter Lombard in a discussion in the fourth book of his *Sentences* of the question of whether souls without bodies could feel the pain of fire: 'Dum ergo peccatorum divitem damnatum in ignibus Veritas perhibet, quis sapiens reproborum animas teneri ignibus neget?' ('when indeed Truth adduces the rich sinner damned in fire, who that is wise could deny that the souls of the reprobate are held in fire?') (distinction 44, 7, *PL* 192: 947). The fourth book of Lombard's *Sentences* was 'the *locus classicus* for discussion of the resurrection' by the late twelfth century (Bynum, *The Resurrection of the Body*, 121).

While *PC* acknowledges the point of view that dead souls will be given bodies of air (lines 3080–5), Thomas Aquinas explicitly refuted the idea that we might rise with celestial, rather than our own fully corporeal bodies (Bynum, *The Resurrection of the Body*, 258).

3060–1 This gloss depends on *Compendium*, 4. 22.

3088–205 Most writers on purgatory held that purgatorial punishment included fire, on the authority of 1 Cor. 3: 10–15.

3094–9 The comparison derives from *Les Peines*, ll. 131–5. In lines 3102–19, the *PC* poet elaborates upon *Les Peines*' much briefer comparison of thrusting one's naked foot into the fire with the pain suffered by the soul once stripped of the body in purgatory (cf. *Les Peines*, ll. 135–8).

3128–85 The poet expands the discussion of purgatorial fire from *Les Peines* with this interpolation derived from *Compendium*, 7. 3. The nature of purgatorial fire was much discussed, but the great scholastic authors were in agreement that the fire of purgatory was real (Le Goff, *The Birth of Purgatory*, 156, 246).

3131–3 Cf. *Compendium*, 7. 3: 'Sicut enim anima secundum ordinem naturae vnitur corpori vt instituat vitam, sic merito secundum ordinem iustitiae vnitur igni a quo suscipiat poenam' ('for just as the soul according to the order of nature is joined with the body to establish life, so deservedly according to the order of justice it is joined with fire from which it receives punishment').

3134–41 The *Compendium* distinguishes material fire ('ignis corporeus') in two aspects: as an instrument of nature ('instrumentum naturae', *PC*'s 'thurgh kynde'), according to which it acts on the body, and as an instrument of God's justice ('instrumentum diuinae iustitiae', *PC*'s 'instrument of Goddes ryghtwysnes'), according to which it acts on the soul (cf. Köhler, 204). The phrase 'instrument of goddis ryghtwysnes' also appears in the fifteenth-century *Revelation of Purgatory* (57/4–7). The context in which the phrase occurs here suggests that it was likely taken from *PC*, an extract of which appears with the *Revelation* in Lincoln Cathedral Library, MS 91: 'þis is an instrument of Goddis ry3twisnesse to purge 30w of 30ur sin in purgatory'. Cf. *PC*'s 'An instrument of Goddes ryghtwysnes, / Thurgh wilk þe saule most clensed be / In purgatory'.

3142–62 Cf. *Compendium*, 7. 3.

3164–7 'It is necessary that as much pain be suffered, as there was love; for the more strongly someone's will adhered to venial sins, the longer he will be tormented.' 'Necesse est . . . amor': ultimately from Augustine, *De Civitate Dei*, 21. 26 (*PL* 41: 746), but the poet has derived the quotation from *Compendium*, 7. 3 (Hahn, 23; Köhler, 205). 'Tanto . . . forcius': not in fact Augustine, but the passage in the *Compendium* which follows the same citation from Augustine. The poet has a habit of incorporating such contextual material from his intermediate sources into his quotations from authorities; cf. lines 4057–60, 4171–6, 5494–5, 5682–3. For the idea that the punishment suffered in purgatory would be commensurate with the pleasure taken in the sin whilst alive, cf. *Gy*, ll. 399–402: 'For, als men may in bokes rede, / Clerkes sais that it es nede / That penaunce alls fer pas, / Als lykyng here in the syn was.'

3178–85 Cf. *Compendium*, 7. 3 (as noted Köhler, 204–5). The passage is based on 1 Cor. 3: 10–15, a central text in developing the concept of purgatory. Exegesis of this text typically compared the wood, hay, and straw to different degrees of venial sins (see Le Goff, *The Birth of Purgatory*, 218).

3201 'gold fyned': Tribulation which tests or purifies the soul is frequently likened in the Bible to the purification of gold in fire; cf. Job 23: 10, Prov. 17: 3, Wisd. 3: 6, Ecclus. 2: 5, Zach. 13: 9, Mal. 3: 3, 1 Pet. 1: 7.

3206–45 Cf. *Les Peines*, ll. 159–72. Line 3223, 'to purchace', echoes *Les Peines*, 'kar la ne est tens ne liu a merite porchacer' ('for that is not the time or the place to purchase merit') (ll. 165–6). *PC*'s lines 3224–7, anticipating the poet's own later discussion of suffrages for the dead, have no equivalent in *Les Peines*.

3235 'fourty wynter': 'cent aunz' in *Les Peines*, but the figures are interchangeable, both referring to indefinite but extended periods of time.

3246–71 Cf. *Les Peines*, ll. 179–88. As Relihan shows (*Les Peines*, 84–5), this passage again suggests that the *PC* poet was using the Anglo-Norman, not the Latin version of *Les Peines*, since he correctly translates the Anglo-Norman 'tregrant pluies' as 'smert stormes als of wynd and rayn' (3257), whereas the Latin refers to great lamentation and weeping ('tantis lamentacionibus et fletibus').

3266–71 For absence of the face of God as the greatest pain of purgatory, cf. *Orologium Sapientiae*, 363. In Part 6, the *PC* poet says that the greatest pain of hell is loss of the sight of God (ll. 7294–307). Purgatory was conceived as a place in which there were two kinds of pain: the pain of loss of the sight of God, and physical pains. Most other-world visions dwell on the latter, and *PC* is somewhat unusual, therefore, in its emphasis, both here and in its discussion of the pains of hell, on the loss of the sight of God as the most intolerable of all the pains.

3283 'als in þis part byfor wryten es': In lines 3120–3.

3300–8 Cf. *Les Peines*, ll. 77–81.

3312–18 Origen, for instance, thought that all men would be tried by fire after death because none is entirely pure; see Le Goff, *The Birth of Purgatory*, 54.

3352–7 The ultimate source for the sins listed here is Caesarius of Arles, *Sermones*, ii. 275. The text was of particular interest in the Middle Ages thanks to its erroneous attribution to Augustine. The *PC* poet's list of venial sins which are punished in purgatory in lines 3440–90, as Relihan shows, seems to be drawn from Caesarius through the intermediary of *Les Peines*; the two texts share one omission from and three expansions of Caesarius' list. However, the list of deadly sins punished in hell in lines 3363–73 is not included in *Les Peines*; it must have been drawn either directly from the list in Caesarius which it closely resembles, or from another source.

3358–9 Caesarius explains (*Sermones*, ii. 725) that although many are confident that their sins will be purged after death, the fire described in 1 Cor. 3: 10–15 purges only venial, not 'capital' sins.

3363–73 Cf. the very similar list in Caesarius, *Sermones*, ii. 725. The poet's qualifications to the inclusion of wrath ('If it be halden in hert lang') and drunkenness ('If it be over-continuele') reflect similar qualifications in Caesarius: 'et, si longo tempore teneatur, iracundia, ebrietas, si assidua sit'. Bloomfield (*The Seven Deadly Sins*, 177) discusses the passage in *PC* with some puzzlement but without apparently realizing its ultimate source.

3398–411 'ten thynges sere': Similar lists of remedies for venial sins appear in the works of two of the authorities on purgatory named by the poet in lines 3940–51, Raymund of Peñaforte and Hostiensis (*Summa*, 3. 34. 58; *Summa aurea*, 5, 'De penitentiis et remissionibus', 8, *s.v.* 'De quibus peccatis facienda est'). Neither of these lists, however, includes all the items found in *PC*, and a third text (though one not acknowledged by the poet) seems to us the likeliest direct source. William of Pagula's *Summa summarum* (BodL, MS Bodley 293, f. 221$^{va–b}$) collates the lists of Raymund and Hostiensis and adds a final item which is not found in either of the two original texts but which is included as the tenth item in *PC*'s list, last anointing.

   The list of remedies for venial sins from this part of *PC* appears in excerpt under the title 'Decem remedia contra peccata venialia' in Trinity Cambridge MS O.2.40, f. 104a, along with the list of venial sins enumerated in lines 3440–90 (Britton; Lewis–McIntosh, E 1).

3418–19 'From the smallest grains is made a great load for the horse.' Walther, no. 5090. Also quoted in *Speculum Vitae*, ll. 5869–70.

3432–3 Prov. 24: 16: 'A just man shall fall seven times [a day]', in the Vulgate 'Septies enim cadet iustus'. *PC*'s version of the quotation appears in *Piers Plowman* and elsewhere: see Alford, *Piers Plowman: A Guide*, 58.

3440–90 As Relihan shows, this list of venial sins, derived ultimately from Caesarius, corresponds closely to the version found in *Les Peines*, ll. 208–40. Both *Les Peines* and *PC* omit one sin listed by Caesarius, excessive enjoyment of sumptuous food when others are hungry. Both *PC* and *Les Peines* also contain the same expansions of two of the items in Caesarius' list, lateness in attending church and tardiness in visiting the sick and incarcerated; cf. *PC*'s lines 3454–9 and 3464–71 with *Les Peines*, ll. 216–19, 222–6 and see further Relihan's discussion (*Les Peines*, 76–9).

The same list of venial sins, also attributed to Augustine, appears in Chaucer's *Parson's Tale*, *Canterbury Tales*, X. 371–80. Chaucer's list is certainly independent of that in *PC*; he includes speaking more than necessary, which *PC* omits.

3512–59 These lines are similar to, but not identical with, the discussion of remedies for sin and tribulation in *Les Peines*, and in Caesarius, the ultimate source. It seems more likely that the *PC* poet is working from *Les Peines* rather than directly from Caesarius. In his discussion of tribulation (cf. *PC* ll. 3518 ff.), Caesarius specifies the death of husband, wife, or child, or the loss of worldly goods: 'quotiens maritus aut uxor aut filius moritur, vel substantia nobis . . . aufertur' ('as often as our husband or wife or son dies, or our possessions are carried off') (*Sermones*, ii. 726). *Les Peines* translates this as 'perte de nos chateaus ou de charneaus ami' ('loss of our possessions or of living friends') (l. 244), and *PC* follows this more generalized translation in line 3521, 'Losse of catelle or of frendes þat lyves'.

3554 'werkes of mercy': Cf. the poet's account of the Judgement in lines 6137–218, when those who performed the works of mercy will be honoured and those who failed to perform them shamed.

3566–8 Many texts which relate visions of purgatory emphasize the efficacy of prayers and good works performed for the dead by their 'frendes', either their relations or their spiritual supporters; see, for instance, Dante, *Purgatorio*, 3, ll. 136–45 and 4, ll. 133–5. Gy's spirit in *The Gast of Gy* reveals that it is being helped by a particular friar for whom he himself provided while living. Gy explains that masses and saying the seven penitential psalms help speed the dead through purgatory (ll. 1024–46).

3570–1 'It is not to be denied that the souls of the dead can be relieved through the piety of their own living relations.' Augustine, *Enchiridion* 110 (*PL* 40: 283). For Augustine's view of suffrages for the dead see Le Goff, *The Birth of Purgatory*, 81–2. As noted by Trudel (*Speculum huius vite*, ii.

426), *De Abundantia exemplorum* contains the same quotation in a slightly different form (see part 3, 'De suffragiis').

3576–611 A close translation of *Compendium*, 7. 4 (Köhler, 205; Hahn, 24).

3624–797 Cf. *Compendium*, 7. 5 (Hahn, 24).

3668–79 Expands *Compendium*'s 'sicut patet in dantem domino iusto eleemosinam per seruum malum' ('as is seen in the giving of alms by a just lord through a wicked servant').

3680–1, 3696–9 The *PC* poet adds these qualifications, which are not found in his source. He seems cautious about condoning too lax an attitude towards morality, especially among the clergy, whilst at the same time setting out the orthodox position upholding the efficacy of the office, notwithstanding the moral standing of the person performing that office. Just such a position, of course, would later be denied by Lollard writers.

3706 ff. The *Compendium* makes explicit that in order for suffrages to be effective, certain things are required on the part of the agent and the recipient. The *PC* poet here turns to consider the recipients of suffrages but without making this point explicit.

3718–39 The *PC* poet inherits from the *Compendium* the unusual argument that suffrages can benefit those in heaven, by augmenting their numbers and thus increasing their glory, and those in hell, by decreasing the number of the damned, which reduces their misery. The *Compendium* thus distinguishes three different types of influence, on those in purgatory 'per modum purgatoris', in heaven 'per modum coniunctionis', and in hell 'per modum diminutionis' (7. 5). It was more usual to insist, as both Bonaventure and Aquinas did, that suffrages for those in heaven had no effect because there was no need for them, and for those in hell were useless because nothing could end their suffering (although the *PC* poet seems ultimately to come to rest at this more usual argument in lines 3740–5). See Le Goff, *The Birth of Purgatory*, 255, 275. Le Goff (p. 266) finds the *Compendium*'s argument (and by extension *PC*'s) 'specious as regards the saved [and] absurd as regards the damned'.

3754–61 Cf. *Compendium*, 7. 5. *PC*'s lines 3762–83 are an addition to this source.

3776–83 In his tract *De Cura pro mortuis gerenda*, Augustine put forward an argument like *PC*'s, that since the fate of the individual soul is unknown, prayers should be said for all the dead so that those able to benefit from them would do so (Le Goff, *The Birth of Purgatory*, 81–2). The *PC* poet had perhaps encountered this argument as it appeared in Raymund's *Summa*, 3. 34. 57.

3784–91 The *Compendium* (7. 5) explains that mass-singing for infants is not done out of necessity, but as an act of thanksgiving ('non sit propter illorum indigentium . . . sed propter gratiarum actionem').

3798–939 Hahn (24, following Köhler, 205) cites *Compendium*, 7. 6 as the source of lines 3798–879 (and the poet indeed himself names this work as one of his sources in lines 3940–51). But unlike *PC*, the *Compendium* is almost exclusively concerned with insisting upon the pope's power to grant indulgences to the dead whilst emphasizing that lay people who have been granted indulgences may not transfer them to another, whether living or dead. Because, the author argues, an indulgence is a release from punishment rather than a benefit, it is a non-thing and therefore may not be transferred to another. Moreover, the laity do not possess the authority to grant indulgences, though their acts of charity may benefit the dead. For the *Compendium*'s treatment of the topic, see Le Goff, *The Birth of Purgatory*, 266. For *PC*'s rather more straightforward treatment, see Swanson, *Indulgences in Medieval England*, 328–9, esp. 329: 'This is very clearly a work aiming to transmit the basic academic analysis for wider consumption, offering a clear statement which does not draw attention to points of contention.' For the poet's sources in this section of the text, see further 3940–51n.

3808–9 Indulgences required that their recipients be confessed and contrite (Swanson, *Indulgences in Medieval England*, 17).

3819–35 The doctrine of the treasury of merits, developed during the thirteenth century although not officially propounded until 1343, held that Christ's passion and the martyrdom of the saints have earned a superabundant supply of merit, administered by the pope and his bishops (Swanson, *Indulgences in Medieval England*, 16).

3846–9 Matt. 16: 19: 'Whatsoever thou shalt bind upon earth, it shall be bound also in heaven: and whatsoever thou shalt loose on earth, it shall be loosed also in heaven.' The poet intrudes 'et' before 'in celis'.

3856–7 It is unclear to which particular 'exposicion' the poet might be referring here, but he in any case simply states the orthodox interpretation of Matt. 16: 19, that the power of the keys given to Peter was passed to all subsequent popes.

3859–79 The pope was the most important figure in the administration of indulgences; he alone could offer indulgence for crusades and he alone could grant plenary indulgence of sins at death. The indulgence that bishops and archbishops were permitted to grant was restricted to forty days (Swanson, *Indulgences in Medieval England*, 30, 32).

3927–39 Hostiensis (named as a source by the poet in line 3944) had recommended that remission acquired in this life should be 'stockpiled' for use in purgatory, because even a day's punishment there would be like a hundred on earth (*Summa aurea*, 5, 'De remissionibus', 7, *s.v.* 'Ad quid valent'). Cf. Swanson, *Indulgences in Medieval England*, 292.

3940–51 The poet cites four sources for his treatment of suffrages and the value of indulgences for the dead in purgatory. In addition to the book 'Veritas Theologie' (i.e. the *Compendium*, for which see 3798–939n), the poet names as his authorities on this topic 'Innocent', 'Hostyen', and 'Raymund'. 'Innocent' (3944) is probably not, as Köhler supposed, Innocent III but rather Innocent IV, whose commentary on the *Decretales* of Gregory IX (i.e. *Liber Extra*) includes a discussion of whether or not indulgences may benefit the dead (for discussion of which see Shaffern, *The Penitents' Treasury*, 167). Innocent doubted that pardons could benefit those in purgatory, because they were outside the jurisdiction of the church, although prayers, almsgiving, and fasting might benefit them. Ultimately, however, he falls back on the position that since the pope grants indulgences for the dead, their efficacy cannot be denied; see *In quinque libros Decretalium*, 5, De penitentiis et remissionibus, 4, *s.v.* 'suo judice'.

'Hostyen' (3944) is Hostiensis, who argued in his *Summa aurea* that indulgences could not benefit the dead because the power of the keys did not extend to purgatory; the suffrages of the church could, however, in his view, benefit the dead (*Summa aurea*, 5, De remissionibus, 6, *s.v.* 'Quibus prosint'; cf. Shaffern, *The Penitents' Treasury*, 166).

'Raymund' (3946) is Raymund of Peñaforte. Hahn (p. 22) notes that his *Summa* was often named the 'Summa Raimundi' ('a boke þat es called his name'). According to Raymund, dead souls could be released from purgatory if the wording of the indulgence so allowed (*Summa*, 3. 34. 64).

It is possible that the *PC* poet indeed consulted these three authors directly, but he might also have consulted a source in which their various opinions on indulgences were combined. William of Pagula's *Summa summarum*, possibly the source of the poet's list of remedies for venial sins in lines 3398–411, cites all three authors in its treatment of the question of whether indulgences could benefit the dead (BodL, MS Bodley 293, f. 221[ra]).

3948 'Thomas Alqwyn': The *Compendium Theologicae veritatis* which the poet here attributes to Thomas Aquinas, and which is also attributed to Albert the Great, is in fact the work of Albert's disciple, Hugh Ripelin of Strasbourg (written *c.*1268). The attribution to Thomas is perhaps understandable, given that Aquinas was also a disciple of Albert, and he also wrote a *Compendium Theologicae* in addition to his better-known *Summa*. The *Compendium*'s account of purgatory is discussed by Le Goff, *The Birth of Purgatory*, 264–6.

PART 5

In his account of the Last Days the poet makes eclectic use of a number of sources in Latin, Anglo-Norman, and, just possibly, in English. The main sources of Part 5 are the *Compendium* and the life of Antichrist by Adso Dervensis, which together provide the poet's treatment of Antichrist (the latter also supplying the discussion of the renovation of the world at the end of Part 5). Humbert of Romans's *Tractatus de Abundantia exemplorum* provides the poet's lists of the accusers at the Judgement and the things for which account must be rendered. The *Elucidarium* was perhaps the source of lines 6017–70 on the Judgement. A small section of this part of the poem, lines 5404–21, probably came from *Les Peines*; Part 5, the longest of our poet's parts, greatly expands upon the brief treatment of the Last Judgement in the Anglo-Norman source. Innocent III's account of the Judgement in his *De Miseria*, the source of much Part 1, also provides a brief passage in Part 5.

In his overall outline, presenting the general signs of impending judgement from the gospel of Matthew, followed by a life of Antichrist, the fifteen signs before doomsday attributed to Jerome, and an account of the Judgement which concludes with a rendering of Matt. 25: 32–46, our poet offers the same sequence of materials as the similar description of the world's seventh age in *Cursor Mundi*. However, as will become clear below, the two English poets differ in the specific versions of these popular topics which they have brought together. *Cursor* may have provided our poet with his inspiration for combining a life of Antichrist with an account of the fifteen signs, but as Thompson has shown (*The* Cursor Mundi, 169), other compilers had previously combined the same materials, and the manuscript in which the *PC* poet obtained his copy of Adso may have inspired his combination of materials in Part 5 if, like several of the surviving manuscripts, it also contained a version of the fifteen signs.

4004 ff. Cf. loosely with the similar account in *Cursor*, 21859–76.

4014–24 Matt. 24: 3–5, 7–8, 12: 'Tell us . . . what shall be the sign of thy coming, and of the consummation of the world? And Jesus answering, said to them: Take heed that no man seduce you: for many will come in my name saying, I am Christ: and they will seduce many . . . For nation shall rise against nation, and kingdom against kingdom; and there shall be pestilences, and famines, and earthquakes in places. Now all these are the beginnings of sorrows . . . And . . . iniquity will abound, [and] the charity of many shall grow cold.' The poet has 'Dic nobis signum . . . consummacionem' for Vulgate 'Dic nobis quando haec erunt et quod signum . . . consumationis'. *PC* also has 'contra gentem' for Vulgate 'in gentem' and 'et habundabit iniquitas, et refrigescet caritas' for Vulgate 'quoniam abundabit iniquitas refrigescet caritas'.

4047–648 *PC*'s life of Antichrist may be compared with the similar English version in *Cursor Mundi*, which our poet surely knew. Indeed, Morris claimed that lines 4153–215 of *PC* were taken from *Cursor*, lines 22005–116 (Morris, 265–8, printing the corresponding passages). However, as Hahn indicates, our poet in fact draws for his account of Antichrist on two Latin sources, the tenth-century *De ortu et tempore Antichristi* by Adso Dervensis (see Emmerson, 76–7) and the *Compendium* (the parallels, first noted by Köhler (p. 205), are listed in summary form by Hahn, 25–6). The poet supplements what he took from these two main sources with additional materials from conventional exegesis and from the 'pseudo-Methodius' tradition on Antichrist (for which see 4197–224n). The poet's dependence upon his two major Latin sources is indicated not only by close parallels of detail and phrasing but also, in places, by clear errors in the poet's reproduction of the Latin. In addition to Hahn, see the brief summary of the poem and its sources in Emmerson, 161–2.

Morris's erroneous notion that the *PC* poet took his account of Antichrist directly from *Cursor Mundi* is understandable, for *Cursor* also draws on Adso's life of Antichrist. However, the *PC* poet used a different version of Adso from that used by the author of *Cursor*. The *Cursor* poet used an expanded version of Adso attributed to Alcuin and edited by Verhelst as number 5, *Vita Antichristi*, 115–28 (cf. Thompson, *The* Cursor Mundi, 167; Verhelst distinguishes each version with a different title, a practice we follow here). This version contains a number of interpolations not found in the other versions of Adso or in *PC*, for example a passage which refutes the opinion that Antichrist will be born of the union of a bishop and a nun (see 4157–86n). The interpolated text used by *Cursor* also omits some material included in the other Adso versions and transmitted by the *PC* poet; l. 4163 of *PC*, for instance, translates a passage from Adso (*Tractatus de Antichristo*, 23/27–31) which has no parallel in the corresponding lines in *Cursor* (ll. 22035–80).

Of the eight versions edited by Verhelst, it seems most likely that the *PC* poet used the *Descriptio cuiusdam sapientis*, which lacks the original prologue and the attribution to Adso and which also differs in some small readings (edited as Verhelst's number 2, 43–9, and cited as *Descriptio* in the notes below). At *PC* lines 4170–86, where the poet incorporates part of Adso's Latin alongside a biblical quotation from that source, the original Adso text (version 1, *Tractatus de Antichristo*) reads 'per semitas iusticiae' for *PC*'s 'per semitam iusticie' ('þe way of rightwysnes'). 'Per semitas' is the reading of version 2. The same reading is also found in versions 3, 5, 6, 7, and 8, but these versions can all be eliminated as *PC*'s source on the basis of variations from the original Adso text not shared by *PC*.

4051–128 These lines are taken from *Descriptio*, 46/105–47/148 (cf. Hahn, 26). Most discussions of Antichrist agree, on the basis of 2 Thess. 2: 1–6, that he will not appear until the Roman empire has fallen (Emmerson, 88). The discussion of this sign of his imminent arrival comes *after* the discussion of his conception and birth in Adso (ll. 4157 ff. in *PC*), but the *PC* poet (perhaps influenced by the order of presentation in the *Compen-*

dium) moves this material to its proper chronological sequence and following his account of the general signs of approaching judgement from the gospel of Matthew. *Cursor* retains the order of exposition found in Adso.

4057–60 'For unless there come a revolt first, etc, that is, unless all kingdoms first separate from Roman imperium, which before were subject to it; not before this will Antichrist come'. 'Quoniam . . . primum': 2 Thess. 2: 3, taken from Adso. As the 'id est' which follows might indicate, the poet has added contextual material from Adso as if it were part of the biblical quotation. The passage from Adso reads as follows:

> *Quoniam, nisi uenerit discessio primum et reuelatus fuerit homo peccati et filius perditionis* . . . Inde ergo dicit Paulus apostolus, Antichristum non antea in mundum esse uenturum, nisi primum uenerit discessio, id est, nisi prius discesserint omnia regna a Romano imperio, que prius subdita erant.

> (For unless there come a revolt first, and the man of sin be revealed, the son of perdition . . . From that cause therefore Paul the apostle says that Antichrist will not come into the world unless there first come a revolt, that is unless all kingdoms first separate from Roman imperium, which before were subject to it) (*Descriptio*, 46/109–20)

The poet also incorporates material from Adso as if part of the biblical text at 4171–6. Trudel (*Speculum huius vite*, i. 98) notes that in adapting *PC*, the *Speculum huius vite* removes the accretion of Adso's commentary and restores the full quotation from 2 Thess. 2: 3 at this point.

2 Thess. 2: 3 was typically taken to mean that the Roman empire would collapse prior to the arrival of Antichrist. Emmerson, 38–9, provides a convenient summary of standard commentary on 2 Thess. 2: 3–11, one of the central sources of the medieval tradition on Antichrist.

4069–72 Whilst it was generally agreed that Roman power would collapse prior to the coming of Antichrist, as Emmerson indicates, 'Rome' could refer to both imperial and ecclesiastical authority. Adso seems to have the Roman empire in mind, since he says the authority of Rome will not be completely destroyed as long as the kings of France remain. The *PC* poet repeats Adso's prediction that the nations formerly subject to Roman imperial authority will fall away, but adds that the authority of the church of Rome will be lost as well (cf. Emmerson, 88–9).

4074 'Es now destruyed a grete party'. *PC*'s wording here appears close to *Cursor*'s parallel 'struid es grete parti' (l. 22246), but in fact both English poets are following the almost identical phrasing of their different Latin sources, 'ex maxima parte destructum' (*Descriptio*, 46/121–2); 'ex maxima parte iam destructum' (*Vita Antichristi*, 123/137–8).

4085 'an sal come': Cf. Adso, 'unus ex regibus Francorum' (*Descriptio*, 46/

125–6). Adso develops the legend of the Last World Emperor to argue that a French king will take control of the Roman empire to rule as the last and greatest of all the kings. *PC* suppresses mention of the French origin of this last emperor, although *Cursor* does specify that this future king will be 'o france' (l. 22254). Possibly the idea of a future French world emperor was less palatable to an English poet by the middle of the fourteenth century than it was at the beginning, although of course it is *Cursor* which has gained notoriety for the pro-English sentiments of its prologue.

4104 'Daniel': Not mentioned by Adso, but the book of Daniel was 'the most important Old Testament source of the Antichrist tradition' (Emmerson, 43), and the poet could have had in mind here several passages which were taken to refer to Antichrist in standard exegesis. The ten toes of the statue in Nebuchadnezzar's dream in Dan. 2 were taken to represent the ten future kings from whom Antichrist would originate, while the deeds of Antiochus Epiphanes in Dan. 11 were frequently discussed in connection with the future tyranny of Antichrist (Emmerson, 44–5).

4106 'þat saynt Paul calles "þe man of syn"': In 2 Thess. 2: 3.

4109–12 Cf. Adso, *Descriptio*, 47/136: 'non per naturam, sed per imitationem'. Most commentators took Antichrist to be the son of the devil not literally (since he was often, although not invariably, taken to be born of human parents, as in *PC* 4158) but metaphorically (Emmerson, 82). Antichrist is 'þe devels son' not biologically, but through imitation of the devil's example.

4139–46 Cf. Adso, *Descriptio*, 43/7–9, 17–21 (Hahn, 26). The meaning of Antichrist's name was expounded in an influential discussion by Isidore of Seville, who played on the distinction between 'ante' and 'anti' to point out that although Antichrist would come before Christ's second coming, his name really means 'contrary to Christ' in Greek (Emmerson, 76). The idea that there were multiple antichrists and that anyone who opposed 'Goddes wille' could be called an antichrist is perhaps most familiar from polemical texts (Wyclif notoriously identified the pope with Antichrist; see Hudson, *The Premature Reformation*, 334) but had its roots in earlier exegesis. The view that any false Christian could be called an antichrist was quite orthodox and can be found, for instance, in the work of Augustine. See Emmerson, 62–73.

4154–6 The poet is fond of such threefold divisions; cf. his three-part division of the ages of man in Part 1.

4157–86 Based on Adso, *Descriptio*, 43/22–44/36 (Hahn, 26), although Adso does not give Corozaim as the place of Antichrist's birth (see further 4197–224n). On the tradition surrounding Antichrist's birth, see Emmerson, 79–83. The most common view held that Antichrist would be born of human parents, as other mortals, although the devil would enter his mother's womb upon his conception. Adso specifically repudiates the alternative view, that Antichrist would be born, in parody of Christ, of a virgin. The *PC* poet suppresses any mention of this alternative tradition. But the interpolated version of Adso used by *Cursor Mundi* contains an expansion refuting the further alternative view that Antichrist will be born of the union of a bishop and a nun (*Vita Antichristi*, 118/31), a passage found in *Cursor* (l. 22028) but absent from *PC*. The idea that at Antichrist's conception the devil will enter his mother's womb depends, as Emmerson indicates, not on any biblical text, but on the idea that Antichrist represents a parodic inversion of Christ. As Adso (but not the *PC* poet) goes on to discuss explicitly, just as the Holy Spirit came upon the Virgin at Christ's conception, so Antichrist's mother is possessed by an evil spirit at his conception. See Emmerson, 75, 81.

4167 'Of a woman of þe kynred of Dan': Medieval tradition held that Antichrist would be born of the Jewish tribe of Dan, also the tribe of the mother of the expected Jewish messiah (Emmerson, 79).

4171–6 'Let Dan be a snake in the way, a serpent in the path, that biteth the horse's heels that his rider may fall backward. That is, Antichrist, as a serpent, will sit in the path, and will be in the way, so that he might snatch those who walk by the path of justice, and with his venom maliciously kill them.' 'Fiat Dan . . . eius retro': Gen. 49: 17, taken from Adso. As Hahn indicates (26), the poet (as at lines 4057–60) has incorporated the subsequent gloss from Adso ('Hoc est sicut . . . malicie occidat') as if it were part of the biblical citation (cf. *Descriptio*, 43–4/26–30). For the traditional identification of the serpent of Gen. 49: 17 with Antichrist, see Emmerson, 80.

4188–96 The poet here turns from Adso to the second major source of his life of Antichrist, the *Compendium*, 7. 7 (Hahn, 25).

4197–224 The poet's main source for Antichrist's early life is Adso's *Descriptio*, 44/47–45/66 (cf. Hahn, 26). His phrase 'nurist and mast conversand' echoes Adso's 'in ciuitatibus Bethsaida et Corazaim *nutriri* et *conseruari* dicitur' (*Descriptio*, 44/55–6); see Textual Note for 'conversand' as the poet's mistranslation of 'conseruari'. But *PC* is also conflating a second source. Whereas according to Adso, Antichrist will be born in Babylon, *PC* follows a second tradition concerning Antichrist's birth. According to the *Revelations* attributed to Methodius, Antichrist will be born in Chorozaim, raised in Bethsaida, and rule in Capernum (Emmerson, 48). *PC* follows this alternative tradition in lines 4197–210; compare the Middle English version *þe Bygynnyng of þe World and þe Ende of Worldes* in Trevisa, *Dialogus* (109/5–9).

4205–6 Matt. 11: 21, 23: 'Woe to thee, Corozain, woe to thee, Bethsaida . . . [Woe to thee], Capharnaum.' In the Vulgate, 'Vae tibi Corozain, vae tibi Bethsaida . . . et tu Capharnaum'.

4217–24 It was generally argued on the basis of 2 Thess. 2: 4 that Antichrist would rebuild the Temple in Jerusalem and proclaim himself to be God (Emmerson, 38).

4217 'thurgh ledyng of þe fende': Nothing in the immediately parallel passage in the source corresponds to this phrase, though it echoes the 'inspirante diabolo' used slightly earlier by Adso, *Descriptio*, 44/59. The *PC* poet adds similar phrases at lines 4304 and 4543, making his Antichrist an emphatically diabolical figure.

4225–30 *PC* here follows *Compendium*, 7. 8.

4231–41 Cf. *Compendium*, 7. 8. As Hahn indicates (p. 25) *PC*'s use of the *Compendium* is indicated definitively here by an error in lines 4237–8, which are not, in fact, a quotation from Daniel as the poet asserts. The relevant passage in *Compendium* reads:

> Antichristus erit luxuriosus, *et in concupiscentiis foeminarum*, vt habetur Dan 11. In aperto tamen per hipocrisum simulabit sanctitatem, vt facilius decipere possit.

> (Antichrist shall be lascivious, *and he shall follow the lust of women*, as Daniel 11 says. Nevertheless outwardly through hypocrisy he shall feign sanctity, in order that he might more readily deceive.)

The italicized phrase above, not the one cited by the poet, is a quotation from Dan. 11: 37. The poet evidently misinterpreted 'vt habetur Dan 11' as referring to the following, not the preceding, words.

4237–8 'Nevertheless outwardly through hypocrisy he shall feign sanctity, so that he might the more easily deceive.' See preceding note.

4243–8 *PC* here returns to Adso, *Descriptio*, 45/67–70 (cf. Hahn, 26). Both Adso and *PC* emphasize that Antichrist first seduces the powerful and '*thurgh þam*' ('per illos') converts the masses. *Cursor*'s version (ll. 22127–30) lacks the causal connection.

4249–54 Cf. *Compendium*, 7. 8.

4255–4412 This discussion of the four means Antichrist will use to convert the people is based upon *Compendium*, 7. 9, 'De quatuor modis quibus decipiet' (cf. Hahn, 25). The quotations in lines 4355–6 and 4365–6 and the reference to Haymo (l. 4391) are all taken from this source, although *PC* adds some details not found in the *Compendium* but present in other sources. Adso discusses only three means employed by Antichrist, fear, rewards, and miracles ('terrore, muneribus et miraculis', *Descriptio*, 45/89). But later writers typically added the fourth method found in the *Compendium* and *PC*, false teaching (for which compare Matt. 24: 11, 24, Mark 13: 22). See Emmerson, 91–2 and n. 56.

4279–82 No equivalent for these lines appears in the *Compendium*. The wording is similar to *Cursor*, ll. 22139–40: 'Fra est to west, fra north to soth, / He sal do mak his sermun cuth.' But the poet has apparently at this point returned to Adso's account: 'Predicatio autem eius et potestas tenebit a mari usque ad mare, ab oriente usque ad occidentem, ab aquilone usque ad septentrionem' ('Moreover his preaching and his power will hold from coast to coast, from east to west, from the north to the south'); *Descriptio*, 45/71–3.

4284–332 Conventional exegesis on Rev. 13 held that Antichrist would perform miracles, including bringing fire from heaven in a parody of Pentecost (Emmerson, 24, 40; Rev. 13: 13). *PC* omits a discussion of the source in biblical commentary found in this part of the *Compendium*.

4288 'I sal tel yhou sum': The poet omits predicting the future from the list enumerated by the *Compendium*.

4303 'on þe thred day': A detail not specified in the *Compendium* but an obvious enough addition based on the analogy between Christ and Antichrist, and a common feature of the Antichrist tradition (Emmerson, 91).

4315 'growe and florisshe fayre': In the *Compendium*, 'cito florere, et arescere' ('at once to flourish, and dry up'), but the poet was perhaps working from a text which read 'cito florere, et crescere'.

4328–9 This explanation of the apparent miracles of Antichrist is not in the *Compendium*, although the *PC* poet could have derived it from, for instance, *Elucidarium* 3, 34: 'diabolus eius maleficio corpus alicuius damnati intrabit et illud apportabit et in illo loquetur, quasi vivum videatur' ('the devil in his wickedness will enter the body of one of the damned and shall carry it and speak in it, as if it were alive'). As Emmerson notes, our poet takes care to explain that Antichrist is unable to work true miracles like Christ. Adso, too, insists that Antichrist's apparent miracles are false (*Descriptio*, 45/80–2). For other writers, however, 'Antichrist's miracles are very real indeed' (Emmerson, 93).

4330–1 No equivalent in *Compendium* but cf. Adso, *Descriptio*, 45/84–6.

4355–6 Matt. 24: 21, 24: 'There shall be . . . great tribulation . . . insomuch as to deceive, if possible, even the elect.' The quotation is taken from the *Compendium*.

4365–6 Rev. 1: 15: 'His feet like unto fine brass, as in a burning furnace'. The quotation is taken from the *Compendium*.

4391 'Haymo': The poet takes the reference to Haymo from the *Compendium*: 'Et dicit Haymo super Apocalypsim, "Illa tentatio non per partes, sed simul totum examinabit mundum"' ('And Haymo upon the Apocalypse says, "That temptation will test not in parts but the whole world at once"'). The *Expositio in Apocalypsim* attributed to Haimo of Halberstadt describes how Antichrist will gain power (cf. Emmerson, 91–2 and n. 56). For the

Compendium's citation, cf., perhaps, 'in omnibus mundi partibus sancti tunc temporis interficientur' ('in all parts of the world in that time he will kill the holy') (*PL* 117: 1074). The *PC* poet's 'tyrauntry' (4392) is an echo of his earlier 'anticrist sal be þe mast tyraunt' (4381), rather than a direct translation of 'tentatio' in the Latin source.

4399–410 The tradition that those deceived by Antichrist will wear his mark, and that those without the mark will be unable to buy or sell, is based on Rev. 13: 16–17 (Emmerson, 40).

4413–50 Based on *Compendium*, 7. 10 (cf. Hahn, 25).

4417–18 Rev. 12: 4: 'His tail drew the third part of the stars of heaven, and cast them to the earth.' The quotation is taken from the *Compendium*.

4423–30 This explanation is not in *Compendium*, but the poet drew on a 'long tradition' in which the tail of the dragon described in Rev. 12 (named as the devil) was interpreted as Antichrist (Emmerson, 22 and 246 n. 29). The poet could have found the identification of the tail with Antichrist in, for instance, the commentary of Berengaud which often appeared in illuminated Apocalypses; see *PL* 17: 876. The *PC* poet was certainly familiar with some form or forms of Apocalypse with commentary, since he draws on their conventions in his moralized description of the city of heaven in Part 7, lines 9048–190.

4441–50 Cf. *Compendium*, 7. 10.

4448 'afterwarde': See lines 4491 ff.

4451–90 Based on *Compendium*, 7. 11 (cf. Hahn, 25). The version of Adso used by our poet does not discuss Gog and Magog. *Cursor Mundi* (ll. 22315–60) presents a different account, according to which Gog and Magog are peoples formerly contained by Alexander the Great. (The *Cursor* poet took his account from an interpolation in the expanded version of Adso he used as his source.) The release of Gog and Magog was typically expected as one of the signs of the end, although different sources present different views as to whether they will appear before or after Antichrist. Some accounts interpret Gog and Magog as specific peoples; others interpret them allegorically as symbols of the wicked in general. As Emmerson notes, *PC* (following the *Compendium*) provides three different interpretations: that Gog and Magog are a specific people enclosed beyond the Caspian sea (ll. 4457–8); that they are the host of Antichrist (ll. 4474–6); that they are all those who oppose the church (ll. 4479–88). See Emmerson, 42, 84–8, and for comment on *PC*'s treatment, 270 n. 40.

4473, 4479 'þe glose': Rev. 20: 7, together with Ezek. 38 and 39, was the source for Gog and Magog as the armies of Antichrist (Emmerson, 42). Jerome was the originator of an interpretation based on the etymologies of Gog and Magog as 'tectum' (roof) and 'de tecto' (from the roof). Augustine said that Gog referred to evil people in general who conceal the devil within them as under a roof; Magog emerges from these people as if uncovered (Emmerson, 85). In the interlinear gloss on 'Gog et Magog' in Rev. 20: 7 in the *Glossa Ordinaria*, 4, 'Gog' is glossed as 'tectum' (roof) and Magog as 'detectio' (an uncovering). The marginal gloss on 'Magog' reads: 'detectos, id est omnes persecutores diabolum in se tegentes et tandem ad apertam persecutionem procedentes' ('uncovered, that is all the persecutors concealing the devil in themselves and finally proceeding to open persecution') (cf. *PC*'s lines 4485–7). Cf. *Compendium*, 7. 11: 'Per Gog enim secundum glossa illi, per quos latenter Diabolus persequetur fideles, designantur. Per Magog illi per quos aperte ecclesia opprimetur' ('For by Gog, according to the gloss, are signified those by whom the devil will persecute secretly the faithful. By Magog those through whom he will openly attack the church').

4491–568 Based on *Compendium*, 7. 12 (cf. Hahn, 25). The quotations in lines 4505–6 and 4515–16 are both taken from this source.

4505–6 Mal. 4: 6: '[They] shall turn the heart[s] of the fathers to the children.' The quotation is taken from the *Compendium*. Mal. 4: 5–6, together with Rev. 11: 3–13 (cf. l. 4523), is the authority for the widespread belief that Enoch and Elijah would return in the last days and preach against Antichrist for 1,260 days, following which they would be killed by Antichrist but restored to life and raised to heaven. Not all writers expected the literal return of the Old Testament figures, but more popular accounts generally do (Emmerson, 41, 95–101). *PC*'s references to the Apocalypse and the gloss thereon in lines 4523–6 are taken from *Compendium*. The interlinear gloss in the *Glossa Ordinaria*, 4, for Rev. 11: 3 reads: 'id est tribus annis et dimidio sicut ipse Christus predicauit' ('that is three and a half years as Christ himself preached').

4515–16 'They shall take the faith which they had themselves.' The 'gloss' is cited from *Compendium*, 7. 12: 'Glossa: quia suscipient fidem quam illi habuerunt.' See the marginal gloss of the *Glossa Ordinaria*, 3, on Mal. 4: 5–6.

4569–86 Based upon *Compendium*, 7. 13 (cf. Hahn, 25).

4570 Three and a half years was usually considered to be the duration of Antichrist's tyranny, based on the analogy with Christ's ministry (Emmerson, 20).

4573–4 Matt. 24: 22: 'Unless those days had been shortened, no flesh should be saved.' The quotation is taken from *Compendium*, 7. 13.

4579–80 'Because God sees our weakness, the evil days which he brings one by one he will shorten mercifully.' Ultimately from Gregory, *Moralia in Job*, 32. 15 (*PL* 76: 650), but the poet has taken the quotation from the *Compendium*, 7. 13.

4588–9 'twa and thretty yhere / And an half': Although the biblical account (cf. Luke 3: 23) implies Jesus lived for thirty-three and one-half years, the poet later gives Jesus's age at death as thirty-two years and three months (see 4987–8 and n). Antichrist's life is a parodic imitation of Christ's.

4597–648 Based on *Compendium*, 7. 14 (cf. Hahn, 25).

4598 'withouten any repentance': Not in the source but a natural enough assumption and consistent with the penitential emphasis of the poem.

4609–10 Not in *Compendium*, but a commonplace of the Antichrist tradition, based upon 2 Thess. 2: 8: 'et tunc relevabitur ille iniquus quem Dominus Iesus interfecit spiritu oris sui' ('And then that wicked one shall be revealed whom the Lord Jesus will kill with the spirit of his mouth'), a passage which is also quoted, for instance, in the *Elucidarium*, 3, 35 and by Adso, *Descriptio*, 48/186–91. The poet's hesitations over the exact manner of Antichrist's death ('Bot howswa it be . . .', line 4611) reflect some uncertainty in the tradition on the exact interpretation of 'the spirit of Christ's mouth'. It was generally thought to designate some agent of Christ, rather than to imply that Christ himself would actually appear at this point (Emmerson, 102–3). Michael was usually identified as this agent, although like our poet (line 4612), Adso insists that it is by Christ's power that Antichrist will be killed, even if that power is deputed to Michael. *Cursor Mundi* presents a more graphic account of Antichrist's death based upon the interpolated version of Adso.

4625 'þe glose of Danyel' is also cited as an authority here by the *Compendium*. Dan. 12: 11–12 was the basis of the belief that a forty-five day period of peace would follow the death of Antichrist before the Second Coming. Adso gives a different figure, forty days (*Descriptio*, 49/196). See Emmerson, 104–5 and the interlinear gloss on Dan. 12: 12 in the *Glossa Ordinaria*, 3.

4635–6 John 10: 16: 'And there shall be one fold and one shepherd', intruding 'et' before 'unus'. The text is not cited in the *Compendium*, but it is alluded to in a Welsh prose description of the last days which also discusses the peace that will follow the death of Antichrist ('Description', 117).

4657–8 Acts 1: 7: 'It is not for you to know the times or moments, which the father hath put in his own power.'

4671–4 'Whether I eat, whether I drink, whether I do anything else, it always seems to me that the trumpet sounds in my ears, "rise you dead, come to the judgement".' Cf. *Regula monachorum*, 30, *PL* 30: 417 (as noted Hahn, 27) and see Heist, *The Fifteen Signs*, 40–1 n. 21.

4691–8 Luke 21: 25–7: 'There shall be signs in the sun, and in the moon, and in the stars; and upon the earth distress of nations, by reason of the confusion of the roaring of the sea and of the waves; men withering away for fear, and expectation of what shall come upon the whole world. For the powers of heaven shall be moved; and then they shall see the Son of man coming in [the clouds], with great power and majesty.' The poem has 'nubibus' for Vulgate 'nube'.

4715–16 The poet perhaps means that he has derived his list of signs from one source and his explanation of them from another; certainly, his list conforms to one type of fifteen-sign versions but incorporates some materials from an alternative tradition. See 4742–5n.

4719–23 Acts 2: 19–20: 'And I will show wonders in the heaven above, and signs on the earth beneath: blood and fire, and vapour of smoke. The sun shall be turned into darkness, and the moon into blood, before the great and manifest day of the Lord come.' Cf. Joel 2: 30.

4738–817 There are numerous versions of the fifteen signs supposed to occur before Doomsday and spuriously attributed to Jerome. Of the four main types distinguished by Heist, the version contained in *PC* belongs to the 'pseudo-Bede' type: see *PL* 94: 555 (translated Heist, *The Fifteen Signs*, 26). *PC* is the only extant English version belonging to this particular group. For *PC*'s treatment of the legend, see Heist, 131–3 (*PC* is Heist's no. 44).

In its presentation of a version of the fifteen signs after a life of Antichrist based in part upon Adso, *PC* resembles in outline *Cursor*, which also follows up its life of Antichrist with a version of the fifteen signs. *Cursor*, however, uses a very different version of the fifteen signs deriving from a French original (Thompson, *The* Cursor Mundi, 169, *Cursor*, ll. 22427–710; Heist no. 35). In both cases, the English poets may have been influenced, in their combination of a version of Adso with a version of the fifteen signs, by the manner in which they encountered their source materials, possibly in the form of compilations by earlier writers. As Thompson indicates (169–70), manuscripts of Adso frequently also contain versions of the fifteen signs.

PC's version of the fifteen signs is well known for being depicted in fifteenth-century stained glass in All Saint's Church, North Street, York; see *Inventory*, iii. 8 and plates 98 and 103, and, for a recent discussion of the glass and its relation to the text of the poem, Powell, 'All Saints' Church'.

4742–5 This passage does not appear in the ps.-Bede type and belongs rather to the closely related type which appears in Peter Comestor's *Historia Scholastica*: 'sed utrum continui futuri sint dies illi, an interpolatim, non expressit' ('but whether these will fall on successive days, or with other days interspersed, it does not say') (*PL* 198: 1611; Heist, 26, 132). This introductory passage from the 'Comestor-type' may regularly have appeared in texts of other types, for it also occurs in *Cursor*, ll. 22443–6.

4790–3 As Heist indicates (p. 132), *PC*'s account of the earthquakes of the ninth day also seems to incorporate detail from the 'Comestor-type' of the legend: the poet's phrase 'Generaly in ilka contre' echoes Comestor's 'fiet *generalis* terrae motus' (our italics), where ps.-Bede reads simply 'erit terrae motus'.

There is a Welsh text, 'A Description of the Day of Judgement', in BL MS Cotton Titus D xxii which contains the same detail from Comestor in what is otherwise a ps.-Bede version. As Heist points out (pp. 140–2), this text also has a more general similarity to *PC* in presenting its fifteen signs together with an account of the general signs of the end from the gospels, a life of Antichrist, and an account of the Judgement, and he suggests that the two texts share a common source. However, the general similarity between the Welsh tract and Part 5 of *PC* to which Heist points is rather superficial. Although the rest of the Welsh tract has similarities with *PC* in containing a life of Antichrist, followed by the fifteen signs and an account of the Judgement, there are significant differences in their handling of these materials. The Welsh text is emphatic, for instance, that whoever says that Antichrist is the product of a natural union between a man and a woman is deceived ('Description', 109; contrast *PC*'s treatment in lines 4157–8). The Welsh description also contains a different version of the Gog and Magog legend, according to which—as in *Cursor*, but not as in *PC*— Gog and Magog are peoples bound by Alexander. If indeed, as Heist surmises, there is a single source for *PC*'s Part 5, it would not seem likely that it is the same source used by the Welsh author.

4824–36 Luke 17: 26–30, 'And as it came to pass in the days of Noe, so shall it be also in [the coming] of the Son of man. They did eat and drink, they married wives, and were given in marriage, until the day that Noe entered into the ark: and the flood came and destroyed them all. Likewise as it came to pass, in the days of Lot: they did eat and drink, they bought and sold, they planted and built. And in the day that Lot went out of Sodom, [and suddenly] it rained fire and brimstone from heaven, and destroyed them all. Even thus shall it be in the day when the Son of man shall be revealed', with 'erit adventus' for biblical 'erit et in diebus'; 'ad diem' for 'in diem', 'similiter' for 'similiter sicut', and 'hoc' for 'haec'. The poet intrudes 'et' after 'plantabunt' and 'autem' after 'secundum'.

4857–956 *PC*'s description of the fire that will burn the world in the last days is taken in the main from *Compendium*, 7. 15 (Köhler, 206, Hahn, 28), but with some additional details.

4875–6 'four maneres': Cf. *Compendium*: 'Ignis autem iste habebit officium quatuor ignium.'

4895–8 The *Compendium* does not include this comparison with the height of the waters of the Flood, but the poet could have found it in the description of the burning of the world in *Elucidarium*, 3, 77, or in the *Legenda Aurea*, i. 18.

4917–18 Ps. 96: 3: 'A fire shall go before him, and shall burn his enemies round about.' This and the following quotation do not appear in the *Compendium*.

4937–8 Ps. 49: 3: 'A fire shall burn before him: and a mighty tempest shall be round about him.'

4950 'aftirward': Cf. lines 6219–36.

4959–64 Hahn (p. 28) compares Matt. 24: 31, 'et mittet angelos suos cum tuba et voce magna, et congregabunt electos eius a quattuor ventis, a summis caelorum usque ad terminos eorum' ('And he shall send his angels with a trumpet, and a great voice: and they shall gather together his elect from the four winds, from the farthest parts of the heavens to the utmost bounds of them').

4973–4 1 Cor. 15: 51, 52: 'All [shall rise] in a moment, in the twinkling of an eye, at the last trumpet.' The Vulgate reads 'omnes quidem resurgemus . . . in momento', etc.

4979–5024 Two alternative sources for this passage have been put forward by previous commentators. Morris believed lines 4779–5020 were taken from the similar account of the resurrection of the body in *Cursor Mundi*, ll. 22816–952 (Morris, 269–72, printing the relevant passage). Hahn suggested (p. 28) that 4979–5030 were probably based upon *Compendium*, 7. 16. Lines 4993–5000 are certainly similar to *Cursor* ll. 22921–3: 'For þof his bodi al war brint, / And blaun ouer al þe puder tint, / Yett mai godd gedir it al again.' However, the *Cursor* poet says that the resurrected will be 30 years old, a figure at odds with that given in *PC*. The *Compendium*'s account of how the resurrected body will be corrected of its deformities and returned to the soul which once animated it is also similar. But again the *Compendium*, which states that the resurrected bodies will be aged 'secundum aetatem plenitudinis Christi' ('according to the age of Christ's maturity'), does not provide support for *PC*'s unusual figure of thirty-two years and three months (for which see 4983–92n). The poet may therefore be using another source as yet unidentified. In describing how the dead shall rise in their own bodies, and that their bodies shall be reassembled even if dispersed or disintegrated, *PC* states, of course, a thoroughly orthodox view (Bynum, *The Resurrection of the Body*, 276).

4983–92 Augustine suggested in one passage of *De Civitati Dei* that all would rise aged 30, an age traditionally considered the peak of human development (Bynum, *The Resurrection of the Body*, 98). Christ's age at his resurrection (more usually said to be thirty-three years) was also taken as a model. Rolle puts the age of the resurrected at thirty-two years (*Super novem lectiones*, ii. 271/16–19). The figure of thirty-two years and three months for Christ's age at death appears in BL MS Royal 17 C.xxxviii and in Richard Pynson's print of the defective version of *Mandeville's Travels* (see *The Book* *of John Mandeville*, 38/641–2; *The Defective Version of Mandeville's Travels*, 29).

5005–6 Luke 21: 18: 'A hair of your head shall not perish.'

5035–41 1 Thess. 4: 16–17: 'For the Lord himself shall come down from heaven with commandment, and with the voice of an archangel, and with the trumpet of God: and the dead who are in Christ, shall rise first. Then we who are alive, who are left, shall be taken up together with them in the clouds to meet Christ, into the air, and so shall we be always with the Lord', with 'voce' for Vulgate 'in voce' and 'Christo in aere, sic' for Vulgate 'Domino in aera, et sic'.

5064–71 Rev. 6: 15–16: 'The kings of the earth, and the princes, and tribunes, and the rich, and the strong, and every bondman, and every freeman, hid themselves in the dens and in the rocks of mountains: and they say to the mountains and the rocks: Fall upon us, and [to the hills] hide us from the face of him that sitteth upon the throne and from the wrath of the Lamb.' The poet intrudes 'collibus'.

5086–8 'Lord, when you will come to judge the earth, where will I hide myself from the face of your ire, for I have sinned excessively in my life?' The response for the third lection of the Office of the Dead (*Breviarium*, ii. 275; cf. *Prymer*, 60).

5095–8 Job 14: 13: 'Who will grant me this, that thou mayst protect me in hell, and hide me till thy wrath pass?' Like the previous quotation, this is derived from the Office of the Dead (sixth lection). The poem follows the form of the quotation in the Office rather than in the Bible, with 'et abscondas' for biblical 'ut abscondas' (cf. *Breviarium*, ii. 278; *Prymer*, 64).

5115–16 Zach. 14: 5: '[Behold] the Lord . . . shall come, and all [his] saints with him.' The Vulgate has 'venit Dominus Deus meus omnesque sancti cum eo'.

5122–5 'As lightning cometh out of the east, and appeareth . . . into the west: so shall also the coming of the Son of man be: sudden, flashing, and dreadful.' 'Sicut . . . hominis': Matt. 24: 27–8, omitting biblical 'enim' after 'sicut' and biblical 'usque' after 'paret'. 'subitus, choruschans, et terribilis': compare Luke 17: 24, 'nam sicut fulgur coruscans de sub caelo in ea quae sub caelo sunt fulget ita erit filius hominis in die sua' ('For as the lightning that lighteneth from under heaven, shineth unto the parts that are under heaven, so shall the Son of man be in his day').

5138–41 Acts 1: 11: 'This Jesus who is taken up from you into heaven, shall so come, as you have seen him going into heaven.'

5153–4 Joel 3: 2: 'I will gather together all nations, and will bring them . . . into the valley of Josaphat', with 'adducam' for biblical 'deducam'.

5159–62 Joel 3: 12: '[They shall] arise, and [all] the nations [shall] come up into the valley of Josaphat: for there I will sit to judge all nations.' The Vulgate has 'Consurgant et ascendant gentes in vallem'.

5169–70 The discussion of the name of Josephat here is commonplace: cf. *Elucidarium* 3, 52: 'Vallis Josaphat dicitur vallis judicii' ('the vale of Josephat is called the vale of judgement'); *Compendium*, 7. 17: 'Iosephat autem, quod interpretatur iudicium, designat iusticiam' ('Moreover Josephat, which is interpreted as judgement, designates justice'); and *Cursor*, ll. 22985–90.

5175–6 'Behold our Lord shall appear upon a white cloud!' Cf. Rev. 14: 14: 'et ecce nubem candidam et super nubem sedentem similem Filio hominis' ('and behold a white cloud; and upon the cloud one sitting like to the Son of man').

5181–226 Cf. *De Abundantia exemplorum*, part 4, 'De loco iudicii'. As Hahn indicates (p. 29), of four reasons given in the source the poet includes only the first two: the vale of Josephat is in the middle of the earth, and Christ will be able to point to the places where he was born and crucified. The further reasons adduced in this source are for the consternation of the Jews, who delighted to see Christ's death, and because Antichrist pretended to ascend into heaven from the same place.

5193–222 Christ's speech corresponds to a passage in *De Abundantia exemplorum*, part 4, 'De loco iudicii' (quoted in full by Hahn, 30).

5227–32 Hahn (30) compares *Compendium*, 7. 17.

5235–40 Cf. *Compendium*, 7. 18.

5247–8 John 5: 22–3: '[The Father] hath given all judgement to the Son, that all men may honour the Son, as they honour the Father.' The poet omits biblical 'omnes' before 'honorificent'.

5279–367 Based on *De Abundantia exemplorum*, part 4, 'De terribilibus iudicii' (see Hahn, 30–1, quoting the relevant passage). The quotations from Augustine and John Chrysostom at 5317–24 and 5361–3 are taken from this source. The poet expands upon Humbert's brief mention of the signs of Christ's passion in lines 5292–300, and where *De Abundantia exemplorum* alludes to Matt. 24, he substitutes a text from the liturgy for the Feast of the Invention of the Cross. After line 5367, the *PC* poet inserts two passages taken from Innocent's *De Miseria* and probably from *Les Peines* (see 5404–21n) before returning to *De Abundantia exemplorum* at that point where he had left off.

5281–2 'This sign of the cross shall be in heaven, when the Lord shall come to the judgement.' Invention of the Cross, Matins, Lectio 1, V. *Breviarium*, iii. 277.

5287–90 Cf. *Elucidarium*, 3, 55, explaining that what will appear is not the cross on which Christ was actually crucified, 'sed lux in modum crucis splendidior sole' ('but light in the form of a cross, more splendid than the sun').

5317–24 'Perhaps our Lord has kept his wounds in his body, so that he might reproach his enemies in the Judgement, so that convicting them he might say: behold the man whom you crucified; behold the God and man in whom you would not believe; look at the wounds which you inflicted; observe the side which you punctured, which for you is open and which you would not enter.' Ultimately from Augustine, *Sermo de symbolo*, 8 (*PL* 40: 647), but as Hahn indicates (p. 30), *PC* follows the paraphrase in *De Abundantia exemplorum* rather than the original Augustine.

5332 'atteyn' is legal diction; see Alford, *Piers Plowman: A Glossary*, *s.v.* 'atteinte': 'convicted, attainted'.

5361–3 'Then there shall not be a place of defence, when they shall see Christ showing testimonies and signs of his passion.' John 'with the gilden mouth' refers to John Chrysostom, alluding to the Greek etymology of his surname, but the poet took the quotation from *De Abundantia exemplorum*.

5368–401 Cf. Innocent, *De Miseria*, 3. 14 (227–9) (noted Hahn, 31). The quotations in lines 5384–7 and 5396–7 have been taken from this source.

5384–7 'If the pillars of heaven tremble, and dread at [Christ's coming], and the angels of peace shall weep bitterly, what then shall sinners do?' 'columpne celi . . . Christi': Job 26: 11, in the Vulgate 'columnae caeli contremescunt et pavent ad nutum eius'. 'angeli . . . flebunt': Isa. 33: 7. The *PC* poet has combined two separate biblical quotations along with some contextual material from his source, *De Miseria*, as if a single biblical passage. The original passage in Innocent reads as follows: 'Nam si "columpne celi contremiscunt et pavent adventum eius," et "angeli pacis amare flebunt," peccatores autem quid facient?'

5396–7 1 Pet. 4: 18: 'If the just man shall scarcely be saved, where shall the ungodly and the sinner appear?' The poet has taken the quotation from *De Miseria*. The quotation also appears in the *Dies Irae* and frequently in Latin grammars (Alford, *Piers Plowman: A Guide*, 81). As Alford points out, *PC*'s interpretation of 'vix salvabitur', that 'Ryhtwys men . . . *Sal* be saf' (5402–3), is the same as given by Ymaginatif in *Piers Plowman* B.12.281–2: '*Salvabitur vix Iustus in die Iudicij;/Ergo salvabitur.*'

5404–21 Probably derived from *Les Peines*, ll. 292–304, whose diction it echoes (cf. *PC*'s 'þe erthe . . . sal . . . *tremble* and *whake*' with 'la terre aval *tremblera* de *terremot*' in *Les Peines*, our emphasis), although there are many similar descriptions of these terrors; cf. especially *Compendium*, 7. 17, also known to our poet, as well as *Legenda Aurea*, i. 23 and Rolle's *Super novem lectiones*, ii. 202/11–203/3.

5422–611 This description of the fifteen accusers at the Judgement is taken from *De Abundantia exemplorum*, part 4, 'De terribilibus judicii', which presents the same accusers, with the same biblical quotations, in the same order (Hahn, 31). The poet resumes at the same point in this source where he had left off at line 5367.

5446 Dan. 7: 10: 'The judgement sat, and the books were opened', also quoted in the source.

5451 'The consciences will be revealed to all.' The poet has taken the quotation from *De Abundantia exemplorum*. It seems to derive ultimately from the marginal gloss on Dan. 7: 10, 'conscientiae et opera singularam . . . omnibus reuelantur' ('their consciences and all their works . . . will be revealed before all') (*Glossa Ordinaria*, 3).

5460–1 This comparison with a thief appears in the source.

5494–5 '[Lord], thou writest bitter things against me, that is, you allow bitter sins to be written against me'. Cf. Job 13: 26: 'Scribis enim contra me amaritudines.' The poet takes this quotation from a later point of the same section of *De Abundantia exemplorum* (Hahn, 32). As the 'id est' indicates, the poet has added to the quotation from Job the gloss which follows it in *De Abundantia exemplorum*: 'Scribis enim contra me amaritudines, id est, permittis scribi peccata.' This passage from Job forms part of the fourth lection of the Office of the Dead (*Breviarium*, ii. 276; cf. *Prymer*, 63).

5514 'Assys' is legal diction; cf. Alford, *Piers Plowman: A Glossary*, s.v. sese, 'An assize, a trail in which sworn assessors or jurymen (sisours) decide questions of fact; a judicial inquest.'

5530–1 Rev. 6: 10: 'How long, O Lord (holy and true) dost thou not . . . revenge our blood on them that dwell on the earth?' with 'non vindicas' for biblical 'non iudicas et vindicas'. The text is alluded to, although not quoted in full, in *De Abundantia exemplorum*.

5550–1 Ecclus. 41: 10: 'The children will complain of an ungodly father, because for his sake they are in reproach.' The poet has taken the quotation from *De Abundantia exemplorum*.

5560–77 Cf. *De Abundantia exemplorum*, 'Item pauperes divites quorum aurum et argentum erugini et tinea demolitus est ipsis afflictis fame et inopia et erit erugo in testimonium contra ipsos Jacobus 5' ('Also the poor will complain upon the rich whose gold and silver rust and moths have destroyed, while they were afflicted by hunger and poverty, and the rust will bear testimony against them, as James chapter 5[: 2–3] says'). The ultimate source, alluded to by *De Abundantia exemplorum*, is Jas. 5: 2–3.

5592–5 'The cross will argue against you, Christ with his wounds will allege against you, his wounds will speak against you, the nails will complain about you.' This quotation is similarly attributed to Jerome in *De Abundantia exemplorum*.

5612–829 The poet now omits some material from his source (although he takes from the omitted section the quotation from Job which he inserts in lines 5494–6) and takes up again at a later point in *De Abundantia exemplorum*'s discussion of the Judgement. All the quotations in this part of the poem with one exception (see 5766–7n) are taken from this source in the order in which they appear there (Hahn, 32). The ultimate sources for this discussion of the account which must be rendered at the Judgement are, of course, two biblical parables, the parable of the unjust steward in Luke 16 and the parable of the talents in Matt. 25. Thomas Wimbledon's well-known sermon on the Judgement, with which *PC*'s account may broadly be compared (see Wilson, 'Langland's "Book of Conscience"') takes the former as its *thema*; the same text also forms an important part of Will's self-presentation in *Piers Plowman* C.5 and is quoted in C.9.274.

Like the previous one, this section of *PC* is essentially a list, in which the poet enumerates all the things for which an account must be given: for each moment of time (5644 ff.); for idle words (5664 ff.); idle thoughts (5674 ff.); idle works (5698 ff.); for the deeds of youth as well as age (5700 ff.); for sin committed unwittingly (5723 ff.); for bad deeds which appeared good at the time (5742 ff.); for good deeds not done, and the further good that might have come out of them (5760 ff.); for the soul (5776 ff.) and for the body (5814 ff.). The items in the list and the supporting citations for each are taken from *De Abundantia exemplorum*. The poet adds the discussion of the account that must be rendered for body and soul together in the following lines (5830–57).

5612–21 Cf. lines 5404–21.

5628–9 Ps. 49: 4: 'He shall call heaven from above, and the earth, to judge his people.' The poet derived the quotation from *De Abundantia exemplorum*. The explanation of the psalm which follows also comes from this source (quoted Hahn, 32).

5654–7 'Just as no hair from your head shall perish, so shall there be no moment from all time about which there shall be no account certainly rendered.' Also attributed to Bernard in *De Abundantia exemplorum*. The quotation also appears in *The Parson's Tale, Canterbury Tales* X.253–54, and *Speculum Christiani*, 55/12–13. See *Riverside Chaucer*, 958 n. 253–4.

5668–9 Matt. 12: 36: 'For each idle word an account shall be rendered on the day of judgement.' The poet takes the quotation from *De Abundantia exemplorum*.

5672 'Reson', i.e. an account. 'Reson' is the usual Middle English rendering of Latin 'ratio'; cf. Alford, 'The Idea of Reason'.

5682–3 'I [know] their works . . . I come that I may gather them together with all nations in order to judge them as I judge men.' 'Ego cogitationes eorum venio ut congregem cum gentibus' is Isa. 66: 18, taken from *De*

Abundantia exemplorum. The poet has incorporated the gloss which follows the biblical text in his source, 'scilicet ad iudicantium sicut iudicabo gentes', as if it were part of the biblical quotation.

5690–3 'Therefore God so knows the ways of all that not the least thoughts, which we were accustomed to think, will remain unexamined.' Ultimately from Gregory, *Moralia in Job* (*PL* 76: 194), but the poet has taken the quotation from *De Abundantia exemplorum.*

5706–11 Eccles. 11: 9: 'Rejoice therefore, O young man, in thy youth, and let thy heart be in that which is good in the days of thy youth, and walk in the ways of thy heart, and in the sight of thy eyes: and know that for all these [the Lord] will bring thee into judgement.' The quotation is taken from *De Abundantia exemplorum.*

5722 Job 13: 26: 'And wilt consume me for the sins of my youth.' The quotation is taken from *De Abundantia exemplorum*, although, like that in lines 5494–5, it also forms part of the fourth lection of the Office of the Dead (*Breviarium*, ii. 276; cf. *Prymer*, 63).

5731–2 Eccles. 12: 14: '[Man will be brought] into judgement for every error, whether it be good or evil.' The quotation is taken from *De Abundantia exemplorum.*

5739 Ps. 24: 7: 'And my ignorances do not remember.' The quotation is taken from *De Abundantia exemplorum.*

5748–9 'Sometimes what is dirty in the eyes of the judge shines in the eyes of the listener.' The quotation is taken from *De Abundantia exemplorum*, which reads 'hominis' for *PC*'s 'auditoris'; the poet must have used a manuscript which contained this erroneous reading.

5754–5 Ps. 74: 3: 'When I shall take a time, I shall judge justices.' Taken from *De Abundantia exemplorum.*

5766–7 Matt. 25: 42: 'I was hungry, and you gave me not to eat: I was thirsty, and you gave me not to drink', with 'Esurivi' for biblical 'esurivi enim', 'dedidistis' for biblical 'dedistis' and 'bibere' for 'potum' ('bibere' is the reading of the parallel verse, Matt. 25: 35). This quotation is not in *De Abundantia exemplorum*; as the poet indicates in line 5768, he is here anticipating his own later account of the conclusion of the Judgement at lines 6127–210, based upon Matt. 25.

5780–800 This analogy is taken from *De Abundantia exemplorum.*

5806–7 Deut. 4: 9: 'Keep . . . thy soul carefully.' The quotation is taken from *De Abundantia exemplorum.*

5820–1 The comparison with a castle is also taken from *De Abundantia exemplorum*, although the soul as a house or a castle that must be protected by governing the senses is familiar from vernacular texts as well, including *Piers Plowman* B.9.1–24 and *Ancrene Riwle*, 44/2–10.

5826–7 'He keeps a good castle who keeps his body.' The quotation is taken from *De Abundantia exemplorum*. The ultimate source is Bernard, *In Assumptione B. V. Mariae*, sermo 2 (*PL* 183: 418).

5830–57 The poet interpolates his own addition of the confession to be rendered by body and soul together, before returning to *De Abundantia exemplorum*.

5858–959 This discussion of how each man will have to give account not only on his own behalf but also for those in his care is again taken from *De Abundantia exemplorum*, part 4, 'De terribilibus iudicii' (Hahn, 23). Again, the items in the list and all the quotations in this section are taken from *De Abundantia exemplorum* in the order in which they appear there.

5876–7 'The rod of correction shall drive away folly bound up in the heart of a child.' Cf. Prov. 22: 15.

5888–9 Ezek. 34: 10: 'Behold . . . I will require my flock at [the hand of my shepherd].'

5896–909 In the source, 'de bonis a deo receptis siue sit bonum spirituale, vt bonum anime naturalia et acquisita et infusa, siue bonum corporale, vt fortitudo corporis pulcritudo agilitas, siue sit bonum temporale vt sunt diuitie delectationes honores' ('concerning the goods received from God, whether they be spiritual goods, as goods of the soul, both natural and acquired and infused, or bodily goods, such as strength of body or beauty or agility, or whether they be temporal goods, like wealth, pleasures and honours'). The *PC* poet expands on *De Abundantia*'s version in his own account. These three goods of 'kynde', fortune ('hap'), and grace are a popular topic in pastoral literature. For some other vernacular examples see Rolle, *Form of Living*, 11/344–45; *Canterbury Tales* X.449–54; *Book of Vices and Virtues*, 19/23–21/10.

5913 'arrirage': A legal term, 'An unpaid debt . . . the condition of being behind in payments or short in one's account' (Alford, *Piers Plowman: A Glossary*, s.v. arrerage). The same word is used in *Piers Plowman* C.9.274 alongside a quotation from Luke 16: 2, the parable of the unjust steward.

5924–5 'For we are all one body'. Cf. 1 Cor. 10: 17, 12: 13. *PC* follows the form of the quotation in *De Abundantia exemplorum*.

5954–5 1 Pet. 4: 10: 'As every man hath received grace, [he ought to minister] the same one to another.'

5962–3 Matt. 10: 8: '[What] freely have you received, freely give.' The poet intrudes 'quod'. For medieval commentary on this passage, used to support the idea that knowledge was a gift of God and could not be sold, see Post et al., 'The Medieval Heritage'.

6017–70 Cf. the similar discussion in *Elucidarium* 3, 59–68. An Anglo-Norman poem ('The Last Judgement') on the Last Judgement in Lambeth

Palace Library, MS 522 also contains a description which broadly resembles that in *PC*. Like *PC* this poem also includes a passage based on Zeph. 1: 15–18 (in this case taken from another Anglo-Norman poem, 'Le Petit Sermon'), and an account of Christ's words at the Judgement based upon Matt. 24.

6017–33 Cf. *Elucidarium* 3, 59: 'Unus ordo est perfectorum cum Deo judicantium. Alter justorum, qui per judicium salvantur. Tertius impiorum sine judicio pereuntium. Quartus malorum, qui per judicium damnantur' ('One group is the perfect judging with God. Another the just, who are saved by judgement. The third, the impious, condemned without judgement. The fourth the wicked, who are damned by judgement'). *PC*'s 'parfit men with God prive' (6025) echoes *Elucidarium*'s 'perfectorum cum Deo judicantium'. *Compendium*, 7. 19 has a similar scheme but it also distinguishes the purely good, the purely bad, the bad mixed with some good, and the good mixed with some (venial) bad. Hahn (p. 34) cites Petrus Pictaviensis, *Sententiarum quinque libris*, 5.19 (*PL* 211: 1268), but the resemblance does not seem very close.

6034–48 'apostels and other ma' echoes *Elucidarium* 3, 60: 'Apostoli, martyres, monachi, virgines'. The poet's account of those who 'forsuke þe worldes solace . . . þat for his luf tholed angre and wo' is similar to the discussion in the Anglo-Norman poem on the Last Judgement in Lambeth Palace Library, MS 522:

> E guerpirent tuit honur
> Terrien por Deu amur
> E chescun terrien delit.
>
> . . .
>
> Por Deu suffrirent feim e freit

(And forsook all earthly honour for the love of God, and each earthly delight . . . For God suffered hunger and cold)

('The Last Judgement', lines 131–7)

6042–4 Matt. 19: 28: 'You, who have followed me . . . shall sit . . . on twelve seats judging the twelve tribes of Israel.' The Vulgate reads 'Sedebitis et vos super sedes', etc. The passage is quoted, although not in full, in *Elucidarium* 3, 58.

6051 'þat blethely wirk wald þe werkes of mercy': Cf. *Elucidarium* 3, 62: 'Qui opera misericordiae in legitimo conjugo exercuerunt' ('who performed the works of mercy in lawful matrimony').

6055–8 Cf. *Elucidarium* 3, 68: 'Judaei qui ante adventum Christi sub lege peccaverunt et mali christiani qui malis operibus Deum negaverunt' ('Jews who before the coming of Christ sinned under the law and wicked Christians who deny God through their wicked deeds'), and the Anglo-

Norman 'The Last Judgement': 'E ne garderent pas sa ley/Mais hardi furent de pecher/E tardis de amender' ('And did not keep the law, but were bold to sin and slow to amend') (lines 182–4).

6061 'þat had na law': Cf. *Elucidarium* 3, 65: 'Qui "sine lege peccaverunt", pagani scilicet et illi Judaei qui fuerunt post passionem Christi' ('who "sinned without the law", that is pagans and Jews who lived after the passion of Christ'), alluding to the same biblical text (Rom. 2: 12) as our poet cites in lines 6069–70.

6065–6 Rom. 2: 12: 'Those who sin without the law, shall perish without the law.' In the Vulgate, 'Quicumque enim sine lege peccaverunt, sine lege et peribunt'. The text is quoted, although not in full, in *Elucidarium* 3, 65.

6096–113 These lines are ultimately based upon Zeph. 1: 15–18, but bear a close resemblance to a similar description of the Judgement that forms part of an Anglo-Norman poem incorporated into many manuscripts of *Le Manuel des Pechiez*, 'Le Petit Sermon':

> Jour de grant amerté
> Jour de grant cheitifté
> Jour de ire, jour de corouz,
> Jour de pleynte grevouz,
> Jour de lermes et de plour,
> Jour de peyne et de dolour,
> Jour de oscur et de tonere,
> Jour de angusce et de grant escleire,
> Quant touz pecchés puniz serrent . . .

> (Day of great bitterness
> Day of great wretchedness
> Day of wrath, day of anger
> Day of heavy complaint
> Day of tears and of weeping
> Day of pain and dolour
> Day of darkness and of thunder
> Day of anguish and great thunderbolts
> When all sins will be punished)
>   (lines 435–43)

The Anglo-Norman poem on the Last Judgement in Lambeth Palace Library, MS 522 also contains these lines from 'Le Petit Sermon'. *PC*'s 'pleynyng' (l. 6101) may perhaps derive from 'pleynte grevouz' in 'Le Petit Sermon'; it has no parallel in the Vulgate original. The passage in *PC* clearly impressed medieval readers: it is excerpted in BodL, MS Rawlinson C.285 and its two derivatives, Cambridge University Library, MS Dd.5.55 and Ff.5.40 (Lewis–McIntosh, E 8, E 2, E 3). The popularity of such set-pieces based on Zeph. 1 may be due to the presence in the Requiem Mass of the sequence *Dies Irae* (based on the same biblical passage). Alternatively, they may be inspired by the first versicle of the ninth lection of the Office of the Dead, also based on the same biblical original: 'Dies illa dies irae calamitatis et miseriae: dies magna et amara valde. Quando caeli movendi sunt et terra' (*Breviarium*, ii. 279; cf. *Prymer*, 69: 'þilke dai is a dai of wraþþe, & of chalenge, & of wrecchidnesse; a greet dai, & a ful bitter, whanne heuene & erþe schulen be moued'). There is a very similar passage in *The York Plays* (Play 47, The Merceres (Doomsday), ll. 239–42), which includes one line almost identical to the passage in *PC*, 'þe day of bale and bittirnes' (l. 239). 'Bitter bale' is, however, a common collocation: see quotations in *MED s.v.* 'bale' n. (1), 2a, 3.

6127–210 Based upon Matt. 25: 32–46.

6132 'pastur strayte': Heaven is sometimes imagined as a pasture: cf., for instance, Ezek. 34: 14: 'in pascuis uberrimis pascam eas' ('I will feed them in the most fruitful pastures'). The poet apparently extends the figurative use of 'pasture' to include any other-worldly place of reward or punishment. Heaven, presumably, is imagined by the poet as a wide, abundant pasture and hell as a narrow, confined one (although this might seem to strain the literal sense of a pasture as a space in which animals are let loose to graze).

6141–3 Matt. 25: 34: 'Come, ye blessed of my Father, possess you the kingdom prepared for you from the foundation of the world.'

6180–2 Matt. 25: 41: 'Depart from me, you cursed, into everlasting fire which was prepared for the devil and his angels', with 'preparatus' for 'paratus'.

6249–56 For the idea that the Judgement would be concluded in the blink of an eye, compare 1 Cor. 15: 52.

6269–70 Ps. 148: 5: 'For he spoke, and they were made: he commanded, and they were created.' Cf. also Ps. 32: 9.

6313–14 'Just as a spark of fire in the middle of the sea, so is all the wrong of man before the mercy of God.' Cf. *Piers Plowman* B.5.283a. Gray, 'Langland's Quotations', 59, cites Serlo's *Summa de poenitentia* as a close parallel. See also Alford, *Piers Plowman: A Guide*, 47 for the origin of the passage in Augustine, *Enarrationes in Psalmos*, *PL* 37: 1861 and for its status as a 'commonplace' of fourteenth-century preaching.

6335–6 Pss. 32: 5, 118: 64: 'The earth is full of the mercy of the Lord.'

6345–398 *PC*'s account of the renovation of the world is based on *Compendium*, 7. 20 (Hahn, 34). The detail that the sun will shine seven times brighter than now seems to have been added from *Compendium*, 7. 28; cf. also *Elucidarium* 3, 78.

PART 6

The poet seems to have drawn upon a variety of sources for his account of hell, the most important of which are the *Elucidarium* and *Les Peines*. Together, these provide the poet with his sources for his list of the fourteen pains of hell. In beginning with infernal punishments in Part 6 and moving to the joys of heaven in Part 7, *PC* follows not only the sequence of *Les Peines* but also the typical structure of popular other-world visions such as *St Patrick's Purgatory* and *The Vision of Tundale*, which generally move from the places of other-worldly punishment to the places of rest and reward.

6437–52 As Hahn indicates (34–5), the comparison of the world with an apple or an egg occurs in the thirteenth-century Old French encyclopedia in dialogue form *Sydrac*, (named as a source by the poet in line 7726), question 184 (102).

6445–6 On the location of hell, compare the discussion of the location of purgatory (also within the earth) in lines 2786–828. For discussions of the location of hell in visionary literature, see Gurevich, *Medieval Popular Culture*, 130–1. Dante's hell is in the centre of the earth, which is also the lowest point of the universe (*Inferno*, 32).

6460–76 That the pains of hell could not be adequately described was a commonplace of medieval discussions; cf. for instance Dante, *Inferno*, 28, ll. 1–3 and Chaucer's *Friar's Tale*, *Canterbury Tales*, III.1645–52. *PC*'s discussion, however, is particularly close to that found in the *Visio Sancti Pauli*, 80: 'si essent c viri loquentes ab inicio mundi et uniusquisque ciiij linguas ferreas haberent, non possent dinumerare penas inferni' ('if there were a hundred men talking since the beginning of the world, and each of them had one hundred and four tongues of iron, they could not tell all the pains of hell') (Silverstein, *Visio Sancti Pauli*, 65–6). Redactions 1, 4 (the version cited here), 5, and 8 of the *Visio Sancti Pauli* all contain this passage, which derives ultimately from *Aeneid* 6. 616–27. The same motif of tongues of steel appears in *Sawles Warde* (*Middle English Prose for Women*, 92/21–3); it was, according to Silverstein, particularly common in late medieval England. Cf. also the English version of the *Visio Sancti Pauli* in Oxford, Jesus College MS 29, titled 'The xi pains of hell' (*An Old English Miscellany*, 154, ll. 265–70).

6483–546 With this discussion of those who have been to hell and returned to tell the tale, Hahn (p. 35) compares *De Abundantia exemplorum*, part 2, 'De inferno', which also discusses, in the same sequence as in *PC*, Lazarus, the sons of Simeon, and other visitors to the other world described 'in gestis sanctorum'. The passage Hahn quotes from this source includes the same quotation from Wisd. 2: 1 found in lines 6491–2. The discussion however, is much briefer than that in *PC* and cannot be treated as the poet's sole direct source. It is possible that, as in lines 2242–97, *De Abundantia exemplorum* provided the initial suggestion which our poet, following good preacher's practice, expanded with his own materials from elsewhere.

6491–2 Wisd. 2: 1: 'No man hath been known to have returned from hell.' The poet has 'reversus est' for Vulgate 'sit reversus', as in *De Abundantia exemplorum*.

6503–24 For the legend surrounding Lazarus that had grown up by the fourteenth century, see Gallagher, 'The *Visio Lazari*'. The raising of Lazarus from the tomb is described in John 11, but as Gallagher suggests, what Lazarus did afterwards seems most to have interested medieval writers. In the biblical account, he is only briefly mentioned as being present, after his resurrection, at the occasion on which Mary Magdalene anoints Christ's feet (John 12: 1–2). But ps.-Augustine had suggested that on this occasion Lazarus recounted the torments of hell (*PL* 39: 1929). We have not located a source for *PC*'s statement that Lazarus lived for fifteen years after being raised from the dead; according to the life of Mary and Martha by Hrabanus Maurus, Lazarus lived for twenty-four more years (*PL* 112: 1490; see Voigt, *Beiträge zur Geschichte der Visionenliteratur*, 18).

6525–42 The account of the harrowing of hell by Leucius and Karinus appears in chapters 17–28 of the apocryphal *Gospel of Nicodemus*, a hugely popular and influential work which describes the trial and death of Jesus, the resurrection, and the harrowing of hell. The version current in England in the Middle Ages was the Late Latin Recension, which includes Pilate's letter concerning these events. Vernacular versions appear from the thirteenth century and English versions exist in stanzas, couplets, and prose (for which see Frances A. Foster, 'Saints' Legends', in Wells, *A Manual*, ii. 448–9, 640–1 [312]); the stanzaic version was copied by the scribe who also copied *PC* in BL, MS Harley 4196. From *PC*'s brief precis it is not possible to be certain which particular version he may have used; possibly he knew of several, including the Latin. *Cursor* (ll. 17781–18584) includes a much fuller account, but it seems likely that the *PC* poet worked independently from this earlier version; in *Cursor*, as in the Latin original, Pilate's letter is sent to 'Claudi' (l. 18524), whereas *PC* says the letter was sent to Tiberius.

6535–6 At the end of their account of the harrowing of hell, Karinus and Leucius say that they are not permitted to reveal any more of the divine mysteries (27: 1).

6540 In the Latin original the letter is said to be sent to Claudius (28. 1). However, it seems to have been a common perception that the letter was sent to Tiberius, the emperor at the time of the Crucifixion. According to the English version of *The Gospel of Nicodemus* in BL MS Egerton 2658 and

Stonyhurst College MS B.xliii (*Harrowing*, p. xlvi n. 4), as well as according to *De Abundantia exemplorum*, the letter is said to have been sent to Tiberius.

6543–6 The poet could have had in mind any of a number of visions of infernal punishments; for overviews of these, of which the best known is the fourth-century *Visio Sancti Pauli*, see Patch, *The Other World*, 80–133 and Easting, *Visions of the Other World*. Since *PC* refers to accounts of hell by those 'þat war dede', the poet perhaps has in mind those accounts in which the protagonist actually or nearly dies and returns to life to recount what he has seen, such as the vision of Fursa told by Bede in his *Ecclesiastical History* as well as in *Handlyng Synne* (ll. 2473–534) and its source, the *Le Manuel des pechiez* (ll. 2831–98); the vision also appears in exemplum form in a fifteenth-century Northern manuscript, BodL, MS Ashmole 751 (Hanna, *The English Manuscripts*, 125–7). Similar are Bede's account of the vision of Dryhthelm (*Ecclesiastical History*, 3. 19, 5. 12 (268–77, 488–98)), *The Vision of Tundale*, and *The Revelation of the Monk of Eynsham* (17/190–202).

6547–7291 Of the fourteen pains of hell described here, nine, as indicated by Hahn (pp. 35–6), derive ultimately from Book 3 of the *Elucidarium* of Honorius Augustodunensis; as Hahn shows, the quotations attributed to 'Augustine' and 'Flos scientie' in lines 6659, 6874, 6923, 7034, 7136, and 7200–3 all come from this source. Of the remaining five pains, four— hunger, thirst, weeping, and despair—are probably based upon the corresponding pains in chapter 4 of *Les Peines*, a work itself dependent for some of its own list of nine pains on the *Elucidarium* (see Relihan's discussion, *Les Peines*, 58–60). For the remaining pain, goading by the 'worm of conscience', we have identified no definite source. The discussion of the worm of conscience in Innocent III's *De Miseria* is very broadly similar and includes the same supporting quotation from Wisd. 5 as appears in the corresponding passage from *PC*. The suggestion for the poet's treatment might alternatively have come from *Compendium*, 7. 22 (see 6973–94n) or from Humbert of Romans's *De Abundantia exemplorum*. But the idea was commonplace, and the poet may well have improvised this discussion from his knowledge of the general tradition (for which see 7045–92n).

The *PC* poet supplements his two major sources with a variety of expansions and citations from other sources, chiefly biblical. It is possible that the poet found his list of fourteen pains 'whole' in some other source, but such a list has not thus far to come to light. The fourteen pains of hell described in Anselm's *De Moribus*, the ultimate source for *PC*'s list of fourteen joys of heaven and corresponding pains of the damned in Part 6, are not the same, although they may lie somewhere behind the notion here that the pains are fourteen in number. Fourteen is indeed a rather unusual number; the *Elucidarium* provides only nine pains, and accounts based on the *Visio Sancti Pauli* list eleven. Although the exact form in which the *PC* poet encountered his list of fourteen pains remains somewhat uncertain, it is clear that the list proved useful to medieval readers, perhaps because it seemed unusually comprehensive in listing such a large number of punishments: a prose redaction of the poem's treatment appears on ff. 53^v–55 of BodL, MS Laud misc. 23 (see Wood, 'A Prose Redaction').

Morris, pp. ix–xii, prints the corresponding portion of *Cursor Mundi*, ll. 23195–350, which has a nine-pain scheme also taken from the *Elucidarium*. The *PC* poet, if he knew *Cursor*'s version, must have worked from the Latin original of the *Elucidarium*, however, since he includes a number of direct quotations of the Latin; *Cursor* contains no such Latin quotations.

6580–4 'aftir þai er worthy': That punishments in hell would fit the sins committed is the premiss of many other-world visions, including most memorably Dante's *Inferno* (where it is called 'contrapasso'). Here, for instance, schismatics' bodies are split open, those who attempted to predict the future have their heads turned backwards, and perpetrators of violence boil in a river of blood (*Inferno*, 28, ll. 34–6; 20, ll. 37–9; 12, ll. 46–8). Similarly, in the *Visio Sancti Pauli* unchaste women, for instance, have their breasts sucked by adders and their feet gnawed by hounds (see the English version in Oxford, Jesus College MS 29, *An Old English Miscellany*, 151, ll. 135–7). The idea had biblical warrant in Wisd. 11: 17, 'Per que peccat homo, per hec et torquetur' ('by what things a man sinneth, by the same also he is tormented'). Innocent III quotes this biblical passage in support of his discussion of how the damned will be punished in those limbs with which they sinned (*De Miseria*, 3. 5, 211–13).

In the *Elucidarium*, question 14 describes the pains, while question 15 describes how each fits a particular sin committed in this life. *PC* combines the material from the two questions, so that the discussion of the corresponding sin follows the discussion of each individual pain. *Cursor* preserves the arrangement in the *Elucidarium*, so that the account of the appropriateness of each pain to the various sinful behaviours on earth follows the complete list of pains.

6591–630 For this discussion of fire, cf. *Elucidarium* 3, 14–15 (1st pain).

6595–8 'A fire is kindled in my wrath, and shall burn even to the lowest hell, that is, even to eternity.' 'Ignis . . . novissima': Deut. 32: 22. 'id est . . . in eternum': cf. the gloss on the same biblical passage in *Glossa Ordinaria*, 1, 'vsque in eternum puniendo' ('punishing right up to eternity'). This quotation is not found in the *Elucidarium*.

6611–26 The discussion of how the fire of hell exceeds in ferocity the fire of earth as material fire exceeds a painted one is found in the *Elucidarium*: 'cuius ardor sic istum materialem vincit ignem, ut iste pictum ignem' ('whose intensity so surpasses a material fire, as material fire a painted fire'). *Cursor* and *PC* contain the same expansion on the original by specifying a painting 'on a waghe' (cf. *Cursor*, l. 23216).

6621–2 'As the fire of the earth is hotter than a painted fire, so the fire of hell surpasses the heat of the world.' Source unidentified. The quotation is not in the *Elucidarium*.

6628 'fole yhernyngs', i.e. sinful desires, translates 'concupiscentia' in the *Elucidarium*. Cf. *Cursor*, ll. 23271–2, 'For þat þai war won to brin, / In catel wit couetise to win.'

6631–2 These lines have been removed from the text; this note refers to the collations. 'It is a place of shame, where the fire is not extinguished, and neither those who are tortured, nor those who torture, will die.' *Sermones centum*, sermo 67 (*PL* 177: 1111). The lines are not translated in the poem itself and are probably spurious; see Britton, review, 317. The distich seems to have been commonplace: see Walther, no. 7578. It is alluded to in an English sermon preached by Richard Alkerton at St Mary Spital in London in 1406 (*Middle English Sermons*, 65/277–66/278).

6633–70 For this discussion of cold, cf. *Elucidarium* 3, 14–15 (2nd pain).

6649 'to eke þair payne': Cf. *Les Peines*, ll. 312–13, 'por agreger leur peine'. The *Elucidarium* does not discuss this alternation of heat and cold, but it is commonplace in visionary literature. Dryhthelm sees a valley with fire on one side and ice on the other, and men being tossed from side to side, although strictly this is purgatory, not hell (*Ecclesiastical History*, 488–91). On the alternation of hot and cold, cf. also *Tundale*, ll. 425–36; *Revelation of the Monk of Eynsham*, 17 (49/759–66); and *A Revelation of Purgatory* (20/362–79), in which priests and their mistresses are plunged into icy water and then into fires.

6655–6 Job 24: 19: '[They shall pass] from the snow waters to excessive heat.' Also quoted *Elucidarium* 3, 15 and *Les Peines*, ll. 315–16.

6661–4 'For the wicked are said to glow outside with heat like iron in a furnace, and inside with cold like ice in winter.' 'Austyn' is really Honorius, the author of the ultimate source of this passage, *Elucidarium* 3, 15.

6671–94 On the stench of hell, cf. *Elucidarium* 3, 14–15 (4th pain). The *Elucidarium* provides little elaboration: 'Quarta est fetor incomparabilis' ('Fourth is incomparable stench'). Our poet found in this source only his discussion of the appropriateness of stench to those who on earth indulged in the filth of lechery. On stench in hell, see Seiler, 'Filth and Stink'. Dryhthelm smells a 'fetor incomparabilis' coming from a flame-filled pit (*Ecclesiastical History*, 490–1); Tundale sees foul-smelling fire coming from a deep dale (*Tundale*, l. 376). Dante describes the stench of hell in *Inferno*, 10, ll. 133–6 and 11, ll. 4–12.

6675–6 'There is inextinguishable fire, and intolerable stench.' 'Ierom' is really Honorius Augustodunensis, *Speculum Ecclesiae* (*PL* 172: 1039). The quotation is not in the *Elucidarium*. A similar statement is attributed to Gregory in *De Abundantia exemplorum*, part 2, 'De qualitate poenarum'.

6691–4 Cf. *Elucidarium* 3, 15: 'Quia autem hic fetore luxuriae dulciter delectabantur, juste ibi fetore putrido atrociter cruciantur' ('Because here they sweetly delighted in the filth of lechery, it is just that there they should be painfully punished with putrid stench'). Cf. *Cursor*, l. 23283: 'And for þai her war wont to li / In þair stincand licheri . . .'. The *Elucidarium* does not specify that the stench comes from 'brunstane and pyk'. Brimstone and boiling pitch were familiar parts of the other-world landscape, however; cf. *Tundale*, l. 569; *A Revelation of Purgatory*, 60/31; *Revelation of the Monk of Eynsham*, 16 (45/685–6); and the lake of boiling pitch in the English version of the *Visio Sancti Pauli* in Oxford, Jesus College MS 29 (*An Old English Miscellany*, 149, ll. 75–7).

6695–728 Hunger is not listed in the *Elucidarium*. *PC*'s account derives from the discussion of hunger in the list of pains in *Les Peines*, ll. 339–48 (5th pain). This includes the same biblical quotations in the same order as those in *PC*, as well as at least one passage which appears to be directly translated in *PC* (6711–16n).

6707–8 Ps. 48: 15: 'Death shall feed upon them.' Also quoted *Les Peines*, ll. 343–4.

6711–16 The same comparison occurs in *Les Peines*, ll. 344–6. For the desire for death of those in hell, cf. also Dante, *Inferno*, i, ll. 115–17.

6719–20 Rev. 9: 6: 'They shall desire to die, and death shall fly from them', quoted *Les Peines*, ll. 347–8, and again by our poet in lines 7275 and 7384–5.

6723–8 *PC* here expands upon the brief warning to gluttons which appears at the end of the discussion of the hunger and thirst of hell in *Les Peines*, ll. 358–9: 'Ceo dussent glotons bien penser e por ceo sobreté amer' ('This gluttons ought well to think on, and for this reason ought to love sobriety').

6729–90 *PC*'s discussion of the thirst of hell is based on *Les Peines*, ll. 348–59 (6th pain).

6739–40 Ps. 10: 7: 'Fire and brimstone and storms of winds shall be the portion of their cup.' The quotation is from *Les Peines*, ll. 351–2.

6749–50 Deut. 32: 33: 'Their wine is the gall of dragons, and the venom of asps, which is incurable', quoted *Les Peines*, ll. 353–4.

6763–4 Cf. *Les Peines*, ll. 356–7: 'si come li enfaunt zouche la mamele sa mere' ('as the infant sucks the breast of its mother').

6767–8 Job 20: 16: '[They] shall suck the head of asps', as quoted in *Les Peines*, l. 358.

6773–80 Again, *PC* expands upon the brief warning against gluttony and drunkenness in *Les Peines*, ll. 358–9.

6787–8 'In hell there shall be endless hunger and endless thirst.' Source unidentified. The same quotation appears, also attributed to 'Ierom', in *Speculum Christiani*, 121/18–19.

6791–2 These lines have been removed from the text; the following note refers to the collations. 'The pains of hell are these: worms and darkness, fire, a crowd of devils, stench and cold, hunger, thirst, dread.' Source unidentified. The lines are untranslated by the poet, and since they list only nine pains they are an incongruous intrusion partway through a fourteen-pain scheme. They are most likely a marginal note derived from a nine-pain scheme in another source that was mistakenly incorporated into the text at some stage in its transmission.

6793–836 *PC*'s account of the sixth pain, darkness, is derived from *Elucidarium* 3, 14–15 (6th pain).

6803–4 'They shall grope darkness at noon, as at midnight.' Cf. Job 5: 14: 'per diem incurrent tenebras et quasi in nocte sic palpabunt in meridie' ('They shall meet with darkness in the day, and grope at noonday as in the night'). Not in *Elucidarium*.

6819–20 Job 10: 21: '[That I not turn] to a land that is dark', with 'ut' for biblical 'et'. The *Elucidarium* 3, 14 paraphrases Job 10: 21–2 quoted here and in 6825–6. Both verses form part of the ninth lection of the Office of the Dead (*Breviarium*, ii. 279; cf. *Prymer*, 69).

6825–6 Job 10: 22: 'Where . . . no order, but everlasting horror dwelleth'. In the Vulgate 'ubi umbra mortis et nullus ordo et sempiternus . . .', etc.

6829–35 Cf. *Elucidarium* 3, 15: 'Quia tenebras vitiorum hic amaverunt et ad lucem Christum venire noluerunt, ideo horridis tenebris ibi obscurabuntur, ut dicitur: "In aeternum non videbunt lumen"' ('Because they here loved the darkness of vices and would not come to the light of Christ, therefore they shall be hidden in terrible darkness there, as it says: "They shall never see light"'). *PC*'s line 6835 paraphrases the biblical passage alluded to in the *Elucidarium*, Ps. 48: 20, 'in aeternum non videbit lumen'.

6837–90 *PC*'s seventh pain is based on *Elucidarium* 3, 14–15 (8th pain).

6867–8 'In hell they shall see those, face to face, whose works they loved on earth.' Source unidentified, but the quotation is a parody of 1 Cor. 13: 12.

6875–8 'They shall see demons by the spark of the fire, and hear the miserable noise of those weeping and lamenting.' *Elucidarium* 3, 14.

6885–90 Cf. *Elucidarium* 3, 15. *PC*'s 'reson and right' translates *Elucidarium*'s 'juste'; for this common doublet, see Alford, *Piers Plowman: A Glossary*, s.v. 'resoun'.

6891–7004 For this discussion of his eighth pain, the poet seems to have combined material from both his major sources: cf. *Elucidarium* 3, 14–15 (3rd pain) and *Les Peines*, ll. 316–36 (3rd pain). Vermin and venomous creatures are a ubiquitous feature of other-world visions; Tundale, for instance, is gnawed by dragons, adders, and vermin in the beast Acheron (*Tundale*, ll. 561–4); Guinevere's mother appears from purgatory covered in serpents and toads in *The Awntyrs off Arthure*, ll. 120–1. Cf. also *Revelation of the Monk of Eynsham*, 16 (45/687–8).

6899–902 Cf. *Les Peines*, ll. 332–4, 'ke les mangeront en leur menbres e les peneront ou eaus avoient delit encountre la volunté Deu en leur vies' ('who will chew on their limbs and torment them where during their lives they took pleasure contrary to the will of God'). *PC*'s 'delite' (l. 6900) echoes the diction of the Anglo-Norman source.

6907–8 Deut. 32: 24: 'I will send the teeth of beasts upon them, with the fury of creatures that trail [in] the ground, and of serpents', with 'in terram' for biblical 'super terram'. The quotation is not in either *Les Peines* or *Elucidarium*. This is the poet's third quotation from Deut. 32, where Moses tells Israel the curses that await it; cf. 6595–8, 6749–50nn.

6919–20 Isa. 66: 24: 'Their worm shall not die, and their fire shall not be quenched.' Also quoted *Les Peines*, ll. 316–19.

6925–6 'The worms of hell are immortal, who, like fishes in water, live in fire.' From *Elucidarium* 3, 14. The same passage from the *Elucidarium*, attributed to 'le seint', is cited in *Les Peines*, ll. 334–6. Cf. also *Cursor*, ll. 23231–2: 'Als we se fixs in water suim, / Sua liue þai in þat lou sa dim.'

6947–8 Isa. 14: 11: 'Under thee shall the moth be strewed, and worms shall be thy covering.' The quotation is taken from *Les Peines*, ll. 320–1. 'Nabogodonosor' (l. 6945) is not mentioned in *Les Peines*, which correctly attributes the passage to 'Ysaie le prophete'; the poet seems to be thinking of Daniel's prophetic interpretation of Nabuchodonosor's dream.

6961–4 Judith 16: 21: '[The Lord] will give fire, and worms into their flesh, that they may burn, and may feel for ever.' Not in *Elucidarium* or *Les Peines*. The Vulgate has 'Dabit enim ignem', etc.

6973–94 Cf. *Compendium*, 7. 22, which argues that there will be no creatures left apart from man, and that the worms of hell alluded to in Scripture must therefore be of a non-material kind: 'Vermis autem Dominus in Isaia comminatur, nequaquam materialis est: quia nullam animal praeter hominem remanebit. Erit autem ibi vermis conscientiae rodens animam, et non corpus' ('But the worm the lord threatens in Isaiah is by no means material: because no animal except man will remain. Nevertheless there will be there the worm of conscience, gnawing the soul, not the body'). For the worm of conscience, see further 7045–92n.

6986 'devels in vermyn lyknes': Cf. *Les Peines*, ll. 325–7: 'Mes quele manere de vermine la serra, ou deables en semblaunce de vermine ou autre manere, nous ne trovum pas escrist apertement' ('But what kind of vermin there will be there, or whether devils in the likeness of vermin or other kind, we do not find clearly written').

6994 'sone afterward': At lines 7045 ff., the tenth pain.

6999–7004 Cf. *Elucidarium* 3, 15.

7005–44 *PC*'s ninth pain is based upon *Elucidarium* 3, 14–15 (cf. 5th pain). 'Dyngyng of devels with hamers glowand' (l. 7010) perhaps suggests that the poet mistook 'flagra' (whips) for 'flagrantes' (burning, glowing) in the *Elucidarium*, or that his copy contained an error: 'Quinta flagra caedentium, ut mallei ferrum percutientium' ('Fifth beating with whips, like hammers striking iron') (3, 14). Hammering of souls is a frequent feature of other-world visions; see, for instance, *The Vision of William of Stranton*: 'fendys bettyng on them wyth brynnyng hamerys' (*St Patrick's Purgatory*, 95) and *Tundale*, ll. 1045–1118, where smiths beat souls with hammers and tongs. Cf. *Cursor*, ll. 23237–8: 'Als it war dintes on a steþi, / þat smythes smittes in a smeþey.' *Cursor*'s 'Als' shows that, unlike our poet, he read 'ut mallei ferrum percutientium' correctly: in the original, the hammers are, unlike in *PC*, merely metaphorical.

7017–20 'As a catapult strikes the walls of a city, so devils, although more bitterly and cruelly, shall whip the bodies and souls of the wicked after the judgement.' Source unidentified. Not in *Elucidarium*.

7035–6 'Judgements are prepared for blasphemers, and for beaters with hammers the bodies of fools.' Actually not Augustine but Prov. 19: 29, quoted *Elucidarium* 3, 15. In the original the Latin reads 'Parata sunt derisoribus iudicia et mallei percutientes stultorum corporibus' ('Judgments are prepared for scorners: and striking hammers for the bodies of fools'). The *Elucidarium*, like *PC*, reads 'blasphematoribus' for Vulgate 'derisoribus'.

7045–92 The worm of conscience is not listed as one of the pains of hell in either the *Elucidarium* or *Les Peines*. The poet's treatment may be compared loosely with that in Innocent, *De Miseria*, 3. 2 (207–9), which includes the same biblical quotation found in lines 7059–64. However, the idea was a familiar one in late medieval culture and the poet may have been drawing on the general tradition, for which see Harley, 'Last Things First'. The worm of conscience figures prominently in the fifteenth-century *Revelation of Purgatory*. In this text the nun Margaret reveals that the worm of conscience is the greatest pain of purgatory and of hell (65/199–203). The worm of conscience also figures in a sermon preached by Richard Alkerton (*Middle English Sermons*, 65/271–2), as well as in three sources used elsewhere by our poet: ps.-Bernard, *Meditationes*, 3. 10 (*PL* 184: 492), *Compendium*, 7. 22 (see 6973–94n), and *De Abundantia exemplorum*, part 2, 'De qualitate damnatorum'. The worm of conscience accuses the soul at death in Guillaume de Deguileville's *Pèlerinage de l'âme*; cf. the Middle English version, *The Pilgrimage of the Soul*, chapters 19–21. Conceived as a *stimulus conscientiae*, the idea of the worm of conscience is obviously central to *PC*.

7059–64 Wisd. 5: 8–11: 'What hath pride profited us? . . . what . . . the boasting of riches . . . ? All those things are passed away like a shadow, and like a post that runneth on, and as a ship that passeth through the waves . . . [and] as when a bird flieth through the air, of the passage of which no mark can be found.' In the Vulgate, 'aut quid divitiarum iactatio contulit nobis', 'illa tamquam umbra', 'navis quae pertransit flutuantem', and 'aut avis quae transvolat in aere nullum invenitur argumentum itineris illius'. The passage was a popular one in works dealing with death and the *contemptus mundi* theme; it is also alluded to, for instance, in *Orologium Sapientiae*, 359 and in Rolle's *Super novem lectiones*, ii. 145/4–7.

7093–130 Tears are not listed in the *Elucidarium*. *PC*'s account probably derives chiefly from *Les Peines*, ll. 336–9, which includes the same comparison between the tears that will be shed in hell and the drops of water in the sea.

7096 'thurgh smoke': The poet may be thinking of an aside in the *Elucidariam*'s discussion of its second pain, cold, in which it is said that the smoke from the fire of hell will make the eyes of the damned water (3, 14).

7113–14 'In hell more tears will be poured out than there are drops in the sea.' The same comparison appears in *Les Peines*: 'E saunz fin lermerount ceaus ke la serrunt, e saunz ceo uncore un soul homme plorra plus de lermes ke goutes sount de eaue en tot le mund' ('And those who are there will weep without end, and still a single man will weep without end more tears than there are drops of water in the whole world) (ll. 336–9) (in the Latin version, 'unus homo plures lacrimas quam modo sunt gutte aquarum in toto mundo effundet'). Trudel (*Speculum huius vite*, ii. 438) points out that the same quotation appears in *Speculum Christiani*, 121/19–20: 'Augustinus: In inferno plures effundentur lacrime, quam sunt in mari gutte.' The same comparison also appears in *A Treatise of Ghostly Battle* (*Yorkshire Writers*, ii. 428), probably also derived from *Les Peines*.

7118–24 Scalding tears which burn like fire also appear in *The Vision of Tundale*, ll. 567–8.

7131–68 *PC*'s account of 'schame and schenshepe' is derived from *Elucidarium* 3, 14–15 (7th pain).

7137–8 'All will be visible before all, and they shall not be able to hide themselves.' From *Elucidarium* 3, 14.

7149–50 Ps. 43: 16: 'All the day long my shame is before me: and the confusion of my face hath covered me.' Not in *Elucidarium*, but the presence of the passage here suggests a concordance-trained mind; it echoes *Elucidarium*'s key word, 'confusio'.

7169–228 With *PC*'s thirteenth pain, compare *Elucidarium* 3, 14–15 (9th pain).

7187–8 Matt. 22: 13: 'Bind his hands and feet, and cast him into the exterior darkness.' In the Vulgate, 'Ligatis pedibus eius et manibus, mittite eum', etc. Not in *Elucidarium*.

7202 '*Flos sciencie*': We have not identified the work to which the poet is here referring. The quotation that follows is ultimately from the *Elucidarium*, but the poet could well have obtained it via an intermediate compilation 'Of sere questyons of divinite' of the kind he here describes. And he may have (mis)read a citation like *Elussidarie* as *Flos scī-e* (i.e. the abbreviation for *scienci-*).

7207–8 'Their heads, he says, shall be turned upside down, their feet erect upwards, and stretched on all sides with pains.' From *Elucidarium* 3, 16.

7229–91 The major source for *PC*'s fourteenth pain is probably *Les Peines*, ll. 359–66, 371–74 (9th pain). This contains the same English proverb (cited in English amidst the Anglo-Norman) as in *PC*, line 7262.

7233–4 Prov. 2: 19: 'None that go in unto her shall return again, neither shall they take hold of the paths of life.' Not in *Les Peines* or *Elucidarium*.

7245–6 'Because in hell there is no redemption'. Cf. Job 7: 9. The same quotation also appears in line 2833; see note.

7261–6 Cf. *Les Peines*, ll. 371–4: 'L'en dit en engleis: ȝif hope ne were, herte tobroste. Mes la serra ke queor de homme crever ne porra, ke saunz nul fin vivront e jammés relees de peyne n'averont' ('It is said in English, "If there were no hope, the heart would burst". But there the heart of man will not be able to burst, because they will live without end and never have release from their pain'). The same proverb, probably also from *Les Peines*, appears in the account of the pains of hell in *A Treatise of Ghostly Battle*, *Yorkshire Writers*, ii. 428. For the English proverb, see Whiting, *Proverbs*, H475; cf. also Whiting H463, 'Of alle thinges that I can fynde, / Hope dothe help the carefull mynd.'

7275 Rev. 9:6: 'Death shall fly from them.' Also quoted in lines 6719–20 and 7384–5.

7285 'Als . . . in swowne fall': Cf. lines 8153–5.

7294–307 To the fourteen pains just outlined, the poet adds one final pain, the greatest of all: loss of the sight of God. 'Carentia visionis diuinae' is listed as one of the pains of hell in *Compendium* 7, 22.

7309 'Als þe boke says': It is difficult to identify any definite source for the poet's concluding account of the 'general' pains of hell; the details could have been inspired by any number of infernal visions. The analogues cited below are representatives of the general tradition rather than specific sources.

7324–7 Cf. *A Treatise of Ghostly Battle*, *Yorkshire Writers*, ii. 428: 'Sende thyne herte in to helle and ther shale thou fynde all that that thou hatest here, that ys a fawte of alle goodys, and plente off alle euylles.' It is possible that the *Treatise* might be derived from *PC* at this point, as well as for part of its description of heaven; see 1036n.

7331–3 Cf. 'Le Petit Sermon', ll. 575–6: 'Et maudirrent trestot lour eé / Que nee furent et engendré' ('And they will curse their life, that they were born and conceived').

7334 Gnashing of teeth in hell has biblical warrant in Matt. 22: 13.

7344–53 On the noise of hell, cf. Dante, *Inferno*, 3, ll. 22–30; 5, ll. 25–7 and pseudo-Bernard, *Meditationes*, 3. 10: 'Nihil aliud ibi audietur nisi fletus et planctus, gemitus et uluatus, moerores atque stridores dentium' ('Nothing else will be heard there except weeping and lamenting, groaning and wailing, grieving and gnashing of teeth') (*PL* 184: 492). The passage is quoted, attributed to Bernard, in *Speculum Christiani*, 121/20–2). See also *Visio Sancti Pauli*, 75: 'alii flent, alii ululant, alii gemunt' ('some weep, some wail, some moan').

7354–65 For devils pressing the wicked into ovens, cf. *The Vision of Tundale*, where there is an oven-like house (ll. 741–3); *Revelation of the Monk of Eynsham*, 16 (45/683), and *St Patrick's Purgatory*, where souls are roasted on a gridiron (*Owayne Miles*, stanza 79, *St Patrick's Purgatory*, 15). In *A Revelation of Purgatory*, men and women are roasted on spits (75/547–9). For souls packed one on top of the other, cf. *Visio Sancti Pauli*, 78: 'Et erat anima una super alteram quasi oves in ovili' ('And there was one soul on top of the other like sheep in a sheep-pen') (contrast John 10: 16, promising a single sheepfold, quoted in lines 4635–6).

7374–5 Tundale also scratches his own face with his nails (*The Vision of Tundale*, ll. 571–2).

7384–5 Rev. 9: 6: 'They shall desire to die, and death shall fly from them.' Also quoted in lines 6719–20 and 7275.

7403–6 Cf. lines 8415–26.

7408 Cf. the English version of the *Visio Sancti Pauli* in BodL, MS Douce 302 (*An Old English Miscellany*, 214, ll. 108–9).

7411–21 Cf. Innocent, *De Miseria*, 3. 9 (219): 'Maledicent Altissimo et blasphemabunt Excelsum, conquerentes eum esse malignum qui creavit illos ad penam et nunquam inclinatur ad veniam' ('They will curse the Almighty and blaspheme the Highest, accusing him of being malignant who created them for punishment and will never be moved to leniency'). For those in hell blaspheming God and cursing their birth and parents, cf. Dante, *Inferno*, 3, ll. 103–5 and 5, ll. 34–6.

7428–31 Cf. lines 6460–76 and n.

7436–55 For the idea that there would be a punishment in hell to fit each sin committed on earth, cf. 6580–4n.

7472–81 Cf. Hugh of St Victor, *De Anima*, 4. 13 (*PL* 177: 186): 'Ibi vidi omnia genera tormentorum, quorum minimum est majus omnibus his tormentis quaecunquae in hoc saeculo' ('There I saw all kinds of torment, of which the least is greater than all the torments of this world').

PART 7

The poet's major source in Part 7 is *Les Peines*, chapters 5 and 6, which provides the basis of his discussion of the fourteen beatitudes and their contrary pains. This discussion, however, the poet expands with a range of materials, including the ps.-Augustinian sermon *De triplici habitaculo* and a moralized description of the city of heaven based ultimately upon the book of Revelation and drawing on the conventions of Apocalypse commentaries such as Berengaud's *Expositio super septem visiones libri apocalypsis*. The poet also draws on sources he has employed elsewhere in the poem, including Bartholomaeus Anglicus's *De Proprietatibus rerum*, which, together with Moses Maimonides's *Guide for the Perplexed* and the Old French *Sydrac*, provides his cosmological description at the beginning of this part of the poem.

7536–45 Cf. the Prologue, lines 139–43 and n. This final part of the poem contains several such recapitulations of its opening.

7552–5 The poet's account of the different heavens is in part based upon Book 8 of Bartholomaeus Anglicus, *De Proprietatibus rerum* (Köhler, 202; Hahn, 36), also his source for the account of the world at the beginning of Part 2. In naming only three different heavens (line 7566), rather than Bartholomaeus's seven, however, the poet may be drawing on the tripartite scheme found in *Sydrac*, question 229 (113), a work named as a source by the poet in line 7726. Cf. also the three heavens in *Elucidarium* I, 11, upon which *Sydrac* is based. In Dante's *Paradiso* there are nine material heavens, with the Empyrean heaven above all.

According to Bartholomaeus (*De Proprietatibus*, 8. 2; Trevisa, *Properties*, i. 448/15–30), the heaven called *firmamentum* is the source of generation and corruption in the world; it is constantly moving. Cf. line 7582 on the motion of the firmament around the earth.

7568 'þe sterned heven': According to Bartholomaeus (*De Proprietatibus*, 8. 6), the stars are contained within the sphere of heaven, which moves around the earth (cf. Trevisa, *Properties*, 456/26–457/20).

7571–9 Cf. *De Proprietatibus*, 8. 3, 'Sextum celum aqueam siue cristallinum' ('Sixth the water or crystalline heaven'; cf. Trevisa, *Properties*, i. 453/5).

7582–9 See introductory note to Part 2. The poet expresses the characteristic medieval view of the cosmos, in which the earth, at the centre of the universe, is also the lowest point in the universe; hell, in the middle of the earth, is the lowest point of all. Earth is made of material coarser than that of the heavens, whose matter is purer the further away they are from the earth. Compare Dante's *Paradiso*, 22, ll. 133–8, where Dante looks down upon the seven spheres and smiles because the earth looks so wretched. In *Paradiso* 28, ll. 49–51, Dante says that the heavens are more divine the further they are from the centre, i.e. the earth.

7590–614 Cf. *De Proprietatibus*, 8. 2 (Trevisa, *Properties*, i. 450/35–451/40).

7622–38 These seven planets, their motions, and their characteristics are treated at length by Bartholomaeus, *De Proprietatibus*, 8. 11–17, beginning with Saturn and ending with the moon.

7639–43 For the heaven called 'aereum', cf. *De Proprietatibus*, 8. 2 (Trevisa, *Properties*, i. 447/5–10).

7648–83 As Hahn indicates (36), 'Rabby Moyses' is the twelfth-century philosopher Moses Maimonides, *Guide for the Perplexed*, 3. 14 (456): 'The distance between the center of the earth to the highest part of the sphere of Saturn is one that could be covered in approximately eight thousand and seven hundred years of three hundred and sixty-five days each, if each day a distance is covered of forty of our legal miles, of which each has two thousand of the cubits used for working purposes.'

7668–79 Cf. *Cursor*'s description of the fall of Lucifer, ll. 502–10: 'Bot bede sais fra erth to heuen / es seuen thusand yeir and hundret seuen, / Bi iornes qua þat gang it may, / Fourti mile on ilk a day.'

7686–7 Cf. Wisd. 11: 21: 'Thou hast ordered all things in measure, number, and weight.'

7714–19 Hahn (36) compares *Early South-English Legendary*, 311, ll. 397–8: 'for þe leste steorre is / In heouene, ase þe bok us tellez: more þane al þe eorþe, i-wis.'

7726–45 Cf. *Sydrac*, question 231 (113) (as noted Hahn, 37).

7758–67 Cf. *De Proprietatibus*, 8. 4: 'Celum empireum est primum et summum celum locus angelorum regio et habitaculum beatorum. Et dicitur a pir quod est ignis quasi totum igneum sic dictum non ab ardore sed pocius a lumine et splendore vt dicit Ysidorus' ('The empyrean heaven is the first and highest, the place of angels and the region and dwelling of the blessed. And it is named from 'pir', that is fire, as if it were totally firey; it is so called not from heat but more from light and brightness, as Ysidore says'). Cf. Trevisa, *Properties*, i. 454/27–30.

7780–801 Cf. *Compendium* 7, 31 (as noted Köhler, 207, Hahn, 37–8): 'Tot igitur, et tanta sunt ibi gaudia, quod omnes arithmetici huius mundi non possent ea numerare, nec geometrici mensurare, nec grammatici, dialectici, rhetorici, aut theologi explicare: quia nec oculus vidit, nec auris audiuit, nec in cor et cetera' ('For so many and so great are the joys there, that all the mathematicians of this world could not number them, nor geometers measure them, nor grammarians, logicians, rhetoricians, or theologians expound them: because eye hath not seen, nor ear heard, neither into the heart . . ., etc.'). The passage in the *Compendium* is accompanied by a tag citation of the verse from 1 Cor. 2: 9 quoted in *PC*, lines 7786–9: 'That eye hath not seen, nor ear heard, neither hath it entered into the heart of man, what things God hath prepared for them that love him.' The Vulgate reads 'quae praeparavit Deus his qui diligunt illum'.

7810–21 As Hahn indicates (p. 211), this series of antitheses is similar to that in Hugh of St Victor's *De Anima*, 4. 16 (*PL* 177: 189). Alternatively, the poet may have been using the similar list which appears in *Compendium* 7, 31.

7856–65 On the sight of God in heaven, cf. the response for the first lection of the Office of the Dead: 'Et in carne mea videbo Deum Salvatorem meum' ('And in my body I shall see God, my saviour') (*Breviarium*, ii. 274 [cf. Job 19: 26]; *Prymer*, 59), and *Parson's Tale*, *Canterbury Tales*, X.1079. See Kolve, *Chaucer and the Imagery of Narrative*, 27.

7872–8629 Relihan (*Les Peines*, 50–1) identifies five distinct Anselmian or ps.-Anselmian works dealing with the seven joys of the body and seven joys of the soul and their contrary pains: chapter 25 of Anselm's *Proslogion* (*Opera Omnia*, i. 89–139); Eadmer of Canterbury's *De beatitudine perennis vitae*; the *Dicta Anselmi*; *De humanis moribus*, chapters 48–71 (all in *Memorials of St Anselm*); and chapters 47–71 of the *Liber de sancti Anselmi similitudinibus* (*PL* 159: 627–43). Of particular interest in the present context is a sixth version, an expanded text of chapter 5 of the *Dicta Anselmi* found in English, Latin, and French versions alongside a copy of *PC* in Lichfield Cathedral Library, MS 16, edited as *De quatuordecim partibus beatitudinis* by Avril Henry and D. A. Trotter, and known in English as 'The Fourteen Parts of Blessedness'.

Not all of these works, however, present the joys in the same manner as *PC*, alternating with their corresponding pains. The *Proslogion* does not discuss the pains at all, while *De beatitudine* and the *Dicta Anselmi* present the pains as a group separately at the end of the work. In 'The Fourteen Parts of Blessedness' only the joys are treated in the main body of the work, although there is a chapter at the end offering a 'Recapitulatio brevis' of the beatitudes and the corresponding pains of the damned.

Of all the Anselmian texts the closest version to *PC*'s, as Hahn recognized (p. 39), is the *De Similitudinibus* (itself really a version of *De humanis moribus* expanded with material from *De beatitudine*). This version alone contains several passages which are reflected in *PC*. Thus although Henry and Trotter are correct in saying in their edition that 'the Anselmian treatment of the seven Dowers of the Body and seven Dowers of the Soul that forms *De quatuordecim partibus beatitudinis* is also found in Part 7 of *The Prick of Conscience*' (p. 9), their statement is potentially misleading if taken to mean that *PC* presents the same version of 'the Anselmian treatment' of this topic. *PC*'s treatment derives from a different version, although probably the distinction between versions was too fine to have been recognized by the producers of Lichfield Cathedral Library, MS 16, who undoubtedly combined *PC* with *De quatuordecim partibus beatitudinis* because of its closely similar 'Anselmian' materials.

Although *PC*'s treatment ultimately derives from the 'Anselmian' discussion in *De Similitudinibus*, however, Relihan convincingly argues (*Les Peines*, 79–82) that *PC*'s immediate source is the translation of this Anselmian text in chapters 5 and 6 of *Les Peines*. Relihan argues for *PC*'s dependence on *Les Peines* rather than on Anselm on the basis of three factors: firstly, both *PC* and *Les Peines* retain the comparison between the joys of heaven and the pains of hell but eliminate Anselm's presentation of this present life as an intermediate state in which neither complete joy nor complete pain is experienced. Secondly, lines 7956–75 and 8004–19 are, as Relihan persuasively argues, 'solely adaptations' of the corresponding passages in *Les Peines*. Thirdly, lines 7956–75 transmit an error found in some manuscripts of *Les Peines*. Relihan demonstrates his claims only in relation to lines 7956–75, the third physical beatitude of strength, but his argument for the dependence of *PC* upon *Les Peines* is confirmed by several expansions in *PC*'s treatment, noted below, which appear only in *Les Peines* and not in the original Anselmian work. The closeness with which the English poet follows the French source is indicated by several places in which his choice of diction echoes that of *Les Peines*.

Guy Trudel (*Speculum huius vite*, ii. 439–40) refutes Relihan's claim by citing three biblical quotations which, he says, appear in *PC* and its abbreviated version, *Speculum huius vite*, and which are found in *De Similitudinibus* but not in *Les Peines*. The first of these, in *PC*, lines 7786–9, is also in the *Compendium*, whence the poet seems to have drawn it together with its surround (see 7786–9n). The second, in *Speculum*, lines 2416a–b, 'Justi autem in perpetuum vivent, et apud Dominum est merces, et cetera', we do not find in *PC*. For the third, see 8286–7n. The presence of this single biblical quotation in Anselm and in *PC*, lines 8286–7 does not seem sufficient evidence to overturn Relihan's argument, especially since *PC* also contains several biblical quotations, as noted below, which occur in equivalent passages in *Les Peines* but not in Anselm, as well as non-biblical expansions on the text of Anselm which are found only in the French text.

7950 'swa hevy, charged with syn': Cf. *Les Peines*, l. 412: 'serront taunt chargés des peynes' ('they will be so weighted down with punishments'). *De Similitudinibus* has 'tanto poenarum pondere premetur' ('[the wicked] shall be so pressed down with the weight of pains') (*PL* 159: 629).

7958 'þof þai feble here and wayke ware': Cf. *Les Peines*, l. 418: 'adonke ja si feble ne seit ore' ('be they never so feble now'). Not in *De Similitudinibus*.

7963 'ilka mountayne and ilka hill': As Relihan indicates, *PC* here follows an expansion in *Les Peines*. *De Similitudinibus* reads 'ut etiam, si velit, terram commovere possit' ('that indeed if he wished he could move the earth') (*PL* 159: 631), where *Les Peines* reads 'totes les muntaynes du munde' (all the mountains of the earth') (l. 419).

7974 'teres' : Relihan argues that *PC* here transmits an error found in some manuscripts of *Les Peines*. Where *De Similitudinibus* reads 'ut nec etiam vermes amovere queat ab oculis suis', one family of manuscripts of *Les Peines* erroneously translates with 'lermes' (tears) for correct 'vermes' (worms). The association between eyes and tears seems sufficiently strong for this to be an error that could have been made independently by the *PC* poet from the original 'vermes' in *De Similitudinibus* . But the error is much more likely to have been made in French, where vermes/lermes are orthographically similar, than in English, and it seems easiest to suppose that the *PC* poet inherited the mistake from a manuscript of *Les Peines* related to this particular family.

7988 *PC*'s list is closer to an expansion in *Les Peines* than to the original in *De Similitudinibus*; cf. *Les Peines*, ll. 429–31: 'Ne nule chose ne lui porra desturber ne defendre de ceo qu'il fere vodra, ne mur, ne feer, ne pere, ne terre, ne closture, ne element' ('And nothing will be able to disturb or prevent them in doing what they wish; neither wall, iron, stone, earth, fence, or element'). The equivalent passage in *De Similitudinibus* reads 'non erit aliquod obstaculum quod nos retardet, nulla clausura quae nobis ullatenus obstet, non elementum quod nobis ad velle nostrum pervium omnino non exstet' ('There shall not be anything that can hinder us, no enclosure which will stand against us, no element that will not stand entirely penetrated at our will') (*PL* 159: 631).

8006 *PC*'s 'grevaunce' echoes the diction of *Les Peines*, ll. 441–2: 'nule peine ne maladie ne corupçoun ne pesauntime jammés ne *grevera* le corps' ('no pain or malady or corruption or heaviness will ever afflict the body') (our emphasis).

8012–19 *De Similitudinibus* contains no mention of purgatory. The discussion here derives from *Les Peines*, ll. 444–9, where the author refers his reader back to his earlier discussion of the pains of purgatory (cf. *PC*'s own treatment of this subject, ll. 2982 ff.).

8040–9 This comparison with a vessel is not found in *De Similitudinibus* and is one of the clearest indications that *PC* depends on the version in *Les Peines*, which contains the same comparison in ll. 458–63.

8050–9 *De Similitudinibus* does not specify the torments. *Les Peines* lists fire, sulphur, and vermin. The *PC* poet adds 'devels þat ay salle þam smyte' (l. 8057) from his own earlier treatment of the pains of hell.

8076–145 These lines have no parallel in *Les Peines* or in *De Similitudinibus*, and the biblical quotations they contain are found in neither source.

8076–7 Ps. 89: 4: 'For a thousand years in thy sight are as yesterday, which is past.'

8092–3 Ps. 83: 11: 'Better is one day in thy courts above thousands.'

8110–27 'Saint Austyn': Hahn (p. 40) compares with the ps.-Augustinian work, *De triplici habitaculo*, 3 (*PL* 40: 993).

8154–5 Again, *PC*'s comparison with the man in a trance depends on an expansion in *Les Peines*. *De Similitudinibus* has simply 'non nisi moriendo vivere tunc poterit' ('he cannot live then except in dying'), where *Les Peines*, ll. 477–9 expands with 'ke leur vie semble plus mort ke vie, kar il serront aussi come genz ki gisent en trauns e jammés parfitement morront' ('for their life resembles more death than life, for they shall be like people who lie in a trance and they shall never perfectly die').

8189–91 The poet here gives the conventional attributes of each of the three persons of the Trinity; cf. lines 1–3.

8204–73 Again, not in *Les Peines* or *De Similitudinibus*. Hahn (p. 40) again compares *De triplici habitaculo*, 6 (*PL* 40: 996–8), which contains the same comparison between the things we see in a mirror, and the three kinds of knowledge the saved will have 'per speculum divinae claritatis'. See also chapter 4 in the same work (*PL* 40: 994). For 8213, 'a myroure', cf. 1 Cor. 13: 12.

8286–7 Ps. 81: 6: 'I have said: You are gods and all of you the sons of the most High.' Not in either *Les Peines* or Anselm's original at this point, although cited later in *De Similitudinibus* (*PL* 159: 639) and alluded to later in *Les Peines* (l. 573: 'si come les fitz e les files Dieu'). For Trudel, this quotation is evidence that the *PC* poet worked from the original Anselmian text rather than from *Les Peines*, but the poet could easily have supplied the quotation on the suggestion of *Les Peines*, or even have had a manuscript in which, as with some other passages, the biblical text alluded to by the author has been 'filled in' by a copyist.

8300 'Saint Anselme þus answers to þis': Cf. *Les Peines*, ll. 500–1: 'Seint Anselme vous respount.' The dialogic mode originates with *De Similitudinibus*, where Anselm poses the question of an imagined interlocutor which he goes on to answer himself. The Latin version of *Les Peines* differs from *PC* in naming 'Johannes Evangelista' at this point.

8323–4 Drunkenness is mentioned only in the Latin version of *Les Peines*, but this version does not mention *PC*'s 'barnhede', 'kant vous futes en berz' in *Les Peines* (l. 510).

8350–1 Ps. 88: 2: 'The mercies of the Lord I will sing for ever.' This quotation is found in the corresponding discussion in *Les Peines* but not in *De Similitudinibus*.

8438–9 Ps. 57: 11: 'The just shall rejoice when he shall see the revenge.' Quoted in the corresponding passage in *Les Peines*, but not in *De Similitudinibus*.

8482 'þe ferth blys': *PC* reverses the order of the fourth and fifth blisses and corresponding pains as found in *Les Peines* and *De Similitudinibus*.

8500–1, 8516–17 Luke 14: 11: 'He that humbleth himself, shall be exalted', 'Every one that exalteth himself, shall be humbled'. The poet reverses the order of the two statements from the biblical original. Not quoted in either *Les Peines* or *De Similitudinibus*.

8536–7 Ps. 138: 17: 'Thy friends, O God, are made exceedingly honourable.' The quotation is in *Les Peines* (although in Anglo-Norman, not in Latin as here), but not in *De Similitudinibus*.

8578–81 *De Similitudinibus* does not mention devils. Cf. *Les Peines*, l. 593: 'les debles hidus irrount e vendrunt sur eaus' ('hideous devils will go and come on them').

8590–1 'The terrible ones shall go and come upon [them].' Job 20: 25. The quotation is taken from the equivalent passage in *Les Peines*; it is not cited in *De Similitudinibus*.

8632–43 Cf. *Compendium* 7, 31 (Köhler, 208; Hahn, 40): 'Gaudebunt enim sancti supra se de Dei visione, infra se de celi et aliarum creaturarum corporalium pulchritudine, intra se de corporis glorificatione, extra se de angelorum et hominum associatione' ('For the blessed will rejoice at the sight of God above them; at the beauty of heaven and of other bodily creatures beneath them; within them, at the glorification of the body; outside them, at the coming together of angels and men'). *De Similitudinibus*, ch. 71 has a shorter version, which does not list these *causes* of this all-encompassing joy but only states that there will be joy within and without, above and below and all around, so again there is no evidence that the *PC* poet knew the Anselm text except through *Les Peines*.

The poet now begins a lengthy description of the fourteenth beatitude, perfect joy, which departs from the account offered in *Les Peines*. He has not entirely abandoned the original scheme of the joys and their corresponding pains, however, to which he returns at line 9384.

8646–737 As Hahn indicates (p. 40), there is a very similar listing of the inhabitants of heaven in Hugh of St Victor's *De Anima*, 4. 14 (*PL* 177: 187).

PC's 'wedded men þat lyfes wele here' (l. 8731) is apparently the poet's own addition, in keeping with the 'lewed' audience he imagines for his poem. With lines 8670–5, compare 1 Cor. 13: 12 and 8204–73n.

8691 The Nine Orders of Angels are depicted in stained glass in All Saints' Church, North Street, York, also home to the well-known '*Prick of Conscience* window'. The subject appears to have been a popular one in York stained glass of the period: the East Window of York Minster by John Thornton depicts the Nine Orders in the tracery lights, and according to Marks, the All Saints' window is very similar to the one in the Minster, as is the depiction of the Nine Orders at St Michael Spurriergate. The remains of a Nine Orders window at Thornhill in West Yorkshire are also, in Marks's view, 'unmistakably York work' (Marks, *Stained Glass*, 182, 185).

8780–1 John 14: 2: 'In my Father's house there are many mansions.'

8790–1 Rev. 21: 2: 'And I saw the holy city, the new Jerusalem, coming down out of heaven from God, prepared as a bride adorned for her husband.' The poet omits Vulgate 'a Deo' after 'de celo'.

8866–89 Morris's gloss on the poet's introduction to his description of the heavenly Jerusalem, 'an imaginary description out of his "own head"', is potentially misleading. As Morris of course knew, the poet's description of the heavenly city is not an 'imaginary' one in the modern sense of an original fiction; it is clearly based on the description of the new Jerusalem in Rev. 21, although the poet adds his own 'imaginary' details and embellishments. By 'imaginary' we must here understand 'imagination' in the medieval sense of 'that faculty that can form an image independent of immediate visual stimulus'; '*imaginativa* includes both the power to recall the forms of sense experience as images, separate from their material identities, *and the power to combine such forms into forms of things never experienced*' (Kolve, *Chaucer and the Imagery of Narrative*, 20–3, our emphasis). The poet can only 'imagine' the city of heaven for his reader, not because he lacks written authorities for its description, but because it must necessarily be outside of ordinary human experience, like 'na cete þat on erth may stand'. Compare the definition of imagination in a work the poet certainly knew, the *Compendium*, 2, 37: 'Ista autem virtus scilicet imaginatio, thesaurus formarum vocatur: quia in ea, sicut dictum est, formae a particularibus sensibus receptae retinentur' ('This power, that is imagination, is called a treasury of forms: because in it, as it is said, are retained the forms received from the individual senses').

The Prologue to the Anglo-Norman prose *Apocalypse* with commentary (also in a Middle English translation, cited here) which the poet may have known (Dean, *Anglo-Norman Literature*, nos. 475, 477, 478) provides a useful gloss on what the poet might mean by saying that his description is 'imagined'. In introducing John's vision, the author distinguishes three different types of 'vision':

for oo. siȝth is bodilich . . . þat oþere is gostlich als it were a semblaunce whan we seen in sleep oiþer wakyng semblaunt of any þing þat oþere þinges ben bitokned by . . . þe þrid manere of siȝth is cleped intellectuel. þat is when þe [holy] gost aliȝtteþ þe vndirstondyng of þe soules & dooþ hem seen on niȝttes þe spirites & þe priuetes of god. (*Apocalypse*, 3/29–37; we have corrected the text by comparison with the Anglo-Norman and following Fridner's notes)

While St John's vision clearly belongs to the last category described here, the poet was perhaps thinking of the second when he referred to his description as 'imagined'; 'gostlich' in the English renders 'espiritele ou ymagenerie' in the Anglo-Norman. Again, 'imagination' here refers to that which makes images or similitudes. It is this sense of 'imagination', similitude-making, to which our poet is referring, for he says that he will 'lyken' heaven, unknown to direct sensory experience, to earthly images or similitudes (ll. 8879–85)—and also that he will offer exegetical 'likenesses' by glossing the spiritual sense ('gastly understandyng') of each of his imagined items. Of course, the book of Revelation itself is understood as communicating by similitudes or symbols; for heaven *likened* to a city, cf. the commentary on Rev. 21 by Berengaud (*PL* 17: 946): 'civitatem Dei *sub figura* Hierusalem' ('the city of God under the figure of Jerusalem', our emphasis).

8891–907 The poet's description of the heavenly city is based on that in Rev. 21: 10–25, although with some 'medievalizing' embellishments. It is clear from the allegorization of the architectural details which follows that the poet was familiar with one or more of the glossed Apocalypse versions, although the allegorical significances he offers are apparently his own. The poet's description may have been inspired by the lavish illustrations which accompanied the text and commentary in the illuminated Apocalypse books popular *c*.1250–1350; for depictions of John being shown the heavenly city in some of these illustrated Apocalypse books, see Lewis, *Reading Images*, 192–4 and figures 163, 165, and 166. A similar visionary structure, also apparently inspired by Rev. 21: 10–25, appears in *The Vision of Tundale* as a wall made of precious stones (ll. 2081–95).

8893 'Opon a mote sett': The poet evidently thinks of the heavenly city as a medieval castle, although the 'mote' also responds in part to the biblical source, in which John is transported 'in montem magnum et altum' ('to a great and high mountain') (Rev. 21: 10). 'Beryll' is mentioned as one of the precious stones which adorn the twelve foundations of the city walls in the biblical description (Rev. 21: 20).

8894–6 The biblical description mentions only twelve foundations and twelve gates; the poet dispenses with the number symbolism and adds the architectural details of 'wardes', 'turrettes', and 'garettes'.

8897 'ryche perre': In the biblical account, each of the twelve gates has a pearl (Rev. 21: 21). Pearl symbolism is of course central to the Middle English poem *Pearl*, which also presents a vision of the heavenly city inspired by the description in the book of Revelation.

8898 'cristall schene': In John's vision, the heavenly city is bright 'as crystal' (Rev. 21: 11). There is 'a ful glorious walle of crystal' in *The Revelation of the Monk of Eynsham*, 55 (161/2802).

8904 'All schynand als gold bryght burnyst': In Rev. 21: 18 and 21: 21 the city and its streets are described as being of pure gold.

8907 'precyouse stanes': Compare *Pearl*, ll. 81–2, where the gravel at the dreamer's feet is made of pearls.

8917 'savours swete': For the sweet smell of heaven, cf. the vision of heaven in Bede's account of Dryhthelm (*Ecclesiastical History*, 494–5); *the Vision of Tundale*, l. 1785; *Revelation of the Monk of Eynsham*, 49 (147/2544–5). See also *PC*, ll. 9273 ff.

8922–77 Cf. *Elucidarium* 3, 90–103 (Köhler, 209–11, Hahn, 40). The list corresponds to the fourteen blessednesses of heaven described above, which the author of the *Elucidarium* also used as a source.

8944–7 In the original, 'Moyses, cujus nunquam dens est motus nec caligavit oculus' ('Moses, none of whose teeth were moved nor his eyes dimmed' (*Elucidarium* 3, 95)). Cf. Deut. 34: 7.

9020–47 Cf. *Elucidarium* 3, 106–18 (Köhler, 209–11, Hahn, 40). In the *Elucidarium*, these comparisons are combined with a version of Anselm's discussion of the fourteen beautitudes. The *Elucidarium* does not, however, as *PC* does, alternate these with the corresponding pains (which are listed separately at the conclusion, 3, 119). There is a shorter set of comparisons in *Compendium*, 7, 31, with only Solomon, Absalon, Asahel, Sampson, Methuselah, and Augustus.

9048–190 The poet now returns to his earlier description of the heavenly city to take up the allegorical significance of the various architectural features he describes. He was undoubtedly familiar with similar allegorized readings in commentaries on the Apocalypse, such as the *Glossa Ordinaria*, the *Bible Moralisée*, the popular commentary by Berengaud (extracts of which appear in the majority of the illuminated Apocalypse books that appeared from the mid-thirteenth century), or the Anglo-Norman/Middle English prose Apocalypse version. The poet's own allegorical meanings do not coincide exactly with any of these sources, however—in part because he has added his own embellishments to the biblical account in describing the architecture. The poet seems to have felt free to invent his own architectural details and his own moralizations in keeping with the general tradition of allegorical buildings (for which see Mann). The poet's treatment is an example of the rather static nature of such allegories, as discussed by Mann ('Allegorical Buildings', 191) and extensively by Aers, *Piers Plowman*: moralized labels are simply applied to or 'read off' from each item in turn. The poet's allegory nevertheless has affinities with the more dynamic treatment of the genre in examples such as Langland's 'Castle of Kynde' in *Piers Plowman* B.10 or Chaucer's *House of Fame*.

9054–61 According to both the *Glossa Ordinaria* and Berengaud (*PL* 17: 945–6), the hill from which John sees his vision (Rev. 21: 10) symbolizes Christ, upon whom the church is founded. The Middle English/Anglo-Norman prose version is rather closer to the poet's idea of the hill as 'haly thoght': 'þat þe Aungel led seint Iohan to a grete hyll and an heiȝ . . . bitokneþ hem þat þorouȝ þe grace of god ben led in to heiȝe lijf forto haue knoweyng of þe blis þat holy chirche abideþ after' (*Apocalypse*, 185/1–4). Alternatively, the poet may be thinking of the interpretation given to 'beryll clene' in the *Glossa Ordinaria*'s commentary on Rev. 21: 19, which explains that beryl is a bi-coloured jewel, its green signifying contemplation and its pallor earthly/active life. Berengaud's interpretation of beryl may also be relevant: he emphasizes beryl's clarity, symbolizing those men of pure living who sequester themselves from any earthly corruption (*PL* 17: 954–5).

9070–1 For precious stones as good works, compare Berengaud on Rev. 21: 14 (*PL* 17: 950). In the Anglo-Norman/Middle English prose and the *Bible Moralisée*, the precious stones which decorate the foundations of the city in Rev. 21: 19 signify that the patriarchs were filled with virtues (*Apocalypse*, 189/ 3–5; cf. *Bible Moralisée*, 4, plate 622 (MS Harley 1527, f. 151)). The gold in Rev. 21: 18 is interpretated as 'sapientia' in both the *Glossa Ordinaria* and Berengaud's commentary (*PL* 17: 953). In the Middle English/Anglo-Norman prose commentary, gold signifies the wisdom of God in holy writ (*Apocalypse*, 187/29–30). For gold as charity, see also 9167–8n.

9074–109 'turrettes', 'wardes', and 'garettes' are the poet's own embellishments on the architecture described in Rev. 21, and so his interpretations of these items have no direct parallels in the Apocalypse commentaries. The closest allegorizations found in those sources are the interpretations given to the walls mentioned in Rev. 21: 12, which in all the commentaries signify Christ or faith in Christ. The poet here adapts the technique of allegorical readings of architecture to suit his own interests, so that the 'wardes', for instance, are the 'strenthe, power, and myght' which he has already described in his account of the fourteen blessednesses of heaven.

9094–7 For the gates as humility, compare the *Glossa Ordinaria*, where the gates of Rev. 21: 12 are the patriarchs, whose example led others to the faith. In the Anglo-Norman/Middle English prose version the twelve gates are the twelve apostles (*Apocalypse*, 186/9). Berengaud compares with the three gates of the temple in Ezek. 46, which he interprets as the Virgin Mary and the Old and New Testaments (*PL* 17: 947–8). Humility, of course, suits the poet's emphasis on humility as the virtue which leads to heaven (ll. 139–43, 7538–9). Meekness also forms part of the allegorical landscape in Piers Plowman's description of the journey to the heavenly castle of Truth (*Piers Plowman* B.5.561).

9128–9 'We ask for your mercy, God, that you condescend to give them bright and peaceful dwelling places.' The quotation is one of the responses at Matins in some uses of the Office of the Dead; see Ottosen, *The Responsories*, no. 93.

9148 Matt. 13: 43: 'The just shall shine as the sun.'

9167–8 For the streets and lanes as the holy men who live in the heavenly city, compare the Middle English/Anglo-Norman prose version, in which they symbolize 'þe symple folk in holy churche þat ben abrode in þe werlde & han her wyues & her richesses. þai owen to ben briȝt as þe golde þorouȝ þe werkes of charite' (*Apocalypse*, 191/3–6). In Berengaud's commentary, the street signifies the minds of the faithful, its gold purity (*PL* 17: 958).

9185–7 Pearls, as in the Middle English poem of that name, typically signify purity. Cf. the Middle English/Anglo-Norman Apocalypse commentary, where the twelve pearls in the twelve gates in Rev. 21: 21 'bitokneþ hem þat shullen wissen oþere & techen hem þe riȝth bileue & hou hij owen to be clene of vertu & briȝth' (*Apocalypse*, 193/1–3). In Berengaud's commentary, twelve gates × twelve pearls = the 144 successors of the apostles, whose purity and sanctity of life is indicated by the brightness of the pearls (*PL* 17: 957). The pavements are of gold, not pearl, in the biblical description (as also in *Pearl*, line 1025).

9214 ' byfor neven': Cf. ll. 7856–65, earlier in Part 7. Correspondingly in Part 6, loss of the sight of God is listed as the greatest pain of hell.

9251–72 For music in heaven, and for instruments that play without human hands, cf. *The Vision of Tundale*, ll. 1905–20, 1974–6.

9291–4 For singing in heaven, cf. Bede's account of Dryhthelm (*Ecclesiastical History*, 494–5).

9305–7 Ps. 89: 15: 'We have rejoiced for the days in which thou hast humbled us: for the years in which we have seen evils.' Fidelity to the parallelism of the original would require 'For' for 'In' at the start of line 9310, which may have been attracted to the 'In' at the head of the previous line.

9320–1 Ps. 20: 4: 'Thou hast set on his head a crown of precious stones', with 'super caput' for biblical 'in capite', and intruding 'Domine'.

9366–7 'Their sight is made their food, their work praise, light their covering.' Walther, no. 33802 (with 'sit' for 'fit' and 'lumen' for 'limen').

9372–9 For the sight of the Trinity as the greatest joy of heaven, compare lines 7856–65.

9384–471 After his long enumeration of heavenly joys, the poet finally returns to the paired scheme he inherits from Anselm via *Les Peines*, and to the corresponding pains of hell. For these he draws on his own earlier account in Part 6.

9403 'Als men mught here me byfor say': In Part 6. Though the poet imagines his text being 'heard', his comment suggests that he also imagines a private reader who would be able, unlike an auditor, to refer to the earlier treatment from this cross-reference. Throughout the text is poised between being heard read aloud and being read privately; cf. lines 9579, 9604–5, and see 40n.

9483–511 For love and dread, compare lines 141–2.

9532 The contents were also listed in the Prologue (lines 348–62) but by 'titeld' the poet perhaps also imagines 'rubricated'.

9544–5 Cf. the more aggressive claims for the use of English for men of England in the Prologue of *Cursor*, and see lines 336–9.

9575 'drawen' here and in line 9613 perhaps means both 'to translate' and 'to compile'.

9584–93 The modest submission to the correction of 'clerks' is a common trope; cf., for instance, the *Parson's Prologue, Canterbury Tales*, X.55–60.

APPENDIX 1

UNSUPPORTED VARIANTS OF W, LINES 501–1873

520 rym] ⟨blank⟩inne
531 þus] *om.*
537 swa] sothe
541 sicut] et   volatum] volandum
560–1 *lines om.*
568 fayre] full fayre
592 Bot] Bot þe
598 leste] best
601 And] *om.*
615 þat] þat at   fra] of
624 wille] *after* says
645 graythely] *after* Behalde
651 Nites] *adds* and
652 springes] commes
666–7 quedam arbor] *trs.*
667 cuius] cum
668 est[1,2]] *om.*
669 sunt[1,2]] *om.*
670 a] *om.*
672 es] es a
698 yvels] *adds* and
699 man] men
706 es forth] *trs.*
714 es] he
724 at] ar
737 annorum] *om.*
738 sal] *after* gast
746 to] for to
752 autem] *om.*
753 et[1] . . . dolor] *om.*
788 He] þe
799 And[1]] He es
830 a[2]] to
854 cadavere] corpore
861 mans dede] *trs.*
864 Til] Vnto

875 es wryten] *trs.*
879 þan] all þan
882 Emperour] Paape emperowre
888 in] alle to
905 tendre] *adds* here
906 rote] *adds* here
941 our] hys
954 a] *om.*
984 heir-on] *after* I
1012 to] for
1018 þe³] *om.*
1024 light here] *trs.*
1025 myrk] as myrke
1027 for-] for to
1069 gude] godes
1086 Forþi] Forwhy   to] for to
1090 Many] Full many
1110 by] thorgh
1115 constituitur] constituetur
1116 He says] *om.*
1120 here God] *trs.*
1122 nec] neque
1125 þat²] *om.*
1130 in mundo] *after* quod
1139 honours] honoure
1153 it] yit
1158 a] *om.*
1194 worldes] worldly
1195 I] *om.*
1200 may] sall
1202–4 follow 1210
1203 ut] *om.*
1205 on] þe
1209 nogt] *adds* so
1211 þe] þis
1226 to] vnto
1242 er] are þe
1255 And] *om.*
1275 ay] y
1303 says þus] *trs.*
1304–5 *lines om.*
1312–13 *lines om.*
1322 tokenyng] taken
1324–25 *lines om.*

1330 men] *om.*
1332–33 *lines om.*
1356–57 *lines om.*   *W lacks three leaves and lines 1366–1565*
1570 bifore] *adds* 'and' (*orig.?*)
1574–5 *lines om.*
1583 lykyng] lykyngs
1590 þe] þis
1595 tyll] vnto
1599 and] þat are
1627 after sall] *trs. and adds* þis lyfe be-
1638 in²] *om.*
1640 knaw] kenne
1641 Him] þat hym
1647 grace] þe grace
1654 on] of
1662 sall] *om.*
1718 gayn-] agayne-
1773 sal] sall torne
1797 may] *after* man   knaw] kenne
1823 body . . . saule] *trs. sbs.*
1835 other twa] *trs.*

APPENDIX 2

'THE GENERAL TRADITION', A FULL SUBSTANTIVE COLLATION OF LINES 1–500 IN THE *b* TRADITION

In lines 1–72, As replaces the damaged M.
4 A Godde and] And oure As
5 and us help] helpe vs As
8 alle til] to a L
9 thyng] time As
10 ar] *om.* L
11 tymes] tyme LAs
12 ay] *om. b*
14 in] *om.* L
15 wald] was As   with] *om.* As
16 wyth] *om.* As
17 beyng] begynnyng L
19 nan] *om.* As
20 He] For he L
21 ay] *om.* As   als wys and] *om.* L
22 myghty] myght L
23 myght . . . wytte] *trs. nouns* SAs   -selve] *om.* As
24 For . . . was] Was neuer good As
25 sythyn] *om.* LAs   sythyn was] *trs.* S   þe²] *om. b*
27 *line om.* SAs   als] *om.* L
28 *followed by scribal line* Withouten **ende als he** be schalle As
29–30 *appear after line 32* L
30 es] he es L
31 als] *om.* As   ay] *om.* As
32 he es] *trs.* As   God] *after* es L, *om.* S, *after* he As
34 sal he] *trs.* S   at þe] *om.* As
35 bot] both LAs
36 And¹] *om.* SAs   and²] *om.* L, of SAs   and³] and of SAs
44 nathing] noght SAs
45 and] or L
48 kyndes] kynde As   certayn] sertande L
50 And] *om.* As   has] *om.* S
54 passes it] passed As
55–56 *trs. couplet* L
55 Loves] And lowys L

56 he] ilka creatour L   kynd ryght] *trs.* As
57 þe] þat S
59 aght] aghe S
60 creatur] *om.* S   in] to do in S   *scribal line* To worschipe him in ma⟨ns
k⟩ynde As
67 And] *om.* L
68 here] he L
69 mans] man- SAs   had] has S
70 for] all for L
71 and¹] *om.* As   þe] all þe L
72 made] he made L
74 digne] worthy LM
75 other] þe M
76 hym] hym bathe L   wytte skille] *trs.* M
77 knaw] knaw both M
78 fre] fayre S
80 *after the heading, adds a couplet* How god man mast worthy creatoure | Of
all oþer and gaf hym wit and skyll | And mynd and þerwith a fre will
(cf. 76–8) L
82 And] *om.* M   in²] with M
83 him] hym to L
84 to] for to L
86 Til] To þe M   at þe last to] for to L, he sal M
87 he] he be S
88 Til] To þe SM   þat has nan] withowtyn LM
89 Ilk] And ilk M   mare] bath mare L
90 til] eftyre L
93 to chese als] on hym L
94 wil] wald SM
95 Bot he þat] Wha þat S, Whoso M
96 mon] may L
98 sal] sall he L, he sal M
99 þat] *om.* M
103 him] *om.* S
104 befor sayde] hymself L
105 maste] more M   him] *om.* L
106 þan] Mare þan L   other] *om. b*
107 hight him yit] him y. h. L
108 uele] wile S
109 mys] omyse LM
110 prived] put L   blys] byse L   *after the following heading, adds two
couplets* Wyttys and þe vndyrestandyng | þat he hafs syfin hym in knawyng
| Of all þat es nedfull to hym | And swa may he to hewen wyn L
111 tok] to L   mans] man SM

112 þe] his M   wald] he wald L
114 þat] heuen M
115 God] he (*after* man) SM
116 benyfices] ane ma L   he him] for him he M
118 þat¹] þe M
119 þier . . . mynde] oþer dedys both alde and ȝong L
120 mans] all man M
121 hym] *om.* L
122 es he] *trs.* SM   es he an un-] art þou no L
124 him use] þe ȝeme L   use it] hys S, kepe with M
125 his¹] bi L   despende] spende M
126 es he] art þou L, *trs.* SM   noght] nothyng M
127 kyndly] gudely M
128 self . . . les] is in his frelnes M
130 God] þi god M
135 how²] *om.* L
136 And how hys ryghtwysnes sal ay last SM
137 ilk day] what he SM
138 knaw and] *om. b*
139 til] to þe L
140 theder es þys] þere it ysse M
142 of¹] *om.* L   and²] and of M
143 may be] he M   of] of god M   -dom] -domes L
144 way] *om.* M   na] a S   may com] mans commes L
146 myght] myghtes S   and²] and of S   his²] *om.* M
150 of] of gude M
153 som] *om. (corr.)* M   has] *om.* L   na] *om.* M
154 gude] summe M
155 lere] here L
156 can] knowys L
157 þat] þat thyng þat L
158 To bryng þaire saules owt of drede M
159 þe] *om.* M   es] *om.* L
161 In] Of L
163 noght lere] *trs.* M
165 þat es lest] lest and mest M
166 als] ay as M   unskilwys] vnresonabill L, vnskilful S
167 nother has] *trs.* L   has . . . ne] skil has ne no M   skil witt] *trs.* L
169 excuses noght] may not excuse L
170 his . . . noght] besys not hys wit L
171 Name of þat thyng hymsilf to knaw L   at hym fel] hymself M
172 it] hym L
174 to²] and M
176 hym] *om.* L

180 sal] may L
182 And¹] *om.* LM
184 lere] will lere L
185 bysy . . . and] willi and bisy in SM
188 and lere] gud thyng L   er] ware L   er ful slaw] suld ben faw M
189 -þi] *om.* M
190 þat] *om.* L
191 way] *om.* L
192 way] *om.* M   lef and] *om.* S
193 es] it is M
195 of] and L
197 ilk] es S
199 þe ryght way] ry3t whar M
200 ilk] *om.* SM   man] men SM
201 Suld] And S   ay and] *trs.* M
205 right] *om.* L
206 als] swa L
208 tyttest] titter S   tyttest come] *trs.* L
210 al] are M   sette fast] stedfast M
211 wele] will M (*possibly, in this MS, dialectical only*)
212 was and es] is was M   and¹] *om.* S
213 talde] calde LM
214 man] *om.* L
217 right] *om.* L   ne] and b
218 But he himself ferst can knaw will M
220 knaw] ken M
221 knew] knawe SM
224 day] day of dome L
226 lythernes] lecherynys L
229 knawyng] to knaw L   alle] *om.* L
230 mynd] meng L   til] *om.* LS
231 swa may he] be M
232 þe] *om.* M
235 alle] *om.* b   þis proces] þis part is L
236 man] hym L, mans SM   es] it is M
237 som] *om.* M
239 first suld] *trs.* L   suld] *om.* M
241 of þat] *om.* L   I] þus I L
242 a mans wytt] man L   ofte] oft full L
244 wilk four] *trs.* L   he hymself] *trs.* L
246 And . . . four] Whylk foure er SM
247 -que] *om.* M
249 es] is þe M   þe] *om.* M   and] and þe M
251 a] *om.* S   man] mannes M

252 hymself] *om.* S, þus M
253 insight] sy3t M
254 noght] *om.* SM
256 ful] *om.* M
257 norisches ofte] *trs.* M
258 men] man M
259 in him] *om.* M   in²] *om.* LS
260 Es selden] *after* sen L
261 þat . . . sese] to se L
262 ne] ne þe M   ne vanitese] and vanite L
264 Thynkes . . . of¹] Ne in mynd hafis L, Ne to thynk of SM
265 can noght] ne can S
266 lyfe] werld L
267 men] *om.* M   here] *om.* L   lofes foly] lyfis folyly L
269 in] he in L   his¹] *om.* SM   delytis] delite L   his hert] þare hertes M
270 þis] hys L   ay] euer L
271 him] þaim M
272 to¹] *om.* M   þat . . . mygt] lykyngis þat euer may L   lykyng to hym] hys (þare M) lykyng SM
273 led] lett L   with] by SM
274 þai folow ay] ay folow M   ay] euer L
275 elles] *om.* SM   thynkes] thynk L
276 es] *om.* S
278 in] in þer M
279 And . . . thurgh] þai ere in L
282 þat¹] þat thyng L   mak þam] *trs.* M
283 wald] will L
285 Noluit] Nolunt M
286 ageret] agerent M
288 to¹] for to S   for] *after* Ne L
289 by þam] þai M
292 likyng] lykyngis L
293 Som] 3it some L   understandes] vndyrestandyng L
294 hertes] hert M
295 þat] of thyng þat L
296 nathyng] noght SM   þat þai] þai it L
297 dredful] dulfulle S
300 et] set L
302 And¹] Bot LM   was] wax L, wer M   angred] angre M   in] in þer L
307 Som] Sum men L   buk] bokis L   buk swilk] *trs.* S, summe bokes M thyng] *om.* SM
308 drede] þo dres M
309 it may noght] no3t may M
310 þus] *om.* SM   þe] hys L

313 he says] *om.* L
315 þos says] *trs.* M
320 says] said LS
321 loved] louese M
324 ay] *om.* L
326–7 *couplet om.* SM
327 hald] hafe L
328 noght] *om.* L   noght drede] *trs.* M
330 rede, here] *adds* it (*twice, the first also* M) L
331 þarin] in it L
334 þat] *om.* S   sal . . . þar-] suld consaile here L
336 es] *after* Ynglese M   on] in LM
338 Til] þat L
340 þam] *om.* LS   knaw] to knaw *b*
341 vanytese] vanite L, vices M
343 þai] þaim L   here or] herys any man L
344 sal prikke] saue S
345 þat] swylk L   a] *om.* L
346 heven] heuens S
348 þis] þis is þe M   it-] þi M
350 hafe] hald LS
351 mans] man- S
352 þe²] *om.* L
353 þe] *om.* L   þis] þe L
354–5 Ʒif it suld langere abown herd by | [*the following line in a crease and illegible*] L
360 payns] pyn L
361 þar þe dampned] Whare dampned sawls L, *adds* saules M   evermare] ay M   -mare] *om.* LS
363 þe . . . buk] *trs. phrs.* L   partes] poyntes M   þis] þe L
364 ilka] *om.* L
366 parte] *om.* L   þat] þat þe L, þe S
368 alle . . . wryten] euer is wrytyn befor L
369 als] *om.* LM   an] *om.* S
374 for] *om.* LM
375 forthy] for L   God] god hymself L, he M
378 als] alssua L
379 þat²] in þat L
380 have þan] thynk L
381 þe] *om.* L   sorow] *adds* mak L
386 in] in hys L
387 he es] þat he was L
388 thurgh] of L
389 þat¹] *erased and left blank* M   þat sen] send L

390 voyde] wyde L   þe] *om.* LM
391 war] was S   ilka] euerilka L
392 þe] *om.* L
396 us] þus LM
397 sayd] sais L   þus] *om.* LM
398 parvulus] paruuli SM
400 Bot] Bot if L   he sayde] als he sais L
401 meke] sufferand M
403 Into þe ioy of hewen þat lastys ay L; *cf.* To heuenrike S   sal last] lastes M
404 by-] be be L   ay here] here ay to L, here euer S, euer M
405 þat] That thyng þat L, þat þat S   him] hymself L
406 here] in herth L
408 a] *om.* LM
409 es] *om.* L
410 says] *after* clerk M   now] ȝow *b*
411 es] is a L   bot] here but M
412 brekes] wrekes L, *after* þat M
413 And] *om.* L   þus] *om.* L, *after* God M
414 queso] *om.* L
415 reduces me] red M
416 says] sayd L   thynk] yueli M   þat] *om. b*
417 to] for to L
418 turne me] *trs.* L
420 says] sal M
421 þus] say þus M   shortly] sor'tly L
422 cinis] cineres S
425 in-] *om. b*   turn] *om.* SM
426 a] *om.* M
427 and¹] *om.* SM
428 suld ilk] *trs.* L
430 þat] þan L   sene . . . shewe] schewed . . . se SM
431 þe²] *om.* L
432 mans] mens L
433 þis] *om.* LM
436 þer] The L   thre²] þe L   spaces] space L, partes M   talde] cald M
437 Of . . . man] Of mannes life M
438 mans] *om.* L   þat] þe L
439 mykel] *adds* of L
440 forthir] forth LS
441 yhou] *om.* LM   a] *om.* L
443 þat] *om.* L
444 aftir als] als it L
445 vile] þe L, wilk M   sede] *om.* M   syn] sede L, syn is M

447 awen] *om.* SM
448 Whar] Wharein L
449 þe] *om.* M
450 Ecce] Ecce enim LM   sum] sum etc. *and ends* M
453 wykked-] wrechyd- LS
456 a] *om.* M
461 With . . . was] So was he M   he] I S
463 wame] wabe S
464 werldys] werld SM
465 ne¹] no *after* ne² M   nouther] noþer L
466 Nouther] Noþer L   yhit] *om.* SM
467 Ne] No ȝit L   with¹] on L
468 les] lest M
469 sene] so vn- M
471 Als] Alssa L   Als . . . and] And als-tite SM   and . . . fra] to ryn and
ga L   to] to hand S
472 *end of* L
473 to] for to M
475 and¹ . . . and²] sprewland S, crouland M
476 child] barn M
477 þat it ne] þatten it S   ne] *om.* M
479 or] or elles M
486 E] It M   and þe] if ȝe inlie M
487 þe name of] *om.* SM   þat] þat first M
490 vel] *om.* M
491 þas] þese M   he says] *om.* M   of] of Adam and M
492 þat . . . here] Men or wommen þat M
494 a a] a SM   e e] e SM
499 Omnes] Omnes enim M   miseriam] miseriam etc. *and ends* M

APPENDIX 3

A REVISED LIST OF MANUSCRIPTS OF
THE PRICK OF CONSCIENCE

In the following list, Northern copies appear with a star (*), those of Lewis–
McIntosh's Type I with a '+'. Our notes add references to descriptions and
discussions more contemporary than those provided in Lewis–McIntosh,
whose designation of those manuscripts they knew we reproduce here.

The Main Version (99 Copies)

MV1	Aberystwyth, National Library of Wales, MS Brogyntyn/ Porkington 20, ff. 1–94^v
MV2	Arundel (Sussex), Arundel Castle, The Duke of Norfolk, ff. 1–141^v
+MV3	*olim* Beeleigh Abbey, Maldon, Foyle MS, ff. 1–131^v; now in a private collection, supposedly Paris, Henri Schiller[1]
MV4	Brussels, Bibliothèque Royale de Belgique, MS IV.998, ff. 1–105^v
*+MV5	Cambridge, Fitzwilliam Museum, MS McClean 131, ff. 1–113^{v2}
MV6	—— Gonville and Caius College, MS 386/606, ff. 1–96
MV7	—— Magdalene College, MS F.4.18, ff. 1–110^v
*MV8	—— St John's College, MS D.5 (80), ff. 1–118
+MV9	—— —— MS E.34 (137), ff. 1–113^v
+MV10	—— University Library, MS Dd.xi.89, ff. 9–162
+MV11	—— —— MS Dd.xii.69, ff. 37–97^v
MV12	—— —— MS Ll.ii.17, ff. 2–145
MV13	—— —— MS Additional 6693, ff. 1–179
+MV14	Cambridge, Mass., Harvard University Library, MS English 515, ff. 1–77[3]
MV15	Canterbury, Cathedral, MS Lit. D.13 (66), ff. 1–144^{v}[4]

[1] There is an extensive description, in the sale catalogue, when the book last changed
hands, Christie's, 11 July 2000, pp. 232–3 (lot 77).

[2] This is, of course, the book here presented as **M**, and a more detailed description than
those cited by Lewis–McIntosh appears above—as is also the case for the books here listed
as MV27/**G**, MV34/**H**, MV44/**A**, MV46/**L**, MV49/**S**, MV60As, MV83/**R**, MV96/**W**.

[3] A somewhat truncated description appears at Voigts, 'A Handlist', 17, with a facsimile.

[4] A more detailed description at Ker, *MMBL* ii. 281, also true of the books listed below
as MV19, at ii. 416–18; MV24 and 25, iii. 67–71; MV53, iii. 361; MV54–6, iii. 401–3, 413–
14; MV95, iv. 290–2; SR6–7, iii. 116, 125.

MV16	Charlottesville, Va., University of Virginia Library, MS Hench 10, ff. 1–136^v
MV17	Chicago, Newberry Library, MS 32.9, ff. 1–99^5
MV18	—— —— MS 33, pp. 1–198
*MV19	Douai Abbey, Upper Woolhampton (Reading, Berks.), MS 7, ff. 2–150
+MV20	Dublin, Trinity College, MS 156 (D.4.8), ff. 2–136^v
*MV21	—— —— MS 157 (D.4.11), ff. 1–89
*MV22	—— —— MS 158 (D.4.15), ff. 1–81^v
MV23	Holkham Hall, Wells-next-the-sea (Norfolk), The Earl of Leicester, MS 668, ff. 1–134^v
+MV24	Leeds, Leeds University Library, MS Brotherton 500, ff. 1–147^v
MV25	—— —— MS Brotherton 501, ff. 1–58$^{v\ 6}$
MV26	London, British Library, MS Arundel 140, ff. 41^v–146^v
*+MV27	—— —— MS Cotton Galba E.ix, ff. 76ra–113ra
MV28	—— —— MS Cotton Appendix vii, ff. 3–145^v
*MV29	—— —— MS Egerton 657, ff. 1–95^v
MV30	—— —— MS Egerton 3245, ff. 2–156
MV31	—— —— MS Harley 1205, ff. 1–125
MV32	—— —— MS Harley 2377, ff. 1–106^v
*MV33	—— —— MS Harley 2394, ff. 1–129
*+MV34	—— —— MS Harley 4196, ff. 215^v–258va
*MV35	—— —— MS Harley 6923, ff. 2–117^v
MV36	—— —— MS Lansdowne 348, ff. 2–127^v
MV37	—— —— MS Sloane 1044, item 235 (a single leaf)
MV38	—— —— MS Sloane 2275, ff. 150ra–183rb
MV39	—— —— MS Additional 11304, ff. 71^v–194
MV40	—— —— MS Additional 22283, ff. 243ra–259va
*MV41	—— —— MS Additional 24203, ff. 1–150^v
*MV42	—— —— MS Additional 25013, ff. 1–136
*MV43	—— —— MS Additional 32578, ff. 1–103
*+MV44	—— —— MS Additional 33995, ff. 102ra–155ra
MV45	—— College of Arms, MS Arundel 57, ff. 133ra–175vb
*+MV46	—— Lambeth Palace Library, MS 260, ff. 101ra–136vb (with index ff. 138ra–139^{vc})
MV47	—— —— MS 491, ff. 296–323
MV48	—— —— MS 492, ff. 1–56^v
	—— St Paul's Cathedral, s.n. (fragments)
*+MV49	—— Sion College, MS Arc. L.40.2/E.25 (now a Lambeth Palace deposit), ff. 48–133^v

[5] There are full formal descriptions of these two copies at Saenger, *A Catalogue*, 58–9.
[6] See Pickering, 'Brotherton Collection MS 501'.

MV50   —— Society of Antiquaries, MS 288, ff. 1–120^v
MV51   —— —— MS 687, pp. 5–358
+MV52   Longleat House, Warminster (Wilts.), The Marquess of
              Bath, MS 31, ff. 1–146^v
MV53   Manchester, Chetham's Library, MS 8008, ff. 1–115^v
MV54   —— John Rylands University Library, MS English 50,
              pp. 1–204
MV55   —— —— MS English 51, ff. 5–116^v
MV56   —— —— MS English 90, ff. 2ra–62vb
MV57   New Haven, Conn., Yale University Library, MS Osborn
              a.13, ff. 2–139
MV58   New York City, Pierpont Morgan Library, MS Bühler 13,
              ff. 1–107
              Notre Dame, Ind., University of Notre Dame, printed book
              PR 2321 | S 87 1529 (Thomas More, *Supplication of Souls*,
              STC 18093) (two leaves)[7]
MV59   Oxford, Bodleian Library, MS Ashmole 41, ff. 1–130
+MV60   —— —— MS Ashmole 52, ff. 1ra–65ra
MV61   —— —— MS Ashmole 60, ff. 1–138^v
*MV62   —— —— MS Bodley 99, ff. 1–120^v
MV63   —— —— MS Digby 14, ff. 2–158$^{v\,8}$
MV64   —— —— MS Digby 87, ff. 1–133^v
MV65   —— —— MS Digby 99, ff. 8^v–156^v
MV66   —— —— MS Douce 126, ff. 1ra–68vb
MV67   —— —— MS Douce 141, ff. 1–129^v
MV68   —— —— MS Douce 156, pp. 1–172
MV69   —— —— MS Douce 157, ff. 1–114^v
MV70   —— —— MS Eng. poet. a.1, ff. 265^{rc}–284$^{ra\,9}$
MV71   —— —— MS Junius 56, ff. 1–120^v
MV72   —— —— MS Laud misc. 486, ff. 1–122
MV73   —— —— MS e Musaeo 76, ff. 1–127
MV74   —— —— MS e Musaeo 88, ff. 1–92
MV75   —— —— MS Rawlinson A.366, pp. 1–250
MV76   —— —— MS Rawlinson C.35, ff. 1–117^v
MV77   —— —— MS Rawlinson C.319, ff. 1–140
*MV78   —— —— MS Rawlinson C.891, ff. 1–127
MV79   —— —— MS Rawlinson D.913, f. 9^{rv} (a single leaf)
MV80   —— —— MS Rawlinson D.913, f. 62^{rv} (a single leaf)
MV81   —— —— MS Rawlinson poet. 138, ff. 1–112^v
MV82   —— —— MS Rawlinson poet. 139, ff. 1–119

[7] See Edwards and O'Byrne, 'A New Manuscript Fragment'.
[8] Fuller descriptions of the Digby copies appear in the revised Macray, *Bodleian Library Quarto Catalogues IX*, Appendix 11–12, 49, and 99 respectively.
[9] There is a full facsimile, *Vernon*, also of value for the related MV40.

*+MV83	—— —— MS Rawlinson poet. 175, ff. 1ra–55rb
MV84	—— —— MS Selden supra 102*, ff. 15–16^v (two leaves)
MV85	—— St John's College, MS 57, ff. 1–137^{10}
MV86	—— —— MS 138, ff. 1–126^v
+MV87	—— Trinity College, MS 15, ff. 1–203^v
MV88	—— —— MS 16A, ff. 1–116^v
MV89	—— —— MS 16B, ff. 3–114
+MV90	—— University College, MS 142, ff. 4–125^v
MV91	Philadelphia, University of Pennsylvania Library, MS English 1, ff. 13–118
MV92	—— —— MS English 8, ff. 147ra–159vb
*MV93	Princeton, Princeton University Library, MS Taylor 13, ff. 1–$126^{v\,11}$
*MV94	San Marino, Calif., Henry E. Huntington Library, MS HM 139, ff. 144ra–$187^{ra\,12}$
MV95	Shrewsbury, Shrewsbury School, MS 3, ff. 1–27^v
*+MV96	Wellesley, Mass., Wellesley College Library, MS 8, pp. 12–247
MV97	Hatfield House (Herts.), The Marquess of Salisbury, Deeds 59/1 (two leaves)

The Southern Recension (19 Copies)

SR1	*olim* Beaumont College, Old Windsor (Berks.), MS 9, ff. 3–158; later Oslo and London, Martin Schøyen, MS 689
SR2	Cambridge, Pembroke College, MS 272, ff. 1–143^v
SR3	—— St John's College, MS B.7 (29), ff. 5–119^v
SR4	—— University Library, MS Ee.4.35 (ii), ff. 1–96^v
SR5	Dublin, Trinity College, MS 69 (A.4.4), ff. 65ra–72vb, 83va–123va
SR6	Lichfield, Lichfield Cathedral, MS 16, ff. 35–189^v
SR7	—— —— MS 50, ff. 1–109^v
SR8	London, British Library, MS Harley 1731, ff. 1–133^v
SR9	—— —— MS Harley 2281, ff. 1–64^v
SR10	—— —— MS Royal 18 A.v, ff. 2–126
SR11	—— —— MS Additional 11305, ff. 2–126^v
SR12	Oxford, Bodleian Library, MS Bodley 423, ff. 244–351
SR13	—— —— MS Laud misc. 601, ff. 1–115^v

[10] For these two books, see Hanna, *A Descriptive Catalogue*, 75–7, 201–2, and plate 21 (facing p. 221); for the context in which the first was produced, see Mooney and Matheson, 'The Beryn Scribe'.

[11] Full descriptions of this book and SR 15 will appear in the forthcoming catalogue of Princeton manuscripts, ed. Donald C. Skemer.

[12] For this manuscript, see the full description, Dutschke, *Guide*, 184–5, and for SR16–18, 156–7, 161–3, and 173–4 respectively.

SR14   —— —— MS Lyell empt. 6, ff. 1–116^v
SR15   Princeton, Princeton University Library, MS Garrett 138, ff. 1–130^v
SR16   San Marino, Calif., Henry E. Huntington Library, MS HM 125, ff. 1–100
SR17   —— —— MS HM 128, ff. 1–94
SR18   —— —— MS HM 130, ff. 1–120^v
                Ushaw (Durham), St Cuthbert's College, MS 50 (two fragments of a leaf)[13]

Extracts (about 49 Copies)

E1   Cambridge, Trinity College, MS O.2.40 (1144), ff. 104–5, 117^{rv}
*E2   —— University Library, MS Dd.v.55, f. 101^v [14]
E3   —— —— MS Ff.v.40, ff. 113^v–114
*E4   Lincoln, Lincoln Cathedral, MS 91, ff. 276va–277ra
*E5   London, British Library, MS Royal 17 C.xvii, ff. 117–24
E6   —— —— MS Additional 36983, ff. 159–74^v [15]
E7   —— —— MS Additional 37049, ff. 36, 69, 72[16]
*E8   Oxford, Bodleian Library, MS Rawlinson C.285, f. 39
                Speculum Christiani, 'Septima tabula' (IMEV 1342, extant in about forty copies)[17]
                York, All Saints, North Street, northeast aisle window (verses in stained glass)[18]

'Speculum Huius Vitae' (2 Copies)

S1   Dublin, Trinity College, MS 155 (C.5.7), pp. 149–238
*S2   Oxford, Bodleian Library, MS Add. A.268, ff. 117ra–139rb

[13] See Doyle, 'Ushaw College, Durham, MS 50'.

[14] For descriptions of this book, as well as E3, E4, E7, and E8, and S1, below, see Hanna, *The English Manuscripts*, nos. 12, 15, 36, 41, 94, and 27 respectively.

[15] A description appears at Thompson, *The* Cursor Mundi, 43–5.

[16] This complicated manuscript will repay narrower investigation. It includes several sets of excerpts overlooked in Lewis–McIntosh: lines 3566–72, 3586–9 + six additional lines, 3918–35 (most of *IMEV* 3476) at f. 24^v; lines 9052–61 at f. 67; lines 9360–3, 9368–77, 8648–55, 8678–81, 8686–9 (the bulk of *IMEV* 493) at f. 80^v. In addition, at ff. 37^v–38, IMEV 3478 is an unnoted excerpt from *Speculum Vitae*, lines 12561–658 (with many excisions), 12771–82; cf. *Speculum Vitae*, p. lix.

[17] About one quarter of this 119-line-long poem directly cites *PC*, and much of the remainder is paraphrase or more distant adaption. From the head (we have numbered the lines of the poem sequentially), compare 27–8 with *PC* 948–9, 28–9 with 952–3, 36–7 with 1360–1, 38–9 with 1082–3, 42–3 with 1110–12, 44–5 with 1074–5, etc.

[18] See Powell, 'All Saints' Church'.

Partial Prose Redaction (1 Copy)

Oxford, Bodleian Library, MS Laud misc. 23, ff. 53^v–55^{19}

The Early Printed Editions (2 Copies, both Derived from SR 18 above)

A Little Book of Purgatory (STC 3360; Robert Wyer, [?1534]) (part 4 only)
A New Treatyse deuyded in thre parties (STC 24228; Robert Wyer, [?1542] (parts 1–3 only)[20]

The Latin Version (6 Copies)

L1   Cambridge, Magdalene College, MS F.4.14, ff. 14–31^v
L2   —— Pembroke College, MS 273, ff. 1ra–29vb
L3   —— University Library, MS Dd.iv.50, ff. 57–99
L4   London, British Library, MS Harley 106, ff. 138^{vab}, 344vb
L5   Oxford, Bodleian Library, MS Bodley 159, ff. 161ra–179ra
L6   —— Merton College, MS 68, ff. 74vb–88va [21]

---

[19] See Wood, 'A Prose Redaction'.
[20] See Schulz, 'A Manuscript Printer's Copy' and 'A Middle English Manuscript'.
[21] See Thomson, *A Descriptive Catalogue*, 70–2.

GLOSSARY

A

a, (þe) ta *num. art.* a, a single, one 4, 17, 78, 126, 140 +; **ane, (þe) tane** 259, 775, 965 +

abayste *v. pa. p., adj.* embarrassed, ashamed 1430

abate *v.* to destroy, diminish 692, 1672, 2840, 3089, 3092 +

abyde *v.* to remain, stay, endure, wait for 1997, 2015, 2412, 2933, 5055 +

ac(c)orde *v.* bring to accord 3473

acouped *v. pa. p.* accused 2947

aferd(e), afered *v. pa. p.* afraid, terrified 2303, 2943, 6856

affeccyon *n.* desire 8873

afforce *v. pr. subj.* (refl.?) attempt, exert oneself 2536, 4253

afray *n.* fear, fright 6109

aftir (þat) *conj.* after, following, according as 37, 47, 228, 266, 444 +

agayn *prep.* against, in opposition to, in anticipation of, in return for 168, 1256, 1258, 2907 +; **ogayn(e)** 304, 1642, 1674 +; **agaynes** 1252; **ogayn(e)s** 1677, 4144; **ogayn(e)** *adv.* 391, 1723, 2271 +; **agayn(e)** 113, 418, 421, 425, 811 +

aght *v. pa.* ought, *(impers.)* it is owing/incumbent upon, 59, 1293, 1607, 1679, 1831 +; cf. **awe** *pres.* 2510

ay *adv.* ever, always 12, 15, 20, 21, 31 +

aywhare *adv.* anywhere, everywhere 8196, 9040

aldirfoulest *adj. superl.* most ugly of all things 527; cf. also **alther-**

alkyn *adj.* every sort of 613, 2718, 3248, 4948 +

allege *v.* to alleviate, to accuse 3894, 5584, 5599

all(e)-if *conj.* although 1714, 1726, 1730, 2206, 2536 +; cf. **alleþogh** 6285, 9404; and **þof**

all-weldand *adj.* all-powerful, ruling over all 8863

almus *n. (pl.)* deed of charity or mercy 2848, 3568, 3609, 3653, 3722 +

almusdede *n. (pl.)* deed of charity or mercy 2639, 2648, 2883, 3090, 3226 +

al(l)owes *v. 3 sg. pr.* praises 2467, 2539

als *conj.* as, as if 17, 21, 22 (2x), 27 +; cf. **als** *adv.* also 3257

al(l)sone *adv.* (for **als-sone**) immediately 4102, 4624, 8459; cf. the next

als-tyte *adv.* quickly, directly, immediately 377, 471, 2640, 3244, 3287 +; **tyte** 208, 322, 766, 1914, 2902 +; **titter** *comp.* 2354, 3727; **tit(t)est** *super.* 405, 3703

alswa, allswa *adv.* also 81, 261, 315, 538, 1030 +; occasionally for **als w(h)a** as if he 860n

altherbest *adj. super.* most superlative 2195

altherfeblest *adj. super.* most weak of all 746

altherheghest *adj. super.* the very highest 7723, 7746, 7753

al-wytty *adj.* completely wise 2

ande *n.* the breath 3054

ane, see **a**

angre, anger- *n.* hardship, adversity 691, 698, 1169, 1262, 1269 +

angred, angerd *v. pa. p.* resented, (were) resentful, made angry 302, 799

anguys(e), angwise *n.* pain, torment 2240, 2981, 2991, 3518, 6104 +

an(e)hede *n.* unity, singleness 14, 16, 7842, 8445, 8462 +

an(e)ly *adj., adv.* only, alone 840, 937, 1016, 1338, 2345 +

aioynt *v. pa. p.* enjoined, directed 3302

ap(p)ayre *v.* to harm, injure, become weak 691, 1475, 1503, 3691

aparty, see 1804n; to represent; **a party** *n.* a part, a portion 3278?, 3280?, 3902, 6514; otherwise, arguably to represent; **apartly, apertly** *adv.* openly 1804, 2210, 2334, 2700, 2967 +

ap(p)ert *adj.* open, manifest 4234, 4490, 5743

ap(p)ert(e)ly *adv.* openly 4239, 8228, 8648, 8678, 8738 +

apostyms *n. pl.* ulcers, boils 2995

appropried *v. pa. p.* assigned, given as

an attribute 7879, 7902, 7993, 8146, 8553 +

approves *v. 3 sg. pr.* regards (as certain) 4746

ar(e) *adv., conj.* before, previously 9, 10, 407, 440, 460 +; **here** 147, or 4730

arely *adv.* early, first 723, 724; **arly** 6155

aresoned *v. pa. p.* interrogated, examined 2460, 5772, 5803, 5997

arrirage *n.* arrears, debt (in allusion to Luke 16) 5913

as(s)ethe(-makyng) *n.* 'asset' 3610; *make asethe* square accounts 3747

assayl(e) *v.* to attack 1037, 1248, 1254, 1263, 1267 +

assays *v. pr. pl.* test, try 1399

at *conj.* usually in combination þat at or bot at that (cf. þat þat 279) 56, 171, 732, 2742, 3229; *prep.* (to introduce the infinitive of verbs, usually *at say*) to 3184, 4139, 4181, 4489, 5169 +

atteyn *v.* to attaint, accuse of crime 5332

auctentyke *adj.* authoritative 7112

avayle *v.* to aid, to benefit 1184, 2766, 3584, 3587, 3629 +

avant *v. (refl.)* to advance oneself by boasting 4298

avantage *n.* benefit, profit 1012

avenand *adj.* handsome 5020

avise *v.* to advise, learn 4000, 9560

awe *n.* fear 1870, 2450, 5547, 8508

awe, see also **aght**

awhile *adv.* at various times, from time to time 1263

awkeward *adj.* askew, awry 1541

awsterne (aust-) *adj.* austere, severe 5235, 5406, 6178

B

bale *n.* distress 1167, 6100, 6461

ban *v.* to curse 3484, 3485, 7391, 8469, 9435

band *n.* chain, bond(s) 3209, 3213, 6575, 7170, 7173 +

bar(e) *v. pa.* bore (in its various senses) 5205, 5817, 5979, 7395, 8163 +

barnhede *n.* childhood, youth 8249, 8323

bede *v.* to offer 2847, 5920, 5958, 6190; **bed(de)** *pa.* 5771, 6148; **bed** *pa. p.* 8531

bede *n.* prayer 3722

bedred(en) *v. pa. p., adj.* bed-ridden, immobile from illness 808, 6195

beme *n.* trumpet 4677, 4961, 4978, 4990, 5044

benyfices, benefice *n. pl.* benefits 116, 119, 5436, 5582, 5586

benyssoun *n.* blessing 3405, 3406

betaken *v.* to signify, symbolize 1260

betyme *adv.* quickly, immediately 1589

bycom *v. pa.* became 731, 743, 2339

byd *v.* to ask, pray, command 2069, 2847, 3663, 4963

bidder *n.* one who makes a request 3679

biddyng *n.* request 3658, 3673, 3677, 4607, 5043 +

bydene *adv.* in a company, together, at once 3215, 7965, 8041, 8931

bigg *adj.* powerful, rich 1460

bygged *v. pa.* built, constructed 4850

byggyns, bygyngs *n. pl.* buildings 4782, 8903, 9116

bihyng *n.* redemption 3608

(hym) byhoves *v. 3 sg. pr. (impers.)* it is necessary that he, he is required to 148, 404, 492, 747, 945 +

byhufe *n.* use, profit 70, 1016; **byhove** 937, 939

bylyve, bilyfe *adv.* immediately, quickly 1229, 9552

bymene *v.* to signify, mean 1205, 5511

bytaght *v. pa.* committed, gave 5785, 5796

bytyde *v.* to befall 9408

bla *adj.* livid, bruise-coloured 5261

blere *v.* to cry out, to bellow 2226

bleth(e)ly *adv.* happily, with pleasure 184, 6051, 6773

blyn *v.* to cease 1746, 5350, 6108, 6574, 7046 +

blythe *adj.* happy, joyous 902, 1391, 1636, 5712, 6518 +

boghsom(e) *adj.* obedient 395, 9099; **bughsom(e)** 50, 201, 1973, 4071; **bousom (bow-)** 85, 7512, 8145, 8810

boghsomnes *n.* obedience 7845; **bowsomnes** 9095

boght *v. pa.* bought, redeemed 113, 2725, 3292, 3615, 4849 +

bond *adj.* in a servile condition 884, 5075

bondman *n.* slave, thrall 1155

bot if *conj.* unless (a number of apparent uses represent 'Bot, if') 1569, 1857, 3376, 3426, 3517 +

bourd *n.* jest, play 1593

bousom, bowsom, see **boghsom(e)**

braydes *n. pl.* gestures, feints 2227; cf. **dede-brayde**

brayne-wode *adj.* violently insane 6703

brede *n.* breadth, width 1488, 1495, 5899, 7662, 8908

brekes *v. 3 sg. pr.* breaks, dissipates, turns aside 412, 2078, 7010

brest *v.* to break or burst 1787, 6732, 7010, 7262, 7264; **brast** *pa.* 5299

brethe *n.* odour, aroma, fume or smoke 613, 4727

brydegome *n.* bridegroom 8796, 8806, 8818

bryn(ne) *v.* to burn 3136, 3148, 3181, 3185, 3188 +; **brinned** *pa. p.* 3183

brist *n.* need, want 6202

brunstane *n.* 'brimstone', sulfur 4853, 6689, 6734, 6742, 9416 +; **bronstane** 8053

bughsom(e), see **boghsom(e)**

C

caffe *n.* chaff, straw 3148

caysere *n.* king, conqueror 882

caytefte *n.* wretchedness, sinfulness 455, 529, 551; cf. **kaytif**

can *v. pr.* be able, know (how), understand 121, 156, 162, 173, 175 +; **kun** *inf.* 187, 5459; **couthe** *pa. (subj.)* might, was/should be able 1918, 2092, 2305, 2310, 2447 +

carion *n.* dead flesh, corpse 572, 847, 857; **carayne** 7923

cast(e) *v.* to throw, consider 432, 892, 1193, 1218, 1219 +; **kast** 7257, 8122

catelle *n.* property, money 3521

certayne *adj.* fixed, specific 48, 419, 810, 814, 1007 +

certifie *v.* to officially notify 6542

chace *v.* to drive, impel 4316, 5879, 6999, 8000

chalange *v.* to lay claim to 2011, 2253, 2266

charge *n.* burden, weight 3157, 6398

charges *v. 3 sg. pr.* weighs upon, heeds or attends to, accuses 3333, 5056, 7950

chasty *v.* to chastise, punish 3528, 3549, 5547, 5869, 5874

chaunce *n.* chance, a fortuitous event 1282, 1315, 1317

chede *v.* (for **schede**) to distinguish, separate 5641

chere *n.* countenance, manner, behaviour 791, 1636, 2233, 5406, 6178 +

chese *v.* to choose 79, 93, 100, 191, 199 +; *pa.* ?1583, 2132, 8682

circumcid *v. pa. p.* circumcised 4187

cled(de) *v. pa., pa. p.* clothed, wearing 6166, 8530, 9360, 9369; **clad** 6153

clene *adj.* pure, virtuous or chaste, purified 972, 1209, 2385, 2625, 2634 +; *adv.* neatly, completely 8899, 8930

clenly *adv.* completely 3500, 9082

cler(e) *adj.* clear, transparent, shining 575, 783, 995, 1444, 2781 +; *adv.* brightly 2632, 9072, 9076, 9179

clergy *n.* learnedness 5844, 7430, 7602, 7796, 8204 +

clerk *n.* learned man, cleric 410, 488, 644, 665, 730 +

cleves *v. pr. pl.* adhere 3425

clynges *v. 3 sg. pr.* shrivels 823

clokes *n. pl.* claws 6936

clomsed *v. pa. p., adj.* stupi(fie)d 1651

colke *n.* core 6441

com(e) *v. pa.* came 506, ?508, 901, 2245, 2251 +; **comen** *pa. p.* 1860, 5147, 5775

commelyng *n.* traveller, newcomer 1385

compas *n.* circle, arc, circumference 1497, 7583

condicion *n.* state, behaviour 61, 352, 769, 805, 1075 +

confessours *n. pl.* persons sanctified for their persistence in the good 3826, 8720

consayve *v.* to understand 334, 6853

contene *v.* to contain (in its various senses) 30, 39, 331, 439, 969 +

continance *n.* mien, manner, expression 6538

contrarius *adj.* opposed, different, hostile 1111, 1414, 1591, 4117

controves *v. pr. pl.* contrive, invent 1561

conversand *adj.* resident, familiar 4198

cordes *v. 3 sg. pr.* accords, agrees 316

cornes *n. pl.* grains 3420

corrumped, corrumpnd *v. pa. p., adj.* poisonous, corrupted 850, 2558

costage *n.* expenditure 1522

cotidiene *adj.* daily; *fever cotidiene* a fever that peaks daily, with a daily crisis 2987

countrefette *v.* to imitate 4311

couth v. pr. 'did' (pleonastic) 321,
    possibly also **can** 1126
covaytes v. pr. pl. desire 7530
cover v. to recover 811
covert adj. hidden, secret 4489
covert n. shelter, refuge 1578
covertoure n. blanket, garment 6951
crepe v. to crawl 467, 474, 873, 6931
cry n. outcry 478, 3475, 6222
crop(pe) n. top 663, 1906
curall n. coral 8901, 9102

D

dalk n. hollow (place) 6443
dased v. pa. p. numbed, cold-hearted
    6643
dasednes n. indifference, lack 4906
daunger n. domination, resistance 7979;
    in daunger under domination 8519,
    8520
dauntes v. 3 sg. pr. dominates, controls
    1078
debate n. strife, contention 3473, 4092,
    7388, 9422
ded(e) n. death 112, 263, 355, 487, 815 +
dede n. for **dette** 3813
dede-brayde n. the attack or onset of
    death 1750, 1805, 1925
dede-stour n. onslaught of death 5812
dede-thraw n. the throes of death 2099,
    2101
defaut n. lack, absence, failure 279, 295,
    3248, 5015, 5016 +; defaute of kynd a
    natural defect
defautles adj. without lack, faultless 8696
defendes v. 3 sg. pr. forbids, prohibits
    3537
defygurd v. pa. p. disfigured 2340
deghe v. to die 813, 1939, 6921, 6928,
    7279; **digh(e), dieghe** 869, 1747, 1748,
    1942, 2045 +; **dey(g)hed** pa. 1780,
    5262; **dieghed** 5596; **dighed** 6529,
    deghed 7081
degyse n. a strange manner of dress
    1518, 1524
degre n. social rank 5883, 6123, 7434,
    7633, 8702 +
dele n. part, portion 7478
dele v. to apportion, share out 3883; dele
    in bed have sex 3460
delices n. pl. delights 1628, 2979, 4615,
    7828 +; **delyce** 7847

delytable adj. delightful 5239, 7561,
    8622, 8643, 8753, 8762 +
delyver v. imp. free, release, hand over
    1749, 2363, 2825, 2830, 2951 +
delyveraunce n. release, rescue 2886,
    3585, 6097
delyvernes n. agility 5900
deme v. to judge, understand 569, 1995,
    2095, 2306, 2419 +
departe v. to separate 1697, 3710, 6130
departyng n. separation 1847, 6110
dere adj. beloved 2978, 4299, 5797,
    8532 +; adv. at great expense 3292
dere v. to harm, hurt 1232, 1469, 2168,
    2290, 2552 +
desayvable adj. deceitful 1088, 4232
despende (dis-) v. to expend, use 125,
    2435, 5915
despite n. scorn, contempt 376
desputed v. pa. p. argued (over) 2581;
    disput v. 2926
digh(e), dieghe, see **deghe**
dight v. pa. p. prepared, adorned,
    dressed or arrayed 448, 909, 6146,
    6184, 6428 +
digne adj. worthy 74, 5853
dyng v. to hammer, beat 7011, 7027,
    7032
dyngyng n. striking, blows 6567, 7006,
    7347
dyntes n. pl. blows, strokes 5418, 7013,
    7015
discucion n. examination, investigation
    2582
discus(s)e v. to examine, investigate
    2415, 2419, 2550, 5752, 6072 +
dysy adj. giddy, dizzy 771
distance n. argument, strife 8397
divised v. pa. p. divided 349, 987
do v. to do, in its various senses, incl. to
    perform, to put or place, to cause
    (4290, 4315, 4317, etc.) 108, 136, 288,
    291, 473 +; **dos(e)** 3 sg. pr. 131, 137,
    695 +; **dus** 2470, 2525, 3091 +; **duse**
    6380; **dyd(de)** pa. 116, 120, 1779 +;
    don(e) pa. p. 67, 109, 136 +
doct(o)urs n. pl. persons sanctified for
    their holy learning 2278, 3830, 8721
dole, dule n. sorrow, mourning 2922,
    3218, 5382, 6883
doleful, duleful adj. sorrowful 1166,
    1840, 6107, 6873, 6889 +
dolefuly adv. sorrowfully 6710

dom(e) *adj.* without speech 49, 4323

dome *n.* judgement 264, 358, 1859, 2584, 2600 +

domesman *n.* justice, judge 4930, 5030, 5059, 5061, 5083 +

domland *adj.* dark, cloudy 1443

dotes *v. 3 sg. pr.* dotes, acts like a fool 785

doungangyng *n.* going down, sunset 4779

dout(e) *n.* fear, doubt 580, 810, 1285, 1694, 1772 +

doutes *v. 3 sg. pr.* fears 2965

draw(e) *v.* to draw (in its various senses, incl. to entice) 240, 341, 807 +; drogh(e) *pa.* 2249, 4419, 5527; dru 9613; drawen *pa. p.* translated 336

drede *v.* to fear, be afraid 190, 277, 291, 328, 355 +; dredande *pr. p., adj.* fearful 282, 1669, 2332, 2567; dred *pa. p., adj.* 1666; drede 6715

dredful *adj.* fearful, causing fear 297, 2616, 4680, 5083, 5101 +

dreghe, drighe *v.* to endure, suffer 2044, 2235, 2754, 3540, 6519 +

drery *adj.* sorrowful 791, 1455

dry *adj.* dry, dried out 1439, ?4707, 7608

drighe, see dreghe

droghe, see drawe

droppes *v. 3 sg. pr.* drips, dribbles 775

dropsy *n.* the disease 700, 2991

droves *v. 3 sg. pr.* agitates, torments 1319

druryes *n. pl.* treasures, pleasures 7822

dubbed *v. pa. p.* adorned 8787

dul(e)ful, see doleful

dungen *v. pa. p.* struck, beaten 3256

dungeon *n.* fortress, prison 456, 463, 2835

dur *v.* to dare 4135, 4548; durst *pa.* 6515, 6855, 7164

dusching *v.* dashing (down), striking 7347

dwelle, duel(le) *v.* to live, stay, remain, tarry 81, 294, 309, 361, 382 +

dwyne *v.* to shrivel, languish 703, 707, 727

E

eese *v.* to soothe, comfort 1469, 7371

eft(e) *adv.* again, in turn 1279, 6519, 6650

egged *v. pa.* incited, encouraged 5483

eggyng *n.* encouragement 5487

eghe *n.* eye 818, 819, 1128; eghen *pl.* 575, 781

eghtild *v. pa.* intended, planned 5784, 5800

eke *v.* to increase 3256, 6236, 6649, 6813 +; heke 3546

eld(e) *n.* (old) age 742, 801, 1479, 1502, 1513 +; held 756; cf. helde

elles *adv.* otherwise 122, 126, 149, 275, 409 +

empiry *adj.* empyrean; *heven . . . empiry* the fiery heaven 7758

enchesoun *n.* reason 5311?, 5790

endlang *adv.* from end to end, in all directions 8579

engyne *n.* siege-engine 7015, 7021

enioynt *v. pa. p.* commanded, prescribed 3906, 3908, 3917; cf. ioynt

ententyfly *adv.* attentively, carefully 624, 2550

entre *n.* entry, gate, prologue 369, 1720, 1763, 2120, 8895 +

environs *v. 3 sg. pr.* surrounds, encloses 7605

erred *v. pa. p.* done wrongfully 5733

erres *n. pl.* wounds, scars 5327, 5600

erth(e)-dyn *n. pl.* earthquake 4036, 4790, 4792

es, esse *v. 3 sg. pr.* is 12, 22, 30, 32, 52 +; er *pr. pl.* are 49, 50, 152, 185, 188 +

et(t)e *v.* to eat 3446, 3453, 4675, 4841, 6188 +; *pa.* 4841, 4848

even *adj.* just, flat, level 4521, 4795, 4797, 6345, 6392 +

even *adv.* exactly, so far as, straightway, in succession 393, 992, 2625, 3379, 4218 +

F

fail *v.* to fail, cease, lack, be lacking 1071, 1463, 1501, 3628, 3636 +

fayn(e) *adj.* happy, joyful 4552, 8432

fayn(e) *adv.* eagerly, preferably 5060, 7376, 7380

fayntise *n.* faintness, slacking 3519

fair(e) *adj.* beautiful 104, 568, 579, 690, 694 +

fayrnes *n.* beauty 249, 702, 8688, 8689, 8694 +

falle *v.* to fall, befall, happen, occur,

pertain or belong (to) 228, 553, 754,
758, 800 +; (hym) fel *v. pa.* it befell
him, it behoved him 171, 377, 379;
felle 383; *als falles* as is appropriate
1052, 2581
fals(h)ed(e) *n.* falsehood, deception 1176,
3522, 5541
fand(e), see fynde
fande *v.* to test, try out 1463, 2228, 3534
fandyng *n.* temptation 314
fantome *n.* vanity, deceit 1197
fare *v.* to travel, behave, live, result 270,
509, 599, 1343, 1774 +
faste *adv.* firmly, steadily, near at hand
210, 269, 684, 1342, 1476 +
faulde *n.* sheepfold 9003
feyn *v.* to show oneself, pretend, feign
4233, 4240, 4302, 4304; feyned *pa. p.,*
adj. imitative, imagined 2556
fel(e) *v.* to experience, perceive 132, 217,
287, 616, 900 +; fel(l)ed *pa.* 2025,
3076; feled *pa. p.* 2749, 3023, 3053 +
fel(l)e *adj.* fierce 1743, 1820, 2453, 2571,
2736 +
felle *n.* skin 4967; *flesshe and felle* (man's)
physical being 82, 739, 3077
felly *adv.* fiercely 4449, 7024, 9454
felony *n.* crime, sinfulness 2947, 5346,
8402
felouns *n. pl.* deep boils 2995
fen *n.* filth, excrement 565, 655, 6685
fende *n.* devil 36, 547, 1253, 1703,
2218 +
ferd *adj.* afraid, terrified 6946; cf. fere,
forferde
ferd(e)layk *n.* terror 2915, 6423
ferdnes *n.* terror, fear 2231, 2321, 2354
fere *v.* to terrify 2227, 2291, 3325; feer
6429; ferd *pa. p., adj.* afraid, terrified
6946
ferforthe *adv.* far; *als ferforthe als* sos far
as, to the extent that 3814, 8273
ferly *n.* marvel, wonder 2211, 2955, 3296,
7740, 8584
fervor *n.* eagerness, enthusiasm 250
fest *v.* to fasten 1907, 5295, 6769, 6933,
8382
fygur(e) *n.* shape, form 2320, 2331, 4322,
6862
fykell *adj.* deceitful, unsteadfast 949,
1088, 1621
file *v.* to defile, pollute 1198, 1210, 2341,
2348, 2349 +

fylyng *n.* defilement, pollution 2345
fynde *v.* to find (in its various senses)
241, 364, 865 +; fand(e) *pa.* 4749,
4753, 4754; fonden, funden *pa. p.*
4608, 5460, 7172, 7785, 8183
fyndynges *n. pl.* discoveries, provisions
1557, 1580
fyne *v.* to refine, purify 2632, 2634, 2720,
3201, 3202 +
firmament *n.* sky, heaven 664, 7553
flay *v.* to frighten, terrify 1268, 2244,
2247, 2316, 2549; flayne *pa. p.* skinned
9517
flaying *n.* terror 6109
flayre *n.* aroma, odour 9014
flemed *v. pa. p.* driven away, exiled
2977, 6054
flesshe, see felle
flesshe-lykyng *n.* carnal desire 1135 (cf.
flesschly lykyng 7224)
flit(e) *v.* to pass, depart 2257, 2433, 3762
flode *n.* flood, current 4706, 4845, 4894,
4895
foly *n.* sin, sinfulness, folly 267, 335, 357,
1170, 1355 +
fon(e) *adj.* few 530, 762, 764, 1184,
2465 +; fune 6420; *comp.* foner 765,
3731, 3732
fonstane, see funstane
forbard *v. pa. p.* prohibited, shut out 957
forbere *v.* tolerate, spare 7403
forbisens *n. pl.* examples 1027
fordo *v.* to destroy 3395, 4254, 4898,
4900, 6320 +; fordus *pr. pl.* 3399,
3504; fordid *pa.* 4846; fordon(e) *pa. p.*
3391, 3500, 4623 +
forferde *v. pa. p.* grievously frightened
6860, 7341
forga *v.* forsake 1842, 8567
forgangers *n. pl.* those who proceed,
purveyours 4152
forluke *v.* to foresee, foretell 1946
formefader *n.* ancestor 483
forsake *v.* to cease, leave off, abandon,
renounce 192, 902, 1571, 1588, 1637 +;
forsuke *pa.* 6036; forsoke 8331;
forsaken *pa. p.* 1571, 4401, 8243
forth-broght *v. pa. p.* extended,
protracted 1513
forthermore (-mare) *adv.* farther
forward 928, 1658, 2892
forþi *adv.* therefore 189, 410, 1947, 2194,

2480 +; **forthy (þat)** *conj.* because 375,
1420, 1796, 1854, 2186 +

forthynkyng *n.* regret, penitential sorrow
3510, 7126, 7508

forthward *adv.* henceforth, in the future
2812

forwhi *adv.* therefore 709, 733, 2118;
conj. because 744, 865, 1249, 1352,
1611 +

forworthes *v. pr. pl.* come to nothing,
fail 780

fraistes *v. pr. pl.* make trial of, seek out
1090, 1358

fraunches *n.* free condition, nobility,
magnanimity 7992

fraward *adj.* contrary, disobedient,
perverse 87, 256, 305, 786, 1604 +

frawardnes *n.* disobedience 1173

fre *adj.* noble, unconstrained, generous
78, 93, 102, 884, 1156 +

fredom *n.* liberty 7976, 7992, 7995, 7997,
8940 +

frely *adv.* generously 2264, 5952, 5958,
5965 (2x), 8340

frende *n.* kinsman, friend 1116, 1453,
2883, 2889, 2978 +

freshe (-ssche) *adj.* new, active, eager
1254, 5307

frete *v.* to eat, gnaw (of animals) 6566,
7047

frett *v. pa. p.* adorned, ornamented 9104

frount *n.* forehead 816, 4410

fruyt *n.* fruit, benefit 631, 649, 659, 660,
923 +

fulfille *v.* to fulfil, perform fully, fill
completely 64, 535, 1035, 3005, 3123 +

funstane *n.* baptismal font 3126;
fonstane 3311

G

ga *v.* walk, pass 193, 466, 470, 777,
928 +; **gan(e)** *pa. p.* 995, 2507, 3750 +

gayn-turnyng *n.* return, coming back
1718

gang *v.* to go, to pass 194, 1396, 1543,
4326, 5914 +; cf. **doun-gangyng**

garettes *n. pl.* watch-towers 8895, 8901,
9098, 9100, 9106

gast(e) *n.* spirit 16, 738, 772, 2272,
2277 +

gast(e)ly *adj.* spiritual 972, 974, 1036,
1037, 1038 +; **gastly** *adv.* spiritually,

in a spiritual (metaphorical) sense 8674,
9070, 9078, 9086, 9094 +

gate *n.* street or way, passage, passing
7072, 8980

gesce, gese *v.* to perceive, judge, discern
1136, 3934, 4340, 5908, 7102 +

gett *n.* fashion 1540

gett(e) *v.* to get (in its various senses),
beget 96, 3463, 6059, 6300; **gat(t)** *pa.*
7395, 8277; **geten** *pa. p.* begotten, born
443, 444, 4157

gilden *adv.* golden; **Iohan wyth þe
gilden mouth** John Chrysostom 5360

gilry *n.* treachery, deception 1176

gys(e) *n.* manner, fashion 1533, 1546,
1550, 1561, 1564 +

glet *n.* slime 459

gnayste *v.* gnash (the teeth), grind 7334

goule *v.* to cry out, yell, howl 477, 7334,
9413

goulyng *n.* howling, lamenting 6106

graythely *adv.* readily, carefully, easily
645, 1074

grape *v.* 'to grope', touch, perceive by
touch 6562, 6795, 6800

greef, see **gryfe**

grege *v.* to increase 2991

gret(e) *v.* to weep 502, 903, 5392, 6882,
7095 +

gretyng *n.* weeping 496, 1451, 6106,
6571, 7093 +

grevaunce *n.* pain 2753, 3019, 8006,
8315

greve, griefe, gryfe *v.* to harm, anger,
lament, be a sorrow for 131, 749, 1564,
1730, 2328 +

gryfe, greef, griefe *adj.* grievous,
painful, deadly 1565, 4260, 8341

grym *adj.* fierce, fearsome 2233, 2250,
6898, 7178, 9401

grymly *adv.* fiercely 2226

gryn *v.* to bear the teeth, snarl 2226,
7407, 7422

grysly, grisely *adj.* terrifying, terrified
911, 1404, 1757, 1934, 2218 +

gryslynes *n.* terrifying mien or
appearance 2310

groches *v. pr. pl.* 'grudge', murmur,
complain 297, 302, 305; **grotchand** *pr.
p.* 3542

gr(o)und *n.* foundation, basis, the bottom
209, 7209; cf. **helle-ground**

gun *v.* a pleonastic auxiliary 'did' 4700,
    9301

H

h-, occasionally introducing roots
    beginning with vowels; see the forms
    lacking **h-**
hayres *n. pl.* hairshirts 4530
halde *v.* to hold, preserve, understand,
    consider, require 79, 119, 327, 374,
    588 +; **halden** *pa. p.* considered 99,
    1596, 1598, 1744 +
hale *adj.* whole, entire, 'hale' or healthy
    1461, 3452, 3933, 4991; **alle hale**
    complete 5837
hale *v.* to heal, make whole 8323, 8344
halghe *n.* saint, holy person 3823, 4650,
    5114, 5118, 5522 +
haly, halely *adv.* wholly, completely 999,
    2416, 2419, 3032, 3710 +
halowes, see **halghe**
hand *n.* 'onde', breath 775
hap(pe) *n.* chance, fortune 1282, 1285,
    1316, 5897, 5908
happy *adj.* fortunate, prosperous 1334,
    1339
hard(e) *adv.* fast, firmly, vigorously,
    harshly 662, 1998, 2031, 2688, 4179;
    hard-haldand *adj.* firmly grasping,
    miserly 790
hardy *adj.* brave, bold 2318, 2912, 6851,
    6857
harn-pane *n.* brain-pan, depths of the
    skull 5298
haterel *n.* the top of the head 1492
hat(e)reden *n.* hatred, wrath, enmity
    3363, 7000, 7390, 8415, 9037 +;
    hatred(e) 519, 8403
haunt *v.* to frequent, dwell, practice
    1079, 1525, 4382, 6341
hawtayne *adj.* proud, haughty 255
hede-syns *n. pl.* principal sins, 'seven
    deadly sins' 3362
heghe(n) *v.* to elevate, exalt 1191, 4119,
    4125, 8503
helde *v.* to grow old 1478; cf. **elde**
heldes *v. pr. pl.* bend down, bow down
    817
hele *n.* health, salvation 757, 1326, 1392,
    2035, 8005 +
helle-ground *n.* the depths of hell 3299
hend *n. pl.* hands 3214, 5602, 7189

hentes *v. 3 sg. pr.* seizes 2722; **hent** *pa.
    p.* dragged away 2803
herber *n.* harbour, lodging 448, 6150,
    6164, 6191, 6202
herber *v.* to lodge, give lodging 6151,
    6165, 6192
heritage *n.* inheritance, patrimony 1013,
    2260
hethen *adv.* from here, hence 509, 835,
    1375, 1586, 2145 +
heved *n.* head 675, 677, 771, 4082 +;
    hede 486, 1715, 3042 +
hevenryke *n.* the kingdom of heaven,
    heaven 403, 1898, 8283, 8524, 8610 +
hewed *v. pa. p.* cut, chopped 3713
hyde *n.* skin 5299
hidos, hydus *adj.* horrible, terrifying
    1744, 2227, 2232, 4773, 4858 +; **ydous**
    2911
hight *v. pa. p.* was promised, was called
    or named 107, 966, 7654, 8833; *pa.*
    6526; **hetes** *3 sg. pr.* 9487
hyng *v.* to hang 675, 1536, 5334, 7206 +;
    hanges *3. sg. pr.* 684; **hanged** *pa. p.*
    5209
hypand *v. pr. p.* hopping 1539
hirde *n.* shepherd 4638, 5892, 6131
honeste *n.* virtue, virtuous behaviour
    5829, 7853
hope *v. 1. sg. pr.* think 2963, 3805, 9598
hordom *n.* adultery, relations without
    marriage 8256
hortel *v.* to collide, cram together 4787
housil *n.* communion, the eucharist 3402
hoven *v. pa. p.* raised, lifted 3126
hoves *v. 3 sg. pr.* hangs in the air, hovers
    7576
hurde *n.* hoard, treasury 5567

I

ilk, ilka, ilkan(e) *adj.* each (one) 53, 89,
    117, 137, 138 +
ille *adj., n.* evil, wrong 77, 80, 92, 94,
    97 +
ille *adv.* evilly, badly 292, 2165, 5407,
    5802, 7083 +
imydward *adv.* at the centre 6443;
    inmyddes 6438, 6441; **in mydward**
    7282; **imyddes** 6639, 7383, 7583; cf.
    midward
inoghe *adv.* aplenty 8992
ynwitt *n.* conscience 5428

irk *v.* to be bored or weary 8915
irkyng *n.* weariness 9356, 9363

J

ianglyng *n.* loose or vain speech 3478
iaunys *n.* jaundice 700
ioly *adj.* lusty, wanton 589
ioynt *v. pa. p.* commanded, prescribed 3900; cf. **enioynt**
iustify *v.* to judge, correct 5987
iuwys *n.* judging or justice, punishment 6103

K

ka *n.* jackdaw 1539
kaytif *n.* wretch 7392; cf. **caytefte**
kele *v.* to cool 6760, 6780
ken *v.* to know, understand, make known or teach, instruct 1074, 4215, 4520, 4703, 5430 +
ken(e) *adj.* fierce 1217, 1223, 1228, 3094, 3258 +
kepe *n.* heed, attention (particularly in the phrase **tas/tuk kepe**) 381, 597, 647, 3231, 8072 +
kepe *v.* to preserve, retain, maintain, serve or attend on 56, 84, 954, 1035, 1138 +
kepyng *n.* preservation, control 3882, 4192, 4196, 5003, 5778 +
kyd(de) *v. pa.* made known, showed 115, 2409, 4342 +; *pa. p.* known 6209, 6213, 6259, 6453 +
kylles *n. pl.* ulcers, boils 2995
kynd(e) *n. pl.* nature, state 48, 52, 54, 56, 58 +
kynd(e)ly *adj.* natural 1686, 2003; *adv.* naturally, intuitively, in nature 127, 221, 1809, 3714, 6377 +
kyngryke *n.* kingdom 5780
knyt *v. pa.* joined 1855, 5843; **knytt** *pa. p.* 3664; **knytted** 7211
knokyng *n.* pounding (the gesture accompanying 'Mea culpa') 3408
konyng, kunnyng *n.* intelligence, knowledge 7203, 9577
kun *v.*, see **can**, cf. **unkunnand**

L

laykyng *n.* play, sport 594, 7836
layn(e)d *v. pa. p.* hidden 5999, 7462, 8201
layt *v.* to seek 6001, 7531

laythede *n.* 'loathhood', loathesomness, uglyness 9021
lakes *v. 3 sg. pr.* criticizes 797
lang-fynger *n.* the middle finger 1489
langly *adv.* for a long time 3188
lapped *v. pa. p.* wrapped 523, 841, 1905, 5199; cf. **umlap**
large *adj.* wide, broad, great, untrammelled or free 1402, 2314, 3159, 3859, 3922 +
lates, lattes *v. 3 sg. pr.* lets, allows 1277, 1567, 3333, 7413
latoun *n.* brass or a compound 4367 (Vulg. auricalco) 4371
latsom *adj.* slow, delayed 793
laverd, see **loverd**
leches *n. pl.* physicians, doctors 5944
lede *v.* to guide, direct, lead 140, 157, 229, 273, 593 +; **lad** *pa. p.* 8979
ledyng *n.* direction, guidance 4217
lef, leve *v.* to leave (behind), abandon, cease 100, 192, 1240, 2003, 3329 +
lefe, leve *adj.* dear, loved 2978, 5797; cf. **lever**
legge *n.* liege, superior; *legge pouste* (prideful) sound mind, full possession of their faculties 5606
lele *adj.* loyal, faithful 1393, 4235, 6048, 8258, 8387 +
lent *v. pa. p.* given, granted 5649, 5951, 5993
ler(e) *v.* to learn, teach 155, 163, 174, 175, 184 +
lered *adj.* learned 117, 2444, 2608, 4414, 5302, 6363 +
leryng *n.* learning, gaining knowledge 170, 177
lese *v.* to lose 2915, 7995
lesyng *n.* lie(s) 4274
lett(e) *v.* to hinder, impede, prevent 238, 243, 253, 261, 953, 3921 +
lettyng *n.* hinderance, impediment, delay 237, 1172, 1996, 2626, 4900 +
leve *n.* permission 2329, 3236, 7031
leve *v.* to live 492, 3355, 8009; life 530, 740; lyf 632; lyves 630, 894, lyfed 729
levenyng *n.* lightning 5125, 5418
lever *adv. comp.* more preferably 3936, 5058, 7505, 9516; cf. **leve**
lewed *adj.* ignorant, unlearned 117, 2444, 2608, 4414, 5302 +; **laude** 338, **lawed** 885
licour(e) *n.* liquid, fluid 6759, 8047

lyf(e)-days *n.* life 2188, 3803, 8498
lyfte *n.* sky, heaven 1444
lygg(e), lygyn *v.* to lie 139, 475, 1398, 3162, 3507 +; **ly** *v.* 849; **lys** *3. sg. pr.* 808; **lyes** 1395; **lyese** *pl.* 3639; **liggen** *pa. p.* 4553
light *adj.* active, easy, happy, frivolous 688, 1454, 3346, 3391, 6009; *adv.* brightly 4368
lyghtly *adv.* easily 786, 1320, 3393, 3482, 4241 +
lightnes *n.* frivolousness 308
liken *v.* to compare 606, 704, 1212, 1213, 1226 +
lykes *v. 3 sg. pr. (impers.)* is pleasing (to) 1119, 7848; **like** *v.* 8511, 8756, 9258 +; **lykand** *pr. p.*, *adj.* pleasant 7831, 8703, 8883
lykyng *pr. p.*, *adj.* pleasing, pleasant 272
lykyng *n.* pleasure, desire 183, 292, 304, 578, 595 +; cf. **flesshe-lykyng**
lym (lym(m)(e)s *pl.)* *n.* limb, member, part of a corporate body 1378, 1912, 2992, 2994, 3041 +
list(e) *v. (impers.)* to be pleasing (to him) 795, 1160, 1635, 2012, 3454 +
lith *n.* limb, member 1917
lither *adj.* perverse, wicked, sinful 1059
lythernes *n.* sinful behaviour? 226
lof *v.* to praise 51, love *imper.* 3535; **loves** 55, 58, 121, 796 +; **loved** 321 (note **lufe** 'love' 115, 1107, 1112, 1124, but **love** 112, **lof(e)** *n.* 345 and 1843, **lofe** *v.* 1470, **loffed** *pa.* 2286—and cf. the use of both verbs at 1346)
loperd *v. pa. p.* coagulated 459
lorn(e) *v. pa. p.* lost, estranged, alienated 547, 4165, 7333, 8246, 8259
louse *v.* loosen, release or pardon, dissolve, resolve 1792, 2182, 3841, 3852, 3853
loverd *n.* lord, God (also as an exclamation) 908, 1384, 2126, 2825, 3669 +; **lord(e)** 4, 935, 941, 1105; **laverd** 416, 420
lovyng *n.* praise 321, 2129, 2137, 3789, 7842 +
lowe *n.* fire 9428
lowted *v. pa.* bowed (to), reverenced 8963
lowtyng *n.* bowing, polite or deferential behaviour 7844
lughe *v. pa.* laughed 6518

luke *v.* to look, seek out, inspect 205, 368, 428, 1128, 1758 +; **loke** 527, 645, 2301 +
lust *n.* delight, desire 1135, 1140, 3462

M

ma *adj.*, *n.* more (in number) 802, 965, 1448, 1591, 1681 +
mayntene *v.* to support, assert 1108, 3080, 4091, 9615
maystre, maistry *n.* lordship, overbearingness 5580, 8486, 8505
malys *n.* 'malease', discomfort 1514
manace *n.* threat, threatening behaviour 4350, 4438
maner(e) *n.* kind, fashion, custom 52, 298, 488, 536, 586 +
manhed(e) *n.* human form (of incarnation) 1779, 2213, 2294, 5131, 5253 +
manyfalde *adv.* multiply, in many forms 1350, 1558, 3250, 4039
mar(e) *adj. comp.*, *n.* greater, more, more persons 65, 89, 156, 175, 380, 381 +; *adv.* including senses longer, further 323, 716, 749, 773 (2x) +
mas(e) *v. 3 sg. pr. pl.* makes 242, 255, 702, 1061, 1064 +
mast *adj. super.*, *n.* greatest, most 4, 66, 74, 101, 105 +
matere, -tir *n.* material, subject or literary materials 331, 337, 365, 373, 376 +
mede *n.* reward 96, 2769, 2771, 2778, 3545 +
medeful *adj.* worthy of reward 9488
meyne *n.* company, retinue 4628; **meigne** 5870
meke *adj.* humble 385, 395, 401, 405, 3408, 3547 +
meke *v.* to make humble 172, 406
mekenes *n.* humility 141, 158, 181, 208, 230 +
melled *v. pa. p.* mixed, mingled 9428
melles *n. pl.* hammers, mauls 6568, 7040, 7044
men *pron. (indef.)* (i.e. **me**) people, one 39, 258, 304, 306, 347 +
mene *v. imp.* remember 5740
meneyng *n.* memory 8317, 8357, 8368
menged *v. pa. p.* mixed 6734, 6744, 8053
mengyng *n.* mixture, confusion 4705

merryng *n.* damage, ruin, affliction 6111
meschyve (mescheefes, myscheves *pl.***)**
n. misfortune 698, 1548, 1565, 5569
meselry *n.* leprosy or a similar skin
disease 3001
messe *n.* (requiem) mass (for souls of the
dead) 2838, 2848, 3090, 3605, 3708 +;
messe-syngyng *n.* 3589
mesur(e) *n.* moderation 1459, 5574, 7687
mete *n.* food, a meal 3058, 6161, 6187,
6712, 6723 +; **meete** 6513, 6702
mette *v.* to measure 1487, 1496; **met** *pa.*
7692
myddyng *n.* dungheap 628; **myddyng-
pytt** 8767
mydlerd(e) *n.* the earth 2302, 6855
midward *n.* the middle 435, 553; cf.
imyd-
myghtfulnes *n.* power, the powerful 754
mykel(l) *adj.* great, a great deal, much
237, 439, 654, 889, 925 +
mynde *n.* consciousness, memory 59, 76,
119, 138, 162 +
myrk *adj.* dark 456, 1025, 1435, 6453,
6817 +
myrknes *n.* darkness, obscurity 194,
1404, 1809, 1811, 2815 +
mys *adv.* wrong(ly) 109, 3288, 3770,
5786, 9555
mysbylyefe *n.* misbelief, absence of
true/Christian belief 5521
myslykyng *n.* displeasure, something
unpleasant 8316, 9025
myspays *v. pr. pl.* displease 1120, 1330,
2562, 3416, 7185
misse *v.* to lack, fail 5266; **mys** 7997,
8039, 8571, 9327 +
myster *n.* need 3447, 3477, 7369
mistyly *adv.* enigmatically 4364
mysturnes *v. pr. pl.* pervert, misdirect
1617, 7223
moghes *n. pl.* moths, maggots 5572
mon *v. pr.* have the power, be able, must
96, 1605, 2598, 7518; **mow** 7933, 7961,
7962 +; **man** 2662; **moght** *pr. (subj.)*
571, 572, 1623, 1642 +; **mught** *pr.*
(subj.), pa. 282, 580, 1076, 1207,
1391 +
mot *v. pr.* must 2933, 4207, 5100, 7393,
7394; **most** 1570, 1671, 2235, 2412,
3140 +
mote *n.* hill 8893
moutes *v. 3 sg. pr.* 'moults', falls out 781

moweld *adj.* mouldy, rotten 5570
mude *v.* animosity 2391
muse *v.* wonder 6263

N

nacyon *n.* people, lineage 2605, 4368,
4498, 6047
nam(e)ly *adv.* particularly, especially 171,
202, 1712, 1936, 2085 +
nedder *n.* serpent 870, 4177, 4182, 6769,
6895, 6912 +
nedly *adv.* necessarily 2864, 3278, 5760
neghe *v.* to approach, come near 1208
neghen *num.* nine 729, 976, 8691;
neghend *ord.* ninth 3988, 4790, 6568,
7005
neghest, see **nest**
nerehande *adv.* nearby, near at hand,
nearly 5202, 8951
nese *n.* nose 626, 775, 820
nes(s)he *adj.* soft 614, 3110, 4949
nest *adv.* nearest (to) 676, 8685; **next**
2685, 2794, 2920 +; **neghest** next
2685, 2794, 2920
neven *v.* to name 969, 2850, 2896, 2903,
4649 +
newed *v. pa.* renewed, repeated 7456
nigremanciens *n. pl.* wizards, magicians
4213
nygromancy *n.* magic, art 4286
nobillay, nobelay *n.* nobility, noble
behaviour or mien 7823, 8529, 8740
noght *n.* nothing, not 46, 54, 61, 126,
163 +
no(u)ther *conj.* neither 167, 465, 466,
1635, 1842 +
nuye *v.* to harm 1184, 1234, 4395
nuyes *n. pl.* hurtful occasions 3538
nurist *v. pa. p.* nurtured, brought up
4198, 4210; **nurysches (nor-)** *v. 3 sg.*
pr. 257, 461, 1020, 7607 +

O

o-, see also **a-**
oboune *prep.* above 5405; **oboven** 849,
1492, 2794 +
occupy *v.* to fill up, take up space 1913,
3025, 3043
ofrace *v.* to tear (apart) 6700; cf. **race**
oftesythe(s) *adv.* often(times), frequently
1272, 3496; *oftsythe als* as often as
7456, 7457; cf. **sythes**

ogayne-stand *v.* to resist, impede 7939
ogayne-standyng *n.* resistance 7966
oght *n.* anything 10, 175, 306, 774, 3520 +
omang *adv.* mixed in, from time to time 2486, 3253, 6560, 7256 +; *prep.* amidst 873, 981, 2240, 3236, 3370 +
onence *prep.* with respect to, opposite, in comparison to 1355, 1704, 2465, 3678, 3679 +
orda(y)ne *v.* to order, establish, arrange, etc. 47, 70, 81, 1016, 1057 +
ordir, ordre *n.* regimen, rank, clerical order 205, 976, 3695, 5882, 7220
or-litel *n.* not enough, too few things 1459
other, (þe) tother *adj.* (the) second, other 72, 75, 106, 156, 215 +
ourw(h)ar *adv.* (i.e. ouwhar) anywhere 4339, 4753, 5062, 6979; cf. **nourwhar(e)** 5057, 6446
outher *conj.* either 494, 1106, 1127, 1651, 2456 +
outrage *n.* excess 1516, 1523, 5011, 6726
outragiouste *n.* excess 5010
outwith *adv.* without, (on the) outside 6665
out-yhetted *v. pa. p.* poured out 7115
over-lightly *adv.* with undue ease, too easily 1403, 3482
over-tyte *adv.* too quickly 7260
overthwert *adv.* across, crosswise 8579
overtures *n. pl.* openings, apertures 627

P

paens *n. pl.* pagans 4120 (poss.), 4124, 5510, 6061
pay *v. (impers.)* to please, be pleasing to, pay or redeem 283, 1734, 2561, 3923, 5675 +
paynes *v. 2. sg. pr.* take pains, exert oneself 3472
pays *n.* weight 7727
para(u)ntere *adv.* perhaps 2562, 5326
parlesy *n.* palsy 2996
parte *v.* to depart, separate, share 1807, 2427, 5575, 5995
party *n.* portion, segment 349, 431, 1804, 2210, 2334 +
partyng *n.* separation 1803, 1840
pas *v.* to pass, surpass, exceed, transgress 54, 314, 440, 714, 764 +; **passand** *pr.*

pa., a. passing (away), transient 717, 723, 725, 844, 1051 +
pases *n. pl.* passes, passages, roads 1239
pees *v.* to pacify 4320
penaunce *n.* hardship, unpleasantness, the sacrament penance 1638, 1725, 2635, 2639, 2648 +
perische (-isshe), perisse *v.* to die, be lost 4078, 5007, 5659, 6068, 7594 +; **peryst(e)** *pa. p.* slain, lost 2943, 3711, 4376, 5003 +
perre *n.* precious stones, gems 8897, 9002, 9178, 9185, 9317
pyk *n.* pitch, tar 3425, 6689, 8054, 9416, 9429
pyn(e) *n.* punishment, torment, pain 88, 1322, 1405, 1456, 1587 +
pyne *v.* to torment, torture 1716, 1928, 2026, 2244, 2988 +; **pynde, pyned** *pa. p.* 3014, 3040, 3046 +
playn(e) *adj.* full, plenary, flat or clear 3839, 3844, 4766, 4795, 4797 +
playnt *n.* complaint, plea 5603
pleyne *v.* to complain, lament 799, 2540, 5552, 5560, 5603 +
pleynyng *n.* lament, complaint 5662, 6101
plenteuouse *adj.* plenteous, manifold 8753, 9283
plenteuously *adv.* plenteously 6338
poynt *n.* point, the smallest part, measure, instant, or detail 820, 2311, 2708, 3303, 3901 +
pompe *n.* pride 226, 257, 1180, 1199, 1517 +
potagre *n.* disease of leg or foot, specifically gout 2993
pouce *n.* pulse 822
poudre *n.* dust 412, 419, 427, 878, 887 +
pouste *n.* power, might 3996, 4090, 4160, 4660, 5606 +
pover, see **pure**
povert *n.* poverty 1193, 1222, 1270, 1341, 1638 +
preson *n.* prisoner 3539
prikke *v.* to pierce, goad, incite 344
prys(e) *n.* value 1142, 9103
pryve *adj.* secret, hidden, furtive 1794, 1940, 2410, 2463, 4493 +
prived *v. pa. p.* deprived 110
prively *adv.* secretly, not openly 4482, 4486

pryvete *n.* secret 2403, 3775, 4651, 5442, 5617 +

pryvyng *n.* depriving, absence 1813

proces *n.* a series of steps, an unfolding procedure, lengthy stage 235, 6246, 6253, 6279

proper *adj.* one's own 3979, 4958, 6862

prove, pruve (profe, prufe) *v.* to test, demonstrate 396, 936, 1017, 1036, 1081 +

pur(e) *adj.* poor 509, 836, 884, 1458, 3450 +; **pover** 1872, 5435, 5560

purchace (-ches) *v.* to gain, acquire 1342, 3223, 3800, 3803, 3807 +

pured *v. pa. p.* purified 2720

Q

qu-, qw-, see also **wh-**

quathes, see **wathe**

quert *n.* health 326

quik, qwyk *adj.* living 38, 1668, 3981, 6387, 6977 +

qwayntys(e) *n.* (vain) ingenuity or elegance 1181, 1348, 4327

qwyken *v.* to be vivified, to come to life 1723

qwyte *v.* to repay, absolve 3920; **qwy(t)te** *pa. p.* 2953, 3327, 3617, 3914, 5679 +

R

race *v.* tear 7375; **rayse** 1916

rayke *v.* to rush, run 4891

rase *n.* rush, onset 8935

raumpe *v.* to rise up threateningly 2225, 2907

raumpyng *n.* rising up 7347

raunson, raunceon *n.* release, redemption, ransom 2263, 2834, 3211, 3619

ravyn *n.* theft 3368; *bestes of ravyn* carnivorous predators 9445

raviss(c)he *v.* to seize (and carry away), to carry off 2222, 2909; **ravyst(e)** *pa. p.* 4309, 5027, 5050, 8976

reche *v.* to extend 554, 992, 3814, 3895, 6308

reco(u)verere *n.* relief, hope 2961, 6091, 7253

red(e) *n.* counsel, advice 1637, 2014, 4303, 4411, 4543 +

reddour, reddure *n.* rigourousness, severity 5357, 5375, 6087, 6094, 6286 +

rede *v.* to counsel, read, explain 307, 329, 330, 343, 347 +; **redde** *pa.* 2216, 2683, 3952 +; **red** *pa. p.* 6414, 6943, 7885 +

reherce *v.* to repeat, summarize, tell 2386, 2390, 2398, 3440, 3442 +

rek *v. 1. sg. pr.* care 9582

reke *n.* smoke 9428

rekles *adj.* negligent, heedless 5546, 5802

reklesly *adv.* negligently 5792

reklesnes *n.* negligence 3909

religiouse *adj. as n.* person in a religious order 1888, 8725

remow(e) *v.* to remove, move about 7361, 7962

renoueld *v. pa. p.* renewed 7470

replenyst *v. pa. p.* filled, crammed full 8905

reprove *n.* reproof, threat, danger 5555, 6218

reso(u)n *n.* (just) account, reasonable behaviour 62, 3676, 5672, 5720, 5791 +

reuthe *n.* pity 6725, 8420, 8427, 8429

reve *v. pr. subj.* steal, seize 251, 308, 1239, 2002, 2053

rewarde *n.* regard 1871, 1881, 5855; *to regard of* with respect to, in comparison with 5516, 7480, 7485 +

rewme *n.* kingdom, realm 4033 (2x)

riches, rychese *n.* wealth 250, 1137, 1142, 1197, 1220 +

ryfe *n.* reeve, steward 5785

right *adj.* direct, proper, just 139, 196, 205, 238, 342 +

right *adv.* properly, accurately, directly 56, 124, 217, 254, 418, 459 +

rightly *adv.* properly 1104, 6037

rightwes (-wyse) *adj.* just 135, 511, 1726, 3605, 3670 +; as *n.* 3435

ryghtwisnes *n.* justice, right dealing 1601, 3139, 3579, 3593, 3606 +; *pl.* 2504

rym *n.* membrane 520

ryn(ne) *v.* to run 471, 781, 4318, 4777, 6604 +

ryve *v.* to pierce, tear 888, 1230, 7375

rode *v.* cross 1780, 5209, 5334, 5348, 6529 +; **rode-tre** 5260, 5295

rogge *v.* to tug, tear 1230

rom(i)yng *n.* outcry, roaring 4772, 4774

rosyng *n.* boasting, pomp 7066

rouke *v.* to crouch, sit 6765, 6897

rouncles *v. 3 sg. pr.* becomes wrinkled 773

ruschyng *n.* noise, din 7346

S

sadde *adj.* solid 3189

saghtel *v. pr. pl.* accord, reach a settlement 1470

sake *n.* wrongdoing or sin, account 111, 3515, 3663, 3665, 3666 +

sal *v.* shall, ought (to) 11, 32, 34, 37, 41 +; **suld** *pa.* 118, 138, 173, 175, 190 +; **shuld** 229, 1904, 1975, 1979 +

samen *adv.* together, one another 1849, 9290

sande *n.* message or mission, command, order 3535

sare *adj.* painful, bitter 772, 1461, 1775, 5945, 6968 +; *adv.* severely, painfully 1317, 2999, 3012, 3102, 3234 +

savour *n.* aroma or taste 656, 8917, 8919, 9012, 9013 +

savour *v.* to taste or smell 9279, 9286

sawen *v. pa. p.* sown 445

schende *v.* to harm, injure, corrupt, disgrace 8371; **schent** *pa. p.* 8542

schene *adj.* bright, shining 8898

schen(d)schepe *n.* destruction, shame, disgrace 380, 1171, 5304, 5315, 5341 +

scratte *v.* scratch 7374

sculkes *v. 3 sg. pr.* stalks 1788

se *v.* to see, look upon, inspect 39, 40, 179, 189, 211 +; **saghe** *pa.* 2320; **saw(e)** 582, 628, 911, 2644, 2914 +; **sen(e)** *pa. p., adj.* visible, present, manifest 260, 430, 469, 797, 973 +

se(e) *n.* seat, throne 4220, 7768

seculere *adj. as n.* person living in the world 1888, 8725

sekkes *n. pl.* sacks, rough garments 4530

selcouthe *adj.* wondrous 1518

self *n., adj.* the very, the same 128, 236, 3660

sely *adj.* blessed 5810, 6002, 6006, 7832

selynes *n.* blessedness, happiness 7831

sembland *n.* mien, mode of behaviour 503, 791, 1161, 9299

semely *adj.* fair, beautiful 73, 5012, 5019, 5899

semes *v. 3 sg. pr.* seems, appears 568, 696, 818, 1322, 1406 +

sen *conj.* since, because 57, 101, 389, 938, 1152 +; **syn** 946, 2364

sene, see **se**

sere *adj.* various 48, 146, 337, 346, 352 +

servage *n.* (the condition of) servitude, slavery 1157

setil *n.* seat 6119, 8528

sette *v.* to fix, fasten, establish 95, 97, 210, 269, 952 +

shew(e), schew *v.* to appear, describe or demonstrate, display 118, 430, 441, 504, 570 +

shilde *v. pr. subj.* protect 9468

shille *adj.* resonant, resounding 9267

shire, schyre *adv.* bright 6609, 6930

sho *pron.* she 583, 1275, 1277, 1278

shrife *v.* to confess 2372, 2447, 3380, 3508; **schryve** 7164; **schrafe** *pa.* 8297; **schrywen, shryven** *pa. p.* 2631, 3196, 3300, 3809 +

shryfte *n.* confession 2647, 3404

syde *adj.* trailing, drooping (of clothing) 1534

signes *n. pl.* signs of the zodiac 997, 4803 (the general sense at 1652, 5310)

syker *adj.* certain, secure 1368, 1372, 2512, 7829, 8140 +

sikerly *adv.* securely, confidently 2469, 5810, 7827, 9512

sykernes *n.* security 8554, 9044, 9188

synoghe *n.* nerve, sinew 1917

sythes *n. pl.* times, occasions 2482, 3434, **sythe** 6356; cf. **oftsythes**

sythyn *adv.* afterward, subsequently 25, 731, 743, 745 +; *conj.* since 4138, 4793, 6014 +

skylle *n.* reason, something reasonable 48, 50, 57, 59, 76 +; *by skylle* reasonably, properly 203, 682, 1110, 1212 +

skomfit *v. pa. p.* discomfitted 2269

skoul *v.* to scowl or frown 2225

skryke *v.* to shriek, scream 7343

skrykyng *n.* shrieking 7348

sla *v.* to kill, slay 1769, 3416, 4185, 4606, 7272 +; **sloghe** *pa.* 5526; **slayn(e)** *pa. p.* 1706, 1722, 1740 +; **slane** 708

sleghe, sleyghe, slyghe *adj.* wise, intelligent, skilful 812, 2308, 2662, 7567, 7803

sleght *n.* wisdom, skill, trick, stratagem 1181, 2309, 7686, 7694

sleke(n) *v.* to slacken, abate 3101, 6310,

6554, 6592, 6608 +; cf. **slake** 2107, 6221, 6884 +

slotered *v. pa. p.* dirtied, made filthy 2367

smert *adj.* swift, active, harsh or hurtful 1464, 1837, 2940, 3257, 5878

smertly *adv.* swiftly 3323

smertes *v. 3 sg. pr.* hurts, harms 1317

smored *v. pa. p.* destroyed (lit. smothered) 7598

socours *v. 3 sg. pr.* aids, supports 1190

sodayn(e) *adj.* unexpected, unforeseen 1940, 1951, 4131, 5128

sodanly *adv.* all at once, unexpectedly, immediately 1282, 1989, 2103, 3294, 4476 +

soght *v. pa. p.* sought after, desired 3916; *es soght* has passed away 1512; cf. **soght** to pass, seek 2293, 2393

solace *n.* delight, joy 3205, 3729, 6036, 7479, 7755 +

son(e) *adv.* immediately 68, 706, 714, 788, 1274 +; **over-sone** too quickly 3907

sonder *v.* divide, split 4789

sothefast *adj.* firm in truth, true 135, 5532, 8065 (2×), 8653 (2×); **suthefast** 6125

souches *v. 3 sg. pr.* suspects 788

souke *v.* to suck 6761, 6764, 6770, 6894, 6934 +

sounes *v. 3 sg. pr.* sounds, accords, conduces 4678, 6075; **sownand** *pr. p.* (re)sounding 8913

soverayne *adj.* surpassing 3074, 9504

soverayne *n.* overlord 256, 1061, 5579

soveraynly *adv.* supremely, absolutely 8774

spare *v.* to spare, avoid (doing something) 1711, 1867, 1870, 1872, 2287 +

specify *v.* to make plain, state clearly, identify 1835, 2686, 2899, 3561, 3954 +

spede *n.* success, aid 2882

spede *v.* to make prosper, complete, bring to a conclusion 5, 2709, 3585, 3725, 3740; **sped(de)** *pa. p.* 2682, 3953, 6248, 6255, 9472 +

spendyd *v. pa. p.* expended, used 2431, 5518, 5968, 5993

spers *v. 3 sg. pr.* shuts 3835

spycery *n.* aromatic substances, spices 8921, 9280, 9288

spille *v.* to destroy 1320; **spilt(e)** *pa. p.* 2950, 5558

sprent *v.* to leap out 6810

spryng *v.* to grow, sprout, shoot out, originate 645, 652, 674, 1904, 2473 +

stalworth *adj.* strong, hardy, vigourous 130, 689

stalworthly *adv.* strongly 9081

staynged *v. pa.* pierced 5293

stand *v.* to stand upright, stop, remain 466, 474, 662, 681, 984 +

state *n.* estate, state, condition 693, 716, 883, 1107, 1341 +

sted *v. pa. p.* placed 6170

sted(e) *n.* place 457, 858, 1168, 1701, 1705 +; *stand in stede* to avail, be beneficial, substitute for 2193, 2759, 3648, 3679, 3811

stey *v.* to climb, rise 4306, 4557, 4560; *pa.* 4603, 5131, 5133, 5220, 7692

sterne *n.* star 996, 1015, 4420, 4427, 4703 +

sterned *v. pa. p., adj.* star-filled 993, 7568, 7572, 7700

steven *n.* voice 4559, 5043

styflyer *adv. comp.* more firmly 3173

styk *v.* to stick, stand still, pierce 7630; **styked** *pa.* 5337; **stak** 5602

stille *adj.* silent, inert 822, 1384, 1388, 2437, 3449 +; *adv.* continually 2746, 3308, 3737 +; *outher loud or stille* in whatever circumstance, in any circumstance 3175, 3782, 9604

stynk *n.* stench 460, 634, 657, 6233, 6557 +

stynt *v.* to stop, cease 1630, 6089, 7299

styntyng *n.* stop, ceasing 7013, 7094

styringes *n. pl.* movement 822

styrre *v.* to stir, impel, incite 154, 497; **stir** 157, 181, 342; **styrd** *pa.* 1555, 4710, 7088

stok *n.* stock, trunk 676

stoles *n. pl.* vestments, the cloth bands worn by priests 1536

stonde *n.* space of time 3298

stopp *v.* to plug, block up, fill or cram 6459, 7364, 7355

stoure *n.* onslaught 1838; cf. **dede-stoure**

strayt *adj.* strait, narrow, exact(ing) or fastidious 2376, 2617, 4736, 5613, 5644 +

stra(y)tly *adv.* exactly, narrowly 3330, 5772, 5814, 5832, 5912 +

streyned *v. pa. p.* constrained, bound, ? twisted 7177, 7195, 7212, 7227

strenth(e) *n.* strength 465, 1038, 3106, 5898 +; **strengh** 692, 702, 4033, 7613

strenthy *adj.* powerful 5075

stresced *v. pa. p.* restrained, confined 7998, 8543

strife *v. pr. pl.* contend, engage in strife 1470, 7373, 8406, 9422

strik *adv.* straight, directly, straightway 2623, 3295; **strek** 3378

strykly *adv.* straightly, directly 3288

strivyng *n.* contention 1173

sug(g)ette *n.* subordinate, one who answers one's commands and corrections 5436, 5578, 5584, 5990

suggette *v. pa. p., adj.* subject, at will 1055, 4052

suspecyon *n.* mistrust, distrust, fear 1652, 3487

suthfastnes *n.* truth 4268

sutil(le) *adj.* clever 1794, 3024, 5904, 7688, 9268

swa *adv.* so, thus 28, 32, 34, 208, 231 +

swelt *v. pa.* expired, died 5212

swet (= swette) *v. pa.* sweated, exuded 1781

swylk *adj.* such 155, 273, 307, 324, 658 +

swynacy *n.* quinsy, a disease of the throat 2999

swynk *n.* labour 755, 7968

swippe *v. pr. pl.* pass away, pass quickly 2196, 3322

swythe *adv.* strongly, immediately, quickly 1390, 3426, 5713

T

(þe) ta, (þe) tane, see **a, tane**

tayled *v. pa. p.* carved, shaped 9082

talde, see **telle**

tale *n.* count 6462, 7703

talent *n.* desire 8456

tan(e) *v. pa. p.* taken in its various senses, including assumed, construed, gave, received 23, 58, 964, 1680, 2364 +; **take** *v.* 112, 191, 1957 +; **tas** *3. sg. pr. pl.* 275, 592, 597, 1504, 1522 +; **tok** *pa.* 111; **tuk(e)** 381, 2808, 5804 +; **touke** 5500

tary *v.* to delay 3921

taries *v. 3 sg. pr.* vexes, torments 1189

tariyng *n.* delay 1172, 3269

tast(e) *v.* to taste, experience 1817, 1926, 2156, 8190, 9276 +

tatird *v. pa. p.* tattered or slashed (clothing, conventionally that of a fool) 1537 (2x)

telle *v.* to account, recount 293, 539, 559, 562, 601 +; **talde** *pa.* 213, 436, 556, 802 +

temper, -re *v. pr. pl.* moderate 1022, 7613

tendre *adj.* tender, solicitous 905, 3015, 3110, 3114, 9551

tene *n.* vexation, trouble 7323

tent *n.* attention, care; *tas tent* pay attention 1504

tentes *v. pr. pl.* attend, pay attention (to) 7612

þa *demon.* those 246, 797, 971, 1188, 1223 +; **þas** 491, 1065, 1078, 1080, 2200 +

þar *v. pr.* has need of/to, need 2023, 2167, 2173, 2963, 7335; **thurt** *pa.* 6229

tharlles *n. pl.* thrals, slaves 1064; **thrall** 8078, 8543

tharne *v.* to lack 8506

tharnyng *n.* lack, deprivation, absence 7296, 7304

þeþen *adv.* from that place, thence 1018, 2721, 3124, 5831, 7732

thewes *n. pl.* proper behaviour, virtues 1883, 5548

þir *dem.* these 257, 434, 800, 828, 1006 +; **þer** 253, 259, 363, 436, 461 +; **þere** 1259, 1832; **þier** 119; **þis** 289, 510, 1330, 3306, 4413; **þes** 2966; **þeis** 9575

(þam) thynk *v. 3 sg. pr. (impers.)* seems (to him/them) 306, 750, 1345, 1650, 1784 +; **thoght** *pa.* 2186, 2452, 4669 +; **thogh** 2184, 3932; **thogt** 323 (Most uses represent modern 'think', e.g. contrast 1648 with 1650.)

þof *conj.* although 7669, 7721, 7961; cf. **þogh(e)** 943, 1733, 2185, 2309, 2463 +, and **alle-if**

thole *v.* to suffer, allow 2263, 2724, 2752, 2774, 2783 +

thraw, see **dede-thraw**

thred(de) *ord. num.* third 354, 1659, 1664, 1685, 1826 +

threp *v.* rebuke, quarrel 5407

threst *n.* thirst 3254, 6560, 6730, 6731, 6757 +; therst 6771

threst *v.* to thrust 5296, 8588

thrested *v. pa.* thirsted 5771, 6149, 6189

thretynges *n. pl.* threat(ening gestures) 2230

thurgh-soght *v. pa. p.* scrutinized, searched completely 2442

thurt, see þar

tyde *n.* (space of) time, occasion, sea-tide 379, 1215, 4845, 4933, 5054 +

tilles *v. 3 sg. pr.* entices 1183

tyn(e) *v.* to lose, remove 697, 702, 1457, 2027, 2036 +; tynt *pa.* 4854; *pa. p.* 1631, 6094, 7302

tysyk *n.* phthisic, a disease of the lungs 701

tyte, see als-tyte

titte *n.* tug, jerk 1915

tytted *v. pa. p.* pulled, stretched 7212

tognaw *v.* completely chew up 863

tome *n.* (empty) space, opportunity 6245

touches *n. pl.* grasping or groping (with one's hand) 779

trace *n.* path, track, model 4349, 6037, 6870, 7072

trayste *v.* trust, place trust in 1091, 1359, 1366, 1431, 2469 +

transyng *n.* an unconscious state, trance 8155

tre *n.* tree, wood 646, 649, 652, 656, 658 +

tregettours *n. pl.* contrivers of illusions 4213

trey *n.* trick, deceit, treason 7323

trespas *n.* transgression, sin 2440, 3170, 5262, 6368

trofels *n. pl.* trifles, vanity, foolishness 183

trouthe *n.* faith, belief 295, 2139, 3321, 4193, 4228 +

trowage *n.* tribute (payments) 4053

trow(e) *v.* to believe 11, 296, 301, 303, 313 +

trowyng *n.* belief 789

turne *v.* to turn, in its various senses, including convert 418, 425, 516, 663, 673 +; *turne agayne* to return 418, 425 +

twyn *num.* two (OE twegen) 3594, 3607, 5842

twyn *v.* to separate 1709, 1823, 2209, 2650, 2905

twynyng *n.* separation, estrangement 1687, 1690, 1864

U

ugge *v.* be horrified or terrified 6415

ugly *adj.* horrible, frightful 860, 870, 907, 2344, 2449 +

uglynes *n.* a horrifying image, horror 917, 2364, 6828

umlapp *v.* to enclose, surround 6933

umset *v. pa. p.* surrounded 1250, 5420

unbowsom(e) *adj.* disobedient 1599, 8593

unchasty(e)d(e) *v. pa. p.* unchastised, undisciplined 5434, 5544, 5985

unclen(e) *adj.* lacking virtue, dirty 1206, 1207, 2505, 2568, 9005

uncrysomd *pa. p.*, *adj.* unbaptized 2791

underloutes *n. pl.* subordinates, lit. those who bow beneath them 3877

underlout *v. pa. p.* subject, bowing to 4052, 8943

undiscussed *v. pa. p.* unexamined 5697

uniustyfyed *v. pa. p.* uncorrected 5871

unkynd(e) *adj.* unnatural 122, 943, 2051, 5855

unkynd(e)nes *n.* unnatural behaviour 3522, 5587, 6216

unkun(n)and *adj.* ignorant 152, 177, 338

unkunnyng *n.* ignorance, lack of knowledge 169

unlered *adj.* unlearned, ignorant 5947

unnethes *adv.* scarcely 476, 890, 1419, 2164, 3326 +

unsemely *adj.* ugly, malformed, lacking beauty 5009, 5023

unsiker *adj.* uncertain, changeable 1089, 2466

unsykernes *n.* insecurity, uncertainty 9046

unskylwys *adj.* lacking reason 166

unsleghe *adj.* foolish, unintelligent 1938

unstedfast *adj.* lacking in firmness or commitment 324

unthewed *v. pa. p.*, *adj.* behaving unvirtuously 5873

unto *conj.* until (the usual form) 910, 1212, 1213, 2433, 2443 +

upright *adj.* morally upright, firm, steadfast 1298

upstegher *n.* rider (lit. one who ascends) 4180

uptane *v. pa. p.* raised up, elevated 5142, 8247

use *v.* to use (habitually), practice, accustom (oneself to) 124, 170, 1518, 1535, 1540 +

V

vaile *v.* to avail, benefit, aid 3448, 3646, 3726, 3942

vanite *n.* vanity, sillyness, worldly things, pride 184, 262, 271, 341, 956 +

vauntyng *n.* boasting 1145

velany (vil-) *n.* churlishness, low behaviour 1171, 1528, 1531, 7144, 7853

vengeaunce *n.* retribution 1569, 2857, 4897, 4853, 5528 +

vermyn *n.* foul or monstruous beasts 651, 916, 917, 6565, 6570 +

verray *adj.* true 4310, 4331, 9199; **werray** 4683

verraly *adv.* more accurately or truly 9236, 9237

vilans *adj.* wretched 4412

violent *adj.* harsh, injurious 852, 6754

voyde *adj.* empty 390

vouches save *v. 3 sg. pr.* grants 93, 3002, 3532, 6165, 6507 +

W

w-, frequently in alternation with **wh-** (e.g. **was** 'whose' 23 or **als wa** 'as a person who' 1954) and with **v-** (as in **werray** 'very' 4683)

waghe *n.* wall 6615

wayn *adj.* deficient, lacking 1060

wayt *v.* to watch for, lie in wait for 1186, 1192, 1243, 2908

wake *adj.* weak, frail 129; **wayk(e)** 693, 767, 6154, 7958 +

wake *v. imp.* to wake, watch, be vigilant, keep a penitential vigil 825, 827, 1970, 3514

walaway *interj.* alas 2434, 7054, 7331, 7359

walde, see **wille**

wam(be) *n.* womb 463, 515, 524, 837, 4161 +

wand(e) *n.* stick, rod of correction 5878, 5880

wanhope *n.* despair 2229

want *v. (impers.)* to lack (usually *3. sg. pr.*, lit. it is lacking to him) 593, 5002, 5013, 6191, 8505 +

wantyng *n.* lack, absence 7324

war *v. pr. subj.* afflict 3169

war(e) *v. pa.* were, should be, would be 176, 187, 391, 583, 942 +

wardes *n. pl.* strongholds, fortified areas 8894, 8899, 9080, 9081, 9084 +

warn *v.* to deny 3058, 7985

warn(e) *conj.* if . . . were not 2342, 7260, 7262, 7599, 8357

wast(e) *v.* to dissolve, destroy, vanish 2870, 3143, 3146, 3151 (2×) +

wate *v. pr.* know 1432, 1808, 2115, 2493, 2506 +; **what(e)** 1771, 2516, 2666; **wayte** 1944; **wyst** *pa.* 1782, 2845, 6197, 9513

wathe *n.* peril, danger 4558; **quathes** *pl.* 2102

waxes *v. pr. pl.* grow 305, 766, 767, 770, 772 +

wawes *n. pl.* waves 1218, 1224

weld(e) *v.* to control, govern, enjoy 757, 2259, 5777, 6146, 7357 +

wele *n.* prosperity, plenty, riches 1002, 1260, 1278, 1279, 2116 +; **welth(e)** 595, 1060, 1261 +

welk *v. pa.* walked 4248, 4390

welkes *v. 3 sg. pr.* dries out, withers 707

welland *v. pr. p.* boiling, molten 7122, 9431; **welled** *pa. p.* boiled 9429

welle *n.* spring, source 4108

wend(e) *v.* to go or pass 87, 233, 835, 1586, 1634 +

wene *v.* to think, expect 1376, 1544, 2154, 3081, 3384 +

wer *adj. comp.* worse (usually **werse**— and **werst** *super.*) 1479

were *n.* doubt 2296, 2510, 8563

wery *v.* to curse 7391, 7418, 8469, 9420 +; *pa. p., adj.* cursed 4202, 6183, 7393, 7394

werk(e) *n.* work, deed 83, 146, 164, 323, 335 +

werld(e) *n.* world 71, 262, 353, 464, 994 + (usually the modern form **world**)

werray *v.* wage war (on/against) 4477, 4683

wethen *adv.* (from) whence 901; **whethen** 5205

wethir *conj.* whichever (of two things),

whether 80, 214, 811, 2116, 2421 +;
   whether 94, 479, 632, 1543 +
wh-, see also **w-** and **qw-** (cf. **whake**, for
   qwake 5411)
whatkyn *adj.* whatever type (of) 856,
   923, 2704, 8853
whilk *adj.* which 144, 159, 210 +; **wilk**
   191, 192, 204 (2×), 244 +; **qwilk** 1165,
   3954, 4265; **quilk** 1354
whil(l)es *conj.* while, so long as 896,
   1256, 1286, 2046, 2050 +; **whils** 524,
   922, 1670 +
whilom *adv.* once, previously 4202, 9028
whyn(e) (for **why ne?**) *adv.* why (. . .
   not) 1207, 6224, 6225, 7419
wyght *adj.* active, vigourous 689
wight *n.* (created) being 1874, 5525, 6183
wyk *adj.* wicked 6690, 8055, 9417
wil(le) *v. pr.* wish(es) 40, 94, 184, 281,
   290 +; *3. sg. pr.* **wild** 1732, 7937, 7965,
   8404; **wald(e)** *v. pa. (subj.)* wished,
   might wish 15, 80, 112, 283, 375 +;
   wyld 6216, 8337, 8478
wyld, see **wille**
wille *n.* (free) will, desire, intention 47,
   63, 78, 93, 95 +
wyn(ne) *v.* to attain, achieve, acquire,
   get, pass 147, 1457, 2112, 2769,
   2804 +; **whyn** 3887
wynk *v.* to shut the eye 4970, 7932, 7969
wirk(e) *v.* to perform, act 335, 2138,
   3134, 3137, 3320 +; **wroght** *pa. p.*
   made, done, performed 9, 45, 53, 373,
   387 +
wysse *v.* to guide, direct, teach 9301,
   9470
witandly *adv.* consciously 5727
wythalle *adv.* completely, likewise,
   indeed, thereby, then 227, 230, 755,
   817, 1308 +
wyt(te) *n.* the senses, intelligence, reason
   2, 21, 23, 50, 76 +
witt(e), wite *v.* to know 813, 1797, 1801,
   2935, 3763 +; **whit** 4775
witty *adj.* wise 588, 880, 1094, 1354,
   1362 +
wlatsom *adj.* nauseating 459, 520, 564,
   583, 610 +
wode *adj.* insane, mad 99, 1608, 1651,
   2224, 2908 +

wodenes *n.* insanity, fury 6911
wolwarde *adv.* dressed in woolens,
   wearing a penitential hairshirt 3514
won(e) *v.* to dwell, remain, live 13, 16,
   997, 1001, 1011 +
wonder *v.* to stare 7409
won(n)yng *n.* dwelling(-place) 980, 1009,
   6823, 7179, 7565 +
won(n)yng-sted *n.* dwelling-place 1372,
   8777, 8782, 9112, 9120 +
world of world *n. phrs.* 'secula
   seculorum', eternity 961
worldysshe *adj.* worldly, transitory 931,
   940, 951, 955, 1065 +; **worldis** 1085;
   worldes 1339, 1353
worow *v.* to throttle 1229
wors(c)hepe *n.* honour 596, 604, 955,
   1139, 1194 +
worshepe *v.* to honour 55, 60, 83, 8739
wrang *adv.* wrongly, amiss 193, 2421,
   2435, 2487
wrangwysly *adv.* sinfully, with sin 3865
wrath(e) *adj.* angry, angered 786, 3482,
   4541, 5479; **wrahte** 5406
wreghe *v.* to reveal 5460, 5462
wreke *n.* vengeance 5538, 5601, 6098
wrenkes *n. pl.* tricks, treachery 1360
wreth(e) *v.* to anger 1551, 5606, 9495
wreth(e) *n.* anger 787, 1552, 1556, 3370,
   5081 +
wrynchand *v. pr. p.* twisting, turning
   (affectedly) 1538
wroght, see **wirk**

Y

yhed *v. pa.* went 4851; **yhode** 6530
yheld(e) *v.* to give, return, render 1826,
   2272, 2277, 2378, 2428 +; **yholden** *pa.
   p.* 5672
yhemed *v. pa.* heeded, cared for 5792
yherne *adv.* eagerly 6701
yhern(e) *v.* to desire 1649, 2176, 2182,
   2188, 4010 +
yhernyng *n.* desire 1127, 1128, 1134,
   1136, 1579 +
yhit(te) *adv.* yet, still, in addition 22,
   105, 109, 152, 180 +; **yit** 107
yhouthede *n.* youth 5713, 5718

INDEX OF QUOTATIONS
AND ALLUSIONS

Entries marked 'n' refer to discussions in the Textual Commentary, usually to sources extensively used but not always marked in the text.

A. BIBLICAL QUOTATIONS AND ALLUSIONS

Genesis
  1: 28   1152
  3: 19   422–3
  6: 3   734–7
  49: 17   4171–3
Deuteronomy
  4: 9   5806–7
  32: 22   6595–7
  32: 24   6907–8
  32: 33   6749–50
Judith
  16: 21   6961–4
Job
  1: 21   512–13
  5: 7   540–1
  5: 14   cf. 6803–4
  7: 9   cf. 2833, 7245–6
  10: 9   414–15
  10: 20   760–1
  10: 21   6819–20
  10: 22   6825–6
  13: 26   5494–5, 5722
  14: 1   532–3
  14: 2   710–11
  14: 13   5095–8
  20: 16   6767–8
  20: 25   8590–1
  21: 26   876–7
  24: 19   6655–6
  26: 11   5384–7
  34: 15   422–3
Psalms
  6: 6   2080–1
  9: 15   2124–5
  10: 7   6739–40
  20: 4   9320–1
  24: 7   5739
  32: 5   6335–6
  35: 4   285–6
  38: 13   1382–3
  43: 16   7149–50

  48: 15   6707–8
  48: 20   cf. 6835
  48: 21   602–3
  49: 3   4937–8
  49: 4   5628–9
  50: 7   450–1
  57: 11   8438–9
  74: 3   5754–5
  80: 13   1574–5
  81: 6   8286–7
  81: 7   2058–9
  83: 11   8092–3
  88: 2   8350–1
  89: 4   8076–7
  89: 6   720–1
  89: 10   752–3
  89: 15   9305–7
  96: 3   4917–18
  105: 12–13   317–19
  105: 24–5   299–300
  105: 29   1554–5
  118: 64   6335–6
  138: 17   8536–7
  148: 5   6269–70
Proverbs
  2: 19   7233–4
  19: 29   7035–6
  22: 15   cf. 5876–7
  24: 16   3432–3
Ecclesiastes
  7: 2   2190–1
  11: 9   5706–11
  12: 1   2070–1
  12: 14   5731–2
Wisdom
  2: 1   6491–2
  5: 8–11   7059–64
  11: 21   cf. 7686–7
Ecclesiasticus
  2: 5 etc.   3201n
  7: 40   2655–7

9: 20   1892–3
10: 13   866–7
41: 1   1932–3
41: 10   5550–1
Isaiah
    5: 20   1612–13
    14: 11   6947–8
    33: 7   5386
    64: 6   2502–3
    66: 18   5682–3
    66: 24   6919–20
Lamentations
    1: 3   2238–9
Ezekiel
    4: 6   2762–3
    33: 11   1736–7
    34: 10   5888–9
Daniel
    2   4104n
    7: 10   5446
    11   4104n
Joel
    3: 2   5153–4
    3: 12   5159–62
Zephaniah
    1: 15–18   6096–113n
Zechariah
    14: 5   5115–16
Malachi
    4: 6   4505–6
Matthew
    6: 24   1100–3
    7: 18   660–1
    10: 8   5962–3
    11: 21, 23   4205–6
    12: 36   5668–9
    13: 43   9148
    16: 19   3846–9
    18: 3   398–9
    19: 28   6042–4
    22: 13   7187–8, cf. 7334
    23: 16   1612–13
    24: 3–5, 7–8, 12   4014–24
    24: 21   4355–6
    24: 22   4573–4
    24: 24   4355–6
    24: 27–8   5122–5
    25: 32–46   6127–210 passim
    25: 42   5766–7
Luke
    8: 13   311–12
    12: 2   2406–7

14: 11   8500–1, 8516–17
16: 19–25   3056–79
17: 26–30   4824–36
21: 18   5005–6
21: 25–7   4691–8
John
    5: 22–3   5247–8
    10: 16   4635–6
    12: 31   1084
    14: 2   8780–1
    14: 30   1084
    16: 11   1084
Acts
    1: 7   4657–8
    1: 11   5138–41
    2: 19–20   4719–23
Romans
    2: 12   6065–6
1 Corinthians
    2: 9   7786–9
    3: 10–15   3088–3205n, 3178–85n
    3: 19   1356–7
    10: 17, 12: 13   cf. 5924–5
    13: 12   cf. 6867–68
    15: 51, 52   4973–4
Philippians
    1: 23   2180–1
1 Thessalonians
    4: 16–17   5035–41
2 Thessalonians
    2: 3   4057, 4106n
Hebrews
    13: 14   1370–1
James
    4: 4   1114–15
    5: 2–3   5560–77
1 Peter
    4: 10   5954–5
    4: 18   5396–7
1 John
    2: 15   1122–3
    2: 16   1130–3
Revelation
    1: 15   4365–6
    6: 10   5530–1
    6: 15–16   5064–71
    9: 6   6719–20, 7275, 7384–5
    12: 4   4417–18
    14: 13   2198–9
    14: 14   cf. 5175–6
    21: 2 and ff.   8790–91 and ff.

B. SOURCES AND ALLUSIONS IN CLASSICAL AND PATRISTIC AUTHORS

Adso Dervensis
  De ortu et tempore Antichristi 4047–
    648n, 4058–60, 4171–6
Anselm of Bec
  Meditatio 1 (through *Les Peines*) 2424–
    57n
ps.-Anselm of Bec
  De similitudinibus (through *Les Peines*)
    7872–8629n
Augustine
  De Civitate Dei
    1. 11   2150–3
    21. 26 (through Hugh)   3164–7
  De Disciplina Christiana
    12   2160–1
  Enarratio in Psalmos
    120   1962–7
    143   cf. 6313–14
  Enchiridion
    110   cf. 3570–1
  Epistola 199. 1   2588–92
  Sermo de symbolo 8 (through Humbert)
    5317–24
  Sermones
    39. 1   1982–5
ps.-Augustine
  De triplici habitaculo
    3   cf. 8110–27n
    6   cf. 8204–73n
  Sermones
    44   2514–15
    48 (through *Les Peines*)   2673
  Speculum peccatoris
    (?)generally   348–69n, 766–99n, 914–
      15, 2242–97n
Bartholomaeus Anglicus
  De Proprietatibus rerum
    8. 1   1164–93n
    8. 2   7552–5n, 7590–614n, 7639–43n
Bernard of Clairvaux
  In Assumptione B. V. Mariae
    sermo 2 (through Humbert)   5826–7
  De conversione ad clericos
    7   1876–9, 1948–9
  De gradibus humilitatis
    1. 2   205–10n
Bernard (through Humbert)   5654–7
lives of Bernard (*PL* 185: 491, 258)   2255–
    67n

ps.-Bernard of Clairvaux
  Meditationes
    1   74n
    3. 7   620–3
    3. 8   247–8, 560–1, 914–15
  *Tractatus de interiori domo seu de
    conscientia*
    19   2542–7
Breviary (see also Mass, Office)
  Invention of the Cross, Matins, Lectio
    1, V   5281–2
Caesarius of Arles (ps.-Augustine)
  Sermones
    1: 277   2038–41
    2: 725   3352–73nn
Disticha Catonis
    4. 22   2170–1
Glossa Ordinaria
    1, on Deut. 32: 22   6597–8
    2, on Esther 7: 1   1982–5
    3, on Dan. 7: 10   5451
    3, on Dan. 12: 12   4625
    3, on Mal. 4: 5–6   4515–16
    4, on Rev. 20: 7   4473, 4479
Gregory the Great
  In septem psalmos poenitentiales
    7   1312–13
  Moralia in Job
    5. 1   1312–13
    21. 5 (through Humbert)   5690–3
    32. 15 (through Hugh)   4579–80
    35. 22   2496–7
Honorius of Regensburg
  Elucidarium
    3. 14–15   6591–630 ff.nn, 6875–8,
      6925–6, 7137–8
    3. 15   6661–4
    3. 16   7207–8
    3. 59 ff.   6017–33 ff.nn
    3. 90–103   8922–77n
    3. 106–18   9020–47n
  Speculum Ecclesiae   6675–6
Hugh Ripelin of Strasbourg
  Compendium veritatis theologiae
    4. 22   2786–828n
    7. 3   2730–1, 3128–85n
    7. 4   3576–611n
    7. 5   3624–797n
    7. 6   3798–939n

7. 8 ('Danielle') 4237–8 and n
7. 9 4255–4412n
7. 10 4413–50n, 4441–50n
7. 11 4451–90n
7. 12 4491–568n
7. 13 4569–86n
7. 14 4597–648n
7. 15 4857–956n
7. 20 6345–398n
7. 31 7780–801n, 7810–21n, 8632–43n
Humbert of Romans
    De Abundantia exemplorum
        part 4 5193–222n, 5279–367n,
            5422–611n, 5612–829n, 5748–9,
            5858–959n
        part 5 1818–31n
Innocent III
    De Miseria condicionis humanae
        1. 2 372–74n, 410–25n
        1. 3 444–55n
        1. 4 456–61n
        1. 5 462–75n
        1. 6 476–507n, 499–501
        1. 7 508–27n
        1. 8 630–87n, 636–43, 666–71
        1. 9 728–801n
        1. 10 538–45n
        1. 14 1339–41n
        1. 17 1362–86n
        1. 18 1245–56n
        1. 25 1506–9
        3. 1 830–79n, 854–5
        3. 14 5368–401n
Isidore of Seville
    Sententiae
        3. 9 2522–3
Jerome
    Commentarium in Joelem prophetam
        1 1295–7
    Regula monachorum

        30 4671–4
        (from Humbert) 5592–5n
John Bromyard
    Summa praedicantium
        Mundus 3. 6 1146–51n
John Chrysostom (through Humbert)
        5361–3
Martin of Braga (ps.-Seneca)
    Formula vitae honestae
        1 1304–5
Mass for the Dead, Offertorium 2822–4
ps.-Methodius
    Revelationes 4197–224n
Office of the Dead
    response of the seventh lection 2833
    response of the third lection 5086–8
    responses at Matins 9128–9
Speculum Christiani (parallels for
    unidentified passages)
        49/24–5 and 209/1–2 2160–1
        121/18–19 ('Ierom') 6787–8
        121/19–20 ('Austyn') 7113–14
        121/24–6 2842–3
        205/30–3 1324–5, 1332–3
        209/9–10 2008–9
Thomas of Ireland
    Manipulus florum
        Mors M 1982–85n
        Mors P 2588–92n
        Mors S 2160–1n
Walther
    Lateinische Sprichwörter
        no. 5090 3418–19
        no. 6845 490
        no. 7578 6631–2
        no. 29074 898–9
        no. 33802 9366–7
        no. 38355 1790–1
William of Pagula
    Summa summarum (BodL, MS Bodley
        293, fo. 221$^{\text{va–b}}$) 3398–3411n

C. VERNACULAR SOURCES

Cursor Mundi
    1 ff., 123 183–92n
    127–8 209n
    221–2 336n
    232–50 336–9n
    269–70 1–8n
    277–8 27–8n
    517–18 372–93n
    567–8 76–80n

    3555–98 766–99n
    17009–12 1840–3n
    22005–116 4047–648n, 4074n
    23333–50 2842–3n
Les Peines de purgatoire
    ll. 28–39 2651–73n
    ll. 45–74 2384–457n
    ll. 74–7 2637–42n
    ll. 77–81 3300–8n

ll. 86–99   2750–83n
ll. 102–88   2897–3273n
ll. 208–40   3440–90n
ll. 292–304   5404–21n
ll. 316–36   6891–7004n
ll. 339–48   6695–728n
ll. 348–59   6729–90n

ll. 359–66, 371–4   7229–91n
ll. 412 ff. ('Anselme')   7950 ff.nn
The Northern Homily Cycle
Prol. 15   76–8on
21–2   125n
61–80   336–9n
81–3   209n

INDEX OF PROPER NAMES

This, unlike the Glossary, offers complete references to those authorities cited by the poet, since these may be of interest in surveying the sources of the work. Line-references to these names within the Latin citations are followed by 'L'. Other references, like those in the Glossary, are restricted to the first five uses.

Abraham   Abraham the patriarch (here as the protector of Lazarus in Luke 16) 3059, 3060, 3063, 3064

Absolon   Absolom, David's son, a paragon of beauty 8924, 9020

Adam   Adam, the first man 483

Affrik   Africa 8966

Alexander   Alexander the Great, the world-conqueror 8965, 9040

Amazons   the legendary tribe of warrior women, usually placed in Scythia/the steppe 4463

Anselme   Anselm of Bec 2424, 7886, 8300

Anticrist   the tyrant king of the last days 3996, 4047, 4060L, 4105, 4147 +; **Onti-** 4475

Aposteles, see *Boke*

Ap(p)ocalip(pe)s(e)   the biblical book Revelation 2197, 4363, 4416, 4523, 4529, 5063, 5529, 5535, 6718, 7383, 8789

Appolyn   Appolo, the classical sun-god 4122

Asy   Asia 8966

Assahel(l)   Asael, David's nephew, famed for his speed of foot (2 Kgs. 2: 18) 8933, 9026

August   Caesar Augustus, the founder of the Roman empire 8941, 9028

Austyn(e)   Augustine of Hippo 1323, 1960, 1981, 2007, 2037, 2149, 2159, 2495, 2587, 2672, 2841, 3163, 3441, 3488, 3561, 3569, 4986, 5316, 6311, 6659, 6874, 6927, 7034, 7111, 7136, 8114, 8204, 8269, 9406

Bernard(e)   Bernard of Clairvaux 245, 559, 562, 619, 913, 1875, 1947, 2057, 2079, 2122, 2248, 2254, 2529, 2540, 2548, 5653, 5825; **Barnard** 2563

Berthelmew(e)   Bartholomaeus Anglicus, OFM, the author of the encyclopedia *De proprietatibus rerum* 966, 1162, 7578; cf. *Boke of Propertese*

Bethleem   Bethlehem, the birthplace of Jesus 5189, 5198

Bethsayda   Galilean village cursed by Jesus (Matt. 11: 21) for failing to heed his signs 4199, 4201, 4205L, 4208

þe Boke of Aposteles Werkes   the biblical book Acts of the Apostles 4656

þe Boke of Propertese of Sere Thinges   Bartholomaeus's *De proprietatibus rerum* 7579–80

þe Buke of Wysdom   the biblical book Wisdom or Sapience 6490

Calvery, þe mount of   Golgotha, site of the Crucifixion 5187, 5208

Capharnaum   Galilean village cursed by Jesus (Matt. 11: 23) for failing to heed his signs 4200, 4201, 4205L, 4208

Caryn   one of the sons of Simeon, supposed to have been released to offer witness to the Harrowing of Hell 6526; cf. **Leutyn**

Caspy   the Caspian Sea; **þe mountes of Caspy** some part of the Caucasus 4458

Caton   Cato, alleged author of the proverbial *Distichs*, a basic grammatical text 2169

Corozaym   Galilean village cursed by Jesus (Matt. 11: 21) for failing to heed his signs 4166, 4202, 4205L, 4207

Crist   both the prophet Jesus of Nazareth and the risen Redeemer 1611, 1779, 2212, 2807, 2942 +; **Criestes** *poss.* 5511; **Cristus** 4018L; **Ihesu Crist** (always in the second sense?) 2258, 2603, 2822L, 5028

Cristen *adj.*   Christian 4225, 4235, 4389, 4452 +; **Cresten** 4317

Cristiante the religion or the world over which it has spread 3117, 3925, 6842, 7427, 7795

Cristendome (Crest-) the Christian faith 3127, 4082, 4168, 4510

Dan Dan, the Israelite tribe descending from Jacob's son of that name (symbolized by a serpent) 4167

Daniel(le) the prophet Daniel 4236, 4625, 5445; *poss.* 4104

David David the king and psalmist 315, 449, 1553, 1573, 1576, 4916, 4935, 5626, 5737, 5756, 6334, 6738, 8349, 8535, 8958, 9036, 9304, 9319; often simply þe prophet(e), e.g. 284, 601, 718 +, and cf. **David þe prophete** 1553

Ebriens authors writing in Hebrew 4750, 4817; **Hebriens** 4754

Egypciens the Egyptians 8962, 9038

Ely Elijah the prophet (Latin Elyas), reft to heaven in 4 Kgs. 2 (here as one of the 'two witnesses' of Rev. 11, also taken to heaven) 4446, 4492, 4557; **Hely** 4566, 8974, 9044

Ennoc, Ennok Enoch the patriarch, reft to heaven in Gen. 5: 24 (here as one of the 'two witnesses' of Rev. 11, also taken to heaven) 4446, 4492, 4557, 4566, 8974, 9044

Europe Europe 8966

Eve Eve, the first woman 487, 491; **Eva** 490L

Ezechyele the prophet Ezechiel 2761, 5887

Filius, see **Son**

þe Flour of Konyng, Flos sciencie an unidentified Latin source 7202, 7203

Gog leader of a savage race serving Antichrist 4454, 4474, 4480, 4489; cf. **Magog**

Gregor Gregory the Great 1311, 1314, 1331, 4578, 5689, 5747

Halghe Thursday Ascension Thursday 7693

Haymo Haymo of Halberstadt, author of a commentary on the *Apocalypse* 4391

He-, see **E-**

Herculy Hercules, the deified classical hero 4122

Hostyen the canonist Henry of Segusio (called 'Hostiensis' from his appointment as cardinal-bishop of Ostia) 3944n

Ingland England 9444

Inglis(e) the English language 2658, 2764, 2814, 3560, 5808, 6493, 6709, 7203, 9445, 9447; **Yngles** 336; **Inglishe** 1205

Innocent Lothario dei Segni, pope Innocent III 498, 635, 665, 853, 1505; pope Innocent IV, a canonistic commentator 3944

Ysay Isaiah the prophet 5681

Ysidre (I-) Isidore of Seville 2501, 2520

Ieremy the prophet Jeremiah 2236

Ierom(e) Jerome of Strido 1294, 4668, 4738, 4745, 4752, 4816, 5591, 6673, 6785

Ierusalem Jerusalem, the holy city 4096, 4218, 4470, 4543, 5185, 5190, 5202; the 'new' city of heaven 8790L, 8793

Iewes the Jews, Jewish people 4444, 4467, 4502, 4511 +; **Iewery** 4509

Ihesu 5141, 6252 +, and see **Crist**; **Ihesus** 4016L, 5137L

Iob(e) the prophet Job 413, 516, 531, 537, 539, 709, 717, 759, 2832, 5094, 5108, 5493, 5721, 6654, 6766, 6799, 6818, 6824, 7244, 8589; **Iope** 5085

Ioel(e) the prophet Joel 4718, 5152

Iohan John the evangelist and (esp.) revelator 2197, 4369, 4424, 5063, 5081, 5246, 7383, 8788, 8797; **Ion** 6717

Iohan wyth þe gilden mouth John Chrysostom 5360

Ionothas Jonathan, son of Saul and David's great friend 8958, 9036

Iosaphat, þe vale of valley near Jerusalem, to be the site of Last Judgement (on the basis of Joel 3: 2) 5150, 5156, 5164, 5169, 5183, 5194, 5225; **valle Iosaphat** 5154L, 5160–1L

Ioseph Joseph, son of Isaac and later ruler in Egypt 8962, 9038

Iubiter Jupiter, the classical ruler of the gods, and the planet 4121, 7626

Iudyth the biblical book of Judith 6960

Lazar Lazarus, the leprous beggar of Luke 16 3058, 3063, 3066, 3070, 3078

Lazar brother of Mary and Martha, raised from the dead by Jesus in John 11 6503

Leutyn one of the sons of Simeon, supposed to have been released to offer witness to the Harrowing of Hell 6526; cf. **Caryn**

Lilyas the Roman Laelius, who narrates his friendship with Scipio Africanus in Cicero's *De amicitia* 8969n, 9042

Loth Lot, whom God saves from the destruction of Sodom 4822, 4830, 4847

Lucifer the fallen angel who became Satan/the devil 377

Luke Luke the evangelist 4823, 5004

Magog leader of a savage race serving Antichrist 4454, 4474, 4484, 4490; cf. **Gog**

Malachy the prophet Malachi 4503

Mary the Blessed Virgin 5195, 5232, 8679

Mary Maudelayne Mary Magdalen 6503, 8332

Mars the planet Mars 7626

Martha sister of Mary Magdalen and Lazarus 6513

Martyn Martin of Tours 2245

Mathew(e) the evangelist Matthew 4354, 4572, 5120, 6128

Matussale Methusalah, the longest lived person in Scripture 8950, 9032

Mercury Mercury, the classical messenger of the gods, and the planet 4121, 7625

Michael the warrior archangel, conqueror of the dragon of Revelation 4606

Moyses the prophet Moses 8945, 9030; see also **Rabby**

Nabogodonosor Nebuchadnezzar, the Babylonian emperor served by Daniel 6945

Noe Noah, the just man of the flood 733, 4822, 4824, 4828, 4843 +

Olyvet(t)(e), þe mount of the Mount of Olives, near Jerusalem, site of the Ascension and of Christ's descent from Heaven at the Last Judgement 4097, 4601, 5130, 5184, 5218

Pater Noster the Lord's Prayer 3403

Paul(e) the apostle Paul 2179, 4056, 4106, 5034; *poss.* 4104; often simply þe apostel, e.g. 1113, 1121 +

Peter, Petre the apostle (and first pope) Peter 3843, 3844, 3855, 5954, 8330

Pilat Pontius Pilate, governor of Judaea and supposed author of the 'Acta Pilati', part of the apocryphal Gospel of Nicodemus 6540

Prik of Conscience the title given the poem 9448

Rab(b)y Moyses 'Rambam', i.e. *R*abbi *M*osheh *b*en *M*aimun (Maimonides) 7655, 7682

Raymund Raymond of Peñaforte, author of a standard treatise on penance 3946

Rome the city and empire of Rome 4050, 4052, 4059L, 4062, 4065 +

Salamon Solomon the wise, king of Israel and author of biblical 'wisdom literature' 1891, 2654, 5705, 5875, 7232, 8938, 8953, 9024, 9034

Sampson Samson (in ME, often **Sampson þe forte**), the strong man of Judges 8929, 9022

Sar(a)zyns Muslims generally 5510, 6061

Saturnus the planet Saturn (the 'highest' or furthest known in the Middle Ages) 7627, 7635, 7668

Scipyon the Roman general Scipio Africanus, devoted friend of Laelius 8969n, 9043

Senek Seneca, the first-century Roman philosopher 1302, 1306

Sydrak the wise philosopher and hero of the French dialogue *Sydrak and Bochas* 7726

Symeon the Jewish priest whose sons, in the apocryphal Gospel of Nicodemus, describe the Harrowing of Hell 6525

Syon the hill Zion, site of the Jewish

Temple (and thus allegorically, the church) 2125L, 2130

Sodome, Sodomis city destroyed with fire for its sins by God in Gen. 18–19 4833L, 4851

þe Son of Man title of a biblical redeemer, assimilated to Jesus 4711; Mans Son 4840, 4856, 5127; Filius Hominis 4836L, 5123L

Thomas Alqwyn Thomas Aquinas, but here referring to the *Compendium*

veritatis theologiae, a tract often ascribed to Thomas, but written by Hugh Ripelin of Strassbourg OP 3948

Tyberius Roman emperor at the time of Jesus, supposed recipient of the epistolary 'Acta Pilati', part of the apocryphal Gospel of Nicodemus 6540

Venus the planet Venus 7625

Wysdom, see *Buke*